Revenue Statistics in Latin America and the Caribbean

1990-2016

Estadísticas tributarias en América Latina y el Caribe

1990-2016

Please cite this publication as:
OECD, et al. (2018), *Revenue Statistics in Latin America and the Caribbean 2018*, OECD Publishing, Paris.
http://dx.doi.org/10.1787/rev_lat_car-2018-en-fr

Por favor, cite esta publicación de la siguiente manera:
OCDE, et al. (2018), *Estadísticas tributarias en América Latina y el Caribe 2018*, OECD Publishing, Paris.
http://dx.doi.org/10.1787/rev_lat_car-2018-en-fr

ISBN 978-92-64-29222-2 (print/impresa)
ISBN 978-92-64-29223-9 (PDF)

Series/*Serie*: Revenue Statistics in Latin America and the Caribbean/*Estadísticas tributarias en América Latina y el Caribe*
ISSN 2410-4728 (print/impresa)
ISSN 2410-4736 (online/en línea)

Corrigenda to OECD publications may be found on line at: *www.oecd.org/about/publishing/corrigenda.htm*.
Las erratas de las publicaciones de la OCDE se encuentran en línea en *www.oecd.org/about/publishing/corrigenda.htm*.

Foreword

Revenue Statistics in Latin America and the Caribbean *is a joint publication by the OECD Centre for Tax Policy and Administration, the OECD Development Centre, the United Nations Economic Commission for Latin America and the Caribbean (ECLAC), the Inter-American Center of Tax Administrations (CIAT) and the Inter-American Development Bank (IDB). It presents detailed, internationally comparable data on tax revenues for 25 Latin American and Caribbean economies, two of which are OECD members. Its approach is based on the well-established methodology of the OECD Revenue Statistics database, which is an essential reference source for OECD member countries. Comparisons are also made with the average tax indicators for OECD economies.*

The term "taxes" in this publication is confined to compulsory, unrequited payments to general government. As outlined in the Interpretative Guide to Revenue Statistics, taxes are "unrequited" in the sense that benefits provided by government to taxpayers are not normally in proportion to their payments. The OECD methodology classifies a tax according to its base: income, profits and capital gains (classified under heading 1000), payroll (heading 3000), property (heading 4000), goods and services (heading 5000) and other taxes (heading 6000). Compulsory social security contributions paid to general government are treated as taxes and classified under heading 2000. Much greater detail on the tax concept, the classification of taxes and the accrual basis of reporting is set out in the Interpretative Guide in Annex A.

Extending the OECD methodology to Latin America and the Caribbean countries enables comparisons of tax systems on a consistent basis both across this region and with OECD countries. In a few cases this methodology differs from the approach used by ECLAC, CIAT and IDB; these differences are noted in the text and in the tables, either with a footnote or an extra row.

The report provides an overview of the main taxation trends in Latin America and the Caribbean. It examines changes in both the level and the composition of taxation plus the attribution of tax collection by sub-level of government between 1990 and 2016.

Presentación

La publicación Estadísticas tributarias en América Latina y el Caribe *ha sido elaborada conjuntamente por el Centro de Política y Administración Tributaria de la OCDE, el Centro de Desarrollo de la OCDE, la Comisión Económica de las Naciones Unidas para América Latina y el Caribe (CEPAL), el Centro Interamericano de Administraciones Tributarias (CIAT) y el Banco Interamericano de Desarrollo (BID). Esta publicación presenta datos detallados comparables a escala internacional sobre los ingresos tributarios de 25 economías latinoamericanas y caribeñas, dos de las cuales son miembros de la OCDE. Su enfoque se basa en la metodología contrastada de la base de datos* "Revenue Statistics" *de la OCDE, que se ha convertido en un referente esencial para los países miembros de la OCDE. Se presentan también comparaciones con la media de medidas tributarias de la OCDE.*

En la presente publicación, el término "impuestos" se circunscribe exclusivamente a los pagos obligatorios sin contraprestación efectuados al gobierno general. Tal y como lo subraya la Guía de Interpretación de Revenue Statistics, los impuestos carecen de contraprestación en el sentido en que, normalmente, las prestaciones proporcionadas por el gobierno a los contribuyentes no guardan relación directa con los pagos realizados por estos. La metodología de la OCDE clasifica los impuestos según la base sobre la que recaen: renta, utilidades y ganancias del capital (categoría 1000); nómina (categoría 3000); propiedad (categoría 4000); bienes y servicios (categoría 5000); y otros impuestos (categoría 6000). Las contribuciones obligatorias a la seguridad social abonadas al gobierno general se tratan aquí como impuestos (categoría 2000). Para mayor detalle sobre el concepto de impuesto, su clasificación y su registro según el criterio de devengo, véase la Guía de interpretación que figura en el Anexo A.

La aplicación de la metodología de la OCDE a América Latina y el Caribe posibilita la comparación de sistemas tributarios a partir de una base coherente en la región, entre los países latinoamericanos, y con los países de la OCDE. Sin embargo, en algunas ocasiones, esta metodología difiere de la empleada por la CEPAL, el CIAT y el BID; en esos casos, las diferencias se han indicado en el texto y los cuadros, sea con una nota a pie de página, o en una línea adicional.

El informe ofrece un panorama general de las principales tendencias en materia tributaria en América Latina y en el Caribe. A tal efecto, examina los cambios registrados entre 1990 y 2016 en el nivel y la composición de la tributación, así como en la atribución de la recaudación tributaria a los diversos subsectores de gobierno.

Acknowledgements

Revenue Statistics in Latin America and the Caribbean has been jointly produced by the Organisation for Economic Co-operation and Development (OECD) Centre for Tax Policy and Administration, the OECD Development Centre, the United Nations Economic Commission for Latin America and the Caribbean (ECLAC), the Inter-American Center of Tax Administrations (CIAT) and the Inter-American Development Bank (IDB). The staff from these organisations with responsibility for producing the publication were: Juan Carlos Benítez and René Orozco of the OECD Development Centre under the supervision of the Director, Mario Pezzini, the Head of the Latin American and Caribbean Unit, Angel Melguizo, and the Coordinator of Revenue Statistics for the Development Centre, Alexander Pick; and Emmanuelle Modica of the OECD Centre for Tax Policy and Administration under the supervision of the Director, Pascal Saint-Amans, Deputy Director, Grace Perez-Navarro, the Head of the Tax Policy and Tax Statistics Division, David Bradbury and the Head of the Tax Data and Statistical Analysis Unit, Michelle Harding; Michael Hanni, Juan Pablo Jimenez, Ignacio Ruelas and Miguel Angel González of the Economic Development Division of UN-ECLAC under the supervision of the Director, Daniel Titelman; and Julio Alberto López from the CIAT Tax Studies and Research Directorate, under the supervision of Director Santiago Díaz de Sarralde; and Luis Fernando Corrales Lara under the supervision of the Principal Technical Leader in Fiscal Economics, Alberto Barreix of the IDB.

The authors would like to thank other staff at the OECD Development Centre and the Centre for Tax Policy and Administration for their invaluable support in completing and improving the 2018 edition of this publication. Elizabeth Nash and Delphine Grandrieux from the OECD Development Centre's Communications and Publications team and Ludivine Baudouin, statistical editor from the OECD Publications and Communications Directorate, ensured the production of the publication, in both paper and electronic form. Michael Sharratt from the OECD Centre for Tax Policy and Administration, Justina La and Antonela Leiva from the OECD Development Centre also assisted production.

Finally, the Centre for Tax Policy and Administration and the Development Centre are also very grateful to our colleagues working in national entities with whom we have consulted regularly. These institutions include the finance ministries and national tax agencies of Argentina, Barbados, Belize, Bolivia, Brazil, Chile, Colombia, Costa Rica, Cuba, Dominican Republic, Ecuador, El Salvador, Guatemala, Guyana, Honduras, Jamaica, Mexico, Nicaragua, Panama, Paraguay, Peru, Uruguay and Venezuela. In addition, CIAT would like to thank their Network of Tax Studies and Research. In particular, we are grateful to Jeferson Luis Bittencourt from the Ministério da Fazenda of Brazil; Jorge Richard Nuñez of Costa Rica´s Ministry of Finance; José Patricio Almeida from the Internal Revenue Service of Ecuador; Luis Alberto Canjura and Luis Antonio Campos from the Ministry of Finance of El Salvador and Gerardo Pérez from the Embassy of El Salvador in France; David Antonio Alvarado from the Secretary of Finances in Honduras; Andrea Gregory and Patricka Wiggan-Chambers from Jamaica´s Tax Administration and Customs agencies; Pedro Galeando from Paraguay´s Finance Ministry and María Victoria Magallanes from the Uruguayan General Taxation Directorate.

Agradecimientos

La publicación *Estadísticas tributarias en América Latina y el Caribe* ha sido elaborada conjuntamente por el Centro de Política y Administración Tributaria de la Organización para la Cooperación y el Desarrollo Económicos (OCDE), el Centro de Desarrollo de la OCDE, la Comisión Económica de las Naciones Unidas para América Latina y el Caribe (CEPAL), el Centro Interamericano de Administraciones Tributarias (CIAT) y el Banco Interamericano de Desarrollo (BID). Las personas de esas organizaciones responsables de redactar la presente publicación han sido: Juan Carlos Benítez y René Orozco del Centro de Desarrollo de la OCDE, bajo la supervisión del director, Mario Pezzini, del Jefe de la Unidad de América Latina y el Caribe Angel Melguizo y el coordinador de Estadísticas tributarias Alexander Pick; Emmanuelle Modica del Centro de Política y Administración Tributaria de la OCDE, bajo la supervisión del director, Pascal Saint-Amans, la sub-directora Grace Perez-Navarro y el Jefe de la División de Políticas y Estadísticas Tributarias, David Bradbury y la Jefe de la Unidad de Análisis de Datos Tributarios y Estadísticas, Michelle Harding; Michael Hanni, Juan Pablo Jiménez, Ignacio Ruelas y Miguel Angel González de la División de Desarrollo Económico de la CEPAL, bajo la supervisión del director Daniel Titelman; Julio Alberto López de la Dirección de Estudios e Investigaciones Tributarias del CIAT, bajo la supervisión del Director Santiago Díaz de Sarralde; y Luis Fernando Corrales Lara, bajo la supervisión del Líder Técnico Principal en Economia Fiscal del BID, Alberto Barreix.

Los autores desean agradecer a otros colegas del Centro de Desarrollo de la OCDE, del Centro de Política y Administración Tributaria de la OCDE por su invaluable contribución a la mejora y finalización de la edición 2018 de esta publicación. En particular, Elizabeth Nash y Delphine Grandrieux, del equipo de Comunicaciones y Publicaciones del Centro de Desarrollo de la OCDE, y Ludivine Baudouin, editora estadística del equipo de Publicaciones y Comunicaciones de la OCDE, que aseguraron la producción de la publicación, tanto fisica como en formato electrónico. Michael Sharratt del Centro de Política y Administración Tributaria, Justina La y Antonela Leiva del Centro de Desarrollo de la OCDE también colaboraron con la traducción y producción de esta publicación.

Por último, El Centro de Política y Administración Tributaria y el Centro de Desarrollo de la OCDE hacen partícipes de nuestro agradecimiento a nuestros colegas de entidades nacionales, a los que hemos consultado con frecuencia. Entre esas instituciones, se cuentan los ministerios de finanzas y las agencias tributarias nacionales de Argentina, Barbados, Belice, Bolivia, Brasil, Chile, Colombia, Costa Rica, Cuba, Ecuador, El Salvador, Guatemala, Honduras, México, Nicaragua, Panamá, Paraguay, Perú, República Dominicana, Uruguay y Venezuela. Asimismo, CIAT también desea agradecer La Red de Estudios e Investigaciones Tributarias. En particular, estamos agradecidos con Jeferson Luis Bittencourt del Ministério da Fazenda de Brasil; Jorge Richard Nuñez del Ministerio de Hacienda de Costa Rica; José Patricio Almeida del Servicio de Rentas Internas de Ecuador;

Luis Alberto Canjura y Luis Antonio Campos del Ministerio de Hacienda de El Salvador y Gerardo Pérez de la Embajada de El Salvador en Francia; David Antonio Alvarado de la Secretaría de Finanzas de Honduras; Andrea Gregory y Patricka Wiggan-Chambers de la Administración Tributaria y la Agencia de Aduanas de Jamaica; Pedro Galeando del Ministerio de Hacienda Paraguayo y a María Victoria Magallanes de la Dirección General de Impuestos de Uruguay.

Table of contents

Índice

LIST OF TABLES/LISTA DE CUADROS

Chapter 1/Capítulo 1
Tax revenue trends, 1990-2016/Tendencias tributarias, 1990-2016

Chapter 2/Capítulo 2
Special feature/Sección especial

Chapter 3/Capítulo 3

Special feature/Sección especial

Chapter 4/Capítulo 4

Tax levels and tax structures, 1990-2016/
Niveles impositivos y estructuras tributarias, 1990-2016

LIST OF FIGURES/LISTA DE GRÁFICOS

Chapter 2/Capítulo 2
Special feature/Sección especial

Chapter 3/Capítulo 3

Special feature/Sección especial

Executive summary

Revenue Statistics in Latin America and the Caribbean provides internationally comparable data on tax levels and tax structures for 25 Latin American and Caribbean (LAC) countries: Argentina, the Bahamas, Barbados, Belize, Bolivia, Brazil, Chile, Colombia, Costa Rica, Cuba, the Dominican Republic, Ecuador, El Salvador, Guatemala, Guyana, Honduras, Jamaica, Mexico, Nicaragua, Panama, Paraguay, Peru, Trinidad and Tobago, Uruguay and Venezuela.

In this publication, "taxes" are defined as compulsory, unrequited payments to general government. Taxes are "unrequited" in the sense that benefits provided by government to taxpayers are not normally in proportion to their payments. Compulsory social security contributions (SSCs) paid to general government are classified as taxes. More information on the tax classification and the basis of reporting is set out in the Interpretative Guide in Annex A.

Tax-to-GDP ratios in the LAC region

The tax-to-GDP ratio is measured as tax revenues, including SSCs paid to general government, as a proportion of GDP. In 2016, the average tax-to-GDP ratio in the LAC region was 22.7%. Tax-to-GDP ratios varied widely between countries, ranging from 12.6% in Guatemala to 41.7% in Cuba. Most countries' tax-to-GDP ratios were between 17% and 26%. All LAC countries had a tax-to-GDP ratio below the OECD average of 34.3% except for Cuba.

Between 2015 and 2016, the average LAC tax-to-GDP ratio decreased by 0.3 percentage points, whereas the OECD average tax-to-GDP ratio increased by 0.3 percentage points over the same period. As a result, the gap between the OECD and LAC average tax-to-GDP ratios increased from 10.9 percentage points in 2015 to 11.5 percentage points in 2016.

The decrease in the tax-to-GDP ratio in the LAC region reflects the overall economic environment in the Latin American region, where real GDP growth has been slowing since 2012, and where there has been an absence of structural tax reforms in most countries. This decrease is likely to reverse in future years with the improving economic climate in 2017 and 2018. In particular, commodity prices are recovering and the LAC region is expected to achieve GDP growth of between 2% and 2.5% in 2018.

Commodity prices continue to be an important driver for tax revenue trends in most LAC countries. The drop in the average LAC tax-to-GDP ratio in 2016 was driven by a decrease of 0.2 percentage points in revenue from income taxes. This decline was largely attributable to a decrease in corporate income tax (CIT) receipts of the same amount. The decrease in CIT revenue in Trinidad and Tobago by 8.1 percentage points – due to the collapse of the prices of hydrocarbons together with reduced production – has driven the decline in CIT revenue in the LAC region average.

Tax revenues declined in about half of the countries included in this report in 2016. Between 2015 and 2016, 13 countries reported an increase in their tax-to-GDP ratios while 12 recorded a decrease. This represents a large downturn compared with the previous year, when 21 countries experienced an increase between 2014 and 2015 and only four countries recorded a decrease. In 2016, the Bahamas, Belize and Cuba recorded the highest increases (of over 2 percentage points of GDP) while Trinidad and Tobago and Venezuela experienced the largest decreases (of over 6 percentage points).

Between 1990 and 2016, the average tax-to-GDP ratio in LAC countries increased almost continuously from 16.0% to 22.7%. The main contributors to the increase were VAT and taxes on income and profits. VAT revenue as a percentage of GDP in LAC countries increased by 3.8 percentage points between 1990 and 2016, reaching a similar level to the OECD average (6.3% and 6.7% respectively in 2015). Since 1990, nine out of 25 countries included in this report introduced a VAT and additional efforts have been made in most countries to improve the mobilisation of VAT revenue (through an increase of VAT rates, expansion of the taxable base and strengthening of the VAT collection system). Revenues from taxes on income and profits increased by 2.2 percentage points over the same period, mainly driven by the boom in commodity prices.

Tax structures in the LAC region

The average LAC tax mix shifted towards VAT and taxes on income and profits between 1990 and 2016. In 2016, the LAC average tax mix exhibits a relatively high share of revenue from taxes on goods and services, which make up about half of overall tax revenues compared with a third in the OECD (2015 figure). In 2016, there was a further shift in the LAC region towards VAT and away from taxes on income and profits. In 2016, VAT revenue was the principal component of revenue from taxes on goods and services, representing 58% of revenues from this category. At 29.3% of the total tax revenues, VAT is the biggest source of revenue on average in the LAC region, followed by revenues from taxes on income and profits (27.3%) and from other taxes on goods and services (21.2%).

On average, 43% of tax revenues in LAC countries came from taxes on income and profits and SSCs, compared with 60% in the OECD in 2015. Within taxes on income and profits, the revenue share of CIT was higher in the LAC region compared to the OECD, meaning that the revenue share of personal income tax (PIT) was low. In 2015, CIT and PIT accounted for 15.9% and 9.5% of total tax revenues respectively, compared with 8.9% and 24.4% in the OECD. Similarly, the average share of SSCs in total tax revenues was about 10 percentage points lower in the LAC region than the OECD average (16.0% compared with 25.8%).

VAT revenue ratios

In the LAC region, the VAT revenue ratio (VRR) in 2015 ranged from 32% in Mexico to 91% in Bolivia and Paraguay, with an average VRR of 58%. A VRR of 100% suggests no loss of VAT revenue due to exemptions, reduced rates, fraud, evasion or tax planning. The design of VAT partly explains this variation: Mexico has exemptions and a zero-rate for a large number of goods and services whereas Bolivia does not apply any reduced rates and has a broad VAT base. In comparison, the OECD average in 2014 was 56%.

Tax revenues by level of government

For the 15 LAC countries with available sub-national data in 2015, receipts by central governments accounted for more than two-thirds of tax revenues, whereas the corresponding figure for OECD countries was about 60%. The share of sub-national tax revenues as a proportion of total tax revenue was lower than 8% except in Argentina, Brazil and Colombia, where it reached more than 15% of total tax revenue (over 30% in Brazil). These figures reflect that sub-national governments in LAC countries tend to have a relatively narrow range of taxes under their jurisdiction compared to OECD countries.

Special features

The report contains two special features. The first identifies trends in the fiscal revenues from non-renewable natural resources for 12 commodity-exporting countries in the LAC region in 2016 and 2017. These revenues have continued to fall, from 3.5% of GDP in 2015 to 2.3% of GDP in 2016, thereby affecting revenues from CIT, taxes on goods and services, and non-tax revenues. This was driven by decreases in hydrocarbon-related revenues (from 5.0% of GDP in 2015 to 3.4% of GDP in 2016 in the ten countries that levied this type of revenues) as a result of exceptionally weak profits, a contraction in regional production and the gradual decline of crude oil prices. Although key commodity prices increased in 2017, hydrocarbon revenues are projected to dip slightly to 3.3% of GDP in 2017 and mining revenues are projected to remain steady at around 0.4% of GDP.

The second special feature examines income taxes in selected countries in Latin America over the last seven decades. Analysis of country data from 2015 demonstrates that the redistributive impact of PIT in Latin America remains weak compared to its impact in the European Union. This partly reflects a comparatively low PIT collection in the Latin American region. Several factors contribute to the low PIT collection in Latin America, including a gradual reduction of the progressivity of tax systems and relatively high tax evasion rates from the richest taxpayers. However, in recent years, Latin American countries have undertaken reforms to improve this performance, such as through higher tax rates and an expansion of the tax base.

Resumen ejecutivo

La publicación *Estadísticas tributarias en América Latina y el Caribe* proporciona datos internacionales comparables sobre los niveles y estructuras de recaudación tributaria para 25 países de América Latina y el Caribe (ALC): Argentina, Las Bahamas, Barbados, Belice, Bolivia, Brasil, Chile, Colombia, Costa Rica, Cuba, la República Dominicana, Ecuador, El Salvador, Guatemala, Guyana, Honduras, Jamaica, México, Nicaragua, Panamá, Paraguay, Perú, Uruguay, Trinidad y Tobago y Venezuela.

En esta publicación, el término "impuestos" se refiere a pagos obligatorios sin contraprestación efectuados al gobierno general. Los impuestos carecen de contraprestación en el sentido que normalmente los bienes y servicios brindados por los gobiernos a los contribuyentes no tienen relación directa con los pagos efectuados por estos últimos. Las contribuciones a la seguridad social (CSS) pagadas al gobierno general se clasifican como impuestos. Se proveen mayores detalles sobre la clasificación de los impuestos y su criterio de registro en la Guía en el Anexo A.

La recaudación tributaria sobre PIB en la región de ALC

La proporción de recaudación tributaria sobre PIB se mide como los ingresos tributarios, incluyendo CSS pagadas al gobierno general, como proporción del PIB. En 2016, el promedio de recaudación tributaria sobre PIB para la región de ALC fue del 22.7%. Los ratios varian significativamente entre los países, de 12.6% en Guatemala a 41.7% en Cuba. En la mayoría de países la recaudación sobre PIB oscila entre el 17% y el 26%. Todos los países de ALC, excepto Cuba, tuvieron una relación de ingresos tributarios con respecto al PIB inferior al promedio de 34.3% de la OCDE.

Entre 2015 y 2016, la recaudación tributaria como proporción del PIB en ALC disminuyó de 0.3 puntos porcentuales, mientras que el promedio de la OCDE aumentó en 0.3 puntos porcentuales durante el mismo período. Esto tuvo como resultado un aumento de la brecha entre los promedios de los ratios de la recaudación tributaria con respecto al PIB de la OCDE y de ALC, pasando de 10.9 puntos porcentuales en 2015 a 11.5 puntos porcentuales en 2016. La disminución en la relación impuestos con respecto al PIB en la región de ALC refleja el entorno económico general de la región de América Latina, donde el crecimiento real del PIB se ha desacelerado en la mayoría de los países desde 2012, y donde ha habido una ausencia de reformas tributarias estructurales. Es probable que esta disminución se revierta en los próximos años con la mejora del clima económico en 2017 y 2018. Los precios de las materias primas se están recuperando y se espera que la región ALC alcance un crecimiento del PIB de entre 2% y 2.5% en 2018.

Los precios de las materias primas siguen siendo un importante motor para las tendencias de los ingresos fiscales en la mayoría de los países de ALC. La caída en el promedio de los impuestos con respecto al PIB de ALC en 2016 fue impulsada por una disminución de 0.2 puntos porcentuales en los ingresos por impuestos a las ganancias. Esta disminución se explica por una disminución en los ingresos provenientes de los impuestos sobre la renta de empresas de la misma cantidad. La disminución de los ingresos provenientes de los impuestos a la renta a las sociedades en Trinidad y Tobago de 8.1 puntos porcentuales, debido al colapso de los precios de hidrocarburos junto a una menor producción, ha impulsado la disminución de los ingresos provenientes de los impuestos a la renta a las sociedades promedio de la región ALC.

En 2016, los ingresos tributarios como proporción del PIB disminuyeron en aproximadamente la mitad de los países analizados de este informe. Entre 2015 y 2016, 13 países reportaron un aumento en sus tasas de recaudación tributaria con respeto al PIB, mientras que 12 registraron una disminución. Esto representa un cambio en comparación con el año anterior, cuando 21 países experimentaron un aumento entre 2014 y 2015 y solo cuatro países registraron una disminución. En 2016, las Bahamas, Belice y Cuba registraron los mayores incrementos (más de 2 puntos porcentuales del PIB), mientras que Trinidad y Tobago y Venezuela experimentaron los mayores descensos (más de 6 puntos porcentuales).

Entre 1990 y 2016, los ingresos tributarios como proporción del PIB en los países de ALC aumentaron casi continuamente, pasando del 16.0% al 22.7%. Los principales contribuyentes al aumento fueron el IVA y los impuestos sobre la renta y utilidades. En los países de la región de ALC, los ingresos del IVA como porcentaje del PIB aumentaron de 3.8 puntos porcentuales entre 1990 y 2016, alcanzando un nivel similar al promedio de la OCDE (6.3% y 6.7% respectivamente en 2015). Desde 1990, nueve de los 25 países cubiertos en este informe introdujeron el IVA y se realizaron esfuerzos adicionales en la mayoría de los países para mejorar la movilización de los ingresos del IVA (a través del aumento de las tasas del IVA, la ampliación de la base imponible y el fortalecimiento del sistema de recaudación del IVA). Los ingresos provenientes de los impuestos sobre la renta, utilidades y las ganancias aumentaron de 2.2 puntos porcentuales durante el mismo período principalmente impulsados por el auge de los precios las materias primas.

Estructuras tributarias en la región

En ALC, la participación en la estructura tributaria (*tax mix*) del IVA y de los impuestos sobre la renta aumentó entre 1990 y 2016. En 2016, el promedio del *tax mix* de ALC tuvo una proporción relativamente alta de ingresos de impuestos sobre bienes y servicios, que representaron aproximadamente la mitad de los ingresos fiscales generales comparado con un tercio en la OCDE (cifra de 2015). En 2016, el aumento de la proporción del IVA y de los impuestos sobre la renta, utilidades y ganancias, se acentuó en la región de ALC. Los ingresos provenientes del IVA fueron el principal componente de los ingresos provenientes de las contribuciones tributarias sobre bienes y servicios, ya que representan el 58% de los ingresos de esta categoría. Con un 29.3% de los ingresos tributarios totales, el IVA es la mayor fuente de ingresos en promedio en la región ALC, seguido por los ingresos provenientes de los impuestos a la renta, utilidades y las ganancias (27.3%) y de otros impuestos sobre bienes y servicios (21.2%).

En promedio, en 2015 el 43% de todos los ingresos tributarios en los países ALC provino de impuestos sobre la renta y utilidades y las CSS, en comparación con 60% en la OCDE. La proporción del impuesto sobre la renta de sociedades, dentro de la categoría de impuestos sobre la renta y utilidades, fue más alta en la región ALC que en la OCDE, lo que significa que la participación del impuesto sobre la renta de personas físicas en los ingresos del impuesto a la renta fue baja. En 2015, la proporción de los ingresos del impuesto sobre la renta de sociedades y sobre personas físicas fue respectivamente de 15.9% y de 9.5% de la recaudación tributaria total comparada con 8.9% y 24.4% en la OCDE. De igual forma, las CSS como proporción de los ingresos tributarios totales fue más baja de 10 puntos porcentuales que el promedio de la OCDE (16.0% comparado con 25.8%).

Ratio de recaudación del IVA

En América Latina y el Caribe, el ratio de recaudación del IVA (VRR por sus siglas en inglés) en 2015 varió desde 32% en México hasta 91% en Bolivia y Paraguay, con un VRR promedio de 58%. Un VRR del 100% sugiere que no hay pérdidas en la recaudación del IVA debido a exenciones, tasas reducidas, fraude, evasión o planificación fiscal. El diseño del IVA explica parcialmente estas diferencias: México tiene exenciones y una tasa cero del IVA para un número importante de bienes y servicios, mientras que Bolivia no aplica tasas reducidas y tiene una base amplia. En comparación, el promedio de la OCDE en 2014 fue del 56%.

Ingresos tributarios por niveles de gobierno

Para los 15 países de ALC con datos subnacionales disponibles en 2015, los ingresos tributarios a nivel del gobierno central constituyen dos tercios o más de la recaudación tributaria total. El monto correspondiente en países de la OCDE es del 60%. Los ingresos tributarios subnacionales, como proporción de los ingresos totales, fueron menores al 8% excepto en Argentina, Brasil y Colombia, países en los cuales alcanzaron más del 15% de la recaudación tributaria total (30% en el caso de Brasil). Estas cifras demuestran que los gobiernos subnacionales en ALC tienden a contar con un escaso número de impuestos bajo su jurisdicción en comparación con lo observado en los países miembros de la OCDE.

Secciones especiales

El Informe contiene dos secciones especiales. La primera identifica tendencias en los ingresos fiscales provenientes de recursos naturales no renovables de 12 países exportadores de materias primas en la región de ALC en 2016 y 2017. Estos ingresos han seguido disminuyendo, pasando del 3.5% del PIB en 2015 al 2.3% del PIB en 2016, lo que también afecta los ingresos sobre la renta de empresas y utilidades, los impuestos sobre los bienes y servicios y los ingresos no tributarios. Esto fue impulsado por la disminución de los ingresos relacionados con los hidrocarburos (del 5.0% del PIB en 2015 al 3.4% del PIB en 2016, en los diez países que recaudaron este tipo de ingresos) como resultado de ganancias excepcionalmente bajas, de una contracción de la producción regional y de la disminución gradual de los precios del petróleo crudo. Aunque los precios de las materias primas claves han aumentado en 2017, se prevé que los ingresos provenientes de hidrocarburos bajen ligeramente hasta llegar al 3.3% del PIB en 2017 y se prevé que los ingresos provenientes de la minería se mantengan estables en torno al 0.4% del PIB.

La segunda sección especial examina los impuestos directos sobre la renta en países seleccionados de América Latina en las últimas siete décadas. El análisis de datos de países de 2015 demuestra que el impacto redistributivo de los impuestos sobre la renta de personas en América Latina sigue siendo débil en comparación con su impacto en la Unión Europea. Esto refleja en parte una recaudación tributaria de impuestos sobre la renta de personas físicas comparativamente baja en la región de América Latina. Varios factores contribuyen a la baja recaudación tributaria de los impuestos sobre la renta de personas físicas en América Latina, lo que incluye una reducción gradual de la progresividad de los sistemas impositivos y tasas de evasión fiscal relativamente altas de los contribuyentes más ricos. Sin embargo, en los últimos años, los países de América Latina han emprendido reformas para mejorar este sistema, tales como tasas más altas y una expansión de la base tributaria.

Chapter 1

Tax revenue trends, 1990-2016

Capítulo 1

Tendencias tributarias, 1990-2016

Chapter 1

Tax revenue trends, 1990-2016

Tax ratios

The tax-to-GDP ratio reflects the collection of taxation revenue by governments to finance public goods and services and to invest in infrastructure. Raising revenue through taxes is important to ensure a country's economic development (OECD, 2014). Taxation provides a predictable and sustainable source of government revenue, in contrast with development assistance and volatile non-tax revenues generated by commodities.

This report presents internationally comparable data on the tax revenues of 25 Latin American and Caribbean countries. This chapter discusses several key tax indicators in these countries: the tax-to-GDP ratio, the tax structure and the share of tax revenue by level of government. The discussion supplements detailed country information found in Chapter 5.

Tax ratios in 2016

The average tax-to-GDP ratio in Latin America and the Caribbean (LAC) amounted to 22.7%[1] in 2016 (Figure 1.1). The tax-to-GDP ratio is measured as tax revenues (including social security contributions paid to the general government) as a proportion of gross domestic product (GDP). Tax-to-GDP ratios varied widely in the region, ranging from 12.6% in Guatemala to 41.7% in Cuba. With the exception of Cuba, all LAC countries had a tax-to-GDP ratio below the OECD average[2] of 34.3%.

Figure 1.1. **Tax-to-GDP ratios (total tax revenue as % of GDP) in LAC countries, 2016**

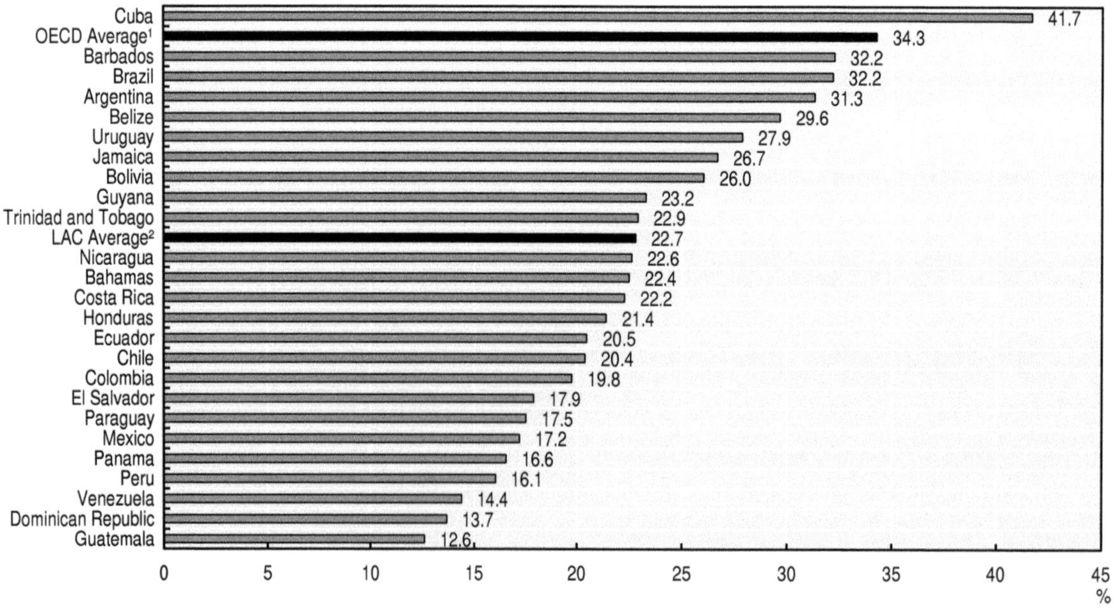

Note: The figures exclude local government revenues for Argentina (but include provincial revenues), the Bahamas, Barbados, Cuba, Dominican Republic, Honduras and Venezuela as the data are not available.

1. Represents OECD member countries. Chile and Mexico are also part of the OECD (35) group.
2. Represents the unweighted average of the 25 Latin American and Caribbean countries.

Source: OECD/ECLAC/CIAT/IDB (2018), Table 4.1.

StatLink http://dx.doi.org/10.1787/888933684599

The highest tax-to-GDP ratios in LAC were in Cuba (41.7%), Barbados (32.2%) and Brazil (32.2%). The countries with the lowest tax-to-GDP ratios were Guatemala (12.6%), the Dominican Republic (13.7%) and Venezuela (14.4%).

In 2016, the average LAC tax-to-GDP ratio was 0.3 percentage points lower than the previous year (Figure 1.2). This decline reflects in part the overall economic environment in the LAC region, and the absence of structural tax reforms in most countries. In Latin America, the average real GDP growth rate had been slowing down since 2012, and turned negative in 2015 and 2016 (OECD/CAF/ECLAC, forthcoming). This decrease is likely to reverse in future years with the improving economic climate in 2017 and 2018. In particular, commodity prices are recovering and the LAC region is expected to achieve GDP growth of between 2% and 2.5% in 2018.

There is a range of different situations across LAC countries with respect to changes in their tax-to-GDP ratios between 2015 and 2016. Thirteen countries - about half the countries covered by this report - reported an increase in their tax-to-GDP ratio in 2016 while 12 recorded a decrease. This represents a large downturn compared with the previous year, when 21 countries experienced an increase between 2014 and 2015 and only four countries recorded a decrease (Figure 1.2).

In 2016, three countries recorded increases in tax-to-GDP ratios of over 2 percentage points. Cuba reported the largest increase (of 3.1 percentage points), followed by the Bahamas and Belize, whose tax-to-GDP ratios increased by 2.6 and 2.4 percentage points respectively. The categories of tax that drove these increases varied for these three countries. Taxes on goods and services and taxes on income and profits were the main drivers of growth for Cuba. Revenue from taxes on goods and services (and in particular VAT) was the main contributor of the increase in the Bahamas (4.7 percentage points) while excise tax revenues accounted for the main increase in Belize (1.5 percentage points). In contrast, Venezuela and Trinidad and Tobago experienced the largest decreases (more than 6.4 percentage points) over the same period.

Significant tax reforms and the economic context have driven increases between 2015 and 2016 in the Bahamas, Belize and Cuba. The Bahamas introduced VAT in January 2015 and continued its successful implementation (IMF, 2017a), which led to a doubling of VAT revenues as a percentage of GDP compared to 2015. Belize introduced new measures on fuel taxes in March 2016 (IMF, 2017b). Higher tourist arrivals in Cuba in 2016 may have contributed to the increase in the tax-to-GDP ratio between 2015 and 2016.

The decreases in Trinidad and Tobago and Venezuela are mainly explained by the economic context. Trinidad and Tobago – as an oil revenue dependent country – levies the major part of its corporate income tax (CIT) revenues from hydrocarbons companies. The collapse of hydrocarbons prices together with reduced production were the main reasons for the large decrease in CIT revenues (8.1 percentage points) (see special feature Chapter 2). Venezuela has seen a decrease in its tax-to-GDP ratio of 6.4 percentage points. All tax revenue categories were affected with the largest decreases in revenues from taxes on goods and services (4.4 percentage points) and taxes in income and profits (1.4 percentage points). Hyperinflation, decreases in domestic consumption and imports, and decreases in oil production in Venezuela have affected the revenues from related taxes such CIT, VAT and excises.

The main driver of the decline in the average tax-to-GDP ratio of the LAC countries covered in this report in 2016 was a decrease in revenue from taxes on income and profits. The average annual decrease of this category between 2015 and 2016 was 0.2 percentage points followed by a decrease in revenues from other taxes on goods and services (mainly excises, customs and import duties) by 0.1 percentage points over the same period (Figure 1.3).

Figure 1.2. **Changes in tax-to-GDP ratios in LAC countries in 2014-15 and 2015-16 (percentage points of GDP)**

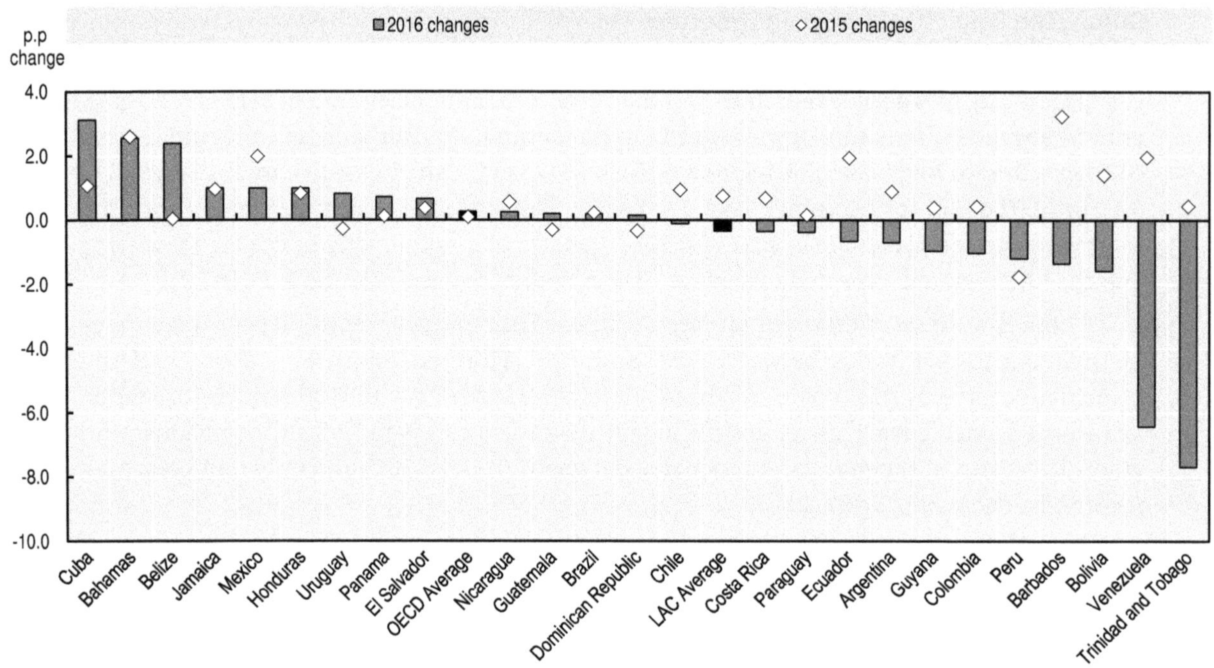

Source: Authors' calculations based on OECD/ECLAC/CIAT/IDB (2018), Table 4.1.

StatLink http://dx.doi.org/10.1787/888933684618

Figure 1.3. **2015-16 changes in tax-to-GDP ratios by type of tax categories (percentage points of GDP)**

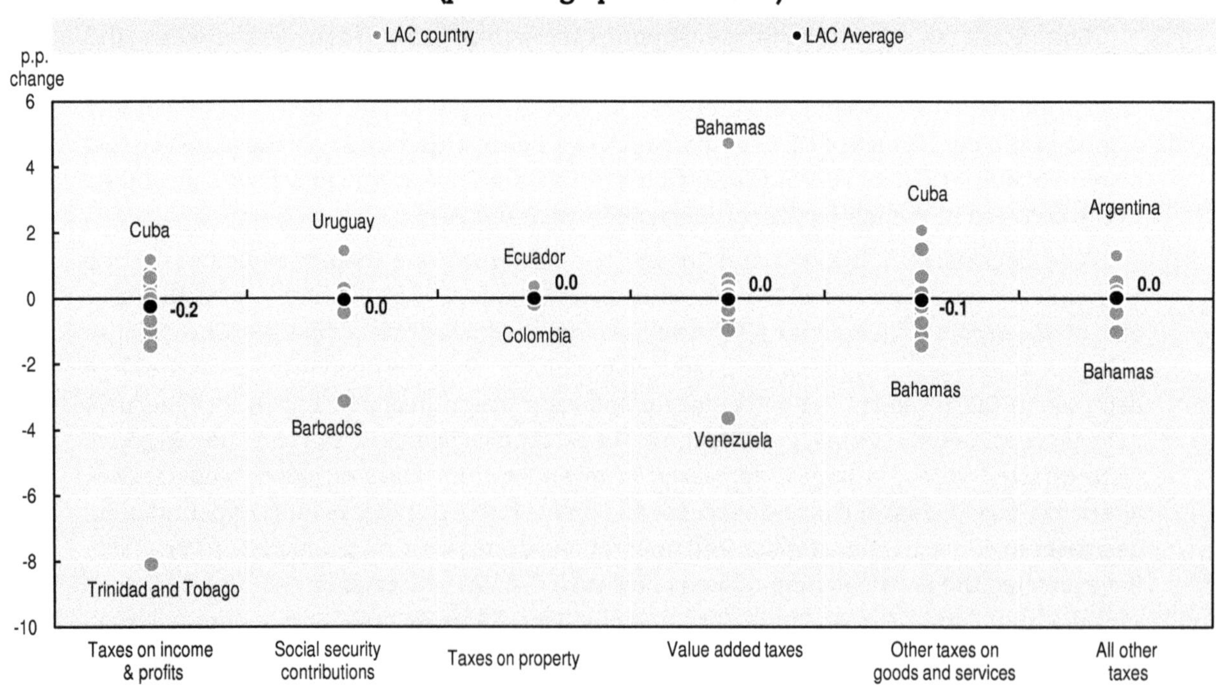

Source: Authors' calculations based on tables in Chapter 4 of OECD/ECLAC/CIAT/IDB (2018).

StatLink http://dx.doi.org/10.1787/888933684637

Changes in revenue from taxes on goods and services and from taxes on income and profits showed the largest variations among countries (Figure 1.4). Changes to revenue from taxes on goods and services and changes to revenue from taxes on income and profits were the main driver for changes in the tax-to-GDP ratios in eleven countries each.

Figure 1.4. **2015-16 changes in tax revenues by category of largest change in LAC countries, as % of GDP (percentage points)**

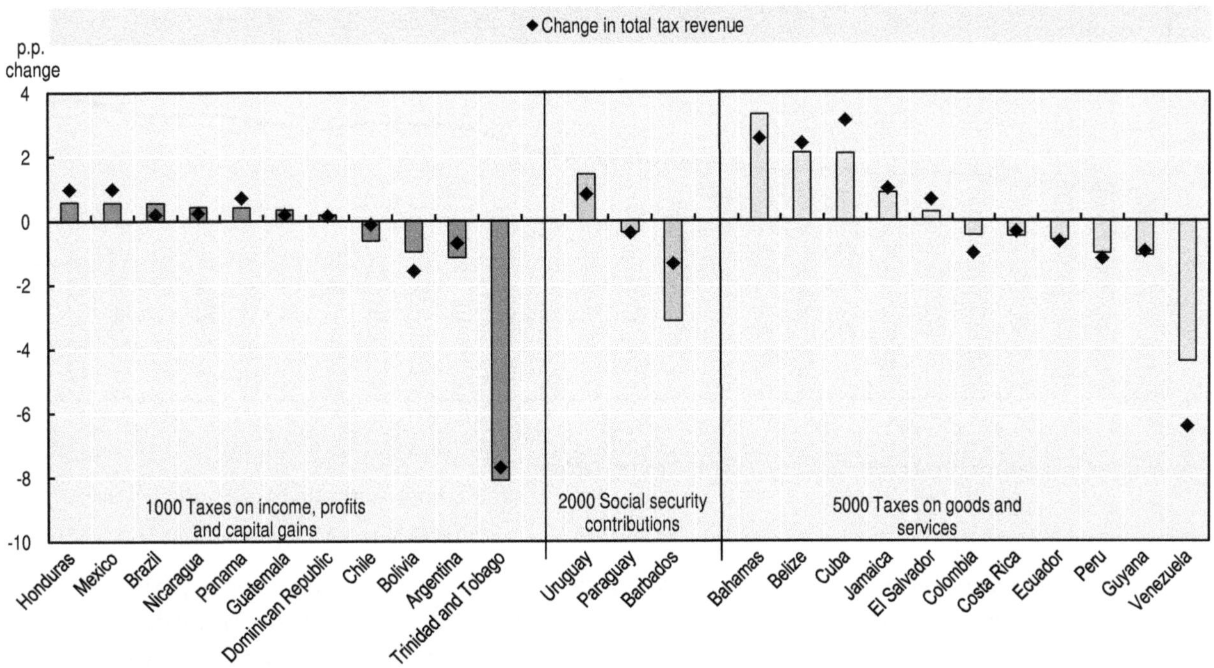

Note: The annual changes in revenue from taxes on goods and services for Venezuela should be interpreted with caution as they have been affected by the high rate of inflation.

Source: Authors' calculations based on tables in Chapter 4 of OECD/ECLAC/CIAT/IDB (2018).

StatLink *http://dx.doi.org/10.1787/888933684656*

Evolution of tax ratios since 2000

With the exception of 2008, 2009 and 2016, the average tax-to-GDP ratio in LAC countries rose continuously since 1990 (Figure 1.5). It increased by more than six percentage points, from 16.0% in 1990 to 22.7% in 2016. This growth reflects favourable macroeconomic conditions, changes in tax system design and strengthening of tax administrations. This trend contrasts with that in the OECD area, where the ratio has been relatively stable; the OECD tax-to-GDP ratio reached 34.3% in 2016, 2.3 percentage points above its level in 1990.

The difference between the LAC and OECD average tax-to-GDP ratios narrowed between 1990 and 2009, and then remained relatively steady (Figure 1.5). The gap in the average tax-to-GDP ratio between LAC and the OECD decreased from 15.9 percentage points in 1990 to about 11.5 percentage points in 2009 and stayed stable at that level until 2014. The gap reached its lowest point in 2015 at 10.9 percentage points and increased in 2016, attaining its pre-2015 level of 11.5 percentage points.

Figure 1.5. **Tax-to-GDP ratios, LAC and OECD averages, 1990-2016**

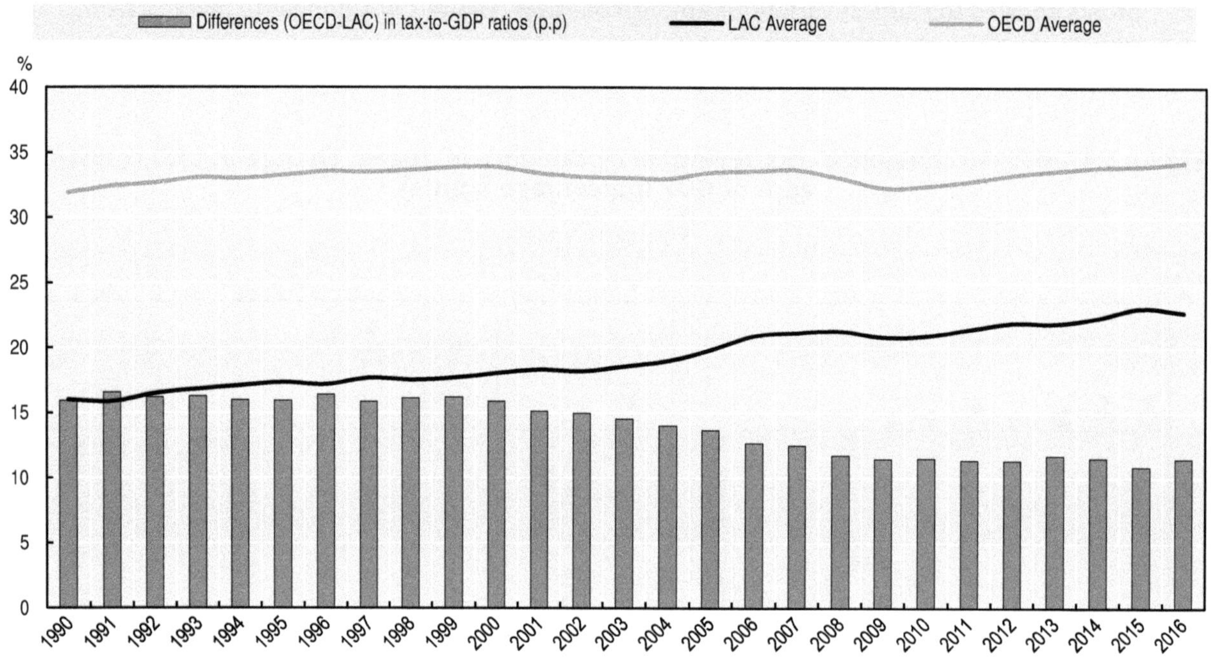

Source: Authors' calculations based on OECD/ECLAC/CIAT/IDB (2018), Table 4.1.

StatLink http://dx.doi.org/10.1787/888933684675

Tax-to-GDP ratios in LAC countries increased in the early 1990s after a period of macroeconomic instability during the previous decade. During the 1980s, countries ran large fiscal imbalances and at the same time some resorted to alternative ways of financing expenditure (borrowing or printing money). This caused rapid inflation across the region, which eroded the real value of countries' tax revenues. Reforms in the 1990s focused on price stability, trade liberalisation and fiscal discipline. Most LAC governments both reduced spending and implemented policies aimed at increasing tax revenues; budget management and fiscal balances improved considerably. Policy makers implemented reforms to tax policy and administration to reinforce tax systems against inflationary episodes by shortening collection lags and indexing tax liabilities.

Significant efforts were undertaken to modernise tax administrations and tax systems over the last two decades. New information technology systems were implemented, the structures of tax administrations were rationalised, tax collection systems became more efficient and staff gained in expertise (IDB, 2013). In addition, some LAC countries simplified their tax systems by broadening their tax bases. They reduced the number of exemptions and tax incentives granted to certain activities and sectors principally to incentivise foreign investment. Tax reforms included the introduction or development of simplified regimes for small taxpayers and the taxation of property based on presumed incomes. Since 2010, various income tax reforms were introduced in LAC countries, which have included rate increases and broadening of the tax base. These measures had a positive effect on revenues in a number of countries thanks to the expansion of taxation to all labour and capital income, including dividends (e.g. Colombia, Dominican Republic, Guatemala, El Salvador, Nicaragua, Panama and Peru). Reforms have also included the establishment of minimum taxes, taxes on financial transactions and the gradual reduction in the real income level taxed at the top marginal rate, as well as additional controls on transfer prices (ECLAC, 2013).

The introduction of VAT was the most significant tax reform in LAC in the 1980s and early 1990s. After this period, reforms relating to VAT have concentrated on increasing the tax rate and widening the tax base. Between 1990 and 2016, revenue from VAT as a percentage of GDP more than doubled for LAC countries on average, from 2.4% of GDP in 1990 to 6.2% in 2016 (Figure 1.6). Over the same period, revenues from other taxes on goods and services (excises, customs and import duties) in LAC decreased as a percentage of GDP. This decline was associated with trade liberalisation, as a result of which LAC countries changed the way they taxed imported and exported goods as well as specific goods and services. These changes included a reduction of import tariffs, narrowing the base of products and services subject to excises (for example by focusing on products such as alcoholic beverages, fuel and tobacco) and the elimination of taxes on exports. One important exception is Argentina, where taxes on exports were re-established in 2002; however, the government established in December 2015 has abolished export taxes on almost all agricultural products (World Grain, 2016 and IMF, 2016).

Figure 1.6. **Revenue from taxes on income and profits, VAT and other taxes on goods and services as a percentage of GDP in the LAC region, 1990-2016**

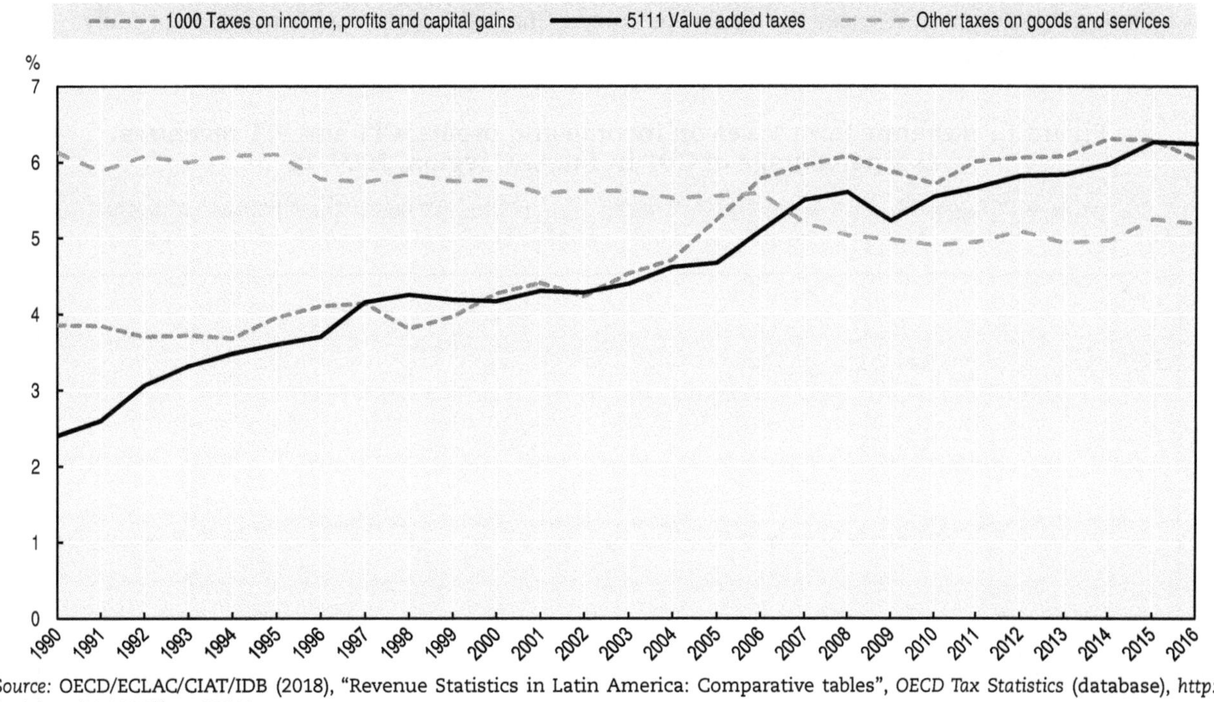

Source: OECD/ECLAC/CIAT/IDB (2018), "Revenue Statistics in Latin America: Comparative tables", *OECD Tax Statistics* (database), *http://dx.doi.org/10.1787/data-00641-en.*

StatLink *http://dx.doi.org/10.1787/888933684694*

The main contributor to growth in the average tax-to-GDP ratio in LAC was VAT between 1990 and 2002 and both VAT and taxes on income and profits between 2002 and 2016. VAT revenue as a percentage of GDP increased by 1.9 percentage points between 1990 and 2002 whereas revenue from taxes on income and profits increased by 0.4 percentage points over the period (Figure 1.6). Revenue from taxes on income and profits as a percentage of GDP caught up with VAT revenues between 2002 and 2016, increasing by

1.8 percentage points over this period. One of the elements that contributed to this result was the recovery of LAC economic activity and the commodity price boom following 2003 that increased CIT revenue (Barreix et al, 2017). Changes in revenue from taxes on goods and services, taxes on income and profits and social security contributions have contributed to the recovery in the LAC tax-to-GDP average following the global financial crisis.

Revenue from taxes on incomes and profits as a percentage of GDP has increased since 2007 with an interruption during the global financial crisis and a further decrease in 2016 of 0.2 percentage points (Figure 1.7). The increase in revenues from taxes on income and profits was driven by CIT. CIT revenues grew faster than personal income tax (PIT) revenues since 1990, reflecting a significant increase in tax revenues from companies in the natural resources sector (ECLAC, 2014). It was also a result of tax policies that reduced tax incentives in free-trade zones, the introduction of minimum taxes for corporations, reforms in international taxation and agreements between countries to fight tax evasion.

Revenues from CIT have reflected the economic cycle in the region. Between 2008 and 2010, CIT revenue as a percentage of GDP in the LAC region dropped by 0.3 percentage points (Figure 1.7). It stayed steady at 3.8% between 2011 and 2014 then recorded a decrease of 0.2 percentage points in 2015, which was followed by a further drop of 0.2 percentage points in 2016. The decrease in 2016 can partly be explained by the drop in CIT revenue from non-renewable commodities (see the special feature in Chapter II of this publication), especially in Trinidad and Tobago.

Figure 1.7. **Revenue from taxes on income and profits, CIT and PIT revenues as a percentage of GDP in the LAC region, 2007-16**

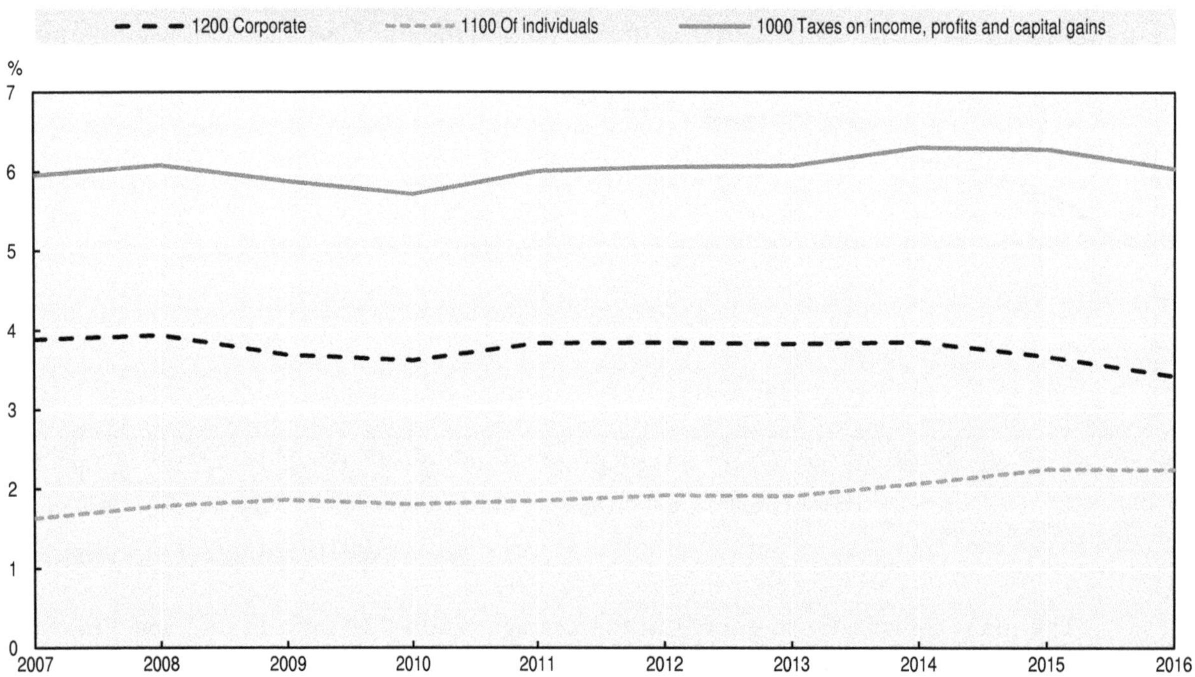

Note: Ecuador, Nicaragua and Venezuela are excluded from the LAC averages for CIT revenue as a percentage of GDP and PIT revenue as a percentage of GDP as more than a third of their revenue from taxes on income and profits cannot be allocated to CIT revenue (1200) or PIT revenue (1100).

Source: OECD/ECLAC/CIAT/IDB (2018), "Revenue Statistics in Latin America: Comparative tables", *OECD Tax Statistics* (database), *http://dx.doi.org/10.1787/data-00641-en.*

StatLink *http://dx.doi.org/10.1787/888933684713*

By contrast, PIT as a percentage of GDP in LAC has been increasing steadily since 2011. It reached its highest-ever level in 2015 (2.2% of GDP) and stayed at this level in 2016. From 2012, growth in PIT revenues as a percentage of GDP was higher than that of CIT revenues, partially due to the subdued economic environment and lower commodity prices. The LAC averages for CIT and PIT revenue as a percentage of GDP should be interpreted with caution: Ecuador, Nicaragua and Venezuela are excluded from the calculation as more than a third of their revenue from taxes on income and profits cannot be allocated to either corporate income tax (1200) or to personal income tax (1100).

Changes in income tax revenues - in particular from CIT - as a percentage of GDP between 2015 and 2016 show large variations across countries (Figure 1.8). Although the LAC average for revenue from taxes on income and profits has decreased by 0.2 percentage points between 2015 and 2016, revenue from this tax category only declined in five countries over this period: Argentina, Bolivia, Chile, Colombia and Trinidad and Tobago. In 2016, Trinidad and Tobago recorded a decrease of 7.7 percentage points in revenue from taxes on income and profits as a percentage of GDP, due to a substantial decline in CIT receipts (8.1 percentage points). This decline was caused by the fall of hydrocarbons prices and a reduced production. In the other four countries, revenues from taxes on income and profits decreased by between 0.3 and 1.1 percentage points.

Figure 1.8. **2015-16 changes in revenue from taxes on income and profits, CIT and PIT as a percentage of GDP in LAC countries**

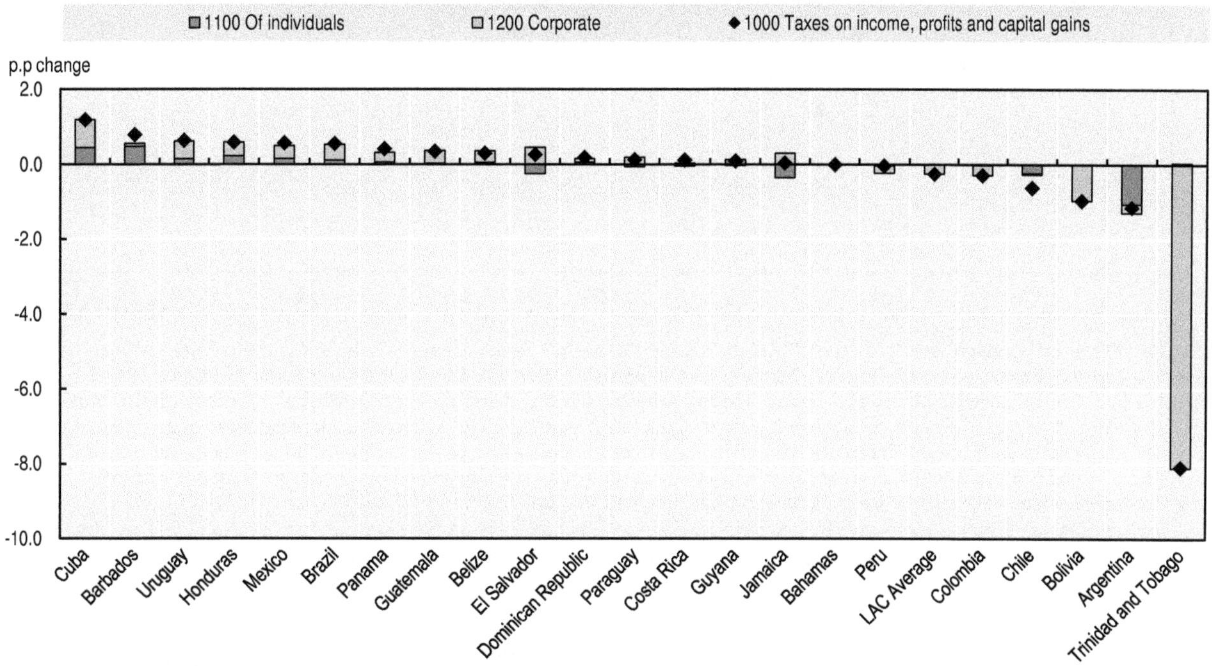

Note: Ecuador, Nicaragua and Venezuela are excluded as more than a third of their revenue from taxes on income and profits cannot be allocated to CIT revenue (1200) or PIT revenue (1100).

Source: OECD/ECLAC/CIAT/IDB (2018), "Revenue Statistics in Latin America: Comparative tables", *OECD Tax Statistics* (database), *http://dx.doi.org/10.1787/data-00641-en*.

StatLink http://dx.doi.org/10.1787/888933684732

Factors influencing tax-to-GDP ratios

Differences between the LAC and OECD average tax-to-GDP ratios are consistent with the tendency for higher income countries to have higher tax-to-GDP ratios. The data implies a positive correlation between GDP per capita (a measure of the level of income of a country or its level of development) and tax-to-GDP ratios (Figure 1.9). In general, OECD countries have higher average incomes than the LAC countries and collect higher tax revenues. Argentina, Barbados, Brazil, Trinidad and Tobago and Uruguay show similar tax-to-GDP ratios and levels of income to some OECD countries. Empirical analysis suggests that stronger tax collection, accompanied by better institutions, education and skill and economic diversification allowed many OECD countries to evade the *middle-income trap*, in contrast to LAC (Melguizo et al., 2017).

Figure 1.9. **GDP per capita in PPP (USD) and tax-to-GDP ratios for countries in the LAC region, the OECD, and a group of African and Asian countries, 2015**

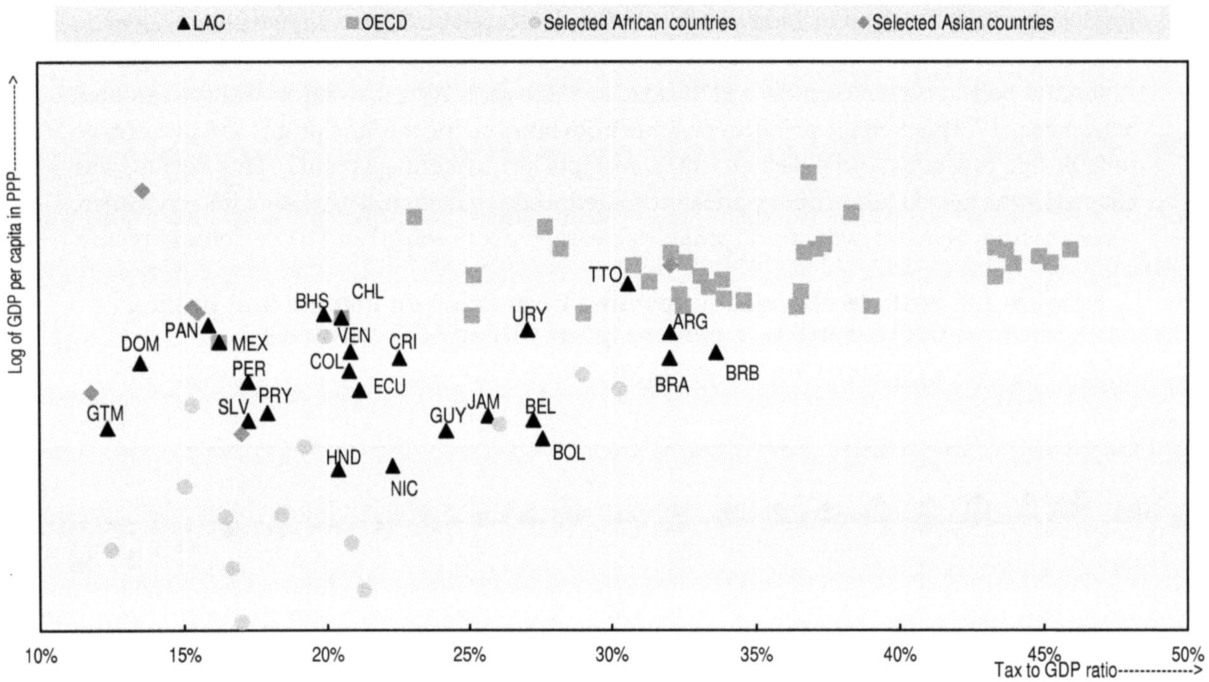

Note: The year of comparison is 2015 as the 2016 data for the tax-to-GDP ratios are not available for the selected African and Asian countries. The purchasing-power-parity (PPP) between two countries is the rate at which the currency of one country needs to be converted into that of a second country to ensure that a given amount of the first country's currency will purchase the same volume of goods and services in the second country as it does in the first. The implied PPP conversion rate is expressed as national currency per current international dollar. An international dollar has the same purchasing power as the US dollar has in the United States. An international dollar is a hypothetical currency that is used as a means of translating and comparing costs from one country to the other using a common reference point, the US dollar (Definitions derived from IMF, 2016b and WHO, 2015).

Source: IMF (2017c), *World Economic Outlook*, October 2017, International Monetary Fund for figures of GDP per capita. Tax-to-GDP ratios are sourced from the regional Revenue Statistics publications (*www.oecd.org/tax/tax-policy/revenue-statistics-comparable-tax-revenue-data.htm*).

StatLink http://dx.doi.org/10.1787/888933684751

Tax-to-GDP ratios are influenced by economic and structural factors. GDP per capita, openness to trade, the extent of the informal economy, natural resource endowments and the importance of agriculture in the economy are all factors that can influence tax-to-GDP ratios. Socio-demographic determinants are also key, such as the level of education or the level of female participation in the labour force. The power of tax administrations, the levels of corruption and tax morale (or willingness of people to pay taxes) are also strongly linked to the level of tax revenues (OECD, 2014). Finally, geographic location and historical factors can also influence tax-to-GDP ratios: for example, landlocked countries are less able to impose taxes on goods and services at the port of entry than coastal countries. In addition, international factors, including the tax policies of other countries, can impact tax-to-GDP ratios.

The extent of state participation in financing social security is another important factor underlying the level of tax ratios in the LAC region. From the 1980s onwards, many LAC countries have privatised healthcare, pension and social security to greater or lesser degrees. Chile, El Salvador and Mexico for example have shifted their public pension provision to a mostly private, fully funded system. In Colombia and Peru, the private and public programmes compete and employees opt for one of them (ECLAC, 2010; OECD/IDB/CIAT, 2015; OECD/IDB/World Bank (2014). On the other hand, Argentina, Brazil and Uruguay follow a model where the public and private systems are complementary. In these three countries substantial reforms were undertaken to extend the coverage of social security systems to those previously excluded. This has also been instrumental in the increase of tax revenues (ECLAC, 2014).

Informality hinders tax revenue collected in LAC countries as it significantly reduces the taxable base (OECD, 2008 and Gómez Sabaini et al. 2010). In Latin America[3] the rate of informality[4] was around 55% on average in 2013 (Bosch et al., 2013) and has remained relatively stable since. Bolivia, Guatemala, Honduras, Nicaragua, Paraguay and Peru have the highest rates of informality exceeding 65% and Brazil, Chile, Costa Rica and Uruguay have rates of informality of less than 40%. These levels were higher in the 1990s, prompting governments to introduce simplified tax systems for small taxpayers that were to some extent successful in integrating informal workers into the formal sector. These simplified systems varied greatly in success depending on the type of taxpayers covered and the actual capacity of tax administrations (ECLAC, 2014; OECD/IDB/CIAT, 2016).

Tax structures

The tax structure (defined as the share of major tax types in total tax revenue) depicts the composition of tax revenues by different tax types. This is a second important indicator, since different taxes have different economic and social effects. Across the countries in this publication, the composition of taxes varies widely, reflecting their different policy choices, economic structures and conditions, tax administration capabilities and historical factors.

Evolution of tax structures

The average LAC tax mix shifted towards value added taxes and taxes on income and profits between 1990 and 2016, with a slight shift toward value-added taxes and away from taxes on income and profits between 2015 and 2016. The revenue share of VAT taxes reached 29.3% of total tax revenues in 2016, corresponding to an increase of 13.0 percentage points between 1990 and 2016, whereas the revenue share of other taxes on goods and services (excises, customs and import duties) declined by 17.3 percentage points over the same period (Figure 1.10). The share of revenues from taxes from incomes and profits grew by 4.5 percentage points (from 22.8% to 27.3% of total tax revenues) between 1990 and 2016, mainly as a result of much higher collection levels in the late 2000s. The share of social security contributions in total tax revenues increased by 3.3 percentage points over the last 26 years, reaching 15.9% in 2016.

These two opposing trends reflect the growing importance of VAT and the diminishing role of other taxes on goods and services. VAT was adopted early by the economies of the region (twelve[5] countries had implemented it by 1980). From the early 1990s, VAT has represented a growing source of revenue for LAC countries and has been consolidated by the implementation of cumulative adjustments to the tax base and statutory rates, as well as the strengthening of tax administrations. The reforms also focused on the simplification of tax systems, with most countries reducing the number of items with zero or reduced rates, moving towards single-rate VAT schemes in several cases.

Figure 1.10. **Average tax structure in the LAC region, 1990 and 2016**

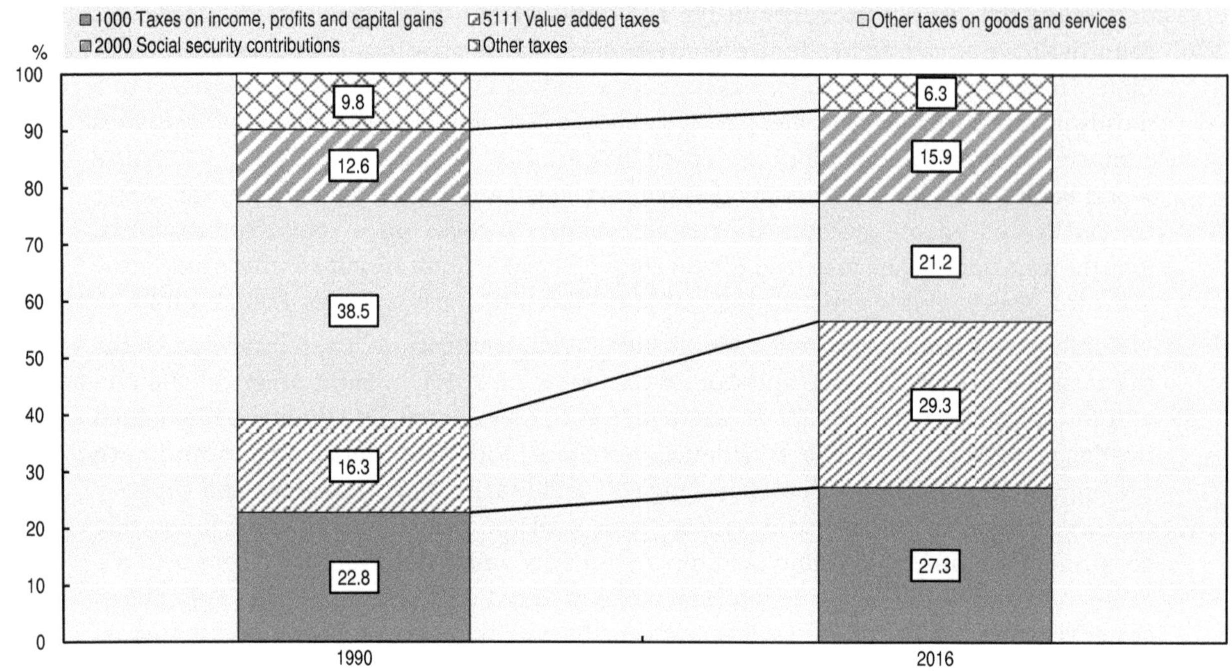

Source: Authors' calculations based on tables in Chapter 4 of OECD/ECLAC/CIAT/IDB (2018).

StatLink http://dx.doi.org/10.1787/888933684770

Figure 1.11. **Average tax structure in the LAC region, 1990-2016**

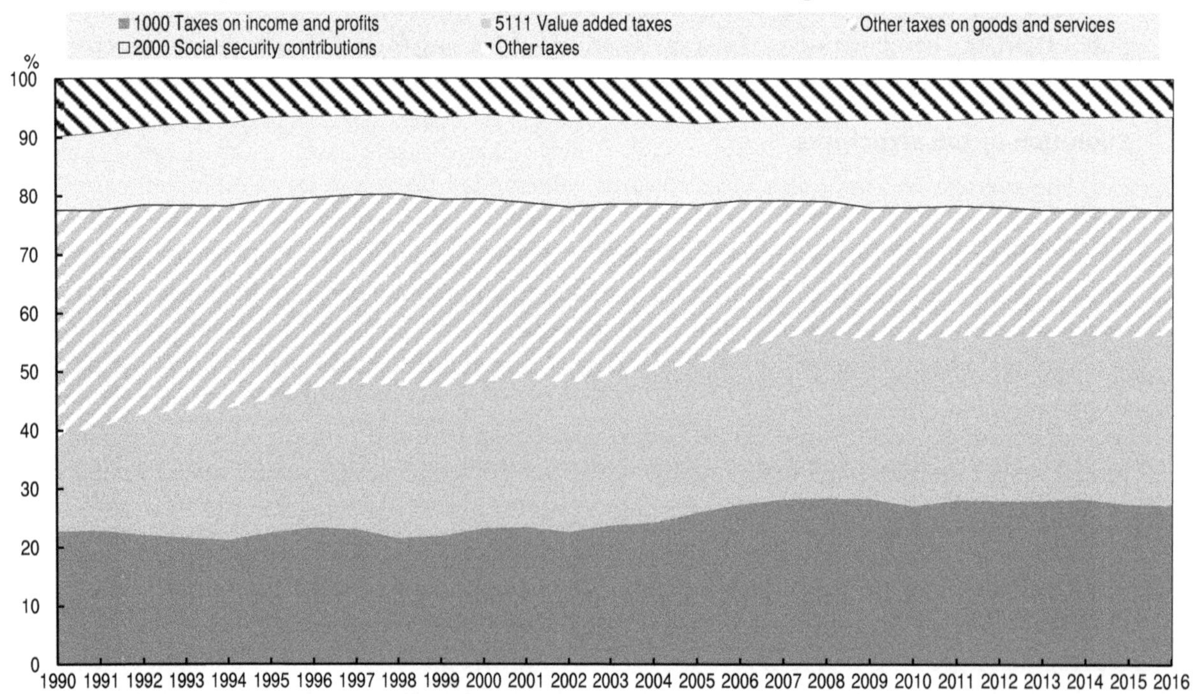

Source: OECD/ECLAC/CIAT/IDB (2018), "Revenue Statistics in Latin America: Comparative tables", *OECD Tax Statistics* (database), *http://dx.doi.org/10.1787/data-00641-en.*

StatLink http://dx.doi.org/10.1787/888933684789

In the LAC region, revenue from taxes on goods and services is the largest source of revenues as a share of total tax revenues and represents half of total taxation. Revenues from taxes on goods and services are the main source of revenue for all LAC countries except for Trinidad and Tobago, Mexico and Panama. Revenue from taxes on income and profits represented the largest share for Mexico and Trinidad and Tobago whereas revenue from social security contributions is the most important source of tax revenue for Panama. Trinidad and Tobago sourced nearly 50% of its tax revenue from taxes on income and profits in 2016 (Figure 1.12).

Figure 1.12. **Tax structure in LAC countries, 2016**

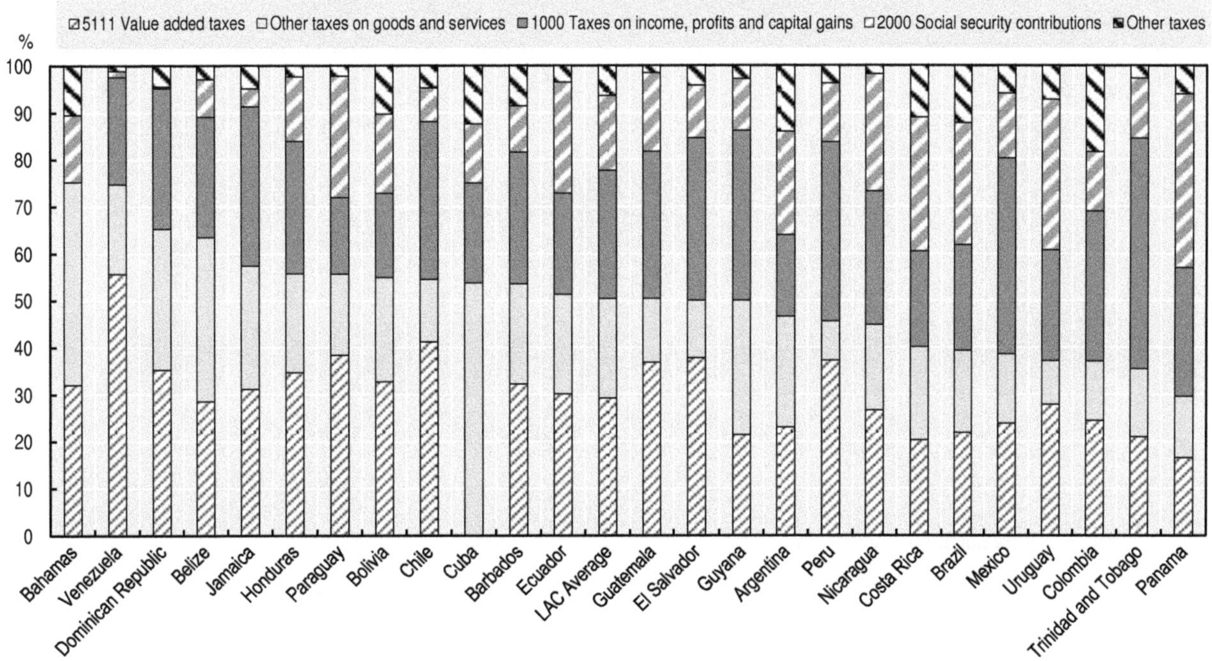

Note: The revenue shares of the different tax categories for Venezuela should be interpreted with caution as they have been affected by the high rate of inflation.

Source: Authors' calculations based on tables in Chapter 4 of OECD/ECLAC/CIAT/IDB (2018).

StatLink http://dx.doi.org/10.1787/888933684808

VAT revenue and VAT revenue ratio

On average in 2016, 29.3% of total tax revenues in LAC countries came from VAT. However there is wide heterogeneity within the region. The contribution of VAT to total revenues ranges from 16.6% in Panama to 55.8% in Venezuela. As a percentage of GDP, Barbados, Belize and Bolivia levied the highest amount of VAT revenue (at 10.4% in Barbados and 8.5% in both Bolivia and Belize). There is no VAT system operating in Cuba. The wide variation across countries is also the result of differences in the design of VAT: rates and tax bases differ significantly across the region. For example, Mexico does not apply VAT on food, medicines or numerous other products, resulting in a relatively narrow tax base. ECLAC (2014) suggests that the tax loss from these particular exemptions ranges between 1.1% and 2.5% of GDP.

VAT revenue ratio

The VAT revenue ratio (VRR) measure is calculated for selected[6] LAC countries. OECD (2016) explains that "the VRR measures the difference between the VAT revenue actually collected and what would theoretically be raised if VAT was applied at the standard rate to the entire potential tax base in a "pure" VAT regime and all revenue was collected". This section shows the VRR levels in Latin American and the Caribbean countries in 2015 and analyses three countries in greater depth: Bolivia, Paraguay and Panama.

Figure 1.13. **Revenue from VAT as % of total tax revenue and as % of GDP in LAC countries, 2016**

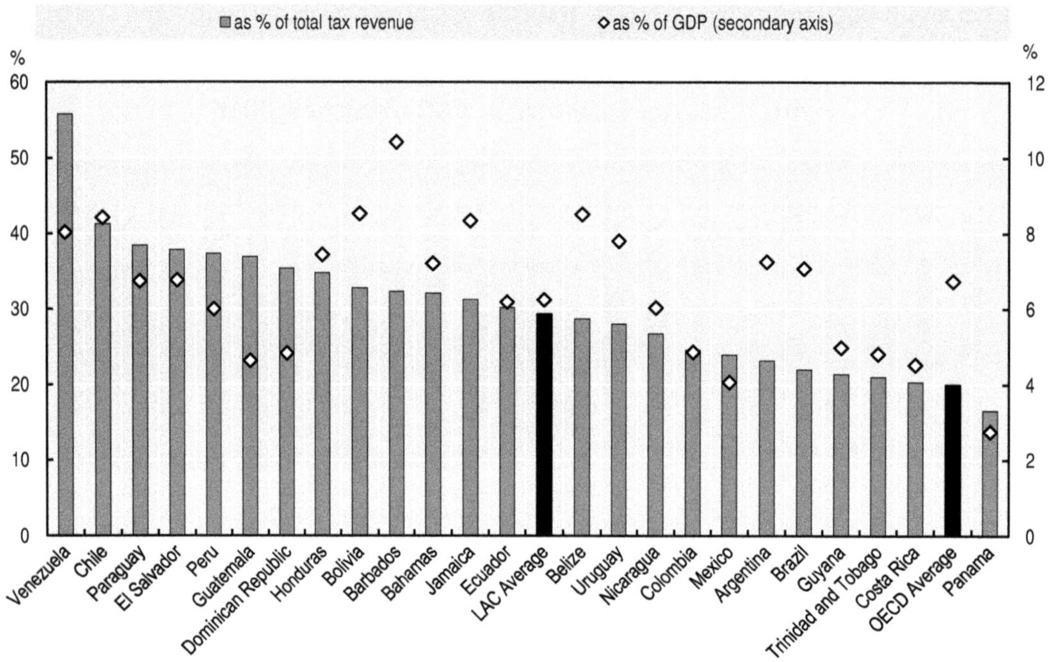

Note: Cuba does not operate a VAT system.

Source: Authors' calculations based on OECD/ECLAC/CIAT/IDB (2018), Table 4.10.

StatLink http://dx.doi.org/10.1787/888933684827

There was a wide disparity of VRRs in Latin American and the Caribbean countries in 2015 (Figure 1.14) with an average VRR of 58%. In comparison, the OECD average in 2014 was 56%. In 2015, Mexico and Guyana had the lowest VRR ratios at 32% and 38% respectively whereas Bolivia and Paraguay had the highest (both at 91%). OECD (2016) explains that several factors may explain the low VRR in Mexico, such as the scope of VAT exemptions, the application of a domestic zero rate to numerous goods and services, a reduced VAT rate (11%) at border areas as well as a low compliance rate. A VAT reform was implemented in January 2014 that replaced the reduced rate of 11% with the standard rate of 16%. The reform also removed the zero rate on hotels and related services to foreigners, now taxed at the standard rate, and adjusted the regime of inward processing arrangements (maquiladores) to reduce the risk of fraud. The VRR in Mexico increased by 0.4 percentage points between 2013 and 2014.

Guyana introduced VAT later than other countries. Since its introduction in 2007, Guyana has seen a reduction in VAT compliance which may be due to a deterioration of the compliance management (Schlotterbeck, 2017). Between 2007 and 2016, VAT revenue as percentage of GDP declined from 6.1% to 5.0%. Zero-rated supplies in Guyana accounted for 52.5% of taxable supplies.

The Bahamas and the Dominican Republic have relatively low VAT revenue ratios. The Bahamas introduced VAT in 2015 at 7.5% (with no reduced rates), one of the lowest rates in the LAC region where the average standard VAT rate stands at 13.7%. In the Bahamas, the

VAT system is a broad-based VAT with a limited number of exemptions, so the VRR is likely to increase as the system becomes more established. The amount of VAT revenue raised in 2016 was three times more than the amount in 2015 and the VRR in 2016 is also likely to be higher.

Figure 1.14. **VAT revenue ratio (VRR) in LAC countries, 2015**

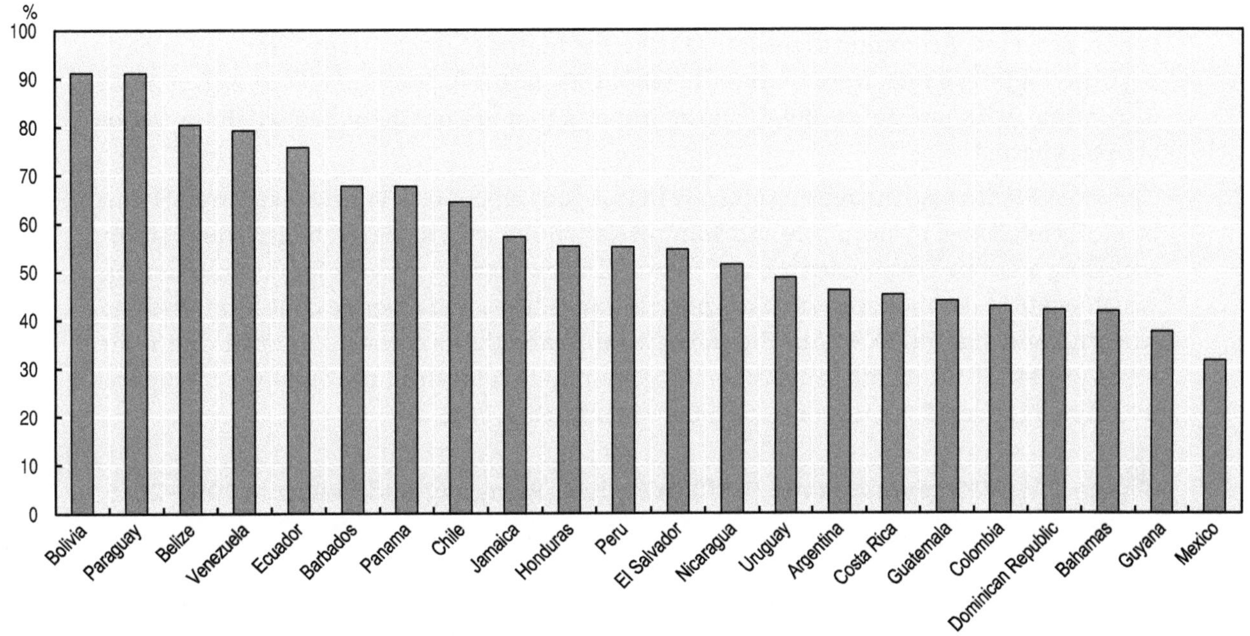

Note: Brazil, Cuba and Trinidad and Tobago are excluded. Brazil operates a multiple-rate system with tax levied at different rates for each sub-national level. Some underlying information was not available for Trinidad and Tobago since 2009; Cuba did not operate a VAT system in 2015.2014 data for Panama as the final consumption expenditure data are not available for 2015.

Source: The VAT rates are sourced from the CIAT, Trading Economics and Deloitte websites, the final expenditure consumption figures from the United Nations Statistics Division website and VAT revenues from the country tables in Chapter 5.

StatLink http://dx.doi.org/10.1787/888933684846

Bolivia's VRR exceeded 90% in 2015. A VRR of 90% suggests very low loss of VAT revenue as a consequence of exemptions, reduced rates, fraud, evasion or tax planning. However, the high level of VRR may be partly explained by other factors. First, Bolivia applies a standard VAT rate of 13% to the final price of a good or service (including VAT) leading to a VAT effective rate (14.94%) higher than the standard rate. The VRR measure is reduced from 91% to 79% in 2015 when the VAT effective rate is used rather than the standard rate. Secondly, Bolivia applies VAT to a wide range of goods and products and does not have reduced rates (Ernst & Young, 2014). High levels of informality can also affect VRR ratios, although it is unclear if this is the case in Bolivia.

The VRR in Bolivia has been increasing since 1990 although this growth was interrupted between 1997 and 2000. A public sector reform adopted in 2000 that included strengthening of the inspection, control process and procedures for VAT refunds may have contributed to the recovery in 2000. According to Zuleta (2008) "the changes in processes and procedures for VAT refunds have had a significant positive impact during the institutional reform". This was evident in a decrease in VAT evasion of 13 percentage points from 42%[7] in 2001 to 29% in 2004 and a decrease in VAT refunds both as a percentage of exports and of VAT revenue. Zuleta (2008) suggests that these results indicate that corruption in the process of VAT refunds had been reduced. Over the same period, the VRR improved by 13 percentage points from 51% to 64%. Between 2004 and 2013, the VRR continued to increase (except during the financial crisis period). However, little evidence is available to explain this; measurement of VAT non-compliance over time or of the impact of informality on VAT may provide more conclusive findings.

Along with Bolivia, Paraguay had the highest VRR among the selected group of LAC countries in 2015 at 91%. It is very unlikely that only 9% of Paraguay's potential VAT revenue is not recovered. According to the IMF (2010), the "high VAT productivity"[8] reflects in large part the high revenues from re-exports (about 2% of GDP). Much of the re-export trade is informal, with payments of VAT on the imports that are not deducted when the goods are re-exported.

The VRR has been increasing steadily in Paraguay since 2002. The increase in 2004 may be partly explained by tax policy and administration reforms. A comprehensive tax reform, including measures to broaden the VAT base and a new legal framework for tax and customs which enabled the modernisation of controls, procedures and revenue collection systems, was implemented in 2004 with the objective to make the tax system simpler and more efficient (IMF, 2010). At the same time, the government addressed the endemic corruption which had hindered tax revenue collection (Franks et al, 2005).

Figure 1.15. **VAT revenue ratio (VRR) in Bolivia, Paraguay and Panama, 1990-2015**

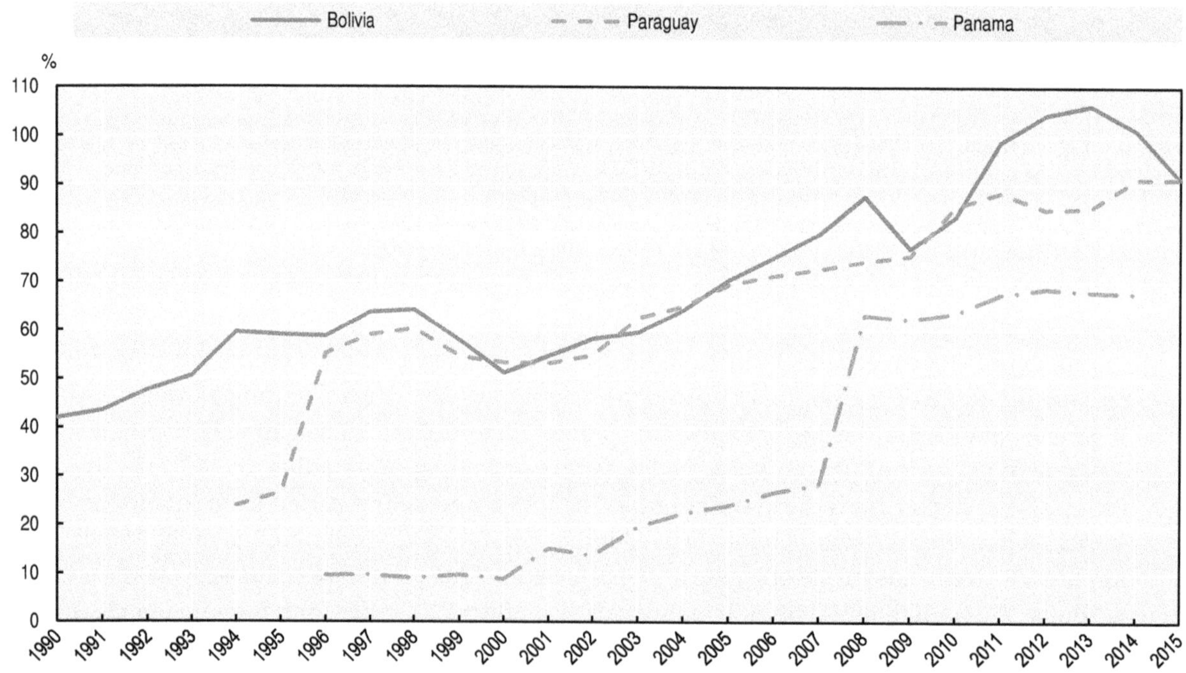

Note: Final consumption expenditure figures to compile the VRR were not available for Panama prior to 1996 and for Paraguay in 2015. There is no VRR between 1990 and 1993 for Paraguay as VAT was implemented in mid-1993.

Source: VAT rates are sourced from the CIAT, Trading Economics and Deloitte websites, the final expenditure consumption figures from the United Nations Statistics Division website and VAT revenues from the country tables in Chapter 5.

StatLink *http://dx.doi.org/10.1787/888933684865*

In 2014, Panama had a VRR at 68% and has had a VRR above 60% since 2008. Panama recorded a substantial rise in the VRR in one year, from 28% in 2007 to 63% to 2008. This followed an extensive audit in 2008 by the Direction General of Taxes to end VAT revenue loss from businesses failing to report VAT charged to customers to the tax authorities. Following this audit, in the first quarter of 2008, VAT revenue receipts increased by 22% compared to the whole year in 2007 (The Panama Investor Blog, 2008). As a percentage of GDP, VAT revenue more than doubled between 2007 and 2008 from 1% to 2.1%.

Taxes on income and profits and social security contributions

In 2016, the share of revenues from taxes on incomes and profits amounted to 27.3% of total tax revenues in the LAC region. Corporate income revenue represented the main share of revenues from taxes on incomes and profits at 15.4% whereas PIT revenues amounted to 9.7% of total tax revenue (Figure 1.16).[9] The LAC average tax structure shifted towards a greater revenue share from PIT and a lower revenue share from CIT.

Figure 1.16. **Average tax structure in the LAC region, 2007 and 2016**

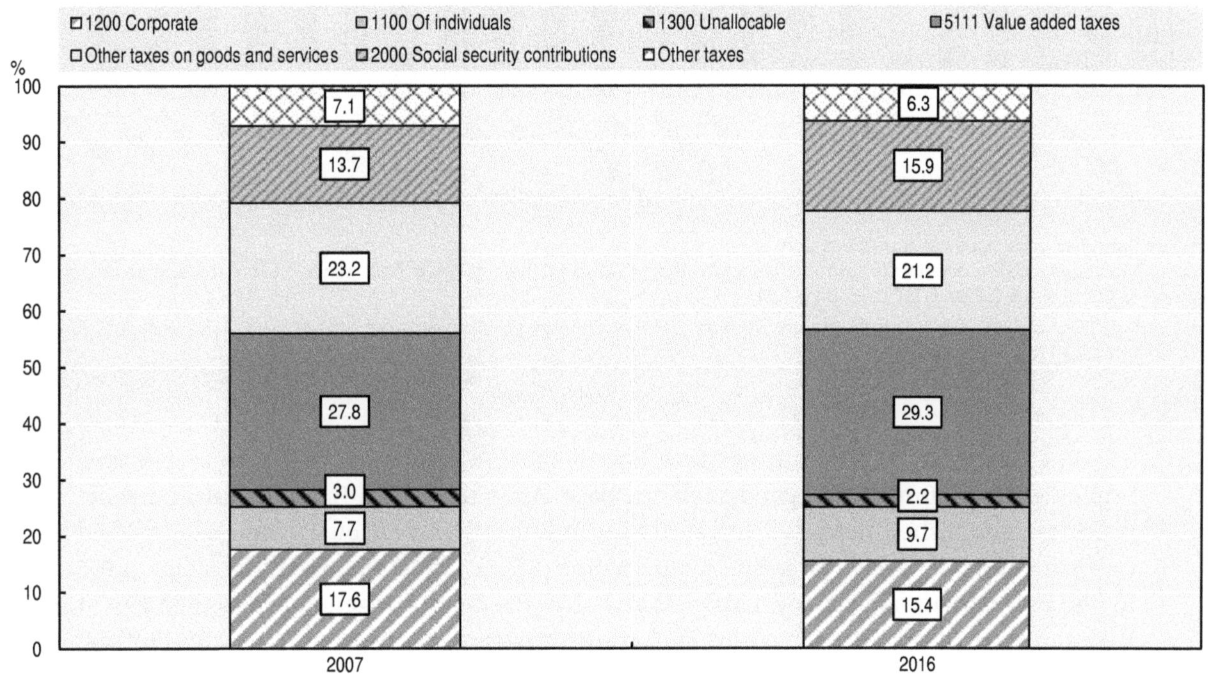

Note: The LAC corporate income tax revenue and personal income tax revenue as a percentage of GDP should be interpreted with caution as Ecuador, Nicaragua and Venezuela are excluded in the calculation.

For these countries, more than a third of their revenue from taxes on income and profits cannot be allocated to corporate income tax revenue (1200) or personal income tax revenue (1100). Excluding these countries, a small proportion from revenue from taxes on income and profits remains unallocable.

Source: OECD/ECLAC/CIAT/IDB (2018), "Revenue Statistics in Latin America: Comparative tables", *OECD Tax Statistics* (database), *http://dx.doi.org/10.1787/data-00641-en.*

StatLink *http://dx.doi.org/10.1787/888933684884*

There is a wide heterogeneity in the LAC region. In 2016, Colombia had the highest share of CIT revenue with 24.6% of total tax revenues being generated from this source and Barbados had the lowest share at 8.2%. The Bahamas is the only country covered in this report that does not have an income tax (corporate or personal) regime. As a percentage of GDP, CIT revenues were highest in Cuba (6.3%) and Trinidad and Tobago (5.4%).

Figure 1.17. **Revenue from CIT as % of total tax revenue and as % of GDP in some LAC countries, 2016**

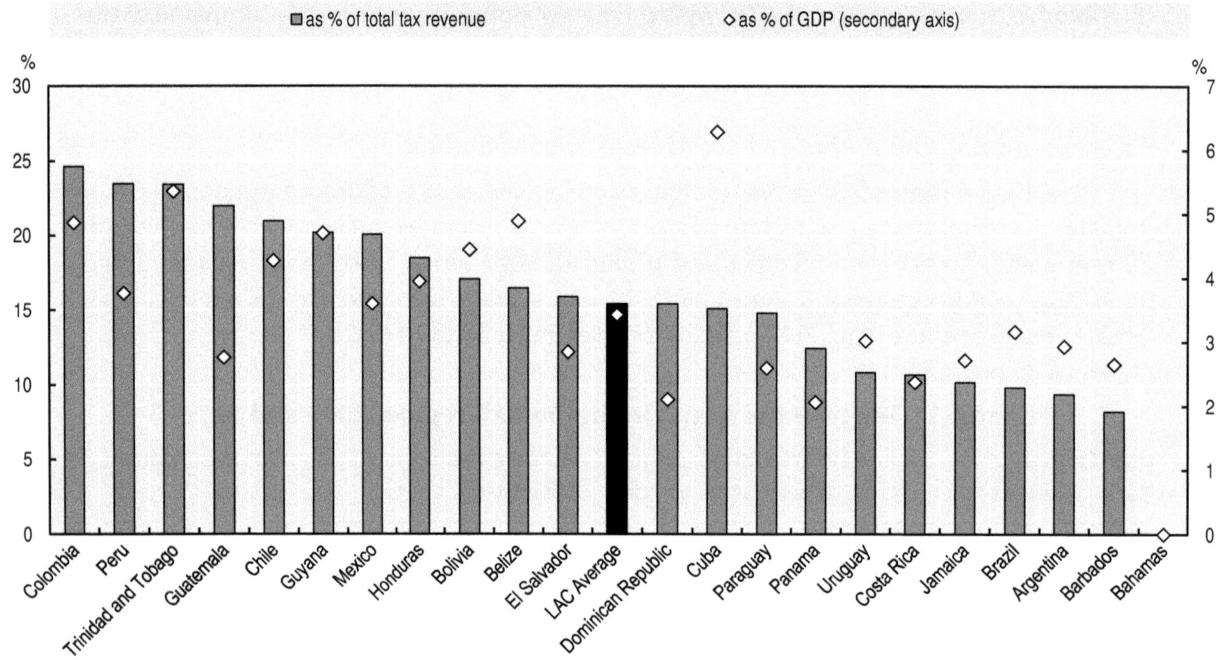

Note: The Bahamas does not operate a CIT system.
Ecuador, Nicaragua and Venezuela are excluded as more than a third of their revenue from taxes on income and profits cannot be allocated to *CIT* revenue (1200) or *PIT* revenue (1100).

Source: OECD/ECLAC/CIAT/IDB (2018), "Revenue Statistics in Latin America: Comparative tables", *OECD Tax Statistics* (database), *http://dx.doi.org/10.1787/data-00641-en.*

StatLink *http://dx.doi.org/10.1787/888933684903*

The share of PIT revenue remains low in the LAC region despite some countries implementing reforms to expand their tax base. After the global financial crisis, several countries established flat rates on capital income that had previously been exempt and implemented progressive rates on labour income (ECLAC, 2014). However, the share of PIT in LAC countries remains modest: more than half of the countries generate less than 10% of their tax revenue from this source. In 2016, the PIT revenue shares range from 0.8% (Bolivia) to 22.8% (Trinidad and Tobago) of total tax revenue excluding the Bahamas which does not operate a PIT system (Figure 1.18). Previous OECD studies (OECD, 2008 and Daude et al., 2010) suggest that the share of labour income in GDP is low in LAC countries. There are also relatively few taxpayers, given the concentration of income earners at low income levels: only 10% of the population in Latin America are registered taxpayers (IDB, 2013). Moreover, several studies (Barreix et al, 2017, IDB, 2015, ECLAC, 2014, ECLAC, 2010 and Gómez Sabaini et al., 2010) mention additional factors: a limited taxable base that is comprised primarily of wages, as tax privileges are granted to returns on capital, and high levels of evasion. IDB (2013) explains that "about half of potential revenue from PIT is lost through evasion" in Latin American countries. A thorough analysis and discussion of PIT revenue in selected Latin American countries are included in the special feature in Chapter 3 of this publication.

The share of social security contributions in total tax revenues increased by 3.3 percentage points since 1990, reaching 15.9% in 2016 (Figure 1.16). This rise reflects two major factors working simultaneously. First, rising personal incomes have had an upward impact on the amounts collected. Second, the full or partial privatisation of social security that occurred in many countries in the region has offset the first factor. In countries with public or mixed social security schemes (including Argentina, Brazil, Costa Rica, Mexico, Panama, Paraguay and Uruguay), social security contributions still have a significant weight (more than 20% of total tax revenues). In Argentina, the figures reflect the introduction of funded schemes in 1994 and their subsequent nationalisation in 2008. Meanwhile, in Colombia and Peru, where private and public programmes compete, social security contributions amount to around 12% of total tax revenue.

Figure 1.18. **Revenue from PIT as % of total tax revenue and as % of GDP in some LAC countries, 2016**

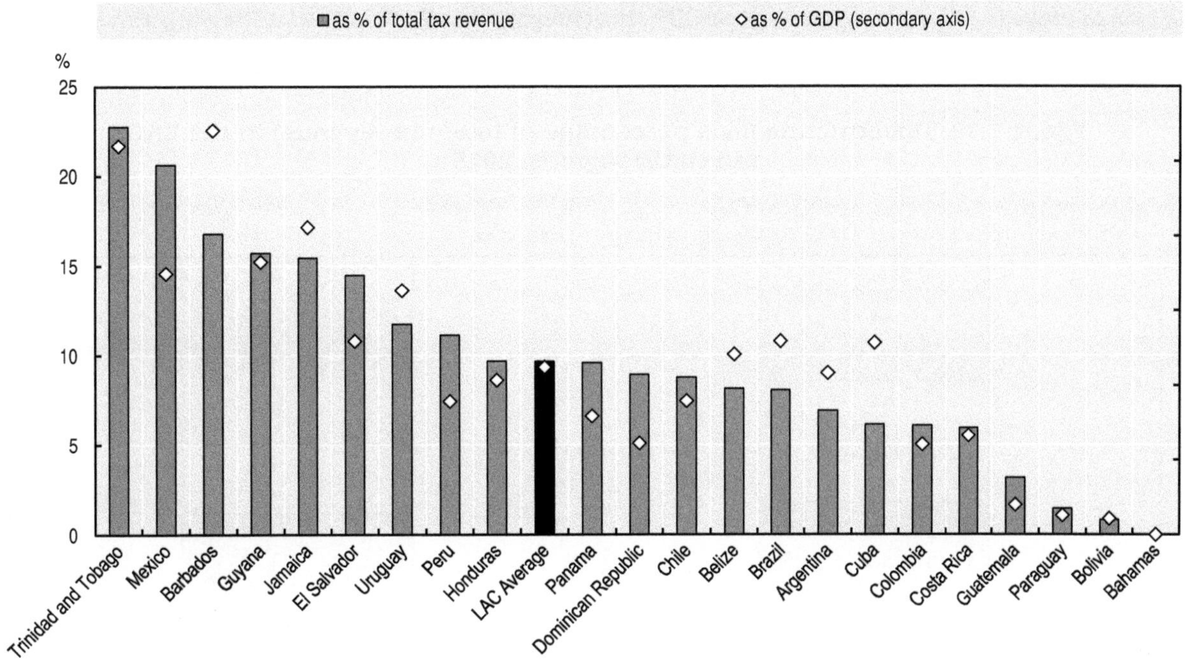

Note: The Bahamas does not operate a PIT system.

Ecuador, Nicaragua and Venezuela are excluded as more than a third of their revenue from taxes on income and profits cannot be allocated to *CIT* revenue (1200) or *PIT* revenue (1100).

Source: Authors' calculations based on tables in Chapter 4 of OECD/ECLAC/CIAT/IDB (2018).

StatLink http://dx.doi.org/10.1787/888933684922

Comparison with the OECD

Relative to the OECD average, the LAC average tax mix exhibits a relatively low direct-tax take, counterbalanced by high indirect-tax receipts (Figure 1.19). In particular, LAC countries on average rely heavily on taxes on goods and services, which make up more than half of overall tax revenues compared with around one-third in OECD economies on average. However, as a percentage of GDP, revenue from taxes on goods and services stood at a similar level for the LAC and OECD averages, at 11.5% and 10.9% respectively in 2015.[10] The level of VAT revenue as a percentage of GDP was also very similar, at 6.3% for the LAC average and 6.7% for the OECD.

On average, less than 44% of tax revenues in LAC countries came from a combination of taxes on income and profits and social security contributions, compared with 60% in the OECD region in 2015. As a percentage of GDP, these two categories amounted to 10% in the LAC region, which represented half of the amount levied in OECD countries on average (20.5%).

The share of social security contributions in total tax revenues was about 10 percentage points lower in the LAC average than in the OECD average (16.0% compared with 25.8%). The tendency towards private provision of social security in many countries in the LAC region explains some of the differences for this category. The contribution of taxes on income and profits to total tax revenues in LAC was 6.7 percentage points lower than the OECD average (27.4% versus 34.1%).

CIT revenue as a share of total tax revenue was 15.9% in the LAC region compared to 8.9% in the OECD area. This corresponds to respectively 3.7% and 2.8% as a percentage of GDP (Figures 1.19 and 1.20). Revenue from PIT contributed 24.4% of the total taxes, on average, in the OECD area in 2015, while this category had a considerably lower share in LAC countries on average (9.5%). As a percentage of GDP, this category was 2.2% in the LAC region, almost four times lower than the average in the OECD (8.4%).

Figure 1.19. **Tax structure (as a percentage of total tax revenue) in the LAC and OECD regions, 2015**

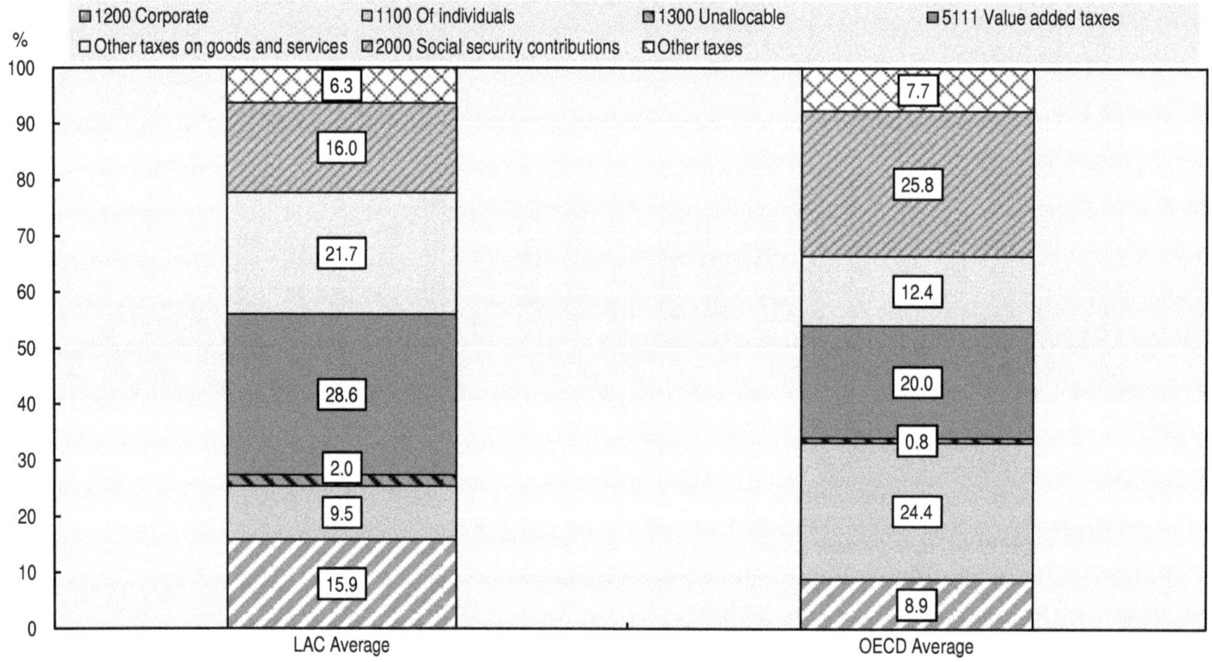

Note: The year of comparison is 2015 as the 2016 data for the OECD average are not available.
Nicaragua and Venezuela are excluded from the LAC averages for CIT and PIT revenue as more than a third of their revenue from taxes on income and profits cannot be allocated to CIT revenue (1200) or PIT revenue (1100).

Source: OECD/ECLAC/CIAT/IDB (2018), "Revenue Statistics in Latin America: Comparative tables", *OECD Tax Statistics* (database), *http://dx.doi.org/10.1787/data-00641-en.*

StatLink *http://dx.doi.org/10.1787/888933684941*

VAT represents a higher proportion of total tax revenues in the LAC region than in the OECD. In 2015, this category accounted for 28.6% of the total tax revenues in the LAC region whereas the corresponding figure in the OECD area was 20.0%. Similarly the revenue share of taxes on other goods and services was higher in LAC countries, amounting to 21.7% on average compared to 12.4% in the OECD area.

Figure 1.20. **Tax structure (as a percentage of GDP) in the LAC and OECD regions, 2015**

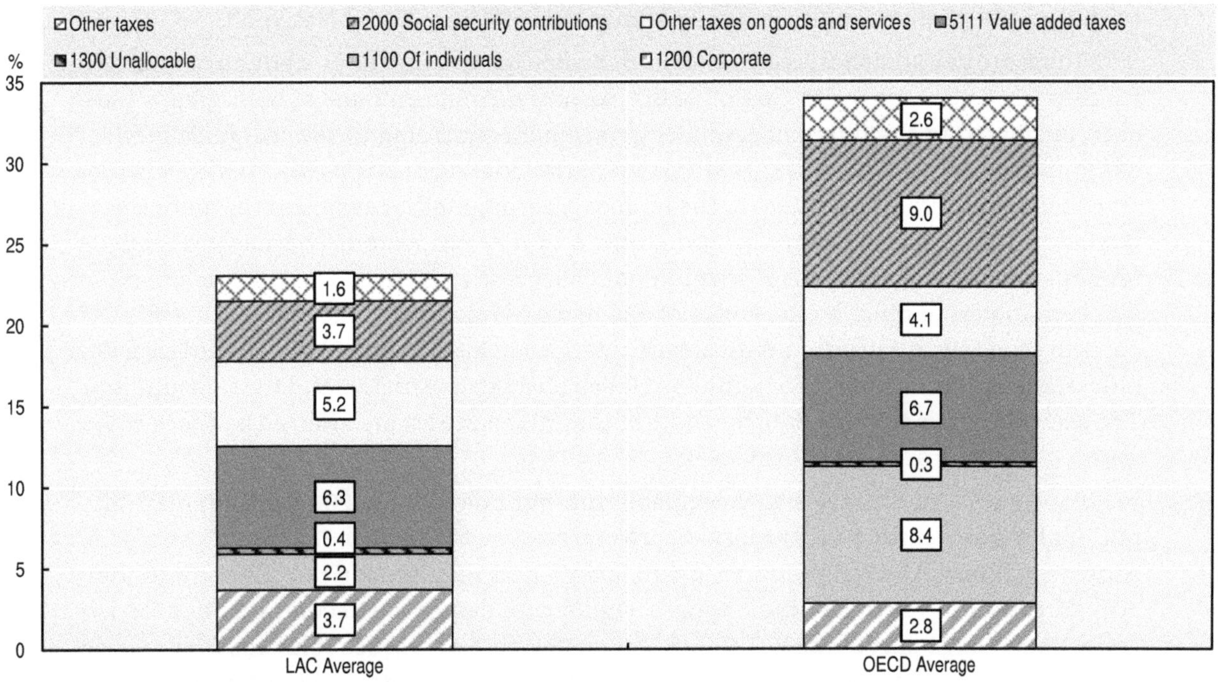

Note: The year of comparison is 2015 as the 2016 data for the OECD average are not available.

Ecuador, Nicaragua and Venezuela are excluded from the LAC averages for CIT and PIT revenue as more than a third of their revenue from taxes on income and profits cannot be allocated to CIT revenue (1200) or PIT revenue (1100).

Source: OECD/ECLAC/CIAT/IDB (2018), "Revenue Statistics in Latin America: Comparative tables", *OECD Tax Statistics* (database), *http://dx.doi.org/10.1787/data-00641-en*.

StatLink *http://dx.doi.org/10.1787/888933684960*

Taxes on immovable property and payroll (comprised within the category "other taxes") are less important sources of revenue for LAC countries. The difficulties experienced by sub-national governments in collecting their own taxes are exemplified by the low revenue-generating capacity of property taxes, which are generally the main source of revenue for local governments in the LAC region (Brossio and Jiménez, 2012), although missing data at the sub-national level makes analysis of this category difficult. The share of payroll taxes is negligible over the whole period. The revenue shares of property and payroll taxes as a proportion of total tax revenue in the LAC region stood at 6.3% of total tax revenue, compared with 7.7% for the OECD average.

Taxes by level of government

Since the mid-1980s, LAC countries have transferred some government functions from the central government to sub-national entities. In the first stage, decentralisation mainly focused on strengthening the democratic role of local authorities. This has been followed by a gradual trend towards a higher share of public expenditure being executed at sub-national level. Nonetheless, tax revenues appear to be collected predominantly by the central or federal entities, with sub-national activities relying more heavily on a system of transfers from upper to lower levels of administration than is the case in OECD countries. In all LAC countries for which sub-national data is available, tax revenues collected by central governments accounted for two-thirds or more of the total collected whereas the corresponding figure for the OECD countries was about 60%. Brazil is a notable exception as the central government tax revenue amounted to 44% in 2015[11] (Table 1.1).

There are two statistical issues to consider when comparing the attribution of revenues for these LAC countries with that of OECD members. First, revenues of both groups have been attributed to the different levels of government according to revised guidelines set out in to the final version of the 2008 System of National Accounts (SNA). This means that revenues are generally attributed to the level of government that exercises the authority to impose the tax or has the final discretion to set and vary the tax rate. This has implications for situations where one level of government collects tax revenues and transfers them in whole or in part to other levels. Regional examples of this type of mechanism are the Co-participation Law in Argentina, federal participations in Mexico (mandated in the Fiscal Co-ordination Law), and participation funds in Brazil (defined in Article 159 of the Constitution). The second issue is that the data for some of the LAC countries are affected by a lack of tax revenue statistics at sub-national level.

For the 15 LAC countries with available sub-national data in 2015, the share of sub-national tax revenues as a proportion of total tax revenue is lower than 8% except in Argentina, Brazil and Colombia. In Brazil, states and municipalities collect more than 30% of total tax revenues, indicating a significant degree of decentralisation of tax collection. A large part of the VAT (ICMS – imposto sobre operações relativas à circulação de mercadorias e prestação de serviços de transporte interestadual e intermunicipal e de comunicação) is collected at the state level. Sub-national tax revenue in Argentina and Colombia represent more than 15% of total tax revenue. Argentina has a significant collection at state level, which is explained in part by the provincial sales tax (impuesto sobre los ingresos brutos). Between 2000 and 2015, the share of revenue raised by sub-national levels of government declined in seven countries and rose in seven countries. The largest decline was in Uruguay (3.9 points) and the highest increase was in Brazil (1.7 points).

These figures reflect the fact that sub-national governments in LAC countries tend to have a relatively narrow range of taxes under their jurisdiction. The taxes most frequently assigned to sub-national entities are property taxes, motor-vehicle licences, taxes on specific services and municipal fees. The revenue-generation potential of these instruments is relatively limited compared with the tax bases under central jurisdiction, such as VAT and income taxes. In 2015, the entire subnational tax revenue in Belize, Guatemala, Jamaica, Trinidad and Tobago and more than 50% of the tax revenue collected at the sub-national level in Paraguay, Peru and Uruguay was sourced from property taxes. All other countries rely principally on revenue from taxes on goods and services. Mexico is the only country that also collected revenue from different tax bases. In 2015, 41% of the sub-national tax revenue in Mexico came from payroll taxes. In OECD member countries, sub-national entities tend to have much broader potential tax bases. A substantial proportion of the revenue collection for sub-national governments in OECD countries is through income taxes and profits (representing more than a third of the total collected amount at sub-national level on average).

Low tax revenues at the sub-national level in LAC countries may also result from a lack of administrative and technical capacity. Property taxes – a common source of sub-national revenue – require sophisticated systems and information since the collection of this revenue is expensive. In addition, appropriate property registers are lacking in many countries and when they exist they are rarely updated (IDB, 2012). As a result, tax authorities have little access to accurate valuations of land and buildings and real estate registries are often reluctant to share this information. Property tax also suffers from a high level of informality: buildings are constructed without permits, properties are not registered and reported prices of some real estate transactions are falsified. As property tax is one of the most controversial taxes with citizens and has high political costs, local politicians are often unwilling to invest the appropriate resources to levy this revenue (IDB, 2015).

Figure 1.21. **Tax mix of the sub-national tax revenue in LAC countries, 2015**

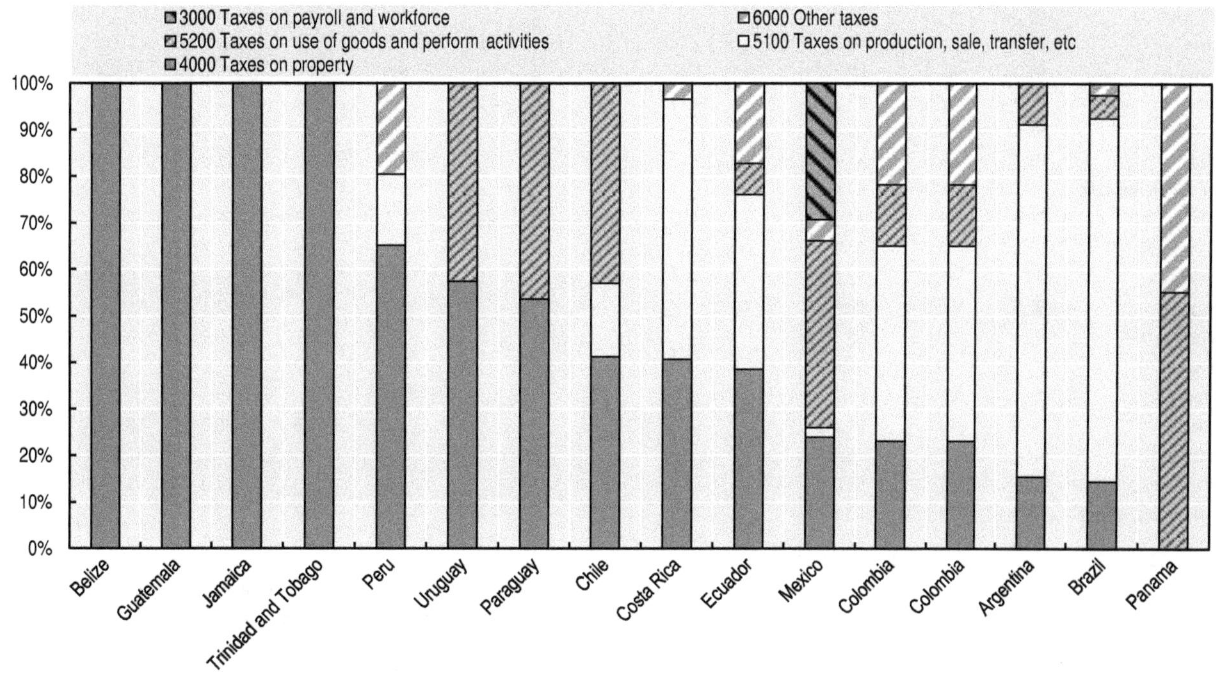

Note: The year of comparison is 2015 as the 2016 data for Mexico are not available.

The Bahamas, Barbados, Bolivia, Cuba, Dominican Republic, El Salvador, Honduras, Nicaragua, Paraguay and Venezuela as either the sub-national tax revenue data or the breakdown of sub-national tax revenue data by the main type of tax category are not available. The figures exclude local government revenues for Argentina (but include provincial revenues).

Source: Authors' calculations based on tables in Chapter 6 of OECD/ECLAC/CIAT/IDB (2018).

StatLink *http://dx.doi.org/10.1787/888933684979*

Between 1995 and 2000, the share of revenue raised by social security funds fell in eight LAC countries, sometimes due to full or partial privatisation. The largest decreases were in Argentina and Ecuador (by around 7.6 and 13.4 percentage points respectively). Argentina adopted a model in 1994 in which some compulsory contributions were directed to individual capital accounts run by privately managed pension funds. Between 2000 and 2015, the share of revenue raised by social security funds increased in 15 of the 25 LAC countries. Argentina and Ecuador recorded the largest increases between 2000 and 2015 (Table 1.1). In Argentina, the compulsory model adopted in 1994 was reversed in 2008 and compulsory contributions previously collected by privately managed pension funds were moved to the public pension system.

Table 1.1. **Attribution of tax revenues to sub-sectors of general government as a percentage of total tax revenue**[1]

	Central government			State or regional government			Local government			Social Security funds		
	1995	2000	2015	1995	2000	2015	1995	2000	2015	1995	2000	2015
Federal countries												
Argentina	59.0	66.4	61.0	17.5	17.8	16.8	..	..	..	23.4	15.8	22.2
Brazil	44.7	47.8	43.7	26.8	25.3	24.4	3.7	3.4	5.9	24.8	23.5	25.9
Mexico	73.9	79.3	80.4	2.8	2.5	4.2	1.5	1.0	1.6	21.8	17.2	13.9
Venezuela	94.6	94.6	97.0	..	..	..	..	..	..	5.4	5.4	3.0
Regional countries												
Colombia[2]	63.2	68.6	71.7	5.5	5.6	4.6	8.6	9.4	11.6	22.7	16.4	12.1
Unitary countries												
Bahamas	89.1	88.1	85.2				..	..	..	10.9	11.9	14.8
Barbados	85.3	84.3	81.2				..	..	..	14.7	15.7	18.8
Belize	93.2	93.5	91.3				0.5	0.7	0.6	6.3	5.8	8.1
Bolivia	95.0	86.4	80.2				5.0	6.3	4.1	0.0	7.3	15.7
Chile	89.9	87.8	86.9				6.5	7.9	7.6	3.6	4.4	5.6
Costa Rica	68.4	66.8	63.4				..	2.0	3.3	30.0	31.2	33.3
Cuba	88.7	89.6	87.1				..	..	..	11.3	10.4	12.9
Dominican Republic	99.3	98.9	99.6				..	..	..	0.7	1.1	0.4
Ecuador	70.5	86.1	73.6				4.0	1.8	2.5	25.5	12.1	23.9
El Salvador	85.9	83.4	87.2				..	..	1.9	14.1	16.6	10.9
Guatemala	83.7	83.6	82.2				0.6	0.9	1.1	15.6	15.5	16.6
Guyana	92.6	88.6	89.6				..	..	..	7.4	11.4	10.4
Honduras	90.1	89.4	85.5				..	..	..	9.9	10.6	14.5
Jamaica	..	99.3	94.5				..	0.7	1.7	..	0.0	3.8
Nicaragua	84.1	80.0	69.8				..	..	..	15.9	20.0	23.5
Panama	62.0	59.8	61.5				..	2.2	1.6	38.0	38.0	36.9
Paraguay	..	82.7	76.4				..	..	4.0	..	17.3	19.6
Peru	88.1	87.8	85.0				..	..	..	11.9	12.2	12.0
Trinidad and Tobago	94.5	91.7	90.1				2.4	1.9	0.7	3.1	6.4	9.3
Uruguay	61.4	62.0	67.9				8.4	8.4	4.5	30.1	29.6	27.6

1. The figures exclude local government revenues for Argentina (but include provincial revenues), the Bahamas, Barbados, Bolivia (prior to 1994), Cuba, the Dominican Republic, El Salvador (prior to 2015), Honduras, Jamaica (prior to 1998), Nicaragua, Panama (prior to 1998), Paraguay (prior to 2004), Peru (prior to 2001) and Venezuela as the data are not available.
2. Colombia is constitutionally a unitary country with high autonomy of its territorial entities.

Source: OECD/ECLAC/CIAT/IDB (2018), Table 4.11.

StatLink http://dx.doi.org/10.1787/888933685397

Notes

1. Figures for Venezuela and Argentina in 2016 should be interpreted with caution as they have been affected by the high rate of inflation from the previous year. Excluding Venezuela and Argentina, the average tax-to-GDP ratio for the remaining LAC countries was 22.7% in 2016.
2. The figure is provisional and has been calculated by applying the unweighted average percentage change for 2016 in the 33 countries providing data for that year to the overall average tax-to-GDP ratio in 2015.
3. In the IDB publication, the Latin American average represents the average of 19 countries: Argentina, Bolivia, Brazil, Chile, Colombia, Costa Rica, Dominican Republic, Ecuador, Guatemala, Honduras, Jamaica, Mexico, Nicaragua, Panama, Peru, Paraguay, El Salvador, Uruguay and Venezuela.
4. Informality is defined as the percentage of non-contributors to pension systems over total employed in Latin America and the Caribbean.
5. This includes Argentina, Brazil, Bolivia, Chile, Colombia, Costa Rica, Ecuador, Honduras, Mexico, Nicaragua, Panama and Peru.
6. The VRR could not be compiled or was not applicable for Cuba and Trinidad and Tobago.

7. VAT evasion is calculated as the loss of VAT revenue as a percentage of expected VAT revenue.
8. The IMF compiled a C-efficiency measure. The C-efficiency is similar in concept to the VRR but uses a slightly different methodology. More information on the differences is available on OECD (2016).
9. Around 2% of total tax revenue is revenue from taxes on income and profits that cannot be allocated between corporate income tax and personal income tax.
10. The year of comparison is 2015 as the 2016 data for the OECD average are not available.
11. The year of comparison is 2015 as the 2016 data for Mexico are not available.

References

Barreix, A., J. Benítez and M. Pecho (2017), "Revisiting personal income tax in Latin America: Evolution and impact", *OECD Development Centre Working Papers* No. 338, OECD Publishing, Paris, *http://dx.doi.org/10.1787/16d42b4a-en.*

Bosch, M., A. Melguizo and C. Pagés (2013), *Better Pensions, Better Jobs: Towards Universal Coverage in Latin America and the Caribbean*, Inter-American Development Bank, Washington, DC.

Brossio, G. and J.P. Jiménez (2012), *Decentralization and Reform in Latin America: Improving Intergovernmental Relations*, Edward Elgar, in press, Cheltenham, UK and Northampton, MA.

Daude, C., Á. Melguizo and A. Neut (2010), "Fiscal Policy in Latin America: Countercyclical and Sustainable at Last?", *OECD Development Centre Working Papers* No. 291, OECD Publishing, Paris, *http://dx.doi.org/10.1787/5km8zdcp7j41-en.*

ECLAC (2014), *Tax policy in Latin America: Assessment and guidelines for a second generation of reforms*, Economic Commission for Latin America and the Caribbean, Santiago de Chile.

ECLAC (2013), *Fiscal Panorama of Latin America and the Caribbean: tax reform and renewal of the fiscal covenant*, Economic Commission for Latin America and the Caribbean, Santiago de Chile

ECLAC (2010), "La Hora de la igualdad. Brechas por cerrar, caminos por abrir", (LC/G.2432(SES.33/3)), Economic Commission for Latin America and the Caribbean, Santiago de Chile.

Ernst & Young (2014), "Worldwide VAT GST and sales tax guide 2014", Ernst & Young Global Limited, *www.ey.com/Publication/vwLUAssets/Worldwide-VAT-GST-and-sales-tax-guide-2014/$FILE/Worldwide-VAT-GST-and-sales-tax-guide-2014.pdf.*

Franks J.R., R. Benelli, V. Mercer-Blackman and R. Sab (2005), "Paraguay: Corruption, Reform, and the Financial System", International Monetary Fund, Washington, DC.

Gómez Sabaini, J.C., J.P. Jiménez and A. Podestá (2010), "Evasión y equidad en América Latina", Project documents, No. 309 (LC/W.309/ Rev.1), ECLAC, Santiago de Chile.

IDB (2015), "Decentralizing Revenue in Latin America Why and How", Inter-American Development Bank, Washington, DC.

IDB (2013), "More than revenues, Taxation as a development tool", Inter-American Development Bank, Washington, DC.

IDB (2012), "Sub-national Revenue Mobilization in Peru", *IDB Working Paper Series* No. 299, Inter-American Development Bank, Washington, DC.

IMF (2017a), "The Bahamas: 2017 article IV consultation—press release and staff report", IMF Country Report No. 17/314, International Monetary Fund, Washington, DC, *www.imf.org/en/Publications/CR/Issues/2017/10/06/The-Bahamas-2017-Article-IV-Consultation-Press-Release-and-Staff-Report-45310.*

IMF (2017b), "Belize: 2017 Article IV Consultation-Press Release; Staff Report; Informational Annex; Statement by the Executive Director for Belize", *IMF Country Report* No. 17/286, International Monetary Fund, Washington, DC, *www.imf.org/en/Publications/CR/Issues/2017/09/19/Belize-2017-Article-IV-Consultation-Press-Release-Staff-Report-Informational-Annex-Statement-45264.*

IMF (2017c), *World Economic Outlook Database, October 2017 Edition*, International Monetary Fund, Washington, DC.

IMF (2017d), "Guyana : 2017 Article IV Consultation-Press Release; Staff Report; and Statement by the Executive Director for Guyana", *IMF Country Report* No. 17/175, International Monetary Fund, Washington, DC, *www.imf.org/en/Publications/CR/Issues/2017/06/28/Guyana-2017-Article-IV-Consultation-Press-Release-Staff-Report-and-Statement-by-the-45010.*

IMF (2016a), "Argentina 2016 Article IV Consultation", *IMF country report* No. 16/346, International Monetary Fund, Washington, DC.

IMF (2016b), *World Economic Outlook Database, October 2016 Edition*, International Monetary Fund, Washington, DC.

IMF (2010), "Paraguay: Selected Issues", IMF Country Report No. 10/170, International Monetary Fund, Washington, DC, *www.imf.org/external/pubs/ft/scr/2010/cr10170.pdf*.

Melguizo, A., S. Nieto-Parra, J.R. Perea and J.A. Perez (2017), "No sympathy for the devil! Policy priorities to overcome the middle-income trap in Latin America", *OECD Development Centre. Working Papers*, No. 340, OECD Publishing, Paris, *http://dx.doi.org/10.1787/26b78724-en*.

OECD (2016), *Consumption Tax Trends 2016: VAT/GST and excise rates, trends and policy issues*, OECD Publishing, Paris, *http://dx.doi.org/10.1787/ctt-2016-en/*.

OECD (2014), *Development Co-operation Report 2014: Mobilising Resources for Sustainable Development*, OECD Publishing, Paris, *http://dx.doi.org/10.1787/dcr-2014-en*.

OECD (2008), *Latin American Economic Outlook 2009*, OECD Publishing, Paris, *http://dx.doi.org/10.1787/leo-2009-en*.

OECD/CAF/ECLAC (2018, forthcoming), *Latin American Economic Outlook 2018: Rethinking Institutions for Development*, OECD Publishing, Paris, *http://dx.doi.org/10.1787/leo-2018-en*.

OECD/IDB/CIAT (2016), *Taxing Wages in Latin America and the Caribbean 2016*, OECD Publishing, Paris, *http://dx.doi.org/10.1787/9789264262607-en*.

OECD/CIAT/ECLAC/IDB (2015), *Revenue Statistics in Latin America and the Caribbean 1990-2013*, OECD Publishing, Paris, *http://dx.doi.org/10.1787/rev_lat-2015-en-fr*.

OECD/IDB/The World Bank (2014), *Pensions at a Glance: Latin America and the Caribbean*, OECD Publishing, Paris, *http://dx.doi.org/10.1787/pension_glance-2014-en*.

Panama Investor Blog (2008), Audit uncovers millions in unpaid sales taxes, *http://primapanama.blogs.com/_panama_residential_devel/2008/06/audit-uncovers.html*.

World Grain (2016), "Reforms boost Argentine grain industry", *www.world-grain.com/articles/news_home/Features/2016/05/Reforms_boost_Argentine_grain.aspx?ID=%7BAE4EE339-0D46-43EF-A962-5ED9DEF72B53%7D*.

Zuleta, J.C (2008), "Combating corruption in the revenue service: the case of VAT refunds in Bolivia", Anti-Corruption Resource Centre, *www.U4.no/themes/pfm*.

Revenue Statistics in Latin America and the Caribbean 2018/
Estadísticas tributarias en América Latina y el Caribe 2018

Capítulo 1

Tendencias tributarias, 1990-2016

Proporciones de ingresos tributarios

La relación de impuestos y el producto interno bruto (PIB) refleja el recaudo tributario de los gobiernos para financiar la provisión de bienes y servicios públicos y la inversión en infraestructura. La movilización de recursos fiscales mediante impuestos es importante para asegurar el desarrollo económico de los países (OCDE, 2014). Los impuestos constituyen una fuente predecible y sostenible de ingresos para los gobiernos, en contraste con la asistencia al desarrollo y la volatilidad de los ingresos no-tributarios por materias primas.

Este reporte presenta datos internacionales comparables sobre recaudo tributario para 25 países de América Latina y el Caribe. Este capítulo analiza varios indicadores tributarios claves en estos países: el recaudo tributario total en relación al PIB, la estructura impositiva y la proporción de ingresos tributarios por nivel de gobierno. Esta discusión suplementa la información detallada de países que se encuentra en el capítulo 5.

Proporciones de ingresos tributarios en 2016

El promedio del recaudo tributario como proporción del PIB en América Latina y el Caribe (ALC) fue del 22.7%[1] en 2016 (véase el gráfico 1.1). La proporción tributaria en relación al PIB se mide como el recaudo tributario (incluidas las contribuciones a la seguridad social) como proporción del PIB. El ratio de impuestos con respecto al PIB varió ampliamente en la región, desde 12.6% en Guatemala a 41.7% en Cuba. A la excepción de Cuba, todos los países de ALC tuvieron ingresos tributarios en proporción al PIB inferiores al promedio de la OCDE de 34.3%[2].

Las proporciones más altas de ingresos tributarios respecto al PIB se dieron en Cuba (41.7%), Barbados (32.2%) y Brasil (32.2%). Los países con los ingresos tributarios como proporción del PIB más bajos fueron Guatemala (12.6%), República Dominicana (13.7%) y Venezuela (14.4%).

En 2016, el promedio del recaudo tributario sobre PIB de ALC fue 0.3 puntos más bajo que en el año previo (véase el gráfico 1.2). Esta caída refleja en parte la coyuntura económica de la región ALC y la ausencia de reformas tributarias estructurales en casi todos los países. En promedio, las tasas de crecimiento del PIB han experimentado una desaceleración desde 2012, y en 2015 y 2016 se volvió negativa (OCDE/CAF/CEPAL de próxima publicación). Es probable que esta disminución se revierta en los próximos años con la mejora del clima económico en 2017 y 2018. Los precios de las materias primas se están recuperando y se espera que la región ALC alcance un crecimiento del PIB de entre 2% y 2.5% en 2018.

Existe una amplia gama de situaciones en los países de ALC en cuanto a los cambios en los ratios ingresos tributarios en proporción del PIB entre 2015 y 2016. Trece países – alrededor de la mitad de los países analizados en este informe– registraron un incremento en sus ingresos tributarios como proporción del PIB en 2016 cuando 12 de ellos registraron un descenso. Esto representa una gran disminución en comparación con el año pasado, en donde 21 países registraron un aumento entre 2014 y 2015 y solo cuatro países registraron una disminución (véase el gráfico 1.2).

Gráfico 1.1. **Relación de ingresos tributarios y el PIB (Ingresos tributarios totales como % del PIB) en los países ALC, 2016**

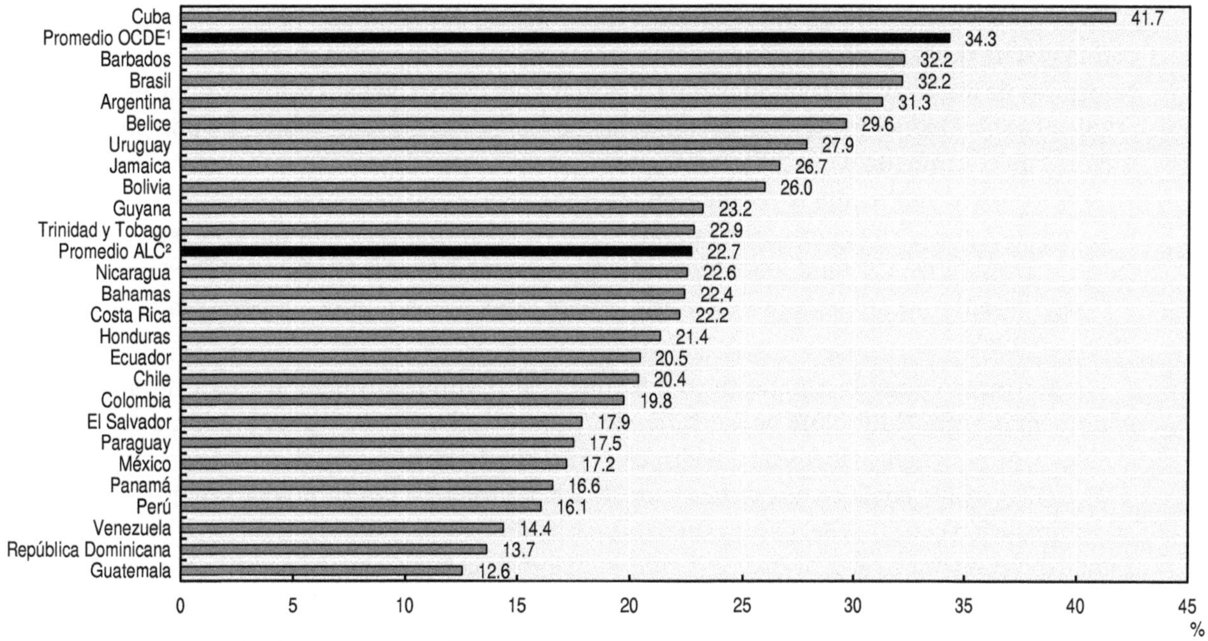

Nota: Las cifras excluyen los ingresos subnacionales de Argentina (aunque se incluyen los ingresos de las provincias), Las Bahamas, Barbados, Cuba, República Dominicana, Honduras y Venezuela dado que los datos no se encuentran disponibles.

1. Representa el promedio de los países miembros de la OCDE. Chile y México forman también parte del promedio del grupo de la OCDE (35).
2. Representa el promedio no ponderado de 25 países de América Latina y el Caribe.

Fuente: OCDE/CEPAL/CIAT/BID (2018), Cuadro 4.1.

StatLink http://dx.doi.org/10.1787/888933684998

Gráfico 1.2. **Cambios en 2014-15 y 2015-16 de los ratios de ingresos tributarios con respecto al PIB en los países ALC (puntos porcentuales del PIB)**

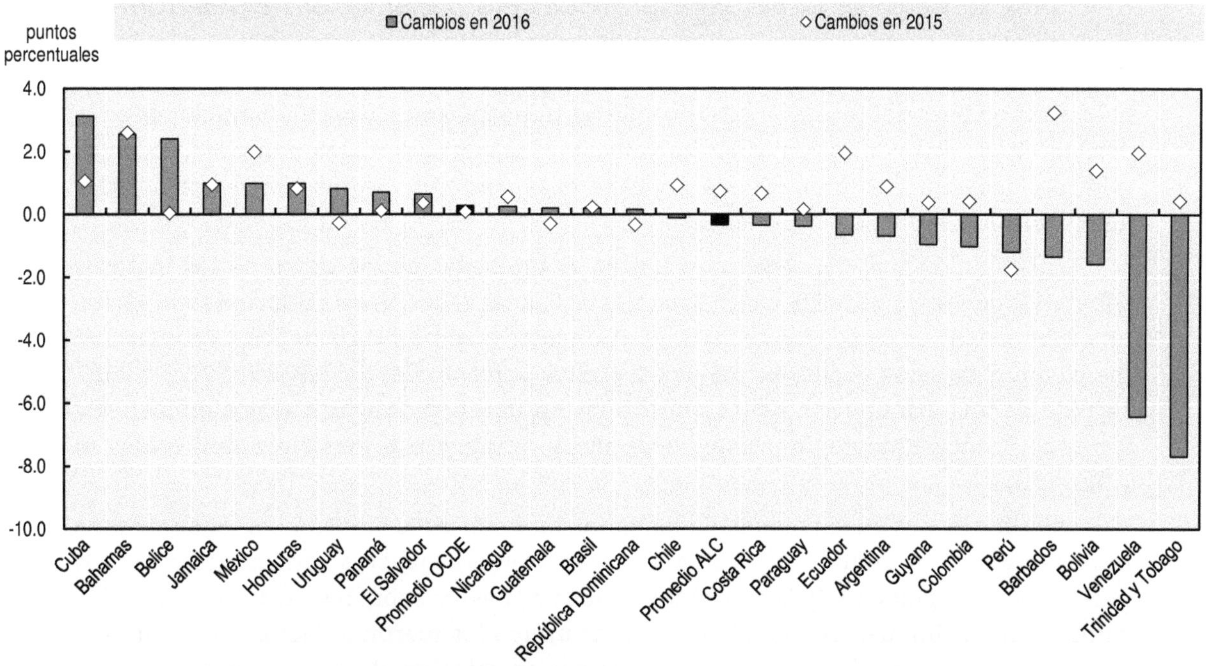

Fuente: Elaboración propia basada en OCDE/CEPAL/CIAT/BID (2018), Cuadro 4.1.

StatLink http://dx.doi.org/10.1787/888933685017

En 2016, tres países registraron aumento de más de dos puntos porcentuales en el cociente de las tasas de impuesto con respecto al PIB. Cuba registró el aumento más importante (de 3.1 puntos porcentuales), seguido por Bahamas y Belice, cuyas proporciones de impuestos con respecto al PIB aumentaron respectivamente de 2.6 y 2.4 puntos de porcentuales. Las categorías de impuestos que impulsaron estos aumentos variaron para estos tres países. Los impuestos sobre bienes y servicios así como los impuestos sobre la renta fueron los principales motores de crecimiento para Cuba. Los ingresos provenientes de los impuestos sobre bienes y servicios (particularmente el IVA) fueron los principales contribuyentes al aumento en las Bahamas (4.7 puntos de porcentaje) mientras que en Belice fueron los impuestos especiales los que contribuyeron al aumento (1.5 puntos de porcentaje). En cambio, Venezuela y Trinidad y Tobago registraron un descenso muy importante (más de 6.4 puntos de porcentaje) en el mismo período.

Reformas tributarias significativas aunadas a la coyuntura económica han llevado a incrementos entre 2015 y 2016 en las Bahamas, Belice y Cuba. Las Bahamas introdujeron un impuesto al valor agregado (IVA) en enero de 2015 y continuaron su implementación exitosa (FMI, 2017a), lo que conllevó una duplicación de los ingresos del IVA como porcentaje del PIB en comparación con 2015. Belice introdujo nuevas medidas relativas a los impuestos sobre los combustibles en marzo de 2016 (FMI, 2017b). El aumento de la frecuentación turística en Cuba en 2016 habrá contribuido al aumento en el ratio impuestos con respecto al PIB entre 2015 y 2016.

Las disminuciones en Trinidad y Tobago y Venezuela se explican principalmente por el contexto económico. Trinidad y Tobago, como país dependiente de los ingresos derivados del petróleo, recauda la mayor parte de sus ingresos por impuestos a las ganancias corporativas de las compañías de hidrocarburos. El colapso de los precios de los hidrocarburos junto con la reducción de la producción fueron las razones principales de la gran disminución de los impuestos a las ganancias corporativas (8.1 puntos porcentuales) (véase el capítulo especial 2). Venezuela ha visto una disminución de 6.4 puntos porcentuales de sus impuestos con respecto al PIB. Todas las categorías de ingresos tributarios se vieron afectadas por las importantes disminuciones de los ingresos provenientes de los impuestos sobre los bienes y servicios (4.4 puntos porcentuales) y los impuestos sobre los ingresos y las ganancias (1.4 puntos porcentuales). La hiperinflación, las disminuciones del consumo interno y de las importaciones, y las disminuciones en la producción de petróleo en Venezuela han afectado los ingresos provenientes de impuestos relacionados como los impuestos a las ganancias corporativas, los impuestos al valor agregado y los impuestos especiales.

El factor principal de la disminución en el promedio de los ratios de los ingresos tributarios con respecto al PIB en los países de ALC, analizados en este informe en 2016, fue una disminución en el recaudo de los impuestos sobre la renta y los beneficios. La variación media anual de estos impuestos fue de 0.2 puntos porcentuales del PIB entre 2015 y 2016, seguido de una disminución de 0.1 puntos porcentuales de otros impuestos en bienes y servicios (principalmente, impuestos específicos, aduaneros e importaciones) (véase el gráfico 1.3).

Las variaciones en el recaudo de los impuestos sobre los bienes y servicios y de los impuestos sobre la renta y las utilidades mostraron las mayores variaciones entre los países (véase el gráfico 1.4). Los cambios en los impuestos sobre bienes y servicios y los cambios en los impuestos sobre la renta y las utilidades fueron el factor principal para cambios en los ratios de los ingresos tributarios en relación al PIB en once países para cada categoría.

Gráfico 1.3. **Cambios en 2015-16 de los ingresos tributarios en relación al PIB por tipo de impuesto (puntos porcentuales de PIB)**

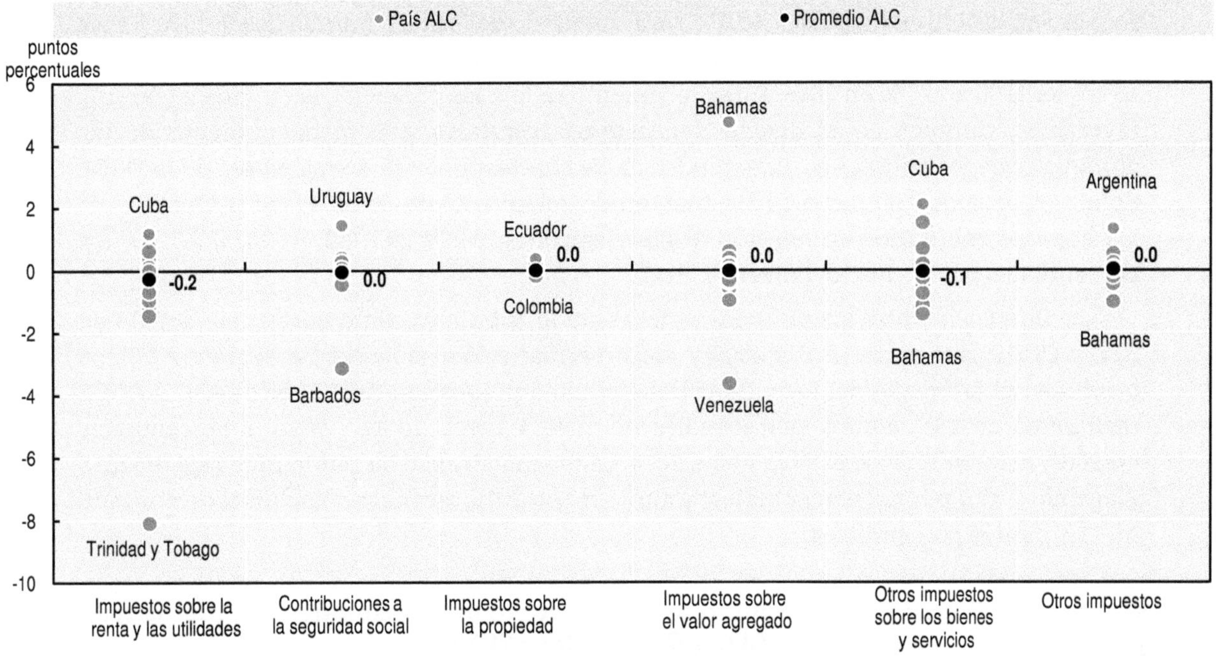

Fuente: Elaboración propia basada en los cuadros en el Capítulo 4, OCDE/CEPAL/CIAT/BID (2018).

StatLink http://dx.doi.org/10.1787/888933685036

Gráfico 1.4. **Cambios en 2015-16 en el recaudo tributario por cambio más importante en los países ALC como % del PIB (puntos porcentuales del PIB)**

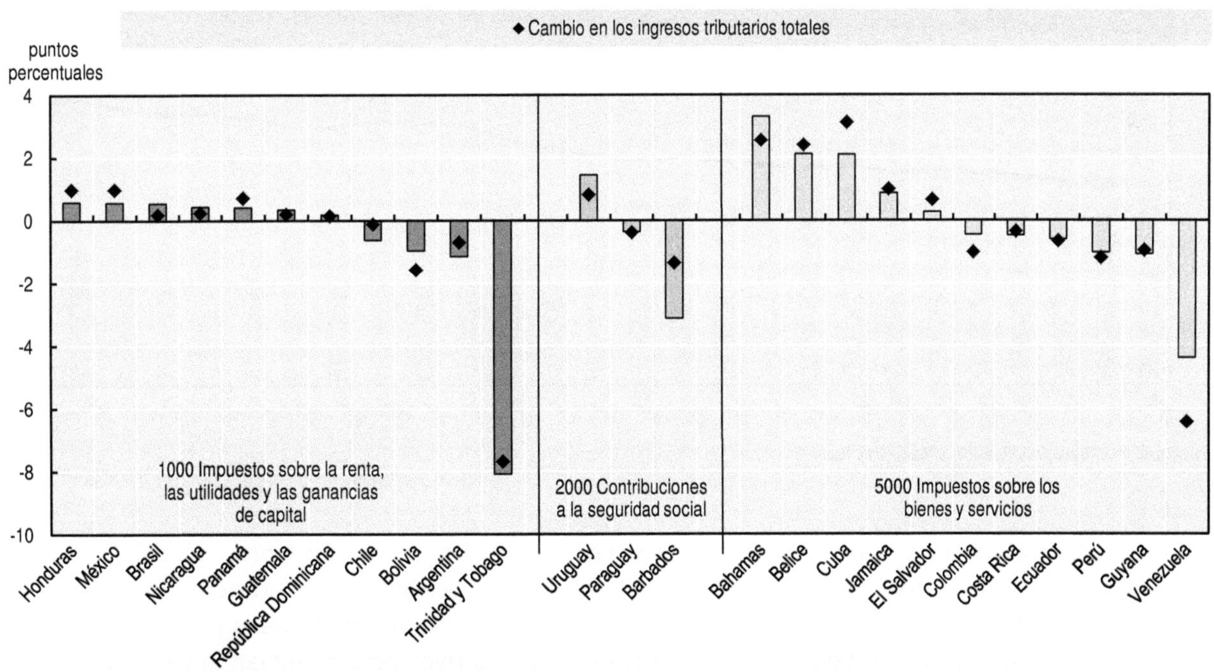

Nota: el cambio interanual en el recaudo de los impuestos sobre bienes y servicios de Venezuela debe ser interpretado con cautela dado los altos índices de inflación que los han afectado.

Fuente: Elaboración propia basada en los cuadros presentados en el Capítulo 4, OCDE/CEPAL/CIAT/BID (2018).

StatLink http://dx.doi.org/10.1787/888933685055

Evolución del recaudo tributario desde el 2000

Con la excepción de 2008, 2009 y 2016, el promedio del recaudo tributario como proporción del PIB en los países de ALC ha aumentado de forma continua desde 1990 (véase el gráfico 1.5). Durante este lapso ha incrementado en más de seis puntos porcentuales desde 16.0% en 1990 a 22.7% en 2016. Este crecimiento refleja las condiciones macroeconómicas favorables, cambios en el diseño del sistema tributario y el fortalecimiento de las administraciones tributarias. Esta tendencia se contrasta con la de los países de la OCDE donde el recaudo tributario se ha mantenido relativamente estable; los promedios de los ingresos tributarios en relación al PIB alcanzaron 34.3% del PIB en 2016, 2.3 puntos porcentuales por encima del nivel de 1990.

La diferencia entre los promedios del recaudo tributario como porcentaje del PIB de ALC y OCDE cayó entre 1990 y 2009 y luego permaneció estable (véase el gráfico 1.5). La brecha en el promedio del recaudo tributario como proporción del PIB entre ALC y OCDE disminuyó de 15.9 puntos porcentuales en 1990 a cerca de 11.5 puntos porcentuales en 2009, manteniéndose estable hasta 2014. La brecha alcanzó su punto más bajo en 2015 (llegando a 10.9 puntos porcentuales) y aumentó en 2016, alcanzando su nivel de pre-2015 de 11.5 puntos porcentuales.

Gráfico 1.5. **Brechas en el recaudo tributario como proporción del PIB, promedios ALC y OCDE 1990 - 2016**

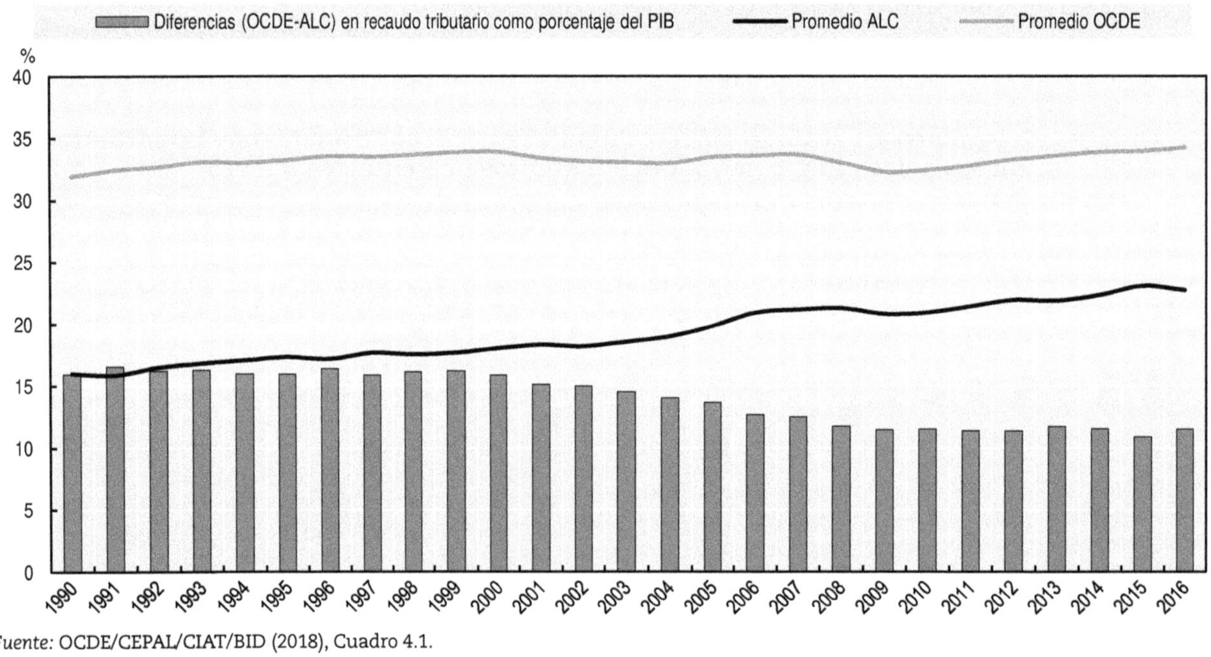

Fuente: OCDE/CEPAL/CIAT/BID (2018), Cuadro 4.1.

StatLink http://dx.doi.org/10.1787/888933685074

Los ratios del recaudo tributario en los países de ALC aumentaron a principios de los años noventa luego de un período de inestabilidad macroeconómica experimentado en la década anterior. Durante los años ochenta, los países mantuvieron grandes desbalances fiscales y al mismo tiempo recurrieron a métodos alternativos para financiar su gasto (vía deuda y emisión de moneda). Lo anterior conllevó a un proceso inflacionario acelerado en la región, lo cual erosionó el valor real de sus ingresos tributarios. Las reformas de los años noventa estuvieron enfocadas a la estabilidad de precios, el libre comercio y la disciplina fiscal. La mayoría de gobiernos de ALC disminuyeron el gasto público e implementaron políticas con miras al incremento del recaudo tributario, lo que derivó en una mejora del manejo presupuestario y de los balances fiscales. Las autoridades implementaron reformas de política y administración para reforzar sistemas tributarios contra episodios inflacionarios. Esto se logró disminuyendo los tiempos de recaudo y mediante la indexación de las obligaciones tributarias.

Durante las últimas dos décadas se llevaron a cabo esfuerzos significativos para modernizar las administraciones y los sistemas tributarios. Se implementaron nuevos sistemas de tecnologías de información, se racionalizó la estructura de las administraciones tributarias y los sistemas de recaudo tributario se tornaron más eficientes mientras que el personal adquirió mayor experiencia (BID, 2013). Aunado a ello, algunos de los países de ALC simplificaron sus sistemas tributarios y ampliaron sus bases impositivas, lo que puede haber contribuido al aumento de los recibos de impuestos. Redujeron los números de las exenciones e incentivos tributarios otorgados a ciertas actividades y sectores, especialmente orientados hacia la atracción de inversión extranjera. Las reformas incluyeron la introducción o el desarrollo de regímenes simplificados para pequeños contribuyentes y la imposición sobre la propiedad basada en criterios de rentas presuntas. Desde 2010 varias reformas sobre el impuesto a la renta se implementaron en los países de ALC, las cuales han incluido aumentos de las tasas y la ampliación de la base tributaria. Estas medidas han tenido un efecto positivo en varios países gracias a la expansión del impuesto para que abarque todas las rentas del trabajo y del capital, incluyendo dividendos (ej. Colombia, República Dominicana, Guatemala, El Salvador, Nicaragua, Panamá y Perú). Las reformas también han establecido impuestos mínimos, impuestos sobre las transacciones financieras, la reducción gradual del nivel de renta real gravado al tipo máximo marginal tanto como controles adicionales sobre los precios de transferencia (CEPAL, 2013).

La introducción del IVA fue la reforma más significativa en los países de ALC en los años ochenta y principios de los años noventa. Las reformas subsecuentes relacionadas al IVA se han centrado en su extensión y fortalecimiento, mediante el aumento de la tasa y la ampliación de su base. De 1990 a 2016, los ingresos del IVA como proporción del PIB se duplicaron, pasando de 2.4% del PIB en 1990 a 6.2% del PIB en 2016 (véase el gráfico 1.6). Durante el mismo período, en los países ALC los ingresos tributarios, provenientes de impuestos sobre los bienes y servicios (los impuestos específicos y los derechos sobre las aduanas y las importaciones) disminuyeron como porcentaje del PIB. Esta caída fue asociada con la liberalización del comercio que trajo consigo un cambio en la forma en la que se gravan los bienes importados y exportados y también los productos y servicios específicos. Estos cambios incluyeron una reducción de los aranceles a la importación, la reducción de la base y de los productos y servicios sujetos a impuestos específicos (por ejemplo, focalizándose en productos como bebidas alcohólicas, tabaco y petróleo) y la eliminación de los impuestos sobre las exportaciones. Una importante excepción es en Argentina, país en el cual los impuestos sobre las exportaciones fueron re-establecidos en 2002. No obstante, el gobierno abolió este impuesto sobre casi todos los productos agropecuarios en 2015 (World Grain y FMI, 2016).

Los principales contribuyentes al crecimiento en el recaudo tributario en ALC fueron el IVA desde 1990 hasta 2002 y entre 2002 y 2016 el IVA y los impuestos sobre la renta y las utilidades. Los ingresos tributarios provenientes del IVA aumentaron en 1.9 puntos porcentuales del PIB desde 1990 hasta 2012, mientras que los ingresos del impuesto a las rentas y utilidades aumentaron 0.4 puntos porcentuales durante el mismo periodo (véase el gráfico 1.6). Los ingresos del impuesto sobre la renta y utilidades aumentaron a la par con el IVA entre 2002 y 2016; el aumento fue de 1.8 puntos porcentuales del PIB durante este periodo. Uno de los elementos que contribuyó a esta tendencia es la recuperación de la actividad económica en ALC y el boom en el precio de las materias primas luego de 2003, que contribuyó al aumento en el recaudo del impuesto sobre las rentas y utilidades de sociedades (Barreix et al, 2017). Cambios en los ingresos provenientes de los impuestos sobre bienes y servicios, impuestos sobre las rentas y utilidades y las contribuciones a la seguridad social han contribuido a la recuperación en el promedio de los ingresos tributarios en relación al PIB en la región ALC después de la crisis financiera.

Gráfico 1.6. **Recaudo de los impuestos sobre la renta y las utilidades, el IVA y otros impuestos sobre bienes y servicios como porcentaje del PIB en la región ALC, 1990 - 2016**

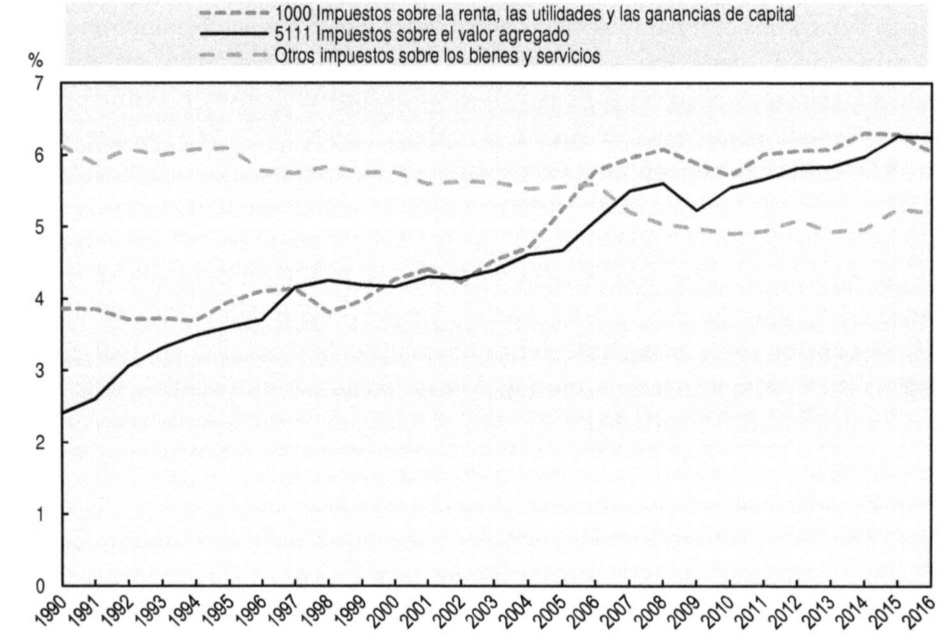

Fuente: OCDE/CEPAL/CIAT/BID (2018), "Estadísticas tributarias en América Latina: tablas comparativas", OCDE Estadísticas tributarias (base de datos) *http://dx.doi.org/10.1787/data-00641-en.*

StatLink *http://dx.doi.org/10.1787/888933685093*

Los ingresos tributarios, como porcentaje del PIB, del impuesto a las rentas y utilidades han incrementado desde 2007 con una interrupción durante la crisis financiera y una nueva disminución en el año 2016 de 0.2 puntos porcentuales. Este incremento se explica por el aumento en los ingresos provenientes de los impuestos sobre las sociedades. Desde 1990, el impuesto sobre sociedades creció mucho más rápido que el impuesto sobre la renta de personas físicas y este incremento refleja los aumentos en los ingresos tributarios derivados de compañías en los sectores de recursos naturales (CEPAL, 2014). También fue el resultado de políticas tributarias que redujeron los incentivos en zonas de libre-comercio, la introducción de impuestos mínimos a las empresas y reformas en el ámbito de la imposición internacional y acuerdos entre países para combatir la evasión.

Los ingresos provenientes del impuesto sobre la renta y utilidades de empresas han reflejado el ciclo económico de la región. Entre 2008 y 2010, los impuestos sobre la renta de empresas como porcentaje del PIB en la región ALC se redujo de 0.3 puntos porcentuales (véase el gráfico 1.7). Se mantuvo estable a un nivel de 3.8% entre 2011 y 2014. En 2015, experimentó una caída de 0.2 puntos porcentuales y en 2016 experimentó una fuerte nueva caída de 0.2 puntos porcentuales. Esta disminución en 2016 puede ser explicada parcialmente por la caída en el recaudo del impuesto sobre la renta y utilidades de las empresas que trabajan en el sector de las materias primas no renovables (véase el capítulo especial II de esta publicación), particularmente en Trinidad y Tobago.

Por el contrario, el recaudo del impuesto a la renta de personas como porcentaje del PIB en la región ALC ha estado incrementando continuamente desde 2011. Alcanzó su máximo nivel en 2015 (2.2% del PIB) y quedó a ese nivel en 2016. Desde 2012, la tasa de crecimiento del impuesto sobre la renta de personas físicas ha sido mayor que la del impuesto que recae sobre las empresas, especialmente debido al mejoramiento de la coyuntura económica y los bajos precios de las materias primas. Los promedios del recaudo de los impuestos sobre la renta y utilidades de empresas y personas físicas deben ser interpretados con cautela dado que Ecuador, Nicaragua y Venezuela han sido excluidos de la estimación en vista que más de un tercio del recaudo no puede ser atribuido al impuesto a la renta de empresas (1200) o al impuesto sobre la renta de personas físicas (1100).

Gráfico 1.7. **Recaudo de impuesto sobre la renta y utilidades, el impuesto sobre la renta de sociedades y el impuesto sobre la renta de personas, como porcentaje del PIB en ALC 2007-16**

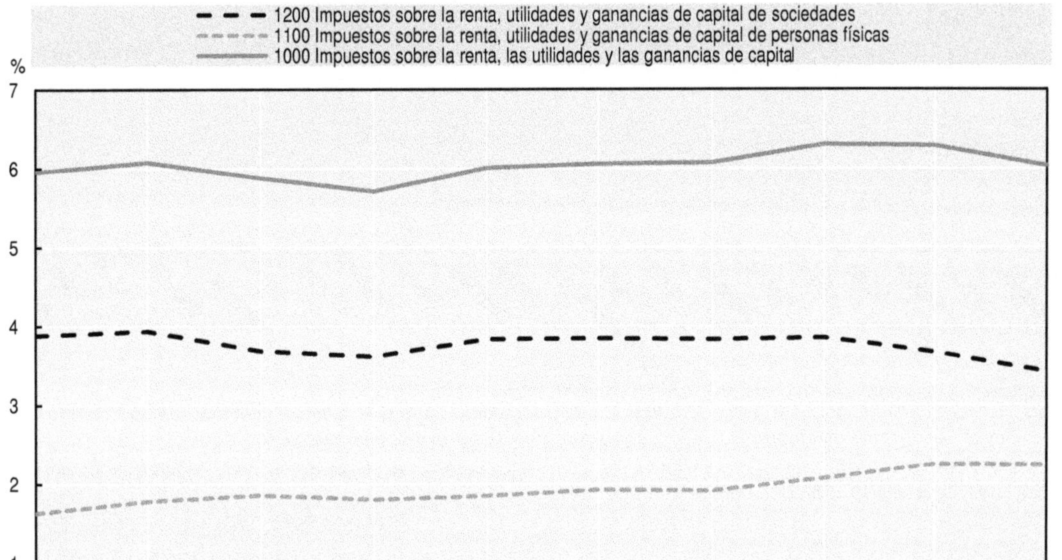

Nota: Ecuador, Nicaragua y Venezuela han sido excluidos de los promedios de los impuestos sobre la renta de empresas y personas físicas dado que más de un tercio de su recaudo no puedo ser atribuido a las categorías de renta de empresas (1200) o impuesto sobre la renta de personas (1100).

Fuente: OCDE/CEPAL/CIAT/BID (2018), "Estadísticas tributarias en América Latina: tablas comparativas", *Estadísticas tributarias de la OCDE* (base de datos), *http://dx.doi.org/10.1787/data-00641-en*.

StatLink *http://dx.doi.org/10.1787/888933685112*

Los cambios en el recaudo del impuesto – especialmente los impuestos sobre la renta de empresas – como porcentaje del PIB experimentados entre 2015 y 2016 muestran amplias variaciones entre los países (véase el gráfico 1.8). Aunque el promedio de la región ALC para los ingresos provenientes de los impuestos sobre la renta y utilidades registró una caída de 0.2 puntos porcentuales entre 2015 y 2016, los ingresos provenientes de esta categoría de impuestos han caído en solo cinco países en este periodo: Argentina, Bolivia, Chile, Colombia y Trinidad y Tobago. En 2016, Trinidad y Tobago registró una caída de 7.7 puntos porcentuales en el recaudo del impuesto sobre la renta y utilidades, explicado principalmente por un desplome del recaudo del impuesto sobre la renta de empresas (8.1 puntos porcentuales). Esta caída fue causada por el desplome de los precios de los hidrocarburos y una disminución de la producción. En los otros cuatro países, los ingresos provenientes del impuesto a la renta y utilidades cayeron entre 0.3 y 1.1 puntos porcentuales.

Gráfico 1.8. **Cambios en 2015-16 de los ingresos provenientes del impuestos sobre la renta y utilidades, impuesto sobre la renta de sociedades y sobre la renta de personas en los países ALC, 2016 (puntos porcentuales del PIB)**

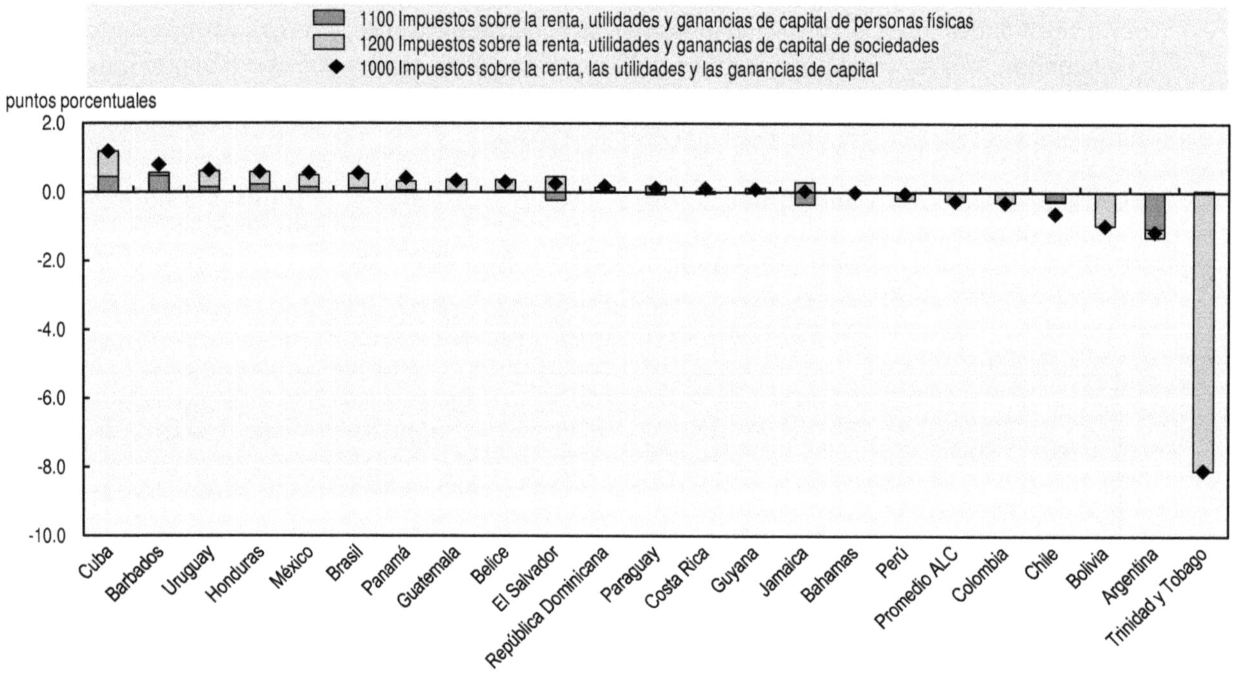

Nota: Ecuador, Nicaragua y Venezuela han sido excluidos de los promedios dado que más de un tercio de su recaudo no puedo ser atribuido a las categorías de renta de empresas (1200) o impuesto sobre la renta de personas (1100).

Fuente: OCDE/CEPAL/CIAT/BID (2018), "Estadísticas tributarias en América Latina: tablas comparativas", *Estadísticas tributarias de la OCDE* (base de datos), *http://dx.doi.org/10.1787/data-00641-en*.

StatLink *http://dx.doi.org/10.1787/888933685131*

Factores que han influenciado los niveles de recaudo tributario

Las diferencias entre los promedios de recaudo tributario, como porcentaje del PIB, entre ALC y la OCDE son consistentes con la tendencia de que los países con una mayor renta per cápita tienen mayores niveles de recaudo tributario. La data muestra una correlación positiva entre el PIB per cápita (una medida del nivel de ingreso de los países o su grado de desarrollo) y las relaciones entre los ingresos tributarios y el PIB (véase el gráfico 1.9). En general, los países de la OCDE tienen ingresos más altos que los países de ALC y también recaudan más en impuestos. Argentina, Barbados, Brasil, Trinidad y Tobago y Uruguay muestran niveles de recaudo tributario similares a los de la OCDE pese a niveles de ingreso por debajo del promedio de países de la OCDE. Los análisis empíricos sugieren que una recaudación tributaria más fuerte, acompañada por mejores instituciones, educación y habilidades y una diversificación económica, han permitido a varios países de la OCDE de evadir la *trampa del ingreso medio*, lo que contrasta con la región ALC (Melguizo et al., 2017)

Gráfico 1.9. **PIB per cápita en PPP (USD) y recaudo tributario (como porcentaje del PIB) en países de América Latina y el Caribe, la OCDE y un grupo de países de África y Asia, 2015**

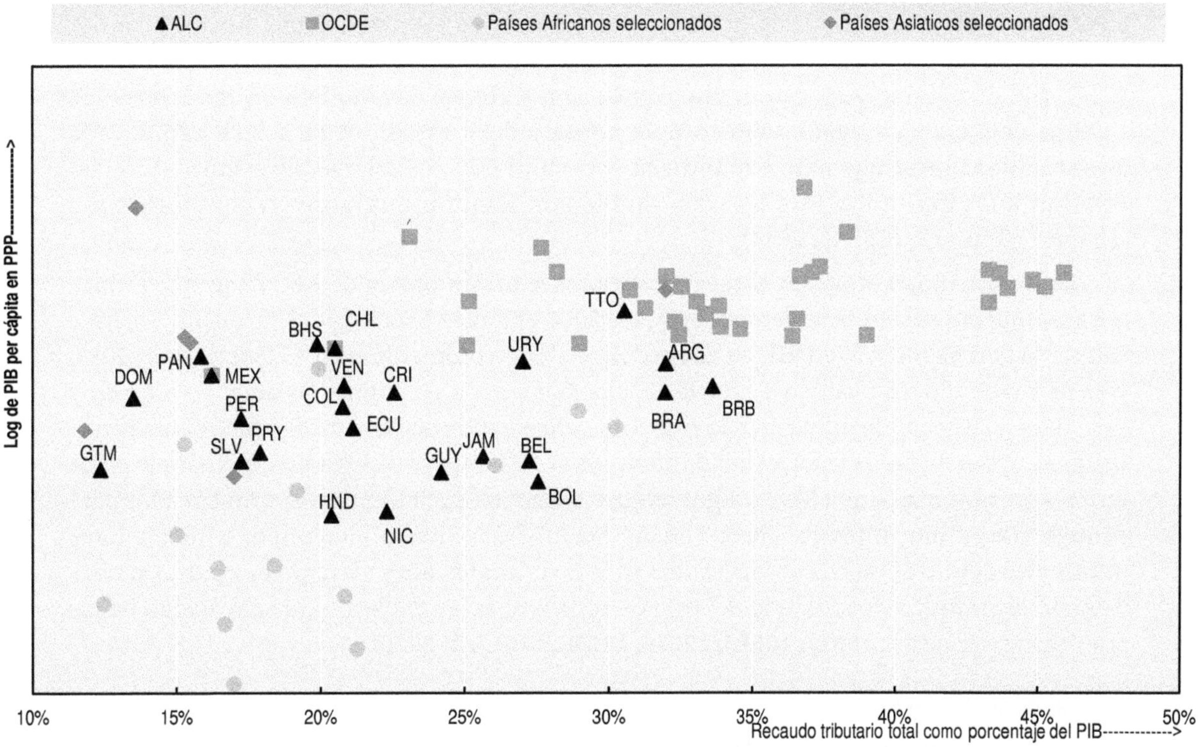

Nota: El año de comparación es 2015 ya que los datos de 2016 en cuanto los promedios de los ingresos tributarios con relación al PIB no estaban disponibles para los países seleccionados de África y Asia. La paridad de poder de compra (PPP) entre dos países es la tasa a la cual la moneda de un país necesita ser convertida en la de un segundo país para asegurar que el mismo volumen de bienes y servicios puedan ser adquiridos en ambos países. El tipo de conversión PPP implícito se expresa como moneda nacional por dólar internacional actual. Un dólar internacional tiene el mismo poder adquisitivo que el dólar estadounidense en los Estados Unidos. Un dólar internacional es una moneda hipotética que se utiliza como medio para convertir y comparar los costos de un país a otro utilizando un punto de referencia común, el dólar estadounidense (Definiciones derivadas del FMI, 2016b y OMS, 2015).

Fuente: FMI (2017c), *Perspectivas de la economía mundial, octubre de 2017*, Fondo Monetario Internacional para cifras del PIB per cápita. Las proporciones entre los ingresos tributarios y el PIB se obtienen de las publicaciones regionales de estadísticas de tributarias (*www.oecd.org/tax/tax-policy/revenue-statistics-comparable-tax-revenue-data.htm*).

StatLink *http://dx.doi.org/10.1787/888933685150*

El recaudo tributario, como porcentaje del PIB, depende de factores económicos y estructurales. El PIB per cápita, la apertura comercial, el tamaño de la economía informal, la dotación de recursos naturales y la importancia del sector agrícola en la economía son todos factores que pueden influenciar el nivel de recaudo tributario. Los determinantes socio-demográficos son también claves, por ejemplo el nivel de educación o el grado de participación femenina en la fuerza de trabajo. El poder de las administraciones tributarias, el nivel de corrupción y la moral fiscal (o la disposición de la gente para pagar impuestos) son todos factores que están fuertemente vinculados al nivel de recaudo (OCDE, 2014). Finalmente, la ubicación geográfica y factores históricos también inciden en la recaudación. Por ejemplo, la posibilidad de gravar bienes y servicios en el puerto de entrada es menor en países sin costa marítima. Adicionalmente, factores internacionales, incluyendo las políticas tributarias adoptadas por otros países, pueden tener un impacto en los niveles de recaudo tributario.

El grado de participación del estado en el financiamiento de la seguridad social es otro factor importante para explicar los niveles de recaudo tributario en la región de ALC. Desde 1980 en adelante, muchos países de ALC privatizaron sus sistemas sanitarios, previsionales y de seguridad social en mayor o menor medida. Chile, El Salvador y México son ejemplos de países que han migrado sus esquemas previsionales a programas de cuentas individuales administrados por el sector privado. En Colombia y Perú, los sistemas públicos y privados compiten y los empleados pueden determinar su afiliación a uno u otro (CEPAL, 2010; OCDE/BID/CIAT, 2014; OCDE/BID/Banco Mundial, 2014). Por otra parte, Argentina, Brasil y Uruguay siguen un modelo en los cuales los sistemas públicos y privados son complementarios. En estos tres países se han llevado a cabo sendas reformas para expandir la cobertura de los sistemas de seguridad social e incluir a los excluidos. Esto ha sido también un factor importante en el aumento del recaudo tributario (CEPAL, 2014).

La informalidad erosiona el recaudo tributario en los países de ALC dado que reduce la base impositiva significativamente (OCDE, 2008 y Gómez Sabaini et al. 2010). En América Latina[3] la tasa de informalidad[4] fue alrededor de 55% en promedio en 2013 (Bosch et al., 2013) y ha permanecido relativamente estable. Bolivia, Guatemala, Honduras, Nicaragua, Paraguay y Perú tienen las tasas de informalidad más altas, excediendo el 65%. Brasil, Chile, Costa Rica y Uruguay tienen tasas de informalidad inferiores al 40%. Estos niveles eran aún más elevados en los años noventa, lo que llevó a algunos gobiernos introducir impuestos simplificados para pequeños contribuyentes que fueron en alguna medida exitosos en integrar a trabajadores informales dentro del sector formal. Estos sistemas simplificados variaron en cuanto al nivel de éxito alcanzado dependiendo del tipo de contribuyentes cubiertos y la capacidad de las administraciones tributarias (CEPAL, 2014; OCDE/BID/CIAT, 2016).

Estructuras tributarias

La estructura impositiva (definida como la proporción de los principales tipos de impuestos en los ingresos fiscales totales) muestra la composición del recaudo tributario por sus diferentes tipos de impuestos. Este es un indicador importante dado que los impuestos tienen efectos económicos y sociales diferentes. Las estructuras tributarias varían en los países incluidos en esta publicación, lo que refleja diferentes opciones de política, estructuras económicas, condiciones coyunturales, capacidades de las administraciones tributarias y factores históricos.

Evolución de las estructuras tributarias

En promedio, la proporción de impuestos al valor agregado y los impuestos sobre la renta y utilidades aumentó entre 1990 y 2016. Hubo un ligero cambio hacia los impuestos al valor agregado y una reducción en los impuestos sobre los ingresos y las ganancias entre 2015 y 2016. La proporción del impuesto al valor agregado alcanzó los 29.3% del total de los ingresos tributarios en 2016, lo que corresponde a un aumento de 13.0 puntos porcentuales entre 1990 y 2016, mientras que la proporción de los ingresos tributarios provenientes de otros impuestos sobre bienes y servicios (impuestos especiales, derechos de aduana y derechos de importación) disminuyó de 17.3 puntos porcentuales durante el mismo periodo (véase el gráfico 1.10). La proporción de impuestos sobre las rentas y utilidades creció de 4.5 puntos porcentuales (de 22.8% a 27.3% del recaudo tributario total) entre 1990 y 2016, como resultado de los mayores niveles de recaudo experimentado en la segunda mitad de los años 2000. Las contribuciones a la seguridad social como porcentaje del recaudo tributario total aumentaron en 3.3 puntos durante los últimos 26 años, alcanzando 15.9% en 2016.

Gráfico 1.10. **Estructura tributaria promedio en la región ALC, 1990 y 2016**

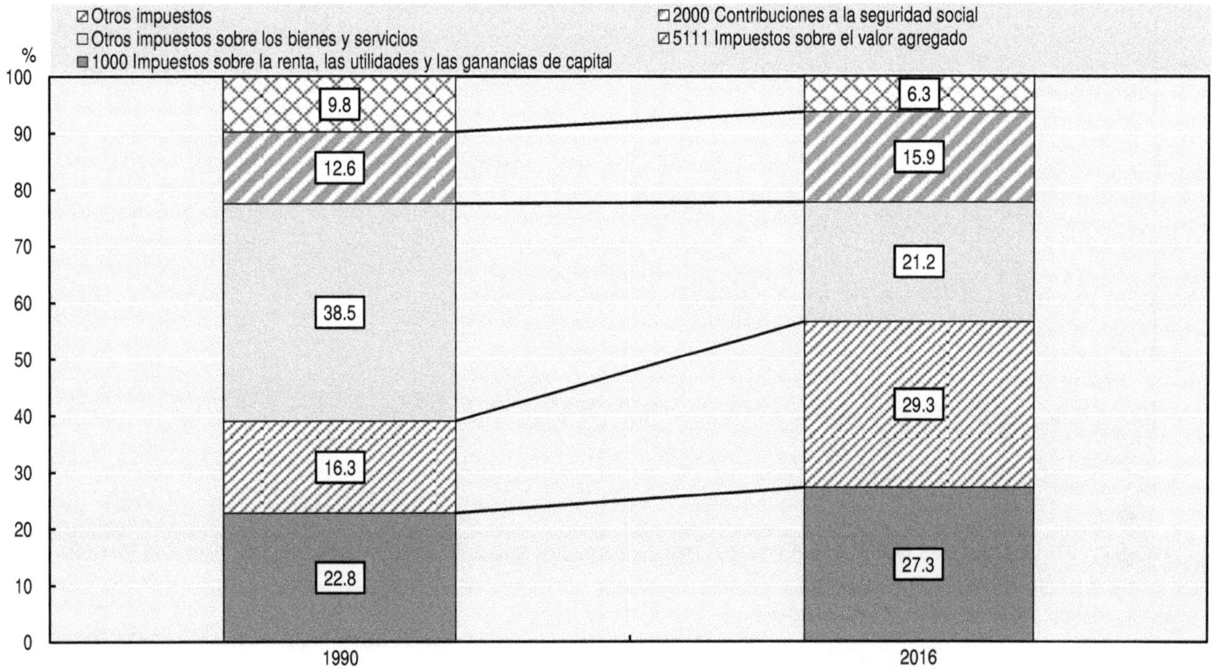

Fuente: Elaboración propia basada en los cuadros presentados en OCDE/CEPAL/CIAT/BID (2018), Capítulo 4.

StatLink http://dx.doi.org/10.1787/888933685169

Las tendencias opuestas experimentadas dentro de los impuestos a los bienes y servicios evidencian la importancia cada vez mayor del IVA y la caída en el papel que juegan los otros impuestos sobre bienes y servicios. El IVA fue adoptado de forma temprana por las economías de la región en los años ochenta (doce[5] países lo habían implementado para el año 1980). Desde los años noventa significó una fuente creciente de recaudo tributario para la región de ALC, rol que ha sido consolidado mediante la implementación de ajustes a la base del impuesto y a sus tasas, así como al fortalecimiento de las administraciones tributarias. Las reformas también se focalizaron en la simplificación del sistema tributario, en la medida que muchos países redujeron el número de productos gravados a tasa cero y a tasas reducidas, avanzando hacia sistemas de una sola tasa del IVA en muchos casos.

En la región ALC, el recaudo de los impuestos sobre bienes y servicios es la mayor fuente de ingresos como proporción del recaudo tributario total y representa la mitad de los impuestos totales. El recaudo de los impuestos sobre los bienes y servicios fue la principal fuente de recaudo en todos los países de ALC con la excepción de Trinidad y Tobago, México y Panamá. Los ingresos provenientes de impuestos sobre la renta y utilidades fueron la principalmente fuente de recaudo para México y Trinidad y Tobago mientras que las contribuciones a la seguridad social fueron la fuente más importante para Panamá. Para Trinidad y Tobago casi 50% de sus ingresos tributarios proviene de los impuestos a la renta y a las utilidades en 2016 (véase el gráfico 1.12).

Gráfico 1.11. **Estructura tributaria promedio en la región ALC, 1990-2016**

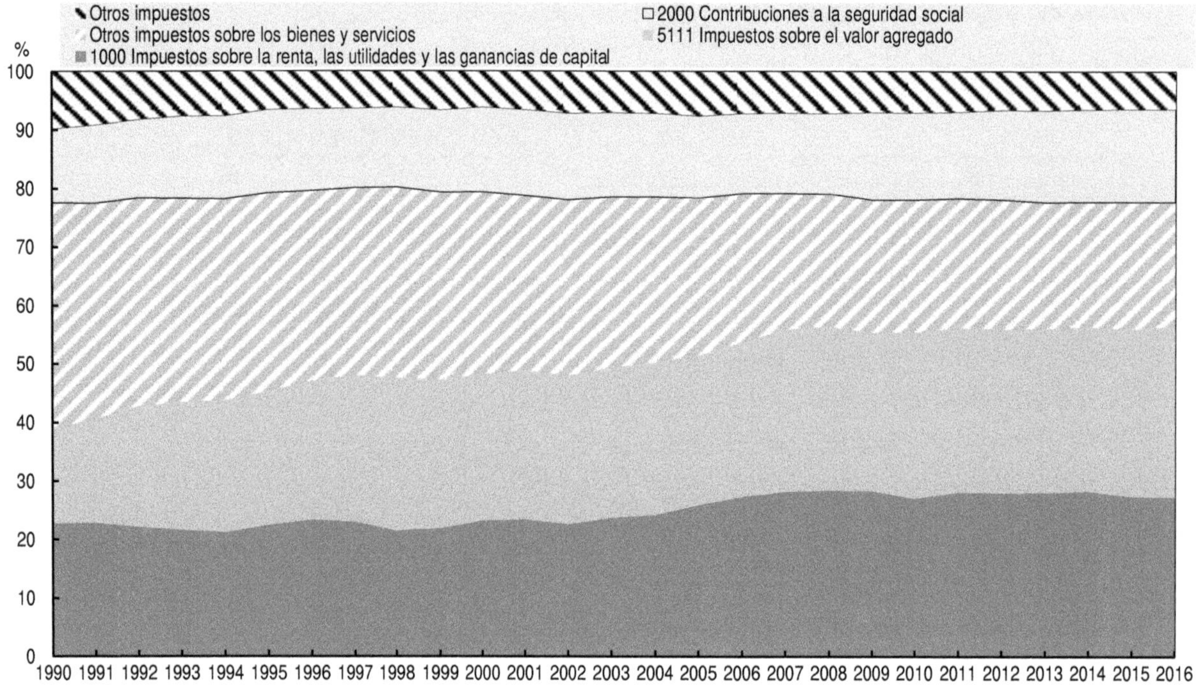

Fuente: OCDE/CEPAL/CIAT/BID (2018), "Estadísticas tributarias en América Latina: tablas comparativas", *Estadísticas tributarias de la OCDE* (base de datos), *http://dx.doi.org/10.1787/data-00641-en.*

StatLink http://dx.doi.org/10.1787/888933685188

Gráfico 1.12. **Estructura tributaria en los países ALC, 2016**

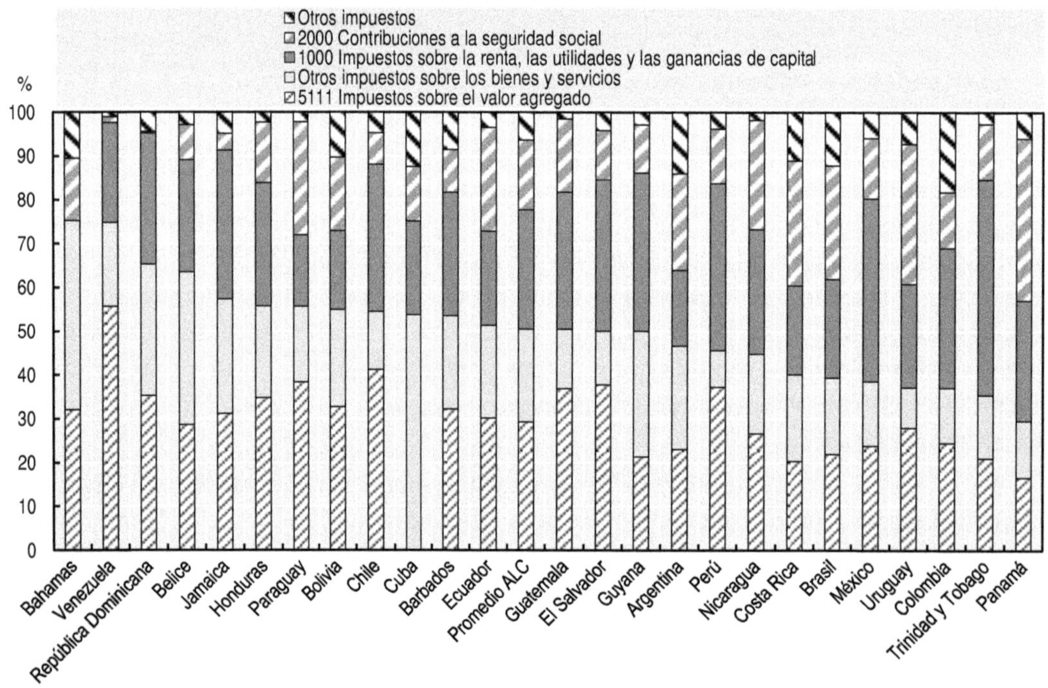

Nota: Las proporciones tributarias de las distintas categorías impositivas deben ser interpretadas con cautela en Venezuela dado que los altos índices de inflación las han afectado.

Fuente: Elaboración propia basada en los cuadros presentados en OCDE/CEPAL/CIAT/BID (2018), Capítulo 4.

StatLink http://dx.doi.org/10.1787/888933685207

En promedio en 2016, el 29.3% del recaudo total procedió del IVA en los países de América Latina. No obstante, existe mucha heterogeneidad en la región. El IVA, como porcentaje del recaudo total, varía de 16.6% en Panamá hasta 55.8% en Venezuela. Como porcentaje del PIB, Barbados, Belice y Bolivia obtuvieron la mayor cantidad de ingresos del IVA (10.4% en Barbados y 8.5% tanto en Bolivia como en Belice). No existe IVA Cuba. La amplia variación entre los países es también un resultado de los diferentes diseños del IVA: las tasas y bases varían ampliamente en la región. Por ejemplo, México no grava los alimentos, medicinas y números otros productos lo que se traduce en una base estrecha. CEPAL (2014) sugiere que las pérdidas tributarias de estas exenciones pueden ir desde 1.1% hasta 2.5% del PIB (véase el gráfico 1.13).

Gráfico 1.13. **Recaudo del IVA como porcentaje del ingreso tributario total y como porcentaje del PIB en los países ALC, 2016**

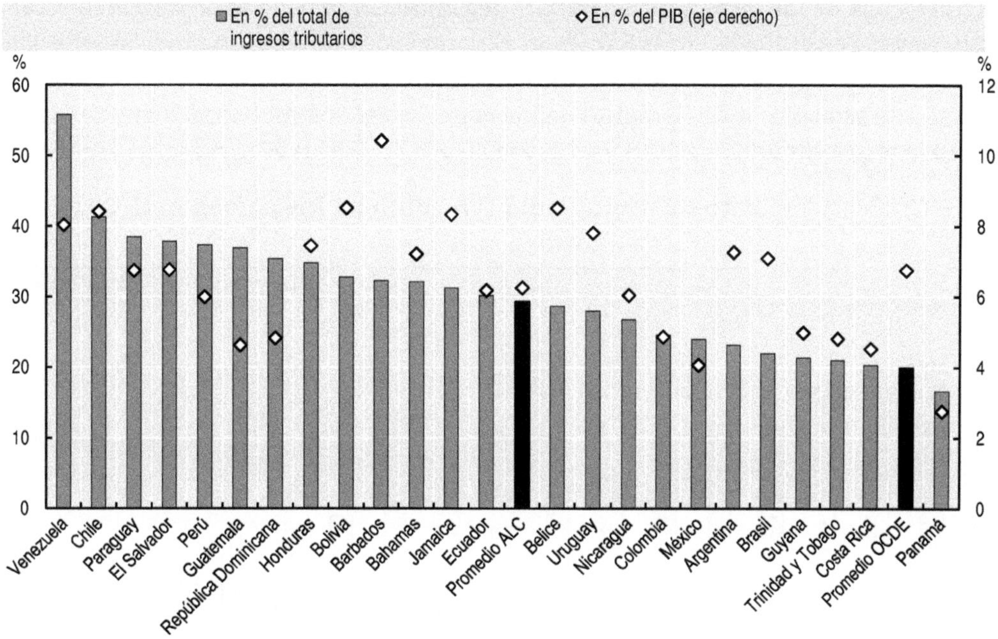

Nota: Cuba no tiene un sistema de IVA.
Fuente: OCDE/CEPAL/CIAT/BID (2018), Cuadro 4.10.

StatLink http://dx.doi.org/10.1787/888933685226

Ratio de recaudo del IVA

La medida del ratio de recaudo del IVA (VRR por sus siglas en inglés) ha sido calculada para los países seleccionados de América Latina[6]. OCDE (2016) explica que el VRR mide la diferencia entre el recaudo observado del IVA y el recaudo teórico o potencial del IVA si este fuese aplicado a una tasa única a toda la base impositiva en un régimen de IVA "puro". Esta sección muestra los niveles del VRR en América Latina y el Caribe en 2015 y analiza tres países a mayor profundidad: Bolivia, Paraguay y Panamá.

Existe una notable disparidad en los VRRs de los países de América Latina y el Caribe en 2015 (véase el gráfico 1.14) con un VRR promedio de 58%. En comparación, el promedio de la OCDE en 2014 fue del 56%. En 2015, México y Guyana tuvieron los índices más bajos de VRR (en 32% y 38% respectivamente) mientras que Bolivia y Paraguay tuvieron los niveles más altos (los dos en 91%). La OCDE (2016) señala que existen varios elementos que explican un bajo VRR en México, como el alcance de las exenciones al IVA, la aplicación de una tasa cero a un gran número de bienes y servicios, una tasa reducida del 11% en zonas fronterizas y también un bajo nivel de cumplimiento. Una reforma al IVA se implementó en enero de 2014 que extendió la tasa estándar de 16% a las zonas fronterizas, eliminando las tasas diferenciadas. La reforma también eliminó la tasa cero sobre hoteles y sobre los servicios provistos a extranjeros, que ahora se encuentran gravados a la tasa estándar, y se ajustó el régimen de las maquiladoras para reducir el riesgo al fraude. El VRR en México se incrementó 0.4 puntos entre 2013 y 2014.

Guyana introdujo el IVA más tarde que otros países. Desde su introducción en 2007, Guyana ha visto una reducción en la conformidad del IVA que puede deberse al deterioro de la gestión del cumplimiento (Schlotterbeck, 2017). Entre 2007 y 2016, los ingresos del IVA como porcentaje del PIB disminuyeron del 6.1% al 5.0%. Además, Schlotterbeck (2017) explica que los suministros con calificación cero en Guyana representaron el 52.5% de los suministros imponibles.

Las Bahamas y la República Dominicana tienen índices de ingresos provenientes del IVA relativamente bajos. Las Bahamas introdujeron el IVA estándar en 2015 a un 7.5% (sin tasas reducidas), una de las tasas más bajas en la región ALC, donde la tasa promedio estándar del IVA se sitúa en el 13.7%. En las Bahamas, el sistema de IVA tiene una base amplia con un número limitado de exenciones, por lo que es probable que el VRR aumente a medida que el sistema se establece más. El monto de los ingresos del IVA recaudados en 2016 fue tres veces mayor que el monto en 2015 y es probable que el VRR en 2016 también sea más alto.

Gráfico 1.14. **Ratio de recaudo del IVA (VRR) en los países ALC, 2015**

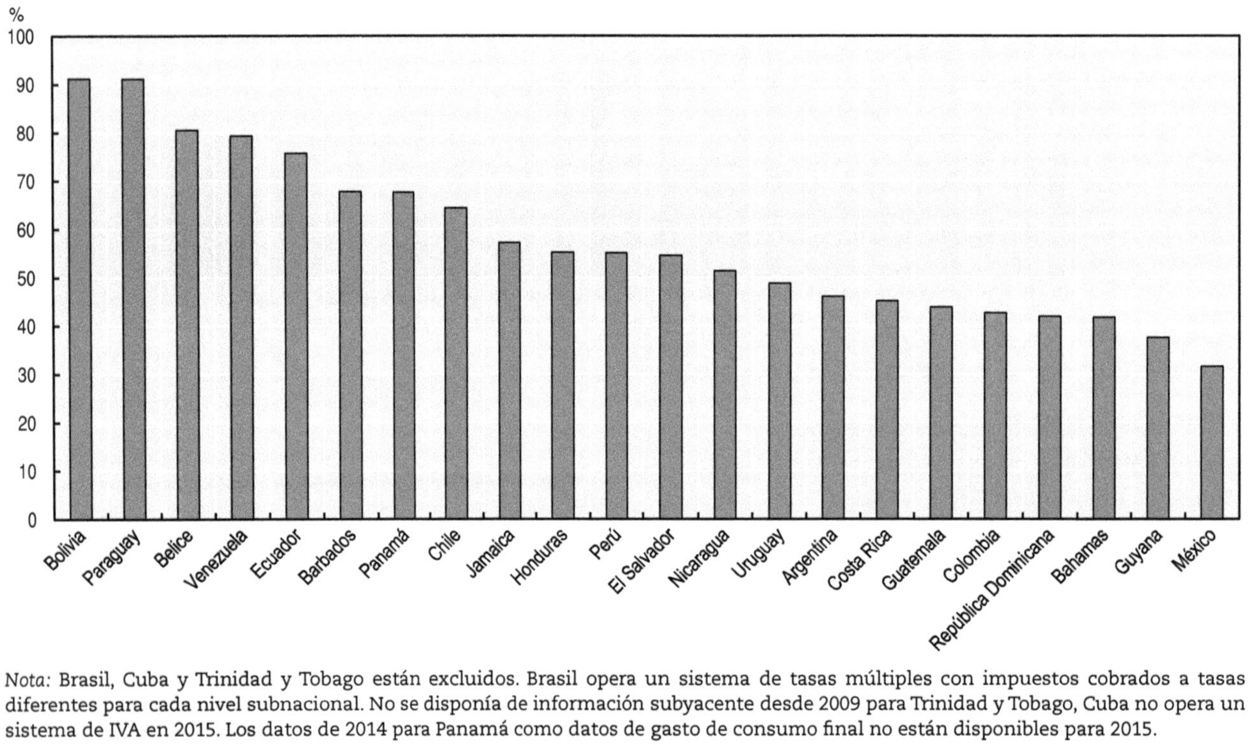

Nota: Brasil, Cuba y Trinidad y Tobago están excluidos. Brasil opera un sistema de tasas múltiples con impuestos cobrados a tasas diferentes para cada nivel subnacional. No se disponía de información subyacente desde 2009 para Trinidad y Tobago, Cuba no opera un sistema de IVA en 2015. Los datos de 2014 para Panamá como datos de gasto de consumo final no están disponibles para 2015.

Fuente: Las tasas de IVA provienen de los sitios web CIAT, Trading Economics y Deloitte, las cifras de consumo final de gastos del sitio web de la División de Estadística de las Naciones Unidas y los ingresos del IVA de las tablas de países del capítulo 5.

StatLink http://dx.doi.org/10.1787/888933685245

El VRR de Bolivia excedió el 90% en 2015. Una tasa del VRR de un 90% sugiere que solo existe una pequeña pérdida en los ingresos del IVA como consecuencia de exenciones, tasas diferenciadas reducidas, fraude, evasión o planificación fiscal. No obstante, el alto nivel del VRR puede ser parcialmente explicado por otros factores. Primero, Bolivia aplica una tasa estándar de 13% al producto final de un bien o un servicio que ya incluyen el IVA, lo que lleva a una tasa efectiva de 14.94%, más alta que la tasa nominal. Al utilizar la tasa efectiva la medida del VRR cae de 91% hasta 79% en 2015. Segundo, Bolivia no tiene tasas reducidas y aplica el IVA a una amplia gama de productos y servicios (Ernst & Young, 2014). Los altos índices de informalidad pueden afectar los niveles del VRR, pero es claro si este es el caso en Bolivia (véase el gráfico 1.15).

El VRR de Bolivia ha estado aumentando desde 1990 aunque este crecimiento fue interrumpido entre 1997 y el 2000. Una reforma del sector público en 2000 incluyó el fortalecimiento de los procesos de inspección y control de las devoluciones del IVA puede haber contribuido a la mejora del indicador a partir del año 2000. De acuerdo a Zuleta (2008), "los cambios en los procesos y los procedimientos para la devolución del IVA han tenido un impacto positivo durante la reforma institucional". Esto se evidenció en la caída en la evasión del IVA en 13 puntos porcentuales, pasando de 42%[7] en 2001 a 29% en 2004. También disminuyeron las devoluciones del IVA como porcentaje de las exportaciones y del recaudo total del IVA. Estas tendencias muestran que la corrupción en los procesos de devolución del IVA han sido reducidos (Zuleta, 2008). Dentro del mismo período, el VRR mejoró 13 puntos porcentuales, pasando de 51% a 64%. Por otra parte, entre 2004 y 2013, el VRR continuó incrementando (excepto durante el período de la crisis fiscal). No obstante, existe poca evidencia para explicarlo: la medición del incumplimiento en el pago del IVA durante el tiempo o los niveles de informalidad en IVA pueden ser útiles para llegar a conclusiones más robustas.

Junto con Bolivia, Paraguay tuvo el VRR más alto dentro del grupo de países seleccionados de ALC, puntuando 91% en 2015. Es muy poco probable que solo 9% de los posibles ingresos provenientes del IVA no se recupere. Según el FMI (2010), "la alta productividad del IVA"[8] refleja, en gran parte, el alto recaudo que se obtiene de las re-exportaciones (cercanas a 2% del PIB). Mucho del comercio de las re-exportaciones son informales, razón por la cual los pagos al IVA en las importaciones no son deducidos cuando los bienes vuelven a ser exportados.

El VRR ha estado incrementando en Paraguay desde 2002. El aumento en 2004 puede ser parcialmente explicado por las reformas de política y administración. Una reforma tributaria exhaustiva que incluya medidas para la ampliación de la base impositiva del IVA y un nuevo marco legal para mejorar el control, procedimientos y sistemas de recaudo sobre impuestos y aduanas se implementó en 2004. La reforma perseguía un sistema tributario mucho más simple y eficiente (FMI, 2010). Al mismo tiempo, el gobierno atacó la corrupción que había estado obstaculizando una mayor recaudación tributaria (Franks, et al., 2005).

Panamá ha tenido un VRR sobre el 60% desde 2008 y tuvo un VRR en 68% en 2014. Panamá tuvo un alza significativa en el VRR de un año a otro, pasando de 28% en 2007 hasta 63% en 2008. Esto fue precedido de una amplia auditoría realizada por Dirección General de Impuestos en 2008 con la finalidad de detener las pérdidas en el IVA por la falta de cumplimiento de las empresas en declarar el IVA cobrado a clientes. Luego de esta auditoría, llevada a cabo en el primer trimestre de 2008, los ingresos provenientes del IVA aumentaron de 22% en comparación con todo el año de 2007 (The Panama Investor Blog, 2008). El IVA, como porcentaje del PIB, se duplicó entre 2007 y 2008, pasando de 1% a 2.1%.

Impuestos sobre las rentas y utilidades y contribuciones a la seguridad social

En 2016, los ingresos provenientes de los impuestos sobre las rentas y utilidades se situaron en 27.3% como proporción de todos los ingresos en la región ALC. El impuesto sobre la renta de empresas representó la proporción más grande de los impuestos sobre la renta y utilidades en 15.4%, del recaudo tributario total mientras que el impuesto sobre la renta de personas representó 9.7%[9] del recaudo tributario total (véase el gráfico 1.16). La estructura impositiva en ALC incluye una mayor participación del impuesto sobre la renta de personas y una menor del impuesto sobre la renta de empresas.

Gráfico 1.15. **Ratio de recaudo del IVA (VRR) en Bolivia, Paraguay y Panamá, 1990 – 2015**

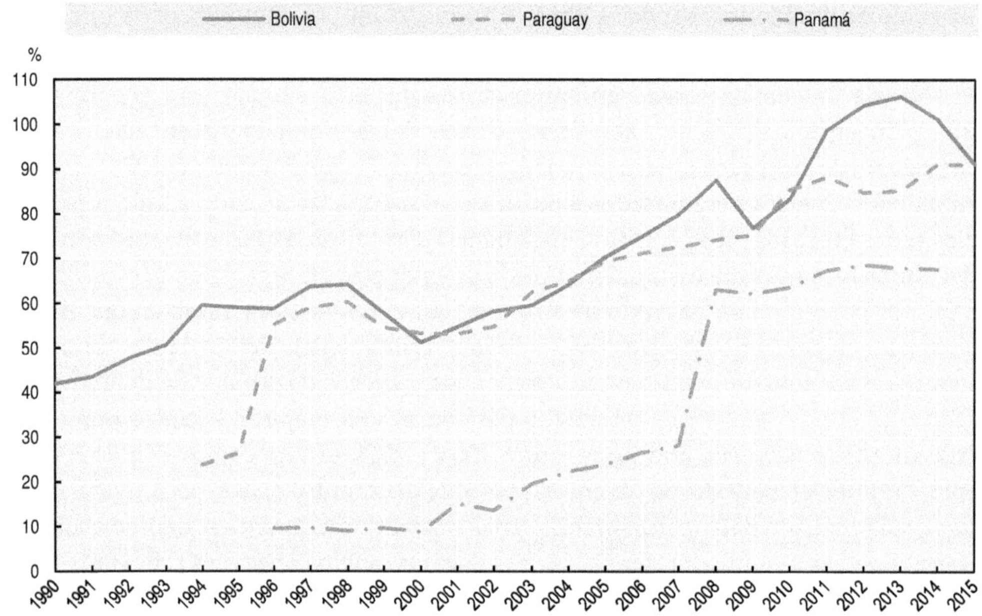

Nota: Las cifras del gasto de consumo final utilizadas para compilar el VRR no estaban disponibles para Panamá antes de 1996 y antes de 2015 para Paraguay. En Paraguay, el IVA fue implementado a mediados de 1993, por lo que no hay VRR entre 1990 y 1993.

Fuente: Las tasas de IVA provienen de los sitios web CIAT, Trading Economics y Deloitte, las cifras de consumo final del sitio web de la División de Estadística de las Naciones Unidas y los ingresos por IVA de las tablas de países del capítulo 5.

StatLink *http://dx.doi.org/10.1787/888933685264*

Gráfico 1.16. **Estructura tributaria promedio en la región ALC, 2007 y 2016**

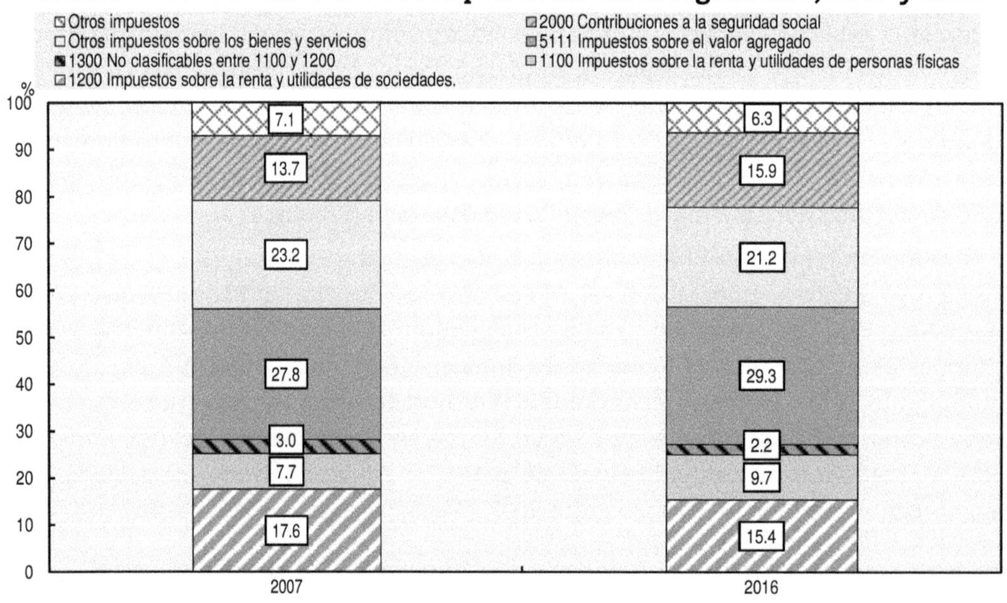

Nota: Los ingresos del impuesto sobre la renta de las personas físicas de ALC y los ingresos del impuesto sobre la renta de las personas físicas como porcentaje del PIB deben ser interpretados con cautela ya que Ecuador, Nicaragua y Venezuela están excluidos en el cálculo. Para estos países, más de un tercio de sus ingresos provenientes de los impuestos sobre la renta y utilidades no pueden ser atribuidos a los ingresos del impuesto sobre la renta de las sociedades (1200) ni a los ingresos del impuesto sobre la renta de las personas físicas (1100). Excluyendo a estos países, una pequeña proporción de los ingresos procedentes de los impuestos sobre la renta y las utilidades sigue sin poder atribuirse.

Fuente: OCDE/CEPAL/CIAT/BID (2018), "Estadísticas Tributarias en América Latina: tablas comparativas", *Estadísticas tributarias de la OCDE* (base de datos), *http://dx.doi.org/10.1787/data-00641-en*.

StatLink *http://dx.doi.org/10.1787/888933685283*

Existe una gran heterogeneidad en la región ALC. En 2016, Colombia tuvo los ingresos del impuesto sobre la renta de sociedades más altos, con 24.6% como porcentaje del ingreso total, y Barbados tiene la tasa más baja de 8.2% (véase el gráfico 1.17). Las Bahamas es el único país en este reporte que no opera un impuesto sobre la renta (de personas o sociedades). En Cuba y Trinidad y Tobago los impuestos sobre la renta son los más elevados como porcentaje del PIB, correspondiendo a 6.3% para Cuba y 5.4% para Trinidad y Tobago.

Gráfico 1.17. **Recaudo del impuesto sobre la renta de sociedades como porcentaje del recaudo total y como porcentaje del PIB en algunos países de ALC, 2016**

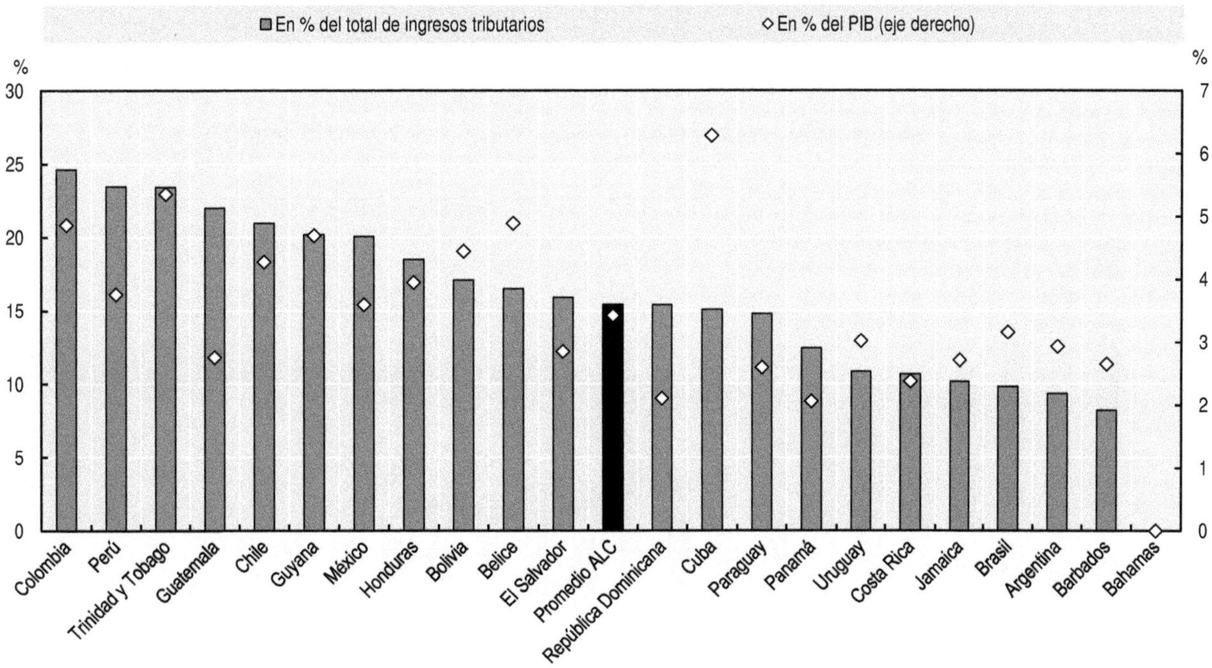

Nota: Las Bahamas no tiene un sistema de impuestos sobre la renta de las empresas. Ecuador, Nicaragua y Venezuela están excluidos de este gráfico ya que más de un tercio de sus ingresos provenientes de los impuestos a la renta y utilidades no pueden ser asignados al impuesto sobre la renta de las empresas o al impuesto a la renta de personas físicas (1100).

Fuente: OCDE/CEPAL/CIAT/BID (2018), "Estadísticas tributarias en América Latina: tablas comparativas", *Estadísticas tributarias de la OCDE* (base de datos), *http://dx.doi.org/10.1787/data-00641-en*.

StatLink http://dx.doi.org/10.1787/888933685302

La proporción de ingresos del impuesto sobre la renta de personas sigue siendo baja en ALC a pesar de las reformas implementadas por algunos países para expandir su base tributaria. Luego de la crisis financiera mundial varios países implementaron tasas proporcionales al capital, que previamente no se gravaban, e introdujeron esquemas progresivos para gravar las rentas del trabajo (CEPAL, 2014). No obstante, la proporción de ingresos provenientes de impuestos sobre la renta de personas físicas sigue siendo modesta en ALC: más de la mitad de los países generan menos del 10% de su recaudo total de esta fuente. En 2016, el recaudo del impuesto a la renta de personas físicas, como proporción de los ingresos tributarios totales, varía desde 0.8% (Bolivia) hasta 22.8% (Trinidad y Tobago) excluyendo a las Bahamas que no opera un sistema de impuestos a la renta de personas físicas (véase el gráfico 1.18).

Estudios de la OCDE (OCDE, 2008 y Daude et al., 2010) sugieren que la proporción de rentas del trabajo en el PIB es baja en los países de ALC. También hay pocos contribuyentes con obligación tributaria, lo que implica que la contribución tributaria sea baja en vista de los niveles de ingresos relativamente bajos de la región: solo el 10% de la población en América Latina es un contribuyente tributario registrado (BID, 2013). Otros estudios (Barreix, et al., 2017; BID, 2015; CEPAL, 2014; CEPAL, 2010 y Gómez Sabaini et al., 2010) atribuyen el bajo recaudo del impuesto a la renta de personas físicas a factores adicionales: una base imponible limitada de salarios, dados algunos beneficios otorgados a las rentas del capital, y altos niveles de evasión. BID (2013) estima que "más de la mitad del potencial de recaudación del impuesto se pierde a través de la evasión" en los países de América Latina. Un análisis exhaustivo del impuesto a la renta de personas físicas en países seleccionados de América latina está incluido en el capítulo especial 3 de esta publicación.

Gráfico 1.18. **Recaudo del impuesto sobre la renta de personas físicas, como porcentaje del recaudo total y como porcentaje del PIB en algunos países de ALC, 2016.**

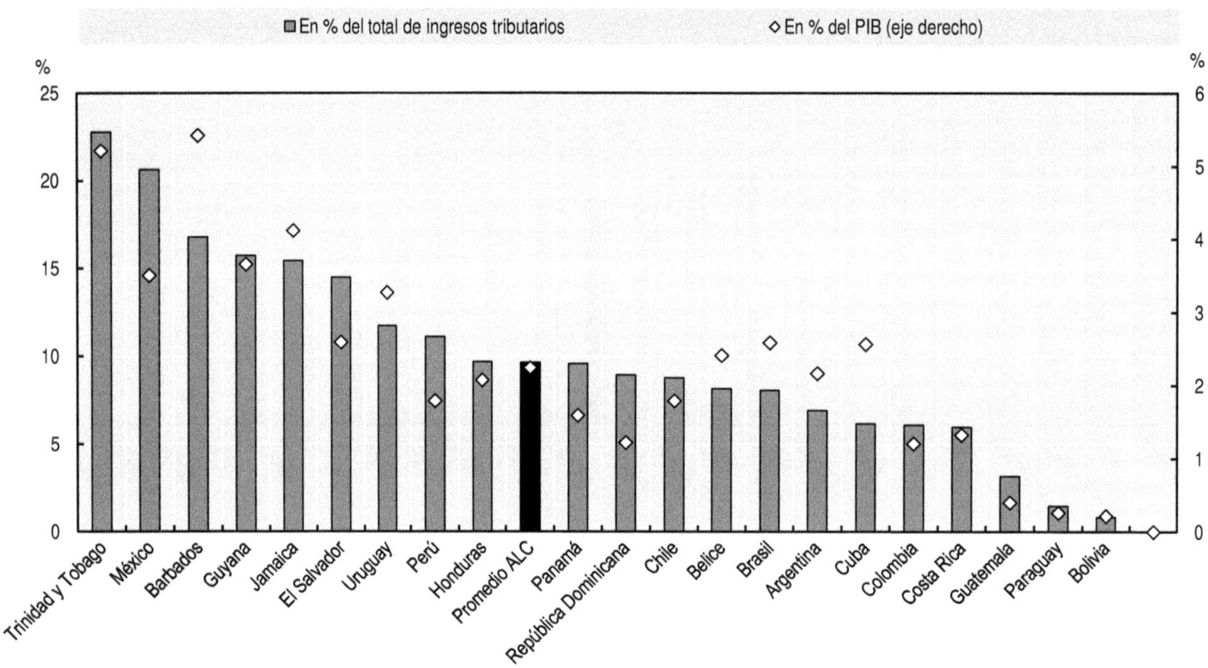

Nota: Las Bahamas no tienen un sistema de impuestos sobre la renta de las personas físicas. Ecuador y Venezuela están excluidos ya que más de un tercio de sus ingresos provenientes de los impuestos sobre la renta y utilidades no pueden asignarse al impuesto sobre la renta de empresas o al impuesto sobre la renta de personas físicas (1100).

Fuente: Elaboración propia basada en los cuadros presentados en OCDE/CEPAL/CIAT/BID (2018), Capítulo 4.

StatLink http://dx.doi.org/10.1787/888933685321

La participación de las contribuciones a la seguridad social dentro de los ingresos tributarios totales aumentó 3.3 puntos porcentuales desde 1990, alcanzando 15.9% en 2016 (véase el gráfico 1.16). Esto refleja dos factores trabajando de forma paralela. Primero, el aumento en la renta per cápita ha tenido un impacto positivo sobre el recaudo. Segundo, los procesos de privatización total o parcial de los sistemas de seguridad social en varios países de la región que lo contrarrestaron. En aquellos países con sistemas públicos o mixtos, incluidos Argentina, Brasil, Costa Rica, México, Panamá, Paraguay y Uruguay, las contribuciones a la seguridad social continúan teniendo un peso significativo (más del 20% del recaudo total). En Argentina, las cifras muestran la introducción de cuentas de capitalización privadas en 1994 y su subsiguiente nacionalización en 2008. Mientras tanto, en Colombia y en Perú, donde los sistemas previsionales público y privado compiten, el recaudo tributario del sistema público se sitúa en torno al 12% del recaudo total.

Comparaciones con la OCDE

La estructura tributaria (*tax mix*) en los países de ALC muestra un recaudo bajo a partir de impuestos directos, con un recaudo alto de impuestos indirectos relativo al promedio observado en OCDE (véase el gráfico 1.19). En particular, los países de ALC dependen fuertemente de los impuestos sobre bienes y servicios, los cuales constituyen más de la mitad de todos los ingresos tributarios, comparado a cerca de un tercio en promedio para economías de la OCDE. Sin embargo, como porcentaje del PBI, los ingresos por impuestos sobre bienes y servicios se mantuvieron en un nivel similar para los promedios de ALC y OCDE, en 11.5% y 10.9% respectivamente en 2015[10]. El nivel de ingresos del IVA como porcentaje del PIB también fue muy similar, con 6.3% para el promedio de ALC y 6.7% para la OCDE.

En promedio, menos del 44% del recaudo tributario total proviene de la suma de impuestos sobre la renta y utilidades y contribuciones a la seguridad social, comparado con 60% para el grupo OCDE en 2015. Como porcentaje del PIB, estas dos categorías sumaron el 10% de la región ALC, lo que representó la mitad del monto promedio recaudado por los países de la OCDE (20.5%). La participación de las contribuciones a la seguridad social dentro del recaudo total fue 10 puntos porcentuales del PIB más baja en ALC que el promedio de la OCDE (16.0% comparado con 25.8%). La existencia de esquemas previsionales y sanitarios privados en la región de ALC explica en alguna medida esta disparidad. La diferencia de la contribución de los impuestos sobre la renta y las utilidades a los ingresos tributarios totales en ALC fue de 6.7 puntos porcentuales más bajos que el promedio en la OCDE (27.4% comparado con 34.1%).

Gráfico 1.19. **Estructura impositiva (como porcentaje del recaudo total) en ALC y en la OCDE, 2015**

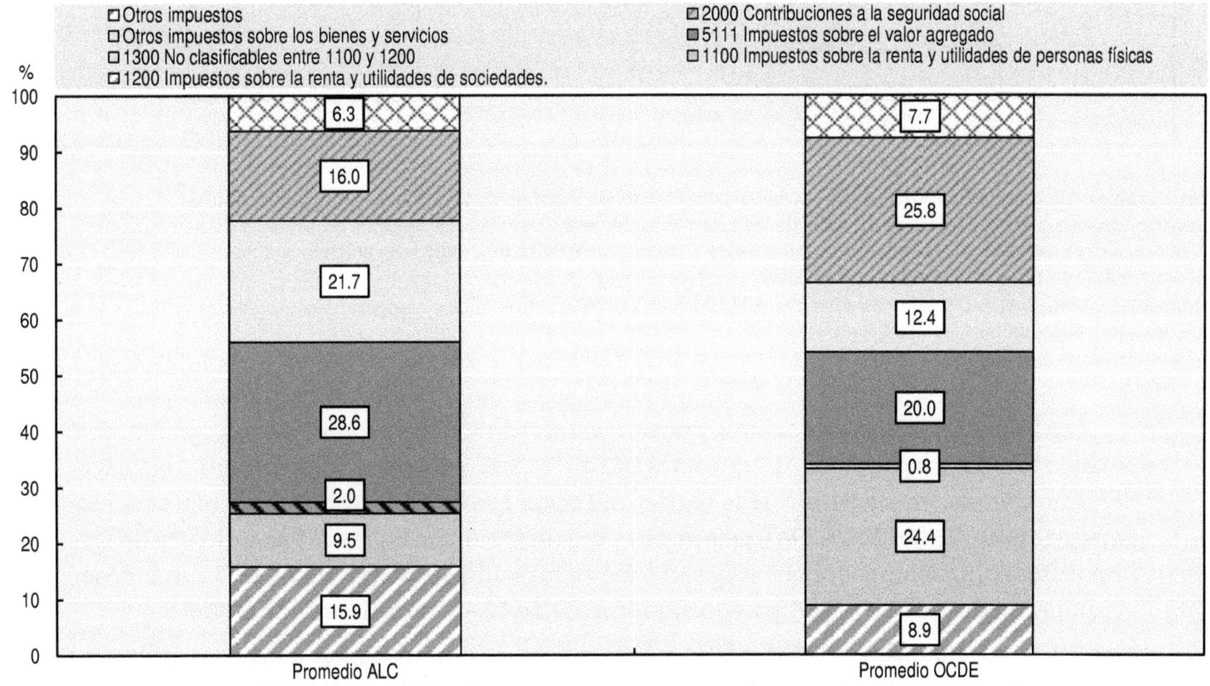

Notas: El año de comparación es 2015 ya que los datos de 2016 para el promedio de la OCDE no estaban disponibles. Ecuador, Nicaragua y Venezuela esta excluidos de los promedios del impuesto sobre la renta de empresas y de personas físicas en ALC ya que más de un tercio de sus ingresos tributarios sobre la renta y utilidades no pueden ser asignados a los ingresos de los impuestos sobre la renta de empresas o personas físicas (1100).

Fuente: OCDE/CEPAL/CIAT/BID (2018), "Estadísticas Tributarias en América Latina: tablas comparativas", *Estadísticas tributarias de la OCDE* (base de datos), *http://dx.doi.org/10.1787/data-00641-en*.

StatLink http://dx.doi.org/10.1787/888933685340

La participación del impuesto sobre la renta y utilidades de sociedades dentro del recaudo total es 15.9% en ALC comparado a 8.9% en el grupo de la OCDE. Esto corresponde respectivamente a 3.7% y 2.8% como porcentaje del PIB (véanse los gráficos 1.19 y 1.20). El recaudo del impuesto sobre la renta de personas representó el 24.4% del recaudo total en la OCDE en 2015, mientras que esta proporción ha sido considerablemente más baja en los países de ALC: 9.5% en promedio. Como porcentaje del PIB esta categoría fue de 2.2% en la región ALC, o sea casi cuatro veces más baja que el promedio de la OCDE (8.4%).

Gráfico 1.20. **Estructura tributaria (como porcentaje del PIB) en la región ALC y en la OCDE, 2015**

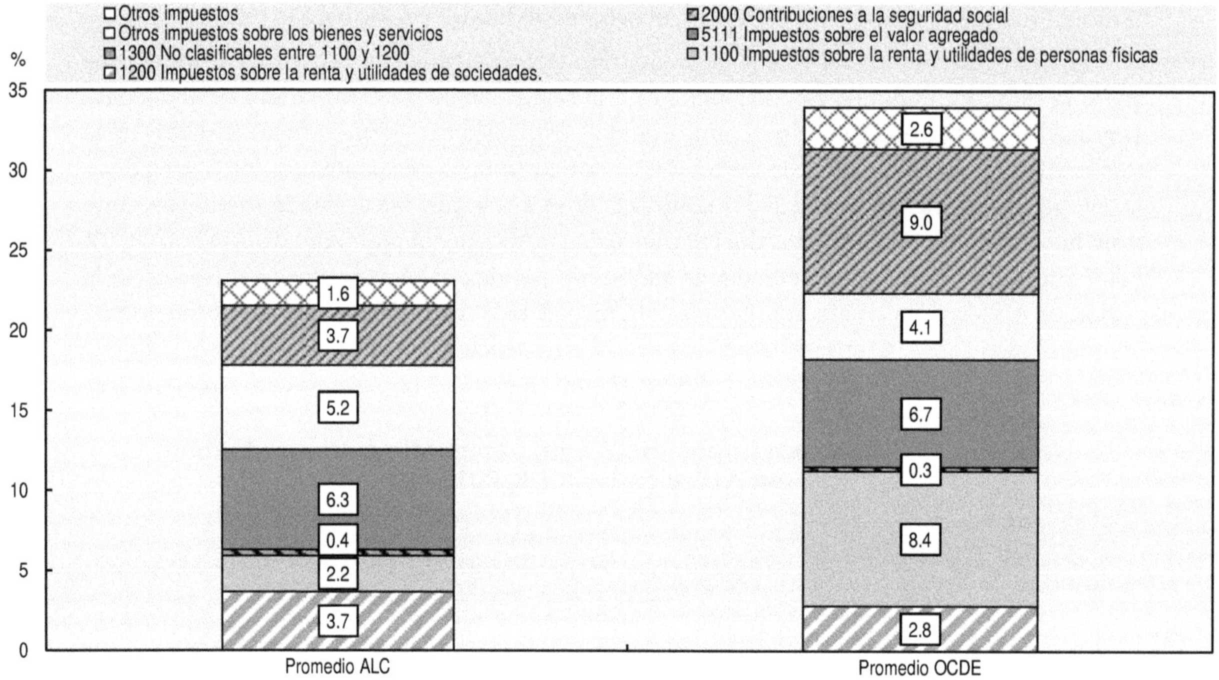

Notas: El año de comparación es 2015 ya que los datos de 2016 para el promedio de la OCDE no estaban disponibles.
Ecuador, Nicaragua y Venezuela esta excluidos de los promedios del impuesto sobre la renta de empresas y de personas físicas en ALC ya que más de un tercio de sus ingresos tributarios sobre la renta y utilidades no pueden ser asignados a los ingresos de los impuestos sobre la renta de empresas o personas físicas (1100).

Fuente: OCDE/CEPAL/CIAT/BID (2018), "Estadísticas Tributarias en América Latina: tablas comparativas", *Estadísticas tributarias de la OCDE* (base de datos), *http://dx.doi.org/10.1787/data-00641-en*.

StatLink *http://dx.doi.org/10.1787/888933685359*

Los impuestos generales sobre el consumo representan una proporción más grande del recaudo total en los países de ALC que en la OCDE. En 2015, esta categoría representó el 28.6% del recaudo total en los países de la región, mientras que la cifra correspondiente para los países de la OCDE fue 20.0%. De forma similar, la proporción de ingresos provenientes de los impuestos específicos sobre bienes y servicios es más alta en los países de ALC situándose en un promedio de 21.7%, comparado al promedio de 12.4% en países de la OCDE.

Los impuestos sobre la propiedad inmueble y sobre la nómina (agrupados en la categoría "otros impuestos") son una fuente de ingresos poco importante en los países de ALC. Las dificultades que tienen los gobiernos subnacionales en el recaudo de sus propios impuestos queda patentado en el bajo recaudo de los impuestos sobre la propiedad, los cuales son por lo general la fuente principal de los gobiernos subnacionales en la región (Brossio y Jiménez, 2012). No obstante, debe reconocerse que la falta de datos a nivel subnacional dificulta el análisis. Por otra parte la participación de los impuestos sobre la nómina es insignificante para todo el período. La participación de los impuestos sobre la propiedad y la nómina como proporción de los ingresos fiscales totales en la región de LAC se situaron en el 6.3% de los ingresos fiscales totales, en comparación con el 7.7% del promedio de la OCDE.

Impuestos por nivel de gobierno

Desde mediados de los años ochenta, los gobiernos centrales en países de ALC han transferido algunas funciones hacia los gobiernos subnacionales. En una primera etapa, la descentralización se centró en el fortalecimiento del rol democrático de las autoridades locales. Esto fue seguido por el aumento gradual en la ejecución de una mayor proporción del gasto público a nivel subnacional. No obstante lo anterior, el recaudo tributario es recolectado sobre todo a nivel del gobierno central o federal, siendo las transferencias el principal mecanismo del cual dependen los gobiernos subnacionales a diferencia de lo registrado en los países de la OCDE. Para los países en los cuales se dispone de datos de recaudo subnacional en ALC, los ingresos tributarios a nivel del gobierno central constituyen dos tercios o más de todo el recaudo. El monto correspondiente en países de la OCDE es de 60%. Brasil es una excepción notable dado que el gobierno central recaudó un 44% de todos los ingresos totales en 2015[11] (véase el cuadro 1.1).

Existen dos elementos estadísticos que deben considerarse cuando se compara la atribución del recaudo para los países de ALC y el de países miembro de la OCDE. Primero, los ingresos tributarios de ambos grupos han sido atribuidos a diferentes niveles de gobierno de acuerdo a las guías revisadas en la versión final del Sistema de Cuentas Nacionales (SCN). Esto implica que los ingresos son generalmente atribuidos al nivel del gobierno que ejerce la potestad de aplicar el impuesto o tiene la potestad de imponer o modificar la tasa del impuesto. Esto tiene implicaciones en situaciones en las que un nivel del gobierno recauda el impuesto y transfiere lo recaudado parcial o totalmente a otros niveles de gobierno. Algunos ejemplos de este tipo de mecanismos son la Ley de Coparticipaciones en Argentina, y las Participaciones Federales en México (regida por la Ley de Coordinación Fiscal), y la participación de los fondos en Brasil (definida en el artículo 159 de la constitución). El segundo elemento es que los promedios en ALC pueden verse afectados por la falta de datos a nivel subnacional en algunos países.

El porcentaje de ingresos tributarios totales recaudado por los gobiernos subnacionales es inferior al 8%, exceptuando a Argentina, Brasil y Colombia, para los 15 países de ALC para los que se dispone datos en 2015. En Brasil, los estados y las municipalidades recaudan más de un 30% de todos los ingresos tributarios, lo que indica un alto grado de descentralización tributaria. Una gran parte del IVA (ICMS - imposto sobre operações relativas à circulação de mercadorias e prestação de serviços de transporte interestadual e intermunicipal e de comunicação) es recaudado a nivel del estado. El recaudo subnacional en Argentina y Colombia representa más del 15% del recaudo nacional total. Argentina tiene un recaudo sustancial a nivel provincial, el cual se explica en gran parte por el impuesto sobre los ingresos brutos. Entre 2000 y 2015, el recaudo tributario a nivel subnacional disminuyó en 7 países y aumentó en 7. La mayor caída de se dio en Uruguay (3.9 puntos porcentuales) y el incremento más grande fue en Brasil (1.7 puntos porcentuales).

Estas cifras reflejan el hecho de que los gobiernos subnacionales en los países de ALC tienden a tener bajo su jurisdicción impuestos de bases estrechas. Los impuestos que con mayor frecuencia son asignados a los gobiernos subnacionales son los impuestos sobre la propiedad, sobre vehículos automotores e impuestos sobre servicios específicos y tasas municipales. El potencial de los ingresos tributarios de estos impuestos es mucho más limitado si se compara con los impuestos bajo la jurisdicción de gobiernos centrales o federales, tales como el IVA o los impuestos sobre la renta. En 2015, todo el recaudo subnacional de Belice, Guatemala, Jamaica y Trinidad y Tobago y más del 50% del recaudo subnacional en Paraguay, Perú y Uruguay provino de los impuestos sobre la propiedad. Todos los otros países dependen del recaudo proveniente de los impuestos sobre bienes y utilidades. México es el único país que utiliza bases tributarias diferentes a las descritas anteriormente. En 2015, el 41% del recaudo subnacional en México procedió de impuestos sobre la nómina (véase el gráfico 1.21). En los países miembros de la OCDE, las entidades subnacionales tienden a tener impuestos cuyas bases son mucho más amplias. Una proporción significativa del recaudo de los gobiernos subnacionales en los países de la OCDE tuvo origen en los impuestos sobre la renta y utilidades (representó más de un tercio del recaudo promedio total a nivel subnacional).

Gráfico 1.21. **Estructura de los ingresos tributarios subnacionales en países de ALC, 2015**

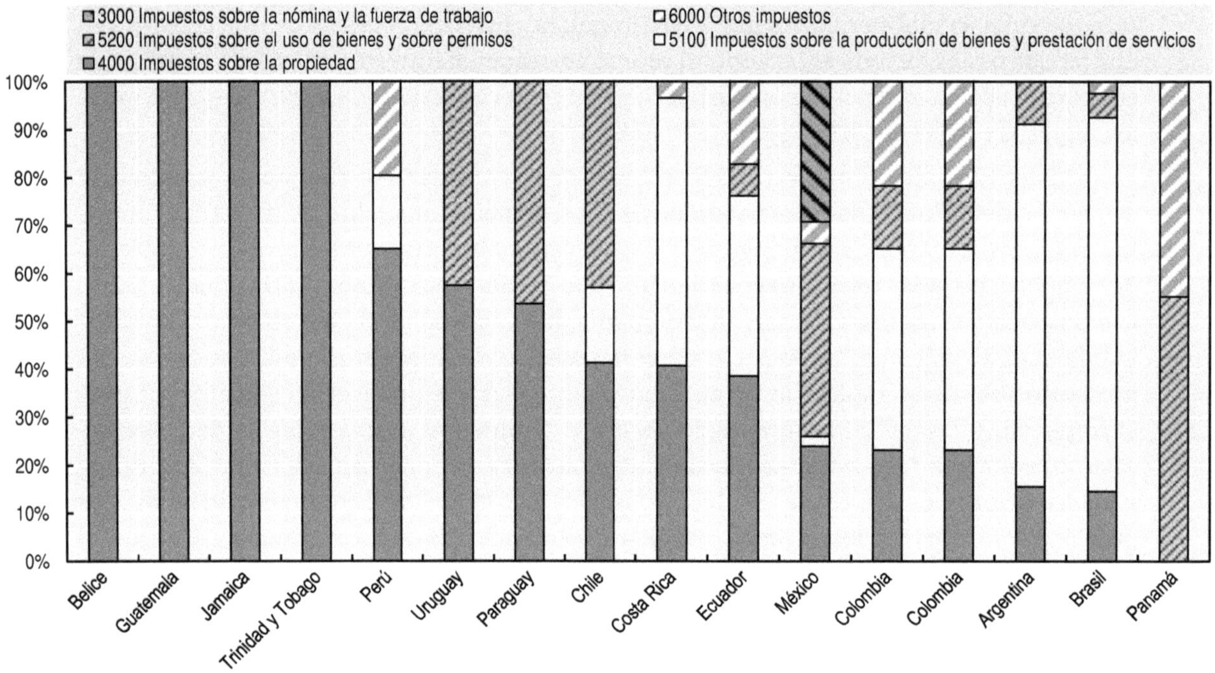

Nota: El año de comparación es 2015 ya que los datos de 2016 no estaban disponibles para México. Las Bahamas, Barbados, Bolivia, Cuba, República Dominicana, El Salvador, Honduras, Nicaragua, Paraguay y Venezuela no se encuentran incluidos dado que los datos de los ingresos impositivos subnacionales o el desglose de los mismos por tipos de categorías tributarias principales no están disponibles. Las cifras excluyen los ingresos del gobierno local para Argentina (pero incluyen ingresos provinciales).

Fuente: Elaboración propia basada en los cuadros presentados en OCDE/CEPAL/CIAT/BID (2018), Capítulo 6.

StatLink http://dx.doi.org/10.1787/888933685378

Los bajos niveles del recaudo subnacional en ALC pueden también ser el resultado de una capacidad administrativa y técnica reducida. Los impuestos sobre la propiedad requieren sistemas sofisticados de información, lo que aumenta el costo de recaudo de este impuesto. Además, los registros catastrales están ausentes en varios países y cuando existen rara vez se actualizan (BID, 2012). Como resultado, las autoridades tributarias no pueden acceder a valoraciones precisas de tierras y edificios, aunado a ello, las agencias de bienes y raíces no siempre están dispuestas a compartir esta información. Los impuestos sobre la propiedad también son susceptibles de sufrir altos niveles de informalidad: los edificios son muchas veces construidos sin los permisos adecuados, muchas propiedades no se encuentran registradas y los precios de venta de los bienes inmuebles son muchas veces falsificados. El impuesto sobre la propiedad es uno de los impuestos más controversiales en los ojos del ciudadano y conlleva altos costos políticos, por lo que las administraciones de gobiernos locales rara vez están dispuestas a invertir en los recursos necesarios para recaudar este impuesto (BID, 2015).

La proporción del recaudo realizada por los sistemas de seguridad social cayó en ocho países ALC, en algunos casos debido a la privatización de estos esquemas entre los años de 1995 y el 2000. Las caídas más grandes tuvieron lugar en Argentina y en Ecuador (cerca de 7.6 y 13.4 puntos porcentuales respectivamente). Argentina adoptó un modelo mixto en 1994 en el cual una parte de las contribuciones obligatorias a los sistemas previsionales se destinaban a cuentas de capitalización individuales administradas por fondos de pensiones privadas. Entre los años 2000 y 2015, la proporción de ingresos derivados de la seguridad social incrementaron en 15 de los 25 países de la región ALC. Argentina y Ecuador fueron los dos países que experimentaron la caída más abrupta en la proporción de ingresos de la seguridad social; registraron las mayores alzas entre 2000 y 2015 (véase el cuadro 1.1). En Argentina, el modelo mixto adoptado en 1994 fue abolido en 2008 y las contribuciones obligatorias a los fondos privados fueron trasladadas al sistema público de pensiones.

Cuadro 1.1. **Atribución de los ingresos tributarios por subsector del gobierno general, como porcentaje del recaudo tributario total[1]**

	Gobierno central			Gobierno estatal o regional			Gobierno local			Fondos de Fondos de seguridad social		
	1995	2000	2015	1995	2000	2015	1995	2000	2015	1995	2000	2015
Países federales												
Argentina	59.0	66.4	61.0	17.5	17.8	16.8				23.4	15.8	22.2
Brasil	44.7	47.8	43.7	26.8	25.3	24.4	3.7	3.4	5.9	24.8	23.5	25.9
México	73.9	79.3	80.4	2.8	2.5	4.2	1.5	1.0	1.6	21.8	17.2	13.9
Venezuela	94.6	94.6	97.0	..	..	..	..	..	..	5.4	5.4	3.0
País régional												
Colombia[2]	63.2	68.6	71.7	5.5	5.6	4.6	8.6	9.4	11.6	22.7	16.4	12.1
Países unitarios												
Bahamas	89.1	88.1	85.2				..	..	..	10.9	11.9	14.8
Barbados	85.3	84.3	81.2				..	..	..	14.7	15.7	18.8
Belice	93.2	93.5	91.3				0.5	0.7	0.6	6.3	5.8	8.1
Bolivia	95.0	86.4	80.2				5.0	6.3	4.1	0.0	7.3	15.7
Chile	89.9	87.8	86.9				6.5	7.9	7.6	3.6	4.4	5.6
Costa Rica	68.4	66.8	63.4				..	2.0	3.3	30.0	31.2	33.3
Cuba	88.7	89.6	87.1				..	..	..	11.3	10.4	12.9
República Dominicana	99.3	98.9	99.6				..	..	..	0.7	1.1	0.4
Ecuador	70.5	86.1	73.6				4.0	1.8	2.5	25.5	12.1	23.9
El Salvador	85.9	83.4	87.2				..	..	1.9	14.1	16.6	10.9
Guatemala	83.7	83.6	82.2				0.6	0.9	1.1	15.6	15.5	16.6
Guyana	92.6	88.6	89.6				..	..	..	7.4	11.4	10.4
Honduras	90.1	89.4	85.5				..	..	..	9.9	10.6	14.5
Jamaica	..	99.3	94.5				..	0.7	1.7	..	0.0	3.8
Nicaragua	84.1	80.0	69.8				..	..	..	15.9	20.0	23.5
Panamá	62.0	59.8	61.5				..	2.2	1.6	38.0	38.0	36.9
Paraguay	..	82.7	76.4				..	..	4.0	..	17.3	19.6
Perú	88.1	87.8	85.0				..	..	..	11.9	12.2	12.0
Trinidad y Tobago	94.5	91.7	90.1				2.4	1.9	0.7	3.1	6.4	9.3
Uruguay	61.4	62.0	67.9				8.4	8.4	4.5	30.1	29.6	27.6

1. Las cifras excluyen los ingresos del gobierno local para Argentina (pero incluyen ingresos provinciales), Las Bahamas, Barbados, Bolivia (antes de 1994), Cuba, República Dominicana, El Salvador (antes de 2015), Honduras, Jamaica (antes de 1998), Nicaragua, Panamá (antes de 1998), Paraguay (antes de 2004), Perú (antes de 2001) y Venezuela dado que los datos no se encuentran disponibles.
2. Colombia es constitucionalmente un país unitario con alta autonomía de sus territorios.

Fuente: OCDE/CEPAL/CIAT/BID (2018), Cuadro 4.11.

StatLink http://dx.doi.org/10.1787/888933685416

Notas

1. Las cifras para Venezuela y Argentina en 2016 tienen que ser interpretadas con precaución ya que han sido afectadas por las altas tasas de inflación del año pasado. Si se excluye a Venezuela y a Argentina del cálculo el promedio de ingresos tributarios en relación al PIB para el resto de los países ALC fue de 22.7% en 2016.
2. Esta cifra es provisional y se ha calculado aplicando el porcentaje de cambio promedio no ponderado para 2016 en los 33 países que proporcionan datos para ese año a la relación entre el impuesto promedio general y el PIB en 2015.
3. En la publicación del BID, el promedio de América Latina incluye 19 países: Argentina, Bolivia, Brasil, Chile, Colombia, Costa Rica, El Salvador, Ecuador, Guatemala, Honduras, Jamaica, México, Nicaragua, Panamá, Perú, Paraguay, República Dominicana, Uruguay y Venezuela.
4. La informalidad se define como el porcentaje de individuos que no contribuyen a sistemas previsionales sobre el total de la fuerza de trabajo en ALC.
5. Estos países son Argentina, Brasil, Bolivia, Chile, Colombia, Costa Rica, Ecuador, Honduras, México, Nicaragua, Panamá y Perú.
6. El VRR no pudo ser estimado para, Cuba y Trinidad y Tobago.
7. La evasión del IVA se calcula como la pérdida de IVA en términos del recaudo esperado del IVA.
8. El FMI estima una medida de eficiencia sobre el consumo, que es un concepto similar al VRR, pero que usa un método ligeramente diferente. Un detalle más amplio sobre las diferencias se presenta en OECD (2016).
9. Aproximadamente 2% de todos los ingresos tributarios provenientes de impuestos sobre la renta y utilidades no pueden ser atribuidos al impuesto a la renta de empresas o de personas físicas.
10. El año de comparación es 2015 ya que los datos de 2016 para el promedio de la OCDE no estaban disponibles.
11. El año de comparación es 2015 ya que los datos de 2016 no estaban disponibles para México.

Referencias

Barreix, A., J. Benítez y M. Pecho (2017), "Revisiting personal income tax in Latin America: Evolution and impact", *OECD Development Centre Working Papers* No. 338, OECD Publishing, Paris, *http://dx.doi.org/10.1787/16d42b4a-en.*

Bosch, M., A. Melguizo y C. Pagés (2013), *Mejores pensiones, mejores trabajos: hacia la cobertura universal en América latina y el Caribe*, Banco Interamericano de Desarrollo, Washington, DC.

Brossio, G. y J.P. Jiménez (2012), *Decentralization and Reform in Latin America: Improving Intergovernmental Relations*, Edward Elgar, in press, Cheltenham, UK and Northampton, MA.

Daude, C., Á. Melguizo y A. Neut (2010), "Fiscal Policy in Latin America: Countercyclical and Sustainable at Last?", *OECD Development Centre Working Papers* No. 291, OECD Publishing, Paris, *http://dx.doi.org/10.1787/5km8zdcp7j41-en.*

CEPAL (2014), *Tax policy in Latin America. Assessment and guidelines for a second generation of reforms*, CEPAL, Santiago de Chile.

CEPAL (2013), *Fiscal Panorama of Latin America and the Caribbean: tax reform and renewal of the fiscal covenant*, CEPAL, Santiago de Chile.

CEPAL (2010), "La Hora de la igualdad. Brechas por cerrar, caminos por abrir" (LC/G.2432 (SES.33/3)), CEPAL, Santiago de Chile.

Ernst & Young (2014), "Worldwide VAT GST and sales tax guide 2014", Ernst & Young Global Limited, *www.ey.com/Publication/vwLUAssets/Worldwide-VAT-GST-and-sales-tax-guide-2014/$FILE/Worldwide-VAT-GST-and-sales-tax-guide-2014.pdf.*

Franks J. R., R. Benelli, V. Mercer-Blackman y R. Sab (2005), "Paraguay: Corruption, Reform, and the Financial System", International Monetary Fund, Washington, DC.

Gómez Sabaini, J.C., J.P. Jiménez y A. Podestá (2010), "Evasión y equidad en América Latina", Project documents, No. 309 (LC/W.309/ Rev.1), CEPAL, Santiago de Chile.

BID (2015), "Decentralizing Revenue in Latin America Why and How", Banco Interamericano de Desarrollo, Washington, DC.

BID (2013), "More than revenues, Taxation as a development tool", Banco Interamericano de Desarrollo, Washington, DC.

BID (2012), "Sub-national Revenue Mobilization in Peru", *IDB Working Paper Series* No. IDB-WP-299, Banco Interamericano de Desarrollo, Washington, DC.

FMI (2017a), "The Bahamas: 2017 article IV consultation—press release;and staff report", IMF Country Report No. 17/314, Fondo Monetario Internacional, Washington, DC, *https://www.imf.org/en/Publications/CR/Issues/2017/10/06/The-Bahamas-2017-Article-IV-Consultation-Press-Release-and-Staff-Report-45310.*

FMI (2017b), "Belize : 2017 Article IV Consultation-Press Release; Staff Report; Informational Annex; Statement by the Executive Director for Belize", *IMF Country Report* No. 17/286, Fondo Monetario Internacional, Washington, DC, *https://www.imf.org/en/Publications/CR/Issues/2017/09/19/Belize-2017-Article-IV-Consultation-Press-Release-Staff-Report-Informational-Annex-Statement-45264.*

FMI (2017c), *World Economic Outlook Database, October 2017 Edition*, Fondo Monetario Internacional, Washington, DC.

FMI (2017d), "Guyana : 2017 Article IV Consultation-Press Release; Staff Report; and Statement by the Executive Director for Guyana", *IMF Country Report* No. 17/175, Fondo Monetario Internacional, Washington, DC, *https://www.imf.org/en/Publications/CR/Issues/2017/06/28/Guyana-2017-Article-IV-Consultation-Press-Release-Staff-Report-and-Statement-by-the-45010.*

FMI (2016a). "Argentina 2016 Article IV Consultation", *IMF country report* No. 16/346, Fondo Monetario Internacional, Washington, DC.

FMI (2016b), *World Economic Outlook Database, October 2016 Edition*, Fondo Monetario Internacional, Washington, DC.

FMI (2010), "Paraguay: Selected Issues", IMF Country Report No. 10/170, Fondo Monetario Internacional, Washington, DC, *https://www.imf.org/external/pubs/ft/scr/2010/cr10170.pdf.*

Melguizo, A., S. Nieto-Parra, J.R. Perea y J.A. Perez (2017), "No sympathy for the devil! Policy priorities to overcome the middle-income trap in Latin America", *OECD Development Centre. Working Papers* No. 340, OECD Publishing, París, *http://dx.doi.org/10.1787/26b78724-en.*

OCDE (2016), *Consumption Tax Trends 2016: VAT/GST and excise rates, trends and policy issues*, OECD Publishing, París, *http://dx.doi.org/10.1787/ctt-2016-en.*

OCDE (2014), *Development Co-operation Report 2014: Mobilising Resources for Sustainable Development*, OECD Publishing, París, *http://dx.doi.org/10.1787/dcr-2014-en.*

OCDE (2009), *Perspectivas Económicas de América latina 2009*, OECD Publishing, París, *http://dx.doi.org/10.1787/leo-2009-es.*

OCDE/CAF/CEPAL (de próxima publicación), *Perspectivas económicas de América Latina 2018: Repensando las instituciones para el desarrollo*, OECD Publishing, París, *http://dx.doi.org/10.1787/leo-2018-es.*

OCDE/BID/CIAT (2016), *Taxing Wages and Taxing Wages in Latin America and the Caribbean*, OECD Publishing, París, *http://dx.doi.org/10.1787/9789264262607-en.*

OCDE/BID/CIAT (2015), *Estadísticas tributarias en América Latina y el Caribe 1990-2013*, OECD Publishing, París, *http://dx.doi.org/10.1787/rev_lat-2015-en-fr.*

OCDE/BID/Banco Mundial (2015), *Un Panorama de las Pensiones en América Latina y el Caribe*, Banco Interamericano de Desarrollo, Washington, DC, *http://dx.doi.org/10.1787/9789264233195-es.*

Panama Investor Blog (2008), Audit uncovers millions in unpaid sales taxes. *http://primapanama.blogs.com/_panama_residential_devel/2008/06/audit-uncovers.html.*

Schlotterbeck, S. (2017), "Tax Administration Reforms in the Caribbean "Challenges, Achievements, and Next Steps"", *IMF Working paper* WP/17/88, International Monetary Fund, Washington, DC, *https://www.imf.org/en/Publications/WP/Issues/2017/04/04/Tax-Administration-Reforms-in-the-Caribbean-Challenges-Achievements-and-Next-Steps-44800.*

World Grain (2016), "Reforms boost Argentine grain industry", *www.world-grain.com/articles/news_home/Features/2016/05/Reforms_boost_Argentine_grain.aspx?ID=%7BAE4EE339-0D46-43EF-A962-5ED9DEF72B53%7D.*

Zuleta, J.C (2008), "Combating corruption in the revenue service: the case of VAT refunds in Bolivia", Anti-Corruption Resource Centre, *www.U4.no/themes/pfm.*

Chapter 2

SPECIAL FEATURE

Fiscal revenues from non-renewable natural resources in Latin America and the Caribbean

Capítulo 2

SECCIÓN ESPECIAL

Ingresos fiscales provenientes de recursos naturales no renovables en América Latina y el Caribe

Revenue Statistics in Latin America and the Caribbean 2018/
Estadísticas tributarias en América Latina y el Caribe 2018

Chapter 2

SPECIAL FEATURE

Fiscal revenues from non-renewable natural resources in Latin America and the Caribbean

Key findings

Overall trends for 2016 and 2017

Despite a year-end up-tick in the price of many key commodities, fiscal revenues associated with non-renewable natural resources continued to fall in 2016. Combined revenues from hydrocarbons and mining contracted on average from 3.5% of GDP in 2015 to 2.3% of GDP for 12 commodity-exporting countries in Latin America and the Caribbean (excluding Venezuela).[a] In contrast to previous years this decline exacerbated a fall in revenues from other sources (tax and non-tax revenue). There has been a sharp decline in the dependence on non-renewable natural resources, reflecting the decline in these resources as well as higher mobilisation of revenues from other sources.

Non-renewable natural resource revenues are not projected to increase sharply, relative to GDP, in 2017. Although international prices for many key commodities have trended higher, they remain significantly lower than their recent highs. Likewise, financial conditions at the region's principal producing companies remain challenging, though they are improving. As a result, hydrocarbons revenues are projected to dip slightly from 3.4% of GDP in 2016 to 3.3% of GDP in 2017 in the ten countries that levied this type of revenue.[b] Mining revenues are expected to hold steady at around 0.4% of GDP in the ten countries that levied this type of revenue.[c]

Developments in non-renewable natural resources revenues in 2016

Hydrocarbon-related revenues fell from a revised average of 5.0% of GDP in 2015 to 3.4% of GDP in 2016 in the ten countries that levied this type of revenues (including Venezuela). Exceptionally weak profits at several of the region's largest hydrocarbons producers led to a sharp contraction in tax revenues, principally corporate income tax (CIT) payments, as well as in non-tax revenues such as dividends. Other non-tax revenues, mainly royalties and other participations in the commercial value of production, fell as the price of crude oil remained soft and regional production contracted.

Mining revenues registered a very modest decline (from 0.37% of GDP in 2015 to 0.35% of GDP in the ten countries that levied this type of revenues), with significant differences among countries. Tax revenues continued to trend lower as financial losses in 2015 significantly impacted CIT receipts in 2016, especially in Chile. A year end bump in prices coupled with higher production in some countries boosted non-tax revenues – mainly royalties – especially in gold-producing countries.

a. Argentina, Bolivia (Plur. State of), Brazil, Chile, Colombia, Dominican Republic, Ecuador, Jamaica, Mexico, Peru, Suriname and Trinidad and Tobago.

b. Argentina, Bolivia (Plur. State of), Brazil, Colombia, Ecuador, Mexico, Peru, Suriname, Trinidad and Tobago and Venezuela.

c. Argentina, Bolivia (Plur. State of), Brazil, Chile, Colombia, Jamaica, Mexico, Peru, Dominican Republic and Suriname.

Overall trends in non-renewable natural resources revenues for Latin America and the Caribbean in 2016 and 2017

Revenues from non-renewable natural resources in Latin America and the Caribbean continued to contract in 2016, weighed down by weak global growth and soft international prices for the region's principal export commodities. Combined revenues from hydrocarbons and mining in 12 commodity-exporter countries – not covering Venezuela due to lack of comparable statistics – fell to an average 2.3% of GDP in 2016, compared to 3.5% of GDP in 2015 (Figure 2.1). This marked the fifth consecutive year of decline. Revenues from renewable natural resources, while not included in this analysis, also trended lower (Box 2.1). Unlike in previous years, the fall in non-renewable natural resources revenues in 2016 was accompanied by a reduction in other revenues reflecting the negative impact of a second consecutive year of economic recession in the region on tax revenues more generally.

Figure 2.1. **Principal non-renewable natural resources producers in Latin America and the Caribbean (12 countries): Disaggregation of general government total revenues, 2010-16[a]**

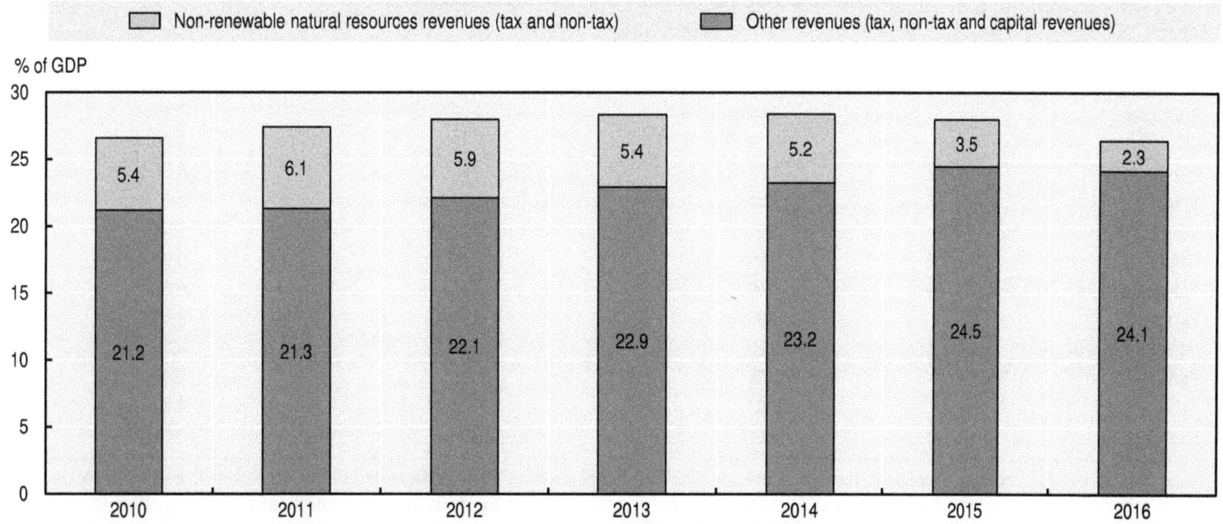

Note: Includes Argentina, Bolivia (Plur. State of), Brazil, Chile, Colombia, Dominican Republic, Ecuador, Jamaica, Mexico, Peru, Suriname and Trinidad and Tobago. Excludes Venezuela (Bol. Rep. of) due to a lack of a revised data series for total revenues during the period considered. Total revenues for Argentina and Ecuador refer to the non-financial public sector, for Mexico to the federal public sector.

a. Simple averages. The simple averages cover the 12 countries cited above (excluding Venezuela) and cannot be compared with the simple averages shown in Tables 2.4 and 2.9 that cover different countries.

Source: Economic Commission for Latin America and the Caribbean (ECLAC), based on official figures.

StatLink http://dx.doi.org/10.1787/888933685435

Box 2.1. **Fiscal revenues from renewable natural resources in Latin America and the Caribbean**

While the role that non-renewable natural resource revenues plays in the region's fiscal accounts is well established, there is less information related to revenues that derive from the exploitation of renewable resources. These revenues can take a variety of forms, but can perhaps be most associated with activities related to agriculture, livestock, hunting, forestry and fishing activities, or with the use of services provided by renewable natural resources (hydroelectricity, transportation, etc.). Relative to revenues from non-renewable natural resources, there is significantly less statistical information available.

Available data suggests that fiscal revenues accruing to the region's governments from the rent created by the exploitation of renewable natural resources tend to be modest, despite the important role Latin American countries play in global agricultural and food exports. Of the countries considered in Box 2.1, only in Argentina and Paraguay are these revenues relatively sizeable (at 0.45% of GDP and 0.16% of GDP in 2016, respectively). In the case of Argentina these revenues are larger than those from mining (0.02% of GDP in 2016). In other countries these revenues are relatively modest compared to revenues from non-renewable natural resources: Brazil (0.01% of GDP, compared to 0.1% of GDP for mining and 1.2% for

Box 2.1. **Fiscal revenues from renewable natural resources in Latin America and the Caribbean** *(cont.)*

hydrocarbons), Chile (0.01% of GDP, although this excludes payment of CIT due to a lack of statistical data, compared to 0.4% of GDP for mining) and Peru (0.03% of GDP, compared to 0.3% of GDP for mining and 0.8% of GDP for hydrocarbons). While these revenues are susceptible to volatility arising from climatic conditions or changes in world production for specific products, their relative size limits their impact on overall fiscal accounts.

Table 2.1. **Selected fiscal revenues from agriculture, livestock, hunting, forestry and fishing in Latin America, 2014-16**

(Percentages of GDP)

Country/instrument	2014	2015	2016
Argentina	0.82	0.73	0.45
CIT	0.10	0.12	0.08
Export duties	0.72	0.61	0.37
Brazil	0.01	0.01	0.01
CIT	0.01	0.01	0.01
Chile	0.00	0.01	0.01
Fishing rights	0.00	0.01	0.01
Paraguay	0.20	0.20	0.16
IMAGRO/IRAGRO	0.20	0.20	0.16
Peru	0.04	0.03	0.03
CIT	0.04	0.03	0.03
Fishing rights	0.01	0.01	0.01

Note: Revenues for fishing rights in Peru are estimated based on central government transfers to subnational governments for the component of the fishing canon that deals with fishing rights; this figure is then doubled reflecting the distribution of these revenues between levels of government. A disaggregation of corporate income tax payments by economic activity was not available for Chile.
Source: ECLAC, based on official figures.

StatLink http://dx.doi.org/10.1787/888933685815

Public revenues related to services associated with the use of renewable natural resources in the region can be important, but are limited to a select group of countries. Examples include central government revenues from the operations of the Panama Canal, which reached 1.9% of GDP in 2015 (0.7% as canal tolls and 1.2% as dividends from the Canal Authority). In Paraguay, royalties and compensations from the Itaipú and Yacyretá hydroelectric plants are also sizeable, at 1.5% of GDP in 2016. These revenues can also be a source of significant volatility in these countries, reflecting their susceptibility to exogenous shocks such as changes in global economic conditions as well as changing climatic conditions from year to year.
Source: Economic Commission for Latin America and the Caribbean (ECLAC).

Despite the downward trend in non-renewable natural resources revenues in the region, total revenues have remained relatively stable, averaging 27.6% of GDP between 2010 and 2016 for this group of 12 countries (2 percentage point fall between 2014 and 2016). During this period, commodity-producing countries in the region enacted a significant number of tax reforms to compensate for the decline in hydrocarbons and mining revenues. As a result, these other revenues rose from an average of 21.2% of GDP in 2010 to a high of 24.5% of GDP in 2015, before declining in 2016. There were significant increases in tax and other revenues over the period in Argentina, Bolivia, Chile, Ecuador, Mexico and Trinidad and Tobago.

Consequently, dependence on revenues from non-renewable natural resources has fallen sharply in the region. As Figure 2.2 shows, in 2010 hydrocarbon and mining revenues accounted for more than 30% of total revenues in Trinidad and Tobago (42%), Bolivia (36%), Ecuador (34%), Mexico (33%) and Suriname (33%). By 2016, the contribution of these revenues had fallen to near 20%, and in the case of Trinidad and Tobago even lower (9%). Similarly, countries that previously had moderate dependence on commodities-related revenues, such as Chile, Colombia and Peru – where hydrocarbon and mining revenues accounted for between 10% and 20% of total revenues in 2010 – also registered a sharp reduction (to around 5% or lower).

Figure 2.2. **Principal non-renewable natural resources producers in Latin America and the Caribbean (12 countries): Share of non-renewable natural resource revenues in general government total revenues, 2010 and 2016[a]**

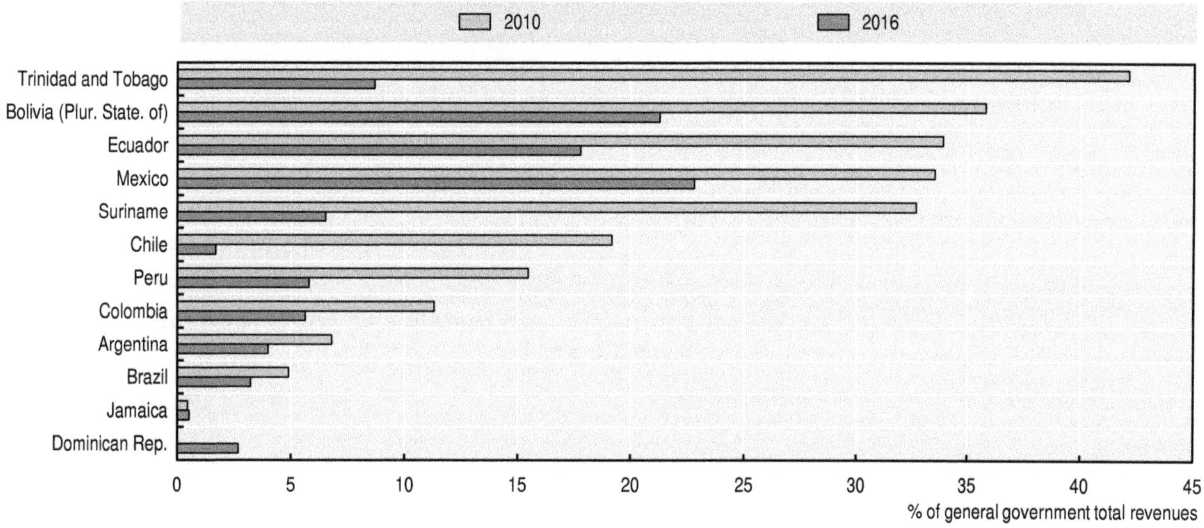

Note: Total revenues for Argentina and Ecuador refer to the non-financial public sector, for Mexico to the federal public sector.
a. Excludes Venezuela due to lack of official data on total revenues of the central government.
Source: Economic Commission for Latin America and the Caribbean (ECLAC), based on official figures.

StatLink http://dx.doi.org/10.1787/888933685454

While increased revenue generation from other sources and reduced dependence on non-renewable natural resource revenues are positive developments, the prevailing fiscal context remains exceptionally challenging. Public spending growth has outstripped that of public revenues in the region, leading to a significant expansion in fiscal deficits (Figure 2.3). Regaining this lost fiscal space will require continued efforts to strengthen domestic resource mobilisation to generate the long-term financing necessary to meet the Sustainable Development Goals.

Consolidation efforts in the region aimed at regaining fiscal space continued to gain pace in 2017, though with little support in the way of higher revenues from non-renewable natural resources. Although international prices for crude oil and a number of minerals and metals are forecast to rise, they remain well below the levels registered in previous years (Figure 2.4). Spot prices for crude oil are forecast to advance 14% in 2017, nevertheless they would still be 49% below 2014 levels. Prices for a basket of minerals and metals are projected to rise 16.8%, the first increase since 2011. Furthermore, financial conditions among producing companies remain challenging – though with signs of improvement – limiting a rebound in revenues from instruments tied to income and profits.

Figure 2.3. **Principal non-renewable natural resources producers in Latin America and the Caribbean (12 countries): General government overall fiscal balance, 2016**

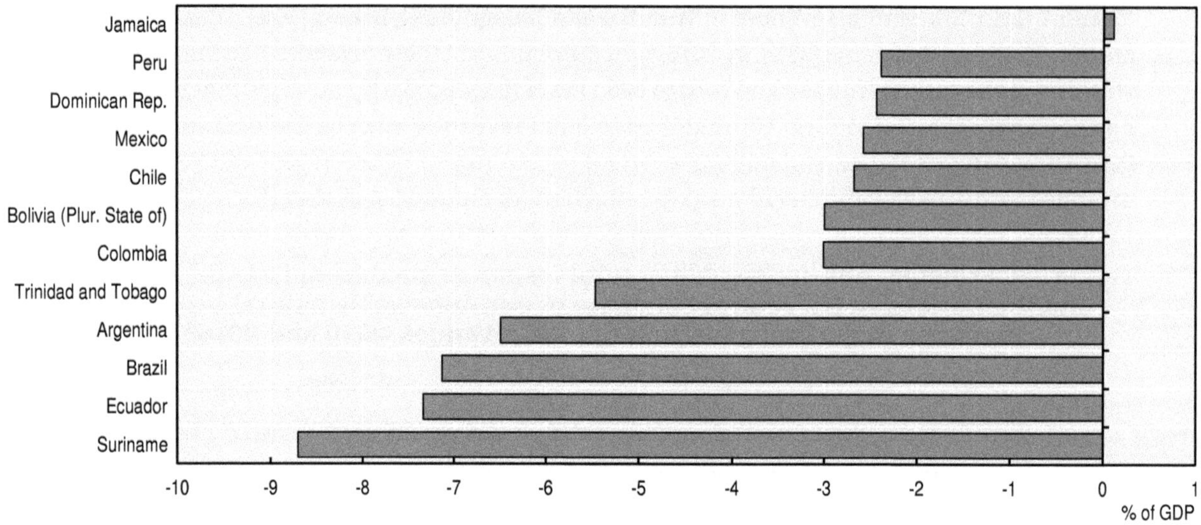

Note: a. Simple averages. Data for Argentina and Ecuador refer to the non-financial public sector, for Mexico to the federal public sector.
Source: Economic Commission for Latin America and the Caribbean (ECLAC), based on official figures.
StatLink http://dx.doi.org/10.1787/888933685473

Figure 2.4. **Price forecasts for minerals and metals and spot crude oil, 2011-17**

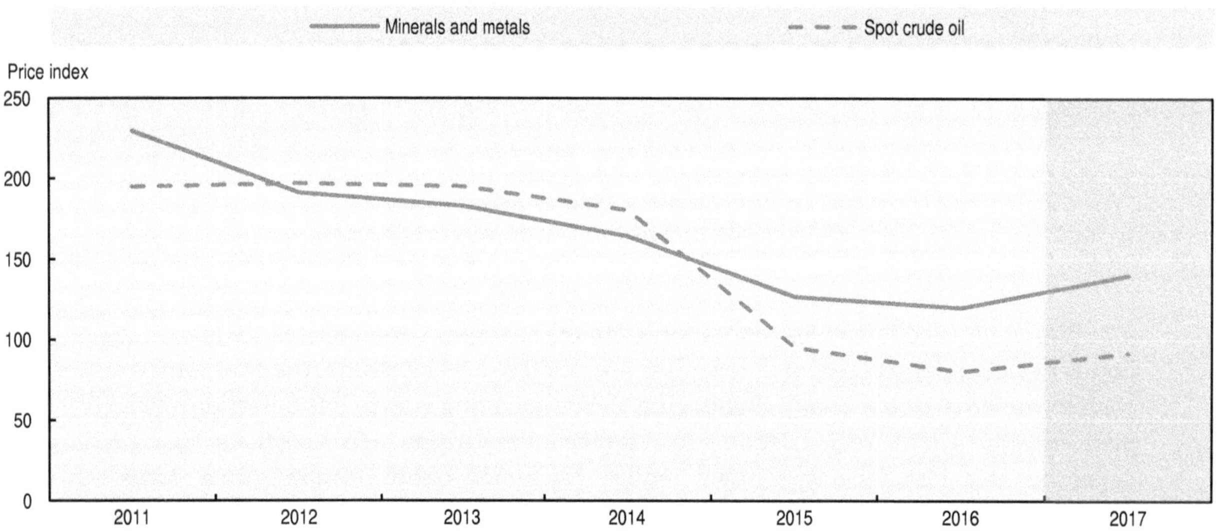

Note: 2005 = 100, on the basis of world export weights.
Source: International Monetary Fund (IMF, 2017), commodities price forecasts with actual data until 13 July 2017, accessed 13 July 2017.
StatLink http://dx.doi.org/10.1787/888933685492

As a result, hydrocarbon revenues are expected to stabilise – relative to GDP – in 2017, slipping to an average of 3.3% of GDP compared to 3.4% of GDP in 2016 (Figure 2.5). Nevertheless, in contrast to 2016, this downward trend is less generalised, with some countries potentially seeing their hydrocarbon revenues stabilising relative to GDP or even increasing very slightly. Mining revenues, which broke a four-year downward streak in 2016, are expected to hold steady at 0.4% of GDP on average for the countries considered. In particular, mining revenues in Chile and Peru are projected to increase, though by less than

0.3 percentage points of GDP, as corporate tax payments by the sector have rebounded after registering sharp declines in 2016.

Figure 2.5. **Principal non-renewable natural resources producers in Latin America and the Caribbean (13 countries): Fiscal revenues from hydrocarbons and mining, 2010-17[a]**

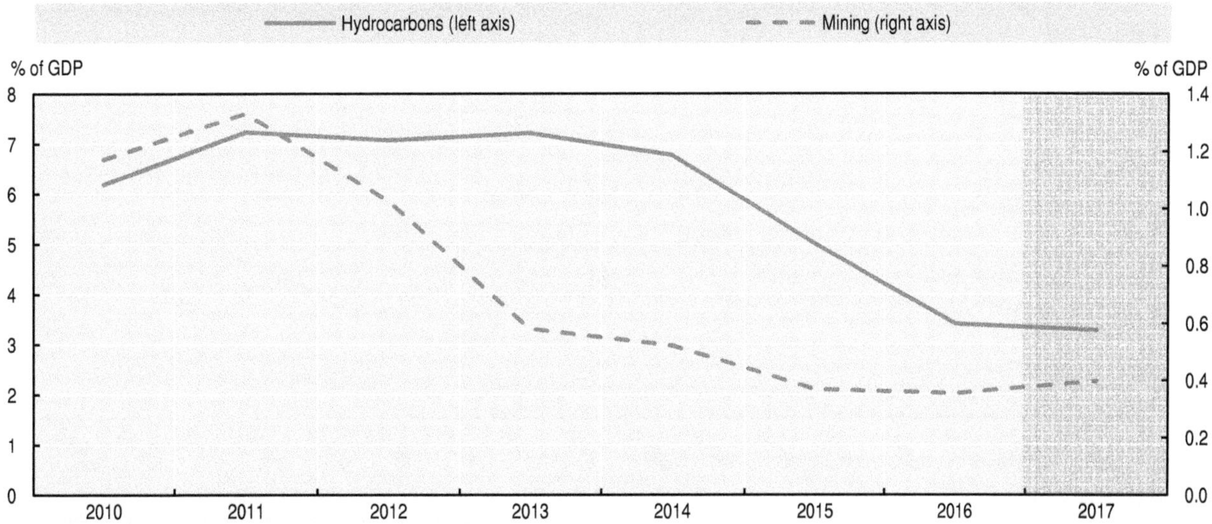

Note: Mining includes: Argentina, Bolivia (Plur. State of), Brazil, Chile, Colombia, Jamaica, Mexico, Peru, Dominican Republic and Suriname. Hydrocarbons include: Argentina, Bolivia (Plur. State of), Brazil, Colombia, Ecuador, Mexico, Peru, Suriname, Trinidad and Tobago and Venezuela (Bol. Rep. of). Values for 2017 are based on official government estimates from 2018 budget documents or from preliminary annual figures. When figures for 2017 were not available they were estimated using monthly data (typically for the first three quarters of the year). When monthly data was not available revenues were estimated by applying the year-on-year change in the price for the most representative product – or basket of products in the case of mining – for the country, expressed in national currency terms, to 2016 revenues.

a. Simple averages. Data for Venezuela (Bol. Rep. of) based on information reported by PDVSA (2017) and Bolivarian Republic of Venezuela (2017).

Source: Economic Commission for Latin America and the Caribbean (ECLAC), based on official figures.

StatLink http://dx.doi.org/10.1787/888933685511

Developments in non-renewable natural resource revenues in 2016

Hydrocarbons

Low international crude oil prices and slumping regional production undercut hydrocarbons revenues in Latin America and the Caribbean. The global oil market remained nominally oversupplied in 2016, which continued to put downward pressure on prices (IEA, 2017). Demand for oil rose more moderately in 2016 (1.4% to 96.1 million barrels per day) compared to the 2.1% increase (to 94.8 million barrels per day) in 2015. Weak macroeconomic fundamentals and a smaller price effect on oil demand than in the previous year depressed the pace of growth.

Crude oil supply also slowed, registering a year-on-year increase of just 0.4% (to 97.0 million barrels per day) compared to a 3.1% increase (to 96.6 million barrels per day) in 2015. In part this reflected the impact of low prices on higher-cost production, especially in the United States. Despite this slower pace of growth, supply remained marginally above demand, placing the market in a surplus position of roughly 0.9 million barrels per day. However, this was substantially lower than the surplus of 1.8 million barrels per day registered in 2015.

Because of these trends, crude oil prices in global spot markets edged lower, falling 15.7% on average in 2016 to reach USD 43 per barrel (Figure 2.6). While this represents a significantly smaller decline than that registered in 2015 (47.2%), the cumulative drop in crude oil prices between 2014 and 2016 reached a staggering 55.5%. Nevertheless, monthly data highlights a progressive – if slow – increase in prices, particularly in the first and fourth quarters of the year.

Figure 2.6. **Spot crude oil price, 2014-16**

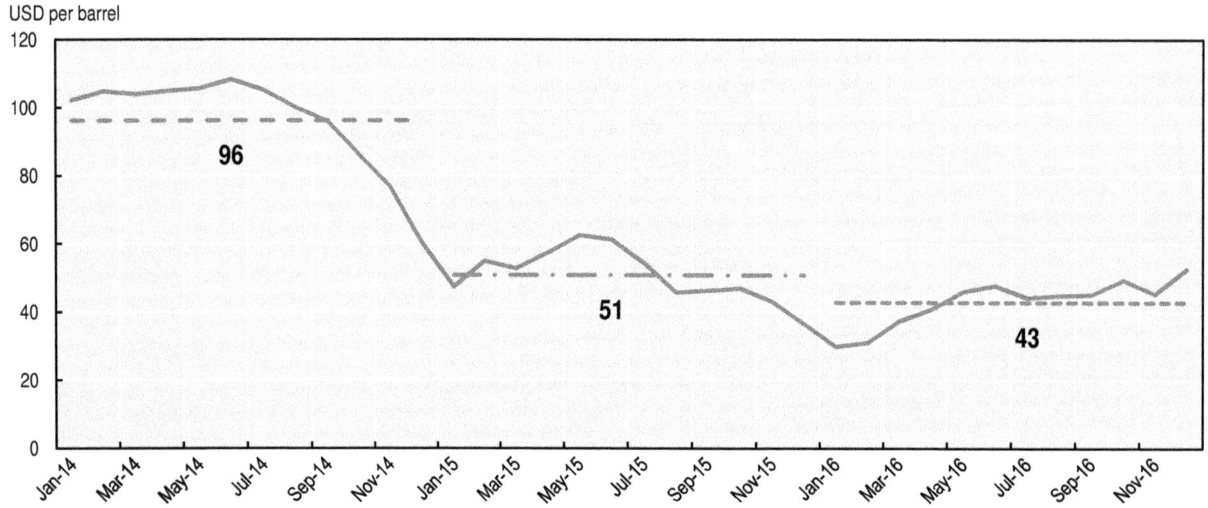

Source: Economic Commission for Latin America and the Caribbean (ECLAC), based on data from UNCTADstat.

StatLink http://dx.doi.org/10.1787/888933685530

Weak global prices for crude oil were compounded in Latin America and the Caribbean by slumping regional hydrocarbons production. According to OPEC (2017), oil production fell 5.1% year-on-year in 2016 in Latin America and the Caribbean, from 9.7 million barrels per day to 9.2 million barrels per day (Table 2.2). There were particularly large declines – both in absolute and percentage terms – in Colombia (12.2%), Venezuela (10.6%) and Mexico (5.0%). Natural gas production rose modestly (0.8%) – principally due to a strong rebound in Trinidad and Tobago (6.1%) – to reach 222.7 million standard cubic meters. However, even with this increase, the combined production of natural gas, assuming a standard conversion for cubic meters to barrels of oil equivalent, and crude oil still fell 3.2% year-on-year.

Table 2.2. **Latin America: hydrocarbons production, 2015-16**

(Units)

Country	Crude oil production by country (1 000 b/d)		Marketed production of natural gas by country (m standard cu m)	
	2015	2016	2015	2016
Latin America	**9 715**	**9 222**	**221 004**	**222 692**
Argentina	532	512	36 400	36 546
Bolivia	n.a.	n.a.	22 597	23 501
Brazil	2 437	2 510	20 411	20 619
Chile	5	4	n.a.	n.a.
Colombia	1 006	883	12 807	12 935
Ecuador	543	549	497	530
Mexico	2 267	2 153	45 984	41 227
Peru	58	40	13 512	14 454
Suriname	17	16	n.a.	n.a.
Trinidad and Tobago	79	71	40 875	43 374
Venezuela	2 654	2 373	26 004	27 718
Others	117	110	1 917	1 789

Source: Economic Commission for Latin America and the Caribbean (ECLAC), based on data from OPEC (2017) and Staatsoile (2017).

StatLink http://dx.doi.org/10.1787/888933685834

As a result of these trends in global prices and regional production levels, fiscal revenues deriving from hydrocarbons in Latin America and the Caribbean registered a 17.9% year-on-year decline in 2016, falling from USD 149.1 billion in 2015 to USD 122.4 billion (Table 2.3). From the standpoint of the hydrocarbons value-chain, revenues from the exploration and extraction of hydrocarbons – so called up-stream activities – fell 23.8%, from USD 111.2 billion in 2015 to USD 84.7 billion. In contrast, revenues related to the commercialisation and sale of hydrocarbons – down-stream activities – fell marginally (0.6%), from USD 37.9 billion in 2015 to USD 37.7 billion, reflecting some slippage in demand but also a more moderate reduction in the prices of refined products.

Table 2.3. **Latin America and the Caribbean: Year-on-year variation in fiscal revenues derived from hydrocarbons, 2015-16**

(Percentage)

Country	Hydrocarbons revenues	
	National currency	US dollars
Argentina	19.3	-25.2
Bolivia (Plur. State of)	-41.8	-41.8
Brazil	-7.1	-11.2
Colombia	-52.0	-56.9
Ecuador	-14.9	-14.9
Mexico	0.3	-14.8
Peru	-12.9	-17.8
Suriname	-100.0	-100.0
Trinidad and Tobago	-71.5	-72.7
Venezuela (Bol. Rep. of)	259.0	-11.2
LAC-10	...	*-17.9*
Upstream	...	*-23.8*
Downstream	...	*-0.6*

Source: Economic Commission for Latin America and the Caribbean (ECLAC), based on official figures.

StatLink http://dx.doi.org/10.1787/888933685853

At the level of individual countries there was significant heterogeneity in the evolution of hydrocarbons revenues, both when expressed in US dollars or in national currency. While several countries registered declines in line with the variation in the price of oil, other countries experienced more dramatic declines. For example, in Colombia and Trinidad and Tobago hydrocarbons revenues fell more than 50% year-on-year in US dollar terms. In Suriname payments of income taxes and dividends by the State-owed producer, Staatsoile, fell to zero.

As in 2015, currency depreciations in some countries softened the impact of declining hydrocarbons revenues when expressed in national currency terms. In Argentina and Mexico revenues increased year-on-year in national currency terms. In contrast, in Colombia the 11.4% depreciation of the peso provided little relief as it was greatly outpaced by the magnitude of the decline in US dollars. In Bolivia – whose currency is on a tight crawling peg – and Ecuador – which is dollarised – there was no relief from the impact of falling oil prices on hydrocarbons revenues.

Despite the cushioning effect provided by currency depreciations, hydrocarbon revenues relative to GDP continued to slide sharply in 2016. As shown in Table 2.4, overall revenues fell from an average of 5.0% of GDP in 2015 to 3.4% of GDP in the ten countries that levied this type of revenues. Disaggregated by type of revenue instrument, both tax and non-tax revenues trended lower during the year. Tax revenues retreated from an average of 1.7% in 2015 of GDP to 0.8% of GDP, reflecting the collapse of these revenues in Trinidad and Tobago and to a lesser degree in Colombia. Non-tax revenues registered a similar decrease, falling from 3.3% of GDP in 2015 to 2.6% of GDP, led by sharp declines in the Plurinational State of Bolivia.

Table 2.4. **Latin America and the Caribbean: fiscal revenues derived from hydrocarbons, 2015-16**

(Percentage of GDP)

	Total			Tax revenues			Non-tax revenues		
	2015	2016	Δ	2015	2016	Δ	2015	2016	Δ
Argentina	1.6	1.4	-0.2	1.3	1.1	-0.2	0.4	0.3	0.0
Bolivia (Plur. State of)	10.4	5.9	-4.5	2.4	1.8	-0.7	7.9	4.1	-3.8
Brazil	1.3	1.1	-0.1	0.9	0.9	0.0	0.4	0.3	-0.1
Colombia	2.5	1.1	-1.4	1.3	0.7	-0.7	1.1	0.4	-0.7
Ecuador	6.3	5.4	-0.9	0.0	0.0	0.0	6.3	5.4	-0.9
Mexico	5.9	5.5	-0.4	1.3	1.4	0.2	4.6	4.1	-0.6
Peru	1.0	0.8	-0.2	0.5	0.5	-0.1	0.4	0.3	-0.1
Suriname	0.8	0.0	-0.8	0.4	0.0	-0.4	0.3	0.0	-0.3
Trinidad and Tobago	9.1	2.7	-6.4	8.0	1.3	-6.6	1.1	1.3	0.2
Venezuela (Bol. Rep. of)	11.2	10.2	-1.0	0.8	0.7	-0.1	10.4	9.5	-0.9
LAC-10	5.0	3.4	-1.6	1.7	0.8	-0.9	3.3	2.6	-0.7

Note: The LAC-10 average covers only the ten countries included in the table and cannot be compared with the simple averages shown in Figure 2.1 and Table 2.9 that cover different countries.

Source: Economic Commission for Latin America and the Caribbean (ECLAC), based on official figures.

StatLink http://dx.doi.org/10.1787/888933685872

Tax revenues from hydrocarbons tax revenues were significantly reduced by the sector's weak profits. Pre-tax profits of the region's major producers remained exceptionally weak in 2016. Pre-tax profits for a selected group of producers in the region reached USD 1.8 billion in 2016, which represented an improvement from the overall loss of USD 33.2 billion reported in 2015 (Figure 2.7). Despite returning to positive territory, profits in 2016 remain very far from the levels registered during 2011-2013, when they averaged USD 107.9 billion per year.

Figure 2.7. **Selected regional oil producers: Pre-tax income, 2011-16**

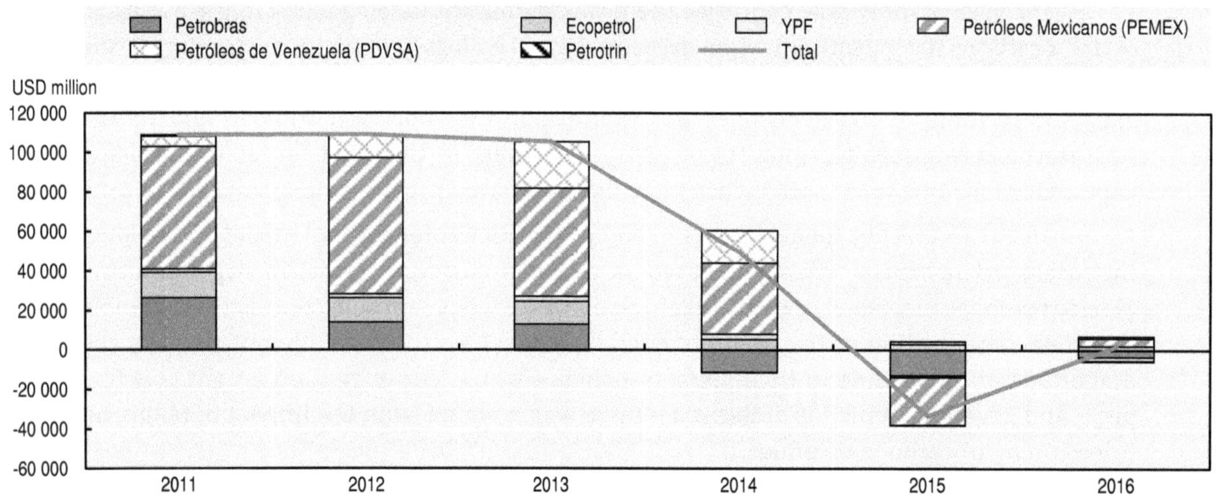

Source: Economic Commission for Latin America and the Caribbean (ECLAC), based on data from Bloomberg.

StatLink http://dx.doi.org/10.1787/888933685549

Weak profits translated into a further decline in hydrocarbons tax revenues in 2016. In particular, tax revenues associated with upstream activities – exploration and extraction – fell sharply, from an average of 1.2% of GDP in 2015 to 0.3% of GDP (Table 2.5). In Colombia corporate tax payments fell sharply reflecting in part the pre-tax financial loss registered by EcoPetrol in 2015. Likewise, in Trinidad and Tobago CIT payments – which represent the majority of overall hydrocarbons revenues – plummeted as low prices reduced earnings and production slumped when major energy companies took units out of production while work proceeded on upstream developments (Ministry of Finance of Trinidad and Tobago, 2016).

Table 2.5. **Latin America and the Caribbean: tax revenues derived from hydrocarbons, by value-chain segment, 2015-16**

(Percentage of GDP)

Country	Tax revenues			Upstream			Downstream		
	2015	2016	Δ	2015	2016	Δ	2015	2016	Δ
Argentina	1.3	1.1	-0.2	0.3	0.1	-0.2	1.0	0.9	0.0
Bolivia (Plur. State of)	2.4	1.8	-0.7	1.0	0.3	-0.8	1.4	1.5	0.1
Brazil	0.9	0.9	0.0	0.0	0.0	0.0	0.9	0.9	0.0
Colombia	1.3	0.7	-0.7	0.9	0.3	-0.6	0.4	0.4	0.0
Ecuador	0.0	0.0	0.0	0.0	0.0	0.0	0.0	0.0	0.0
Mexico	1.3	1.4	0.2	0.0	0.0	0.0	1.2	1.4	0.2
Peru	0.5	0.5	-0.1	0.2	0.1	-0.1	0.4	0.4	0.0
Suriname	0.4	0.0	-0.4	0.4	0.0	-0.4	0.0	0.0	0.0
Trinidad and Tobago	8.0	1.3	-6.6	8.0	1.3	-6.6	0.0	0.0	0.0
Venezuela (Bol. Rep. of)	0.8	0.7	-0.1	0.7	0.7	0.0	0.1	0.0	-0.1
LAC-10	1.7	0.8	-0.9	1.2	0.3	-0.9	0.5	0.6	0.0

Source: Economic Commission for Latin America and the Caribbean (ECLAC), based on official figures.

StatLink http://dx.doi.org/10.1787/888933685891

Downstream revenues, principally related to the consumption of hydrocarbons in producing countries, were little changed in 2016 compared to their 2015 levels (Table 2.5). Revenues from the Special Tax on Production and Services (IEPS, for its initials in Spanish) on fossil fuels in Mexico rose from 1.2% of GDP in 2015 to 1.4% of GDP as a result of a significant change in the tax adopted in November 2015. Prior to the reform the IEPS tax on fuels served as a tax or as a subsidy depending on the evolution of international prices. The new law adopts a fixed rate by product that can be modified when prices fall outside a price band that is modified monthly.

Non-tax revenues from hydrocarbons trended lower on the back of weaker global prices and slumping regional production. Hydrocarbons non-tax revenues in the region largely arise from instruments that reserve a share of the commercial value of production for the State. These typically take the form of royalties or other production levies. The evolution of these revenues is therefore closely linked to that of prices and production levels. Figure 2.8 highlights this tight relationship and further reveals that the decline in hydrocarbons non-tax revenues in the region in 2016 was exacerbated by the substantial contraction in regional oil production as highlighted above. This was in sharp contrast to previous years, where the variation in overall production played little or no role.

While the slide in non-tax revenues from hydrocarbons was generalised during the year, it was most notable in Bolivia, which registered a decline of 3.8 percentage points of GDP (Table 2.4). In the case of Bolivia, this decline largely reflects the impact of the pricing structure for its natural gas exports to Argentina and Brazil, which includes a price adjustment mechanism that operates with a quarterly lag. Thus, prices for exports in the first quarter of 2016 reflected the exceptionally low crude oil price observed at the end of 2015.

Figure 2.8. **Year-on-year variation of crude oil price, crude oil production and hydrocarbons non-tax revenues, 2010-16**

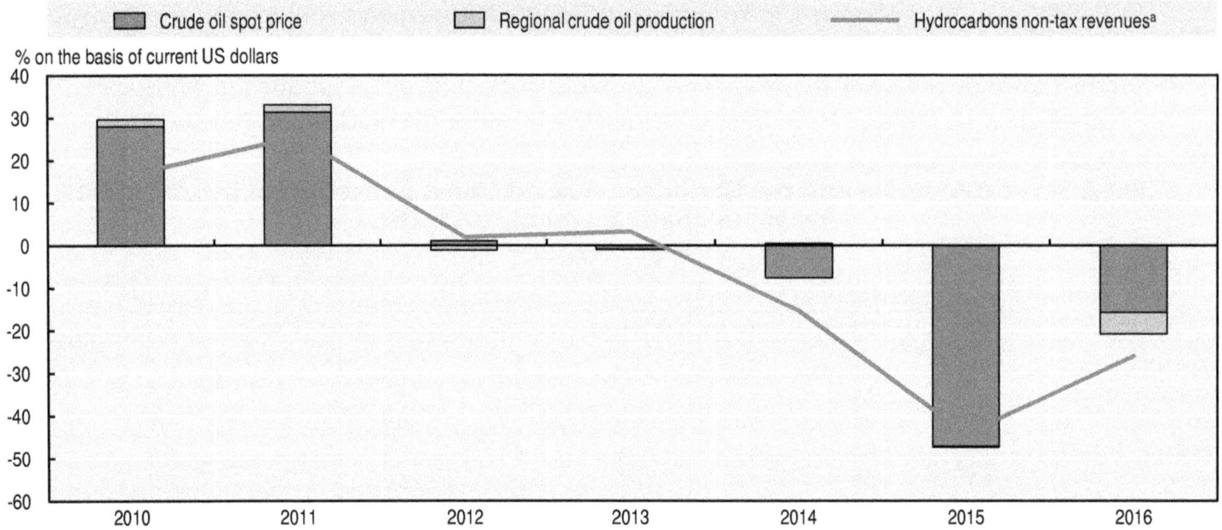

Note: a. Excludes extraordinary non-tax revenues in Venezuela.

Source: Economic Commission for Latin America and the Caribbean (ECLAC), based on official figures.

StatLink http://dx.doi.org/10.1787/888933685568

Non-tax hydrocarbon revenues also include other types of property rents that are more closely related to operating profits. The most common of these are dividend payments made by hydrocarbons producers to their shareholders, in this case the State. In Colombia, the decline in non-tax revenues relative to GDP (from 1.1% of GDP in 2015 to 0.4% of GDP) was largely due to a decline in dividend payments (which fell from 0.5% of GDP in 2015 to 0.1% of GDP) received by the State from Ecopetrol. Likewise, in Suriname dividend payments to the central government by the State-owned oil producer Staatsoile dwindled in 2016 as profits fell to near zero.

Mining

Metals and minerals prices began to show signs of recovery in 2016, bolstering mining revenues in Latin America and the Caribbean. Metals prices, as measured by a weighted basket of the principal globally exported industrial metals, slipped a further 5% in 2016, though this represented a significantly smaller decline than that registered in the previous year (Table 2.6). During the year there was a gradual easing in the downward trajectory of prices, with a number of minerals and metals registering positive year-on-year gains in the second half of the year, especially in November and December. This was especially apparent in the case of the prices for iron ore and coal, which posted large double-digit year-on-year gains in the fourth quarter (50% and 78%, respectively). In contrast, despite an end of year rally, the price of copper – a key metal exported by the region – still fell 12% compared to its 2015 average level.

The up-tick in international prices during the year largely reflected an increase in demand for minerals and metals, especially in China where the government enacted a large-scale economic stimulus program. Chinese import volumes for a number of key minerals and metals registered strong increases during the year (Figure 2.9). Copper ore and concentrate imports were exceptionally strong, rising at double digit rates for much of the year, resulting in an annual increase of 28.0% over 2015 levels. Refined copper imports surged early in the year before wavering mid-year, ending the year with an annual increase of 2.7%. Iron ore imports also snapped a year-long slump and began showing increased dynamism in 2016, rising 7.5% over 2015 levels.

Table 2.6. **Year-on-year variation in metals and minerals prices, 2015-16**

(Percentage)

Product	2015	2016				
	Year	1	2	3	4	Year
Metals	-23.1	n.a.	n.a.	n.a.	n.a.	-5.0
Copper	-19.7	-19.9	-21.8	-9.3	8.1	-11.7
Aluminium	-10.9	-16.0	-11.2	1.7	14.5	-3.6
Iron Ore	-42.4	-24.0	-3.0	5.6	49.9	4.3
Tin	-26.6	-16.0	8.4	22.0	38.0	11.6
Nickel	-29.8	-40.9	-32.4	-3.0	14.5	-19.1
Zinc	-10.6	-19.4	-12.6	22.2	56.0	8.2
Lead	-14.7	-4.0	-11.6	9.1	27.2	4.4
Coal	-17.2	-20.2	-12.9	11.9	78.0	11.8

Source: Economic Commission for Latin America and the Caribbean (ECLAC), based on data from IMF (2017).

StatLink http://dx.doi.org/10.1787/888933685910

Figure 2.9. **China: Year-on-year variation in import volumes of selected metals and minerals, 2014-16**

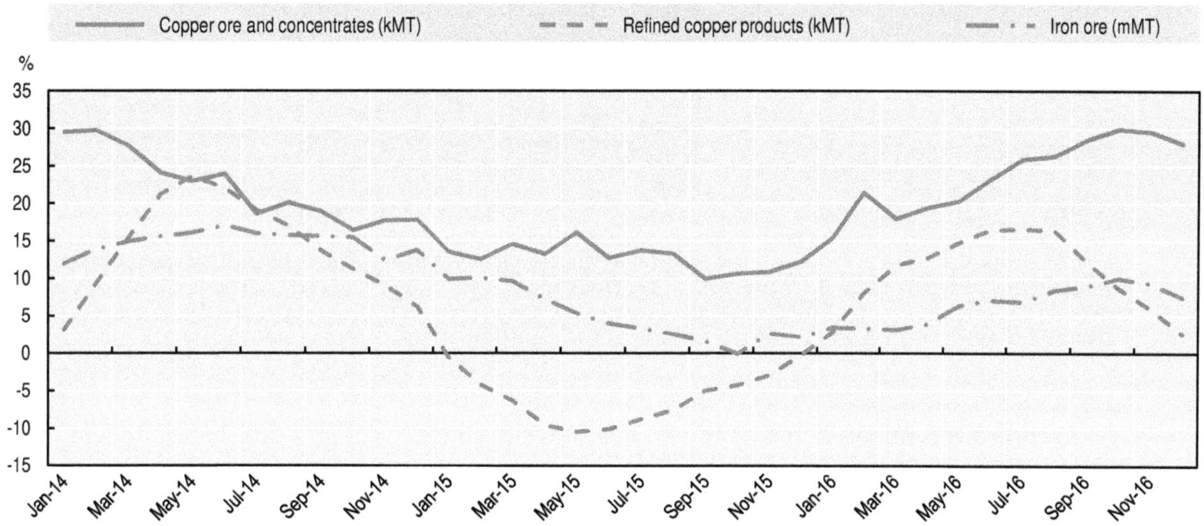

Note: Based on a rolling 12 month accumulated basis.

Source: Economic Commission for Latin America and the Caribbean (ECLAC), based on data from Bloomberg.

StatLink http://dx.doi.org/10.1787/888933685587

Supply-side considerations also supported higher prices, due to mine closures and policy measures that constrained supply, especially in Asia (World Bank, 2017). This was somewhat at odds with mine production trends in Latin America and the Caribbean, where a number of countries registered significant increases. Perhaps no country experienced a greater change in mining output than Peru, where copper production surged 38.4% (Table 2.7). During the year the new Las Bambas mine (MMG/CITIC Metal) began production and the newly expanded Cerro-Verde mine (Freeport-McMoRan) ramped up its output. As a result of this increase Peru overtook China as the second-largest copper producer in the world.

Table 2.7. **Latin America and the Caribbean: Mine production and prices of selected products, 2015-16**

(Units and percentages)

Minerals and metals	Market price (2016-15 %)	Mine production			
		Country	2015	2016	% change
Copper (kMT)	-11.7	Chile	5 772.1	5 552.6	-3.8
		Peru	1 700.8	2 353.9	38.4
		Mexico	485.5	491.0	1.1
Iron ore (mMT)	4.3	Brazil	397.0	391.0	-1.5
Silver (kKg)	8.9	Peru	4 101.6	4 374.4	6.7
		Mexico	4 959.4	4 109.6	-17.1
		Chile	1 504.3	1 501.4	-0.2
		Bolivia	1 306.1	1 353.0	3.6
Zinc (kMT)	8.2	Peru	1 421.2	1 336.8	-5.9
		Bolivia	442.2	487.0	10.1
		Mexico	454.6	384.2	-15.5
Bauxite (kMT)	-3.6	Jamaica	9 628.8	8 540.1	-11.3
Tin (kMT)	11.6	Brazil	25.0	26.0	4.0
		Peru	19.5	18.8	-3.7
		Bolivia	20.1	17.8	-11.6
Lead (kMT)	4.4	Peru	315.5	314.2	-0.4
		Mexico	213.0	159.0	-25.3
		Bolivia	75.3	89.5	18.9
Gold (kKg)	7.6	Peru	146.8	153.0	4.2
		Mexico	123.4	116.9	-5.2
		Colombia	59.2	61.8	4.4
		Chile	42.5	46.3	9.0
		Dominican Republic[a]	29.7	36.3	22.4
		Surinam[b]	9.4	9.7	3.3
		Bolivia	6.0	5.0	-16.4
Coal (kMT)	11.8	Colombia	85 548.0	90 512.0	5.8

Source: Economic Commission for Latin America and the Caribbean (ECLAC), based on data from CEPALstat (prices), Instituto Nacional de Estadística de Bolivia (INE) (2017), Ministerio de Minería de Chile (2017), Ministerio de Minas y Energía de Colombia (2016, 2017), Barrick Gold (2017), Jamaica Bauxite Institute (2017), Instituto Nacional de Estadística y Geografía de México (INEGI) (2017), Ministerio de Energía y Minas del Perú (2016, 2017) and IAMGOLD (2017).

StatLink http://dx.doi.org/10.1787/888933685929

Results were mixed among the region's other producers. On the one hand, Bolivia registered significant increases in production, especially of lead (18.9%) and zinc (10.1%), as higher international prices made low-grade operations profitable again. Production of coal in Colombia, the principal generator of royalty revenues in the country, rose strongly (5.8%). Likewise, gold production rose in several countries reflecting strong prices and demand.

In contrast, the production of iron ore in Brazil fell (by 1.5%), as output from the Samarco mine slowed due to a fatal mine disaster caused by the collapse of the facility's tailings pond. Copper production in Chile, the world's largest producer, slipped 3.8% as a number of mines reported declining ore grades (Consejo Minero, 2017). Mining production in Mexico also slowed across a number of categories: silver (-17.1%), zinc (-15.5%), lead (-25.3%) and gold (-5.2%).

These differing trends in prices and production were also manifest in the evolution of mining revenues in the region. For example, these revenues rose in US dollar terms in Bolivia (62.6%), Brazil (10.2%), Dominican Republic (19.4%) and Suriname (58.4%) (Table 2.8). In contrast, there were sharp declines in mining-related revenues in Argentina (-70.1%),

Chile (-68.7%), Jamaica (-10.3%), Mexico (-14.9%) and Peru (-20.2%). Colombia also registered a decline in US dollar terms (-2.8%), but this flipped to a moderate increase (8.3%) when expressed in national currency terms.

Table 2.8. **Latin America and the Caribbean: Year-on-year variation in fiscal revenues derived from mining, 2015-16**

(Percentages)

Country	Mining revenues	
	National currency	US dollars
Argentina	-52.4	-70.1
Bolivia (Plur. State of)	62.6	62.6
Brazil	15.3	10.2
Chile	-67.6	-68.7
Colombia	8.3	-2.8
Dominican Republic	22.1	19.4
Jamaica	-4.0	-10.3
Mexico	0.2	-14.9
Peru	-15.4	-20.2
Suriname	188.8	58.4
LAC-10	...	*-30.0*

Source: Economic Commission for Latin America and the Caribbean (ECLAC), based on official figures.

StatLink http://dx.doi.org/10.1787/888933685948

Relative to GDP, however, mining revenues held relatively stable in 2016, reflecting in part the diminished contribution of these revenues in US dollar and national currency terms (Table 2.9). For the ten countries considered in this sample the simple average slipped from 0.37% of GDP in 2015 to 0.35% of GDP. The effect of the significant decline in mining revenues in Chile (from 1.26% of GDP in 2015 to 0.39% of GDP) on the average was largely offset by rising revenues in Bolivia (0.50% of GDP in 2015 to 0.79% of GDP) and Suriname (0.46% of GDP in 2015 to 0.98% of GDP). In general, the reduction in mining revenues was concentrated in tax revenues, which fell from 0.19% of GDP in 2015 to 0.12% of GDP. Non-tax revenues, in contrast, posted a very modest gain, rising from 0.18% of GDP to 0.20% of GDP in 2016.

Table 2.9. **Latin America and the Caribbean: Fiscal revenues derived from mining, 2015-16**

(Percentages of GDP)

	Total			Tax revenues			Non-tax revenues		
	2015	2016	Δ	2015	2016	Δ	2015	2016	Δ
Argentina	0.1	0.0	0.0	0.1	0.0	0.0	0.0	0.0	0.0
Bolivia (Plur. State of)	0.5	0.8	0.3	0.1	0.3	0.3	0.4	0.5	0.0
Brazil	0.1	0.1	0.0	0.0	0.0	0.0	0.0	0.0	0.0
Chile	1.3	0.4	-0.9	0.9	0.0	-0.9	0.4	0.4	0.0
Colombia	0.3	0.3	0.0	0.1	0.1	0.0	0.2	0.2	0.0
Jamaica	0.2	0.2	0.0	0.0	0.0	0.0	0.2	0.2	0.0
Mexico	0.2	0.2	0.0	0.2	0.2	0.0	0.0	0.0	0.0
Peru	0.4	0.3	-0.1	0.2	0.2	-0.1	0.1	0.1	0.0
Dominican Republic	0.3	0.4	0.0	0.3	0.3	0.0	0.1	0.1	0.0
Suriname	0.5	1.0	0.5	0.1	0.4	0.3	0.4	0.6	0.2
LAC-10	0.4	0.4	0.0	0.2	0.2	0.0	0.2	0.2	0.0

Note: The LAC-10 average covers only the ten countries included in the table and cannot be compared with the simple averages shown in Figure 2.1 and Table 2.4 that cover different countries.

Source: Economic Commission for Latin America and the Caribbean (ECLAC), based on official figures.

StatLink http://dx.doi.org/10.1787/888933685967

The retreat in mining tax revenues was driven by a continued contraction in CIT payments by the sector. Financial information for a sample of major mining companies operating in the region reveals that pre-tax income remains exceptionally weak. Although pre-tax income returned to positive territory (USD 12.3 billion for this sample of companies) in 2016, it remained well below the average of USD 26.6 billion per year during 2006-2014 (Figure 2.10). More importantly, a number of major companies reported financial losses in 2015 and this continued to have a significant effect on 2016 collections.

Figure 2.10. **Selected regional mining companies: Pre-tax income, 2006-16**

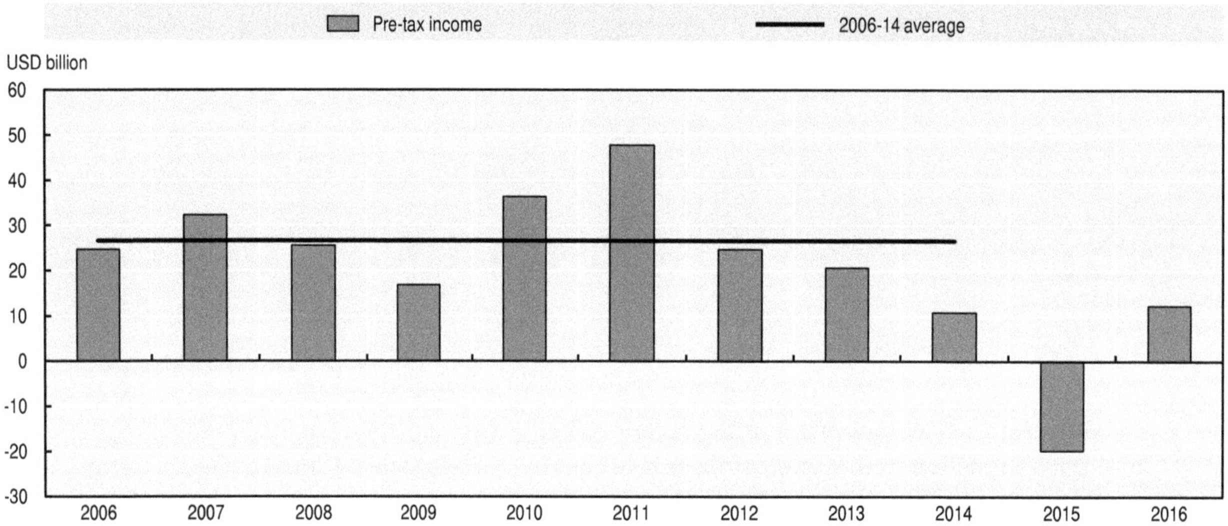

Note: Data corresponds to Antofagasta PLC, Compañía de Minas Buenaventura SAA, Codelco, Fresnillo PLC, Grupo México SAB de CV, Hochschild Mining PLC, Industrias Penoles SAB de CV, Minera Frisco SAB de CV, Minsur SA, Sociedad Minera Cerro Verde SAA, Vale SA, Volcán Compañía Minera SAA.

Source: Economic Commission for Latin America and the Caribbean (ECLAC), based on data from Bloomberg.

StatLink http://dx.doi.org/10.1787/888933685606

In Chile, tax revenues from mining fell from 0.9% of GDP in 2015 to just 0.02% of GDP. Payments of CIT and the special mining tax (calculated on the basis of operating income) for the largest private producers and CODELCO (the state-owned producer) fell to near zero. Likewise, mining tax receipts in Peru slipped – though less dramatically, from 0.24% of GDP to 0.18% of GDP – reflecting in part the expanded use of an accelerated depreciation tax benefit in line with the opening of a number of new investments (Banco Central de Reserva del Perú, 2017). In Argentina the retreat in mining tax revenues, from 0.05% of GDP to 0.01% of GDP, was due to a decrease in CIT payments – as an increasing number of producers reported financial losses – and a significant drop in export duties paid by the sector (AFIP, 2017).

Non-tax revenues, largely in the form of property rents such as royalties, rose in a number of countries as a result of improving prices and higher production. Stronger royalty payments were especially noteworthy in the Plurinational State of Bolivia, Dominican Republic and Suriname. It is important to highlight that in the latter two countries these royalties are entirely or nearly entirely associated with the production of gold. Non-tax revenues in Peru fell, from 0.15% of GDP in 2015 to 0.13% of GDP, despite a significant increase in production, especially of copper. This was due to a sharp decline in collections of the special mining levy (GEM, for its initials in Spanish), which is calculated on the basis of operating income. By contrast, revenues from traditional mining royalties, calculated as a share of the commercial value of production, rose sharply (by 32.7% in national currency terms).

References

AFIP (2017), *Anuario Estadísticas Tributarias 2016*, Administración Federal de Ingresos Públicos de Argentina.

Banco Central de Reserva del Perú (2017), *Memoria 2016*, Banco Central de Reserva del Perú , Lima.

Barrick Gold (2017), *Annual Report 2016*, Barrick Gold Corporation, Toronto.

Bolivarian Republic of Venezuela (2017), *Annual Report on Form 18-K to the United States Securities and Exchange Commission*, Bolivarian Republic of Venezuela, Caracas.

Consejo Minero (2017), *Reporte Anual 2016*, Consejo Minero, Toronto.

IAMGOLD Corporation (2017), *Annual Report 2016*, IAMGOLD Corporation, Toronto.

IEA (2017), *Oil Market Report* [online], International Energy Agency, Paris, *www.iea.org/oilmarketreport/omrpublic/*.

IMF (2017), "Prices & Forecasts", *IMF Primary Commodity Prices Forecasts* [online], International Monetary Fund, Washington, DC, *www.imf.org/external/np/res/commod/index.aspx*.

INE (2017), Estadísticas por Actividad Económica, [online], Instituto Nacional de Estadística de Bolivia, *https://www.ine.gob.bo/index.php/estadisticas-por-actividad-economica*.

INEGI (2017), Banco de Información Económica (BIE) [online], Instituto Nacional de Estadística y Geografía, *http://www.inegi.org.mx/sistemas/bie/*.

Jamaica Bauxite Institute (2017), "Total Bauxite Production Data" [online], *http://www.jbi.org.jm/*.

Ministerio de Energía y Minas del Perú (2017), *Reporte Anual Producción Minera 2016*, Lima.

Ministerio de Energía y Minas del Perú (2016), *Reporte Anual Producción Minera 2015*, Lima.

Ministerio de Minas y Energía de Colombia (2017), "Anexos minas", *Memorias al Congreso de la República 2016-2017*, Bogotá.

Ministerio de Minas y Energía de Colombia (2016), "Anexos minas", *Memorias al Congreso de la República 2015-2016*, Bogotá.

Ministerio de Minería de Chile (2017), *Anuario de la minería de Chile 2016*, Santiago.

Ministry of Finance of Trinidad and Tobago (2016), *Review of the Economy 2016*, Government of the Republic of Trinidad and Tobago, Port of Spain.

OPEC (2017), *Annual Statistical Bulletin 2017*, Organization of the Petroleum Exporting Countries.

PDVSA (2017), *Informe de Gestión Anual 2016*, Petróleos de Venezuela, S.A.

Staatsolie (2017), *Company Profile 2017*, available online at: *www.staatsolie.com/media/34837/companyprofile2017.pdf*.

Staatsolie (2016), *Annual Report 2015*.

World Bank (2017), "Commodity Markets Outlook: Investment Weakness in Commodity Exporters", January.

Revenue Statistics in Latin America and the Caribbean 2018/
Estadísticas tributarias en América Latina y el Caribe 2018

Capítulo 2

SECCIÓN ESPECIAL

Ingresos fiscales provenientes de recursos naturales no renovables en América Latina y el Caribe

Principales hallazgos

Tendencias generales para 2016 y 2017

Pese a un repunte en los precios de materias primas, los ingresos fiscales asociados con los recursos naturales no renovables continuaron cayendo en 2016. Los ingresos combinados de los hidrocarburos y la minería se contrajeron en promedio del 3.5% del PIB en 2015 a 2.3% del PIB para 12 países exportadores de materias primas en América Latina y el Caribe (excluyendo Venezuela).[a] A diferencia de años anteriores, este descenso agravó la caída de los ingresos de otras fuentes (otros ingresos tributarios y no tributarios). Ha habido una fuerte disminución de la dependencia de los ingresos provenientes de recursos naturales no renovables, lo que refleja la disminución de estos recursos, así como una mayor movilización de los ingresos procedentes de otras fuentes.

No se prevé que los ingresos fiscal provenientes de los recursos naturales no renovables aumenten notablemente, en relación con el PIB, en 2017. Si bien los precios internacionales de muchos productos claves han tendido al alza, siguen siendo significativamente más bajos que sus máximos recientes. Del mismo modo, las condiciones financieras de las principales compañías productoras de la región enfrentan dificultades, no obstante en los últimos años han mejorado. Como resultado, se proyecta que los ingresos provenientes de hidrocarburos caerán levemente de 3.4% del PIB en 2016 a 3.3% del PIB en 2017, en los diez países que recaudaron este tipo de ingresos.[b] Se espera que los ingresos de la minería se mantengan estables en torno al 0.4% del PIB, en los diez países que recaudaron este tipo de ingresos.[c]

Evolución de los ingresos por recursos naturales no renovables en 2016

Los ingresos relacionados con hidrocarburos se redujeron de un promedio revisado de 5.0% del PIB en 2015 a 3.4% del PIB en 2016 en los diez países que recaudaron este tipo de ingresos (incluido Venezuela). Las excepcionalmente débiles utilidades registradas por los mayores productores de hidrocarburos de la región provocaron una fuerte contracción en los ingresos tributarios asociados con el sector, principalmente en el impuesto a las ganancias corporativas, así como en los ingresos no tributarios, como los dividendos. Otros ingresos no tributarios, principalmente regalías y otras participaciones en el valor comercial de la producción, cayeron a medida que el precio del petróleo crudo se mantuvo blando y la producción regional se contrajo.

Los ingresos de la minería registraron un descenso ligero (de 0.37% del PIB en 2015 a 0.35% del PIB en los diez países que recaudaron este tipo de ingresos), con diferencias significativas entre países. Los ingresos tributarios continuaron registrando una tendencia a la baja, reflejando el hecho de que las pérdidas financieras en 2015 afectaron significativamente los ingresos por impuestos a la renta de las empresas en 2016, especialmente en Chile. El repunte de los precios al fin de año junto con una mayor producción en algunos países impulsó los ingresos no tributarios, principalmente las regalías, especialmente en los países productores de oro.

a. Argentina, Bolivia (Est. Plur. de), Brasil, Chile, Colombia, Ecuador, Jamaica, México, Perú, República Dominicana, Surinam y Trinidad y Tobago.

b. Argentina, Bolivia (Est. Plur.de), Brasil, Colombia, Ecuador, México, Perú, Surinam, Trindad y Tobago y Venezuela (Bol. Rep. of).

c. Argentina, Bolivia (Est. Plur.de), Brasil, Chile, Colombia, Jamaica, México, Perú, República Dominicana y Surinam.

Las tendencias generales de los ingresos fiscales provenientes de recursos naturales no renovables en América Latina y el Caribe para 2016 y 2017

Los ingresos provenientes de recursos naturales no renovables en América Latina y el Caribe continuaron contrayéndose en 2016, afectados por el débil crecimiento global y por la caída en los precios internacionales para las principales materias primas de exportación de la región. Los ingresos combinados de hidrocarburos y minería en los 12 países exportadores de materias primas, sin incluir a Venezuela por falta de estadísticas comparables, cayeron a un promedio del 2.3% del PIB en 2016, en comparación con el 3.5% del PIB en 2015 (véase el gráfico 2.1). Esto marcó el quinto año consecutivo de declive. Los ingresos provenientes de recursos naturales renovables, aunque no se incluyen en este análisis, también registraron un descenso durante el año (véase el recuadro 2.1). A diferencia de años anteriores, la caída en los ingresos de recursos naturales no renovables en 2016 estuvo acompañada por una reducción en ingresos de otras fuentes (otros ingresos tributarios y no tributarios), lo que refleja el impacto negativo sobre los ingresos fiscales de un segundo año consecutivo de recesión económica en la región.

Gráfico 2.1. **Principales productores de recursos naturales no renovables en América Latina y el Caribe (12 países): desglose de los ingresos totales del gobierno general, 2010-16[a]**

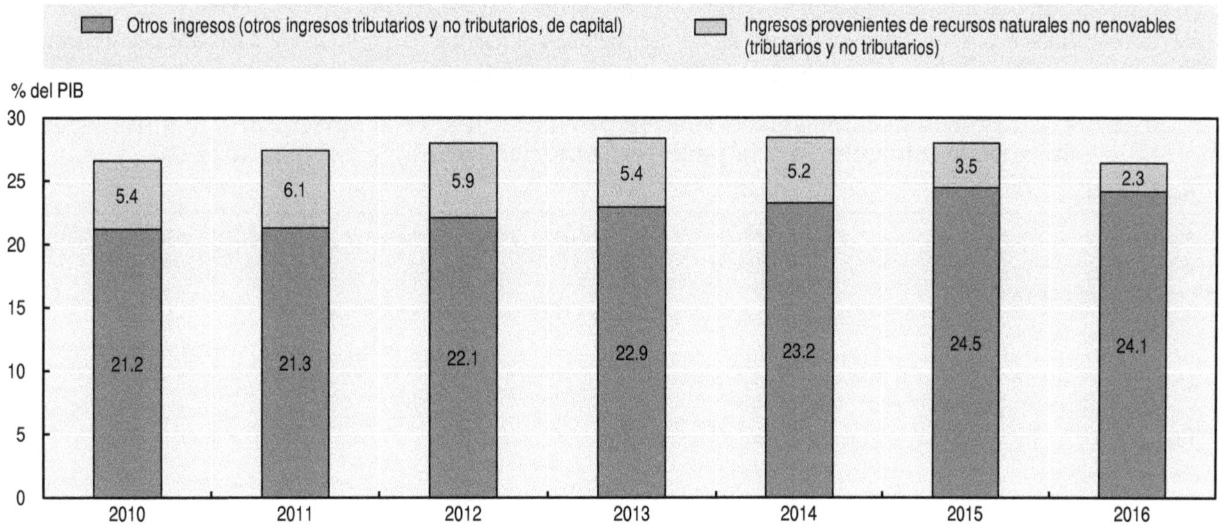

Nota: Incluye Argentina, Bolivia (Est. Plur. de), Brasil, Chile, Colombia, Ecuador, Jamaica, México, Perú, República Dominicana, Surinam y Trinidad y Tobago. Excluye a Venezuela (Rep. Bol. De) debido a la falta de una serie de datos revisada para los ingresos totales durante el período considerado. Los ingresos totales para Argentina y Ecuador se refieren al sector público no financiero, para México al sector público federal.

a. Promedios simples. Los promedios simples cubren los 12 países citados anteriormente (excluyendo a Venezuela) y no se pueden comparar con los promedios simples que se muestran en los cuadros 2.4 y 2.9 que cubren diferentes países.

Fuente: Comisión Económica para América Latina y el Caribe (CEPAL), sobre la base de cifras oficiales.

StatLink http://dx.doi.org/10.1787/888933685625

A pesar de la tendencia a la baja en los ingresos de recursos naturales no renovables en la región, los ingresos totales se han mantenido relativamente estables, con un promedio del 27.6% del PIB entre 2010 y 2016 para este grupo de 12 países (2 p.p. de caída entre 2014 y 2016). Durante este período, los países productores de productos básicos de la región promulgaron un número importante de reformas tributarias para compensar la disminución de los ingresos de los hidrocarburos y la minería. Como resultado, estos otros ingresos aumentaron de un promedio de 21.2% del PIB en 2010 a un máximo de 24.5% del PIB en 2015, antes del descenso en 2016. Hubo aumentos significativos en los ingresos tributarios y de otro tipo durante el período en Argentina, Bolivia, Chile, Ecuador, México y Trinidad y Tobago.

Recuadro 2.1. **Ingresos fiscales de recursos naturales renovables en América Latina y el Caribe**

Si bien el papel que juegan los ingresos de recursos naturales no renovables en las cuentas fiscales de la región está bien establecido, existe menos información sobre los ingresos que se derivan de la explotación de los recursos naturales renovables. Estos ingresos pueden tomar una variedad de formas, pero tal vez se asocien más con actividades relacionadas con la agricultura, la ganadería, la caza, la silvicultura y la pesca, o con el uso de servicios proporcionados por recursos naturales renovables (hidroelectricidad, transporte, etc.). En contraste con los ingresos provenientes de recursos naturales no renovables, hay significativamente menos información estadística disponible.

Las cifras disponibles sugieren que los ingresos fiscales para los gobiernos de la región provenientes de la renta generada por la explotación de recursos naturales renovables tienden a ser modestos, a pesar del importante papel que juegan los países latinoamericanos en las exportaciones agrícolas y alimentarias mundiales. De los países considerados en el cuadro 2.1, solo en Argentina y Paraguay estos ingresos son relativamente considerables (en 0.45% del PIB y 0.16% del PIB en 2016, respectivamente). Es de destacar que, en el caso de Argentina, estos ingresos son mayores que los de la minería (0.02% del PIB en 2016). En los otros países estos ingresos son relativamente modestos en comparación con los ingresos de recursos naturales no renovables: Brasil (0.01% del PIB, comparado con 0.1% del PIB para la minería y 1.2% para los hidrocarburos), Chile (0.01% del PIB, aunque esto excluye el pago del IRPJ por falta de datos estadísticos, en comparación con el 0.4% del PIB para la minería) y Perú (0.03% del PIB, en comparación con el 0.3% del PIB para la minería y el 0.8% del PIB para hidrocarburos). Si bien estos ingresos son susceptibles a la volatilidad que surge de las condiciones climáticas o cambios en la producción mundial de productos específicos, su tamaño relativo limita su impacto en las cuentas fiscales generales.

Cuadro 2.1. **Ingresos fiscales seleccionados provenientes de la agricultura, la ganadería, la caza, la silvicultura y la pesca en América Latina, % del PIB, 2014-16**

País/instrumento	2014	2015	2016
Argentina	0.82	0.73	0.45
IRPJ	0.10	0.12	0.08
Derechos de exportación	0.72	0.61	0.37
Brasil	0.01	0.01	0.01
IRPJ	0.01	0.01	0.01
Chile	0.00	0.01	0.01
Derechos de pesca	0.00	0.01	0.01
Paraguay	0.20	0.20	0.16
IMAGRO/IRAGRO	0.20	0.20	0.16
Perú	0.04	0.03	0.03
IRPJ	0.04	0.03	0.03
Derechos de pesca	0.01	0.01	0.01

Nota: Los ingresos por derechos de pesca en Perú se estiman en base a las transferencias del gobierno central a los gobiernos subnacionales, por el componente del canon de pesca que trata de los derechos de pesca. Esta cifra se duplica al reflejar la distribución de estos ingresos entre niveles de gobierno. No se dispuso de un desglose de los pagos del impuesto a la renta corporativo por actividad económica para Chile.

Fuente: Comisión Económica para América Latina y el Caribe (CEPAL), sobre la base de cifras oficiales.

StatLink http://dx.doi.org/10.1787/888933685986

Los ingresos públicos relacionados con los servicios asociados con el uso de recursos naturales renovables en la región pueden ser importantes, pero están limitados a un grupo selecto de países. Los ejemplos incluyen los ingresos del gobierno central de las operaciones del Canal de Panamá, que alcanzaron 1.9% del PIB en 2015 (0.7% como peajes de canales y 1.2% como dividendos de la Autoridad del Canal). En Paraguay, las regalías y compensaciones de las plantas hidroeléctricas de Itaipú y Yacyretá también son considerables, con un 1.5% del PIB en 2016. Estos ingresos también pueden ser una fuente de volatilidad significativa en estos países, reflejando su susceptibilidad a choques exógenos como cambios en condiciones económicas globales, así como las condiciones climáticas cambiantes de año en año.

Fuente: Comisión Económica para América Latina y el Caribe (CEPAL).

En consecuencia, la dependencia de los ingresos de los recursos naturales no renovables ha disminuido considerablemente en la región. Como muestra el gráfico 2.2, en 2010 los ingresos por hidrocarburos y minería representaron más del 30% de los ingresos totales en Trinidad y Tobago (42%), Bolivia (36%), Ecuador (34%), México (33%) y Surinam (33%). Para el 2016, la participación de estos ingresos había caído a cerca del 20%, y en el caso de Trinidad y Tobago, aún más baja (9%). Del mismo modo, los países que previamente habían tenido un nivel moderado de dependencia de estos ingresos, como Chile, Colombia y Perú – todos los cuales tenían participaciones entre el 10% y el 20% en 2010 – también registraron una fuerte reducción (en torno al 5% o más bajo).

Gráfico 2.2. **Principales productores de recursos naturales no renovables de América Latina y el Caribe (12 países): participación de los ingresos de recursos naturales no renovables en los ingresos totales del gobierno general, 2010 y 2016[a]**

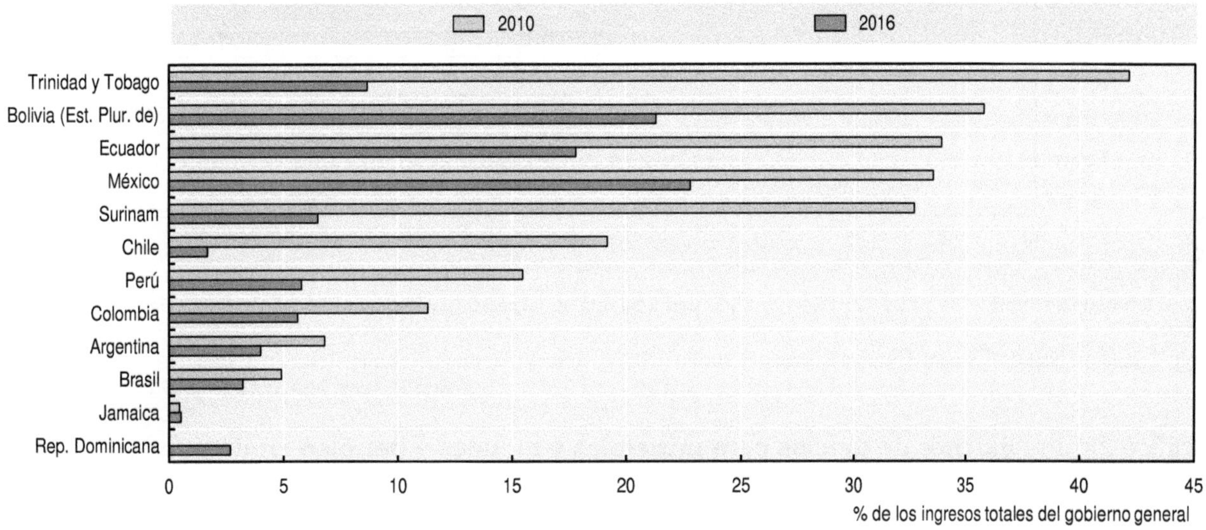

Nota: Los ingresos totales para Argentina y Ecuador se refieren al sector público no financiero, para México al sector público federal.
a. Excluye a Venezuela debido a la falta de datos oficiales sobre los ingresos totales del gobierno central.
Fuente: Comisión Económica para América Latina y el Caribe (CEPAL), sobre la base de cifras oficiales.
StatLink http://dx.doi.org/10.1787/888933685644

Aunque la mayor generación de recursos de otras fuentes y una menor dependencia de los ingresos de recursos naturales no renovables son acontecimientos positivos, el contexto fiscal sigue siendo excepcionalmente difícil. El crecimiento del gasto público ha superado al de los ingresos públicos en la región, lo que ha llevado a una expansión significativa del déficit fiscal (véase el gráfico 2.3). La recuperación de este espacio fiscal perdido requerirá esfuerzos para fortalecer la movilización de recursos domésticos para generar la financiación a largo plazo necesario para cumplir con los Objetivos de Desarrollo Sostenible.

Los esfuerzos de consolidación en la región dirigidos a recuperar el espacio fiscal siguieron aumentando en 2017, aunque con poco apoyo en términos de mayores ingresos provenientes de recursos naturales no renovables. Aunque se pronostica un aumento de los precios internacionales del petróleo crudo y una serie de minerales y metales, se mantienen muy por debajo de los niveles registrados en años anteriores (véase el gráfico 2.4). Para el 2017, se espera que los precios spot del petróleo crudo aumenten un 14%; sin embargo, con este aumento esperado, los precios aún estarían un 49% por debajo de los niveles de 2014. Por otro lado, se prevé que los precios de una canasta de minerales y metales aumenten un 16.8%, lo cual sería el primer incremento desde 2011. Además, las condiciones financieras entre las empresas productoras siguen enfrentando dificultades, aunque con signos de mejora, lo cual limita el repunte de los ingresos de instrumentos vinculados a ingresos y ganancias.

Gráfico 2.3. **Principales productores de recursos naturales no renovables en América Latina y el Caribe (12 países): balance fiscal del gobierno general, 2016[a]**

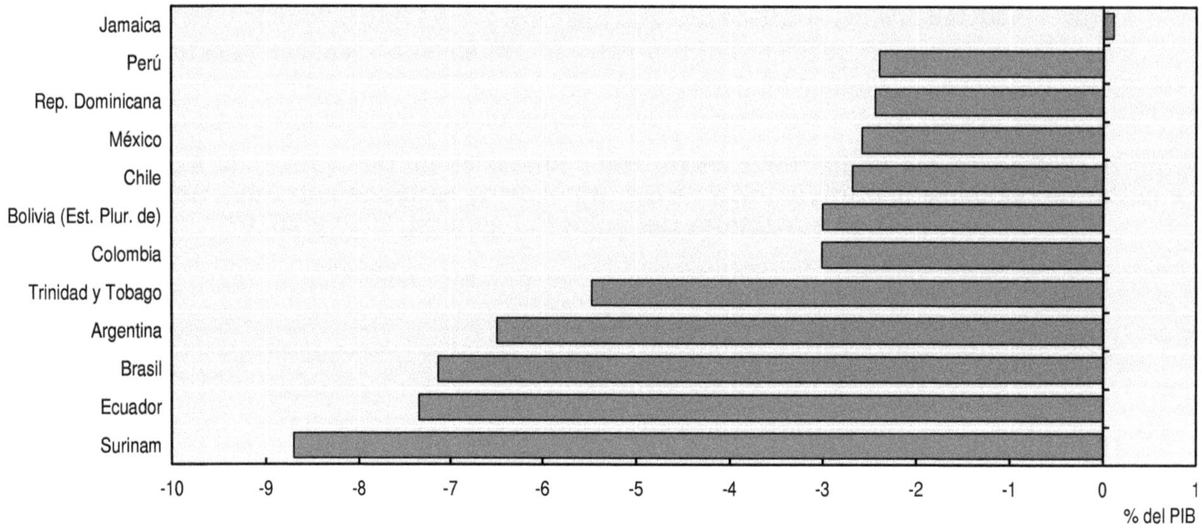

Nota: a. Promedios simples. Los datos para Argentina y Ecuador se refieren al sector público no financiero, para México al sector público federal.

Fuente: Comisión Económica para América Latina y el Caribe (CEPAL), sobre la base de cifras oficiales.

StatLink http://dx.doi.org/10.1787/888933685663

Gráfico 2.4. **Previsiones de precios para minerales y metales y petróleo crudo puntual, 2011-17**

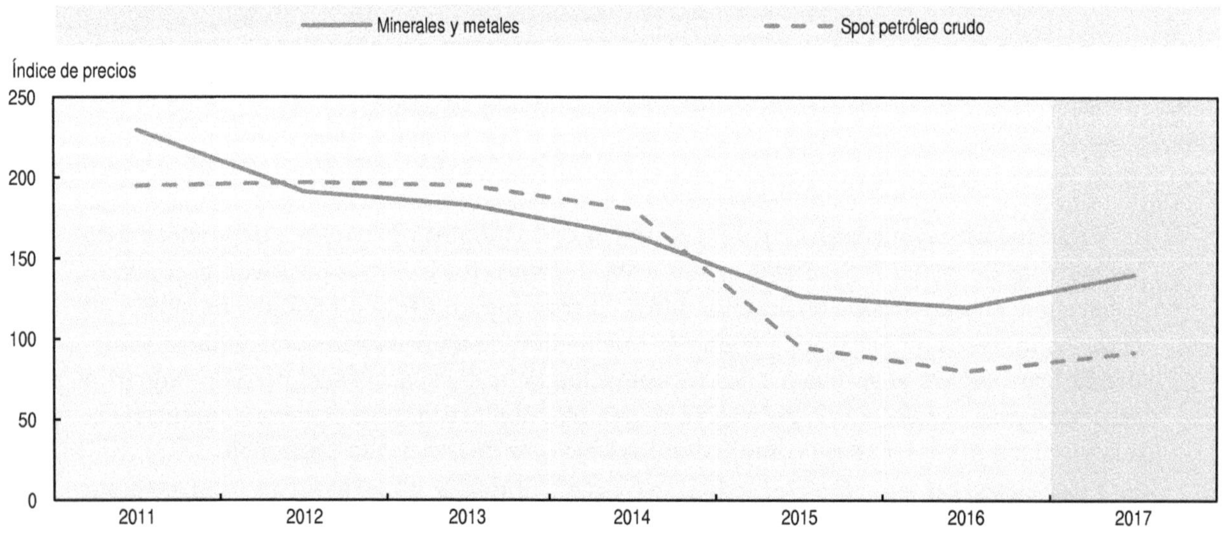

Nota: 2005 = 100, sobre la base de los pesos mundiales de exportación.

Fuente: Fondo Monetario Internacional (FMI, 2017), pronósticos de precios de los productos básicos con precios efectivos hasta el 13/07/2017.

StatLink http://dx.doi.org/10.1787/888933685682

Como resultado, se espera que los ingresos de hidrocarburos se estabilicen – en relación con el PIB – en 2017, cayendo a un promedio de 3.3% del PIB en comparación con 3.4% del PIB en 2016 (véase el gráfico 2.5). Sin embargo, en contraste con 2016, esta tendencia a la baja es menos generalizada, ya que en algunos países los ingresos de hidrocarburos podrían estabilizarse en relación con el PIB o incluso aumentar levemente. Se espera que los ingresos de la minería, que rompieron una racha de cuatro años a la baja en 2016, se mantengan estables en un 0.4% del PIB en promedio para los países considerados. En particular, se prevé que los ingresos de la minería en Chile y Perú aumenten, aunque en menos de 0.3 puntos porcentuales del PIB, ya que los pagos de impuestos corporativos del sector se han empezado a recuperar después de las fuertes caídas registradas en 2016.

Gráfico 2.5. **Principales productores de recursos naturales no renovables en América Latina y el Caribe (13 países): ingresos fiscales de hidrocarburos y minería, 2010-17[a]**

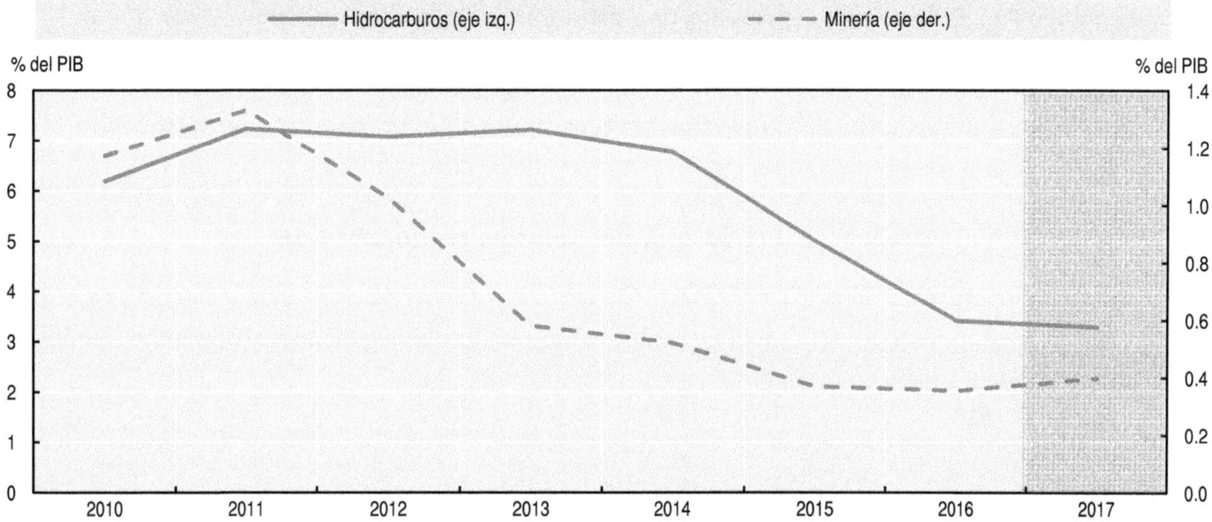

Nota: La minería incluye: Argentina, Bolivia (Estado Plurinacional de), Brasil, Chile, Colombia, Jamaica, México, Perú, República Dominicana y Surinam. Los hidrocarburos incluyen: Argentina, Bolivia (Estado Plurinacional de), Brasil, Colombia, Ecuador, México, Perú, Surinam, Trinidad y Tobago y Venezuela (Bol. Rep. De). Los valores para 2017 se basan en estimaciones oficiales del gobierno a partir de documentos presupuestarios del 2018 o de cifras anuales preliminares. Cuando las cifras para 2017 no estaban disponibles, se calcularon utilizando datos mensuales (por lo general, durante los primeros tres trimestres del año). Cuando los datos mensuales no estaban disponibles, los ingresos se estimaron aplicando el cambio interanual en el precio del producto más representativo (o cesta de productos en el caso de la minería) para el país, expresado en términos de moneda nacional, para los ingresos de 2016.

a. Promedios simples. Datos para Venezuela (Bol. Rep. De) basados en información reportada en PDVSA (2017) y República Bolivariana de Venezuela (2017).

Fuente: Comisión Económica para América Latina y el Caribe (CEPAL), sobre la base de cifras oficiales.

StatLink http://dx.doi.org/10.1787/888933685701

Evolución de los ingresos provenientes de recursos naturales no renovables en 2016

Hidrocarburos

Los bajos precios internacionales del petróleo crudo y la caída de la producción regional redujeron los ingresos de hidrocarburos en América Latina y el Caribe. El exceso de oferta en el mercado mundial del petróleo se mantuvo en 2016, lo que continuó presionando a la baja los precios (AIE, 2017). La demanda de petróleo aumentó más moderadamente en 2016 (1.4% a 96.1 millones de barriles por día), en comparación con el fuerte incremento de 2.1% (a 94.8 millones de barriles por día) del 2015. Es así que el ritmo de crecimiento de la demanda del sector de hidrocarburos se debió principalmente a los débiles fundamentos macroeconómicos de los países de la región, aunado al efecto de la caída – que vale resaltar fue menor en comparación a años anteriores – de los precios.

El suministro de petróleo crudo también se desaceleró, registrando un incremento interanual de solo 0.4% (a 97.0 millones de barriles por día) en comparación con un aumento de 3.1% (a 96.6 millones de barriles por día) en 2015. En parte, esto reflejaba el impacto de precios bajos en la producción de mayor costo, especialmente en los Estados Unidos. A pesar de este ritmo más lento de crecimiento, la oferta se mantuvo marginalmente por encima de la demanda, colocando al mercado en una posición de superávit de aproximadamente 0.9 millones de barriles por día. Sin embargo, esto fue sustancialmente menor que el superávit de 1.8 millones de barriles por día registrado en 2015.

Debido a estas tendencias, los precios spot del petróleo crudo en los mercados mundiales disminuyeron, cayendo un 15.7% en promedio en 2016 para llegar a USD 43 por barril (véase el gráfico 2.6). Si bien esto representa una disminución significativamente menor que la registrada en 2015 (47.2%), la caída acumulada en los precios del crudo entre 2014 y 2016 alcanzó un asombroso 55.5%. No obstante, los datos mensuales destacan un aumento progresivo, aunque lento, de los precios, especialmente en el primer y el cuarto trimestre del año.

Gráfico 2.6. **Precio spot del petróleo crudo, 2014-16**

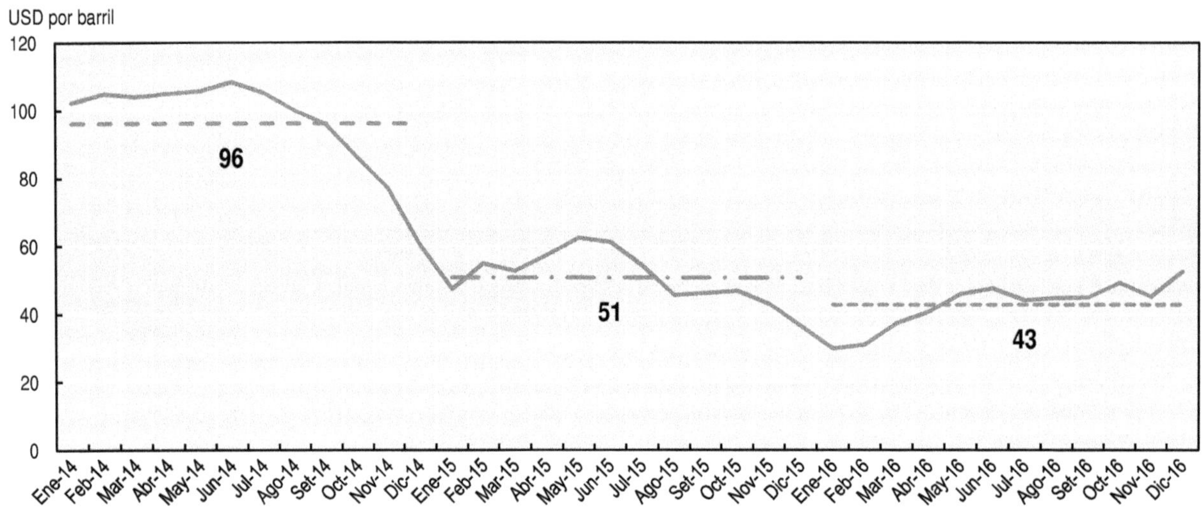

Fuente: Comisión Económica para América Latina y el Caribe (CEPAL), sobre la base de datos de UNCTADstat.

StatLink http://dx.doi.org/10.1787/888933685720

Los débiles precios mundiales del petróleo crudo se vieron agravados en América Latina y el Caribe por la caída de la producción regional de hidrocarburos. Según la OPEP (2017), la producción de petróleo cayó un 5.1% interanual en 2016 en América Latina y el Caribe, de 9.7 millones de barriles por día a 9.2 millones de barriles por día (cuadro 2.2). Hubo caídas particularmente grandes, tanto en términos absolutos como porcentuales, en Colombia (12.2%), Venezuela (10.6%) y México (5.0%). La producción de gas natural aumentó modestamente (0.8%), principalmente debido a un fuerte repunte en Trinidad y Tobago (6.1%), para alcanzar 222.7 millones de metros cúbicos estándar. Sin embargo, incluso con este aumento, la producción combinada de gas natural – suponiendo una conversión estándar de metros cúbicos equivalente a barriles de petróleo – y el petróleo crudo cayeron un 3.2% año con año.

Cuadro 2.2. **América Latina y el Caribe: producción de hidrocarburos, 2015-16**

País	Producción de petróleo crudo (1,000 b / d)		Producción comercializada de gas natural (m estándar cu m)	
	2015	2016	2015	2016
América Latina	9 715	9 222	221 004	222 692
Argentina	532	512	36 400	36 546
Bolivia	n.a.	n.a.	22 597	23 501
Brasil	2 437	2 510	20 411	20 619
Chile	5	4	n.a.	n.a.
Colombia	1 006	883	12 807	12 935
Ecuador	543	549	497	530
México	2 267	2 153	45 984	41 227
Perú	58	40	13 512	14 454
Surinam	17	16	n.a.	n.a.
Trinidad y Tobago	79	71	40 875	43 374
Venezuela	2 654	2 373	26 004	27 718
Otros	117	110	1 917	1 789

Fuente: Comisión Económica para América Latina y el Caribe (CEPAL), sobre la base de datos de la OPEP (2017) y Staatsoile (2017).

StatLink http://dx.doi.org/10.1787/888933686005

Como resultado de estas tendencias en los precios globales y niveles de producción regional, los ingresos fiscales derivados de los hidrocarburos en América Latina y el Caribe registraron una disminución interanual del 17.9% en 2016, cayendo de USD 149.1 mil millones en 2015 a USD 122.4 mil millones (cuadro 2.3). Desde el punto de vista de la cadena de valor de los hidrocarburos, los ingresos por la exploración y extracción de hidrocarburos – los llamados actividades up-stream – cayeron un 23,8%, de USD 111.2 mil millones en 2015 a USD 84.7 mil millones. Por el contrario, los ingresos relacionados con la comercialización y venta de hidrocarburos – actividades down-stream – cayeron marginalmente (0,6%), de USD 37.900 millones en 2015 a USD 37.700 millones, reflejando una disminución en la demanda, pero también una reducción más moderada en los precios de los productos refinados.

Cuadro 2.3. **América Latina y el Caribe: variación interanual en los ingresos fiscales derivados de los hidrocarburos, 2015-16**

(Porcentaje)

País	Ingresos por hidrocarburos	
	Moneda nacional	USD
Argentina	19.3	-25.2
Bolivia (Est. Plur. de)	-41.8	-41.8
Brasil	-7.1	-11.2
Colombia	-52.0	-56.9
Ecuador	-14.9	-14.9
México	0.3	-14.8
Perú	-12.9	-17.8
Surinam	-100.0	-100.0
Trinidad y Tobago	-71.5	-72.7
Venezuela (Rep. Bol. de)	259.0	-11.2
ALC-10	...	*-17.9*
Upstream	...	*-23.8*
Downstream	...	*-0.6*

Fuente: Comisión Económica para América Latina y el Caribe (CEPAL), sobre la base de cifras oficiales.

StatLink http://dx.doi.org/10.1787/888933686024

A nivel de los países, hubo una gran heterogeneidad en la evolución de los ingresos de hidrocarburos, tanto expresados en dólares estadounidenses como en moneda nacional. Mientras que varios países registraron disminuciones en línea con la variación en el precio del petróleo, otros países experimentaron caídas más dramáticas. Por ejemplo, en Colombia y Trinidad y Tobago, los ingresos por hidrocarburos cayeron más de 50% año con año en términos de dólares. En Surinam, los pagos de impuestos sobre la renta y dividendos del productor estatal, Staatsoile, cayeron a cero.

Al igual que en 2015, las depreciaciones cambiarias en algunos países suavizaron el impacto de la disminución de los ingresos de hidrocarburos cuando se expresaron en términos de moneda nacional. En Argentina y México, los ingresos aumentaron año a año en términos de moneda nacional. Por el contrario, en Colombia la depreciación del peso del 11.4% proporcionó poco alivio, ya que fue superada en gran medida por la magnitud de la disminución en los ingresos fiscales de hidrocarburos expresados en dólares estadounidenses. En Bolivia – cuya moneda tiene una paridad móvil ajustada – y Ecuador – que está dolarizado – no hubo alivio por el impacto de la caída de los precios del petróleo sobre los ingresos de los hidrocarburos.

A pesar del efecto de amortiguación proporcionado por las depreciaciones monetarias, los ingresos de hidrocarburos relativos al PIB continuaron cayendo bruscamente en 2016. Como se muestra en el cuadro 2.4, los ingresos totales cayeron de un promedio de 5.0% del PIB en 2015 a 3.4% del PIB, en los diez países que recaudaron este tipo de ingresos. Desagregado por tipo de instrumento de ingresos, los ingresos tributarios y no tributarios tuvieron una tendencia a la baja durante el año. Los ingresos tributarios disminuyeron de un promedio de 1.7% en 2015 del PIB a 0,8% del PIB, reflejando la fuerte disminución de estos ingresos en Trinidad y Tobago y en menor grado en Colombia. Los ingresos no tributarios registraron una disminución similar, al pasar del 3.3% del PIB en 2015 al 2.6% del PIB, liderado por una fuerte reducción en el Estado Plurinacional de Bolivia.

Cuadro 2.4. **América Latina y el Caribe: ingresos fiscales derivados de los hidrocarburos, 2015-16**

(Porcentaje del PIB)

	Total			Ingresos tributarios			Ingresos no tributarios		
	2015	2016	Δ	2015	2016	Δ	2015	2016	Δ
Argentina	1.6	1.4	-0.2	1.3	1.1	-0.2	0.4	0.3	0.0
Bolivia (Est. Plur. de)	10.4	5.9	-4.5	2.4	1.8	-0.7	7.9	4.1	-3.8
Brasil	1.3	1.1	-0.1	0.9	0.9	0.0	0.4	0.3	-0.1
Colombia	2.5	1.1	-1.4	1.3	0.7	-0.7	1.1	0.4	-0.7
Ecuador	6.3	5.4	-0.9	0.0	0.0	0.0	6.3	5.4	-0.9
México	5.9	5.5	-0.4	1.3	1.4	0.2	4.6	4.1	-0.6
Perú	1.0	0.8	-0.2	0.5	0.5	-0.1	0.4	0.3	-0.1
Surinam	0.8	0.0	-0.8	0.4	0.0	-0.4	0.3	0.0	-0.3
Trinidad y Tobago	9.1	2.7	-6.4	8.0	1.3	-6.6	1.1	1.3	0.2
Venezuela Rep. Bol. de	11.2	10.2	-1.0	0.8	0.7	-0.1	10.4	9.5	-0.9
ALC-10	5.0	3.4	-1.6	1.7	0.8	-0.9	3.3	2.6	-0.7

Nota: El promedio ALC-10 cubre solo los diez países incluidos en el cuadro y no se puede comparar con los promedios simples que se muestran en el gráfico 2.1 y el cuadro 2.9 que cubren diferentes países.

Fuente: Comisión Económica para América Latina y el Caribe (CEPAL), sobre la base de cifras oficiales.

StatLink http://dx.doi.org/10.1787/888933686043

Los ingresos fiscales de los hidrocarburos se vieron significativamente socavados por las débiles ganancias del sector. Las utilidades de los principales productores de la región se mantuvieron excepcionalmente débiles en 2016. Las ganancias antes de impuestos para un grupo seleccionado de productores en la región alcanzaron USD 1.800 millones en 2016, lo que representó una mejora con respecto a la pérdida USD 33.2 mil millones reportados en

2015 (gráfico 2.7). Sin embargo, a pesar de ser nuevamente positivas, las ganancias en 2016 se mantienen muy lejos de los niveles registrados durante 2011-13, cuando promediaron USD 107.9 mil millones por año.

Gráfico 2.7. **Productores seleccionados de petróleo regionales: utilidades antes de impuestos, 2011-16**

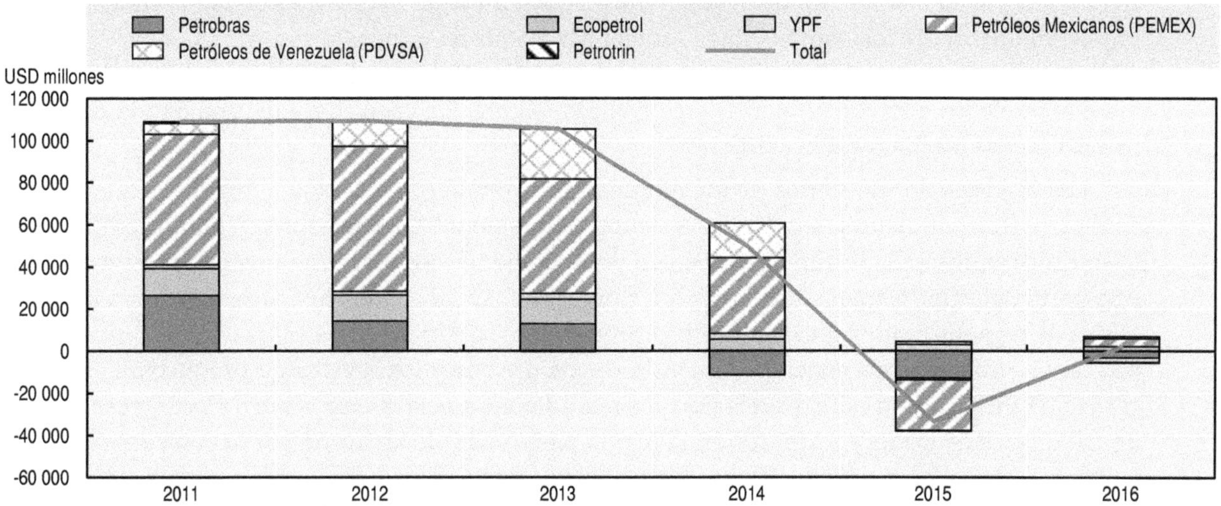

Fuente: Comisión Económica para América Latina y el Caribe (CEPAL), sobre la base de datos de Bloomberg.

StatLink http://dx.doi.org/10.1787/888933685739

Las débiles ganancias se tradujeron en una nueva disminución de los ingresos tributarios de hidrocarburos en 2016. En particular, los ingresos tributarios asociados con actividades up-stream – exploración y extracción – se redujeron substancialmente, de un promedio de 1.2% del PIB en 2015 a 0.3% del PIB (véase el cuadro 2.5). En Colombia, los pagos de impuestos corporativos cayeron bruscamente, reflejando en parte la pérdida financiera antes de impuestos registrada por EcoPetrol en 2015. Asimismo, en Trinidad y Tobago los pagos del impuesto a las ganancias corporativas – que representan la mayoría de los ingresos totales de hidrocarburos – cayeron drásticamente, reflejando el hecho de que las principales compañías de energía sacaron de producción varias unidades asignadas a nuevos proyectos de actividades up-stream que ya estaban en desarrollo (Ministry of Finance of Trinidad and Tobago, 2016).

Cuadro 2.5. **América Latina y el Caribe: ingresos fiscales derivados de los hidrocarburos, por segmento de la cadena de valor, 2015-16**

(Porcentaje del PIB)

País	Ingresos tributarios			Upstream			Downstream		
	2015	2016	Δ	2015	2016	Δ	2015	2016	Δ
Argentina	1.3	1.1	-0.2	0.3	0.1	-0.2	1.0	0.9	0.0
Bolivia (Est. Plur. de)	2.4	1.8	-0.7	1.0	0.3	-0.8	1.4	1.5	0.1
Brasil	0.9	0.9	0.0	0.0	0.0	0.0	0.9	0.9	0.0
Colombia	1.3	0.7	-0.7	0.9	0.3	-0.6	0.4	0.4	0.0
Ecuador	0.0	0.0	0.0	0.0	0.0	0.0	0.0	0.0	0.0
México	1.3	1.4	0.2	0.0	0.0	0.0	1.2	1.4	0.2
Perú	0.5	0.5	-0.1	0.2	0.1	-0.1	0.4	0.4	0.0
Surinam	0.4	0.0	-0.4	0.4	0.0	-0.4	0.0	0.0	0.0
Trinidad y Tobago	8.0	1.3	-6.6	8.0	1.3	-6.6	0.0	0.0	0.0
Venezuela (Rep. Bol. de)	0.8	0.7	-0.1	0.7	0.7	0.0	0.1	0.0	-0.1
ALC-10	1.7	0.8	-0.9	1.2	0.3	-0.9	0.5	0.6	0.0

Fuente: Comisión Económica para América Latina y el Caribe (CEPAL), sobre la base de cifras oficiales.

StatLink http://dx.doi.org/10.1787/888933686062

Los ingresos provenientes de las actividades down-stream, principalmente relacionados con el consumo de hidrocarburos en los países productores, experimentaron pocos cambios en 2016 en comparación con sus niveles de 2015 (véase el cuadro 2.5). Los ingresos del Impuesto Especial a la Producción y Servicios (IEPS) aplicado a combustibles fósiles en México aumentaron del 1.2% del PIB en 2015 al 1.4% del PIB como resultado de un cambio significativo en el mismo impuesto adoptado en noviembre de 2015. Antes de la reforma, el impuesto IEPS sobre los combustibles funcionaba como un impuesto o como un subsidio dependiendo de la evolución de los precios internacionales. La nueva ley adopta una tasa fija por producto que puede modificarse cuando los precios caen fuera de una banda de precios que se modifica mensualmente.

Los ingresos no tributarios de los hidrocarburos tendieron a la baja a raíz de la caída de los precios mundiales y la caída de la producción regional. Los ingresos no tributarios de los hidrocarburos en la región provienen en gran medida de los instrumentos que reservan una parte del valor comercial de la producción para el Estado. Estos típicamente toman la forma de regalías u otros gravámenes a la producción. La evolución de estos ingresos está, por tanto, íntimamente relacionada con la de los precios y los niveles de producción. El gráfico 2.8 destaca esta estrecha relación y revela además que la disminución de los ingresos no tributarios de los hidrocarburos en la región en 2016 se vio agravada por la contracción sustancial de la producción regional de petróleo, como se destacó anteriormente. Esto contrastaba marcadamente con años anteriores, donde la variación en la producción general tuvo poco o ningún papel.

Gráfico 2.8. **Variación interanual del precio del petróleo crudo, la producción de petróleo crudo y los ingresos no tributarios derivados de los hidrocarburos, 2010-16**

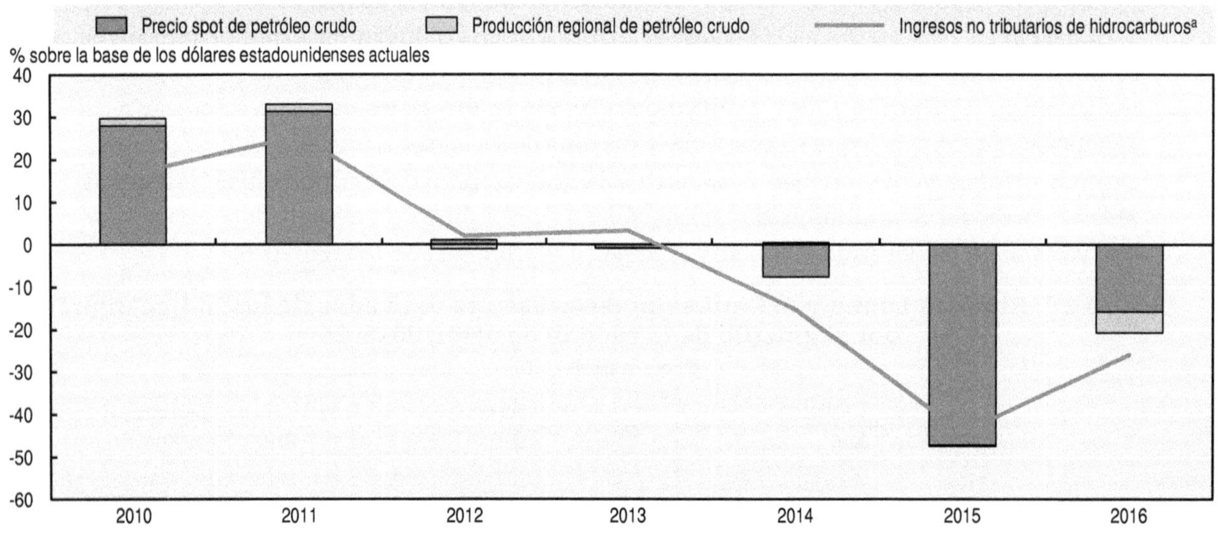

Nota: a. Excluye los ingresos extraordinarios petroleros no tributarios en Venezuela (Bol. Rep. de).

Fuente: Comisión Económica para América Latina y el Caribe (CEPAL), sobre la base de cifras oficiales.

StatLink http://dx.doi.org/10.1787/888933685758

Mientras que la caída en los ingresos no tributarios de los hidrocarburos fue generalizada durante el año, fue más notable en Bolivia, que registró un descenso de 3.8 puntos porcentuales del PIB (véase el cuadro 2.4). En el caso de Bolivia, esta disminución refleja en gran medida el impacto de la estructura de precios para sus exportaciones de gas natural a Argentina y Brasil, que incluye un mecanismo de ajuste de precios que opera con un desfase trimestral. Por lo tanto, los precios de las exportaciones en el primer trimestre de 2016 reflejaron el precio excepcionalmente bajo del petróleo crudo observado a fines de 2015.

Los ingresos no tributarios de hidrocarburos también incluyen otros tipos de rentas de propiedades que están más estrechamente relacionadas con las ganancias operativas. Los más comunes son los pagos de dividendos realizados por los productores de hidrocarburos a sus accionistas, que en este caso, es el Estado. En Colombia, el descenso de los ingresos no tributarios en relación con el PIB (del 1.1% del PIB en 2015 al 0.4% del PIB) se debió en gran medida a una disminución del pago de dividendos (que cayó del 0.5% del PIB en 2015 a 0.1% del PIB) recibido por el Estado de parte de Ecopetrol. Del mismo modo, en Surinam, los pagos de dividendos al gobierno central por parte del productor estatal de petróleo Staatsoile disminuyeron en 2016 debido a que las ganancias cayeron casi a cero.

Minería

Los precios de los metales y minerales comenzaron a mostrar signos de recuperación en 2016, impulsando los ingresos de la minería en América Latina y el Caribe. Los precios de los metales, medido por una cesta ponderada de los principales metales industriales exportados a nivel mundial, cayeron un 5% adicional en 2016, aunque esto representó un descenso significativamente menor que el registrado en el año anterior (cuadro 2.6). Durante el año hubo una disminución gradual en la trayectoria descendente de los precios, con una cantidad de minerales y metales registrando ganancias año a año positivas en la segunda mitad del año, especialmente en noviembre y diciembre. Esto fue especialmente evidente en el caso de los precios del mineral de hierro y el carbón, que registraron grandes incrementos interanuales de dos dígitos en el cuarto trimestre (50% y 78%, respectivamente). En contraste, a pesar del repunte de fin de año, el precio del cobre, un metal clave exportado por la región, aún cayó un 12% en comparación con su nivel promedio de 2015.

Cuadro 2.6. **Variación interanual en los precios de los metales y minerales, 2015-16**

(Porcentaje)

Producto	2015	2016				
	Año	1	2	3	4	Año
Metales	-23.1	n.a.	n.a.	n.a.	n.a.	-5.0
Cobre	-19.7	-19.9	-21.8	-9.3	8.1	-11.7
Aluminio	-10.9	-16.0	-11.2	1.7	14.5	-3.6
Mineral de hierro	-42.4	-24.0	-3.0	5.6	49.9	4.3
Estaño	-26.6	-16.0	8.4	22.0	38.0	11.6
Níquel	-29.8	-40.9	-32.4	-3.0	14.5	-19.1
Zinc	-10.6	-19.4	-12.6	22.2	56.0	8.2
Plomo	-14.7	-4.0	-11.6	9.1	27.2	4.4
Carbón	-17.2	-20.2	-12.9	11.9	78.0	11.8

Fuente: Comisión Económica para América Latina y el Caribe (CEPAL), sobre la base de datos de FMI (2017).

StatLink http://dx.doi.org/10.1787/888933686081

El repunte de los precios internacionales durante el año reflejó en gran medida un aumento en la demanda de minerales y metales, especialmente en China, donde el gobierno promulgó un programa de estímulo económico a gran escala. Los volúmenes de importación de China para varios minerales y metales clave registraron fuertes incrementos durante el año (gráfico 2.9). Las importaciones de mineral de cobre y concentrados fueron excepcionalmente fuertes, aumentando a tasas de dos dígitos durante gran parte del año, lo que resultó en un incremento anual de 28.0% sobre los niveles de 2015. Las importaciones de cobre refinado subieron a principios de año, antes de desacelerar a mediados del mismo, terminando con un incremento anual de 2.7%. Las importaciones de mineral de hierro también interrumpieron la larga caída de un año y comenzaron a mostrar un mayor dinamismo en 2016, aumentando un 7.5% con respecto a los niveles de 2015.

Gráfico 2.9. **China: variación interanual en los volúmenes de importación de metales y minerales seleccionados, 2014-16[a]**

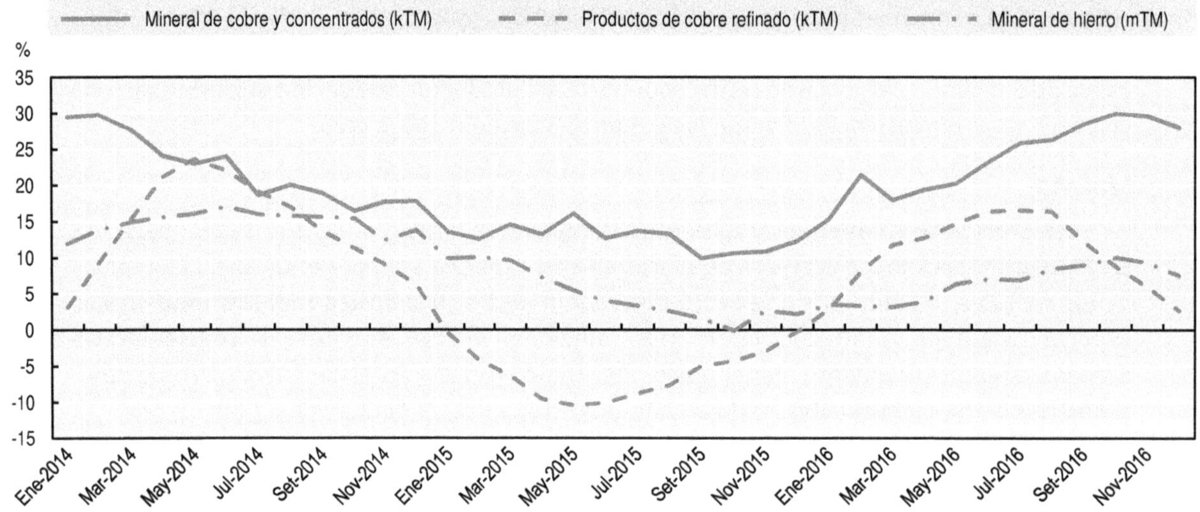

Nota: Sobre la base de una suma móvil de 12 meses.

Fuente: Comisión Económica para América Latina y el Caribe (CEPAL), sobre la base de datos de Bloomberg.

StatLink http://dx.doi.org/10.1787/888933685777

Los factores por el lado de la oferta también respaldaron precios más altos, debido al cierre de minas y medidas de política que restringieron el suministro, especialmente en Asia (Banco Mundial, 2017). Esto contrasta con las tendencias de producción minera en América Latina y el Caribe, donde varios países registraron aumentos significativos. Tal vez ningún país experimentó un cambio mayor en la producción minera como lo hizo Perú, donde la producción de cobre aumentó un 38.4% (véase el cuadro 2.7). Durante el año, comenzó la producción de la nueva mina Las Bambas (MMG / CITIC Metal) y la mina Cerro-Verde (Freeport-McMoRan) aumentó su producción. Como resultado de este aumento, Perú superó a China como el segundo mayor productor de cobre del mundo.

Los resultados fueron mixtos entre los otros productores de la región. Por un lado, Bolivia registró aumentos significativos en la producción, especialmente de plomo (18.9%) y zinc (10.1%), ya que los precios internacionales más altos hicieron que las operaciones de baja ley volvieran a ser rentables. La producción de carbón en Colombia, el principal generador de ingresos por regalías en el país aumentó fuertemente (5.8%). Del mismo modo, la producción de oro aumentó en varios países debido a los fuertes precios y la demanda.

Por el contrario, la producción de mineral de hierro en Brasil cayó (-1.5%), ya que la producción de la mina Samarco se desaceleró debido a un desastre fatal causado por el colapso del estanque de relaves de la instalación. La producción de cobre en Chile, el mayor productor mundial, cayó un 3.8% ya que varias minas reportaron una disminución en las leyes de mineral (Consejo Minero, 2017). La producción minera en México también se desaceleró en varias categorías: plata (-17.1%), zinc (-15.5%), plomo (-25.3%) y oro (-5.2%).

Cuadro 2.7. **América Latina y el Caribe: producción minera y precios de productos seleccionados, 2015-16**

(Unidades y porcentajes)

Minerales y metales	Precio de mercado (2016-15 %)	Producción minera			
		País	2015	2016	%
Cobre (kTM)	-11.7	Chile	5 772.1	5 552.6	-3.8
		Perú	1 700.8	2 353.9	38.4
		México	485.5	491.0	1.1
Mineral de hierro (mTM)	4.3	Brasil	397.0	391.0	-1.5
Plata (kKg)	8.9	Perú	4 101.6	4 374.4	6.7
		México	4 959.4	4 109.6	-17.1
		Chile	1 504.3	1 501.4	-0.2
		Bolivia	1 306.1	1 353.0	3.6
Zinc (kMT)	8.2	Perú	1 421.2	1 336.8	-5.9
		Bolivia	442.2	487.0	10.1
		México	454.6	384.2	-15.5
Bauxita (kTM)	-3.6	Jamaica	9 628.8	8 540.1	-11.3
Estaño (kTM)	11.6	Brasil	25.0	26.0	4.0
		Perú	19.5	18.8	-3.7
		Bolivia	20.1	17.8	-11.6
Plomo (kTM)	4.4	Perú	315.5	314.2	-0.4
		México	213.0	159.0	-25.3
		Bolivia	75.3	89.5	18.9
Oro (kKg)	7.6	Perú	146.8	153.0	4.2
		México	123.4	116.9	-5.2
		Colombia	59.2	61.8	4.4
		Chile	42.5	46.3	9.0
		República Dominicana	29.7	36.3	22.4
		Surinam[b]	9.4	9.7	3.3
		Bolivia	6.0	5.0	-16.4
Carbón (kTM)	11.8	Colombia	85 548.0	90 512.0	5.8

Fuente: Comisión Económica para América Latina y el Caribe (CEPAL), sobre la base de datos de CEPALstat (prices), Instituto Nacional de Estadística de Bolivia (INE) (2017), Ministerio de Minería de Chile (2017), Ministerio de Minas y Energía de Colombia (2016, 2017), Barrick Gold (2017), Jamaica Bauxite Institute (2017), Instituto Nacional de Estadística y Geografía de México (INEGI) (2017), Ministerio de Energía y Minas del Perú (2016, 2017) y IAMGOLD (2017).

StatLink http://dx.doi.org/10.1787/888933686100

Estas tendencias diferentes en precios y producción entre productos y países también se manifestaron en la evolución de los ingresos de la minería en la región. Por ejemplo, estos ingresos aumentaron en términos de dólares estadounidenses en Bolivia (62.6%), Brasil (10.2%), República Dominicana (19.4%) y Surinam (58.4%) (véase el cuadro 2.8). En contraste, hubo fuertes disminuciones en los ingresos relacionados con la minería en Argentina (-70.1%), Chile (-68.7), Jamaica (-10.3%), México (-14.9%) y Perú (-20.2%). Colombia también registró un descenso en términos de dólares estadounidenses (-2.8%), cambio que en términos de moneda nacional significó aumento moderado (8.3%).

Sin embargo, en relación con el PIB, los ingresos de la minería se mantuvieron relativamente estables en 2016, lo que refleja en parte estado debilitado de estos ingresos en dólares estadounidenses y en términos de moneda nacional (cuadro 2.9). Para los diez países considerados en esta muestra, el promedio simple cayó del 0.37% del PIB en 2015 al 0.35% del PIB. El efecto de la disminución significativa de los ingresos mineros en Chile (de 1.26% del PIB en 2015 a 0.39% del PIB) en promedio se compensó en gran medida con el aumento de los ingresos en Bolivia (0.50% del PIB en 2015 a 0.79% del PIB) y Surinam (0.46% del PIB en 2015 a 0.98% del PIB). En general, la reducción de los ingresos de la minería se centró en los ingresos derivados de los instrumentos tributarios, que cayeron de 0.19% del PIB en 2015 a 0.12% del PIB. Los ingresos no tributarios, por el contrario, registraron una ganancia muy modesta, al pasar del 0.18% del PIB al 0.20% del PIB en 2016.

Cuadro 2.8. **América Latina y el Caribe: variación interanual en los ingresos fiscales derivados de la minería, 2015-16**

(Porcentajes)

País	Ingresos de la minería	
	Moneda nacional	USD
Argentina	-52.4	-70.1
Bolivia (Est. Plur. de)	62.6	62.6
Brasil	15.3	10.2
Chile	-67.6	-68.7
Colombia	8.3	-2.8
Jamaica	-4.0	-10.3
México	0.2	-14.9
República Dominicana	22.1	19.4
Perú	-15.4	-20.2
Surinam	188.8	58.4
ALC-10	...	*-30.0*

Fuente: Comisión Económica para América Latina y el Caribe (CEPAL), sobre la base de cifras oficiales.

StatLink http://dx.doi.org/10.1787/888933686119

Cuadro 2.9. **América Latina y el Caribe: ingresos fiscales derivados de la minería, 2015-16**

(Porcentaje del PIB)

	Total			Ingresos tributarios			Ingresos no tributarios		
	2015	2016	Δ	2015	2016	Δ	2015	2016	Δ
Argentina	0.1	0.0	0.0	0.1	0.0	0.0	0.0	0.0	0.0
Bolivia (Est. Plur. de)	0.5	0.8	0.3	0.1	0.3	0.3	0.4	0.5	0.0
Brasil	0.1	0.1	0.0	0.0	0.0	0.0	0.0	0.0	0.0
Chile	1.3	0.4	-0.9	0.9	0.0	-0.9	0.4	0.4	0.0
Colombia	0.3	0.3	0.0	0.1	0.1	0.0	0.2	0.2	0.0
Jamaica	0.2	0.2	0.0	0.0	0.0	0.0	0.2	0.2	0.0
México	0.2	0.2	0.0	0.2	0.2	0.0	0.0	0.0	0.0
Perú	0.4	0.3	-0.1	0.2	0.2	-0.1	0.1	0.1	0.0
República Dominicana	0.3	0.4	0.0	0.3	0.3	0.0	0.1	0.1	0.0
Surinam	0.5	1.0	0.5	0.1	0.4	0.3	0.4	0.6	0.2
ALC-10	0.4	0.4	0.0	0.2	0.2	0.0	0.2	0.2	0.0

Nota: El promedio ALC-10 cubre solo los diez países incluidos en el cuadro y no se puede comparar con los promedios simples que se muestran en el gráfico 2.1 y el cuadro 2.4 que cubren diferentes países.

Fuente: Comisión Económica para América Latina y el Caribe (CEPAL), sobre la base de cifras oficiales.

StatLink http://dx.doi.org/10.1787/888933686138

El retroceso en los ingresos por impuestos a la minería fue impulsado por una continua contracción en los pagos del impuesto a las ganancias corporativas por parte del sector. La información financiera de una muestra de las principales compañías mineras que operan en la región revela que los ingresos antes de impuestos siguen siendo excepcionalmente débiles. Aunque los ingresos antes de impuestos volvieron a territorio positivo (USD 12.300 millones para esta muestra de empresas) en 2016, se mantuvo muy por debajo del promedio de USD 26.600 millones por año durante 2006-14 (véase el gráfico 2.10). Más importante aún, varias empresas importantes registraron pérdidas financieras en 2015 y esto continuó teniendo un efecto significativo en las recaudaciones de 2016.

En Chile, los ingresos tributarios de la minería disminuyeron del 0.9% del PIB en 2015 a solo el 0.02% del PIB. Los pagos del impuesto sobre la renta corporativa y el impuesto especial a la minería (calculado sobre la base del ingreso operativo) para los productores privados más grandes y para CODELCO (el productor estatal) cayeron a casi cero. Asimismo, los ingresos tributarios mineros en Perú disminuyeron – aunque de manera menos dramática, del 0.24% del PIB al 0.18% del PIB – reflejando en parte el uso expandido de un beneficio fiscal por depreciación acelerada en línea con la apertura de una serie de nuevas inversiones (Banco Central de Reserva del Perú, 2017). En Argentina, el retroceso en ingresos tributarios mineros, del 0.05% del PIB al 0.01% del PIB, se debió a una disminución en los pagos del impuesto a las ganancias corporativas, ya que un número creciente de productores reportó pérdidas financieras, y una caída significativa en los aranceles de exportación pagados por el sector (AFIP, 2017).

Gráfico 2.10. **Compañías mineras regionales seleccionadas: utilidades antes de impuestos, 2006-16**

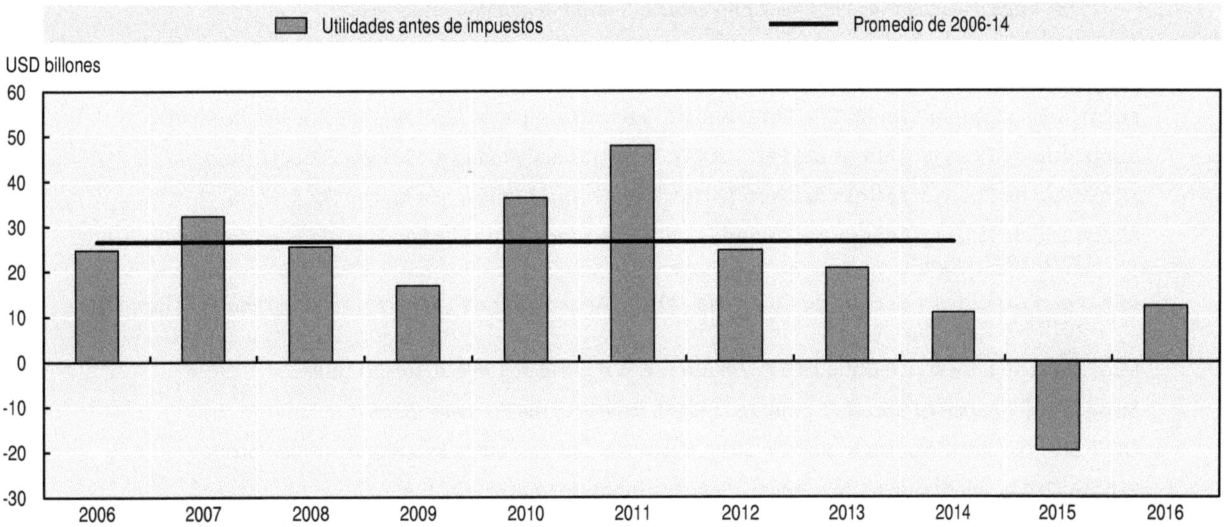

Nota: Los datos corresponden a Antofagasta PLC, Compañía de Minas Buenaventura SAA, Codelco, Fresnillo PLC, Grupo México SAB de CV, Hochschild Mining PLC, Industrias Penoles SAB de CV, Minera Frisco SAB de CV, Minsur SA, Sociedad Minera Cerro Verde SAA, Vale SA, y Volcán Compañía Minera SAA.

Fuente: Comisión Económica para América Latina y el Caribe (CEPAL), sobre la base de datos de Bloomberg.

StatLink http://dx.doi.org/10.1787/888933685796

Los ingresos no tributarios, en gran medida en forma de rentas de propiedades, como regalías, aumentaron en varios países como resultado de la mejora de los precios y el aumento de la producción. Los pagos de regalías más fuertes fueron especialmente notables en Bolivia, República Dominicana y Surinam. Es importante destacar que en los dos últimos países estas regalías están total o casi totalmente asociadas con la producción de oro. Los ingresos no tributarios en Perú disminuyeron, del 0.15% del PIB en 2015 al 0.13% del PIB, a pesar de un aumento significativo en la producción, especialmente del cobre. Esto se debió a una fuerte disminución en las recaudaciones del gravamen especial a la minería (GEM), que se calcula sobre la base de los ingresos de explotación. Por el contrario, los ingresos de las regalías mineras tradicionales, calculados como una parte del valor comercial de la producción, aumentaron considerablemente (32.7% en términos de moneda nacional).

Referencias

AFIP (2017), *Anuario Estadísticas Tributarias 2016*, Administración Federal de Ingresos Públicos de Argentina.

AIE (2017), *Oil Market Report* [en línea], Agencia Internacional de la Energía, *www.iea.org/oilmarketreport/omrpublic.*

FMI (2017), "Prices & Forecasts", IMF Primary Commodity Prices Forecasts [en línea], Fondo Monetario Internacional, *www.imf.org/external/np/res/commod/index.aspx.*

Banco Central de Reserva del Perú (2017), *Memoria 2016*, Banco Central de Reserva del Perú, Lima.

Banco Mundial (2017), "Commodity Markets Outlook: Investment Weakness in Commodity Exporters", enero.

Barrick Gold (2017), *Annual Report 2016*, Barrick Gold Corporation, Toronto.

Bolivarian Republic of Venezuela (2017), *Annual Report on Form 18-K to the United States Securities and Exchange Commission*, Ministry of Finance, Bolivarian Republic of Venezuela, Caracas.

Consejo Minero (2017), *Reporte Anual 2016*, Consejo Minero, Santiago.

IAMGOLD Corporation (2017), *Annual Report 2016*, IAMGOLD Corporation, Toronto.

INE (2017), *Estadísticas por Actividad Económica*, [online], Instituto Nacional de Estadística de Bolivia, La Paz, *https://www.ine.gob.bo/index.php/estadisticas-por-actividad-economica.*

INEGI (2017), *Banco de Información Económica* (BIE) [online], Instituto Nacional de Estadística y Geografía, *www.inegi.org.mx/sistemas/bie.*

Jamaica Bauxite Institute (2017), "Total Bauxite Production Data" [online], *http://www.jbi.org.jm/.*

Ministerio de Energía y Minas del Perú (2017), *Reporte Anual Producción Minera 2016*, Lima.

Ministerio de Energía y Minas del Perú (2016), *Reporte Anual Producción Minera 2015*, Lima.

Ministerio de Minas y Energía de Colombia (2017), "Anexos minas", *Memorias al Congreso de la República 2016-2017*, Bogotá.

Ministerio de Minas y Energía de Colombia (2016), "Anexos minas", *Memorias al Congreso de la República 2015-2016*, Bogotá.

Ministerio de Minería de Chile (2017), *Anuario de la minería de Chile 2016*, Santiago.

Ministry of Finance of Trinidad y Tobago (2016), *Review of the Economy 2016.*

OPEP (2017), *Annual Statistical Bulletin 2017*, Organización de Países Exportadores de Petróleo.

PDVSA (2017), *Informe de Gestión Anual 2016*, Petróleos de Venezuela, S.A.

Staatsolie (2017), *Company Profile 2017*, *www.staatsolie.com/media/34837/companyprofile2017.pdf.*

Staatsolie (2016), *Annual Report 2015.*

Chapter 3

SPECIAL FEATURE

Income tax in Latin America

Capítulo 3

SECCIÓN ESPECIAL

El impuesto sobre la renta en América Latina

Chapter 3

SPECIAL FEATURE
Income tax in Latin America

Key findings

- Over the last seven decades, the collection of taxes on income, profits and capital gains (1000) in Latin America has almost tripled, increasing from roughly 2% of GDP to above 6% in 2016.
- More than 55% of the collection of this tax derives from the income of companies (1200), while 32% corresponds to personal income (1100); the remainder of income taxes cannot be directly attributed to individuals or companies (1300).
- When the average tax structure and level of the Latin American countries is compared with those of the OECD, the main difference is the low collection of the personal income tax (PIT).
- The evolution of maximum and minimum PIT rates shows a narrowing of the taxable base evidenced by a reduction of the maximum rate and increase of the minimum rate, which reduces the progressivity of the tax system.
- Tax evasion rates are high in the countries of the region, reflecting low levels of compliance with the payment of income taxes, both by individuals and companies.
- The redistributive impact of the personal income tax in Latin America is weak, achieving a reduction of just 2% in income inequality, which contrasts markedly with the countries of the European Union, whose distribution improves more than 12% after income taxes.
- In recent years, Latin America has undertaken tax reforms focused on equity; these have shown early progress in terms of collection and improvement in income distribution.

Introduction

The public finances of Latin American countries have traditionally been characterised by a tax system that is biased towards the collection of taxes on consumption and that has a weak redistributive impact. Comparison with the rest of the world indicates that this latter characteristic is explained by low collection of the personal income tax (PIT) (Tanzi, 2000).

PIT usually has advantages with respect to other taxes, not only in macroeconomic terms (as an automatic stabiliser on the revenue side), but also due to its impact on the distribution of income, as shown by most of the work on tax incidence. While revenues from corporate income tax (CIT) are comparable with other regions, Latin America's revenues from PIT are low and achieve a limited macro and redistributive impact.

This chapter will take a closer look at PIT in Latin America. It will analyse the factors that have limited PIT collection and constrained its macro and redistributive impact. The chapter will also examine recent reforms and other developments in this area.

Characteristics of the income tax in Latin American countries

Examining the long-term evolution of income tax revenues in Latin America shows that collection, relative to GDP, grew between 1940 and 1980 for six countries where information is available (Table 3.1). With the debt crises of the 1980s, income tax revenues fell in the majority of these countries; they then stabilised in the 1990s.

Table 3.1. **Latin America (6 countries): Income tax revenues, 1940-2016**

(Percentage of GDP)

Countries	1940-49	1950-59	1960-69	1970-79	1980-89	1990-99	2000-09	2010-16
Argentina	2.3	2.8	1.8	1.4	0.8	2.1	4.3	5.5
Brazil	1.9	2.4	2.0	2.7	4.6	4.7	6.6	6.8
Chile	3.1	4.6	6.7	6.0	4.5	4.3	6.5	7.5
Colombia	2.2	3.6	4.1	4.0	2.9	3.8	4.8	6.1
Mexico	1.7	2.4	2.9	4.4	4.7	4.3	4.6	5.9
Peru	1.9	4.3	4.3	4.4	2.9	2.5	4.9	7.0
Average	2.2	3.4	3.6	3.8	3.4	3.6	5.3	6.5

Note: The 1990-2016 data is from OECD/ECLAC/CIAT/IDB (2018), *Revenue Statistics in Latin America and the Caribbean 2018.*
Source: Authors' calculations based on OECD/ECLAC/CIAT/IDB (2018), *Revenue Statistics in Latin America and the Caribbean 2018* and Gómez Sabaini, Jiménez and Rossignolo (2012), "Imposición a la renta personal y equidad en América Latina: nuevos desafíos", *Serie Macroeconomía del Desarrollo*, N° 119 (LC/L.3477-P).

StatLink http://dx.doi.org/10.1787/888933686271

Tax reforms in the 1990s emphasised the application of a general tax on goods and services: the value added tax (VAT). This served as a substitute for tariffs and coincided with the repeal of low-yield taxes, simplification of tax regulations, reduction of the levels and brackets of the income tax and generalisation of the tax bases (although this last aspect related more to the VAT than to taxes on income). In general, tax policy design during this decade was influenced by a tendency across the region to reduce the size of the public sector rather than to increase the level of taxation above historical values.

In the 21st century there has been a significant increase in the collection of income taxes in most Latin American countries. Average revenues from income taxes between 2010 and 2016 (as a percentage of GDP) were double the average collected over the period between 1990 and 1994 (Figure 3.1).

Significant improvements over the last decade are explained by different factors and can be separated into two periods. Between 2005 and 2009, there was greater growth in revenues from CIT. This was associated with a significant increase in revenue from mining and oil companies, as a result of the rise in export prices of primary products and reforms to achieve a greater appropriation of these kinds of rents. From 2010 onwards, there has been a significant increase in PIT revenue. As will be discussed in the last part of this chapter, this was driven by reforms to expand the tax base, especially through strengthened taxation of income from capital. Additionally, changes in rates and in tax brackets were also included and international taxation rules were improved.

Although PIT revenues have increased, growth in CIT revenues accounted for almost two thirds of the total increase of income tax revenues over the period between 1990 and 2016. In Latin America, revenues from CIT accounted for 57% of total income tax receipts in 2015, while PIT contributed 31.9%; the rest is classified as other income taxes (classification 1300). By contrast, in the countries of the OECD, PIT and CIT account for 72% and 26% of income tax revenues respectively. PIT accounts for 79% of income taxes across 15 economies of the European Union (EU-15).

Figure 3.1. **Latin America (selected countries): Structure and evolution of income tax (1000), 1990-2016**

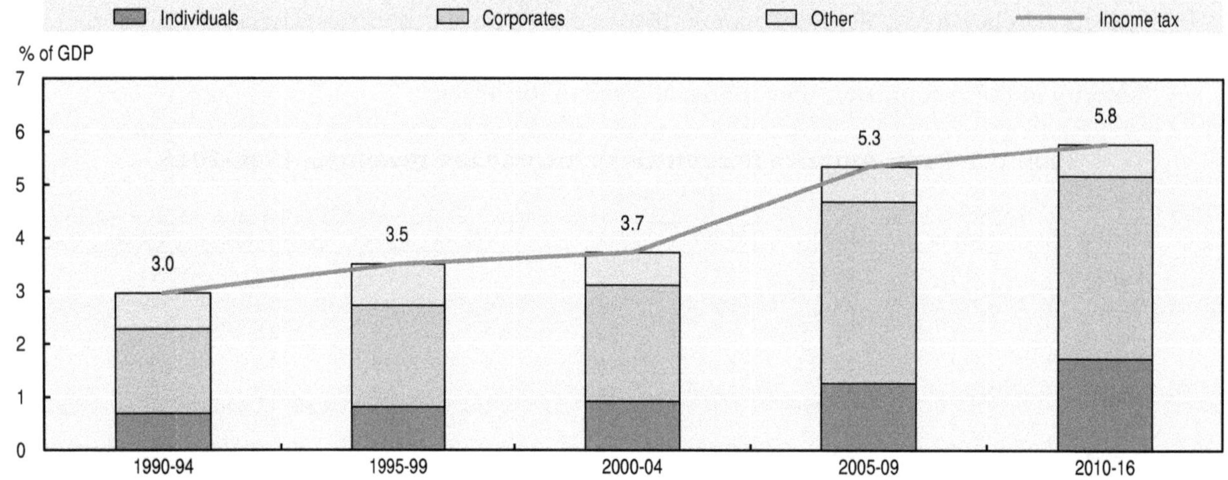

Note: The disaggregation between individuals and companies corresponds to the simple average of 9 countries for which information is available for the period 1990-2016 (Argentina, Brazil, Chile, Colombia, Guatemala, Honduras, Panama, Peru and Uruguay).

Source: Authors' calculations based on OECD/ECLAC/CIAT/IDB (2018).

StatLink http://dx.doi.org/10.1787/888933686157

Table 3.2. **Latin America, OCDE (35) and EU (15): Personal and corporate income revenues, circa 2015**

Countries	Revenues as % of GDP		As a share of total income tax (1000)	
	Individuals (1100)	Corporates (1200)	Individuals (1100)	Corporates (1200)
Argentina	3.2	3.2	48.9	48.3
Bolivia	0.2	5.4	4.0	96.0
Brazil	2.5	2.7	37.1	40.9
Colombia	1.2	5.1	18.5	77.9
Costa Rica	1.4	2.3	31.0	52.9
Dominican Republic	2.8	2.4	47.8	40.3
El Salvador	1.2	2.0	29.7	51.5
Guatemala	0.4	2.4	10.4	67.3
Honduras	1.8	3.6	34.0	66.0
Panama	1.5	1.8	37.1	43.5
Uruguay	3.1	2.5	52.6	42.9
Latin America (11)	1.8	3.0	31.9	57.1
OECD (34)	8.4	2.8	71.6	26.0
EU (15)	10.0	2.7	78.8	21.2

Notes: The disaggregation between individuals and companies corresponds to the simple average of eleven countries for which information is available for the period 1990-2016.

Source: Authors' calculations based on OECD/ECLAC/CIAT/IDB (2018).

StatLink http://dx.doi.org/10.1787/888933686290

An important constraint on PIT in Latin America is that it is collected primarily from the salaries of formal sector workers who are subject to withholding at their source of income. According to Gómez Sabaini, Jiménez and Podestá (2010), 60% (or more) of PIT comes from salaried workers in the countries for which information is available. This unbalanced structure affects the horizontal equity of the tax, since independent workers have greater possibilities of evasion and avoidance. Rents from capital, meanwhile, receive preferential treatment, either because they are usually taxed at a lower rate or because they are often not taxed at all.

Additionally, as discussed in Box 3.1, several countries have introduced mechanisms for simplifying the tax system since the 1990's with the aim of incorporating a larger number of taxpayers into the formal sector. However, these regimes have had the effect of eroding the PIT base.

Factors of income tax collection

In addition to tax reforms (to be analysed later) and notwithstanding improvements in the level of PIT revenues in recent years, three additional factors have constrained the performance of this tax in Latin America (Jiménez and Podestá, 2016; Barreix, Benítez and Pecho, 2017):

1. The evolution of legal rates, which has led to a reduction in the maximum marginal rates applied across the region on average.
2. A narrow taxable base as a result of a large number of allowed exemptions and deductions, the existence of simplified tax regimes, and minimum non-taxable levels, which have combined to render a significant number of taxpayers and income not liable for PIT.
3. A high level of non-compliance (informality, evasion and delinquency) that is observed in almost all countries.

These factors result in tax receipts and effective rates that are substantially lower than is needed to achieve desired economic and redistributive effects. Each of these constraints is analysed in greater detail below.

Figure 3.2. **Latin America (selected countries): Evolution of the maximum and minimum marginal income tax rates for individuals, 1985-2016**

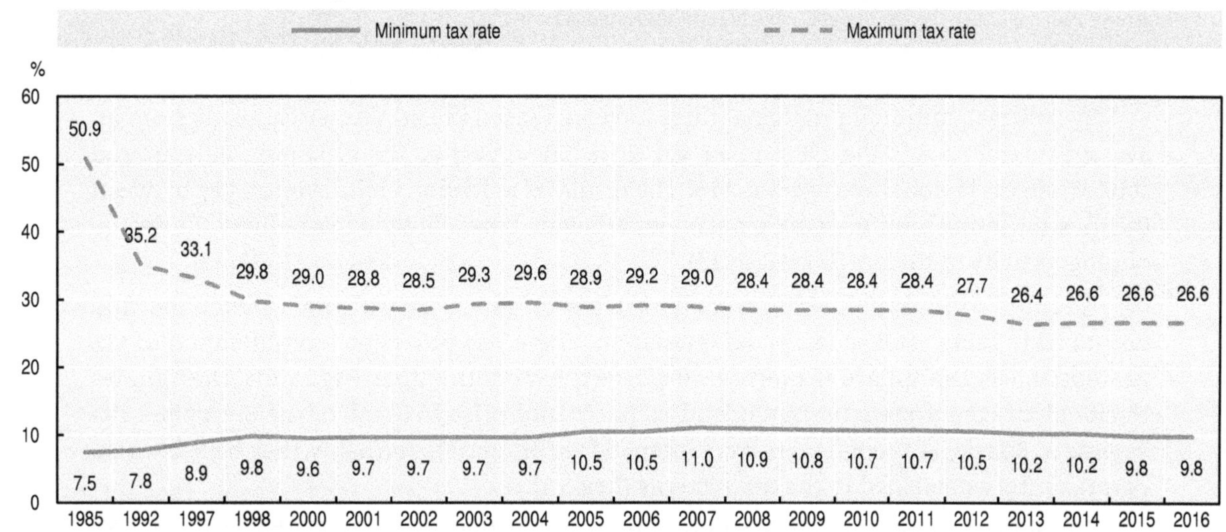

Source: Authors' calculations based on Tanzi (2000), "Taxation in Latin America in the last decade"; and data from CEPALSTAT and the Inter-American Center of Tax Administrations (CIAT).

StatLink http://dx.doi.org/10.1787/888933686176

The regional average of the maximum marginal rate of PIT has decreased in 18 Latin American countries analysed here, from 50.9% in the 1980s to around 35.2% at the beginning of the 1990s and to 26.6% in 2016 (Figure 3.2). This gradual reduction has brought down the maximum rates of some Latin American countries to below international levels. For example, the maximum marginal PIT rate in 2014 was 45% on average for 18 euro-zone economies, or 39.4% for the average of the 28 countries of the European Union. It should be noted that in several European countries (Austria, Belgium, Denmark, Spain, Finland, France, the Netherlands, Portugal and Sweden) these rates are equal to or higher than 50% (European Union, 2014).

Table 3.3. **Latin America: Maximum and minimum marginal rates of income tax on individuals by country, 1985-2016**

Country	1985-86		1992		2000		2008		2016	
	Min	Max	Min	Max	Min	Max	Min	Max	Min	Max
Argentina	16.5	45	15	30	9	35	9	35	9	35
Bolivia	n/a	30	10	10	13	13	13	13	13	13
Brazil	0	60	10	25	15	27.5	15	27.5	7.5	27.5
Chile	0	57	5	50	5	45	5	40	4	40
Colombia	n/a	49	5	30	10	35	19	33	19	33
Costa Rica	5	50	10	25	10	25	10	15	10	15
Dominican Republic	2	73	3	70	15	25	15	25	15	25
Ecuador	19	40	10	25	5	15	5	35	5	35
El Salvador	3	60	10	30	10	30	10	30	10	30
Guatemala	11	48	4	34	15	25	15	31	5	7
Honduras	3	40	12	40	10	25	10	25	15	25
Mexico	3	55	3	35	3	40	1.92	28	1.92	35
Nicaragua	15	50	8	35.5	10	30	10	30	15	30
Panama	13	56	3.5	56	2	30	16.5	27	15	25
Paraguay	n/a	n/a	n/a	n/a	n/a	n/a	n/a	n/a	8	10
Peru	2	56	6	37	15	30	15	30	8	30
Uruguay	n/a	n/a	n/a	n/a	n/a	n/a	10	25	10	30
Venezuela	12	45	10	30	6	34	6	34	6	34
Latin America (18)	7.5	50.9	7.8	35.2	9.6	29.0	10.9	28.4	9.8	26.6

Source: Jiménez y Podestá (2016), "Los impuestos sobre la renta en América Latina".

StatLink http://dx.doi.org/10.1787/888933686309

By contrast, minimum marginal rates have increased in Latin America, rising from an average rate of 7.5% in the 1980s to 9.8% in 2016. They reached their highest value around 2007, when the regional average was 11%. The resultant reduction in the average gap between the maximum and minimum marginal rates of the taxation of individuals reduces the degree of progressivity of the tax (ECLAC, 2017).

Another constraint to PIT revenues relates to generous personal deductions and non-taxable gains established in tax legislation. There has also been a proliferation of tax exemptions and simplified tax regimes (such as the Monotributo in Argentina, the Simples Nacional and the System for the Individual Microenterprise in Brazil or the Simplified Tax Regime in Bolivia). Although these were intended as "bridges" to formality, they have become permanently established in the tax systems (Box 3.1).

Simplified regimes imply a lower tax burden and further erode the PIT base due to their lack of co-ordination. Circumvention and arbitration of taxpayers between two regimes also threatens the horizontal equity of the system, as they discriminate between taxpayers of similar contributory capacity.

In Latin America, the level of income at which PIT begins to be paid is higher than that of the OECD countries, whether measured in terms of GDP per capita (see Jiménez and Podestá, 2016; ECLAC, 2017) or with reference to average salaries (OECD/IDB/CIAT, 2016). The result is that a high proportion of individuals are exempt, which weakens the redistributive potential of the PIT.

Box 3.1. **Informality and tax simplification programmes in Latin America**

Simplified schemes oriented primarily towards small taxpayers have been introduced In Latin America with the aim of promoting the formalisation of taxpayers and simplify tax administration. One of the main features of simplified regimes in the region is that they were not designed with the principal objective of increasing tax collections, but rather to introduce formality to a large sector of taxpayers. The average collection of these regimes, it should be noted, is close to 1% of total tax revenues, although this average hides wide differences between countries.

These special treatment regimes exclude small taxpayers from the general rules of VAT and / or ISR and establish presumptive methods of determination and/or impose lower rates for these workers. It has been one of the region's main strategies for alleviating the workload of the tax administrations and thus improving their oversight capacities.

Simplified tax regimes are commonplace in Latin America; with the exception of El Salvador and Venezuela, all countries in the region have implemented a preferential treatment system for small taxpayers. These regimes have sought to facilitate payment of taxpayers typically characterised as: a) low income b) numerous (which makes official control difficult) c) informal d) not included within well-organised structures and e) highly mobile in terms of entry and exit between regimes. They intend to simplify the rules and administrative procedures associated with tax obligations, aiming to provide a "transitional bridge" to attract workers into the formal sector and, at the same time, improve the management of the resources of the tax administration.

To function effectively as a bridge to the general tax system, simplified tax regimes should limit the requirements they impose and benefits they grant. Tax systems should also seek to gradually reduce the time that taxpayers can spend in simplified regimes, given that general regimes tend to be fairer (both in terms of horizontal and vertical equity) and better respect the principle of tax neutrality.

Source: Cetrángolo et al (2014), "Monotributo en América Latina", *Los casos de Argentina, Brasil y Urugua*; Arenas de Mesa (2016), *Sostenibilidad fiscal y reformas tributarias en América Latina.*

Exemptions at the lower end of the income distribution drive up the threshold at which the maximum marginal rate is applied. While this rate takes effect at incomes around 3 or 4 times GDP per capita in most developed countries, in Latin America this rate takes effect at incomes higher than 7.3 times the per capita income and at rates significantly lower than in developed countries (ECLAC, 2017).

There is significant variation in the minimum and maximum PIT thresholds applied by different countries in Latin America, although practically all of them are reducing the taxable income at which the minimum rate is applied. This is an outcome of reforms in the design of the taxable income brackets and the elimination of exemptions and personal deductions. Between 2007 and 2016, the average exemption level was reduced by 36% as a result (Gómez Sabaini, Jiménez and Martner, 2017; ECLAC, 2017).

Latin American countries use exemptions, deductions, low tax rates, special regimes and other tax expenditures to achieve many different objectives. These include attracting foreign direct investment, stimulating savings, enhancing financial markets, developing underdeveloped regions, promoting exports, industrialisation, employment generation, environmental concerns, the transfer of technology, diversification of the economic structure and formation of human capital. These different forms of tax expenditures eroded the tax base and entailed a cost in terms of foregone revenue collection. The extent to which tax expenditure is an effective or efficient way of achieving these multiple objectives has been questioned and there is a lack of evaluation.

Comparative analysis of tax expenditures is complex since estimation methodologies differ between the countries in the region. However, it can be inferred that their magnitude is significant in most cases; depending on the country, tax expenditure has been calculated to range between 2 and 7 points of GDP and represent between 7% and 40% of overall tax pressure (ECLAC, 2017).

Low levels of compliance and high rates of evasion also constrain revenue collection. Estimates of tax evasion rates for income tax and, in particular, for individuals, are scarce in the region. Available studies (Gómez Sabaini, Jiménez and Podestá, 2010, Pecho, Peláez and Sánchez, 2012, Gómez Sabaini, Jiménez and Martner, 2017) find that the levels of evasion in the region are higher than those from existing estimates for the VAT and that they are higher for CIT than for PIT.[1]

Redistributive potential of income tax

The modest advances in the collection of PIT have a direct impact on the redistributive power of this instrument and the tax system as a whole. In 2013-14, the reduction of the Gini coefficient attributable to PIT averaged 2% for 18 countries in Latin America (Figure 3.3). While this represents an improvement over the period 2004-07, it remains well below the redistributive power registered in the countries of the European Union, whose PIT systems achieve a reduction of the Gini coefficient of over 12% (ECLAC, 2017).

Differences of a similar order of magnitude are found by Lustig (2016), who measures the redistributive effect of taxes and direct transfers according to their impact on the Gini coefficient.[2] For countries in Latin America, the average impact ranges between 2.3 percentage points and 3.7 percentage points, while for countries in the EU the effect is between 7.8 percentage points and 19.1 percentage points, depending on whether pension payments are included in the calculation.[3] Using the Reynolds-Smolensky indicator, which shows the difference between the Gini before and after PIT payment, Barreíx et al. (2017) show that OECD countries achieve improvements four times higher than those attained by countries in Latin America.[4]

The changes in redistributive power observed between 2004-07 and 2013-14 differ between Latin American countries. In Bolivia, Costa Rica, Ecuador, Honduras, Nicaragua, Panama, Peru and Venezuela, there were practically no changes in PIT's impact on the income distribution. On the other hand, improvements were observed in Argentina, Brazil, Chile, the Dominican Republic, El Salvador, Mexico and Uruguay. The positive changes are mainly due to wage growth and modifications to the tax structure.

The low tax burden of the richest taxpayers is also a challenge for tax policy in Latin America. In 2014, the average effective tax rate for the top decile (10) was 4.8% of gross income, far below the 21.3% achieved by countries in the European Union (ECLAC, 2017). One of the main factors underlying this phenomenon is the fact that capital income in the region is taxed at lower rates than labour income (and in some cases is not taxed at all). Moreover, the richest taxpayers can take advantage of aggressive tax planning in order to minimise tax payments in their countries of residence.

OECD/CIAT/IDB (2016) shows a more progressive trend, indicating that households in the top decile in Latin American countries pay more than 25% (depending on the family structure) of labour income in direct taxes on average. This study estimates the level of PIT, social security contributions and payroll taxes paid by employees and employers as a percentage of labour income, though only for the formal sector.

Figure 3.3. **Latin America (18 countries) and European Union (28 countries): Reduction of the Gini coefficient due to personal income tax**

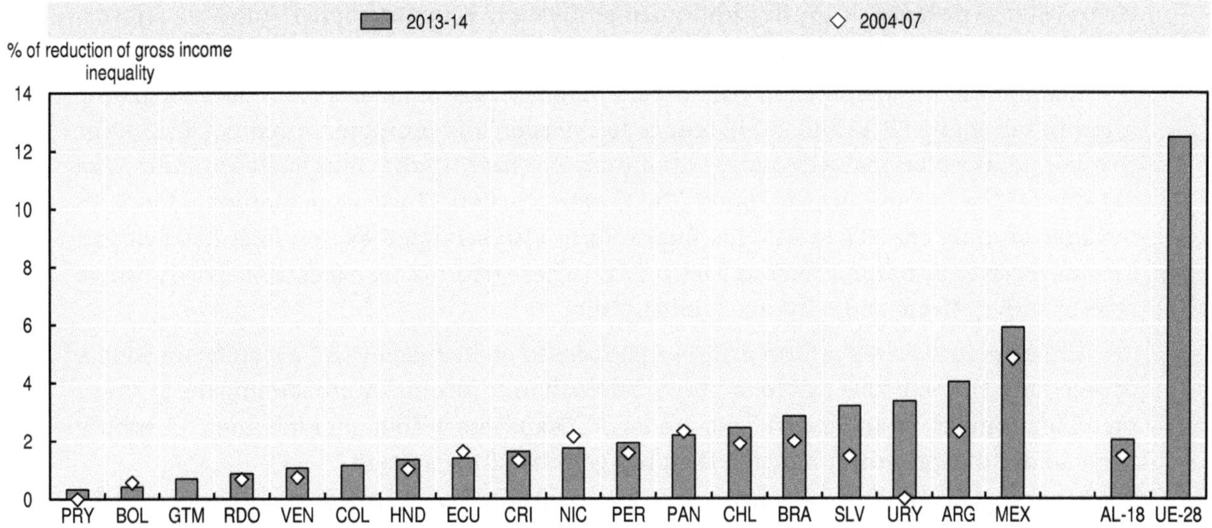

Source: ECLAC on the basis of Household Surveys and EUROMOD.

StatLink http://dx.doi.org/10.1787/888933686195

Another fundamental challenge for most of the countries of the region lies in ensuring the middle class pays PIT. PIT payment in Latin American countries is highly concentrated in the top decile, at approximately 88% of total payments; the corresponding figure for countries in the European Union is below 40% (ECLAC, 2017). The low contribution of the middle class to PIT revenues significantly reduces the revenues collected from this tax and weakens PIT's capacity to reduce inequality. It also means that PIT does not generate a virtuous circle of reciprocity, whereby citizens receive better public goods and services in exchange for paying more in tax.

Recent changes and the relevance of income tax in tax reforms

Tax reforms have been one of the most common and transversal public policies In Latin America over the past decade. Their objective has been to increase tax revenues, generate distributive effects and strengthen fiscal sustainability (Arenas de Mesa, 2016). Between 2010 and 2015, at least 18 countries in the region modified either the level or structure of their taxes (or in some cases both). During this period, 51 tax modifications and 17 tax reforms were recorded.

In 75% of cases, these reforms were directed at taxation on income. They often involved changes in the structure of rates and typically increased rates as well. They also sought to expand the tax base to include capital income and the distribution of dividends. As a result of these measures, the relative share of direct taxes within the tax structure of countries in the region has increased.

A major tax reform undertaken by Uruguay in 2007 was a forerunner of the reforms undertaken across the region between 2010 and 2015. The Uruguayan reform introduced a dual scheme of taxation on income and created a personal income tax (IRPF) to replace the tax on the remuneration of persons (IRP). It also introduced progressive rates of between 3% and 12%.

Among the reforms carried out in recent years across Latin America, those of Colombia (2010, 2012, 2014 and 2016), Mexico (2013) and Chile (2014) stand out. These had a range of objectives: to respond to distributive challenges (Colombia), to finance education reform

(Chile) and to complement broader structural reforms (Mexico). The early indications are that these reforms have led to improvements both in revenue collection and in distributive terms (Arenas de Mesa, 2016). In addition, Argentina and Ecuador implemented tax reforms that focused largely on changes in the CIT in 2017.

Colombia has undertaken a series of reforms since 2010 to increase tax collection (2010), improve tax equity (2012 and 2014), reduce tax evasion and promote formality (2016). Over this period, the National Alternative Minimum Tax (IMAN), the Simplified Minimum Tax (IMAS) and the Income Tax for Equity (CREE) were created. These were eliminated in 2016 in order to unify the PIT rates. This final reform also scrapped exemptions for dividend income received by natural persons (OECD, 2017). These reforms are expected to have positive redistributive effects and reinforce tax neutrality.

Chile approved a tax reform in 2014 that focused on increasing CIT, a significant source of revenues. The objective was to improve distribution of income by broadening the tax base on which companies and individuals are taxed. Taxpayers with higher incomes contribute more under this reform, enhancing the progressivity of the system.

The Chilean reform gradually increased the CIT rate from 20% to 25% between 2014 and 2017 in the integrated system, and from 25.5% in 2017 to 27% in 2018 in the semi-integrated system. It also reduced the maximum marginal rate of income for individuals from 40% to 35% from January 2017. The semi-integrated system allows 65% of CIT paid by employers to be accredited to PIT to reduce the impact on economic growth associated with the tax increase (OECD, 2015). Likewise, the reform repealed the regime included in the existing income tax law that allowed taxpayers to pay no taxes while profits were not withdrawn. Chile's central government intends to increase its revenues by 3% of the GDP through this reform; of this amount, it is estimated that close to 50% of the total will respond to modifications of the income tax, reaching an amount close to 1.46% of GDP.

Mexico's tax reform replaced the CIT and the cash deposit tax with a modified CIT, which includes the tax burden of the two taxes that were eliminated. With regard to the tax on natural persons, a tax of 10% was created on the income of individuals derived from capital gains and distribution of dividends. Likewise, an annual limit was placed on personal deductions and the structure of tax rates was modified, increasing higher income brackets.

The Mexican reform has achieved better-than-expected results. The total effective tax collection in 2014 was 1.1% of GDP, similar to the estimate approved by Congress (1% of GDP); however, in 2015, the effective tax collection reached 2.6% of GDP, which was more than was expected. An important part of this collection came from the special tax on gasoline production and services. Although income tax revenues fell between 2013 and 2014 (by 0.3% of GDP), revenues rose by 1.1% of GDP in 2015 compared with the previous year, which was higher than targeted by Congress (0.5%). As a result of the modifications to income taxes, the Ministry of Finance and Public Credit (SCHP) estimates an improvement in the distribution of income and an associated decrease in the Gini coefficient of 0.032 points.

The tax reform approved in Argentina in 2017 included a gradual reduction of the CIT rate, from 35% to 25% (35% in 2018, 30% in 2019-20, and 25% for 2021 onwards). A withholding tax on the distribution of dividends was introduced with the aim of encouraging the reinvestment of profits. A rate of 7% has been applied for profits accrued in 2018 and 2019, rising to 13% for 2020 onwards.

In addition, a tax on categories of individual income previously exempt from taxation was introduced in Argentina. The special income tax deduction for self-employed workers was increased, whose amount had historically been much lower than the special deduction for dependent workers.

In Ecuador, the Organic Law for the Reactivation of the Economy, Strengthening Dollarization and Modernization of Financial Management was approved in 2017. This included a number of changes to income tax. In the case of companies, the general rate was increased from 22% to 25%, with a reduction of 3 percentage points for microenterprises and exporters. In the latter case, the reduction in the rate only occurs if the company maintains or increases its level of employment. It also introduced certain limits to the reduction of rates for the reinvestment of profits (mainly limiting these incentives to habitual exporters and manufacturing companies). A rate of 22% is offered to companies that enter into investment contracts within the first year of the law, whose projects contribute to the change of the production matrix or are planning mining operations.

The Ecuadorian reform also included benefits for micro-enterprises. A non-taxable minimum of the income tax for micro-enterprises of USD 11 290 was established and new micro-enterprises were exempted from paying the same tax for a period of three years. In the case of income tax on individuals, the reform in Ecuador extended deductible expenses to include expenses for children (without age limit) and dependent parents.

Conclusions and challenges

Although progress has been made in the area of income taxation in recent years, PIT revenues remain low in Latin America, relative both to PIT receipts in developed economies and to receipts from CIT in the region. The structure of this tax also is unbalanced since most of it falls on wages in the formal sector while capital rents benefit from preferential treatment, either because they are generally taxed at a lower rate or because they are simply not taxed.

The shortcomings of PIT in the region reduce the resources available to governments and weaken the macro and redistributive impact of the tax system. It is critical that Latin American countries work towards strengthening the PIT, including through mechanisms to combat tax evasion and avoidance.

A broad and general tax base should be established that covers all the income of taxpayers; capital income should be treated in a similar way to wage income and co-ordination with simplified regimes should be improved. At the same time, preferential treatments should be revised and reduced, as should allowed deductions. In turn, tax brackets of the PIT can be modified so that the maximum marginal rates are levied at lower income levels, as observed in other regions. In several countries, it might also be possible to reduce the exempt minimum so that it is equal to or less than their per capita income and thus expand the tax base.

This integrated approach for different sources of income and different categories of worker would reinforce the stabilising effect of PIT. It would also enhance its impact on equity, both in relation to the principle of capacity to pay (vertical equity) and in ensuring equal tax treatment for those with equivalent income (horizontal equity).

Notes

1. There are also studies for specific countries. For example recent studies are: the Internal Revenue Service of Chile (SII, 2012 a and 2012 b); Ávila and Cruz Lazo for Colombia (2015); Fuentes (2013) for the case of Mexico; Molina and Muñoz (2014) for Costa Rica, ICEFI (2015) for Guatemala and Salim (2011) for the case of the Dominican Republic.
2. Calculated as the difference of the coefficients of inequality (Gini) between market income (understood as the income before fiscal policy) and disposable income (income with which the person has to acquire goods and services after taxes, social contributions and direct transfers).
3. The authors differentiate between income from pensions depending on whether they are considered as deferred income or as a direct transfer, which is why the redistributive effect increases, although this increase is greater in the EU countries.
4. Immervol and Richardson (2011), for example, show that, by mid-2000, the redistributive effect of fiscal policy for OECD countries was 28.7%.

References

Arenas de Mesa, A. (2016), *Sostenibilidad fiscal y reformas tributarias en América Latina*, (LC/G.2688-P), ECLAC, Santiago de Chile.

Barreíx, A., J.C. Benítez and M. Pecho (2017), "Revisiting personal income tax in Latin America: Evolution and impact", *Development Centre Working Paper* No. 338, Paris.

ECLAC (2017), *Fiscal Panorama of Latin America and the Caribbean: Mobilizing resources to finance of sustainable development*, Economic Commission for Latin America and the Caribbean, Santiago, Chile, *http://repositorio.cepal.org/handle/11362/41047*.

Cetrángolo, O., A. Goldschmit, J.C. Gómez Sabaini and D. Morán (2014), "Monotributo en América Latina", *Los casos de Argentina, Brasil y Urugua*, OIT, Lima.

Gómez Sabaini, J.C., J.P. Jiménez and D. Rossignolo (2012), "Imposición a la renta personal y equidad en América Latina: nuevos desafíos", *Serie Macroeconomía del Desarrollo*, N° 119 (LC/L.3477-P), ECLAC, Santiago de Chile.

Gómez Sabaini J.C., J.P. Jiménez and A. Podestá (2010), "Tributación, evasión y equidad en América Latina y el Caribe", in J.P. Jiménez, J.C. Gómez Sabaini and A. Podestá (editors), *Evasión y equidad en América Latina*, ECLAC, Santiago de Chile.

Immervoll, H. and L. Richardson (2011), "Redistribution Policy and Inequality Reduction in OECD Countries: What Has Changed in Two Decades?", *IZA Discussion Paper* No. 6030, October.

Jiménez, J.P. and A. Podestá (2016), "Los impuestos sobre la renta en América Latina", in *Consensos y Conflictos en la política tributaria de América Latina*, J.C. Gómez Sabaini, P. Jiménez, and R. Martner (editors), ECLAC, Santiago de Chile.

Lustig, N. (2016), "The impact of the tax system and social spending on the distribution of income and poverty in Latin America: Argentina, Bolivia, Brazil, Chile, Colombia, Costa Rica, Ecuador, El Salvador, Guatemala, Honduras, Mexico, Peru and Uruguay", *Working document* No. 37, Commitment to Equity Institute (CEQ), Tulane University.

OECD/CIAT/IDB (2016), *Taxing Wages in Latin America and the Caribbean*, OECD Publishing, Paris, *http://dx.doi.org/10.1787/9789264262607-en*.

OECD/ECLAC/CIAT/IDB (2018), Revenue statistics in Latin America and the Caribbean 1990-2016, OECD Publishing, Paris.

OECD/ECLAC/CIAT/IDB (2017), *Tax statistics in Latin America and the Caribbean 2017*, OECD Publishing, Paris, *http://dx.doi.org/10.1787/rev_lat_car-2017-en-fr*.

OECD (2017), *OECD Economic Surveys: Colombia 2017*, OECD Publishing, Paris, *http://dx.doi.org/10.1787/eco_surveys-col-2017-en*.

OECD (2015), *OECD Economic Surveys: Chile 2015*, OECD Publishing, Paris, *http://dx.doi.org/10.1787/eco_surveys-chl-2015-en*.

Pecho, M., F. Peláez and J. Sánchez (2012), "Estimation of tax non-compliance in Latin America 2000-2010", *Working document* No. 3, Tax Studies and Investigations Department, Inter-American Center of Tax Administrations (CIAT).

Tanzi, V. (2000), "Taxation in Latin America in the last decade", document presented at the Conference on fiscal and financial reforms in Latin America, Stanford University, 9 and 10 November.

Revenue Statistics in Latin America and the Caribbean 2018/
Estadísticas tributarias en América Latina y el Caribe 2018

Capítulo 3

SECCIÓN ESPECIAL
El impuesto sobre la renta en América Latina

Principales mensajes del capítulo

- La recaudación del impuesto a los ingresos, utilidades y ganancias del capital (1000) en los países de América Latina se ha casi triplicado en los últimas siete décadas, pasando de montos cercanos al 2% del PIB a cifras superiores al 6% para el 2016. Más del 55% de la recaudación de este impuesto recae sobre la renta de las empresas, mientras que el 32% corresponde a la renta personal, quedando el restante en otros impuestos a la renta que no son directamente imputables a personas físicas o empresas.
- La evolución de las tasas máximas y mínimas del impuesto a la renta personal, muestra una estrechez de la base gravable evidenciada en la reducción de la tasa máxima y el aumento de la tasa mínima, lo que a su vez merma la progresividad del sistema tributario.
- Las tasas de evasión son altas en los países de la región, mostrando tasas que son superiores al 50%, lo que da cuenta de los bajos niveles de cumplimiento de personas físicas y sociedades en el pago del impuesto sobre la renta.
- El impacto redistributivo del impuesto a la renta en América Latina es débil, logrando una reducción de apenas el 2% en la desigualdad de ingresos, que contrasta claramente con lo logrado en los países de la Unión Europea, cuya distribución mejora más del 12% después del cobro de este impuesto.
- En los últimos años, en América Latina se han emprendido reformas tributarias enfocadas en la equidad, lo que ha ido mostrando incipientes avances en materia de recaudación y mejora en la distribución de ingresos.

Introducción

Las finanzas públicas de los países de América Latina se han caracterizado tradicionalmente por un sistema tributario sesgado a la recaudación de impuestos al consumo y por una política impositiva con débil impacto redistributivo. Cuando se compara los sistemas tributarios de la región con los del resto del mundo, la gran brecha es la baja recaudación del impuesto a la renta. Este impuesto se compone principalmente de dos agregados: el impuesto sobre las sociedades y sobre las personas físicas.[1]

El impuesto a la renta suele tener ventajas con respecto a otros tributos, tanto en términos de estabilización macroeconómica, como "estabilizador automático" por el lado de los ingresos fiscales, como en su rol distributivo, por su mayor impacto redistributivo, tal cual se consigna en la mayoría de los trabajos de incidencia impositiva.

Mientras que el impuesto sobre las sociedades registra un nivel recaudatorio relativamente comparable con otras regiones, en el caso del impuesto sobre la renta personal en América Latina ha observado un débil desempeño recaudatorio, así como un bajo impacto macro y redistributivo; motivo por el cual en este capítulo se hace un énfasis particular en este impuesto, analizando los factores que limitaron su recaudación, su impacto macro y redistributivo y sus reformas y evolución reciente.

Características del impuesto a la renta en los países de la región

Al considerar una mirada de largo plazo en la evolución del impuesto sobre la renta, se obtiene evidencia de que, en general, la recaudación proveniente de ese tipo de impuesto creció entre 1940 y 1980 en los países de América Latina sobre los que se dispone de información histórica (véase el cuadro 3.1). Luego, con la crisis de la deuda en los años ochenta, los ingresos fiscales originados en los impuestos sobre los ingresos, las utilidades y las ganancias de capital, medidos en porcentajes del PIB, disminuyeron en la mayoría de los países, al tiempo que en los años noventa, la proporción de estos impuestos en relación con el PIB se mantuvo estable en el promedio de seis países de la región.

Cuadro 3.1. **América Latina (6 países): impuestos sobre los ingresos, utilidades y ganancias de capital, 1940-2016**

(Porcentaje del PIB)

País	1940-49	1950-59	1960-69	1970-79	1980-89	1990-99	2000-09	2010-16
Argentina	2.3	2.8	1.8	1.4	0.8	2.1	4.3	5.5
Brasil	1.9	2.4	2.0	2.7	4.6	4.7	6.6	6.8
Chile	3.1	4.6	6.7	6.0	4.5	4.3	6.5	7.5
Colombia	2.2	3.6	4.1	4.0	2.9	3.8	4.8	6.1
México	1.7	2.4	2.9	4.4	4.7	4.3	4.6	5.9
Perú	1.9	4.3	4.3	4.4	2.9	2.5	4.9	7.0
Promedio	2.2	3.4	3.6	3.8	3.4	3.6	5.3	6.5

Nota: El datos 1990-2016 sobre la base de OCDE/CEPAL/CIAT/BID (2018), Estadísticas tributarias en América Latina y el Caribe 2018.

Fuente: Elaboración sobre la base de OCDE/CEPAL/CIAT/BID (2018), *Estadísticas tributarias en América Latina y el Caribe 2018* y Gómez Sabaini, Jiménez y Rossignolo (2012), "Imposición a la renta personal y equidad en América Latina: nuevos desafíos".

StatLink http://dx.doi.org/10.1787/888933686328

Las reformas tributarias impulsadas en esa década enfatizaron la aplicación de un gravamen general sobre bienes y servicios (el impuesto sobre el valor agregado [IVA]) como sustituto de la imposición arancelaria, la derogación de impuestos de bajo rendimiento, la simplificación de las normas, la reducción de los niveles y tramos del impuesto sobre la renta y la generalización de las bases imponibles, aunque este último aspecto se refería más bien al IVA que a la imposición sobre los ingresos. En líneas generales, el diseño de la política tributaria estuvo influenciado por la creencia de que era más apropiado reducir el tamaño del sector público que aumentar significativamente el nivel de imposición por encima de los valores históricos observados.

En el siglo XXI tiene lugar un importante crecimiento de la recaudación del impuesto sobre la renta en todos los países considerados. El promedio del último quinquenio casi triplica los valores (en porcentajes del PIB) de hace siete décadas.

La tendencia positiva registrada durante este siglo puede separarse en dos periodos explicados por diferentes factores para cada uno. En primer lugar, entre 2005 y 2009 ocurrió un mayor crecimiento del impuesto sobre la renta de las personas jurídicas (ver gráfico 3.1). En esencia, ello estuvo asociado al significativo aumento de la recaudación proveniente de empresas mineras y petroleras, como resultado del auge de los precios de exportación de los productos primarios y de ciertas reformas implementadas para lograr una mayor apropiación fiscal de ese tipo de rentas. En segundo término, y en especial a partir de 2010, se destaca el incremento de la recaudación del impuesto sobre la renta de las personas físicas. En ese sentido, tal como se analizará en la última parte de este capítulo, un factor importante han sido las reformas implementadas por los países de la región que buscaban ampliar las bases imponibles de ese tributo, sobre todo para fortalecer la tributación sobre las rentas de capital. También se incluyeron cambios en las alícuotas y en los tramos de ingresos imponibles y se mejoraron las reglas de tributación internacional.

Gráfico 3.1. **América Latina (países seleccionados): evolución y estructura del impuesto sobre la renta (1000), 1990-2016[a]**

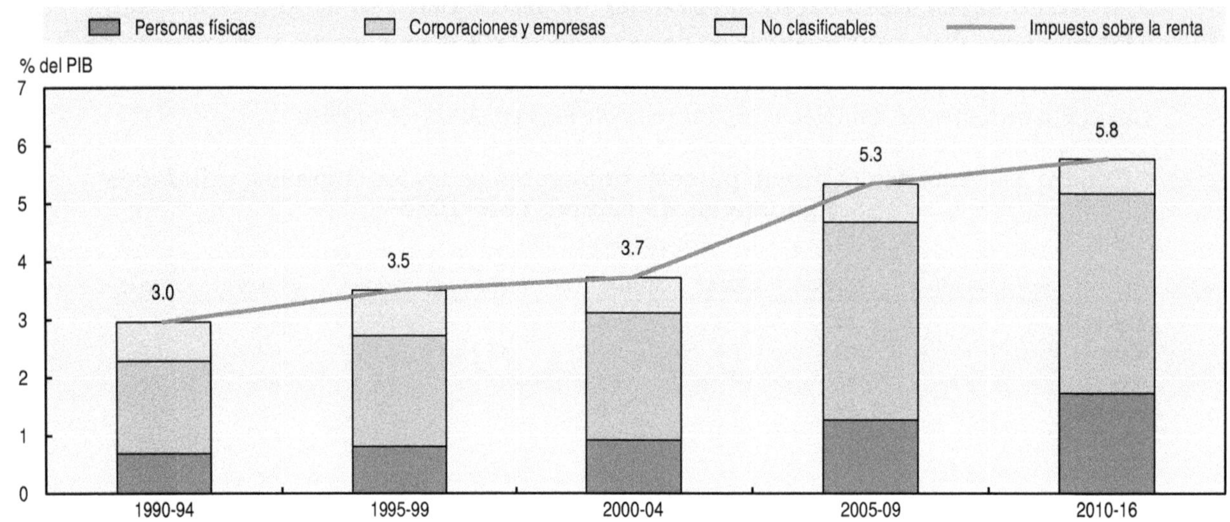

Nota: a. La desagregación entre personas físicas y empresas corresponde al promedio simple de 9 países sobre los que se dispone de información correspondiente al período 1990-2016 (Argentina, Brasil, Chile, Colombia, Guatemala, Honduras, Panamá, Perú and Uruguay).
Fuente: Elaboración propia, sobre la base de información de OCDE/CEPAL/CIAT/BID (2018).

StatLink http://dx.doi.org/10.1787/888933686214

A pesar de que la recaudación de los impuestos sobre la renta personal se ha ido incrementando, el crecimiento de los impuestos que recaen sobre la renta de las sociedades explica casi dos tercios del aumento total de este tipo de tributo en el período 1990-2016. En América Latina, las personas jurídicas (sociedades) aportan más del 55% del total recaudado en concepto del impuesto sobre la renta, mientras que las personas naturales apenas aportan el 31.9%, quedando el resto en otros impuestos a la renta (clasificación 1300). En los países de la Organización de Cooperación y Desarrollo Económicos (OCDE) esas participaciones son inversas: el 72% es aportado por las personas físicas y el 26% por las empresas, mientras que en el promedio de 15 economías de la Unión Europea (UE-15), el impuesto sobre la renta personal alcanza una participación del 79% del total.

Debe observarse que una limitación importante del impuesto sobre la renta personal en América Latina es que se recauda fundamentalmente de los asalariados, es decir, recae sobre los trabajadores formales en relación de dependencia, a quienes se les realiza la retención en su fuente de ingreso. De acuerdo con Gómez Sabaini, Jiménez y Podestá (2010), el 60% (o más) del impuesto sobre la renta personal proviene de trabajadores asalariados en los países sobre los que se dispone de información. Esta estructura desbalanceada afecta la equidad horizontal del impuesto, ya que la mayor parte es soportada por este tipo de trabajadores, mientras que los trabajadores independientes tienen mayores posibilidades de evasión y elusión y las rentas de capital se benefician de un tratamiento preferencial, ya sea porque generalmente tributan a una tasa menor o porque simplemente no se encuentran gravadas.

Adicionalmente, tal como se muestra en el cuadro 3.1, desde la década de los noventa, varios países han introducido mecanismos de simplificación tributaria con la finalidad de incorporar a la formalidad a un amplio sector de contribuyentes, regímenes que han tenido impacto en la erosión de la base imponible del impuesto a la renta personal.

Cuadro 3.2. **América Latina, OCDE (35) y UE (15): recaudación del impuesto sobre la renta de empresas y personas naturales, alrededor del 2015[a]**

Países	Recaudación como % del PIB		Participación en el total de impuesto al ingreso y ganancias (1000)	
	Renta personal (1100)	Empresas (1200)	Renta personal (1100)	Empresas (1200)
Argentina	3.2	3.2	48.9	48.3
Bolivia	0.2	5.4	4.0	96.0
Brasil	2.5	2.7	37.1	40.9
Colombia	1.2	5.1	18.5	77.9
Costa Rica	1.4	2.3	31.0	52.9
El Salvador	1.2	2.0	29.7	51.5
Guatemala	0.4	2.4	10.4	67.3
Honduras	1.8	3.6	34.0	66.0
Panamá	1.5	1.8	37.1	43.5
República Dominicana	2.8	2.4	47.8	40.3
Uruguay	3.1	2.5	52.6	42.9
América Latina (11)	1.8	3.0	31.9	57.1
OCDE (35)	8.4	2.8	71.6	26.0
Promedio EU (15)	10.0	2.7	78.8	21.2

Notas: La desagregación entre las personas naturales y las empresas corresponde al simple promedio de once países para los cuales la información está disponible para el periodo 1990-2016

Fuente: Elaboración propia, sobre la base de información OCDE/CEPAL/CIAT/BID (2018).

StatLink http://dx.doi.org/10.1787/888933686347

Factores que inciden en la recaudación del impuesto sobre la renta

Más allá de las reformas tributarias -más adelante analizadas- y de las mejoras en los niveles de recaudación del impuesto sobre la renta personal de los últimos años, existe consenso en señalar tres factores que han condicionado un mejor desempeño de ese tributo en los países de América Latina (Jiménez y Podestá, 2016; Barreix, Benítez y Pecho, 2017):

1. La evolución de las alícuotas legales, que llevó a una reducción de las tasas marginales máximas aplicadas en el promedio de los países;
2. La estrecha base imponible como consecuencia de un gran número de exenciones y deducciones permitidas, la existencia de regímenes tributarios simplificados, y por los niveles mínimos no imponibles, todo lo cual deja fuera del gravamen una cantidad importante de contribuyentes e ingresos, y
3. Los altos niveles de incumplimiento (informalidad, evasión y morosidad) que se observan en casi todos los países.

Esos factores conllevan la existencia de recaudaciones y tasas efectivas sustancialmente bajas como para lograr los efectos económicos y redistributivos deseados. A continuación se analiza con mayor detalle cada uno de esos condicionantes.

En el gráfico 3.2 se muestra la evolución de las tasas legales máximas y mínimas aplicables a la tributación sobre la renta de las personas físicas en un promedio de 18 países de América Latina.

Los promedios regionales de las alícuotas marginales máximas del impuesto sobre la renta de las personas físicas fueron descendiendo en América Latina, partiendo de tasas del 50.9% en la década de 1980, de alrededor del 35.2% a principios de la década de 1990 y en torno al 26.6% en 2016. Esta reducción paulatina ha hecho que las alícuotas máximas de algunos países latinoamericanos estén por debajo de los niveles internacionales. Por ejemplo, las tasas marginales máximas del impuesto sobre la renta personal llegaron en 2014 al 45% en el promedio de 18 economías pertenecientes a la eurozona, o al 39.4% si se considera el promedio de los 28 países de la Unión Europea. Cabe destacar que en varios países europeos (Austria, Bélgica, Dinamarca, España, Finlandia, Francia, Países Bajos, Portugal y Suecia) estas tasas son iguales o superiores al 50% (Unión Europea, 2014).

Gráfico 3.2. **América Latina (países seleccionados): evolución de las tasas marginales máximas y mínimas del impuesto sobre la renta de personas físicas, 1985-2016**

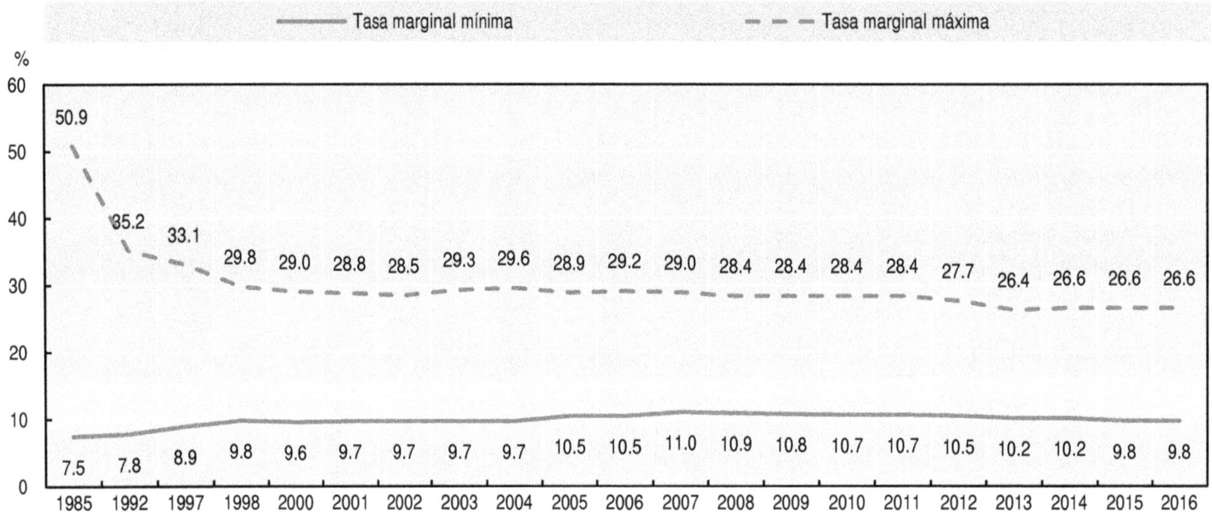

Fuente: Elaboración propia, sobre la base de Tanzi (2000), "Taxation in Latin America in the last decade" y datos de CEPALSTAT y el Centro Interamericano de Administraciones Tributarias (CIAT).

StatLink http://dx.doi.org/10.1787/888933686233

En contraste, las tasas marginales mínimas evidenciaron un incremento en América Latina, al pasar de una tasa media del 7.5% en la década de 1980 a un 9.8% en 2016. Alcanzaron su mayor valor hacia 2007, con una alícuota del 11% para el promedio regional. De esa forma se observa una reducción de la brecha media entre las tasas marginales máximas y mínimas de la imposición a la renta de personas físicas, lo que influye en el grado de progresividad del tributo (ver CEPAL, 2017).

Otra limitante tiene relación con el generoso tratamiento en materia de deducciones personales y ganancias no imponibles establecidos en la legislación impositiva, con los numerosos regímenes de exención o gastos tributarios, así como la proliferación y permanencia de regímenes tributarios simplificados (como el Monotributo en Argentina, el Simples Nacional y el Sistema para el Micro Emprendedor Individual en Brasil o el Regímen Tributario Simplificado en Bolivia) que si bien nacieron como "puentes" de entrada a la formalidad, se han consolidado de manera permanente en los sistemas tributarios (ver recuadro).

La proliferación de regímenes simplificados, que implican una carga tributaria menor, puede significar una erosión adicional a la base imponible de este tributo, en la medida que no estén debidamente coordinados. Las maniobras de elusión y arbitraje de los contribuyentes entre los dos regímenes, si bien puede no ser importante en términos de recursos, atentan contra la equidad horizontal del sistema, en tanto signifiquen un tratamiento discriminatorio entre contribuyentes de similar capacidad contributiva.

En América Latina, el nivel de ingreso a partir del cual comienza a pagarse el impuesto sobre la renta personal es mayor al de los países de la OECD, sea que se mida el ingreso mínimo exento en términos del PIB per cápita (véase Jiménez y Podestá, 2016, CEPAL, 2017); o que se mida en términos del salario promedio (OECD/BID/CIAT, 2016). Más allá de las diferencias metodológicas, la evidencia converge en mostrar altos niveles de tramos exentos, lo que claramente debilita el poder redistributivo del impuesto a la renta.

Cuadro 3.3. **América Latina: Tasas marginales máximas y mínimas del Impuesto sobre la Renta de personas físicas por países, 1985-2016**

País	1985-86		1992		2000		2008		2016	
	Mínimo	Máximo	Mínimo	Máximo	Mínimo	Máximo	Mínimo	Máximo	Mínimo	Máximo
Argentina	16.5	45	15	30	9	35	9	35	9	35
Bolivia	n/a	30	10	10	13	13	13	13	13	13
Brasil	0	60	10	25	15	27.5	15	27.5	7.5	27.5
Chile	0	57	5	50	5	45	5	40	4	40
Colombia	n/a	49	5	30	10	35	19	33	19	33
Costa Rica	5	50	10	25	10	25	10	15	10	15
Ecuador	19	40	10	25	5	15	5	35	5	35
El Salvador	3	60	10	30	10	30	10	30	10	30
Guatemala	11	48	4	34	15	25	15	31	5	7
Honduras	3	40	12	40	10	25	10	25	15	25
México	3	55	3	35	3	40	1.92	28	1.92	35
Nicaragua	15	50	8	35.5	10	30	10	30	15	30
Panamá	13	56	3.5	56	2	30	16.5	27	15	25
Paraguay	n/a	n/a	n/a	n/a	n/a	n/a	n/a	n/a	8	10
Perú	2	56	6	37	15	30	15	30	8	30
República Dominicana	2	73	3	70	15	25	15	25	15	25
Uruguay	n/a	n/a	n/a	n/a	n/a	n/a	10	25	10	30
Venezuela	12	45	10	30	6	34	6	34	6	34
América Latina (18)	7.5	50.9	7.8	35.2	9.6	29.0	10.9	28.4	9.8	26.6

Fuente: Jiménez y Podestá (2016), "Los impuestos sobre la renta en América Latina".

StatLink http://dx.doi.org/10.1787/888933686366

Por otro lado, también resulta difícil justificar el monto desde el que comienza a aplicarse la tasa marginal máxima. Mientras que en los países desarrollados esa tasa se establece a partir de 3 o 4 veces el PIB per cápita, en los países latinoamericanos dicha alícuota comienza a tener efecto a partir de ingresos superiores a 7.3 veces el ingreso per cápita, con tasas significativamente más bajas que en los países desarrollados (CEPAL, 2017).There is significant variation in the minimum and maximum PIT thresholds applied by different País in Latin America, although practically all of them are reducing the taxable income at which the minimum rate is applied. This is an outcome of reforms in the design of the taxable income brackets and the elimination of exemptions and personal deductions. Between 2007 and 2016, the Promedio exemption level was reduced by 36% as a result (Gómez Sabaini, Jiménez and Martner, 2017; ECLAC, 2017).

Cuando se observa en forma desagregada, el panorama entre los distintos países de la región es muy diverso, aunque prácticamente en todos se aprecia una tendencia a reducir el ingreso gravable a partir del cual se aplica la alícuota mínima. Esto es resultado de reformas en el diseño de los tramos de ingresos imponibles y la eliminación de exenciones y deducciones personales, que permitieron reducir el nivel de exención en un 36%, en promedio, entre 2007 y 2016 (Gómez Sabaini, Jiménez y Martner, 2017; CEPAL 2017).

Los altos gastos tributarios en los países de la región constituyen otro factor que reduce las bases imponibles. Mediante el uso de exenciones, deducciones, alícuotas reducidas, regímenes especiales y otros gastos tributarios, los países han buscado lograr diferentes objetivos, como la atracción de la inversión extranjera directa, el estímulo del ahorro, el desarrollo de mercados financieros, el desarrollo de regiones atrasadas, la promoción de exportaciones, la industrialización, la generación de empleo, el cuidado del medio ambiente, la transferencia de tecnología, la diversificación de la estructura económica y la formación de capital humano. Más allá de que la eficacia y la eficiencia en el logro de esos múltiples objetivos ha sido muy cuestionada y escasamente evaluada, lo cierto es que esos gastos tributarios han llevado a una erosión de las bases tributarias y han entrañado un costo en términos de recaudación.

Recuadro 3.1. **La informalidad y los programas de simplificación tributaria en América Latina**

En América Latina, se han introducido esquemas simplificados destinados principalmente a los pequeños contribuyentes con la finalidad de promover su formalización de los contribuyentes y simplificar la administración tributaria. Uno de los principales rasgos que surgen al analizar los regímenes simplificados de los países de la región, es que su instrumentación no ha tenido como objeto primordial la recaudación tributaria, sino incorporar a la formalidad a un amplio sector de contribuyentes. La recaudación promedio de estos regímenes, vale señalar, es cercana al 1% de los ingresos tributarios totales, aunque dicho promedio esconde amplias diferencias entre los países.

El diseño de estos regímenes de tratamientos especiales para gravar a los pequeños contribuyentes, excluyéndolos de las normas generales del IVA y/o ISR, estableciendo métodos presuntivos de determinación y/o imponiéndoles tasas más reducidas, ha sido uno de los principales caminos que han adoptado los países de la región para aliviar la carga de trabajo de las administraciones tributarias y mejorar asi sus capacidades de fiscalización.

En América Latina estos regímenes de tributación simplificada se encuentran ampliamente difundidos, ya que a excepción de El Salvador y Venezuela todos los países de la región han implementado algún sistema de tratamiento preferencial para los pequeños contribuyentes. A partir de su implementación, se ha buscado facilitar el pago de impuestos de contribuyentes cuyas características generalmente responden a: a) bajos ingresos, b) un alto número que dificulta el control oficial, c) informales, d) pobre estructura organizacional y e) alta movilidad de entrada y salida. Lo que se busca es la simplificación de las normas legales y trámites administrativos que tiene el cumplimiento de las obligaciones tributarias, apuntando con ello a brindarles un "puente transitorio" para atraer a la formalidad a los agentes económicos y, al mismo tiempo, mejorar el manejo de los recursos de la administración tributaria.

Resulta importante resaltar la necesidad de que estos instrumentos funcionen efectivamente como un "puente transitorio" entre los regímenes especialmente diseñados para los sectores informales y el cumplimiento voluntario de las normas impositivas generales, acotando los requisitos y beneficios otorgados, procurando la reducción progresiva del tiempo de permanencia de los contribuyentes en estos sistemas, dado que los regímenes generales suelen ser más justos, en términos de equidad horizontal y vertical, y respetan mejor el principio de neutralidad impositiva.

Fuente: Elaboración sobre la base de Cetrángolo et al. (2014), "Monotributo en América Latina", *Los casos de Argentina, Brasil y Urugua*, y Arenas de Mesa (2016), *Sostenibilidad fiscal y reformas tributarias en América Latina.*

Realizar un ejercicio comparativo sobre los gastos tributarios resulta complejo toda vez que las metodologías de estimación difieren entre los países de la región, no obstante se puede inferir que la magnitud de los gastos tributarios resulta significativa en la mayoría de los casos, ya que se sitúan en un rango entre 2 y 7 puntos del PIB y representan entre un 7% y un 40% de la presión tributaria, según el país analizado (ver CEPAL, 2017).

Otro factor limitante de la capacidad de recaudación del impuesto sobre la renta es el bajo nivel de cumplimiento y las altas tasas de evasión. Las estimaciones de las tasas de evasión del pago del impuesto sobre la renta y, en especial, del que recae sobre las personas físicas, son escasas en la región. De los estudios disponibles (Gómez Sabaini, Jiménez y

Podestá, 2010; Pecho, Peláez y Sánchez, 2012; Gómez Sabaini, Jiménez y Martner, 2017), no obstante, se puede señalar que los niveles de evasión en los países de la región son más altos en comparación con las estimaciones existentes para el caso del IVA y, además, mayores en los impuestos sobre la renta de las sociedades que en lo que se refiere a la renta personal.[2]

Potencial redistributivo del impuesto a la renta

Los modestos avances en la recaudación del impuesto sobre la renta tienen incidencia directa en la evolución del poder redistributivo de este instrumento. En años recientes la reducción del coeficiente de Gini debido al impuesto sobre la renta personal alcanzó el 2% en el promedio de 18 países de América Latina, cifra que muestra una mejora respecto a periodos anteriores (2004-07), pero que no obstante sigue muy por debajo del poder redistributivo mostrado en los países de la Unión Europea (UE), cuyo efecto logra disminuciones superiores al 12%, dejando entrever un magro desempeño en esta materia (CEPAL, 2017).

Diferencias en el mismo sentido encuentran Lustig y otros (2016), quienes miden el efecto redistributivo de los impuestos y transferencias directas:[3] el efecto redistributivo para los países de la región ronda entre el 2.3 puntos porcentuales y el 3.7 puntos porcentuales, mientras que para los países de la UE el efecto ronda entre 7.8 puntos porcentuales y 19.1 puntos porcentuales, según sean consideradas las pensiones.[4] Si se toma en cuenta solo el indicador que mide la diferencia entre el gini antes y después del pago al impuesto a la renta (lo que se conoce como el indicador Reynolds-Smolensky), Barreíx y otros (2017) señalan que los países miembros de la OCDE alcanzan mejoras cuatro veces superiores que las que alcanzan los países de la región.[5]

Los cambios en el poder redistributivo son distintos entre los países de la región. Se observan casos, por ejemplo, como el de Bolivia, Costa Rica, Ecuador, Honduras, Nicaragua, Panamá, Perú y Venezuela en donde prácticamente no se han dado cambios en el impacto que tiene el impuesto sobre la renta en la distribución de ingresos. Destacan, por otro lado, los avances en Argentina, Brasil, Chile, El Salvador, México, República Dominicana y Uruguay. Los cambios positivos, se señala, obedecen principalmente a un crecimiento en los ingresos por sueldos y salarios junto con modificaciones en la estructura del tributo.

Gráfico 3.3. **América Latina (18 países) y Unión Europea (28 países): reducción del coeficiente de Gini debido al impuesto sobre la renta**

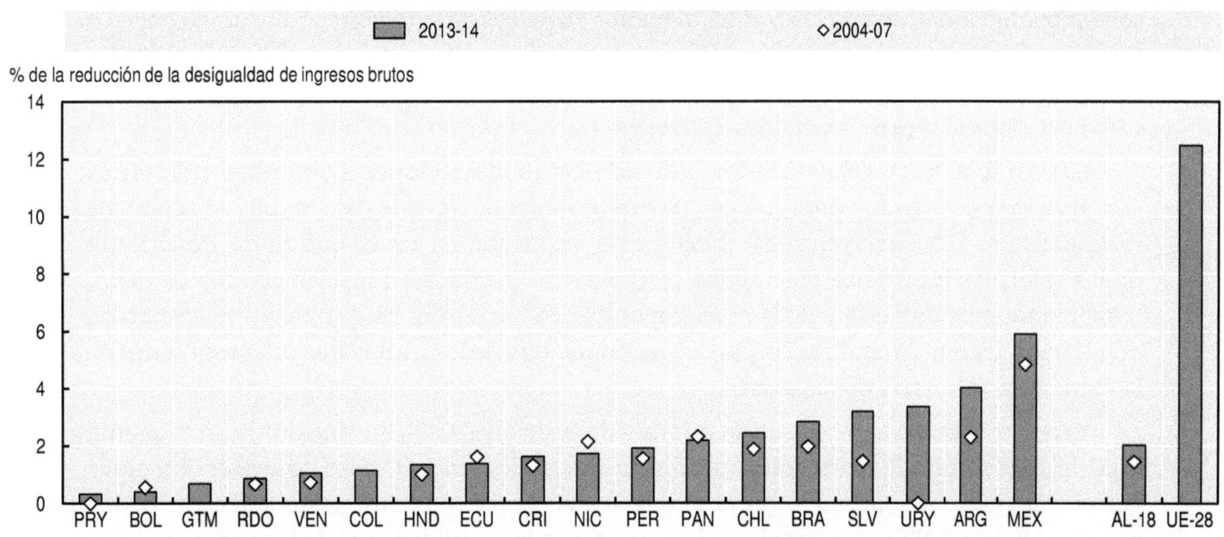

Fuente: CEPAL, sobre la base de Encuesta de Hogares y EUROMOD.

StatLink http://dx.doi.org/10.1787/888933686252

Se suma a los desafíos pendientes la carga tributaria de los contribuyentes más ricos, cuya evidencia muestra que para el 2014 la tasa media efectiva del último decil (10) sólo alcanzó un 4.8% en promedio para la región, cifra que claramente constrasta con el 21.3% alcanzado por los países de la Unión Europea (CEPAL, 2017). Uno de los principales factores que originan este resultado, se argumenta, es el hecho de que los ingresos de capital en la región se gravan a tasas menores que los ingresos laborales o, incluso, no se gravan en algunos países. Aunado a ello, son los contribuyentes más ricos los que pueden aprovechar la planificación tributaria agresiva con el fin de minimizar el pago de impuestos en sus países de residencia.

Es importante agregar que en OCDE/CIAT/BID (2016), se estima la parte (en porcentaje) de los ingresos laborales (sólo se toma el sector formal) que es destinada al pago del impuesto a la renta, las contribuciones a la seguridad social y los impuestos a la nómina que los empleados y empleadores tienen que pagar. Con ello se encuentra una tendencia más progresiva, en donde el decil X, en promedio de los países de América Latina, cubre más del 25% (dependiendo de la estructura familiar) de los costos laborales.

También se ha planteado que otro desafío fundamental para la mayoría de los países de la región se encuentra en la incorporación de la clase media al pago del impuesto sobre la renta. En efecto, el pago del impuesto sobre la renta personal de los países de América Latina está altamente concentrado en el último decil (cerca del 88%), mientras que en los países de la Unión Europea el último decil concentra menos del 40% del pago de este impuesto (CEPAL, 2017). A primera vista, de acuerdo con lo que se ha señalado, esto podría parecer un resultado positivo, pero en realidad esta baja participación de la clase media termina por debilitar el potencial recaudatorio y su capacidad para modificar la distribución del ingreso en términos más generales. Con ello, tampoco se contribuye como debiera a la formación de círculos virtuosos conforme a los cuales los ciudadanos aceptan pagar más impuestos a cambio de más y mejores bienes y servicios públicos.

Cambios recientes y la relevancia del impuesto sobre la renta en las reformas tributarias

En América Latina, las reformas o modificaciones tributarias han sido una de las políticas públicas más extendidas y transversales en la presente década, debido a su potencial para incrementar los ingresos tributarios, generar efectos distributivos y fortalecer la sostenibilidad fiscal. Entre 2010 y 2015, al menos 18 países de la región modificaron el nivel o la estructura de sus impuestos, o incluso ambos. Durante este periodo existen contabilizadas 51 modificaciones tributarias y 17 reformas tributarias; de estas últimas, tres se califican como estructurales (Arenas de Mesa, 2016).[6]

Los cambios más generalizados han sido las modificaciones y reformas tributarias con énfasis en el cambio del impuesto sobre la renta. Es así que del total de los cambios realizados, un 75% incluyeron cambios a este impuesto, en tanto que parte importante de las reformas tributarias efectuadas consideraron cambios en las estructuras de tasas, o bien aumentos de tasas y de la base imponible de las rentas del capital y repartición de dividendos, incrementando así la participación relativa de los impuestos directos dentro de la estructura tributaria de los países.

Vale tomar como antecedente la reforma de Uruguay (2007), que introdujo un esquema dual de imposición a la renta, como una forma parcial de alcanzar todas las rentas obtenidas por el contribuyente. En esa reforma se destaca la creación del impuesto a la renta de las personas físicas (IRPF), en reemplazo del impuesto a las retribuciones de las personas (IRP), con tasas progresivas de entre el 3% y el 12%.

En los últimos años se destacan las reformas de Colombia (2010, 2012, 2014 y 2016), México (2013) y Chile (2014), cuyos objetivos apuntaban a enfrentar desafíos distributivos en un contexto de precios bajos de las exportaciones de las materias primas como en el caso concreto de Colombia, hasta financiar reformas al sistema educativo (Chile) y otras reformas estructurales (México). En términos generales, estas reformas han mostrado incipientes efectos positivos en materia fiscal (recaudación) y distributiva (Arenas de Mesa, 2010). Sumado a ello, vale destacar que recientemente en Argentina (2017) y Ecuador (2017) se han emprendido reformas que también han afectado al impuesto bajo análisis.

En Colombia, desde el 2010, se han emprendido una serie de reformas cuyos propósitos abarcan principalmente al aumento de la recaudación (2010), la mejora de la equidad tributaria (2012 y 2014), la reducción de la evasión y la promoción de la formalidad (2016). En este periodo se crearon el impuesto mínimo alternativo nacional (IMAN), el impuesto mínimo simplificado (IMAS) y el impuesto a la renta para la equidad (CREE), impuestos que para el 2016 fueron eliminados con la finalidad de unificar las tasas del impuesto a la renta.[7] Con esta última reforma (2016) también se ha gravado la distribución de dividendos percibidos por personas naturales que antes se encontraban exentos (OCDE, 2017a). En materia de resultados, se han discutido efectos neutros en cuanto a recaudación, mientras que se han anticipado efectos redistributivos que son positivos.[8]

En Chile, en 2014 se aprobó una reforma tributaria centrada en el alza a la renta de empresas, por su importante recaudación fiscal y porque apunta a cumplir uno de sus principales objetivos: mejorar la distribución del ingreso. La idea central de la reforma consiste en ampliar la base sobre la que tributaban las empresas y las personas, lo que implica que los contribuyentes de mayores ingresos aporten más a la recaudación, de manera tal de potenciar la progresividad del sistema.

En la reforma en Chile se establece un aumento gradual del impuesto a la renta de las empresas, del 20% al 25% entre 2014 y 2017 en el sistema integrado, quedando del 25.5% en 2017 y del 27% en 2018 en el sistema semiintegrado, y la reducción de la tasa marginal máxima de la renta de las personas del 40% al 35% a partir de enero del 2017. El sistema semiintegrado permite la acreditación del 65% del impuesto a la renta de empresas pagado por empresarios sobre su impuesto a la renta personal para reducir los impactos sobre el crecimiento económico derivados del alza del impuesto (OCDE, 2015). Asimismo se derogó, de igual forma, el régimen contemplado de la ley del impuesto a la renta que permitía a los contribuyentes no pagar impuestos mientras no se retiraran las utilidades.

Con la reforma en régimen, se proyecta una recaudación para el gobierno central de Chile del 3% del PIB, de lo cual se estima que cerca del 50% del total responda a las modificaciones del impuesto a la renta, alcanzando por esta dimensión un monto cercano a 1.46% una vez que la reforma esté totalmente en régimen (que sería a partir del 2018 en adelante).[9]

En el marco de la reforma hacendaria de México, se reemplazaron el impuesto sobre la renta de las empresas y el impuesto a los depósitos en efectivo por un impuesto sobre la renta empresarial modificado, que incluyó la carga tributaria de los dos impuestos eliminados. En lo que se refiere al impuesto sobre las personas naturales, se creó un impuesto del 10% sobre los ingresos de las personas naturales derivados de ganancias de capital y distribución de dividendos. Asimismo, se puso un límite anual a las deducciones personales y se modificó la estructura de las tasas del impuesto, aumentando los tramos de más altos ingresos.

En cuanto a los efectos fiscales de la reforma mexicana, en términos agregados el rendimiento tributario efectivo ha estado muy por encima de las cifras inicialmente estimadas.[10] Por el lado del impuesto a la renta, si bien para el 2014 su efecto recaudatorio fue negativo (-0.3% del PIB respecto al 2013), para el 2015 la recaudación efectiva producto de la reforma ascendió a 1.1% del PIB, cifra superior a lo aprobado por el Congreso (0.5%). Producto de las modificaciones a los impuestos sobre la renta, la Secretaría de Hacienda y Crédito Público estima una mejora en la distribución del ingreso, evidenciada con una disminución del coeficiente de Gini de 0.032 puntos.

En Argentina, durante el 2017 se aprobó una reforma tributaria, en la cual se incluyó una reducción gradual de la tasa del Impuesto a las Ganancias aplicado a sociedades, de 35% a 25% (35% en 2018, 30% en 2019-20, y 25% para 2021 y adelante). Con el fin de incentivar la reinversión de utilidades, se introdujo una retención a la distribución de dividendos – con una tasa de 7% para las utilidades devengadas en 2018 y 2019 y de 13% para los años 2020 en adelante – lo que implica que la carga tributaria para ganancias distribuidas se mantiene al mismo nivel.

Se introdujo, además, un impuesto a la renta financiera de personas físicas, cuyas fuentes estaban exentas del impuesto anteriormente. Se aumentó la deducción especial del Impuesto a las Ganancias para trabajadores autónomos, cuyo monto había sido históricamente muy inferior a la deducción especial para trabajadores dependientes.

En Ecuador, por su parte, se aprobó la Ley Orgánica para la Reactivación de la Economía (2017), Fortalecimiento de la Dolarización y Modernización de la Gestión Financiera que abarcó cambios en varios impuestos. Con el fin de generar recursos adicionales la ley incorporó varios cambios al impuesto sobre la renta. En el caso de sociedades, se aumentó la tasa general de 22% a 25%, con una rebaja de 3 puntos porcentuales para microempresas y exportadores. En este último caso la rebaja en la tasa solo se produce si la empresa mantiene o aumenta su nivel de empleo. Se introdujo también ciertas limitaciones a la reducción en la tasa por la reinversión de utilidades (principalmente limitando estos incentivos a exportadoras habituales y empresas manufactureras). Se ofrece una tasa de 22% a las empresas que entran en contratos de inversión dentro del primer año de vigencia de la misma ley, cuyos proyectos contribuyan al cambio de la matriz productiva o contemplen la explotación minera.

También se estableció un mínimo no imponible del impuesto sobre la renta para microempresas de USD 11.290 y se exoneró a las nuevas microempresas del pago del mismo impuesto por un periodo de tres años. En el caso del impuesto sobre la renta de personas físicas, la reforma en Ecuador amplió los gastos deducibles para incluir los gastos por hijos (sin límite de edad) y padres dependientes.

Conclusiones y principales desafíos

Si bien en los últimos años se han registrado avances en materia de imposición a la renta, los países de América Latina siguen presentando una baja recaudación del impuesto sobre la renta personal; tanto si se compara con lo que aporta el impuesto sobre las sociedades en la región, así como con lo que se recauda sobre individuos en las economías desarrolladas. La estructura de este impuesto, además, resulta desequilibrada debido a que la mayor parte recae en los trabajadores asalariados, a quienes se les retiene el impuesto en el momento del pago de su remuneración. Por su parte, las rentas de capital se benefician de un tratamiento preferencial, ya sea porque generalmente tributan a una tasa menor o porque simplemente no se encuentran gravadas.

En efecto, dado que todo lo anterior reduce los recursos disponibles y debilita el impacto macro como redistributivo del sistema tributario, resulta crucial que los países trabajen en pos del fortalecimiento del impuesto sobre la renta de las personas naturales. Para ello es fundamental que se promuevan acciones para combatir la evasión y elusión fiscal y, en especial, en este tributo.

Además se debe tender a una base amplia y general del impuesto, donde se consideren todas las rentas del contribuyente dentro de la base gravable, otorgándose a las rentas de capital un tratamiento similar al aplicado sobre las rentas provenientes del trabajo y coordinando este tributo con los regímenes simplificados. Del mismo modo deben revisarse y reducirse los tratamientos preferenciales como así también las deducciones permitidas. A su vez, se puede reducir el nivel de ingreso a partir del cual aplican las tasas máximas del impuesto sobre la renta personal, en línea con lo observado en otras regiones. En varios países se podría tender también a una reducción del mínimo exento para que sea igual o inferior a su ingreso per cápita y así ampliar la base del impuesto.

Esta mirada integral permitiría reforzar su efecto estabilizador así como su impacto sobre la equidad, ya sea en relación con el principio de la capacidad de pago (equidad vertical) o con un tratamiento impositivo igualitario para aquellos que tengan ingresos equivalentes (equidad horizontal), aunque sean de diferente fuente (salario o capital) o diferente modalidad contractual (asalariado o autónomo).

Notas

1. Tanzi (2000) ha caracterizado a los países de América Latina como "alérgicos" al impuesto a la renta debido a su bajo recaudo.
2. Existen además análisis específicos para los países. Por ejemplo, entre los más recientes destacan: el del Servicio de Impuestos Internos de Chile (SII, 2012 a y 2012 b); el de Ávila y Cruz Lazo para Colombia (2015); el de Fuentes (2013) para el caso de México; el de Molina y Muñoz (2014) para Costa Rica; el de ICEFI (2015) para Guatemala o el de Salim (2011) para el caso de República Dominicana.
3. Efecto que consiste en la diferencia en los coeficientes de desigualdad (gini) entre el ingreso de mercado (entendido como el ingreso antes de la política fiscal) y el ingreso disponible (ingreso con el que cuenta la persona para adquirir bienes y servicios después de impuestos directos, las contribuciones sociales y las transferencias directas).
4. Los autores diferencian el ingreso de las pensiones cuando son parte del ingreso y cuando corresponden a transferencia directa, motivo por el cual el efecto redistributivo aumenta, aunque dicho aumento es mayor en los países de la UE.
5. En Immervol y Richardson (2011), por ejemplo, se muestra que, para mediados del 2000, el efecto redistributivo de la política fiscal para los países de la OCDE fue del 28.7%.
6. Ver Arenas de Mesa (2016), para un análisis más detallado de las reformas.
7. Se unificaron las tasas del impuesto sobre la renta de las empresas, eliminándose el CREE y se estableció una alícuota general del 34% para el 2017, que se reduce al 33% a partir del 2018 (con una sobre tasa del 6% en 2017 y 4% en 2018). Se creó, en la misma línea, un gravamen a los dividendos con tarifas del 5% para quienes reciban más de 18 millones de pesos colombianos al año (pasarlo a dólares) y del 10% para quienes reciban más de 30 millones de pesos colombianos al año (idem.). Asimismo, se racionalizaron los beneficios tributarios, limitando las excenciones y las deducciones al 40% del ingreso total, que en todo caso no puede exceder 160 millones de pesos (dólares). Se simplificó además este impuesto, eliminando el IMAN y el IMAS, con lo cual los contribuyentes sólo deberán diligenciar una declaración. Las sociedades podrán deducir del impuesto sobre la renta el IVA sobre los bienes de capital utilizados en procesos productivos.
8. Ver mayores detalles en Arenas de Mesa (2016).
9. Dentro de sus efectos distributivos, destaca que con la reforma, el 0.1% más rico de los contribuyentes asciende su contribución del 38% (antes de la reforma) al 47.5% del total de los ingresos provenientes del impuesto a la renta. La reforma, en sí, aumentó en gran medida la carga efectiva del impuesto

a la renta en el percentil más alto de la distribución del ingreso, del 12.7% al 18.5%, mientras que para el 90% de la población se mantiene prácticamente constante (Arenas de Mesa, 2016).

10. Por ejemplo, la recaudación total efectiva en 2014 fue del 1.1% del PIB, similar a la estimación aprobada por el Congreso (1% del PIB), no obstante en 2015 la recaudación tributaria efectiva alcanzó el 2.6% del PIB, cifra superior a lo aprobado para ese año en más de un 1% del PIB. Parte importante de esta recaudación, vale aclarar, provino del impuesto especial sobre producción y servicios (IEPS) a las gasolinas.

Referencias

Arenas de Mesa, A. (2016), *Sostenibilidad fiscal y reformas tributarias en América Latina*, (LC/G.2688-P), CEPAL, Santiago de Chile.

Barreíx, A., J.C. Benítez y M. Pecho (2017), "Revisiting personal income tax in Latin America: Evolution and impact", *Development Centre Working Paper* No. 338, París.

ECLAC (2017), *Fiscal Panorama of Latin America and the Caribbean: Mobilizing resources to finance of sustainable development*, CEPAL, Santiago, Chile, *http://repositorio.cepal.org/handle/11362/41047*.

Cetrángolo, O., A. Goldschmit, J.C. Gómez Sabaini y D. Morán (2014), "Monotributo en América Latina", *Los casos de Argentina, Brasil y Urugua*, OIT, Lima.

Gómez Sabaini, J.C., J.P. Jiménez y D. Rossignolo (2012), "Imposición a la renta personal y equidad en América Latina: nuevos desafíos", *Serie Macroeconomía del Desarrollo*, N° 119 (LC/L.3477-P), CEPAL, Santiago de Chile.

Gómez Sabaini J.C., J.P. Jiménez y A. Podestá (2010), "Tributación, evasión y equidad en América Latina y el Caribe", in J.P. Jiménez, J.C. Gómez Sabaini y A. Podestá (editors), *Evasión y equidad en América Latina*, CEPAL, Santiago de Chile.

Immervoll, H. y L. Richardson (2011), "Redistribution Policy and Inequality Reduction in OCDE País: What Has Changed in Two Decades?", *IZA Discussion Paper* No. 6030, Octubre.

Jiménez, J.P. y A. Podestá (2016), "Los impuestos sobre la renta en América Latina", in *Consensos y Conflictos en la política tributaria de América Latina*, J.C. Gómez Sabaini, P. Jiménez y R. Martner (editors), CEPAL, Santiago de Chile.

Lustig, N. (2016), "The impact of the tax system and social spending on the distribution of income and poverty in Latin America: Argentina, Bolivia, Brasil, Chile, Colombia, Costa Rica, Ecuador, El Salvador, Guatemala, Honduras, México, Perú and Uruguay", *Working document* No. 37, Commitment to Equity Institute (CEQ), Tulane University.

OCDE/CIAT/BID (2016), *Taxing Wages in Latin America and the Caribbean*, OCDE Publishing, París, *http://dx.doi.org/10.1787/9789264262607-en*.

OCDE/CEPAL/CIAT/BID (2018), *Estadísticas tributarias en América Latina y el Caribe 1990-2016*, OCDE Publishing, París.

OCDE/CEPAL/CIAT/BID (2017), *Estadísticas tributarias en América Latina y el Caribe 2017*, OCDE Publishing, París, *http://dx.doi.org/10.1787/rev_lat_car-2017-en-fr*.

OCDE (2017), *OCDE Economic Surveys: Colombia 2017*, OCDE Publishing, París, *http://dx.doi.org/10.1787/eco_surveys-col-2017-en*.

OCDE (2015), *OCDE Economic Surveys: Chile 2015*, OCDE Publishing, París, *http://dx.doi.org/10.1787/eco_surveys-chl-2015-en*.

Pecho, M., F. Peláez y J. Sánchez (2012), "Estimation of tax non-compliance in Latin America 2000-2010", *Working document* No. 3, Tax Studies and Investigations Department, Centro Interamericano de Administraciones Tributarias (CIAT).

Tanzi, V. (2000), "Taxation in Latin America in the last decade", document presented at the Conference on fiscal and financial reforms in Latin America, Stanford University, 9 y 10 de noviembre.

Chapter 4

Tax levels and tax structures, 1990-2016

Capítulo 4

Niveles impositivos y estructuras tributarias, 1990-2016

Chapter 4 / Capítulo 4

4.1. Comparative tables, 1990-2016

In all of the following tables a (..) indicates not available. The main series in this volume cover the years 1990 to 2016.

Figures referring to 1991-99, 2001-04 and 2006-09 in Tables 4.1 to 4.2 and Tables 4.15 to 4.17, figures relating to 1991-99, 2001-09 and 2011-14 in Tables 4.5 to 4.10 and figures relating to 1990-94, 1996-99 and 2001-14 in Tables 4.11 to 4.13 have been omitted because of lack of space. Complete series are, however, available on line at *www.latameconomy.org* and in the database OECD/ECLAC/CIAT/IDB (2018), "Revenue Statistics in Latin America: Comparative tables", *OECD Tax Statistics*, *http://dx.doi.org/10.1787/data-00641-en*.

4.1. Cuadros comparativos, 1990-2016

En todos los cuadros siguientes, (..) indica dato indisponible. Las principales series de datos de esta sección cubren el periodo que va de 1990 a 2016.

Las cifras relativas a 1991-99, 2001-04 y a 2006-09 en Cuadros 4.1 hasta 4.2 y Cuadros 4.15 hasta 4.17 y las cifras relativas a 1991-99, 2001-09 y 2011-14 en Cuadros 4.5 hasta 4.10 y las cifras relativas a 1990-94, 1996-99 y 2001-14 en Cuadros 4.11 hasta 4.13 a se han omitido por falta de espacio. Sin embargo, las series completas están disponibles en línea en *www.latameconomy.org* y en la base de datos OCDE/CEPAL/CIAT/BID (2018), "Revenue Statistics in Latin America: Comparative tables", *OECD Tax Statistics*, *http://dx.doi.org/10.1787/data-00641-en*.

Table 4.1. Total tax revenue as % of GDP, 1990-2016
Cuadro 4.1. Total de ingresos tributarios en % del PIB, 1990-2016

	1990	2000	2005	2010	2011	2012	2013	2014	2015	2016
Argentina	13.7	19.8	24.5	29.1	29.3	30.6	31.2	31.1	32.0	31.3
Bahamas[1]	12.3	15.2	13.8	16.1	18.9	17.6	17.0	17.3	19.9	22.4
Barbados	23.2	30.2	29.5	30.6	32.4	33.1	29.5	30.4	33.6	32.2
Belize / Belice[1]	21.8	19.1	22.3	26.6	25.1	25.0	25.7	27.2	27.3	29.6
Bolivia	8.3	17.6	20.0	20.3	22.1	24.4	25.3	26.2	27.6	26.0
Brazil / Brasil	25.5	29.6	32.8	32.4	33.2	32.5	32.4	31.8	32.0	32.2
Chile	16.9	18.8	20.7	19.6	21.1	21.3	19.9	19.6	20.5	20.4
Colombia	10.6	14.6	18.1	18.0	18.8	19.7	20.1	20.4	20.8	19.8
Costa Rica	21.3	18.4	20.0	20.7	21.2	21.2	21.9	21.9	22.6	22.2
Cuba	29.1	37.2	41.1	37.6	38.4	39.7	37.3	37.5	38.6	41.7
Dominican Republic / República Dominicana	7.8	10.8	11.9	12.3	12.3	13.1	13.7	13.8	13.5	13.7
Ecuador[1]	7.3	10.3	12.1	16.6	17.7	19.8	19.6	19.2	21.1	20.5
El Salvador	10.5	12.1	14.2	15.4	15.6	16.4	17.3	16.9	17.2	17.9
Guatemala	8.8	12.4	13.1	12.4	12.8	12.9	13.0	12.7	12.4	12.6
Guyana[1]	20.6	20.8	23.0	24.2	23.4	22.5	22.9	23.8	24.2	23.2
Honduras	16.2	15.3	16.9	17.3	16.9	17.8	18.4	19.6	20.4	21.4
Jamaica	23.1	22.7	23.3	24.9	24.5	24.5	24.9	24.7	25.7	26.7
Mexico / México[2]	12.4	13.1	12.1	13.4	13.3	13.1	13.8	14.2	16.2	17.2
Nicaragua	..	13.0	16.1	19.4	20.3	20.9	21.2	21.8	22.3	22.6
Panama / Panamá	15.9	15.9	13.8	16.7	16.5	16.8	17.1	15.7	15.9	16.6
Paraguay	5.8	12.6	13.8	16.5	16.9	17.7	16.4	17.8	17.9	17.5
Peru / Perú	12.1	14.6	16.4	17.8	18.6	19.3	19.2	19.0	17.2	16.1
Trinidad and Tobago / Trinidad y Tobago	23.4	21.4	26.7	27.5	26.7	27.6	27.7	30.1	30.6	22.9
Uruguay[1]	19.6	21.6	23.9	26.2	26.6	26.9	27.5	27.3	27.0	27.9
Venezuela[1]	18.1	13.6	15.9	11.8	13.4	14.1	14.4	18.9	20.8	14.4
Unweighted average / Promedio no ponderado										
LAC / ALC[3]	**16.0**	**18.0**	**19.8**	**20.9**	**21.4**	**21.9**	**21.9**	**22.4**	**23.1**	**22.7**
OECD / OCDE[4]	**31.9**	**33.9**	**33.5**	**32.5**	**32.8**	**33.3**	**33.6**	**33.9**	**34.0**	**34.3**

Note: The figures exclude local government revenues for Argentina (but include provincial revenues), Bahamas, Barbados, Bolivia (prior to 1994), Cuba, Dominican Republic, El Salvador (prior to 2002), Honduras, Jamaica (prior to 1998), Nicaragua (prior to 2010), Panama (prior to 1998), Paraguay (prior to 2004), Peru (prior to 2001) and Venezuela as the data are not available.

1. The data include the following estimations: Bahamas (social security contributions for 2016), Belize (social security contributions for 2016), Ecuador (local tax revenues for 2016), Guyana (social security contributions in 2015 and 2016), Uruguay (local tax revenues for 2016) and Venezuela (tax revenues from oil profits for 2015 and 2016, and social security contributions from 2011 onward). See the corresponding country tables for more information.
2. The data are estimated for 2016 including expected revenues for state and local governments.
3. Represents a group of 25 Latin American and Caribbean countries. The average is calculated using calendar year data, except for Bahamas and Trinidad and Tobago where fiscal year data are used. Chile and Mexico are also part of the OECD (35) group.
4. Calculated by applying the unweighted average percentage change for 2016 in the 32 countries providing data for that year to the overall average tax to GDP ratio in 2015.

Nota : Las cifras excluyen los ingresos de gobiernos locales en Argentina (pero incluye ingresos de las provincias), Bahamas, Barbados, Bolivia (previo a 1994), Cuba, República Dominicana, El Salvador (previo a 2002), Honduras, Jamaica (previo a 1998), Nicaragua (previo a 2010), Panamá (previo a 1998), Paraguay (previo a 2004), Perú (previo a 2001) y Venezuela dado que los datos no están disponibles.

1. Los datos incluyen las siguientes estimaciones: Bahamas (contribuciones a la seguridad social para 2016), Belice (contribuciones a la seguridad social para 2016), Ecuador (ingresos tributarios de los gobiernos locales para 2016), Guyana (contribuciones a la seguridad social para 2015 y 2016), Uruguay (ingresos tributarios de los gobiernos locales para 2016) y Venezuela (ingresos tributarios sobre la renta petrolera para 2015 y 2016, y contribuciones a la seguridad social desde 2011). Véanse las tablas de país para mayor información.
2. Los datos estimados incluyen ingresos esperados a nivel estatal y local para el 2016.
3. Representa un grupo de 25 países de América Latina y el Caribe. Para la estimación del promedio se utiliza el año calendario, excepto para Bahamas y Trinidad y Tobago donde se utiliza el año fiscal. Chile y México son también parte del grupo OCDE (35).
4. Calculado aplicando el promedio no ponderado en el cambio porcentual para el 2016 en los 32 países con datos disponibles para ese año en el total de ingreso tributario en porcentaje del PIB en 2015.

StatLink http://dx.doi.org/10.1787/888933686385

Table 4.2. Total tax revenue in millions of USD at market exchange rates, 1990-2016
Cuadro 4.2. Total de ingresos tributarios en millones de US dólares a tipos de cambio de mercado, 1990-2016

	1990	2000	2005	2010	2011	2012	2013	2014	2015	2016
Argentina	20 952	61 084	48 885	123 456	154 594	177 582	190 650	175 336	202 079	170 478
Bahamas[1]	505	965	1 060	1 277	1 487	1 480	1 445	1 490	1 761	1 956
Barbados	471	942	1 148	1 360	1 411	1 435	1 288	1 322	1 473	1 468
Belize / Belice[1]	90	159	248	372	373	393	415	465	475	516
Bolivia	402	1 478	1 910	4 008	5 332	6 644	7 809	8 701	9 165	8 852
Brazil / Brasil	126 210	193 921	292 125	714 794	868 041	800 443	801 521	779 902	576 032	578 460
Chile	5 829	14 647	25 484	42 814	53 265	56 969	55 282	51 099	49 738	50 373
Colombia	5 082	14 497	26 498	51 488	62 892	72 757	75 794	76 412	59 920	56 063
Costa Rica	1 247	3 013	4 113	7 794	9 059	9 968	10 970	10 996	12 086	12 919
Cuba	6 265	11 367	17 528	24 201	26 508	29 068	28 804	30 236	33 591	37 377
Dominican Republic / República Dominicana	666	2 775	4 301	6 631	7 178	7 947	8 512	9 039	9 208	9 785
Ecuador[1]	1 105	1 885	5 029	11 568	14 020	17 379	18 631	19 626	21 165	20 021
El Salvador	506	1 585	2 420	3 298	3 621	3 905	4 222	4 229	4 492	4 795
Guatemala	614	2 129	3 561	5 112	6 087	6 498	7 001	7 439	7 882	8 474
Guyana[1]	134	234	302	550	605	643	685	733	774	814
Honduras	494	1 089	1 638	2 725	2 966	3 267	3 379	3 836	4 219	4 565
Jamaica	1 076	2 054	2 619	3 286	3 531	3 621	3 543	3 426	3 649	3 721
Mexico / México	35 937	85 040	104 410	140 315	155 239	155 437	173 186	184 394	185 955	..
Nicaragua	..	663	1 016	1 699	1 982	2 203	2 332	2 586	2 846	2 985
Panama / Panamá	893	1 953	2 257	4 815	5 666	6 721	7 650	7 740	8 268	9 146
Paraguay	284	1 029	1 203	3 302	4 229	4 353	4 754	5 484	4 963	4 810
Peru / Perú	3 432	7 445	12 308	26 337	31 469	36 534	38 015	38 581	33 150	31 306
Trinidad and Tobago / Trinidad y Tobago	1 184	1 747	4 270	6 076	6 842	7 142	7 477	8 056	7 377	5 318
Uruguay[1]	2 011	4 936	4 153	10 565	12 747	13 790	15 809	15 640	14 407	14 604
Venezuela[1]	8 738	16 027	22 753	34 753	44 921	46 777	33 810	40 058	50 513	34 031

Note: The figures are derived by multiplying the total tax revenue data in the tables from Chapter 4 by the exchange rate data in Table 4.17. The figures exclude local government revenues for Argentina (but include provincial revenues), Bahamas, Barbados, Bolivia (prior to 1994), Cuba, Dominican Republic, El Salvador (prior to 2002), Honduras, Jamaica (prior to 1998), Nicaragua (prior to 2010), Panama (prior to 1998), Paraguay (prior to 2004), Peru (prior to 2001) and Venezuela as the data are not available.

1. The data include the following estimations: Bahamas (social security contributions for 2016), Belize (social security contributions for 2016), Ecuador (local tax revenues for 2016), Guyana (social security contributions in 2015 and 2016), Uruguay (local tax revenues for 2016) and Venezuela (tax revenues from oil profits for 2015 and 2016, and social security contributions from 2011 onward). See the corresponding country tables for more information.

Note : Las cifras se obtienen multiplicando el total de ingresos tributarios en las tablas del Capítulo 4 por los datos de tipo de cambio del Cuadro 4.17. Las cifras excluyen los ingresos de gobiernos locales en Argentina (pero incluye ingresos de las provincias), Bahamas, Barbados, Bolivia (previo a 1994), Cuba, República Dominicana, El Salvador (previo a 2002), Honduras, Jamaica (previo a 1998), Nicaragua (previo a 2010), Panamá (previo a 1998), Paraguay (previo a 2004), Perú (previo a 2001) y Venezuela dado que los datos no están disponibles.

1. Los datos incluyen las siguientes estimaciones: Bahamas (contribuciones a la seguridad social para 2016), Belice (contribuciones a la seguridad social para 2016), Ecuador (ingresos tributarios de los gobiernos locales para 2016), Guyana (contribuciones a la seguridad social para 2015 y 2016), Uruguay (ingresos tributarios de los gobiernos locales para 2016) y Venezuela (ingresos tributarios sobre la renta petrolera para 2015 y 2016, y contribuciones a la seguridad social desde 2011). Véanse las tablas de país para mayor información.

StatLink http://dx.doi.org/10.1787/888933686404

Table 4.3. Tax revenue of main headings as % of GDP, 2016
Cuadro 4.3. Ingresos tributarios en las principales partidas en % del PIB, 2016

	1000 Income & profits / Ingresos y utilidades	2000 Social security / Seguridad social	3000 Payroll / Nómina	4000 Property / Propiedad	5000 Goods and services / Bienes y servicios	6000 Others / Otros
Argentina	5.4	6.9	0.0	2.7	14.6	1.6
Bahamas[1]	0.0	3.2	0.0	1.2	16.9	1.1
Barbados	9.0	3.2	0.0	2.1	17.3	0.6
Belize / Belice[1]	7.6	2.4	0.0	0.8	18.8	0.0
Bolivia	4.7	4.4	0.0	0.2	14.3	2.5
Brazil / Brasil	7.2	8.4	0.9	2.0	12.7	1.0
Chile	6.8	1.5	0.0	1.0	11.1	-0.1
Colombia	6.3	2.5	0.3	2.1	7.3	1.1
Costa Rica	4.5	6.3	1.4	0.4	8.9	0.6
Cuba	8.8	5.2	2.7	0.0	22.5	2.4
Dominican Republic / República Dominicana	4.1	0.0	0.0	0.6	8.9	0.0
Ecuador[1]	4.4	4.8	0.0	0.6	10.5	0.1
El Salvador	6.2	2.0	0.0	0.4	9.0	0.3
Guatemala	3.9	2.1	0.0	0.1	6.3	0.1
Guyana[1]	8.4	2.6	0.0	0.5	11.6	0.2
Honduras	6.0	2.9	0.0	0.5	11.9	0.0
Jamaica	9.0	1.0	0.0	0.4	15.3	0.9
Mexico / México[2]	7.3	2.2	0.4	0.3	6.5	0.1
Nicaragua	6.4	5.6	0.0	0.2	10.1	0.2
Panama / Panamá	4.6	6.1	0.2	0.6	4.9	0.2
Paraguay	2.8	4.5	0.0	0.4	9.8	0.0
Peru / Perú	6.1	2.0	0.0	0.4	7.3	0.2
Trinidad and Tobago / Trinidad y Tobago	11.2	2.9	0.0	0.4	8.1	0.2
Uruguay[1]	6.6	8.9	0.0	2.0	10.4	0.0
Venezuela[1]	3.3	0.2	0.0	0.0	10.8	0.1
Unweighted average / Promedio no ponderado						
LAC / ALC[3]	**6.0**	**3.7**	**0.2**	**0.8**	**11.4**	**0.5**
OECD / OCDE[4]	**11.5**	**9.0**	**0.4**	**1.9**	**10.9**	**0.2**

Note: The figures exclude local government revenues for Argentina (but include provincial revenues), Bahamas, Barbados, Bolivia (prior to 1994), Cuba, Dominican Republic, El Salvador (prior to 2002), Honduras, Jamaica (prior to 1998), Nicaragua (prior to 2010), Panama (prior to 1998), Paraguay (prior to 2004), Peru (prior to 2001) and Venezuela as the data are not available.

1. The data include the following estimations: Bahamas (social security contributions for 2016), Belize (social security contributions for 2016), Ecuador (local tax revenues for 2016), Guyana (social security contributions in 2015 and 2016), Uruguay (local tax revenues for 2016) and Venezuela (tax revenues from oil profits for 2015 and 2016, and social security contributions from 2011 onward). See the corresponding country tables for more information.
2. Data for 2015 are used for 3000 and 4000. Federal government data are used for 5000 and 6000.
3. Represents a group of 25 Latin American and Caribbean countries. Chile and Mexico are also part of the OECD (35) group.
4. Represents the unweighted average for OECD member countries. Data for 2015 are used.

Nota : Las cifras excluyen los ingresos de gobiernos locales en Argentina (pero incluye ingresos de las provincias), Bahamas, Barbados, Bolivia (previo a 1994), Cuba, República Dominicana, El Salvador (previo a 2002), Honduras, Jamaica (previo a 1998), Nicaragua (previo a 2010), Panamá (previo a 1998), Paraguay (previo a 2004), Perú (previo a 2001) y Venezuela dado que los datos no están disponibles.

1. Los datos incluyen las siguientes estimaciones: Bahamas (contribuciones a la seguridad social para 2016), Belice (contribuciones a la seguridad social para 2016), Ecuador (ingresos tributarios de los gobiernos locales para 2016), Guyana (contribuciones a la seguridad social para 2015 y 2016), Uruguay (ingresos tributarios de los gobiernos locales para 2016) y Venezuela (ingresos tributarios sobre la renta petrolera para 2015 y 2016, y contribuciones a la seguridad social desde 2011). Véanse las tablas de país para mayor información.
2. Se utilizan los datos de 2015 en 3000 y 4000. Datos del nivel federal se utilizan para 5000 y 6000.
3. Representa un grupo de 25 países de América Latina y el Caribe. Chile y México son también parte del grupo OCDE (35).
4. Representa el promedio no ponderado para los países miembros de la OCDE. Se utilizan los datos de 2015.

StatLink http://dx.doi.org/10.1787/888933686423

Table 4.4. Tax revenue of main headings as % of total tax revenue, 2016
Cuadro 4.4. Ingresos tributarios en las principales partidas en % del total de ingresos tributarios, 2016

	1000 Income & profits / Ingresos y utilidades	2000 Social security / Seguridad social	3000 Payroll / Nómina	4000 Property / Propiedad	5000 Goods and services / Bienes y servicios	6000 Others / Otros
Argentina	17.3	22.1	0.0	8.7	46.7	5.2
Bahamas[1]	0.0	14.3	0.0	5.3	75.3	5.1
Barbados	28.0	9.8	0.0	6.5	53.7	2.0
Belize / Belice[1]	25.6	8.0	0.0	2.9	63.5	0.0
Bolivia	17.9	16.9	0.0	0.7	55.0	9.5
Brazil / Brasil	22.5	26.0	2.7	6.4	39.4	3.1
Chile	33.6	7.2	0.0	5.0	54.6	-0.3
Colombia	31.9	12.7	1.8	10.7	37.2	5.7
Costa Rica	20.4	28.5	6.3	1.9	40.2	2.7
Cuba	21.2	12.6	6.5	0.0	53.9	5.8
Dominican Republic / República Dominicana	29.9	0.3	0.0	4.4	65.3	0.0
Ecuador[1]	21.6	23.7	0.0	2.9	51.3	0.5
El Salvador	34.6	11.2	0.0	2.2	50.1	1.9
Guatemala	31.4	16.7	0.0	0.9	50.5	0.6
Guyana[1]	36.2	11.0	0.0	2.0	50.0	0.8
Honduras	28.2	13.7	0.0	2.3	55.8	0.0
Jamaica	33.9	3.8	0.0	1.5	57.5	3.3
Mexico / México[2]	41.7	13.9	2.4	2.0	38.6	1.5
Nicaragua	28.4	24.9	0.0	0.7	44.9	1.0
Panama / Panamá	27.5	37.0	1.2	3.6	29.6	1.1
Paraguay	16.2	25.8	0.0	2.1	55.8	0.1
Peru / Perú	38.2	12.5	0.0	2.5	45.6	1.2
Trinidad and Tobago / Trinidad y Tobago	49.1	12.7	0.0	1.6	35.5	1.0
Uruguay[1]	23.6	32.0	0.0	7.0	37.3	0.1
Venezuela[1]	22.8	1.3	0.0	0.3	74.8	0.8
Unweighted average / Promedio no ponderado						
LAC / ALC[3]	**27.3**	**15.9**	**0.8**	**3.4**	**50.5**	**2.1**
OECD / OCDE[4]	**34.1**	**25.8**	**1.1**	**5.8**	**32.4**	**0.5**

Note: The figures exclude local government revenues for Argentina (but include provincial revenues), Bahamas, Barbados, Bolivia (prior to 1994), Cuba, Dominican Republic, El Salvador (prior to 2002), Honduras, Jamaica (prior to 1998), Nicaragua (prior to 2010), Panama (prior to 1998), Paraguay (prior to 2004), Peru (prior to 2001) and Venezuela as the data are not available.

1. The data include the following estimations: Bahamas (social security contributions for 2016), Belize (social security contributions for 2016), Ecuador (local tax revenues for 2016), Guyana (social security contributions in 2015 and 2016), Uruguay (local tax revenues for 2016) and Venezuela (tax revenues from oil profits for 2015 and 2016, and social security contributions from 2011 onward). See the corresponding country tables for more information.
2. Data for 2015 are used as the state and local government revenue data for 2016 are not available.
3. Represents a group of 25 Latin American and Caribbean countries. Chile and Mexico are also part of the OECD (35) group.
4. Represents the unweighted average for OECD member countries. Data for 2015 are used.

Nota : Las cifras excluyen los ingresos de gobiernos locales en Argentina (pero incluye ingresos de las provincias), Bahamas, Barbados, Bolivia (previo a 1994), Cuba, República Dominicana, El Salvador (previo a 2002), Honduras, Jamaica (previo a 1998), Nicaragua (previo a 2010), Panamá (previo a 1998), Paraguay (previo a 2004), Perú (previo a 2001) y Venezuela dado que los datos no están disponibles.

1. Los datos incluyen las siguientes estimaciones: Bahamas (contribuciones a la seguridad social para 2016), Belice (contribuciones a la seguridad social para 2016), Ecuador (ingresos tributarios de los gobiernos locales para 2016), Guyana (contribuciones a la seguridad social para 2015 y 2016), Uruguay (ingresos tributarios de los gobiernos locales para 2016) y Venezuela (ingresos tributarios sobre la renta petrolera para 2015 y 2016, y contribuciones a la seguridad social desde 2011). Véanse las tablas de país para mayor información.
2. Se utilizan los datos de 2015 ya que los datos de ingresos del gobierno estatal y local para 2016 no están disponibles.
3. Representa un grupo de 25 países de América Latina y el Caribe. Chile y México son también parte del grupo OCDE (35).
4. Representa el promedio no ponderado para los países miembros de la OCDE. Se utilizan los datos de 2015.

StatLink http://dx.doi.org/10.1787/888933686442

Table 4.5. Taxes on income and profits (1000) as % of GDP and as % of total tax revenue
Cuadro 4.5. Impuestos sobre la renta y las utilidades (1000) en % del PIB y del total de ingresos tributarios

	% of GDP / % del PIB					% of total tax revenue / % del total de ingresos tributarios				
	1990	2000	2010	2015	2016	1990	2000	2010	2015	2016
Argentina	0.7	3.7	4.7	6.6	5.4	5.3	18.5	16.2	20.5	17.3
Bahamas	0.0	0.0	0.0	0.0	0.0	0.0	0.0	0.0	0.0	0.0
Barbados	6.2	9.2	8.6	8.2	9.0	27.0	30.5	28.0	24.6	28.0
Belize / Belice	4.5	4.6	8.9	7.3	7.6	20.8	23.9	33.4	26.8	25.6
Bolivia	0.4	2.3	4.6	5.6	4.7	5.3	13.2	22.5	20.4	17.9
Brazil / Brasil	4.6	5.7	6.7	6.7	7.2	18.1	19.4	20.6	20.9	22.5
Chile	3.9	4.4	7.5	7.5	6.8	23.2	23.3	38.1	36.4	33.6
Colombia	3.2	3.4	4.8	6.6	6.3	29.9	23.3	26.8	31.7	31.9
Costa Rica	2.2	2.6	3.8	4.4	4.5	10.4	13.9	18.4	19.5	20.4
Cuba	0.1	6.0	5.6	7.7	8.8	0.2	16.1	14.9	19.9	21.2
Dominican Republic / República Dominicana	2.0	2.6	2.7	3.9	4.1	25.9	24.0	22.0	28.9	29.9
Ecuador	0.9	1.6	3.4	4.7	4.4	12.4	15.6	20.3	22.2	21.6
El Salvador	2.0	3.1	4.6	5.9	6.2	18.9	25.7	30.2	34.4	34.6
Guatemala	1.6	2.5	3.1	3.6	3.9	18.4	19.9	25.1	29.1	31.4
Guyana	6.9	7.9	8.5	8.3	8.4	33.5	37.8	35.4	34.4	36.2
Honduras	3.4	2.7	4.4	5.4	6.0	21.2	17.8	25.5	26.6	28.2
Jamaica	11.7	10.1	10.3	9.0	9.0	50.9	44.8	41.3	35.1	33.9
Mexico / México[1]	4.2	4.5	5.2	6.8	7.3	34.0	34.4	38.6	41.7	41.7
Nicaragua	..	1.8	4.5	6.0	6.4	..	13.6	23.0	26.8	28.4
Panama / Panamá	3.9	3.9	4.6	4.1	4.6	24.3	24.8	27.4	26.1	27.5
Paraguay	1.2	1.6	2.2	2.7	2.8	21.1	13.1	13.4	15.2	16.2
Peru / Perú	0.7	2.9	6.5	6.2	6.1	5.7	19.5	36.7	35.8	38.2
Trinidad and Tobago / Trinidad y Tobago	12.0	11.8	18.6	19.3	11.2	51.6	55.1	67.6	63.2	49.1
Uruguay	0.9	2.0	5.5	5.9	6.6	4.8	9.4	20.8	21.9	23.6
Venezuela[2]	15.1	5.9	3.6	4.7	3.3	83.7	43.2	30.7	22.7	22.8
Unweighted average / Promedio no ponderado										
LAC / ALC[3]	**3.9**	**4.3**	**5.7**	**6.3**	**6.0**	**22.8**	**23.2**	**27.1**	**27.4**	**27.3**
OECD / OCDE[4]	**12.2**	**12.0**	**10.8**	**11.5**	..	**37.5**	**35.0**	**33.2**	**34.1**	..

Note: The figures exclude local government revenues for Argentina (but include provincial revenues), Bahamas, Barbados, Bolivia (prior to 1994), Cuba, Dominican Republic, El Salvador (prior to 2002), Honduras, Jamaica (prior to 1998), Nicaragua (prior to 2010), Panama (prior to 1998), Paraguay (prior to 2004), Peru (prior to 2001) and Venezuela as the data are not available.

1. Data for 2015 are used in 2016 for the figure in % of total tax revenue as the state and local government revenue data for 2016 are not available.
2. The data include the following estimations: Venezuela for tax revenues from oil profits for 2015 and 2016. See Table 5.25 for more information.
3. Represents a group of 25 Latin American and Caribbean countries. Chile and Mexico are also part of the OECD (35) group.
4. Represents the unweighted average for OECD member countries.

Nota : Las cifras excluyen los ingresos de gobiernos locales en Argentina (pero incluye ingresos de las provincias), Bahamas, Barbados, Bolivia (previo a 1994), Cuba, República Dominicana, El Salvador (previo a 2002), Honduras, Jamaica (previo a 1998), Nicaragua (previo a 2010), Panamá (previo a 1998), Paraguay (previo a 2004), Perú (previo a 2001) y Venezuela dado que los datos no están disponibles.

1. Se utilizan los datos de 2015 en 2016 para la cifra en % del total de ingresos tributarios ya que los datos de ingresos del gobierno estatal y local para 2016 no están disponibles.
2. Los datos incluyen las siguientes estimaciones: Venezuela por los ingresos tributarios sobre la renta petrolera para 2015 y 2016. Véanse el Cuadro 5.25 para mayor información.
3. Representa un grupo de 25 países de América Latina y el Caribe. Chile y México son también parte del grupo OCDE (35).
4. Representa el promedio no ponderado para los países miembros de la OCDE.

StatLink http://dx.doi.org/10.1787/888933686461

Table 4.6. Social security contributions (2000) as % of GDP and as % of total tax revenue
Cuadro 4.6. Contribuciones a la seguridad social (2000) en % del PIB y del total de ingresos tributarios

	% of GDP / % del PIB					% of total tax revenue / % del total de ingresos tributarios				
	1990	2000	2010	2015	2016	1990	2000	2010	2015	2016
Argentina	3.5	3.1	6.2	7.1	6.9	25.3	15.8	21.2	22.2	22.1
Bahamas[1]	1.6	1.8	2.1	2.9	3.2	13.2	11.9	13.1	14.8	14.3
Barbados	3.3	4.7	5.9	6.3	3.2	14.2	15.7	19.3	18.8	9.8
Belize / Belice[1]	1.2	1.1	2.2	2.2	2.4	5.7	5.8	8.1	8.1	8.0
Bolivia[2]	0.0	1.3	1.2	4.3	4.4	0.0	7.3	5.9	15.7	16.9
Brazil / Brasil	6.1	7.0	8.1	8.3	8.4	24.0	23.5	25.0	25.9	26.0
Chile	1.5	1.4	1.3	1.4	1.5	9.0	7.3	6.8	6.9	7.2
Colombia	0.8	2.4	2.1	2.5	2.5	7.9	16.4	11.7	12.1	12.7
Costa Rica	5.7	4.9	5.8	6.3	6.3	26.8	26.9	28.1	28.0	28.5
Cuba	3.2	3.9	4.6	5.0	5.2	11.0	10.4	12.3	12.9	12.6
Dominican Republic / República Dominicana	0.1	0.1	0.1	0.0	0.0	0.8	1.1	0.8	0.4	0.3
Ecuador	1.6	1.2	3.7	5.0	4.8	21.9	12.1	22.0	23.9	23.7
El Salvador	1.4	2.0	1.7	1.9	2.0	13.3	16.6	11.2	10.9	11.2
Guatemala	1.4	1.9	1.9	2.1	2.1	15.8	15.5	15.6	16.6	16.7
Guyana[1]	0.8	2.4	2.2	2.5	2.6	3.7	11.4	9.0	10.4	11.0
Honduras	1.4	1.6	2.9	3.0	2.9	8.8	10.6	16.7	14.5	13.7
Jamaica	0.0	0.0	0.7	1.0	1.0	0.0	0.0	2.9	3.8	3.8
Mexico / México[3]	2.1	2.3	2.1	2.2	2.2	16.8	17.2	15.7	13.9	13.9
Nicaragua	..	2.6	4.3	5.2	5.6	..	20.0	22.3	23.5	24.9
Panama / Panamá	4.8	6.0	5.7	5.8	6.1	30.4	38.0	34.0	36.9	37.0
Paraguay	0.5	3.2	3.7	4.9	4.5	8.3	25.6	22.7	27.3	25.8
Peru / Perú	0.9	1.8	1.9	2.1	2.0	7.7	12.2	10.7	12.0	12.5
Trinidad and Tobago / Trinidad y Tobago	0.9	1.4	1.9	2.8	2.9	3.6	6.4	6.8	9.3	12.7
Uruguay	6.0	6.4	6.2	7.5	8.9	30.5	29.6	23.5	27.6	32.0
Venezuela[1]	0.9	0.7	1.0	0.6	0.2	4.9	5.4	8.1	3.0	1.3
Unweighted average / Promedio no ponderado										
LAC / ALC[4]	**2.1**	**2.6**	**3.2**	**3.7**	**3.7**	**12.7**	**14.5**	**14.9**	**16.0**	**15.9**
OECD / OCDE[5]	**7.4**	**8.6**	**8.8**	**9.0**	..	**22.0**	**24.7**	**26.4**	**25.8**	..

Note: The figures exclude local government revenues for Argentina (but include provincial revenues), Bahamas, Barbados, Bolivia (prior to 1994), Cuba, Dominican Republic, El Salvador (prior to 2002), Honduras, Jamaica (prior to 1998), Nicaragua (prior to 2010), Panama (prior to 1998), Paraguay (prior to 2004), Peru (prior to 2001) and Venezuela as the data are not available.

1. The data are estimated in the following countries: Bahamas (2016), Belize (2016), Guyana (2015 and 2016) and Venezuela (from 2011 onward).
2. Figures for 1990-98 are estimated by the Direction General of Taxes as the methodology they use to calculate social security contributions was not employed until 1999.
3. Data for 2015 are used in 2016 for the figure in % of total tax revenue as the state and local government revenue data for 2016 are not available.
4. Represents a group of 25 Latin American and Caribbean countries. Chile and Mexico are also part of the OECD (35) group.
5. Represents the unweighted average for OECD member countries.

Nota : Las cifras excluyen los ingresos de gobiernos locales en Argentina (pero incluye ingresos de las provincias), Bahamas, Barbados, Bolivia (previo a 1994), Cuba, República Dominicana, El Salvador (previo a 2002), Honduras, Jamaica (previo a 1998), Nicaragua (previo a 2010), Panamá (previo a 1998), Paraguay (previo a 2004), Perú (previo a 2001) y Venezuela dado que los datos no están disponibles.

1. Los datos son estimados en los siguientes países: Bahamas (2016), Belice (2016), Guyana (2015 y 2016) y Venezuela (desde 2011 en adelante).
2. Las cifras de 1990-98 son estimaciones por la Dirección General de Impuestos dado que el empleo de la metodología actual utilizada para calcular las contribuciones a la seguridad social tuvo lugar en 1999.
3. Se utilizan los datos de 2015 en 2016 para la cifra en % del total de ingresos tributarios ya que los datos de ingresos del gobierno estatal y local para 2016 no están disponibles.
4. Representa un grupo de 25 países de América Latina y el Caribe. Chile y México son también parte del grupo OCDE (35).
5. Representa el promedio no ponderado para los países miembros de la OCDE.

StatLink http://dx.doi.org/10.1787/888933686480

Table 4.7. Taxes on payroll (3000) as % of GDP and as % of total tax revenue
Cuadro 4.7. Impuestos sobre la nómina (3000) en % del PIB y del total ingresos tributarios

	% of GDP / % del PIB					% of total tax revenue / % del total de ingresos tributarios				
	1990	2000	2010	2015	2016	1990	2000	2010	2015	2016
Argentina	0.0	0.0	0.0	0.0	0.0	0.0	0.0	0.0	0.0	0.0
Bahamas	0.0	0.0	0.0	0.0	0.0	0.0	0.0	0.0	0.0	0.0
Barbados	0.0	0.0	0.0	0.0	0.0	0.0	0.0	0.0	0.0	0.0
Belize / Belice	0.0	0.0	0.0	0.0	0.0	0.0	0.0	0.0	0.0	0.0
Bolivia	0.0	0.0	0.0	0.0	0.0	0.0	0.0	0.0	0.0	0.0
Brazil / Brasil	0.4	0.6	0.9	0.8	0.9	1.5	1.9	2.6	2.6	2.7
Chile	0.0	0.0	0.0	0.0	0.0	0.0	0.0	0.0	0.0	0.0
Colombia	0.0	0.6	0.7	0.4	0.3	0.0	4.2	4.1	1.7	1.8
Costa Rica	1.4	1.2	1.3	1.4	1.4	6.6	6.4	6.1	6.4	6.3
Cuba	0.0	3.2	6.9	3.2	2.7	0.0	8.5	18.2	8.2	6.5
Dominican Republic / República Dominicana	0.0	0.0	0.0	0.0	0.0	0.0	0.0	0.0	0.0	0.0
Ecuador	0.0	0.0	0.0	0.0	0.0	0.0	0.0	0.0	0.0	0.0
El Salvador	0.0	0.0	0.0	0.0	0.0	0.0	0.0	0.0	0.0	0.0
Guatemala	0.0	0.0	0.0	0.0	0.0	0.0	0.0	0.0	0.0	0.0
Guyana	0.0	0.0	0.0	0.0	0.0	0.0	0.0	0.0	0.0	0.0
Honduras	0.0	0.0	0.0	0.0	0.0	0.0	0.0	0.0	0.0	0.0
Jamaica	0.0	0.0	0.0	0.0	0.0	0.0	0.0	0.0	0.0	0.0
Mexico / México[1]	0.2	0.2	0.3	0.4	0.4	1.8	1.4	2.1	2.4	2.4
Nicaragua	..	0.0	0.0	0.0	0.0	..	0.0	0.0	0.0	0.0
Panama / Panamá	0.0	0.3	0.2	0.2	0.2	0.0	1.9	1.2	1.3	1.2
Paraguay	0.0	0.0	0.0	0.0	0.0	0.0	0.0	0.0	0.0	0.0
Peru / Perú	0.0	0.6	0.0	0.0	0.0	0.0	4.4	0.0	0.0	0.0
Trinidad and Tobago / Trinidad y Tobago	0.0	0.0	0.0	0.0	0.0	0.0	0.0	0.0	0.0	0.0
Uruguay	0.0	0.0	0.0	0.0	0.0	0.0	0.0	0.0	0.0	0.0
Venezuela	0.0	0.0	0.0	0.0	0.0	0.0	0.0	0.0	0.0	0.0
Unweighted average / Promedio no ponderado										
LAC / ALC[2]	**0.1**	**0.3**	**0.4**	**0.3**	**0.2**	**0.4**	**1.1**	**1.4**	**0.9**	**0.8**
OECD / OCDE[3]	**0.3**	**0.4**	**0.3**	**0.4**	..	**1.0**	**1.0**	**1.0**	**1.1**	..

Note: The figures exclude local government revenues for Argentina (but include provincial revenues), Bahamas, Barbados, Bolivia (prior to 1994), Cuba, Dominican Republic, El Salvador (prior to 2002), Honduras, Jamaica (prior to 1998), Nicaragua (prior to 2010), Panama (prior to 1998), Paraguay (prior to 2004), Peru (prior to 2001) and Venezuela as the data are not available.

1. Data for 2015 are used in 2016 as the state and local government revenue data for 2016 are not available.
2. Represents a group of 25 Latin American and Caribbean countries. Chile and Mexico are also part of the OECD (35) group.
3. Represents the unweighted average for OECD member countries.

Nota : Las cifras excluyen los ingresos de gobiernos locales en Argentina (pero incluye ingresos de las provincias), Bahamas, Barbados, Bolivia (previo a 1994), Cuba, República Dominicana, El Salvador (previo a 2002), Honduras, Jamaica (previo a 1998), Nicaragua (previo a 2010), Panamá (previo a 1998), Paraguay (previo a 2004), Perú (previo a 2001) y Venezuela dado que los datos no están disponibles.

1. Se utilizan los datos de 2015 en 2016 ya que los datos de ingresos del gobierno estatal y local para 2016 no están disponibles.
2. Representa un grupo de 25 países de América Latina y el Caribe. Chile y México son también parte del grupo OCDE (35).
3. Representa el promedio no ponderado para los países miembros de la OCDE.

StatLink http://dx.doi.org/10.1787/888933686499

Table 4.8. Taxes on property (4000) as % of GDP and as % of total tax revenue
Cuadro 4.8. Impuestos sobre la propiedad (4000) en % del PIB y del total de ingresos tributarios

	% of GDP / % del PIB					% of total tax revenue / % del total de ingresos tributarios				
	1990	2000	2010	2015	2016	1990	2000	2010	2015	2016
Argentina	1.6	1.3	2.6	2.8	2.7	11.4	6.3	9.0	8.9	8.7
Bahamas	0.5	0.5	1.2	1.2	1.2	3.8	3.3	7.2	6.1	5.3
Barbados	1.0	1.5	1.3	2.1	2.1	4.2	4.9	4.2	6.4	6.5
Belize / Belice	0.8	0.8	0.8	1.0	0.8	3.5	4.2	3.0	3.7	2.9
Bolivia	0.0	0.0	0.3	0.2	0.2	0.1	0.0	1.3	0.7	0.7
Brazil / Brasil	1.7	2.4	1.9	2.0	2.0	6.5	8.1	5.9	6.3	6.4
Chile	1.0	1.3	0.8	0.9	1.0	6.2	7.0	4.1	4.4	5.0
Colombia	0.2	1.0	1.6	2.3	2.1	2.2	6.6	8.7	11.0	10.7
Costa Rica	0.3	0.2	0.3	0.4	0.4	1.4	0.9	1.6	1.9	1.9
Cuba	0.0	0.0	0.0	0.0	0.0	0.0	0.0	0.0	0.0	0.0
Dominican Republic / República Dominicana	0.1	0.2	0.7	0.6	0.6	1.2	1.5	5.5	4.6	4.4
Ecuador	0.1	0.1	0.1	0.2	0.6	1.2	0.6	0.7	1.1	2.9
El Salvador	0.5	0.1	0.1	0.4	0.4	5.1	0.7	0.5	2.4	2.2
Guatemala	0.0	0.1	0.2	0.1	0.1	0.0	1.0	1.5	1.2	0.9
Guyana	0.2	0.3	0.3	0.5	0.5	1.0	1.6	1.4	2.0	2.0
Honduras	0.1	0.2	0.3	0.6	0.5	0.8	1.6	1.9	2.8	2.3
Jamaica	0.2	0.2	0.2	0.4	0.4	0.9	0.7	0.9	1.7	1.5
Mexico / México[1]	0.2	0.2	0.3	0.3	0.3	1.9	1.7	2.2	2.0	2.0
Nicaragua	..	0.0	0.1	0.1	0.2	..	-0.1	0.4	0.7	0.7
Panama / Panamá	0.8	0.5	0.7	0.6	0.6	4.9	3.2	4.4	3.9	3.6
Paraguay	0.3	0.0	0.3	0.3	0.4	4.9	0.0	1.7	1.7	2.1
Peru / Perú	1.9	0.0	0.5	0.4	0.4	15.3	0.0	3.0	2.3	2.5
Trinidad and Tobago / Trinidad y Tobago	0.7	0.5	0.3	0.2	0.4	3.0	2.5	1.1	0.7	1.6
Uruguay	1.6	2.2	2.4	2.1	2.0	8.4	10.3	9.1	7.7	7.0
Venezuela	0.1	0.5	0.0	0.0	0.0	0.3	3.7	0.2	0.2	0.3
Unweighted average / Promedio no ponderado										
LAC / ALC[2]	**0.6**	**0.6**	**0.7**	**0.8**	**0.8**	**3.7**	**2.8**	**3.2**	**3.4**	**3.4**
OECD / OCDE[3]	**1.8**	**1.8**	**1.7**	**1.9**	..	**5.7**	**5.5**	**5.5**	**5.8**	..

Note: The figures exclude local government revenues for Argentina (but include provincial revenues), Bahamas, Barbados, Bolivia (prior to 1994), Cuba, Dominican Republic, El Salvador (prior to 2002), Honduras, Jamaica (prior to 1998), Nicaragua (prior to 2010), Panama (prior to 1998), Paraguay (prior to 2004), Peru (prior to 2001) and Venezuela as the data are not available.

1. Data for 2015 are used in 2016 as the state and local government revenue data for 2016 are not available.
2. Represents a group of 25 Latin American and Caribbean countries. Chile and Mexico are also part of the OECD (35) group.
3. Represents the unweighted average for OECD member countries.

Nota : Las cifras excluyen los ingresos de gobiernos locales en Argentina (pero incluye ingresos de las provincias), Bahamas, Barbados, Bolivia (previo a 1994), Cuba, República Dominicana, El Salvador (previo a 2002), Honduras, Jamaica (previo a 1998), Nicaragua (previo a 2010), Panamá (previo a 1998), Paraguay (previo a 2004), Perú (previo a 2001) y Venezuela dado que los datos no están disponibles.

1. Se utilizan los datos de 2015 en 2016 ya que los datos de ingresos del gobierno estatal y local para 2016 no están disponibles.
2. Representa un grupo de 25 países de América Latina y el Caribe. Chile y México son también parte del grupo OCDE (35).
3. Representa el promedio no ponderado para los países miembros de la OCDE.

StatLink http://dx.doi.org/10.1787/888933686518

Table 4.9. Taxes on goods and services (5000) as % of GDP and as % of total tax revenue
Cuadro 4.9. Impuestos sobre bienes y servicios (5000) en % del PIB y del total de ingresos tributarios

	% of GDP / % del PIB					% of total tax revenue / % del total de ingresos tributarios				
	1990	2000	2010	2015	2016	1990	2000	2010	2015	2016
Argentina	7.5	11.2	15.2	15.2	14.6	55.2	56.5	52.4	47.5	46.7
Bahamas	9.4	11.4	10.0	13.6	16.9	76.4	74.9	62.3	68.3	75.3
Barbados	8.2	14.4	14.0	16.8	17.3	35.2	47.6	45.7	50.0	53.7
Belize / Belice	15.3	12.7	14.8	16.7	18.8	70.0	66.1	55.5	61.4	63.5
Bolivia	6.7	12.7	12.8	15.2	14.3	80.8	72.0	63.3	55.2	55.0
Brazil / Brasil	12.2	13.7	14.0	13.2	12.7	47.7	46.3	43.1	41.4	39.4
Chile	10.6	12.0	10.0	11.1	11.1	62.9	63.8	51.2	54.1	54.6
Colombia	5.7	6.4	7.7	7.8	7.3	53.8	43.8	43.0	37.6	37.2
Costa Rica	10.0	9.1	9.0	9.4	8.9	46.9	49.3	43.5	41.7	40.2
Cuba	25.3	22.0	19.1	20.4	22.5	86.9	59.2	50.8	52.8	53.9
Dominican Republic / República Dominicana	5.4	7.8	8.8	8.9	8.9	69.6	72.3	71.8	66.1	65.3
Ecuador	4.5	7.4	9.1	11.1	10.5	61.7	71.6	54.4	52.6	51.3
El Salvador	5.4	6.9	8.7	8.7	9.0	51.3	57.0	56.2	50.4	50.1
Guatemala	5.5	7.7	7.0	6.5	6.3	62.0	62.4	56.5	52.6	50.5
Guyana	8.7	10.1	12.8	12.7	11.6	42.0	48.6	53.0	52.5	50.0
Honduras	11.2	10.7	9.7	11.4	11.9	69.1	70.0	55.8	56.0	55.8
Jamaica	8.4	11.3	13.0	14.5	15.3	36.4	50.1	52.1	56.3	57.5
Mexico / México[1]	5.4	5.8	5.3	6.3	6.5	44.0	44.3	39.9	38.6	38.6
Nicaragua	..	8.6	10.2	10.5	10.1	..	66.4	52.4	47.1	44.9
Panama / Panamá	6.0	4.7	5.2	4.9	4.9	37.6	29.4	31.4	30.7	29.6
Paraguay	3.0	7.3	10.0	10.0	9.8	51.4	58.0	60.5	55.8	55.8
Peru / Perú	7.9	9.0	8.7	8.3	7.3	65.6	61.4	48.8	48.4	45.6
Trinidad and Tobago / Trinidad y Tobago	9.5	7.5	6.6	7.9	8.1	40.8	35.0	24.1	26.0	35.5
Uruguay	11.1	11.2	12.2	11.5	10.4	56.7	51.7	46.7	42.6	37.3
Venezuela	2.0	6.5	7.2	15.2	10.8	11.1	47.7	61.1	72.8	74.8
Unweighted average / Promedio no ponderado										
LAC / ALC[2]	**8.5**	**9.9**	**10.4**	**11.5**	**11.4**	**54.8**	**56.2**	**51.0**	**50.3**	**50.5**
OECD / OCDE[3]	**10.0**	**10.9**	**10.6**	**10.9**	..	**32.5**	**33.0**	**33.0**	**32.4**	..

Note: The figures exclude local government revenues for Argentina (but include provincial revenues), Bahamas, Barbados, Bolivia (prior to 1994), Cuba, Dominican Republic, El Salvador (prior to 2002), Honduras, Jamaica (prior to 1998), Nicaragua (prior to 2010), Panama (prior to 1998), Paraguay (prior to 2004), Peru (prior to 2001) and Venezuela as the data are not available.

1. In 2016, federal government data are used for the figure as % of GDP. Data for 2015 are used in 2016 for the figure in % of total tax revenue as the state and local government revenue data for 2016 are not available.
2. Represents a group of 25 Latin American and Caribbean countries. Chile and Mexico are also part of the OECD (35) group.
3. Represents the unweighted average for OECD member countries.

Nota : Las cifras excluyen los ingresos de gobiernos locales en Argentina (pero incluye ingresos de las provincias), Bahamas, Barbados, Bolivia (previo a 1994), Cuba, República Dominicana, El Salvador (previo a 2002), Honduras, Jamaica (previo a 1998), Nicaragua (previo a 2010), Panamá (previo a 1998), Paraguay (previo a 2004), Perú (previo a 2001) y Venezuela dado que los datos no están disponibles.

1. En 2016, para la cifra como porcentaje del PIB se utilizan datos del gobierno federal. Se utilizan los datos de 2015 en 2016 para la cifra en % del total de ingresos tributarios ya que los datos de ingresos del gobierno estatal y local para 2016 no están disponibles.
2. Representa un grupo de 25 países de América Latina y el Caribe. Chile y México son también parte del grupo OCDE (35).
3. Representa el promedio no ponderado para los países miembros de la OCDE.

StatLink http://dx.doi.org/10.1787/888933686537

Table 4.10. Value added taxes (5111) as % of GDP and as % of total tax revenue
Cuadro 4.10. Impuesto al valor agregado (5111) en % del PIB y del total de ingresos tributarios

	% of GDP / % del PIB					% of total tax revenue / % del total de ingresos tributarios				
	1990	2000	2010	2015	2016	1990	2000	2010	2015	2016
Argentina	2.1	6.2	7.0	7.4	7.2	15.6	31.1	24.1	23.1	23.1
Bahamas	0.0	0.0	0.0	2.5	7.2	0.0	0.0	0.0	12.4	32.1
Barbados	0.0	8.0	8.5	10.5	10.4	0.0	26.6	27.7	31.4	32.3
Belize / Belice	0.0	0.0	7.1	7.9	8.5	0.0	0.0	26.8	29.0	28.7
Bolivia	3.6	5.7	7.4	9.1	8.5	43.2	32.2	36.7	33.0	32.8
Brazil / Brasil	9.4	8.4	7.6	7.2	7.1	36.9	28.5	23.3	22.5	22.0
Chile	6.3	7.9	7.5	8.4	8.4	37.4	41.8	38.5	40.8	41.3
Colombia	2.4	4.1	5.3	5.2	4.9	22.6	27.7	29.4	25.0	24.6
Costa Rica	4.0	4.4	4.7	4.7	4.5	18.7	24.0	22.7	20.9	20.3
Cuba	0.0	0.0	0.0	0.0	0.0	0.0	0.0	0.0	0.0	0.0
Dominican Republic / República Dominicana	1.2	2.4	4.1	4.8	4.8	15.1	22.1	33.3	35.5	35.4
Ecuador	2.0	4.6	5.6	6.3	6.2	27.3	44.4	33.6	30.0	30.2
El Salvador	0.0	5.4	6.7	6.8	6.8	0.0	45.1	43.4	39.3	37.8
Guatemala	2.4	4.7	5.1	4.8	4.6	27.6	37.9	41.2	38.6	36.9
Guyana	0.0	0.0	5.8	5.4	5.0	0.0	0.0	24.2	22.1	21.4
Honduras	2.7	4.8	5.4	7.1	7.4	16.9	31.5	31.0	34.6	34.8
Jamaica	0.9	5.8	7.1	8.1	8.3	3.8	25.5	28.7	31.7	31.2
Mexico / México[1]	3.2	3.1	3.8	3.9	4.1	26.1	23.6	28.5	23.9	23.9
Nicaragua	..	4.5	5.5	6.0	6.0	..	34.9	28.5	26.7	26.7
Panama / Panamá	1.4	0.6	2.6	2.6	2.7	9.0	3.5	15.9	16.4	16.6
Paraguay	..	4.0	6.3	6.8	6.7	..	32.1	38.3	37.8	38.4
Peru / Perú	1.5	5.4	7.0	7.0	6.0	12.1	37.1	39.1	40.3	37.3
Trinidad and Tobago / Trinidad y Tobago	4.3	3.7	4.3	4.8	4.8	18.4	17.2	15.5	15.7	21.0
Uruguay	5.5	6.5	8.6	7.8	7.8	28.0	30.1	32.7	28.9	28.0
Venezuela	..	4.1	5.5	11.7	8.0	..	30.2	46.7	56.0	55.8
Unweighted average / Promedio no ponderado										
LAC / ALC[2]	**2.4**	**4.2**	**5.5**	**6.3**	**6.2**	**16.3**	**25.1**	**28.4**	**28.6**	**29.3**
OECD / OCDE[3]	**5.2**	**6.4**	**6.4**	**6.7**	..	**16.7**	**19.2**	**20.0**	**20.0**	..

Note: The figures exclude local government revenues for Argentina (but include provincial revenues), Bahamas, Barbados, Bolivia (prior to 1994), Cuba, Dominican Republic, El Salvador (prior to 2002), Honduras, Jamaica (prior to 1998), Nicaragua (prior to 2010), Panama (prior to 1998), Paraguay (prior to 2004), Peru (prior to 2001) and Venezuela as the data are not available.

1. Data for 2015 are used in 2016 for the figure in % of total tax revenue as the state and local government revenue data for 2016 are not available.
2. Represents a group of 25 Latin American and Caribbean countries. Chile and Mexico are also part of the OECD (35) group.
3. Represents the unweighted average for OECD member countries.

Nota : Las cifras excluyen los ingresos de gobiernos locales en Argentina (pero incluye ingresos de las provincias), Bahamas, Barbados, Bolivia (previo a 1994), Cuba, República Dominicana, El Salvador (previo a 2002), Honduras, Jamaica (previo a 1998), Nicaragua (previo a 2010), Panamá (previo a 1998), Paraguay (previo a 2004), Perú (previo a 2001) y Venezuela dado que los datos no están disponibles.

1. Se utilizan los datos de 2015 en 2016 para la cifra en % del total de ingresos tributarios ya que los datos de ingresos del gobierno estatal y local para 2016 no están disponibles.
2. Representa un grupo de 25 países de América Latina y el Caribe. Chile y México son también parte del grupo OCDE (35).
3. Representa el promedio no ponderado para los países miembros de la OCDE.

StatLink http://dx.doi.org/10.1787/888933686556

Table 4.11. Tax revenues of sub-sectors of general government as % of total tax revenue
Cuadro 4.11. Ingresos tributarios por subsector del gobierno general, en % del total de ingresos tributarios

	Central government / Gobierno central			State or Regional government / Gobierno estatal o regional			Local government / Gobierno local			Social Security Funds / Fondos de seguridad social		
	1995	2000	2015	1995	2000	2015	1995	2000	2015	1995	2000	2015
Federal countries / Países federales												
Argentina	59.0	66.4	61.0	17.5	17.8	16.8	..	..	..	23.4	15.8	22.2
Brazil / Brasil	44.7	47.8	43.7	26.8	25.3	24.4	3.7	3.4	5.9	24.8	23.5	25.9
Mexico / México	73.9	79.3	80.4	2.8	2.5	4.2	1.5	1.0	1.6	21.8	17.2	13.9
Venezuela[1]	..	..	..	..	..	..	..	..	..	..	..	..
Regional country / País régional												
Colombia	63.2	68.6	71.7	5.5	5.6	4.6	8.6	9.4	11.6	22.7	16.4	12.1
Unitary countries / Países unitarios												
Bahamas	89.1	88.1	85.2	..	..	..	..	..	..	10.9	11.9	14.8
Barbados	85.3	84.3	81.2	..	..	..	..	..	..	14.7	15.7	18.8
Belize / Belice	93.2	93.5	91.3	..	..	..	0.5	0.7	0.6	6.3	5.8	8.1
Bolivia	95.0	86.4	80.2	..	..	..	5.0	6.3	4.1	..	7.3	15.7
Chile	89.9	87.8	86.9	..	..	..	6.5	7.9	7.6	3.6	4.4	5.6
Costa Rica	68.4	66.8	63.4	..	..	..	1.6	2.0	3.3	30.0	31.2	33.3
Cuba	88.7	89.6	87.1	..	..	..	..	..	..	11.3	10.4	12.9
Dominican Republic / República Dominicana	99.3	98.9	99.6	..	..	..	..	..	..	0.7	1.1	0.4
Ecuador	70.5	86.1	73.6	..	..	..	4.0	1.8	2.5	25.5	12.1	23.9
El Salvador	85.9	83.4	87.2	..	..	..	..	..	1.9	14.1	16.6	10.9
Guatemala	83.7	83.6	82.2	..	..	..	0.6	0.9	1.1	15.6	15.5	16.6
Guyana[1]	92.6	88.6	89.6	..	..	..	0.0	0.0	0.0	7.4	11.4	10.4
Honduras	90.1	89.4	85.5	..	..	..	..	..	..	9.9	10.6	14.5
Jamaica	100.0	99.3	94.5	..	..	..	..	0.7	1.7	0.0	0.0	3.8
Nicaragua	84.1	80.0	69.8	..	..	..	..	..	6.8	15.9	20.0	23.5
Panama / Panamá	62.0	59.8	61.5	..	..	..	0.0	2.2	1.6	38.0	38.0	36.9
Paraguay	100.0	82.7	76.4	..	..	..	..	..	4.0	..	17.3	19.6
Peru / Perú	88.1	87.8	85.0	..	..	..	..	..	3.0	11.9	12.2	12.0
Trinidad and Tobago / Trinidad y Tobago	94.5	91.7	90.1	..	..	..	2.4	1.9	0.7	3.1	6.4	9.3
Uruguay	61.4	62.0	67.9	..	..	..	8.4	8.4	4.5	30.1	29.6	27.6

Note: The figures exclude local government revenues for Argentina (but include provincial revenues), Bahamas, Barbados, Bolivia (prior to 1994), Cuba, Dominican Republic, El Salvador (prior to 2002), Honduras, Jamaica (prior to 1998), Nicaragua (prior to 2010), Panama (prior to 1998), Paraguay (prior to 2004), Peru (prior to 2001) and Venezuela as the data are not available.

1. Social security contributions are estimated for Guyana (2015 and 2016) and Venezuela (from 2011 onward).

Nota : Las cifras excluyen los ingresos de gobiernos locales en Argentina (pero incluye ingresos de las provincias), Bahamas, Barbados, Bolivia (previo a 1994), Cuba, República Dominicana, El Salvador (previo a 2002), Honduras, Jamaica (previo a 1998), Nicaragua (previo a 2010), Panamá (previo a 1998), Paraguay (previo a 2004), Perú (previo a 2001) y Venezuela dado que los datos no están disponibles.

1. Las contribuciones a la seguridad social han sido estimadas en Guyana (2015 y 2016) y Venezuela (desde 2011 en adelante).

StatLink http://dx.doi.org/10.1787/888933686575

Table 4.12. Main central government taxes as % of total tax revenues of central government, 2015
Cuadro 4.12. Impuestos principales del gobierno central en % del total de ingresos tributarios del gobierno central, 2015

	1000 Income & profits / Ingresos y utilidades	2000 Social security / Seguridad social[1]	3000 Payroll / Nómina	4000 Property / Propiedad	5000 Goods and services / Bienes y servicios	6000 Others / Otros
Federal countries / Países federales						
Argentina	33.6	0.0	0.0	10.3	55.5	0.6
Brazil / Brasil	47.8	0.0	6.0	4.3	40.4	1.5
Mexico / México	51.8	0.0	0.0	0.0	47.0	1.2
Venezuela	23.4	0.0	0.0	0.2	75.0	1.3
Regional country / País régional						
Colombia	44.2	0.0	2.3	10.2	42.9	0.4
Unitary countries / Países unitarios						
Bahamas	0.0	0.0	0.0	7.1	80.1	12.7
Barbados	30.2	0.0	0.0	7.8	61.5	0.4
Belize / Belice	29.4	0.0	0.0	3.4	67.3	0.0
Bolivia	25.4	0.0	0.0	0.8	68.9	4.9
Chile	41.9	1.5	0.0	1.3	57.3	-2.1
Costa Rica	30.8	1.6	0.0	0.9	62.7	4.0
Cuba	22.8	0.0	9.4	0.0	60.6	7.2
Dominican Republic / República Dominicana	29.0	0.0	0.0	4.6	66.4	0.0
Ecuador	30.2	0.0	0.0	0.2	69.3	0.3
El Salvador	39.4	0.0	0.0	2.7	57.8	0.0
Guatemala	35.3	0.0	0.0	0.0	63.9	0.7
Guyana	38.4	0.0	0.0	2.3	58.6	0.7
Honduras	31.2	0.0	0.0	3.3	65.5	0.0
Jamaica	37.1	0.0	0.0	0.0	59.6	3.3
Nicaragua	38.4	0.0	0.0	0.9	60.5	0.2
Panama / Panamá	42.3	0.0	2.2	6.3	48.5	0.7
Paraguay	19.9	10.1	0.0	0.0	70.0	0.1
Peru / Perú	42.1	0.0	0.0	0.2	56.4	1.3
Trinidad and Tobago / Trinidad y Tobago	70.2	0.0	0.0	0.0	28.8	1.0
Uruguay	32.3	0.0	0.0	7.5	59.9	0.2

Note: Excluding social security contributions collected by social security funds.

1. These comprise social security contributions collected by central government.

Nota : Se excluyen las contribuciones a la seguridad social que recaudados por los fondos de la seguridad social.

1. Estos comprenden contribuciones a la seguridad social recaudados por el gobierno central.

StatLink http://dx.doi.org/10.1787/888933686594

Table 4.13. Main state government taxes as % of total tax revenues of state government, 2015
Cuadro 4.13. Impuestos principales del gobierno estatal en % del total de ingresos tributarios del gobierno estatal, 2015

	1000 Income & profits / Ingresos y utilidades	2000 Social security / Seguridad social	3000 Payroll / Nómina	4000 Property / Propiedad	5000 Goods and services / Bienes y servicios	6000 Others / Otros
Federal countries / Países federales						
Argentina	0.0	0.0	0.0	15.5	81.1	3.3
Brazil / Brasil	0.0	0.0	0.0	9.1	84.7	6.2
Mexico / México	0.0	0.0	56.8	18.2	19.7	5.2
Venezuela	..	..	..	..	..	..
Regional country / País régional						
Colombia	0.0	0.0	0.0	0.0	53.6	46.4
Unitary countries / Países unitarios						
Bahamas	..	..	..	..	..	..
Barbados	..	..	..	..	..	..
Belize / Belice	..	..	..	..	..	..
Bolivia	..	..	..	..	..	..
Chile	..	..	..	..	..	..
Costa Rica	..	..	..	..	..	..
Cuba	..	..	..	..	..	..
Dominican Republic / República Dominicana	..	..	..	..	..	..
Ecuador	..	..	..	..	..	..
El Salvador	..	..	..	..	..	..
Guatemala	..	..	..	..	..	..
Guyana	..	..	..	..	..	..
Honduras	..	..	..	..	..	..
Jamaica	..	..	..	..	..	..
Nicaragua	..	..	..	..	..	..
Panama / Panamá	..	..	..	..	..	..
Paraguay	..	..	..	..	..	..
Peru / Perú	..	..	..	..	..	..
Trinidad and Tobago / Trinidad y Tobago	..	..	..	..	..	..
Uruguay	..	..	..	..	..	..

StatLink http://dx.doi.org/10.1787/888933686613

Table 4.14. Main local government taxes as % of total tax revenues of local government, 2015
Cuadro 4.14. Impuestos principales del gobierno local en % del total de ingresos tributarios del gobierno local, 2015

	1000 Income & profits / Ingresos y utilidades	2000 Social security / Seguridad social	3000 Payroll / Nómina	4000 Property / Propiedad	5000 Goods and services / Bienes y servicios	6000 Others / Otros
Federal countries / Países federales						
Argentina	..	..	..	..	..	..
Brazil / Brasil	0.0	0.0	0.0	36.7	50.9	12.3
Mexico / México	0.0	0.0	0.0	75.3	1.7	23.0
Venezuela	..	..	..	..	..	..
Regional country / País régional						
Colombia	0.0	0.0	0.0	32.4	37.4	30.3
Unitary countries / Países unitarios						
Bahamas	..	..	..	..	..	..
Barbados	..	..	..	..	..	..
Belize / Belice	0.0	0.0	0.0	100.0	0.0	0.0
Bolivia	0.0	0.0	0.0	0.0	0.0	100.0
Chile	0.0	0.0	0.0	42.4	57.6	0.0
Costa Rica	0.0	0.0	0.0	40.6	59.3	0.1
Cuba	..	..	..	..	..	..
Dominican Republic / República Dominicana	..	..	..	..	..	..
Ecuador	0.0	0.0	0.0	37.8	62.2	0.0
El Salvador	0.0	0.0	0.0	0.0	0.0	100.0
Guatemala	0.0	0.0	0.0	100.0	0.0	0.0
Guyana	0.0	0.0	0.0	0.0	0.0	100.0
Honduras	..	..	..	..	..	..
Jamaica	0.0	0.0	0.0	100.0	0.0	0.0
Nicaragua	0.0	0.0	0.0	0.0	72.7	27.3
Panama / Panamá	0.0	0.0	0.0	0.0	55.3	44.7
Paraguay	0.0	0.0	0.0	41.6	57.6	0.8
Peru / Perú	0.0	0.0	0.0	69.7	15.3	14.9
Trinidad and Tobago / Trinidad y Tobago	0.0	0.0	0.0	100.0	0.0	0.0
Uruguay	0.0	0.0	0.0	57.5	42.5	0.0

StatLink http://dx.doi.org/10.1787/888933686632

Table 4.15. Gross domestic product for tax reporting years at market prices, in millions of national currency
Cuadro 4.15. Producto interno bruto para los años fiscales a precios de mercado, en millones de moneda local

		1990	2000	2005	2010	2011	2012	2013	2014	2015	2016
Argentina	ARS	74 710	308 491	582 538	1 661 721	2 179 024	2 637 914	3 348 308	4 579 086	5 854 014	8 806 974
Bahamas	BSD	4 088	6 328	7 706	7 910	7 890	8 399	8 522	8 618	8 854	8 717
Barbados	BAR	4 070	6 243	7 795	8 893	8 718	8 664	8 742	8 706	8 771	9 104
Belize / Belice	BZD	824	1 664	2 228	2 794	2 973	3 147	3 227	3 413	3 485	3 481
Bolivia	BOB	15 443	51 928	77 024	137 876	166 232	187 154	211 856	228 004	228 031	233 602
Brazil / Brasil	BRL	13	1 199 092	2 170 585	3 885 847	4 376 382	4 814 760	5 331 619	5 778 953	6 000 570	6 266 895
Chile	CLP	10 522 684	42 005 194	68 831 705	111 508 611	122 006 090	129 947 342	137 876 216	148 855 347	158 636 806	167 227 448
Colombia	COP	24 295 234	208 531 000	340 156 000	544 924 000	619 894 000	664 240 000	710 497 000	757 506 000	799 312 000	862 675 000
Costa Rica	CRC	536 380	5 041 731	9 785 862	19 580 719	21 391 917	23 371 406	24 780 859	26 702 680	28 279 440	31 287 380
Cuba	CUP	21 541	30 565	42 644	64 328	68 990	73 141	77 148	80 656	87 133	89 689
Dominican Republic / República Dominicana	DOP	82 484	414 459	1 088 056	1 978 852	2 218 429	2 384 280	2 590 678	2 841 203	3 068 139	3 298 427
Ecuador	USD	15 232	18 319	41 507	69 555	79 277	87 925	95 130	102 292	100 177	97 802
El Salvador	USD	4 801	13 134	17 094	21 418	23 139	23 814	24 351	25 054	26 052	26 797
Guatemala	GTQ	31 176	133 428	207 729	333 093	371 012	394 723	423 098	454 053	488 128	522 594
Guyana	GYD	25 432	205 128	262 250	462 910	525 554	584 783	613 653	635 377	660 226	723 245
Honduras	HNL	12 537	106 654	183 747	299 286	335 028	361 349	376 539	414 634	457 432	491 339
Jamaica	JAM	33 577	387 089	699 989	1 152 737	1 240 327	1 313 729	1 431 098	1 541 719	1 667 193	1 753 010
Mexico / México	MXN	825 100	6 132 389	9 424 602	13 266 858	14 527 337	15 599 271	16 078 960	17 217 016	18 194 758	19 472 074
Nicaragua	NIO	519	64 812	105 777	187 053	219 182	247 994	271 530	308 403	347 463	378 661
Panama / Panamá	PAB	5 632	12 304	16 374	28 917	34 374	39 955	44 856	49 166	52 132	55 188
Paraguay	PYG	6 031 160	28 574 101	53 962 327	94 934 255	105 203 214	108 832 260	125 152 245	137 797 686	144 249 481	155 602 570
Peru / Perú	PEN	5 322	177 918	247 081	418 144	464 833	498 536	534 707	576 380	612 504	658 715
Trinidad and Tobago / Trinidad y Tobago	TTD	21 539	51 371	100 682	141 268	163 008	165 203	170 318	167 764	150 247	145 911
Uruguay	UYU	12 010	276 152	425 018	808 079	926 356	1 041 211	1 178 332	1 330 508	1 455 848	1 581 115
Venezuela	VEF	2 279	79 656	304 087	1 016 835	1 357 488	1 635 450	2 245 844	3 031 242	6 025 330	23 751 850

Source: OECD National Accounts data for Chile and Mexico, CEPALSTAT (ECLAC) for Cuba, the World Economic Outlook (IMF) for Argentina, Bahamas, Barbados, Belize, Jamaica, Panama, Paraguay and Venezuela, official National Accounts data for the other countries.

Fuente : Datos de Cuentas Nacionales de la OCDE para Chile y México, CEPALSTAT (CEPAL) para Cuba, World Economic Outlook (FMI) para Argentina, Bahamas, Barbados, Belice, Jamaica, Panamá, Paraguay y Venezuela, estadísticas oficiales de Cuentas Nacionales para el resto de países.

StatLink http://dx.doi.org/10.1787/888933686651

Table 4.16. Gross domestic product for tax reporting years at market prices, in USD
Cuadro 4.16. Producto interno bruto para los años fiscales a precios de mercado, en US dólares

	1990	2000	2005	2010	2011	2012	2013	2014	2015	2016
Argentina	153 205	308 491	199 273	424 728	527 645	579 667	611 471	563 614	631 621	595 940
Bahamas	4 088	6 328	7 706	7 910	7 890	8 399	8 522	8 618	8 854	8 717
Barbados	2 035	3 122	3 897	4 447	4 359	4 332	4 371	4 353	4 386	4 552
Belize / Belice	412	832	1 114	1 397	1 487	1 574	1 614	1 707	1 743	1 740
Bolivia	4 868	8 385	9 573	19 786	24 135	27 282	30 883	33 237	33 241	34 053
Brazil / Brasil	494 686	655 455	891 635	2 208 698	2 614 031	2 464 050	2 471 720	2 456 051	1 801 480	1 798 618
Chile	34 512	77 876	122 978	218 652	252 381	267 390	278 379	260 859	242 444	247 180
Colombia	47 866	99 078	146 666	286 426	334 352	369 284	378 019	375 403	288 399	283 766
Costa Rica	5 859	16 376	20 525	37 603	42 759	46 984	50 164	50 195	53 514	58 109
Cuba	21 541	30 565	42 644	64 328	68 990	73 141	77 148	80 656	87 133	89 689
Dominican Republic / República Dominicana	8 526	25 613	36 101	53 803	58 304	60 703	62 061	65 322	68 197	71 673
Ecuador	15 232	18 319	41 507	69 555	79 277	87 925	95 130	102 292	100 177	97 802
El Salvador	4 801	13 134	17 094	21 418	23 139	23 814	24 351	25 054	26 052	26 797
Guatemala	6 950	17 187	27 211	41 338	47 655	50 388	53 851	58 722	63 767	67 495
Guyana	652	1 123	1 311	2 276	2 581	2 864	2 988	3 079	3 197	3 503
Honduras	3 049	7 104	9 672	15 730	17 588	18 401	18 372	19 619	20 699	21 367
Jamaica	4 663	9 065	11 228	13 192	14 409	14 761	14 203	13 863	14 218	13 959
Mexico / México	290 451	648 719	865 462	1 050 268	1 168 381	1 186 238	1 259 133	1 293 980	1 146 184	1 045 346
Nicaragua	519	5 110	6 321	8 759	9 774	10 532	10 983	11 880	12 748	13 230
Panama / Panamá	5 632	12 304	16 374	28 917	34 374	39 955	44 856	49 166	52 132	55 188
Paraguay	4 904	8 196	8 735	20 048	25 100	24 595	28 966	30 881	27 715	27 441
Peru / Perú	28 325	50 981	74 948	147 974	168 741	188 969	197 836	202 995	192 243	195 052
Trinidad and Tobago / Trinidad y Tobago	5 068	8 154	15 982	22 113	25 584	25 922	26 948	26 741	24 141	23 258
Uruguay	10 270	22 832	17 398	40 285	47 962	51 266	57 531	57 236	53 275	52 420
Venezuela	48 391	117 676	143 290	294 281	334 069	331 457	234 401	212 347	242 596	236 443

Source: The figures are derived by multiplying the GDP data in Table 4.15 by the exchange rate in Table 4.17.
Fuente : Las cifras se obtienen multiplicando los datos del PIB en el Cuadro 4.15 por el tipo de cambio en el Cuadro 4.17.

StatLink http://dx.doi.org/10.1787/888933686670

Table 4.17. Exchange rates used, national currency per US dollar at market exchange rates
Cuadro 4.17. Tasas de cambio utilizadas, moneda local por US dólares a precios de mercado

		1990	2000	2005	2010	2011	2012	2013	2014	2015	2016
Argentina	ARS	0.488	1.000	2.923	3.912	4.130	4.551	5.476	8.125	9.268	14.778
Bahamas	BSD	1.000	1.000	1.000	1.000	1.000	1.000	1.000	1.000	1.000	1.000
Barbados	BAR	2.000	2.000	2.000	2.000	2.000	2.000	2.000	2.000	2.000	2.000
Belize / Belice	BZD	2.000	2.000	2.000	2.001	1.999	1.999	1.999	1.999	1.999	2.001
Bolivia	BOB	3.172	6.193	8.046	6.968	6.888	6.860	6.860	6.860	6.860	6.860
Brazil / Brasil	BRL	0.000	1.829	2.434	1.759	1.674	1.954	2.157	2.353	3.331	3.484
Chile	CLP	304.899	539.492	559.768	510.249	483.667	486.492	495.311	570.373	654.075	676.940
Colombia	COP	507.565	2 104.716	2 319.263	1 902.497	1 854.018	1 798.725	1 879.526	2 017.846	2 771.548	3 040.092
Costa Rica	CRC	91.553	307.871	476.787	520.724	500.286	497.433	493.998	531.974	528.448	538.426
Cuba	CUP	1.000	1.000	1.000	1.000	1.000	1.000	1.000	1.000	1.000	1.000
Dominican Republic / República Dominicana	DOP	9.674	16.181	30.139	36.780	38.050	39.278	41.744	43.495	44.989	46.021
Ecuador	USD	1.000	1.000	1.000	1.000	1.000	1.000	1.000	1.000	1.000	1.000
El Salvador	USD	1.000	1.000	1.000	1.000	1.000	1.000	1.000	1.000	1.000	1.000
Guatemala	GTQ	4.486	7.763	7.634	8.058	7.785	7.834	7.857	7.732	7.655	7.743
Guyana	GYD	39.006	182.661	200.038	203.392	203.590	204.154	205.394	206.388	206.531	206.477
Honduras	HNL	4.112	15.014	18.998	19.027	19.049	19.638	20.495	21.135	22.099	22.995
Jamaica	JAM	7.201	42.703	62.343	87.382	86.080	89.000	100.760	111.211	117.259	125.583
Mexico / México	MXN	2.838	9.457	10.890	12.629	12.430	13.169	12.770	13.303	15.881	18.689
Nicaragua	NIO	1.000	12.684	16.733	21.357	22.424	23.547	24.723	25.959	27.257	28.621
Panama / Panamá	PAB	1.000	1.000	1.000	1.000	1.000	1.000	1.000	1.000	1.000	1.000
Paraguay	PYG	1 229.845	3 486.347	6 177.714	4 735.348	4 191.363	4 424.975	4 320.660	4 462.216	5 204.830	5 670.441
Peru / Perú	PEN	0.188	3.490	3.297	2.826	2.755	2.638	2.703	2.839	3.186	3.377
Trinidad and Tobago / Trinidad y Tobago	TTD	4.250	6.300	6.300	6.389	6.372	6.373	6.320	6.274	6.224	6.274
Uruguay	UYU	1.169	12.095	24.429	20.059	19.314	20.310	20.482	23.246	27.327	30.163
Venezuela	VEF	0.047	0.677	2.122	3.455	4.064	4.934	9.581	14.275	24.837	100.455

Note: Annual average market exchange rates.

Source: Central banks for most countries included in the report except for Bahamas, Barbados, Belize, Jamaica, Paraguay and Venezuela in which an implied conversion rate was estimated from the GDP figures published by the IMF.

Nota : Se utilizan tasas de cambio de mercado promedios anuales.

Fuente : Bancos centrales de los países incluidos en el reporte excepto para Bahamas, Barbados, Belice, Jamaica, Paraguay y Venezuela, para los cuales se estimo un tipo de cambio implícito a partir de los del PIB publicados por el FMI.

StatLink http://dx.doi.org/10.1787/888933686689

Chapter 5

Country tables, 1990-2016 – Tax revenues

Capítulo 5

Cuadros país, 1990-2016 – Ingresos tributarios

Table 5.1. Argentina
Details of tax revenue / Ingresos tributarios detallados

Million ARS

	1990	2000	2005	2010	2011	2012	2013	2014	2015	2016
Total tax revenue	**10 217**	**61 084**	**142 906**	**483 014**	**638 429**	**808 131**	**1 043 967**	**1 424 523**	**1 872 915**	**2 519 367**
1000 Taxes on income, profits and capital gains	**542**	**11 303**	**29 203**	**78 427**	**110 118**	**140 108**	**185 688**	**269 809**	**384 536**	**436 927**
1100 Of individuals	141	3 937	8 192	23 980	36 870	54 494	79 803	125 503	188 218	174 248
1110 On income and profits	130	3 854	8 151	23 858	36 713	54 279	79 449	125 067	187 663	173 486
1120 On capital gains	11	82	41	122	157	215	354	436	555	762
1200 Corporate	357	6 575	19 602	50 664	68 127	81 938	99 346	132 178	185 725	235 866
1210 On profits	357	6 575	19 602	50 664	68 127	81 938	99 346	132 178	185 725	235 866
Corporate income taxes	198	5 956	18 494	49 012	66 767	80 490	97 614	129 881	183 207	232 608
Tax on assets	160	19	5	4	4	5	3	6	4	12
Tax on assumed minimum income	0	600	1 102	1 648	1 357	1 443	1 728	2 291	2 513	3 246
1220 On capital gains	..	..	..	..	..	..	..	..	..	..
1300 Unallocable between 1100 and 1200	43	792	1 409	3 783	5 121	3 676	6 539	12 128	10 593	26 814
Non resident taxpayers	11	792	1 409	3 783	5 121	3 676	6 539	12 128	10 593	26 814
Other	33	0	0	0	0	0	0	0	0	0
2000 Social security contributions	**2 583**	**9 670**	**17 400**	**102 460**	**137 186**	**179 777**	**236 072**	**307 656**	**415 410**	**556 067**
2100 Employees	..	2 486	3 690	37 990	49 587	69 159	91 779	121 276	163 590	219 274
2110 On a payroll basis	..	2 486	3 690	37 990	49 587	69 159	91 779	121 276	163 590	219 274
2120 On an income tax basis	..	0	0	0	0	0	0	0	0	0
2200 Employers	..	6 069	12 557	54 713	77 596	101 114	132 999	174 965	235 610	314 617
2210 On a payroll basis	..	6 069	12 557	54 713	77 596	101 114	132 999	174 965	235 610	314 617
2220 On an income tax basis	..	0	0	0	0	0	0	0	0	0
2300 Self-employed or non-employed	98	1 115	1 153	9 757	10 003	9 504	11 293	11 416	16 210	22 176
2310 On a payroll basis	98	1 115	1 153	9 757	10 003	9 504	11 293	11 416	16 210	22 176
2320 On an income tax basis	0	0	0	0	0	0	0	0	0	0
2400 Unallocable between 2100, 2200 and 2300	2 485	0	0	0	0	0	0	0	0	0
2410 On a payroll basis	2 485	..	..	..	..	..	..	..	..	..
2420 On an income tax basis	0	..	..	..	..	..	..	..	..	..
3000 Taxes on payroll and workforce	**0**	**0**	**0**	**0**	**0**	**0**	**0**	**0**	**0**	**0**
4000 Taxes on property	**1 164**	**3 867**	**15 997**	**43 538**	**57 537**	**72 374**	**96 679**	**129 065**	**166 182**	**220 014**
4100 Recurrent taxes on immovable property	419	1 809	2 837	5 035	6 099	9 921	14 097	17 547	21 738	29 066
4110 Households	0	0	0	0	0	0	0	0	0	0
4120 Others	419	1 809	2 837	5 035	6 099	9 921	14 097	17 547	21 738	29 066
4200 Recurrent taxes on net wealth	246	1 084	1 867	5 248	6 018	7 408	10 471	14 575	18 538	19 976
4210 Individual	3	1 024	1 813	5 147	5 892	7 263	10 296	14 356	18 210	19 541
Personal assets	0	1 024	1 813	5 147	5 892	7 263	10 296	14 356	18 210	19 541
Recurrent taxes on net wealth	3	0	0	0	0	0	0	0	0	0
4220 Corporate	242	60	55	101	126	145	175	220	327	435
4300 Estate, inheritance and gift taxes	0	0	0	0	0	0	0	0	0	0
4310 Estate and inheritance taxes	..	..	..	..	..	..	..	..	..	..
4320 Gift taxes	..	..	..	..	..	..	..	..	..	..
4400 Taxes on financial and capital transactions	459	904	11 272	33 252	45 420	55 044	72 111	96 943	125 906	170 972
Immovable property transfers	0	54	116	539	775	721	734	912	1 256	2 052
Movable property transfers	44	0	0	0	0	0	0	0	0	0
Bank accounts' credits and debits	205	0	9 434	26 885	36 179	43 931	56 515	76 740	97 480	131 669
Stamp taxes	211	850	1 722	5 829	8 466	10 392	14 862	19 291	27 170	37 251
4500 Non-recurrent taxes	40	70	21	3	0	1	0	0	0	0
4510 On net wealth	0	0	0	0	..	0	..	..	..	..
4520 Other non-recurrent taxes	40	70	21	3	..	1	..	..	..	..
4600 Other recurrent taxes on property	0	0	0	0	0	0	0	0	0	0
5000 Taxes on goods and services	**5 636**	**34 539**	**77 959**	**253 092**	**327 059**	**407 716**	**517 591**	**704 677**	**889 323**	**1 175 652**
5100 Taxes on production, sale, transfer, etc	5 462	34 288	78 555	252 550	326 822	403 294	513 926	703 883	881 120	1 167 594
5110 General taxes	2 384	25 123	51 467	167 534	224 813	281 589	381 630	515 090	671 297	901 799
5111 Value added taxes	1 594	19 009	36 853	116 386	154 237	190 496	249 006	331 203	433 076	583 217
5112 Sales tax	0	0	0	0	0	0	0	0	0	0
5113 Other	791	6 114	14 613	51 148	70 576	91 093	132 624	183 887	238 221	318 582
5120 Taxes on specific goods and services	3 077	9 166	27 088	85 016	102 009	121 704	132 296	188 793	209 822	265 795
5121 Excises	1 866	5 850	10 609	26 208	30 851	40 800	49 680	69 977	92 349	129 790
Alcoholic beverages	25	36	73	238	322	422	525	673	985	1 163
Non alcoholic beverages	25	90	189	501	654	912	1 195	1 586	2 168	2 477
Beers	0	50	131	212	210	332	650	879	1 384	1 171
Tobacco products	425	1 875	3 460	6 884	8 620	10 310	12 343	17 432	26 152	42 183
Liquid fuel and gas	1 073	3 478	6 017	15 269	18 131	25 785	31 010	44 490	56 478	75 664
Electricity	72	205	283	591	616	610	547	607	590	637
Motor vehicles	59	20	0	27	24	153	185	121	88	265
Other	189	96	456	2 485	2 274	2 275	3 225	4 189	4 503	6 229
5122 Profits of fiscal monopolies	0	0	0	0	0	0	0	0	0	0

Table 5.1. Argentina *(cont.)*
Details of tax revenue / Ingresos tributarios detallados

Million ARS

	1990	2000	2005	2010	2011	2012	2013	2014	2015	2016
5123 Customs and import duties	219	1 976	3 877	11 428	14 678	16 640	23 551	30 058	35 512	56 365
Import duties	166	1 938	3 780	11 183	14 373	16 313	23 134	29 482	34 822	55 305
Import fees	53	38	96	246	305	327	416	576	691	1 060
5124 Taxes on exports	724	32	12 323	45 547	54 163	61 316	55 465	84 088	75 939	71 509
5125 Taxes on investment goods	0	0	0	0	0	0	0	0	0	0
5126 Taxes on specific services	163	1 233	150	1 429	1 820	2 227	2 677	3 533	4 420	5 782
Insurance services	42	194	8	21	27	35	46	65	88	118
Financial services	32	855	2	0	0	0	0	0	0	0
Telephone services	82	33	110	936	1 163	1 391	1 605	1 983	2 301	2 911
Other specific services	7	151	31	472	629	801	1 026	1 486	2 031	2 753
5127 Other taxes on internat. trade and transactions	98	74	129	404	497	721	924	1 136	1 601	2 349
5128 Other taxes	8	0	0	0	0	0	0	0	0	0
5130 Unallocable between 5110 and 5120	0	0	0	0	0	0	0	0	0	0
5200 Taxes on use of goods and perform activities	177	833	1 289	3 598	4 928	6 409	9 059	12 010	17 035	23 042
5210 Recurrent taxes	177	833	1 289	3 598	4 928	6 409	9 059	12 010	17 035	23 042
5211 Paid by households: motor vehicles	177	833	1 289	3 598	4 928	6 409	9 059	12 010	17 035	23 042
5212 Paid by others: motor vehicles	0	0	0	0	0	0	0	0	0	0
5213 Paid in respect of other goods	0	0	0	0	0	0	0	0	0	0
5220 Non-recurrent taxes	0	0	0	0	0	0	0	0	0	0
5300 Unallocable between 5100 and 5200	-3	-583	-1 885	-3 056	-4 690	-1 987	-5 394	-11 215	-8 831	-14 983
6000 Other taxes	**292**	**1 704**	**2 347**	**5 497**	**6 527**	**8 157**	**7 937**	**13 316**	**17 463**	**130 706**
6100 Paid solely by business	0	354	757	2 093	2 983	3 825	4 423	4 259	5 624	6 873
Simplified system for small taxpayers	0	354	757	2 093	2 983	3 825	4 423	4 259	5 624	6 873
6200 Other	292	1 351	1 590	3 404	3 544	4 332	3 514	9 056	11 839	123 833
Tax debt payments	135	24	112	293	710	934	-1 313	1 340	1 306	110 721
Special payments	79	6	1	0	0	0	0	0	0	0
Other national level	0	12	7	0	0	0	0	0	0	0
Other provincial level	78	1 309	1 469	3 110	2 833	3 398	4 827	7 716	10 533	13 112

Note: Year ending 31st December.
The data are on a cash basis.
The figures exclude local government tax revenues as the data are not available (but include provincial revenues).
Heading 5212: In ECLAC data, property tax on motor vehicles is classified in category 4000.
Heading 5300: The figures are negative as they represent general reimbursements of exports and specific taxes on goods and services.
Heading 6200: The tax debt payments in 2016 include revenue following the implementation of a new voluntary disclosure regime in July 2016 (Law 27260).

Source: Subsecretaría de Ingresos Públicos, Dirección Nacional de Investigaciones y Análisis Fiscal, Ministerio de Hacienda y Finanzas Públicas (Undersecretary of Public Revenue, National Direction of Research and Fiscal Analysis, Ministry of Finance).

StatLink http://dx.doi.org/10.1787/888933686708

Table 5.2. Bahamas
Details of tax revenue / Ingresos tributarios detallados

Million BSD

	1990	2000	2005	2010	2011	2012	2013	2014	2015	2016
Total tax revenue	**505**	**965**	**1 060**	**1 277**	**1 487**	**1 480**	**1 445**	**1 490**	**1 761**	**1 956**
1000 Taxes on income, profits and capital gains	**0**	**0**	**0**	**0**	**0**	**0**	**0**	**0**	**0**	**0**
1100 Of individuals	0	0	0	0	0	0	0	0	0	0
1110 On income and profits	..	..	..	..	..	..	..	..	..	..
1120 On capital gains	..	..	..	..	..	..	..	..	..	..
1200 Corporate	0	0	0	0	0	0	0	0	0	0
1210 On profits	..	..	..	..	..	..	..	..	..	..
1220 On capital gains	..	..	..	..	..	..	..	..	..	..
1300 Unallocable between 1100 and 1200	0	0	0	0	0	0	0	0	0	0
2000 Social security contributions	**66**	**115**	**136**	**167**	**190**	**203**	**229**	**245**	**260**	**280**
2100 Employees	..	..	..	60	67	74	87	91	98	105
2110 On a payroll basis	..	..	..	..	..	..	..	..	..	..
2120 On an income tax basis	..	..	..	..	..	..	..	..	..	..
2200 Employers	..	..	..	104	120	124	137	149	157	169
2210 On a payroll basis	..	..	..	..	..	..	..	..	..	..
2220 On an income tax basis	..	..	..	..	..	..	..	..	..	..
2300 Self-employed or non-employed	..	..	..	3	4	5	6	6	6	6
2310 On a payroll basis	..	..	..	..	..	..	..	..	..	..
2320 On an income tax basis	..	..	..	..	..	..	..	..	..	..
2400 Unallocable between 2100, 2200 and 2300	66	115	136	0	0	0	-1	-1	-1	-1
2410 On a payroll basis	..	..	..	..	..	..	..	..	..	..
2420 On an income tax basis	..	..	..	..	..	..	..	..	..	..
3000 Taxes on payroll and workforce	**0**	**0**	**0**	**0**	**0**	**0**	**0**	**0**	**0**	**0**
4000 Taxes on property	**19**	**32**	**54**	**92**	**92**	**95**	**115**	**104**	**107**	**104**
4100 Recurrent taxes on immovable property	19	32	54	92	92	95	115	104	107	104
4110 Households	0	0	0	0	0	0	0	0	0	0
4120 Others	19	32	54	92	92	95	115	104	107	104
4200 Recurrent taxes on net wealth	0	0	0	0	0	0	0	0	0	0
4210 Individual	..	..	..	..	..	..	..	..	..	..
4220 Corporate	..	..	..	..	..	..	..	..	..	..
4300 Estate, inheritance and gift taxes	0	0	0	0	0	0	0	0	0	0
4310 Estate and inheritance taxes	..	..	..	..	..	..	..	..	..	..
4320 Gift taxes	..	..	..	..	..	..	..	..	..	..
4400 Taxes on financial and capital transactions	0	0	0	0	0	0	0	0	0	0
4500 Non-recurrent taxes	0	0	0	0	0	0	0	0	0	0
4510 On net wealth	..	..	..	..	..	..	..	..	..	..
4520 Other non-recurrent taxes	..	..	..	..	..	..	..	..	..	..
4600 Other recurrent taxes on property	0	0	0	0	0	0	0	0	0	0
5000 Taxes on goods and services	**386**	**723**	**736**	**795**	**944**	**1 018**	**955**	**986**	**1 203**	**1 472**
5100 Taxes on production, sale, transfer, etc	354	654	657	672	799	868	806	772	993	1 296
5110 General taxes	0	0	0	0	0	0	0	0	219	628
5111 Value added taxes	0	0	0	0	0	0	0	0	219	628
5112 Sales tax	0	0	0	0	0	0	0	0	0	0
5113 Other	0	0	0	0	0	0	0	0	0	0
5120 Taxes on specific goods and services	354	654	657	672	799	868	806	772	775	668
5121 Excises	0	0	0	188	254	331	246	249	262	230
5122 Profits of fiscal monopolies	0	0	0	0	0	0	0	0	0	0
5123 Customs and import duties	289	537	525	364	370	366	350	336	307	264
Import tax	289	435	413	348	354	348	332	336	307	264
Stamp tax from imports duties	0	102	112	15	16	18	18	0	0	0
5124 Taxes on exports	6	13	13	14	13	15	14	10	9	12
Export tax	6	13	13	14	13	15	14	10	9	12
Stamp tax from exports	0	0	0	0	0	0	0	0	0	0
5125 Taxes on investment goods	0	0	0	0	0	0	0	0	0	0
5126 Taxes on specific services	59	104	119	106	162	156	196	178	197	162
Departure tax	27	64	69	70	103	102	144	125	147	135
Gaming tax	27	20	25	10	18	11	10	8	25	26
Hotel occupancy tax	5	20	25	25	41	43	42	45	25	1
5127 Other taxes on internat. trade and transactions	0	0	0	0	0	0	0	0	0	0
5128 Other taxes	0	0	0	0	0	0	0	0	0	0
5130 Unallocable between 5110 and 5120	0	0	0	0	0	0	0	0	0	0
5200 Taxes on use of goods and perform activities	32	69	78	123	145	150	149	214	209	177
5210 Recurrent taxes	32	69	78	123	145	150	149	214	209	177
Motor vehicle tax	10	14	18	21	27	29	28	29	29	30
5211 Paid by households: motor vehicles	0	0	0	0	0	0	0	0	0	0
5212 Paid by others: motor vehicles	0	0	0	0	0	0	0	0	0	0

Table 5.2. Bahamas *(cont.)*
Details of tax revenue / Ingresos tributarios detallados

Million BSD

	1990	2000	2005	2010	2011	2012	2013	2014	2015	2016
5213 Paid in respect of other goods	22	55	61	102	118	121	121	185	180	146
Company fees and registration	0	5	5	5	5	5	5	5	5	6
International business companies	0	17	15	19	17	17	17	17	16	15
Others	22	33	40	78	95	99	99	163	159	125
5220 Non-recurrent taxes	0	0	0	0	0	0	0	0	0	0
5300 Unallocable between 5100 and 5200	0	0	0	0	0	0	0	0	0	0
6000 Other taxes	**33**	**95**	**135**	**223**	**261**	**163**	**145**	**155**	**191**	**100**
6100 Paid solely by business	0	0	0	0	0	0	0	0	0	0
6200 Other	33	95	135	223	261	163	145	155	191	100
All other stamp taxes	37	74	135	162	258	174	160	164	191	100
Incentive acts and other refunds	-8	14	-15	11	-9	-11	-15	-8	0	0
Other taxes	4	7	15	49	12	0	0	0	0	0

Note: Fiscal year ending on 30th June.

The data are on a cash basis.

The data for 2016 are preliminary as indicated and published by the Central Bank of Bahamas.

The figures exclude local government tax revenues as the data are not available.

Heading 2000: The data are estimated for 2016. The breakdown for social security contributions has been introduced since 2010 for the first time in this edition.

Heading 2400: This heading includes refunds of social security contributions as reported by the National Insurance Board (NIB).

Heading 5111: A value added tax was enforced on 1st January 2015.

Source: Ministry of Finance, IDB-CIAT (2015), *Equivalent Fiscal Pressure for Latin America and the Caribbean* and the Central Bank of the Bahamas.

StatLink http://dx.doi.org/10.1787/888933686727

Table 5.3. Barbados
Details of tax revenue / Ingresos tributarios detallados

Million BAR

	1990	2000	2005	2010	2011	2012	2013	2014	2015	2016
Total tax revenue	**942**	**1 884**	**2 297**	**2 719**	**2 822**	**2 869**	**2 576**	**2 643**	**2 947**	**2 936**
1000 Taxes on income, profits and capital gains	**254**	**574**	**639**	**762**	**782**	**744**	**615**	**702**	**723**	**823**
1100 Of individuals	129	289	296	388	419	380	344	429	433	493
1110 On income and profits	129	289	296	388	419	380	344	429	433	493
1120 On capital gains	..	..	..	..	..	..	..	..	..	..
1200 Corporate	111	252	294	327	299	276	191	208	225	241
1210 On profits	111	252	294	327	299	276	191	208	225	241
1220 On capital gains	..	..	..	..	..	..	..	..	..	..
1300 Unallocable between 1100 and 1200	14	33	49	47	64	88	80	65	65	89
2000 Social security contributions	**134**	**295**	**408**	**525**	**526**	**529**	**513**	**532**	**553**	**288**
2100 Employees	..	..	..	..	..	..	..	..	..	..
2110 On a payroll basis	..	..	..	..	..	..	..	..	..	..
2120 On an income tax basis	..	..	..	..	..	..	..	..	..	..
2200 Employers	..	..	..	..	..	..	..	..	..	..
2210 On a payroll basis	..	..	..	..	..	..	..	..	..	..
2220 On an income tax basis	..	..	..	..	..	..	..	..	..	..
2300 Self-employed or non-employed	..	..	..	..	..	..	..	..	..	..
2310 On a payroll basis	..	..	..	..	..	..	..	..	..	..
2320 On an income tax basis	..	..	..	..	..	..	..	..	..	..
2400 Unallocable between 2100, 2200 and 2300	134	295	408	525	526	529	513	532	553	288
2410 On a payroll basis	..	..	..	..	..	..	..	..	..	..
2420 On an income tax basis	..	..	..	..	..	..	..	..	..	..
3000 Taxes on payroll and workforce	**0**	**0**	**0**	**0**	**0**	**0**	**0**	**0**	**0**	**0**
4000 Taxes on property	**39**	**92**	**127**	**114**	**112**	**148**	**125**	**113**	**188**	**191**
4100 Recurrent taxes on immovable property	26	60	76	98	95	133	109	94	173	175
Land tax	26	60	76	98	95	133	109	94	173	175
4110 Households	..	..	..	..	..	..	..	..	..	..
4120 Others	..	..	..	..	..	..	..	..	..	..
4200 Recurrent taxes on net wealth	0	0	0	0	0	0	0	0	0	0
4210 Individual	..	..	..	..	..	..	..	..	..	..
4220 Corporate	..	..	..	..	..	..	..	..	..	..
4300 Estate, inheritance and gift taxes	0	0	0	0	0	0	0	0	0	0
4310 Estate and inheritance taxes	..	..	..	..	..	..	..	..	..	..
4320 Gift taxes	..	..	..	..	..	..	..	..	..	..
4400 Taxes on financial and capital transactions	0	0	0	0	0	0	0	0	0	0
4500 Non-recurrent taxes	13	32	51	16	17	15	16	19	15	16
4510 On net wealth	..	..	..	..	..	..	..	..	..	..
4520 Other non-recurrent taxes	..	..	..	..	..	..	..	..	..	..
4600 Other recurrent taxes on property	0	0	0	0	0	0	0	0	0	0
5000 Taxes on goods and services	**332**	**897**	**1 101**	**1 242**	**1 367**	**1 421**	**1 292**	**1 264**	**1 473**	**1 575**
5100 Taxes on production, sale, transfer, etc	332	793	974	1 092	1 240	1 245	1 187	1 156	1 325	1 425
5110 General taxes	197	501	610	753	897	907	871	823	925	948
5111 Value added taxes	0	501	610	753	897	907	871	823	925	948
5112 Sales tax	197	0	0	0	0	0	0	0	0	0
5113 Other	0	0	0	0	0	0	0	0	0	0
5120 Taxes on specific goods and services	135	292	364	339	343	338	317	333	401	477
5121 Excises	5	159	172	148	159	137	129	122	169	234
5122 Profits of fiscal monopolies	0	0	0	0	0	0	0	0	0	0
5123 Customs and import duties	112	133	192	191	185	200	188	211	232	243
Import duties	112	133	192	191	185	200	188	211	232	243
5124 Taxes on exports	0	0	0	0	0	0	0	0	0	0
5125 Taxes on investment goods	0	0	0	0	0	0	0	0	0	0
5126 Taxes on specific services	18	1	0	0	0	0	0	0	0	0
Hotel and restaurant tax	18	1	0	0	0	0	0	0	0	0
5127 Other taxes on internat. trade and transactions	0	0	0	0	0	0	0	0	0	0
5128 Other taxes	0	0	0	0	0	0	0	0	0	0
5130 Unallocable between 5110 and 5120	0	0	0	0	0	0	0	0	0	0
5200 Taxes on use of goods and perform activities	0	104	127	150	126	176	105	108	148	151
5210 Recurrent taxes	..	104	127	150	126	176	105	108	148	151
5211 Paid by households: motor vehicles	..	0	0	0	0	0	0	0	0	0
5212 Paid by others: motor vehicles	..	0	0	0	0	0	0	0	0	0
5213 Paid in respect of other goods	..	104	127	150	126	176	105	108	148	151
5220 Non-recurrent taxes	..	0	0	0	0	0	0	0	0	0
5300 Unallocable between 5100 and 5200	0	0	0	0	0	0	0	0	0	0
6000 Other taxes	**183**	**26**	**21**	**76**	**36**	**27**	**31**	**32**	**10**	**58**
6100 Paid solely by business	0	0	0	0	0	0	0	0	0	0

Table 5.3. Barbados *(cont.)*
Details of tax revenue / Ingresos tributarios detallados

Million BAR

	1990	2000	2005	2010	2011	2012	2013	2014	2015	2016
6200 Other	183	26	21	76	36	27	31	32	10	58
Levies	86	14	0	61	24	16	21	20	0	49
Stamp duties	98	12	21	15	12	11	10	13	10	9

Note: Year ending 31st December.

The data are on a cash basis.

The data for 2016 are from the "Revised Estimates 2016-2017" published by parliament.

The figures exclude local government tax revenues as the data are not available.

Heading 5213: This heading includes data on tax collection levied on a recurrent basis for which the tax base is not identifiable. In the previous edition these figures were classified under heading 5210.

Heading 6200: This heading includes stamp duties collected by customs, previously classified under heading 5123.

Source: The Central Bank of Barbados, the Inland Revenue Department and Barbados budget estimates 2017-18.

StatLink http://dx.doi.org/10.1787/888933686746

Table 5.4. Belize / Belice
Details of tax revenue / Ingresos tributarios detallados

Million BZD

	1990	2000	2005	2010	2011	2012	2013	2014	2015	2016
Total tax revenue	**179**	**318**	**496**	**744**	**745**	**786**	**830**	**929**	**950**	**1 032**
1000 Taxes on income, profits and capital gains	**37**	**76**	**129**	**248**	**252**	**232**	**245**	**272**	**254**	**265**
1100 Of individuals	21	19	35	52	51	60	64	74	82	84
1110 On income and profits	21	19	35	52	51	60	64	74	82	84
Income tax (PAYE)	20	19	35	52	51	60	64	74	82	84
Income tax on individuals	1	0	0	0	0	0	0	0	0	0
1120 On capital gains	..	..	..	..	..	..	..	..	..	..
1200 Corporate	12	51	90	189	194	164	172	183	159	170
Income tax (companies)	12	1	0	51	48	27	18	16	1	0
Income tax (business tax)	0	51	90	138	133	132	150	167	158	170
Income tax (supplemental petroleum tax)	0	0	0	0	14	6	4	0	0	0
1210 On profits	..	..	..	..	..	..	..	..	..	..
1220 On capital gains	..	..	..	..	..	..	..	..	..	..
1300 Unallocable between 1100 and 1200	4	6	4	7	6	8	10	15	13	10
Income tax (arrears)	4	3	1	1	1	2	2	2	2	2
Income tax (withholding)	0	3	2	6	5	7	8	13	11	9
2000 Social security contributions	**10**	**18**	**50**	**60**	**61**	**65**	**67**	**72**	**77**	**82**
2100 Employees	..	..	..	..	..	..	..	..	..	..
2110 On a payroll basis	..	..	..	..	..	..	..	..	..	..
2120 On an income tax basis	..	..	..	..	..	..	..	..	..	..
2200 Employers	..	..	..	..	..	..	..	..	..	..
2210 On a payroll basis	..	..	..	..	..	..	..	..	..	..
2220 On an income tax basis	..	..	..	..	..	..	..	..	..	..
2300 Self-employed or non-employed	..	..	..	..	..	..	..	..	..	..
2310 On a payroll basis	..	..	..	..	..	..	..	..	..	..
2320 On an income tax basis	..	..	..	..	..	..	..	..	..	..
2400 Unallocable between 2100, 2200 and 2300	10	18	50	60	61	65	67	72	77	82
2410 On a payroll basis	..	..	..	..	..	..	..	..	..	..
2420 On an income tax basis	..	..	..	..	..	..	..	..	..	..
3000 Taxes on payroll and workforce	**0**	**0**	**0**	**0**	**0**	**0**	**0**	**0**	**0**	**0**
4000 Taxes on property	**6**	**13**	**27**	**23**	**26**	**27**	**31**	**35**	**35**	**30**
4100 Recurrent taxes on immovable property	1	2	6	7	7	5	6	6	5	6
4110 Households	1	2	6	7	7	5	6	6	5	6
4120 Others	0	0	0	0	0	0	0	0	0	0
4200 Recurrent taxes on net wealth	0	0	0	0	0	0	0	0	0	0
4210 Individual	..	..	..	..	..	..	..	..	..	..
4220 Corporate	..	..	..	..	..	..	..	..	..	..
4300 Estate, inheritance and gift taxes	0	0	0	0	0	0	0	0	0	0
4310 Estate and inheritance taxes	..	0	0	0	0	0	0	0	0	0
4320 Gift taxes	..	0	0	0	0	0	0	0	0	0
4400 Taxes on financial and capital transactions	5	11	22	16	19	22	25	29	29	23
4500 Non-recurrent taxes	0	0	0	0	0	0	0	0	0	0
4510 On net wealth	..	..	..	..	..	..	..	..	..	..
4520 Other non-recurrent taxes	..	..	..	..	..	..	..	..	..	..
4600 Other recurrent taxes on property	0	0	0	0	0	0	0	0	0	0
5000 Taxes on goods and services	**126**	**211**	**289**	**412**	**406**	**462**	**486**	**550**	**583**	**656**
5100 Taxes on production, sale, transfer, etc.	122	207	282	400	396	443	469	540	571	648
5110 General taxes	0	82	131	199	175	214	237	270	275	296
5111 Value added taxes	0	0	0	199	175	214	237	270	275	296
5112 Sales tax	..	82	131	0	0	0	0	0	0	0
5113 Other	..	0	0	0	0	0	0	0	0	0
5120 Taxes on specific goods and services	122	125	151	200	221	229	232	269	296	352
5121 Excises	35	47	57	31	33	34	35	38	39	160
Revenue replacement duty	18	39	57	7	9	12	13	15	15	1
Excise duties	17	8	0	22	21	20	21	22	23	158
Excise on locally refined petroleum products	0	0	0	0	1	0	0	0	1	1
Excise on locally extracted crude oil	0	0	0	1	2	2	2	1	0	0
5122 Profits of fiscal monopolies	0	0	0	0	0	0	0	0	0	0
5123 Customs and import duties	78	64	80	144	160	165	165	196	221	162
Import duties	50	64	80	123	138	141	140	167	190	130
Environmental tax	0	0	0	21	22	24	25	29	31	32
Imports into EPZs	0	0	0	0	0	0	0	0	0	0
Stamps duties on customs	28	0	0	0	0	0	0	0	0	0
5124 Taxes on exports	0	0	0	0	0	0	0	0	0	0
5125 Taxes on investment goods	0	0	0	0	0	0	0	0	0	0
5126 Taxes on specific services	0	0	0	0	0	0	0	0	0	0

Table 5.4. Belize / Belice (cont.)
Details of tax revenue / Ingresos tributarios detallados

Million BZD

	1990	2000	2005	2010	2011	2012	2013	2014	2015	2016
5127 Other taxes on internat. trade and transactions	8	14	15	25	28	30	32	35	35	30
Goods in transit - administration charge	3	1	1	1	1	1	1	1	1	1
Goods in transit - social fee	0	5	4	8	10	11	11	12	11	10
Taxes on foreign currency transactions	6	8	9	16	16	18	20	22	23	19
5128 Other taxes	0	0	0	0	0	0	0	0	0	0
5130 Unallocable between 5110 and 5120	0	0	0	0	0	0	0	0	0	0
5200 Taxes on use of goods and perform activities	4	4	7	13	10	19	17	10	12	7
5210 Recurrent taxes	4	4	7	13	10	19	17	10	12	7
5211 Paid by households: motor vehicles	2	3	5	3	3	3	4	4	4	4
5212 Paid by others: motor vehicles	0	0	0	0	0	0	0	0	0	0
5213 Paid in respect of other goods	2	1	2	10	7	16	14	6	8	3
5220 Non-recurrent taxes	0	0	0	0	0	0	0	0	0	0
5300 Unallocable between 5100 and 5200	0	0	0	0	0	0	0	0	0	0
6000 Other taxes	**0**	**0**	**0**	**0**	**0**	**0**	**0**	**0**	**0**	**0**
6100 Paid solely by business	..	..	..	..	..	..	..	..	..	..
6200 Other	..	..	..	..	..	..	..	..	..	..

Note: Year ending 31st March. Data are on a April(n-1)/March(n) fiscal year basis. For example, the data for 2016 represent April 2016 to March 2017.
The data are on a cash basis.
The data for 2016 are the expected outturn as presented by the Belize "draft estimates of revenue and expenditures".
Heading 2000: The data for social security contributions are estimated for 2016.

Source: Ministry of Finance of Belize, the Social Security Board and IDB-CIAT (2015), *Equivalent Fiscal Pressure for Latin America and the Caribbean.*

StatLink http://dx.doi.org/10.1787/888933686765

Table 5.5. Bolivia
Details of tax revenue / Ingresos tributarios detallados

Million BOB

	1990	2000	2005	2010	2011	2012	2013	2014	2015	2016
Total tax revenue	**1 277**	**9 155**	**15 369**	**27 929**	**36 722**	**45 577**	**53 571**	**59 689**	**62 871**	**60 722**
1000 Taxes on income, profits and capital gains	**68**	**1 209**	**2 383**	**6 294**	**7 926**	**9 679**	**11 644**	**12 723**	**12 809**	**10 876**
1100 Of individuals	68	214	214	263	277	279	364	439	508	497
1110 On income and profits	68	214	214	263	277	279	364	439	508	497
RC-IVA	62	161	187	237	260	260	333	401	461	442
RC-IVA fiscal notes	6	53	28	26	18	19	31	38	47	55
1120 On capital gains	..	..	..	..	..	..	..	..	..	..
1200 Corporate	0	995	2 169	6 031	7 649	9 400	11 280	12 284	12 302	10 379
1210 On profits	..	995	2 169	6 031	7 649	9 400	11 280	12 284	12 302	10 379
Mining profits	..	0	75	473	616	322	283	82	67	8
Corporate tax	..	546	1 481	3 874	4 724	6 256	6 824	8 026	9 235	6 960
Corporate tax remittances	..	258	315	742	732	718	806	954	959	1 670
Fiscal notes on corporate tax	..	192	286	768	1 451	1 773	3 137	3 150	1 898	1 475
Fiscal notes on mining profits	..	0	11	174	127	331	229	72	143	266
1220 On capital gains	..	..	..	..	..	..	..	..	..	..
1300 Unallocable between 1100 and 1200	0	0	0	0	0	0	0	0	0	0
2000 Social security contributions	**0**	**666**	**936**	**1 645**	**2 665**	**6 339**	**7 276**	**8 694**	**9 842**	**10 251**
2100 Employees	..	..	..	..	..	..	..	..	..	..
2110 On a payroll basis	..	..	..	..	..	..	..	..	..	..
2120 On an income tax basis	..	..	..	..	..	..	..	..	..	..
2200 Employers	..	..	..	..	..	..	..	..	..	..
2210 On a payroll basis	..	..	..	..	..	..	..	..	..	..
2220 On an income tax basis	..	..	..	..	..	..	..	..	..	..
2300 Self-employed or non-employed	..	..	..	..	..	..	..	..	..	..
2310 On a payroll basis	..	..	..	..	..	..	..	..	..	..
2320 On an income tax basis	..	..	..	..	..	..	..	..	..	..
2400 Unallocable between 2100, 2200 and 2300	..	666	936	1 645	2 665	6 339	7 276	8 694	9 842	10 251
2410 On a payroll basis	..	666	936	1 645	2 665	6 339	7 276	8 694	9 842	10 251
2420 On an income tax basis	..	0	0	0	0	0	0	0	0	0
3000 Taxes on payroll and workforce	**0**	**0**	**0**	**0**	**0**	**0**	**0**	**0**	**0**	**0**
4000 Taxes on property	**1**	**3**	**640**	**367**	**401**	**401**	**412**	**433**	**424**	**455**
4100 Recurrent taxes on immovable property	0	0	0	0	0	0	0	0	0	0
4110 Households	..	..	..	..	..	..	..	..	..	..
4120 Others	..	..	..	..	..	..	..	..	..	..
4200 Recurrent taxes on net wealth	0	0	0	0	0	0	0	0	0	0
4210 Individual	..	..	..	..	..	..	..	..	..	..
4220 Corporate	..	..	..	..	..	..	..	..	..	..
4300 Estate, inheritance and gift taxes	1	3	7	20	22	23	28	32	36	15
4310 Estate and inheritance taxes	1	3	7	20	22	23	28	32	36	15
4320 Gift taxes	0	0	0	0	0	0	0	0	0	0
4400 Taxes on financial and capital transactions	0	0	633	347	380	378	384	401	388	440
4500 Non-recurrent taxes	0	0	0	0	0	0	0	0	0	0
4510 On net wealth	..	..	..	..	..	..	..	..	..	..
4520 Other non-recurrent taxes	..	..	..	..	..	..	..	..	..	..
4600 Other recurrent taxes on property	0	0	0	0	0	0	0	0	0	0
5000 Taxes on goods and services	**1 032**	**6 594**	**10 207**	**17 684**	**23 540**	**26 528**	**30 878**	**33 857**	**34 731**	**33 402**
5100 Taxes on production, sale, transfer, etc.	1 032	6 594	10 207	17 684	23 540	26 528	30 878	33 857	34 731	33 402
5110 General taxes	708	3 892	6 768	12 434	16 864	19 508	22 620	24 661	25 220	24 288
5111 Value added taxes	551	2 949	5 314	10 259	14 092	16 306	19 033	20 581	20 757	19 902
VAT internal market	297	1 204	1 937	4 100	5 134	6 555	7 805	9 273	9 914	10 318
VAT imports	178	1 445	2 637	5 193	6 975	7 690	8 709	9 390	9 738	8 458
VAT fiscal notes (internal market)	56	223	584	581	494	623	783	760	666	622
VAT fiscal notes (imports)	20	76	156	385	1 489	1 437	1 736	1 158	438	504
5112 Sales tax	0	0	0	0	0	0	0	0	0	0
5113 Other	157	943	1 455	2 174	2 772	3 202	3 587	4 081	4 463	4 386
5120 Taxes on specific goods and services	324	2 702	3 439	5 250	6 676	7 020	8 258	9 196	9 511	9 114
5121 Excises	118	2 047	2 604	3 658	4 393	4 475	5 012	5 663	5 853	6 040
Excises (Internal)	61	245	209	933	1 204	1 157	1 468	1 365	1 487	1 687
Excises (Imports)	22	298	208	379	642	580	719	1 051	1 109	917
Special tax on hydrocarbons and derivatives	0	1 348	1 529	1 070	2 236	1 144	1 681	1 998	2 581	2 696
Fiscal notes on excises	35	118	309	155	115	290	47	328	262	103
Fiscal notes on special tax on hydrocarb. and deriv.	0	40	350	1 121	196	1 304	1 098	921	415	638
5122 Profits of fiscal monopolies	0	0	0	0	0	0	0	0	0	0
5123 Customs and import duties	204	640	803	1 545	2 218	2 485	2 850	3 102	3 254	2 894
Customs and import duties	163	616	777	1 504	2 074	2 278	2 663	2 879	3 057	2 787
Fiscal notes customs and import duties	41	24	26	41	144	207	186	223	198	107
5124 Taxes on exports	0	0	0	0	0	0	0	0	0	0

Table 5.5. Bolivia (cont.)
Details of tax revenue / Ingresos tributarios detallados

Million BOB

	1990	2000	2005	2010	2011	2012	2013	2014	2015	2016
5125 Taxes on investment goods	0	0	0	0	0	0	0	0	0	0
5126 Taxes on specific services	2	15	32	47	65	60	91	120	127	175
Air departure tax	2	15	32	47	52	51	71	90	102	116
Tax on gambling	0	0	0	0	13	9	20	30	25	59
5127 Other taxes on internat. trade and transactions	0	0	0	0	0	0	306	311	277	6
5128 Other taxes	0	0	0	0	0	0	0	0	0	0
5130 Unallocable between 5110 and 5120	0	0	0	0	0	0	0	0	0	0
5200 Taxes on use of goods and perform activities	0	0	0	0	0	0	0	0	0	0
5210 Recurrent taxes	..	..	..	..	..	..	..	..	..	..
5211 Paid by households: motor vehicles	..	..	..	..	..	..	..	..	..	..
5212 Paid by others: motor vehicles	..	..	..	..	..	..	..	..	..	..
5213 Paid in respect of other goods	..	..	..	..	..	..	..	..	..	..
5220 Non-recurrent taxes	..	..	..	..	..	..	..	..	..	..
5300 Unallocable between 5100 and 5200	0	0	0	0	0	0	0	0	0	0
6000 Other taxes	**177**	**682**	**1 203**	**1 939**	**2 189**	**2 630**	**3 361**	**3 982**	**5 065**	**5 738**
6100 Paid solely by business	4	6	5	12	13	14	17	20	26	35
Simplified tax regime	3	6	4	12	13	14	17	20	25	35
Integrated tax system	1	0	0	0	0	0	0	0	0	0
6200 Other	172	676	1 199	1 927	2 176	2 615	3 344	3 961	5 040	5 703
Unified agricultural regime	0	1	5	14	17	22	23	23	26	27
Fiscal notes on transactions	15	64	250	108	94	56	116	53	28	39
Other	154	37	178	422	556	860	1 241	1 716	2 378	2 696
Fiscal notes on other taxes	3	0	5	3	5	2	9	25	23	63
Municipal taxes	0	575	762	1 381	1 504	1 675	1 955	2 145	2 585	2 879

Note: Year ending 31st December.

The data are on a cash basis.

Heading 2000: The figures have been updated from 2012 to account for the enforcement of renationalisation of the pension system.

Heading 5113: This heading includes the "Impuesto a las Transacciones", a turnover tax previously classified under heading 6200.

Source: Ministerio de Economía y Finanzas Públicas, Ministry of Economy and Public Finance.

Unidad de Análisis de Políticas Sociales y Económicas, Social and Economic Policy Analysis Unit.

StatLink http://dx.doi.org/10.1787/888933686784

Table 5.6. Brazil / Brasil

Details of tax revenue / Ingresos tributarios detallados

Million BRL

	1990	2000	2005	2010	2011	2012	2013	2014	2015	2016
Total tax revenue	**3**	**354 760**	**711 145**	**1 257 564**	**1 453 265**	**1 564 067**	**1 728 920**	**1 835 066**	**1 918 710**	**2 015 517**
1000 Taxes on income, profits and capital gains	**1**	**68 667**	**149 309**	**258 738**	**314 299**	**321 463**	**360 549**	**381 870**	**401 112**	**453 549**
1100 Of individuals	0	3 406	6 981	87 828	104 336	116 342	126 006	140 446	148 858	162 255
1110 On income and profits	0	3 406	6 981	87 828	104 336	116 342	126 006	140 446	148 858	162 255
Withholding taxes on income and profits	0	0	0	71 580	83 821	93 843	101 818	114 664	121 659	133 971
Other personal income taxes	0	0	0	16 248	20 515	22 499	24 188	25 782	27 199	28 285
1120 On capital gains	..	..	..	..	..	..	..	..	..	..
1200 Corporate	0	25 430	73 071	128 255	153 652	148 423	171 003	171 352	164 057	197 941
1210 On profits	0	25 430	73 071	128 255	153 652	148 423	171 003	171 352	164 057	197 941
Corporate income tax	0	16 680	47 832	82 474	94 958	92 589	109 316	109 020	104 910	131 181
Social contribution on net profits (CSLL)	0	8 750	25 239	45 780	58 694	55 834	61 687	62 332	59 147	66 760
1220 On capital gains	..	..	..	..	..	..	..	..	..	..
1300 Unallocable between 1100 and 1200	0	39 831	69 257	42 656	56 311	56 697	63 540	70 072	88 196	93 353
Non-residents	0	39 831	69 257	11 537	13 870	15 207	18 582	19 703	24 669	24 892
Capital	0	0	0	24 887	35 159	33 309	37 121	41 288	53 692	59 404
Others	0	0	0	6 232	7 281	8 182	7 837	9 082	9 836	9 057
2000 Social security contributions	**1**	**83 469**	**168 226**	**313 949**	**360 277**	**402 437**	**441 880**	**478 642**	**497 791**	**523 803**
2100 Employees	..	..	..	..	..	..	..	..	..	..
2110 On a payroll basis	..	..	..	..	..	..	..	..	..	..
2120 On an income tax basis	..	..	..	..	..	..	..	..	..	..
2200 Employers	0	18 709	32 248	64 271	74 979	85 813	98 045	108 782	118 323	124 713
2210 On a payroll basis	0	18 709	32 248	64 271	74 979	85 813	98 045	108 782	118 323	124 713
2220 On an income tax basis	0	0	0	0	0	0	0	0	0	0
2300 Self-employed or non-employed	..	..	..	..	..	..	..	..	..	..
2310 On a payroll basis	..	..	..	..	..	..	..	..	..	..
2320 On an income tax basis	..	..	..	..	..	..	..	..	..	..
2400 Unallocable between 2100, 2200 and 2300	1	64 760	135 978	249 679	285 298	316 625	343 836	369 860	379 469	399 090
2410 On a payroll basis	1	64 760	135 978	249 679	285 298	316 625	343 836	369 860	379 469	399 090
Social security contributions (Federal)	1	59 334	118 869	231 903	266 169	294 578	319 566	341 992	349 787	365 723
Social security contributions (State)	0	4 423	14 682	12 635	13 294	15 551	16 499	19 529	20 797	23 248
Social security contributions (Municipal)	0	1 003	2 427	5 141	5 835	6 496	7 771	8 339	8 885	10 118
2420 On an income tax basis	0	0	0	0	0	0	0	0	0	0
3000 Taxes on payroll and workforce	**0**	**6 749**	**14 468**	**33 090**	**34 399**	**39 206**	**43 391**	**47 724**	**50 399**	**53 537**
PASEP contributions	0	1 312	2 863	9 880	6 958	8 398	8 775	9 491	9 958	12 013
Payroll-based contribution to education	0	2 791	5 906	11 049	13 115	14 775	16 561	18 411	19 039	19 473
"S" System contributions	0	2 646	4 397	9 925	11 858	13 557	15 351	16 884	18 153	18 428
Other	0	0	1 302	2 236	2 467	2 477	2 704	2 938	3 248	3 623
4000 Taxes on property	**0**	**28 818**	**56 274**	**74 377**	**86 700**	**92 085**	**97 817**	**106 597**	**120 378**	**128 247**
4100 Recurrent taxes on immovable property	0	4 753	8 405	17 933	20 276	22 148	25 063	28 739	31 864	38 688
4110 Households	0	0	0	0	0	0	0	0	0	0
4120 Others	0	4 753	8 405	17 933	20 276	22 148	25 063	28 739	31 864	38 688
Tax on rural land property (ITR)	0	234	288	485	571	614	764	900	1 105	1 126
Tax on urban land property (IPTU)	0	4 519	8 117	17 448	19 706	21 533	24 299	27 839	30 760	37 562
4200 Recurrent taxes on net wealth	0	0	0	0	0	0	0	0	0	0
4210 Individual	..	..	..	..	..	..	..	..	..	..
4220 Corporate	..	..	..	..	..	..	..	..	..	..
4300 Estate, inheritance and gift taxes	0	329	821	2 518	2 768	3 409	4 142	4 698	6 469	7 262
4310 Estate and inheritance taxes	0	329	821	2 518	2 768	3 409	4 142	4 698	6 469	7 262
4320 Gift taxes	0	0	0	0	0	0	0	0	0	0
4400 Taxes on financial and capital transactions	0	18 442	36 587	32 559	39 544	39 499	39 380	40 707	45 788	43 284
Tax on financial operations (IOF)	0	3 096	5 974	26 571	31 999	31 002	29 417	29 756	34 681	33 645
Real estate property transfers (ITBI)	0	950	1 593	6 005	7 466	8 497	9 963	10 950	11 107	9 639
Other	0	14 396	29 021	-18	79	0	0	0	0	0
4500 Non-recurrent taxes	0	0	0	0	0	0	0	0	0	0
4510 On net wealth	..	..	..	..	..	..	..	..	..	..
4520 Other non-recurrent taxes	..	..	..	..	..	..	..	..	..	..
4600 Other recurrent taxes on property	0	5 294	10 460	21 367	24 112	27 030	29 232	32 453	36 257	39 013
5000 Taxes on goods and services	**2**	**164 144**	**317 875**	**542 259**	**617 617**	**665 106**	**736 786**	**767 868**	**793 382**	**794 799**
5100 Taxes on production, sale, transfer, etc	2	162 575	312 503	542 259	617 617	665 106	736 786	767 868	793 382	794 799
5110 General taxes	2	154 130	294 251	497 899	564 045	614 568	681 107	711 337	732 495	739 994
5111 Value added taxes	1	100 978	177 589	293 489	324 761	357 190	393 742	419 459	431 904	443 034
Tax on the circulation of goods and services (ICMS)	1	82 279	153 437	268 117	297 419	326 236	363 190	384 287	396 513	412 857
Tax on industrialised products (IPI)	0	18 699	24 153	25 372	27 342	30 954	30 552	35 172	35 391	30 177
5112 Sales tax	0	47 046	105 415	171 653	200 926	213 096	239 290	236 646	242 508	242 338
Contribution to financing social security (COFINS)	0	38 707	86 837	140 939	164 982	175 008	197 545	194 696	199 876	201 517
PIS contribution	0	8 339	18 578	30 714	35 944	38 088	41 745	41 950	42 632	40 821
5113 Other	0	6 106	11 247	32 757	38 358	44 282	48 074	55 232	58 084	54 622

Table 5.6. Brazil / Brasil *(cont.)*

Details of tax revenue / Ingresos tributarios detallados

Million BRL

	1990	2000	2005	2010	2011	2012	2013	2014	2015	2016
5120 Taxes on specific goods and services	0	8 445	18 252	44 360	53 572	50 538	55 679	56 531	60 887	54 805
5121 Excises	..	0	7 683	19 681	22 845	14 587	13 105	14 055	15 929	17 676
Vehicles	..	..	..	5 787	7 150	4 395	3 799	4 940	4 367	3 299
Beverages	..	..	..	2 431	2 992	3 223	3 455	3 401	2 599	2 684
Tobacco	..	..	..	3 704	3 745	4 083	5 117	5 688	5 692	5 692
Fuels	..	..	..	7 759	8 959	2 885	734	26	3 271	6 001
5122 Profits of fiscal monopolies	..	0	0	0	0	0	0	0	0	0
5123 Customs and import duties	..	8 445	8 953	21 119	26 763	31 088	36 974	36 774	38 969	31 448
5124 Taxes on exports	..	0	0	0	0	0	0	0	0	0
5125 Taxes on investment goods	..	0	0	0	0	0	0	0	0	0
5126 Taxes on specific services	..	0	983	2 349	2 457	2 883	3 367	3 204	3 005	2 741
5127 Other taxes on internat. trade and transactions	..	0	0	0	0	0	0	0	0	0
5128 Other taxes	..	0	633	1 212	1 507	1 979	2 233	2 499	2 983	2 940
5130 Unallocable between 5110 and 5120	..	0	0	0	0	0	0	0	0	0
5200 Taxes on use of goods and perform activities	0	1 569	5 372	0	0	0	0	0	0	0
5210 Recurrent taxes	0	1 569	5 372	..	..	..	..	..	..	..
5211 Paid by households: motor vehicles	0	1 569	5 372	..	..	..	..	..	..	..
5212 Paid by others: motor vehicles	0	0	0	..	..	..	..	..	..	..
5213 Paid in respect of other goods	0	0	0	..	..	..	..	..	..	..
5220 Non-recurrent taxes	0	0	0	..	..	..	..	..	..	..
5300 Unallocable between 5100 and 5200	0	0	0	0	0	0	0	0	0	0
6000 Other taxes	**0**	**2 913**	**4 993**	**35 151**	**39 973**	**43 770**	**48 498**	**52 364**	**55 649**	**61 582**
6100 Paid solely by business	0	0	277	0	0	0	0	0	0	0
Revenue service development fund (FUNDAF)	0	0	277	0	0	0	0	0	0	0
6200 Other	0	2 913	4 715	35 151	39 973	43 770	48 498	52 364	55 649	61 582
Other federal taxes	0	941	36	9 610	10 672	10 545	11 743	12 814	12 527	12 648
Other social contributions	0	1 273	1 725	0	0	0	0	0	0	0
Other state taxes	0	322	1 551	17 135	19 825	22 980	25 864	27 352	29 067	32 461
Other municipal taxes	0	377	1 404	8 406	9 476	10 245	10 891	12 198	14 054	16 473

Note: Year ending 31st December.

The data are on a cash basis.

Heading 1100: In this edition, taxes on income and profits collected by the state and local governments have been attributed to the central government. In previous editions these were attributed to state and local governments when they in fact pertained to the central government.

Heading 1300: In this edition, an improved breakdown on unallocable income taxes is provided.

Headings 3000, 5112 and 6200: For years prior to 2000 the PASEP (Program of Formation of the Patrimony of the Public Servants) contributions are combined with PIS (Social Integration Program) contributions in heading 5112.

Headings 5111 and 5121: From 2007 to 2011, a portion of the IPI (Industrial Products Tax) is levied separately as an excise tax on automobiles, beverages, and tobacco products.

Heading 5121: An improved breakdown for excise taxes has been provided since 2007 in this edition.

Heading 6100: From 2008 FUNDAF (Special Fund for Development and Improvement of Auditing Activities) contributions are included in heading 6200.

Heading 5200: From 2009, taxes paid by households: motor vehicles are included in heading 5200.

Source: Secretaria da Receita Federal (Ministry of Finance) in Carga Tributária no Brasil.

StatLink http://dx.doi.org/10.1787/888933686803

Table 5.7. Chile

Details of tax revenue / Ingresos tributarios detallados

Million CLP

	1990	2000	2005	2010	2011	2012	2013	2014	2015	2016
Total tax revenue	**1 777 218**	**7 901 998**	**14 265 265**	**21 845 693**	**25 762 449**	**27 714 772**	**27 381 686**	**29 145 219**	**32 532 354**	**34 099 516**
1000 Taxes on income, profits and capital gains	**412 974**	**1 841 630**	**5 171 293**	**8 329 060**	**10 322 824**	**10 803 031**	**9 520 709**	**9 628 037**	**11 840 521**	**11 444 570**
1100 Of individuals	99 154	604 100	738 620	1 492 837	1 690 230	1 893 620	1 964 172	2 114 296	3 199 876	2 990 653
Second category tax	65 552	490 980	700 150	1 449 099	1 663 293	1 917 675	1 981 699	2 140 345	2 350 120	2 458 249
Global complementary tax	33 603	113 120	38 470	43 738	26 936	-24 055	-17 527	-26 050	-36 757	-213 365
1110 On income and profits	..	..	..	..	..	..	..	..	..	..
1120 On capital gains	..	..	..	..	..	..	..	..	..	..
1200 Corporate	219 586	882 896	3 155 480	4 448 745	6 021 408	7 560 906	6 041 089	6 196 077	6 839 133	7 146 657
First category tax	200 891	815 747	3 040 875	3 913 870	5 254 907	6 770 329	5 473 355	5 182 214	6 183 830	6 689 101
Surtax on state owned enterprises	16 074	47 634	78 267	194 203	116 725	80 084	124 220	100 851	132 352	88 362
Mining tax	0	0	0	298 558	598 790	619 150	324 577	801 647	323 507	105 653
Other	2 621	19 516	36 338	42 114	50 987	91 343	118 937	111 365	199 444	263 541
1210 On profits	..	..	..	..	..	..	..	..	..	..
1220 On capital gains	..	..	..	..	..	..	..	..	..	..
1300 Unallocable between 1100 and 1200	94 233	354 634	1 277 193	2 387 478	2 611 186	1 348 506	1 515 449	1 317 664	1 801 512	1 307 260
Additional tax	59 082	350 301	799 648	1 414 057	1 187 866	1 178 917	1 337 721	1 454 847	1 429 758	1 331 564
Other	35 151	4 332	477 545	973 421	1 423 320	169 589	177 727	-137 183	371 755	-24 304
2000 Social security contributions	**159 559**	**576 758**	**931 717**	**1 493 987**	**1 623 818**	**1 802 468**	**1 968 973**	**2 110 087**	**2 252 489**	**2 441 419**
2100 Employees	154 021	553 937	893 821	1 433 159	1 565 828	1 742 526	1 906 340	2 044 356	2 188 575	2 373 777
2110 On a payroll basis	154 021	553 937	893 821	1 433 159	1 565 828	1 742 526	1 906 340	2 044 356	2 188 575	2 373 777
2120 On an income tax basis	0	0	0	0	0	0	0	0	0	0
2200 Employers	5 538	22 821	37 896	60 828	57 990	59 942	62 633	65 731	63 914	67 642
2210 On a payroll basis	5 538	22 821	37 896	60 828	57 990	59 942	62 633	65 731	63 914	67 642
2220 On an income tax basis	0	0	0	0	0	0	0	0	0	0
2300 Self-employed or non-employed	0	0	0	0	0	0	0	0	0	0
2310 On a payroll basis	..	..	..	..	..	..	..	..	..	..
2320 On an income tax basis	..	..	..	..	..	..	..	..	..	..
2400 Unallocable between 2100, 2200 and 2300	0	0	0	0	0	0	0	0	0	0
2410 On a payroll basis	..	..	..	..	..	..	..	..	..	..
2420 On an income tax basis	..	..	..	..	..	..	..	..	..	..
3000 Taxes on payroll and workforce	**0**	**0**	**0**	**0**	**0**	**0**	**0**	**0**	**0**	**0**
4000 Taxes on property	**109 319**	**554 037**	**901 776**	**898 607**	**1 027 627**	**1 180 307**	**1 133 765**	**1 228 961**	**1 421 274**	**1 711 790**
4100 Recurrent taxes on immovable property	59 968	302 244	416 565	662 368	731 191	788 919	840 842	924 062	1 056 920	1 151 466
4110 Households	..	..	..	..	..	..	..	..	..	..
4120 Others	..	..	..	..	..	..	..	..	..	..
4200 Recurrent taxes on net wealth	0	0	0	0	0	0	0	0	0	0
4210 Individual	..	..	..	..	..	..	..	..	..	..
4220 Corporate	..	..	..	..	..	..	..	..	..	..
4300 Estate, inheritance and gift taxes	3 444	10 906	23 184	39 338	30 876	66 719	45 550	31 340	92 236	100 490
4310 Estate and inheritance taxes	..	..	..	..	..	..	..	..	..	..
4320 Gift taxes	..	..	..	..	..	..	..	..	..	..
4400 Taxes on financial and capital transactions	45 907	240 886	462 027	196 901	265 560	324 669	247 373	273 559	272 118	459 834
4500 Non-recurrent taxes	0	0	0	0	0	0	0	0	0	0
4510 On net wealth	..	..	..	..	..	..	..	..	..	..
4520 Other non-recurrent taxes	..	..	..	..	..	..	..	..	..	..
4600 Other recurrent taxes on property	0	0	0	0	0	0	0	0	0	0
5000 Taxes on goods and services	**1 118 722**	**5 041 769**	**7 346 434**	**11 185 156**	**12 700 180**	**13 873 611**	**14 779 915**	**16 127 855**	**17 597 378**	**18 619 797**
5100 Taxes on production, sale, transfer, etc	1 074 009	4 789 827	6 952 092	10 532 904	11 963 914	13 052 989	13 869 529	15 131 675	16 515 485	17 444 386
5110 General taxes	664 421	3 306 350	5 391 285	8 399 926	9 536 786	10 447 374	11 170 794	12 133 710	13 273 958	14 073 050
5111 Value added taxes	664 421	3 306 350	5 391 285	8 399 926	9 536 786	10 447 374	11 170 794	12 133 710	13 273 958	14 073 050
5112 Sales tax	0	0	0	0	0	0	0	0	0	0
5113 Other	0	0	0	0	0	0	0	0	0	0
5120 Taxes on specific goods and services	409 588	1 483 477	1 560 807	2 132 978	2 427 128	2 605 615	2 698 735	2 997 965	3 241 527	3 371 336
5121 Excises	166 050	816 160	1 107 703	1 561 205	1 750 916	1 892 713	1 987 475	2 224 223	2 412 773	2 568 863
Cigarettes and tobacco	60 604	283 275	382 690	647 637	744 302	783 995	815 991	856 595	981 422	1 009 034
Gasoline and diesel	105 445	532 885	724 803	913 568	1 006 614	1 108 718	1 171 483	1 361 724	1 388 218	1 502 039
Oil stabilisation fund	0	0	210	0	0	0	0	0	0	0
5122 Profits of fiscal monopolies	0	0	0	0	0	0	0	0	0	0
5123 Customs and import duties	222 486	548 571	286 044	267 331	301 828	314 441	303 393	337 839	343 491	308 871
5124 Taxes on exports	0	0	0	0	0	0	0	0	0	0
5125 Taxes on investment goods	0	0	0	0	0	0	0	0	0	0
5126 Taxes on specific services	21 052	118 746	167 060	304 442	374 384	398 461	407 867	435 903	485 263	493 602
5127 Other taxes on internat. trade and transactions	0	0	0	0	0	0	0	0	0	0
5128 Other taxes	0	0	0	0	0	0	0	0	0	0
5130 Unallocable between 5110 and 5120	0	0	0	0	0	0	0	0	0	0
5200 Taxes on use of goods and perform activities	44 714	251 942	394 343	652 252	736 266	820 622	910 386	996 180	1 081 893	1 175 411
5210 Recurrent taxes	44 714	251 942	394 343	652 252	736 266	820 622	910 386	996 180	1 081 893	1 175 411
Motor vehicles	24 469	93 880	139 174	218 219	267 116	301 895	330 754	365 316	397 608	431 888

Table 5.7. Chile *(cont.)*
Details of tax revenue / Ingresos tributarios detallados

Million CLP

	1990	2000	2005	2010	2011	2012	2013	2014	2015	2016
5211 Paid by households: motor vehicles	0	0	0	0	0	0	0	0	0	0
5212 Paid by others: motor vehicles	0	0	0	0	0	0	0	0	0	0
5213 Paid in respect of other goods	20 245	158 062	255 169	434 033	469 150	518 727	579 632	630 864	684 285	743 523
Municipal permits	18 401	136 138	234 460	396 944	425 138	468 938	527 955	578 671	630 943	690 267
Mining patents	3 374	34 730	20 094	36 213	42 944	47 899	50 094	50 448	51 767	51 641
Other	-1 530	-12 806	615	876	1 068	1 890	1 583	1 745	1 575	1 615
5220 Non-recurrent taxes	0	0	0	0	0	0	0	0	0	0
5300 Unallocable between 5100 and 5200	0	0	0	0	0	0	0	0	0	0
6000 Other taxes	**-23 356**	**-112 195**	**-85 954**	**-61 117**	**88 000**	**55 355**	**-21 676**	**50 279**	**-579 308**	**-118 061**
6100 Paid solely by business	0	0	0	0	0	0	0	0	0	0
6200 Other	-23 356	-112 195	-85 954	-61 117	88 000	55 355	-21 676	50 279	-579 308	-118 061

Note: Year ending 31st December.

Headings 1100, 1200 and 1300: In this edition, further discrimination between taxes on dividends paid by individuals and corporations is provided following a tax reform implemented in 2015.

The data are on a cash basis.

Heading 5121: In ECLAC data, figures from the Oil Prices Stabilisation Fund (FEPP) are considered as non-tax revenues.

Source: Servicio de Impuestos Internos (Chile's Tax Service).

StatLink http://dx.doi.org/10.1787/888933686822

Table 5.8. Colombia

Details of tax revenue / Ingresos tributarios detallados

Million COP

	1990	2000	2005	2010	2011	2012	2013	2014	2015	2016
Total tax revenue	**2 579 426**	**30 512 910**	**61 455 845**	**97 954 930**	**116 603 658**	**130 869 983**	**142 457 341**	**154 187 502**	**166 070 450**	**170 436 896**
1000 Taxes on income, profits and capital gains	**771 694**	**7 103 525**	**17 348 618**	**26 218 852**	**33 453 048**	**43 671 856**	**47 743 096**	**50 083 349**	**52 656 876**	**54 326 726**
1100 Of individuals	47 210	1 499 345	3 594 441	5 192 384	6 407 675	6 841 470	7 686 121	8 513 856	9 741 528	10 378 965
1110 On income and profits	47 210	1 499 345	3 594 441	5 192 384	6 407 675	6 841 470	7 686 121	8 513 856	9 741 528	10 378 965
1120 On capital gains	..	..	..	..	..	..	..	..	..	..
1200 Corporate	359 758	5 119 828	13 044 361	20 405 209	26 110 879	35 669 308	38 545 617	40 200 727	41 036 561	41 966 610
1210 On profits	359 758	5 119 828	13 044 361	20 405 209	26 110 879	35 669 308	38 545 617	40 200 727	41 036 561	41 966 610
Income tax	359 758	5 119 828	13 044 361	20 405 209	26 110 879	35 669 308	35 606 038	27 739 252	27 110 392	27 855 875
Pro Equity Income Tax - CREE	0	0	0	0	0	0	2 939 579	12 461 475	13 926 169	14 110 734
1220 On capital gains	..	..	..	..	..	..	..	..	..	..
1300 Unallocable between 1100 and 1200	364 726	484 352	709 816	621 258	934 494	1 161 078	1 511 357	1 368 765	1 878 787	1 981 152
Income tax	364 726	484 352	709 816	621 258	934 494	1 161 078	1 511 357	1 368 765	1 878 787	1 981 152
Pro Equity Income Tax - CREE	0	0	0	0	0	0	0	0	0	0
2000 Social security contributions	**203 596**	**4 989 000**	**7 845 000**	**11 478 085**	**10 303 830**	**11 815 723**	**16 645 000**	**19 272 000**	**20 169 000**	**21 694 000**
2100 Employees	..	..	..	..	..	..	..	..	..	..
2110 On a payroll basis	..	..	..	..	..	..	..	..	..	..
2120 On an income tax basis	..	..	..	..	..	..	..	..	..	..
2200 Employers	..	..	..	..	..	..	..	..	..	..
2210 On a payroll basis	..	..	..	..	..	..	..	..	..	..
2220 On an income tax basis	..	..	..	..	..	..	..	..	..	..
2300 Self-employed or non-employed	..	..	..	..	..	..	..	..	..	..
2310 On a payroll basis	..	..	..	..	..	..	..	..	..	..
2320 On an income tax basis	..	..	..	..	..	..	..	..	..	..
2400 Unallocable between 2100, 2200 and 2300	203 596	4 989 000	7 845 000	11 478 085	10 303 830	11 815 723	16 645 000	19 272 000	20 169 000	21 694 000
2410 On a payroll basis	203 596	4 989 000	7 845 000	11 478 085	10 303 830	11 815 723	16 645 000	19 272 000	20 169 000	21 694 000
2420 On an income tax basis	0	0	0	0	0	0	0	0	0	0
3000 Taxes on payroll and workforce	**0**	**1 286 803**	**2 179 842**	**4 022 503**	**4 479 886**	**4 775 034**	**3 527 459**	**2 627 958**	**2 797 308**	**2 998 237**
4000 Taxes on property	**56 160**	**2 027 654**	**4 838 158**	**8 535 238**	**12 921 501**	**13 668 964**	**15 018 163**	**16 119 572**	**18 306 740**	**18 266 486**
4100 Recurrent taxes on immovable property	56 160	991 070	1 974 213	3 338 935	3 611 383	4 016 860	4 845 576	5 559 528	6 212 601	6 747 288
4110 Households	0	0	0	0	0	0	0	0	0	0
4120 Others	56 160	991 070	1 974 213	3 338 935	3 611 383	4 016 860	4 845 576	5 559 528	6 212 601	6 747 288
4200 Recurrent taxes on net wealth	0	0	462 720	1 970 530	4 240 512	4 183 752	4 274 832	4 118 075	5 352 940	4 440 142
4210 Individual	..	..	462 720	1 970 530	4 240 512	4 183 752	4 274 832	4 118 075	5 352 940	4 440 142
4220 Corporate	..	..	0	0	0	0	0	0	0	0
4300 Estate, inheritance and gift taxes	0	0	0	0	0	0	0	0	0	0
4310 Estate and inheritance taxes	..	..	..	..	..	..	..	..	..	..
4320 Gift taxes	..	..	..	..	..	..	..	..	..	..
4400 Taxes on financial and capital transactions	0	1 036 584	2 401 226	3 225 773	5 069 606	5 468 351	5 897 755	6 441 969	6 741 200	7 079 055
4500 Non-recurrent taxes	0	0	0	0	0	0	0	0	0	0
4510 On net wealth	..	..	..	..	..	..	..	..	..	..
4520 Other non-recurrent taxes	..	..	..	..	..	..	..	..	..	..
4600 Other recurrent taxes on property	0	0	0	0	0	0	0	0	0	0
5000 Taxes on goods and services	**1 388 653**	**13 367 908**	**25 866 553**	**42 156 822**	**49 224 753**	**50 795 912**	**52 393 473**	**57 894 877**	**62 378 051**	**63 375 512**
5100 Taxes on production, sale, transfer, etc	1 388 653	13 367 908	25 866 553	42 156 822	49 224 753	50 795 912	52 393 473	57 894 877	62 378 051	63 375 512
5110 General taxes	672 368	9 585 866	19 934 400	33 333 802	40 024 882	41 862 732	40 598 702	45 330 387	48 721 833	49 506 811
5111 Value added taxes	583 078	8 445 776	17 427 948	28 811 682	35 093 071	36 324 330	34 642 822	38 749 869	41 553 967	41 878 886
5112 Sales tax	89 290	1 140 090	2 506 452	4 522 121	4 931 810	5 538 402	5 955 879	6 580 518	7 167 866	7 627 926
Industry and commerce tax (State)	89 290	1 140 090	2 506 452	4 522 121	4 931 810	5 538 402	5 955 879	6 580 518	7 167 866	7 627 926
5113 Other	0	0	0	0	0	0	0	0	0	0
5120 Taxes on specific goods and services	716 285	3 782 042	5 932 153	8 823 019	9 199 872	8 933 180	11 794 771	12 564 490	13 656 219	13 868 701
5121 Excises	404 699	2 037 944	3 109 633	4 171 020	5 119 156	5 409 860	7 897 587	8 577 766	9 065 288	9 755 514
Oil	141 270	833 004	1 143 308	1 418 766	1 603 227	1 735 062	2 883 410	2 980 883	3 297 392	3 335 157
Tobacco (State)	52 898	213 410	287 379	390 472	499 531	486 282	508 089	493 868	524 357	595 476
Beer (State)	85 722	471 137	867 569	1 432 453	1 764 785	1 900 215	2 031 349	2 108 721	2 305 895	2 549 948
Liquors (State)	124 808	520 393	811 377	929 328	1 251 613	1 288 302	1 292 742	1 345 827	1 253 466	1 574 864
Restaurant, vehicles sale and mobile telephony	0	0	0	0	0	0	1 181 998	1 648 467	1 684 179	1 700 069
5122 Profits of fiscal monopolies	0	0	0	0	0	0	0	0	0	0
5123 Customs and import duties	311 586	1 744 097	2 822 520	4 651 999	4 080 716	3 523 320	3 897 184	3 986 724	4 590 931	4 113 187
Custom duties	180 989	1 744 097	2 822 520	4 651 999	4 080 716	3 523 320	3 897 184	3 986 724	4 590 931	4 113 187
Imports surcharge	130 597	0	0	0	0	0	0	0	0	0
5124 Taxes on exports	0	0	0	0	0	0	0	0	0	0
5125 Taxes on investment goods	0	0	0	0	0	0	0	0	0	0
5126 Taxes on specific services	0	0	0	0	0	0	0	0	0	0
5127 Other taxes on internat. trade and transactions	0	0	0	0	0	0	0	0	0	0
5128 Other taxes	0	0	0	0	0	0	0	0	0	0
5130 Unallocable between 5110 and 5120	0	0	0	0	0	0	0	0	0	0
5200 Taxes on use of goods and perform activities	0	0	0	0	0	0	0	0	0	0
5210 Recurrent taxes	..	..	..	..	..	..	..	..	..	..

Table 5.8. Colombia *(cont.)*
Details of tax revenue / Ingresos tributarios detallados

Million COP

	1990	2000	2005	2010	2011	2012	2013	2014	2015	2016
5211 Paid by households: motor vehicles	..	..	..	..	..	..	..	..	..	..
5212 Paid by others: motor vehicles	..	..	..	..	..	..	..	..	..	..
5213 Paid in respect of other goods	..	..	..	..	..	..	..	..	..	..
5220 Non-recurrent taxes	..	..	..	..	..	..	..	..	..	..
5300 Unallocable between 5100 and 5200	0	0	0	0	0	0	0	0	0	0
6000 Other taxes	**159 323**	**1 738 020**	**3 377 674**	**5 543 430**	**6 220 640**	**6 142 494**	**7 130 151**	**8 189 746**	**9 762 474**	**9 775 935**
6100 Paid solely by business	0	0	0	0	0	0	0	0	0	0
6200 Other	159 323	1 738 020	3 377 674	5 543 430	6 220 640	6 142 494	7 130 151	8 189 746	9 762 474	9 775 935
Stamp tax	0	401 497	633 586	357 160	123 923	58 973	58 378	72 425	105 729	97 492
Other	78 306	79 287	48 498	126 602	143 770	174 845	200 465	260 721	318 271	357 863
Other (sub-national)	81 017	1 257 236	2 695 589	5 059 668	5 952 946	5 908 676	6 871 308	7 856 600	9 338 474	9 320 581

Note: Year ending 31st December.
The data are on a cash basis.
Includes the reported consolidated revenues of the territorial entities (departments and municipalities).
Heading 2000: Before 2013, social security contributions did not include all the contributions entering FOSYGA (Solidarity and Guarantee Fund). Only the portion of the contributions used to finance the subsidised regime (up to 1.5 pp of the 12.5% of the monthly wage paid by employers and employees as an obligatory health contribution) was included. The part of the contributions entering FOSYGA to finance the contributory regime was classified in the social security sector as "other incomes". From 2013 onwards, all of the health contributions entering FOSYGA are classified as social security contributions. The portion of the contributions not entering FOSYGA that is both collected and spent by the health insurers – EPS - is not part of the fiscal accounts.
Headings 1100 and 1200: The data are estimated.

Source: Dirección de Impuestos y Aduanas Nacionales de Colombia, Ministerio de Hacienda y Crédito Público y Banco Central de Colombia. (National Tax and Customs Administration, Ministry of Finance and Public Credit and Central Bank of Colombia).

StatLink http://dx.doi.org/10.1787/888933686841

Table 5.9. Costa Rica
Details of tax revenue / Ingresos tributarios detallados

Million CRC

	1990	2000	2005	2010	2011	2012	2013	2014	2015	2016
Total tax revenue	**114 173**	**927 561**	**1 960 924**	**4 058 696**	**4 532 171**	**4 958 578**	**5 419 339**	**5 849 639**	**6 386 643**	**6 956 107**
1000 Taxes on income, profits and capital gains	**11 820**	**128 805**	**324 224**	**748 093**	**828 691**	**891 669**	**1 014 440**	**1 091 470**	**1 247 308**	**1 416 218**
1100 Of individuals	..	..	16 438	202 849	233 486	307 489	316 894	349 139	386 241	414 247
1110 On income and profits	..	..	16 438	202 849	233 486	307 489	316 894	349 139	386 241	414 247
1120 On capital gains	..	..	..	..	..	..	..	..	..	..
1200 Corporate	..	..	288 355	450 312	486 001	461 481	545 183	574 137	659 951	742 011
1210 On profits	..	..	288 355	450 312	486 001	461 481	545 183	574 137	659 951	742 011
1220 On capital gains	..	..	..	..	..	..	..	..	..	..
1300 Unallocable between 1100 and 1200	11 820	128 805	19 430	94 932	109 204	122 699	152 363	168 194	201 116	259 961
2000 Social security contributions	**30 543**	**249 182**	**497 341**	**1 139 265**	**1 279 856**	**1 399 618**	**1 511 383**	**1 648 831**	**1 785 522**	**1 985 151**
2100 Employees	..	..	..	..	..	..	..	..	..	..
2110 On a payroll basis	..	..	..	..	..	..	..	..	..	..
2120 On an income tax basis	..	..	..	..	..	..	..	..	..	..
2200 Employers	..	..	..	..	..	..	..	..	..	..
2210 On a payroll basis	..	..	..	..	..	..	..	..	..	..
2220 On an income tax basis	..	..	..	..	..	..	..	..	..	..
2300 Self-employed or non-employed	..	..	..	..	..	..	..	..	..	..
2310 On a payroll basis	..	..	..	..	..	..	..	..	..	..
2320 On an income tax basis	..	..	..	..	..	..	..	..	..	..
2400 Unallocable between 2100, 2200 and 2300	30 543	249 182	497 341	1 139 265	1 279 856	1 399 618	1 511 383	1 648 831	1 785 522	1 985 151
2410 On a payroll basis	..	..	..	..	..	..	..	..	..	..
2420 On an income tax basis	..	..	..	..	..	..	..	..	..	..
3000 Taxes on payroll and workforce	**7 484**	**59 129**	**112 082**	**248 259**	**275 775**	**309 804**	**337 696**	**372 869**	**406 296**	**435 328**
4000 Taxes on property	**1 566**	**8 396**	**25 110**	**63 706**	**71 214**	**82 007**	**99 030**	**114 313**	**123 261**	**134 332**
4100 Recurrent taxes on immovable property	1 200	5 390	14 264	48 963	52 161	61 057	70 785	81 613	90 003	97 869
Land tax	0	0	0	0	0	0	0	0	0	0
Additional land tax	0	0	0	0	0	0	0	0	0	0
Tax on sumptuary constructions	0	0	0	0	0	0	0	0	0	0
Immovable property tax	0	0	0	3 527	2 475	2 638	3 998	4 013	4 076	4 098
Municipal immovable property tax	1 200	5 390	14 264	45 436	49 686	58 418	66 787	77 600	85 927	93 771
4110 Households	..	..	..	..	..	..	..	..	..	..
4120 Others	..	..	..	..	..	..	..	..	..	..
4200 Recurrent taxes on net wealth	0	0	0	0	0	0	0	0	0	0
4210 Individual	..	..	..	..	..	..	..	..	..	..
4220 Corporate	..	..	..	..	..	..	..	..	..	..
4300 Estate, inheritance and gift taxes	0	0	0	0	0	0	0	0	0	0
4310 Estate and inheritance taxes	..	..	..	..	..	..	..	..	..	..
4320 Gift taxes	..	..	..	..	..	..	..	..	..	..
4400 Taxes on financial and capital transactions	366	3 007	10 846	14 743	19 053	20 950	28 246	32 700	33 258	36 462
4500 Non-recurrent taxes	0	0	0	0	0	0	0	0	0	0
4510 On net wealth	..	..	..	..	..	..	..	..	..	..
4520 Other non-recurrent taxes	..	..	..	..	..	..	..	..	..	..
4600 Other recurrent taxes on property	0	0	0	0	0	0	0	0	0	0
5000 Taxes on goods and services	**53 509**	**456 851**	**944 623**	**1 766 914**	**1 968 853**	**2 150 384**	**2 302 986**	**2 468 087**	**2 661 902**	**2 794 229**
5100 Taxes on production, sale, transfer, etc	49 867	425 713	884 453	1 600 302	1 802 830	1 958 415	2 092 588	2 222 962	2 388 900	2 508 186
5110 General taxes	21 326	222 775	485 168	920 298	1 029 811	1 145 403	1 212 471	1 306 110	1 368 601	1 420 938
5111 Value added taxes	21 326	222 775	485 168	920 298	1 029 811	1 122 978	1 176 745	1 266 798	1 336 075	1 414 358
5112 Sales tax	0	0	0	0	0	0	0	0	0	0
5113 Other	0	0	0	0	0	22 425	35 726	39 313	32 526	6 580
5120 Taxes on specific goods and services	28 541	202 939	399 286	680 004	773 019	813 013	880 117	916 851	1 020 299	1 087 248
5121 Excises	11 096	157 204	296 222	523 617	596 268	629 423	689 528	706 016	798 412	846 864
Fuels and energy	0	0	172 028	320 638	359 425	354 149	404 210	404 901	457 827	472 644
Alcohol beverages	0	8 229	20 219	28 035	32 936	35 620	35 254	36 293	43 095	43 400
Non alcoholic beverages	0	0	12 491	26 566	27 804	30 205	32 519	34 874	36 353	39 764
Soaps	0	0	573	1 317	1 425	1 487	1 989	1 493	2 562	2 912
Cement	0	0	0	227	250	247	291	340	304	267
Tobacco	0	0	0	0	0	19 852	38 860	32 277	33 681	32 560
Abolished specific taxes on production and consumption	0	0	0	0	0	0	0	0	0	0
Other specific taxes on consumption	11 096	148 975	90 913	146 834	174 428	187 863	176 405	195 838	224 590	255 317
5122 Profits of fiscal monopolies	0	0	0	0	0	0	0	0	0	0
5123 Customs and import duties	15 052	40 485	82 446	126 134	146 511	152 275	154 576	169 120	174 568	185 544
Import duties	13 977	32 336	66 598	103 851	122 355	128 358	130 634	142 226	148 666	158 559
Custom duties	1 075	8 149	15 848	22 284	24 156	23 917	23 942	26 894	25 902	26 986

Table 5.9. Costa Rica *(cont.)*
Details of tax revenue / Ingresos tributarios detallados

Million CRC

	1990	2000	2005	2010	2011	2012	2013	2014	2015	2016
5124 Taxes on exports	2 113	2 238	969	3 973	3 990	3 823	4 877	4 853	4 468	5 073
Export duties	2 113	2 088	830	3 816	3 827	3 663	4 104	3 067	2 701	3 250
Export duties Law 133	0	0	0	0	0	0	0	0	0	0
Export duties Law 5519	0	0	0	0	0	0	0	0	0	0
Tax on banana exports	0	150	139	157	163	160	168	176	156	184
Export duties on ground transportation	0	0	0	0	0	0	605	1 610	1 611	1 638
5125 Taxes on investment goods	0	0	0	0	0	0	0	0	0	0
5126 Taxes on specific services	280	2 929	19 555	24 767	24 190	25 579	28 571	34 081	38 687	44 934
Casinos and gambling	0	225	519	445	288	213	1 019	940	1 455	1 609
Port cargo movements	0	6	13	0	0	0	0	0	0	0
Overseas departure tax	0	0	19 022	24 322	23 902	25 366	27 552	33 141	37 232	43 325
10% on public shows	0	0	0	0	0	0	0	0	0	0
Pro-national airport's stamp tax	0	0	0	0	0	0	0	0	0	0
Stamp tax on the use of borders and ports	280	2 697	0	0	0	0	0	0	0	0
5127 Other taxes on internat. trade and transactions	0	83	94	1 513	2 060	1 913	2 565	2 782	3 093	3 512
5128 Other taxes	0	0	0	0	0	0	0	0	1 071	1 320
5130 Unallocable between 5110 and 5120	0	0	0	0	0	0	0	0	0	0
5200 Taxes on use of goods and perform activities	3 642	31 138	60 170	166 612	166 022	191 968	210 398	245 125	273 003	286 044
5210 Recurrent taxes	3 642	31 138	60 170	166 612	166 022	191 968	210 398	245 125	273 003	286 044
5211 Paid by households: motor vehicles	0	0	0	0	0	0	0	0	0	0
5212 Paid by others: motor vehicles	1 425	15 374	30 918	94 102	85 152	101 903	113 727	130 000	145 894	156 517
Property tax on vehicles, aircraft and boats	1 425	15 374	30 918	94 102	85 152	101 903	113 727	130 000	145 894	156 517
5213 Paid in respect of other goods	2 217	15 763	29 252	72 510	80 870	90 065	96 671	115 125	127 109	129 527
Local taxes	1 262	11 898	27 411	68 808	74 756	85 411	91 163	110 120	122 248	124 862
Hunting and fishing licences	0	0	0	0	0	0	0	0	0	0
Spirits licence	0	0	0	0	0	0	0	0	0	0
Revenue stamps	955	3 866	1 841	3 702	6 114	4 654	5 508	5 005	4 861	4 664
Sport stamp tax	0	0	0	0	0	0	0	0	0	0
5220 Non-recurrent taxes	0	0	0	0	0	0	0	0	0	0
5300 Unallocable between 5100 and 5200	0	0	0	0	0	0	0	0	0	0
6000 Other taxes	**9 251**	**25 198**	**57 545**	**92 460**	**107 782**	**125 097**	**153 803**	**154 069**	**162 355**	**190 850**
6100 Paid solely by business	0	0	0	0	0	0	0	0	0	0
6200 Other	9 251	25 198	57 545	92 460	107 782	125 097	153 803	154 069	162 355	190 850
Transfers of vehicles, aircraft and boats	497	2 530	6 357	12 311	13 672	12 947	17 177	19 099	20 999	23 022
Tax revenue from decentralised units	2 764	15 048	11 985	29 969	37 231	39 172	45 700	46 591	49 334	67 584
Other taxes	5 990	7 620	39 203	50 180	56 879	72 978	90 926	88 379	92 022	100 243

Note: Year ending 31st December.

The data are on a cash basis.

The local government tax revenues data have been expanded and start in 1990 in this edition.

Heading 2000: In ECLAC data, social security contributions also include INA (National Institute of Apprenticeship), IMAS (Joint Social Aid Institute), and FODESAF (Social Development and Family Allowances Fund).

Heading 3000: In Costa Rica and for ECLAC, social security contributions from decentralised institutions are classified under heading 2000.

Heading 5113: This heading includes a turnover tax previously classified under heading 6100.

Heading 5212: In ECLAC data, tax on ownership of vehicles, aircraft and boats is classified in category 4000.

Heading 5213: This includes local tax revenue previously classified under heading 5126 up to 2011 and under heading 5130 between 2012 and 2015.

Heading 6200: The figures have been revised and include the tax revenue of decentralised bodies (other than social security contributions) that was not accounted for in previous editions. The tax revenue of decentralised bodies is classified under central government for this publication. In Costa Rica this revenue is classified under a separate unit (decentralised) considered to be separate from the central government. In ECLAC data, the tax on the transfer of used vehicles Law No. 7088 of 30/11/87 is classified as a property tax.

Source: Secretaría Técnica de la Autoridad Presupuestaria, Ministerio de Finanzas y Contraloría General de la República (Technical Secretary of the Budgeting Authority, Ministry of Finance and National General Comptroller).

StatLink http://dx.doi.org/10.1787/888933686860

Table 5.10. Cuba
Details of tax revenue / Ingresos tributarios detallados

Million CUP

	1990	2000	2005	2010	2011	2012	2013	2014	2015	2016
Total tax revenue	**6 265**	**11 367**	**17 528**	**24 201**	**26 508**	**29 068**	**28 804**	**30 236**	**33 591**	**37 377**
1000 Taxes on income, profits and capital gains	**14**	**1 826**	**2 451**	**3 603**	**4 504**	**4 535**	**5 292**	**5 995**	**6 676**	**7 937**
1100 Of individuals	14	291	326	554	762	873	1 055	1 308	1 848	2 300
1110 On income and profits	..	..	..	..	..	..	..	..	..	..
1120 On capital gains	..	..	..	..	..	..	..	..	..	..
1200 Corporate	0	1 535	2 126	3 049	3 742	3 662	4 237	4 687	4 828	5 637
1210 On profits	..	..	..	..	..	..	..	..	..	..
1220 On capital gains	..	..	..	..	..	..	..	..	..	..
1300 Unallocable between 1100 and 1200	0	0	0	0	0	0	0	0	0	0
2000 Social security contributions	**691**	**1 181**	**1 778**	**2 974**	**2 996**	**3 043**	**3 123**	**3 622**	**4 322**	**4 700**
2100 Employees	..	..	..	..	..	..	..	..	..	..
2110 On a payroll basis	..	..	..	..	..	..	..	..	..	..
2120 On an income tax basis	..	..	..	..	..	..	..	..	..	..
2200 Employers	..	..	..	..	..	..	..	..	..	..
2210 On a payroll basis	..	..	..	..	..	..	..	..	..	..
2220 On an income tax basis	..	..	..	..	..	..	..	..	..	..
2300 Self-employed or non-employed	..	..	..	..	..	..	..	..	..	..
2310 On a payroll basis	..	..	..	..	..	..	..	..	..	..
2320 On an income tax basis	..	..	..	..	..	..	..	..	..	..
2400 Unallocable between 2100, 2200 and 2300	691	1 181	1 778	2 974	2 996	3 043	3 123	3 622	4 322	4 700
2410 On a payroll basis	691	1 181	1 778	2 974	2 996	3 043	3 123	3 622	4 322	4 700
2420 On an income tax basis	0	0	0	0	0	0	0	0	0	0
3000 Taxes on payroll and workforce	**0**	**970**	**2 962**	**4 414**	**4 235**	**4 108**	**3 424**	**2 939**	**2 753**	**2 420**
4000 Taxes on property	**0**	**0**	**0**	**0**	**0**	**0**	**0**	**0**	**0**	**0**
4100 Recurrent taxes on immovable property	..	..	..	..	..	..	..	..	..	..
4110 Households	..	..	..	..	..	..	..	..	..	..
4120 Others	..	..	..	..	..	..	..	..	..	..
4200 Recurrent taxes on net wealth	..	..	..	..	..	..	..	..	..	..
4210 Individual	..	..	..	..	..	..	..	..	..	..
4220 Corporate	..	..	..	..	..	..	..	..	..	..
4300 Estate, inheritance and gift taxes	..	..	..	..	..	..	..	..	..	..
4310 Estate and inheritance taxes	..	..	..	..	..	..	..	..	..	..
4320 Gift taxes	..	..	..	..	..	..	..	..	..	..
4400 Taxes on financial and capital transactions	..	..	..	..	..	..	..	..	..	..
4500 Non-recurrent taxes	..	..	..	..	..	..	..	..	..	..
4510 On net wealth	..	..	..	..	..	..	..	..	..	..
4520 Other non-recurrent taxes	..	..	..	..	..	..	..	..	..	..
4600 Other recurrent taxes on property	..	..	..	..	..	..	..	..	..	..
5000 Taxes on goods and services	**5 443**	**6 732**	**9 844**	**12 283**	**13 696**	**16 232**	**15 588**	**15 911**	**17 742**	**20 135**
5100 Taxes on production, sale, transfer, etc	5 443	6 732	9 844	12 283	13 696	16 232	15 588	15 911	17 742	20 135
5110 General taxes	5 017	6 131	9 036	10 525	11 819	14 511	14 057	14 171	15 611	17 550
5111 Value added taxes	0	0	0	0	0	0	0	0	0	0
5112 Sales tax	5 017	6 131	9 036	10 525	11 819	14 511	14 057	14 171	15 611	17 550
5113 Other	0	0	0	0	0	0	0	0	0	0
5120 Taxes on specific goods and services	426	602	808	1 758	1 876	1 721	1 531	1 740	2 131	2 585
5121 Excises	..	..	..	..	..	..	..	..	..	..
5122 Profits of fiscal monopolies	..	..	..	..	..	..	..	..	..	..
5123 Customs and import duties	..	..	..	..	..	..	..	..	..	..
5124 Taxes on exports	..	..	..	..	..	..	..	..	..	..
5125 Taxes on investment goods	..	..	..	..	..	..	..	..	..	..
5126 Taxes on specific services	..	..	..	..	..	..	..	..	..	..
5127 Other taxes on internat. trade and transactions	..	..	..	..	..	..	..	..	..	..
5128 Other taxes	..	..	..	..	..	..	..	..	..	..
5130 Unallocable between 5110 and 5120	..	..	..	..	..	..	..	..	..	..
5200 Taxes on use of goods and perform activities	0	0	0	0	0	0	0	0	0	0
5210 Recurrent taxes	..	..	..	..	..	..	..	..	..	..
5211 Paid by households: motor vehicles	..	..	..	..	..	..	..	..	..	..
5212 Paid by others: motor vehicles	..	..	..	..	..	..	..	..	..	..
5213 Paid in respect of other goods	..	..	..	..	..	..	..	..	..	..
5220 Non-recurrent taxes	..	..	..	..	..	..	..	..	..	..
5300 Unallocable between 5100 and 5200	..	..	..	..	..	..	..	..	..	..
6000 Other taxes	**117**	**657**	**493**	**927**	**1 078**	**1 150**	**1 378**	**1 769**	**2 098**	**2 185**
6100 Paid solely by business	..	..	..	..	..	..	..	..	..	..
6200 Other	..	..	..	..	..	..	..	..	..	..

Table 5.10. Cuba *(cont.)*
Details of tax revenue / Ingresos tributarios detallados

Note: Year ending 31st December.
The data are on a cash basis.
The figures exclude local government tax revenues as the data are not available.
Heading 5110: For this edition, the disaggregation of heading 5110 has been improved.
The figures for the sub-category under the heading 5120 are not available.

Source: Oficina Nacional de Estadística e Información. Anuario Estadístico de Cuba (National Office of Statistics and Information. Annual Statistical Review of Cuba).

StatLink http://dx.doi.org/10.1787/888933686879

Table 5.11. Dominican Republic / República Dominicana
Details of tax revenue / Ingresos tributarios detallados

Million DOP

	1990	2000	2005	2010	2011	2012	2013	2014	2015	2016
Total tax revenue	**6 439**	**44 898**	**129 639**	**243 872**	**273 132**	**312 148**	**355 314**	**393 157**	**414 245**	**450 325**
1000 Taxes on income, profits and capital gains	**1 670**	**10 782**	**30 042**	**53 643**	**65 453**	**92 850**	**108 853**	**125 098**	**119 819**	**134 804**
1100 Of individuals	..	4 088	7 588	17 088	20 673	21 874	27 147	31 525	35 549	40 193
1110 On income and profits	..	4 070	7 509	16 901	20 220	21 575	26 723	31 119	35 187	39 780
1120 On capital gains	..	18	79	187	453	299	424	406	361	413
1200 Corporate	..	4 679	16 222	21 475	25 125	46 921	58 923	72 865	61 695	69 362
1210 On profits	..	4 605	16 147	21 325	24 913	46 582	58 597	72 628	61 455	69 079
1220 On capital gains	..	74	75	151	212	339	326	238	240	283
Casinos	..	59	73	151	182	213	187	173	184	228
Racetracks	..	15	2	0	0	0	0	0	0	0
Phone gaming	..	0	0	0	30	127	139	64	56	55
1300 Unallocable between 1100 and 1200	1 670	2 015	6 232	15 080	19 655	24 055	22 782	20 708	22 576	25 249
2000 Social security contributions	**53**	**490**	**35**	**1 845**	**1 328**	**1 250**	**1 552**	**1 515**	**1 483**	**1 550**
2100 Employees	..	..	..	..	..	..	..	..	1 321	1 392
2110 On a payroll basis	..	..	..	..	..	..	..	..	..	..
2120 On an income tax basis	..	..	..	..	..	..	..	..	..	..
2200 Employers	..	..	..	..	..	..	..	..	163	158
2210 On a payroll basis	..	..	..	..	..	..	..	..	..	..
2220 On an income tax basis	..	..	..	..	..	..	..	..	..	..
2300 Self-employed or non-employed	..	..	..	..	..	..	..	..	0	0
2310 On a payroll basis	..	..	..	..	..	..	..	..	..	..
2320 On an income tax basis	..	..	..	..	..	..	..	..	..	..
2400 Unallocable between 2100, 2200 and 2300	53	490	35	1 845	1 328	1 250	1 552	1 515	0	0
2410 On a payroll basis	53	490	35	1 845	1 328	1 250	1 552	1 515	..	..
2420 On an income tax basis	0	0	0	0	0	0	0	0	..	..
3000 Taxes on payroll and workforce	**0**	**0**	**0**	**0**	**0**	**0**	**0**	**0**	**0**	**0**
4000 Taxes on property	**74**	**689**	**6 749**	**13 315**	**15 928**	**19 606**	**22 928**	**18 183**	**19 044**	**19 809**
4100 Recurrent taxes on immovable property	9	115	1 710	555	629	686	1 518	1 579	1 755	1 871
4110 Households	9	115	1 710	555	629	686	1 518	1 579	1 755	1 871
4120 Others	0	0	0	0	0	0	0	0	0	0
4200 Recurrent taxes on net wealth	0	0	0	2 449	4 605	7 665	8 666	3 458	3 445	3 544
Tax on assets	..	..	..	2 449	2 790	3 044	3 337	3 454	3 445	3 544
4210 Individual	..	..	..	..	0	0	0	0	0	0
4220 Corporate	..	..	..	..	1 816	4 620	5 329	4	0	0
4300 Estate, inheritance and gift taxes	11	96	84	231	237	227	315	325	418	388
4310 Estate and inheritance taxes	..	..	..	..	..	..	..	..	..	..
4320 Gift taxes	..	..	..	..	..	..	..	..	..	..
4400 Taxes on financial and capital transactions	40	377	4 716	8 658	8 827	9 405	11 209	11 394	12 067	13 265
Tax on checks	0	0	3 133	4 262	4 492	4 852	5 168	5 620	5 951	6 591
Real estate operations	22	217	1 413	3 864	3 763	3 872	5 236	4 876	5 169	5 668
Tax on the transfer of immovable property	18	160	170	533	572	682	805	898	947	1 005
4500 Non-recurrent taxes	3	32	89	488	578	609	412	677	591	681
4510 On net wealth	3	32	89	488	578	609	412	677	591	681
4520 Other non-recurrent taxes	0	0	0	0	0	0	0	0	0	0
4600 Other recurrent taxes on property	11	70	151	934	1 052	1 014	810	751	769	61
5000 Taxes on goods and services	**4 483**	**32 442**	**91 152**	**175 069**	**190 423**	**198 442**	**221 981**	**248 361**	**273 898**	**294 161**
5100 Taxes on production, sale, transfer, etc	4 413	31 724	89 434	168 570	183 720	191 369	214 540	239 526	263 435	281 259
5110 General taxes	970	9 912	40 983	81 226	88 892	92 205	112 731	130 447	147 039	159 212
5111 Value added taxes	970	9 912	40 983	81 226	88 892	92 205	112 731	130 447	147 039	159 212
5112 Sales tax	0	0	0	0	0	0	0	0	0	0
5113 Other	0	0	0	0	0	0	0	0	0	0
5120 Taxes on specific goods and services	3 444	21 812	48 451	87 345	94 828	99 164	101 809	109 080	116 396	122 047
5121 Excises	510	6 614	27 384	56 024	63 634	67 154	68 434	72 399	74 586	77 110
Alcoholic beverages	251	2 451	8 142	15 054	16 240	17 089	17 969	19 779	22 371	23 617
Tobacco products	102	469	2 879	4 529	4 241	4 470	4 356	4 382	4 532	4 117
Petroleum products	105	3 143	14 712	34 598	40 303	42 460	42 222	44 335	29 989	32 697
Other	52	551	1 651	1 843	2 850	3 136	3 887	3 904	17 694	16 679
5122 Profits of fiscal monopolies	0	0	0	0	0	0	0	0	0	0
5123 Customs and import duties	1 548	13 459	14 403	19 455	18 801	18 891	19 043	21 315	25 212	27 286
Custom duties	615	13 456	14 293	19 455	18 801	18 776	18 916	21 238	24 378	26 397
Other	933	3	110	0	0	115	126	76	834	889
5124 Taxes on exports	6	4	46	146	181	264	34	12	8	0
5125 Taxes on investment goods	0	0	0	0	0	0	0	0	0	0

Table 5.11. Dominican Republic / República Dominicana *(cont.)*
Details of tax revenue / Ingresos tributarios detallados

Million DOP

	1990	2000	2005	2010	2011	2012	2013	2014	2015	2016
5126 Taxes on specific services	344	1 590	5 609	11 411	11 822	12 516	13 863	14 956	16 245	17 327
Telecommunications	85	0	3 193	4 886	4 947	5 124	5 897	6 129	6 375	6 607
Insurance premiums	33	584	0	3 088	3 238	3 437	3 674	3 965	4 301	4 828
Travel tickets	204	809	2 414	3 428	3 632	3 951	4 283	4 839	5 535	5 892
Hotels	22	191	0	0	0	0	0	0	0	0
Others	0	7	1	9	6	4	9	24	35	0
5127 Other taxes on internat. trade and transactions	1 037	145	1 010	309	389	338	436	397	346	323
Exchange commission	857	0	0	0	0	0	0	0	0	0
Consular fees	77	32	271	132	138	130	143	142	137	149
Other	103	112	738	176	251	209	293	256	209	174
5128 Other taxes	0	0	0	0	0	0	0	0	0	0
5130 Unallocable between 5110 and 5120	0	0	0	0	0	0	0	0	0	0
5200 Taxes on use of goods and perform activities	69	718	1 718	6 498	6 703	7 073	7 442	8 835	10 463	12 902
5210 Recurrent taxes	69	718	1 718	2 265	2 434	2 568	2 569	2 736	2 958	3 332
5211 Paid by households: motor vehicles	45	268	977	1 277	1 300	1 271	1 073	1 289	1 558	1 932
5212 Paid by others: motor vehicles	0	0	0	0	0	0	0	0	0	0
5213 Paid in respect of other goods	24	450	742	988	1 134	1 297	1 496	1 447	1 400	1 400
Licences to carry firearms	17	237	244	296	253	194	240	200	171	190
Licences to operate gambling houses	0	114	155	211	571	1 076	1 229	1 221	1 208	1 210
Licences to operate slot machines	4	60	102	458	287	0	0	0	0	0
Other	4	39	240	24	23	28	28	26	21	0
5220 Non-recurrent taxes	0	0	0	4 234	4 268	4 505	4 872	6 099	7 505	9 570
Vehicle property registration	..	..	..	4 234	4 268	4 505	4 595	5 683	6 990	8 903
Ecological taxes	..	..	..	0	0	0	277	416	515	667
5300 Unallocable between 5100 and 5200	0	0	0	0	0	0	0	0	0	0
6000 Other taxes	**159**	**495**	**1 661**	**0**	**0**	**0**	**0**	**1**	**1**	**1**
6100 Paid solely by business	0	0	0	..	..	0	0	0	0	0
6200 Other	159	495	1 661	..	..	0	0	1	1	1

Note: Year ending 31st December.
The data are on a cash basis.
The figures exclude local government tax revenues as the data are not available.
Heading 2000: The data exclude social security contributions to general government managed by the private sector. An additional breakdown is available since 2015 to discern between social security contributions paid by employees and those paid by employers.
Heading 4400: The transfer tax, previously classified under heading 5121, has been reclassified under this heading.
Heading 4200: This heading includes taxes on assets and taxes on financial assets. Both taxes were previously classified under heading 4120.
Heading 5220: This heading also includes revenue from vehicle registrations, previously classified as 5121.
Source: Ministerio de Hacienda (Ministry of Finance).

StatLink http://dx.doi.org/10.1787/888933686898

Table 5.12. Ecuador
Details of tax revenue / Ingresos tributarios detallados

Million USD

	1990	2000	2005	2010	2011	2012	2013	2014	2015	2016
Total tax revenue	**1 105**	**1 885**	**5 029**	**11 568**	**14 020**	**17 379**	**18 631**	**19 626**	**21 165**	**20 021**
1000 Taxes on income, profits and capital gains	**138**	**293**	**936**	**2 348**	**3 027**	**3 307**	**3 838**	**4 150**	**4 705**	**4 315**
1100 Of individuals	..	10	27	80	93	113	161	177	192	224
1110 On income and profits	..	..	..	..	..	..	..	..	..	..
1120 On capital gains	..	..	..	..	..	..	..	..	..	..
1200 Corporate	..	53	342	485	869	851	1 023	1 121	1 578	1 377
1210 On profits	..	..	..	..	..	..	..	..	..	..
1220 On capital gains	..	..	..	..	..	..	..	..	..	..
1300 Unallocable between 1100 and 1200	138	231	567	1 783	2 066	2 344	2 654	2 851	2 935	2 714
Unallocable income tax	138	204	854	1 858	2 148	2 422	2 740	2 965	3 034	2 746
Income tax refunds	0	27	-287	-75	-82	-78	-86	-113	-99	-32
2000 Social security contributions	**243**	**228**	**1 109**	**2 549**	**3 971**	**4 752**	**4 547**	**4 718**	**5 055**	**4 741**
2100 Employees	..	..	..	..	..	..	..	..	..	..
2110 On a payroll basis	..	..	..	..	..	..	..	..	..	..
2120 On an income tax basis	..	..	..	..	..	..	..	..	..	..
2200 Employers	..	..	..	..	..	..	..	..	..	..
2210 On a payroll basis	..	..	..	..	..	..	..	..	..	..
2220 On an income tax basis	..	..	..	..	..	..	..	..	..	..
2300 Self-employed or non-employed	..	..	..	..	..	..	..	..	..	..
2310 On a payroll basis	..	..	..	..	..	..	..	..	..	..
2320 On an income tax basis	..	..	..	..	..	..	..	..	..	..
2400 Unallocable between 2100, 2200 and 2300	243	228	1 109	2 549	3 971	4 752	4 547	4 718	5 055	4 741
2410 On a payroll basis	..	..	..	..	..	..	..	..	..	..
2420 On an income tax basis	..	..	..	..	..	..	..	..	..	..
3000 Taxes on payroll and workforce	**0**	**0**	**0**	**0**	**0**	**0**	**0**	**0**	**0**	**0**
4000 Taxes on property	**14**	**11**	**44**	**86**	**104**	**156**	**165**	**194**	**229**	**590**
4100 Recurrent taxes on immovable property	13	10	38	66	73	105	114	115	126	149
4110 Households	0	0	0	0	0	0	0	0	0	0
4120 Others	13	10	38	66	73	105	114	115	126	141
4200 Recurrent taxes on net wealth	0	0	0	0	0	0	0	0	0	202
4210 Individual	..	..	..	..	..	..	..	..	..	..
4220 Corporate	..	..	..	..	..	..	..	..	..	..
4300 Estate, inheritance and gift taxes	0	0	1	5	3	6	9	11	29	15
4310 Estate and inheritance taxes	..	..	1	5	3	6	9	11	29	15
4320 Gift taxes	..	..	0	0	0	0	0	0	0	0
4400 Taxes on financial and capital transactions	1	2	6	15	28	44	42	69	75	84
4500 Non-recurrent taxes	0	0	0	0	0	0	0	0	0	141
4510 On net wealth	..	..	..	..	..	..	..	..	..	..
4520 Other non-recurrent taxes	..	..	..	..	..	..	..	..	..	..
4600 Other recurrent taxes on property	0	0	0	0	0	0	0	0	0	0
5000 Taxes on goods and services	**682**	**1 350**	**2 887**	**6 295**	**6 889**	**9 052**	**9 950**	**10 462**	**11 130**	**10 278**
5100 Taxes on production, sale, transfer, etc	671	1 330	2 786	6 078	6 642	8 771	9 630	10 120	10 774	9 823
5110 General taxes	306	840	1 990	3 926	4 243	5 468	6 118	6 448	6 425	6 124
5111 Value added taxes	302	836	1 975	3 886	4 201	5 415	6 056	6 376	6 352	6 042
5112 Sales tax	0	0	0	0	0	0	0	0	0	0
5113 Other	4	4	15	39	42	53	62	72	73	82
5120 Taxes on specific goods and services	365	490	796	2 152	2 399	3 303	3 512	3 672	4 349	3 699
5121 Excises	90	75	221	530	618	685	744	804	840	827
Alcohol products	..	30	89	..	..	..	..	..	232	229
Soft drinks and mineral water	..	9	15	..	..	..	..	..	59	118
Cigarettes	..	24	71	..	..	..	..	..	195	158
Luxury goods and vehicles	..	11	46	..	..	..	..	..	213	145
Telecomunications	..	0	0	0	0	..	..	1	0	24
Pipeline tax	..	0	0	0	..	..	..	..	0	0
Excise on imports	..	0	0	..	..	..	..	..	142	124
Plastic bottles	..	0	0	..	..	..	..	..	0	28
5122 Profits of fiscal monopolies	0	0	0	0	0	0	0	0	0	0
5123 Customs and import duties	227	217	547	1 152	1 156	1 261	1 352	1 357	2 026	1 633
5124 Taxes on exports	0	0	0	0	0	0	0	0	0	0
5125 Taxes on investment goods	0	0	0	0	0	0	0	0	0	0
5126 Taxes on specific services	8	23	29	470	625	1 358	1 417	1 511	1 402	1 150
Exit taxes	7	17	0	428	558	1 275	1 322	1 406	1 278	1 012
Public shows and events	1	2	3	6	8	8	8	7	8	9
Commercial, industrial and service patents	0	5	26	35	58	73	85	97	115	128
Construction contracts with the public sector	0	0	0	0	0	0	0	0	0	0
Disposal of livestock	0	0	0	1	1	1	1	1	1	1
Lotteries and gambling	0	0	0	0	0	0	0	0	0	0

Table 5.12. Ecuador *(cont.)*
Details of tax revenue / Ingresos tributarios detallados

Million USD

	1990	2000	2005	2010	2011	2012	2013	2014	2015	2016
5127 Other taxes on internat. trade and transactions	40	175	0	0	0	0	0	0	81	90
On capital movements	0	169	..	..	..	..	..	..	..	..
On purchase of foreign exchange	22	4	..	..	..	..	..	..	..	..
On credit operations in national currency	18	2	..	..	..	..	..	..	..	..
5128 Other taxes	0	0	0	0	0	0	0	0	0	0
5130 Unallocable between 5110 and 5120	0	0	0	0	0	0	0	0	0	0
5200 Taxes on use of goods and perform activities	8	13	69	168	191	220	245	260	265	354
5210 Recurrent taxes	8	13	69	168	191	220	245	260	265	354
5211 Paid by households: motor vehicles	2	0	0	0	0	0	0	0	0	112
5212 Paid by others: motor vehicles	5	11	69	168	188	209	231	248	245	219
Annual tax on motor vehicles	3	11	60	156	174	194	214	228	223	195
5213 Paid in respect of other goods	1	1	0	0	3	11	14	12	21	23
5220 Non-recurrent taxes	0	0	0	0	0	0	0	0	0	0
5300 Unallocable between 5100 and 5200	3	8	33	49	56	61	75	81	91	101
6000 Other taxes	**29**	**2**	**53**	**289**	**29**	**112**	**132**	**102**	**45**	**97**
6100 Paid solely by business	0	0	0	0	0	0	0	0	0	0
6200 Other	29	2	53	286	20	105	126	102	45	97
Credit notes	..	..	..	0	0	0	0	0	0	0
Simplified taxation system of Ecuador (RISE)	..	..	..	6	10	12	15	20	20	19
Other reimbursements	..	..	..	0	0	0	0	0	0	-1
Others	..	..	..	280	10	93	111	82	25	79

Note: Year ending 31st December.

The data are on a cash basis.

The 2016 figures include solidarity contributions enforced in this year to finance the reconstruction efforts in the aftermath of the 2015 earthquake. These affect headings 1100, 1200, 4200, 4500, 4600 and 5111. The figures for local government tax revenues have been estimated for 2016. This affects headings 4120, 4400, 5113, 5121, 5126, 5130, 5212, 5213, 5300 and 6200.

Heading 2000: Social security data is recorded at the non-financial public sector level.

Heading 6200: The disaggregation for heading 6200 has been improved for this edition.

Source: Servicio de Rentas Internas (SRI) y Banco Central del Ecuador (Internal Revenue Service and Central Bank of Ecuador).

StatLink http://dx.doi.org/10.1787/888933686917

Table 5.13. El Salvador
Details of tax revenue / Ingresos tributarios detallados

Million USD

	1990	2000	2005	2010	2011	2012	2013	2014	2015	2016
Total tax revenue	**506**	**1 585**	**2 420**	**3 298**	**3 621**	**3 905**	**4 222**	**4 229**	**4 492**	**4 795**
1000 Taxes on income, profits and capital gains	**95**	**407**	**637**	**995**	**1 127**	**1 250**	**1 479**	**1 522**	**1 545**	**1 659**
1100 Of individuals	..	..	312	571	456	697	578	627	739	695
1110 On income and profits	..	..	312	571	456	697	578	627	739	695
1120 On capital gains	..	..	..	..	..	..	..	..	..	..
1200 Corporate	..	..	356	423	631	555	793	693	622	763
1210 On profits	..	..	356	423	631	555	793	693	622	763
1220 On capital gains	..	..	..	..	..	..	..	..	..	..
1300 Unallocable between 1100 and 1200	95	407	-31	0	41	-2	108	201	183	202
Withholding income tax	95	429	0	55	107	66	135	204	213	232
Income tax refunds	0	-22	-31	-55	-66	-68	-27	-3	-30	-31
2000 Social security contributions	**67**	**263**	**282**	**369**	**382**	**404**	**425**	**445**	**488**	**539**
2100 Employees	..	75	76	99	100	106	112	117	130	143
2110 On a payroll basis	..	75	76	99	100	106	112	117	130	143
2120 On an income tax basis	..	0	0	0	0	0	0	0	0	0
2200 Employers	..	176	181	238	245	260	273	286	314	347
2210 On a payroll basis	..	176	181	238	245	260	273	286	314	347
2220 On an income tax basis	..	0	0	0	0	0	0	0	0	0
2300 Self-employed or non-employed	..	13	25	33	36	38	40	42	45	48
2310 On a payroll basis	..	13	25	33	36	38	40	42	45	48
2320 On an income tax basis	..	0	0	0	0	0	0	0	0	0
2400 Unallocable between 2100, 2200 and 2300	67	0	0	0	0	0	0	0	0	0
2410 On a payroll basis	67	..	..	..	..	..	..	..	..	..
2420 On an income tax basis	0	..	..	..	..	..	..	..	..	..
3000 Taxes on payroll and workforce	**0**	**0**	**0**	**0**	**0**	**0**	**0**	**0**	**0**	**0**
4000 Taxes on property	**26**	**12**	**16**	**16**	**16**	**20**	**21**	**24**	**107**	**107**
4100 Recurrent taxes on immovable property	0	0	0	0	0	0	0	0	0	0
4110 Households	..	..	..	..	..	..	..	..	..	..
4120 Others	..	..	..	..	..	..	..	..	..	..
4200 Recurrent taxes on net wealth	16	0	0	0	0	0	0	0	0	0
4210 Individual	16	..	..	..	..	..	..	..	..	..
4220 Corporate	0	..	..	..	..	..	..	..	..	..
4300 Estate, inheritance and gift taxes	0	0	0	0	0	0	0	0	0	0
4310 Estate and inheritance taxes	..	..	..	..	..	..	..	..	..	..
4320 Gift taxes	..	..	..	..	..	..	..	..	..	..
4400 Taxes on financial and capital transactions	10	12	16	16	16	20	21	24	107	107
Property transfers	..	..	..	..	..	..	..	..	20	23
Checks and electronic transfers of funds	..	..	..	..	..	..	..	..	55	54
Withholding for liquidity control	..	..	..	..	..	..	..	..	31	31
4500 Non-recurrent taxes	0	0	0	0	0	0	0	0	0	0
4510 On net wealth	..	..	..	..	..	..	..	..	..	..
4520 Other non-recurrent taxes	..	..	..	..	..	..	..	..	..	..
4600 Other recurrent taxes on property	0	0	0	0	0	0	0	0	0	0
5000 Taxes on goods and services	**259**	**903**	**1 447**	**1 855**	**2 027**	**2 155**	**2 213**	**2 147**	**2 266**	**2 400**
5100 Taxes on production, sale, transfer, etc	259	903	1 447	1 847	2 019	2 146	2 202	2 147	2 254	2 387
5110 General taxes	133	714	1 104	1 433	1 574	1 677	1 731	1 720	1 764	1 813
5111 Value added taxes	0	714	1 104	1 433	1 574	1 677	1 731	1 720	1 764	1 813
5112 Sales tax	0	0	0	0	0	0	0	0	0	0
5113 Other	133	0	0	0	0	0	0	0	0	0
5120 Taxes on specific goods and services	127	189	344	415	445	469	472	427	490	574
5121 Excises	65	49	162	211	229	253	238	224	285	355
Alcoholic beverages	..	..	14	18	23	22	19	14	22	23
Cigarettes	..	..	23	31	38	40	27	22	29	28
Soft drinks	..	..	33	31	35	40	42	43	48	49
Beer	..	..	26	26	29	42	40	32	55	61
Weapons, ammunition and explosives	..	..	1	1	1	1	1	1	1	1
Ad-valorem on fuels	..	..	0	0	0	0	0	0	7	9
Special contribution- Sugar	..	..	1	1	1	1	1	1	1	1
Special contribution- Public transportation	..	..	0	35	35	36	36	37	40	43
Special contribution- FOVIAL	..	..	66	69	69	71	72	74	80	86
Special contribution- Public security	..	..	0	0	0	0	0	0	2	56
5122 Profits of fiscal monopolies	0	0	0	0	0	0	0	0	0	0
5123 Customs and import duties	61	141	181	148	167	180	199	181	194	207
5124 Taxes on exports	0	0	0	0	0	0	0	0	0	0
5125 Taxes on investment goods	0	0	0	0	0	0	0	0	0	0
5126 Taxes on specific services	0	0	0	56	48	36	34	22	11	12
5127 Other taxes on internat. trade and transactions	0	0	0	0	0	0	0	0	0	0
5128 Other taxes	0	0	0	0	0	0	0	0	0	0

Table 5.13. El Salvador *(cont.)*
Details of tax revenue / Ingresos tributarios detallados

Million USD

	1990	2000	2005	2010	2011	2012	2013	2014	2015	2016
5130 Unallocable between 5110 and 5120	0	0	0	0	0	0	0	0	0	0
5200 Taxes on use of goods and perform activities	0	0	0	0	0	0	0	0	12	14
5210 Recurrent taxes	..	..	..	..	..	..	..	..	0	0
5211 Paid by households: motor vehicles	..	..	..	..	..	..	..	..	..	..
5212 Paid by others: motor vehicles	..	..	..	..	..	..	..	..	..	..
5213 Paid in respect of other goods	..	..	..	..	..	..	..	..	..	..
5220 Non-recurrent taxes	..	..	..	..	..	..	..	..	12	14
5300 Unallocable between 5100 and 5200	0	0	0	0	0	0	0	0	0	0
6000 Other taxes	**58**	**0**	**37**	**63**	**69**	**77**	**83**	**91**	**86**	**89**
6100 Paid solely by business	0	0	0	0	0	0	0	0	0	0
6200 Other	58	0	37	63	69	77	83	91	86	89

Note: Year ending 31st December.

The data are on a cash basis.

In this edition, local government tax revenue data have been expanded and start in 2002. These are classified under 6200.

Heading 1000: For 2002 and from 2006 onwards sub-headings 1100 and 1200 are presented on a gross basis i.e. not including income tax refunds. The latter are classified under heading 1300.

Heading 2000: Corresponds to social security contributions paid to the Salvadoran Institute of Social Security and excludes payments to privately managed pension funds (AFPs).

Heading 5121: Special contributions to public security have been included since 2015.

Source: Dirección General de Tesorería, Ministerio de Hacienda. Banco Central de Reserva y el Instituto Salvadoreño del Seguro Social (General Treasury Directorate, Ministry of Finance, Central Reserve Bank and the Salvadoran Social Security Institute).

StatLink http://dx.doi.org/10.1787/888933686936

Table 5.14. Guatemala
Details of tax revenue / Ingresos tributarios detallados

Million GTQ

	1990	2000	2005	2010	2011	2012	2013	2014	2015	2016
Total tax revenue	**2 756**	**16 531**	**27 187**	**41 189**	**47 387**	**50 904**	**55 006**	**57 520**	**60 334**	**65 609**
1000 Taxes on income, profits and capital gains	**507**	**3 295**	**6 049**	**10 319**	**13 100**	**13 907**	**16 093**	**17 752**	**17 534**	**20 572**
1100 Of individuals	25	143	645	1 225	1 462	1 477	1 246	1 784	1 826	2 082
1110 On income and profits	25	143	645	1 225	1 462	1 477	1 246	1 784	1 826	2 082
Personal income tax	25	137	642	1 225	1 462	1 477	1 246	1 784	1 826	2 082
Income from financial products	0	6	4	0	0	1	0	0	0	0
1120 On capital gains	..	..	..	..	..	..	..	..	..	..
1200 Corporate	482	3 149	3 756	6 520	9 013	9 581	11 584	12 426	11 802	14 418
1210 On profits	482	3 149	3 756	6 520	9 013	9 581	11 584	12 426	11 802	14 418
Corporate income tax	482	1 610	3 495	6 132	8 601	9 118	11 529	12 423	11 801	14 417
Income from financial products	0	248	235	386	403	463	52	0	0	0
Commercial and agricultural enterprises	0	1 291	26	2	8	0	3	3	0	1
1220 On capital gains	..	..	..	..	..	..	..	..	..	..
1300 Unallocable between 1100 and 1200	0	2	1 647	2 574	2 625	2 849	3 263	3 543	3 907	4 072
Extraordinary and temporary solidarity tax in support of peace agreements	..	0	1 647	44	54	4	21	9	1	1
Solidarity tax	..	0	0	2 530	2 571	2 845	3 243	3 533	3 906	4 070
Extraordinary and temporary solidarity tax	..	2	0	0	0	0	0	0	0	0
2000 Social security contributions	**436**	**2 569**	**4 072**	**6 408**	**7 125**	**7 858**	**8 617**	**8 157**	**10 034**	**10 974**
2100 Employees	..	..	..	..	..	..	..	..	..	..
2110 On a payroll basis	..	..	..	..	..	..	..	..	..	..
2120 On an income tax basis	..	..	..	..	..	..	..	..	..	..
2200 Employers	..	..	..	..	..	..	..	..	..	..
2210 On a payroll basis	..	..	..	..	..	..	..	..	..	..
2220 On an income tax basis	..	..	..	..	..	..	..	..	..	..
2300 Self-employed or non-employed	..	..	..	..	..	..	..	..	..	..
2310 On a payroll basis	..	..	..	..	..	..	..	..	..	..
2320 On an income tax basis	..	..	..	..	..	..	..	..	..	..
2400 Unallocable between 2100, 2200 and 2300	436	2 569	4 072	6 408	7 125	7 858	8 617	8 157	10 034	10 974
2410 On a payroll basis	436	2 569	4 072	6 408	7 125	7 858	8 617	8 157	10 034	10 974
2420 On an income tax basis	0	0	0	0	0	0	0	0	0	0
3000 Taxes on payroll and workforce	**0**	**0**	**0**	**0**	**0**	**0**	**0**	**0**	**0**	**0**
4000 Taxes on property	**0**	**165**	**350**	**630**	**648**	**743**	**791**	**843**	**713**	**587**
4100 Recurrent taxes on immovable property	..	153	341	620	635	735	780	829	693	565
4110 Households	..	0	0	0	0	0	0	0	0	0
4120 Others	..	153	341	620	635	735	780	829	693	565
Property tax	..	6	1	1	1	1	1	1	1	1
Property tax (municipal)	..	147	341	620	634	734	779	827	692	564
4200 Recurrent taxes on net wealth	..	0	0	0	0	0	0	0	0	0
4210 Individual	..	..	..	..	..	..	..	..	..	..
4220 Corporate	..	..	..	..	..	..	..	..	..	..
4300 Estate, inheritance and gift taxes	..	0	0	0	0	0	0	0	0	0
4310 Estate and inheritance taxes	..	..	..	..	..	..	..	..	..	..
4320 Gift taxes	..	..	..	..	..	..	..	..	..	..
4400 Taxes on financial and capital transactions	..	12	8	10	13	8	10	15	20	23
4500 Non-recurrent taxes	..	0	0	0	0	0	0	0	0	0
4510 On net wealth	..	..	..	..	..	..	..	..	..	..
4520 Other non-recurrent taxes	..	..	..	..	..	..	..	..	..	..
4600 Other recurrent taxes on property	..	0	0	0	0	0	0	0	0	0
5000 Taxes on goods and services	**1 709**	**10 317**	**16 402**	**23 259**	**25 876**	**27 518**	**29 075**	**30 409**	**31 716**	**33 105**
5100 Taxes on production, sale, transfer, etc	1 681	10 131	16 083	22 754	25 317	26 614	27 545	29 089	30 085	31 355
5110 General taxes	762	6 259	10 753	16 980	19 472	20 913	21 874	23 153	23 271	24 215
5111 Value added taxes	762	6 259	10 753	16 980	19 472	20 913	21 874	23 153	23 271	24 215
5112 Sales tax	0	0	0	0	0	0	0	0	0	0
5113 Other	0	0	0	0	0	0	0	0	0	0
5120 Taxes on specific goods and services	919	3 872	5 330	5 773	5 845	5 701	5 671	5 936	6 813	7 140
5121 Excises	258	1 797	1 262	3 101	3 013	3 072	3 372	3 550	4 289	4 422
Tobacco and derivatives	76	205	312	347	259	312	385	405	369	365
Beer	0	97	122	159	176	191	217	243	293	306
Alcoholic beverages	0	77	76	98	101	100	90	56	88	90
Soft drinks	0	15	172	220	245	263	282	300	328	348
Other beverages	77	12	2	2	2	1	1	0	0	1
Cement	0	0	93	99	104	102	100	101	312	117
Oil and derivatives	105	1 389	485	2 179	2 125	2 103	2 297	2 445	2 899	3 195
5122 Profits of fiscal monopolies	0	0	0	0	0	0	0	0	0	0
5123 Customs and import duties	506	1 806	3 715	2 368	2 533	2 311	1 965	2 044	2 157	2 323
5124 Taxes on exports	0	0	0	0	0	0	0	0	0	0
5125 Taxes on investment goods	0	0	0	0	0	0	0	0	0	0

Table 5.14. Guatemala *(cont.)*
Details of tax revenue / Ingresos tributarios detallados

Million GTQ

	1990	2000	2005	2010	2011	2012	2013	2014	2015	2016
5126 Taxes on specific services	155	269	354	304	300	318	334	343	367	395
5127 Other taxes on internat. trade and transactions	0	0	0	0	0	0	0	0	0	0
5128 Other taxes	0	0	0	0	0	0	0	0	0	0
5130 Unallocable between 5110 and 5120	0	0	0	0	0	0	0	0	0	0
5200 Taxes on use of goods and perform activities	28	186	319	505	558	904	1 530	1 320	1 631	1 750
5210 Recurrent taxes	28	186	319	505	558	904	1 530	1 320	1 631	1 750
5211 Paid by households: motor vehicles	0	0	0	0	0	331	694	747	914	967
5212 Paid by others: motor vehicles	28	186	319	505	558	573	836	572	717	782
5213 Paid in respect of other goods	0	0	0	0	0	0	0	0	0	0
5220 Non-recurrent taxes	0	0	0	0	0	0	0	0	0	0
5300 Unallocable between 5100 and 5200	0	0	0	0	0	0	0	0	0	0
6000 Other taxes	**104**	**186**	**315**	**572**	**639**	**878**	**430**	**359**	**337**	**370**
6100 Paid solely by business	0	0	0	0	0	0	0	0	0	0
6200 Other	104	186	315	572	639	878	430	359	337	370
Revenue stamps and stamped paper	104	182	313	572	638	877	430	359	336	370
Other indirect taxes	0	4	1	1	1	1	1	0	0	0

Note: Year ending 31st December.

The data are on a cash basis.

The figures exclude some local government tax revenues as the data are not available. Revenues from the municipal property tax (IUSI) are included.

Heading 2000: Corresponds to social security contributions paid to the Guatemalan Social Security Institute (IGSS) and payments by public employees to the government's pension fund.

Headings 4120 and 4400: For years prior to 2000, the property tax under heading 4120 is included in the total under heading 4400.

Heading 5121: Up to 1999, "Other beverages" contains all alcoholic and non-alcoholic beverages.

Source: Dirección de Análisis de Política Fiscal del Ministerio de Hacienda, Instituto Guatemalteco del Seguro Social y Superintendencia de la Administración Tributaria (Fiscal Policy Analysis Directorate at the Ministry of Finance, the Guatemalan Institute of Social Security and the Tax Administration Superintendency).

StatLink http://dx.doi.org/10.1787/888933686955

Table 5.15. Guyana

Details of tax revenue / Ingresos tributarios detallados

Million GYD

	1990	2000	2005	2010	2011	2012	2013	2014	2015	2016
Total tax revenue	**5 232**	**42 750**	**60 319**	**111 906**	**123 199**	**131 321**	**140 678**	**151 381**	**159 814**	**168 149**
1000 Taxes on income, profits and capital gains	**1 752**	**16 179**	**23 843**	**39 561**	**43 469**	**44 547**	**46 587**	**51 611**	**55 011**	**60 914**
1100 Of individuals	333	7 734	11 139	17 816	19 639	19 530	18 506	21 389	23 300	26 439
1110 On income and profits	333	7 734	11 139	17 816	19 639	19 530	18 506	21 389	23 300	26 439
Personal	306	7 157	11 139	15 419	16 845	16 155	15 199	17 900	19 894	22 300
Self-employed	27	577	0	2 397	2 794	3 375	3 307	3 490	3 407	4 139
1120 On capital gains	..	..	..	..	..	..	..	..	..	..
1200 Corporate	1 375	8 266	12 555	21 427	23 421	24 419	27 622	29 794	31 200	33 965
1210 On profits	..	..	..	..	..	..	..	..	..	..
1220 On capital gains	..	..	..	..	..	..	..	..	..	..
1300 Unallocable between 1100 and 1200	43	179	149	317	409	598	459	428	511	510
2000 Social security contributions	**191**	**4 868**	**6 670**	**10 047**	**10 814**	**11 824**	**13 195**	**14 985**	**16 563**	**18 468**
2100 Employees	..	..	..	..	..	..	..	..	..	..
2110 On a payroll basis	..	..	..	..	..	..	..	..	..	..
2120 On an income tax basis	..	..	..	..	..	..	..	..	..	..
2200 Employers	..	..	..	..	..	..	..	..	..	..
2210 On a payroll basis	..	..	..	..	..	..	..	..	..	..
2220 On an income tax basis	..	..	..	..	..	..	..	..	..	..
2300 Self-employed or non-employed	..	..	..	..	..	..	..	..	..	..
2310 On a payroll basis	..	..	..	..	..	..	..	..	..	..
2320 On an income tax basis	..	..	..	..	..	..	..	..	..	..
2400 Unallocable between 2100, 2200 and 2300	191	4 868	6 670	10 047	10 814	11 824	13 195	14 985	16 563	18 468
2410 On a payroll basis	..	..	..	..	..	..	..	..	..	..
2420 On an income tax basis	..	..	..	..	..	..	..	..	..	..
3000 Taxes on payroll and workforce	**0**	**0**	**0**	**0**	**0**	**0**	**0**	**0**	**0**	**0**
4000 Taxes on property	**53**	**701**	**828**	**1 593**	**1 753**	**1 903**	**2 608**	**2 423**	**3 237**	**3 297**
4100 Recurrent taxes on immovable property	40	681	807	1 562	1 723	1 866	2 572	2 381	3 201	3 258
4110 Households	0	0	0	0	0	0	0	0	0	0
4120 Others	40	681	807	1 562	1 723	1 866	2 572	2 381	3 201	3 258
4200 Recurrent taxes on net wealth	0	0	0	0	0	0	0	0	0	0
4210 Individual	..	..	..	..	..	..	..	..	..	..
4220 Corporate	..	..	..	..	..	..	..	..	..	..
4300 Estate, inheritance and gift taxes	13	20	21	31	30	37	37	42	37	39
4310 Estate and inheritance taxes	..	..	..	..	..	..	..	..	..	..
4320 Gift taxes	..	..	..	..	..	..	..	..	..	..
4400 Taxes on financial and capital transactions	0	0	0	0	0	0	0	0	0	0
4500 Non-recurrent taxes	0	0	0	0	0	0	0	0	0	0
4510 On net wealth	..	..	..	..	..	..	..	..	..	..
4520 Other non-recurrent taxes	..	..	..	..	..	..	..	..	..	..
4600 Other recurrent taxes on property	0	0	0	0	0	0	0	0	0	0
5000 Taxes on goods and services	**2 200**	**20 798**	**27 940**	**59 360**	**65 650**	**71 339**	**76 691**	**81 104**	**83 924**	**84 156**
5100 Taxes on production, sale, transfer, etc	2 162	20 530	27 414	58 846	65 134	70 793	76 072	80 431	83 227	83 147
5110 General taxes	1 399	14 861	21 396	27 044	31 103	34 077	34 317	37 307	35 374	36 968
5111 Value added taxes	0	0	0	27 044	31 103	34 077	34 317	37 307	35 374	35 968
Imports	..	..	..	14 877	17 996	19 297	20 036	20 370	19 366	18 324
Domestic supply	..	..	..	12 168	13 107	14 781	14 281	16 937	16 008	17 644
5112 Sales tax	0	0	0	0	0	0	0	0	0	0
5113 Other	1 399	14 861	21 396	0	0	0	0	0	0	1 000
5120 Taxes on specific goods and services	763	5 669	6 019	31 802	34 031	36 715	41 755	43 124	47 853	46 179
5121 Excises	32	609	1 211	22 070	22 905	23 815	28 343	29 267	33 827	29 862
Imports	0	0	0	18 935	19 077	19 605	24 147	25 044	29 953	25 915
Domestic supply	0	0	0	2 358	2 813	3 139	3 124	3 190	3 377	3 947
Purchase tax - motor cars	32	475	738	0	0	0	0	0	0	0
Environmental tax	0	134	473	777	1 014	1 071	1 072	1 033	496	0
5122 Profits of fiscal monopolies	0	0	0	0	0	0	0	0	0	0
5123 Customs and import duties	544	3 943	3 635	8 302	9 864	11 561	11 866	12 167	12 357	14 259
5124 Taxes on exports	94	7	7	7	10	9	14	14	12	15
5125 Taxes on investment goods	0	0	0	0	0	0	0	0	0	0
5126 Taxes on specific services	92	1 110	1 166	1 423	1 253	1 331	1 532	1 676	1 658	2 042
Entertainment tax	12	27	2	0	0	0	0	0	0	0
Travel tax	80	1 084	1 164	1 423	1 253	1 331	1 532	1 676	1 658	2 042
5127 Other taxes on internat. trade and transactions	0	0	0	0	0	0	0	0	0	0
5128 Other taxes	0	0	0	0	0	0	0	0	0	0
5130 Unallocable between 5110 and 5120	0	0	0	0	0	0	0	0	0	0
5200 Taxes on use of goods and perform activities	38	268	525	514	515	547	620	673	697	1 009
5210 Recurrent taxes	38	268	525	514	515	547	620	673	697	1 009
5211 Paid by households: motor vehicles	27	239	274	475	477	513	587	637	653	913
5212 Paid by others: motor vehicles	0	0	0	0	0	0	0	0	0	0

Table 5.15. Guyana *(cont.)*
Details of tax revenue / Ingresos tributarios detallados

Million GYD

	1990	2000	2005	2010	2011	2012	2013	2014	2015	2016
5213 Paid in respect of other goods	12	29	251	39	38	34	33	35	44	96
Other licences	12	29	251	39	38	34	33	35	44	96
5220 Non-recurrent taxes	0	0	0	0	0	0	0	0	0	0
5300 Unallocable between 5100 and 5200	0	0	0	0	0	0	0	0	0	0
6000 Other taxes	**1 037**	**204**	**1 039**	**1 346**	**1 514**	**1 708**	**1 596**	**1 259**	**1 079**	**1 314**
6100 Paid solely by business	0	0	0	0	0	0	0	0	0	0
6200 Other	1 037	204	1 039	1 346	1 514	1 708	1 596	1 259	1 079	1 314

Note: Year ending 31st December.
The data are on a cash basis.
The data for 2016 are revised budget estimates published by the Ministry of Finance.
The figures for 2015 and 2016 are estimated.
Miscellaneous revenues reported by the Ministry of Finance of Guyana have been excluded as these encompass interest and penalties paid on VAT and excise taxes.

Source: Ministry of Finance, the Central Bank of Guyana and the National Insurance Scheme.

StatLink http://dx.doi.org/10.1787/888933686974

Table 5.16. Honduras
Details of tax revenue / Ingresos tributarios detallados

Million HNL

	1990	2000	2005	2010	2011	2012	2013	2014	2015	2016
Total tax revenue	**2 032**	**16 347**	**31 123**	**51 844**	**56 499**	**64 153**	**69 256**	**81 066**	**93 228**	**104 976**
1000 Taxes on income, profits and capital gains	**431**	**2 907**	**7 037**	**13 232**	**16 668**	**17 309**	**19 366**	**21 347**	**24 843**	**29 584**
1100 Of individuals	157	991	2 312	4 528	5 232	5 745	6 478	7 312	8 451	10 173
1110 On income and profits	157	991	2 312	4 528	5 232	5 745	6 478	7 312	8 451	10 173
1120 On capital gains	..	..	..	..	..	..	..	..	..	..
1200 Corporate	274	1 916	4 725	8 705	11 437	11 564	12 888	14 034	16 392	19 411
1210 On profits	274	1 916	4 725	8 705	11 437	11 564	12 888	14 034	16 392	19 411
Corporate income tax	274	1 916	4 121	7 400	9 447	10 088	11 523	12 756	14 742	17 746
Income tax surcharge	0	0	604	1 305	1 990	1 468	1 352	1 265	1 637	1 653
Special contribution of the cooperative sector	0	0	0	0	0	8	14	13	13	13
1220 On capital gains	..	..	..	..	..	..	..	..	..	..
1300 Unallocable between 1100 and 1200	0	0	0	0	0	0	0	0	0	0
2000 Social security contributions	**179**	**1 727**	**4 416**	**8 671**	**6 955**	**10 854**	**12 529**	**12 467**	**13 524**	**14 402**
2100 Employees	..	..	..	..	..	..	..	..	..	..
2110 On a payroll basis	..	..	..	..	..	..	..	..	..	..
2120 On an income tax basis	..	..	..	..	..	..	..	..	..	..
2200 Employers	..	..	..	..	..	..	..	..	..	..
2210 On a payroll basis	..	..	..	..	..	..	..	..	..	..
2220 On an income tax basis	..	..	..	..	..	..	..	..	..	..
2300 Self-employed or non-employed	..	..	..	..	..	..	..	..	..	..
2310 On a payroll basis	..	..	..	..	..	..	..	..	..	..
2320 On an income tax basis	..	..	..	..	..	..	..	..	..	..
2400 Unallocable between 2100, 2200 and 2300	179	1 727	4 416	8 671	6 955	10 854	12 529	12 467	13 524	14 402
2410 On a payroll basis	179	1 727	4 416	8 671	6 955	10 854	12 529	12 467	13 524	14 402
2420 On an income tax basis	0	0	0	0	0	0	0	0	0	0
3000 Taxes on payroll and workforce	**0**	**0**	**0**	**0**	**0**	**0**	**0**	**0**	**0**	**0**
4000 Taxes on property	**16**	**266**	**631**	**994**	**600**	**1 217**	**1 446**	**2 300**	**2 635**	**2 362**
4100 Recurrent taxes on immovable property	0	0	0	0	0	0	0	0	0	0
4110 Households	..	..	..	..	..	..	..	..	..	..
4120 Others	..	..	..	..	..	..	..	..	..	..
4200 Recurrent taxes on net wealth	0	0	0	0	0	0	0	0	0	0
4210 Individual	..	..	..	..	..	..	..	..	..	..
4220 Corporate	..	..	..	..	..	..	..	..	..	..
4300 Estate, inheritance and gift taxes	0	0	0	0	0	0	0	0	0	0
4310 Estate and inheritance taxes	..	..	..	..	..	..	..	..	..	..
4320 Gift taxes	..	..	..	..	..	..	..	..	..	..
4400 Taxes on financial and capital transactions	0	0	0	0	0	659	903	1 636	2 003	1 738
4500 Non-recurrent taxes	0	0	316	381	0	0	0	0	0	0
4510 On net wealth	..	..	0	0	..	..	..	..	..	..
4520 Other non-recurrent taxes	..	..	316	381	..	..	..	..	..	..
4600 Other recurrent taxes on property	16	266	315	613	600	558	543	664	633	624
5000 Taxes on goods and services	**1 405**	**11 445**	**19 032**	**28 937**	**32 266**	**34 764**	**35 908**	**44 945**	**52 217**	**58 611**
5100 Taxes on production, sale, transfer, etc	1 405	11 445	19 032	28 937	32 266	34 764	35 908	44 945	52 217	58 611
5110 General taxes	344	5 146	9 565	16 050	18 967	20 150	20 637	27 735	32 273	36 521
5111 Value added taxes	344	5 146	9 565	16 050	18 967	20 150	20 637	27 735	32 273	36 521
5112 Sales tax	0	0	0	0	0	0	0	0	0	0
5113 Other	0	0	0	0	0	0	0	0	0	0
5120 Taxes on specific goods and services	1 061	6 299	9 468	12 887	13 299	14 614	15 270	17 211	19 944	22 090
5121 Excises	256	3 600	6 322	8 458	8 670	9 490	10 119	11 588	13 349	14 953
Beer	71	376	338	376	466	503	503	525	668	824
Soft drinks	25	240	268	514	632	675	725	754	838	890
Liquors	32	48	69	121	164	165	165	188	195	190
Petroleum products	43	347	0	0	0	0	0	0	0	0
Cigarettes	57	369	437	607	660	633	495	610	598	564
Fuel tax	0	1 962	4 916	6 288	6 177	6 868	7 613	8 874	10 317	11 594
Other	28	258	295	551	572	646	618	638	735	890
5122 Profits of fiscal monopolies	0	0	0	0	0	0	0	0	0	0
5123 Customs and import duties	498	2 083	2 174	2 505	2 626	2 933	2 651	2 974	3 541	3 998
Petroleum	0	297	0	0	0	0	0	0	0	0
Other	498	1 786	2 174	2 505	2 626	2 933	2 651	2 974	3 541	3 998
5124 Taxes on exports	217	6	0	0	4	62	101	107	84	59
Bananas	39	5	..	..	0	0	0	0	0	0
Coffee	1	0	..	..	0	0	0	0	0	0
Temporary export tax	163	0	..	..	0	0	0	0	0	0
Special contribution of the mining sector	0	0	..	..	4	62	101	107	84	59
Other	15	1	..	..	0	0	0	0	0	0
5125 Taxes on investment goods	0	0	0	0	0	0	0	0	0	0

Table 5.16. Honduras *(cont.)*
Details of tax revenue / Ingresos tributarios detallados

Million HNL

	1990	2000	2005	2010	2011	2012	2013	2014	2015	2016
5126 Taxes on specific services	0	0	0	0	16	92	87	90	91	73
Special contribution of mobile services	..	..	..	..	12	75	66	67	67	51
Special contribution of the food and services sector	..	..	..	..	3	14	18	20	21	19
Special contribution of casino games and slot machines	..	..	..	..	1	3	3	3	3	2
5127 Other taxes on internat. trade and transactions	0	0	0	0	0	0	0	0	0	0
5128 Other taxes	90	610	971	1 924	1 983	2 038	2 312	2 451	2 880	3 007
5130 Unallocable between 5110 and 5120	0	0	0	0	0	0	0	0	0	0
5200 Taxes on use of goods and perform activities	0	0	0	0	0	0	0	0	0	0
5210 Recurrent taxes	..	..	..	..	..	..	..	..	..	..
5211 Paid by households: motor vehicles	..	..	..	..	..	..	..	..	..	..
5212 Paid by others: motor vehicles	..	..	..	..	..	..	..	..	..	..
5213 Paid in respect of other goods	..	..	..	..	..	..	..	..	..	..
5220 Non-recurrent taxes	..	..	..	..	..	..	..	..	..	..
5300 Unallocable between 5100 and 5200	0	0	0	0	0	0	0	0	0	0
6000 Other taxes	**1**	**2**	**7**	**9**	**9**	**10**	**8**	**7**	**8**	**18**
6100 Paid solely by business	0	0	0	0	0	0	0	0	0	0
6200 Other	1	2	7	9	9	10	8	7	8	18

Note: Year ending 31st December.

The data are on a cash basis.

Data for local government tax revenues previously under headings 6000 and 6200 are excluded since they included non-tax revenues and central government transfers for the period 1990-2015. Local government tax revenue is only available for the year 2016 and is not included in this edition to allow comparability over time.

Heading 4520: Taxes levied on the revaluation of assets have been reclassified under heading 4520. In previous editions this tax was classified as 1300.

Heading 4600: Taxes on net assets have been reclassified under heading 4600. In previous editions this tax was classified as 1300.

Source: Secretaria de Finanzas (Ministry of Finance).

StatLink http://dx.doi.org/10.1787/888933686993

Table 5.17. Jamaica
Details of tax revenue / Ingresos tributarios detallados

Million JAM

	1990	2000	2005	2010	2011	2012	2013	2014	2015	2016
Total tax revenue	**7 748**	**87 713**	**163 291**	**287 139**	**303 983**	**322 299**	**356 956**	**381 060**	**427 933**	**467 350**
1000 Taxes on income, profits and capital gains	**3 944**	**39 277**	**69 894**	**118 708**	**122 752**	**126 441**	**129 951**	**134 083**	**149 989**	**158 409**
1100 Of individuals	1 687	17 441	36 043	54 798	62 792	64 315	66 282	70 867	74 537	72 175
1110 On income and profits	1 687	17 441	36 043	54 798	62 792	64 315	66 282	70 867	74 537	72 175
PAYE	1 489	16 515	34 223	50 828	58 851	60 637	62 172	66 645	70 075	67 591
Other individuals	198	926	1 820	3 969	3 940	3 678	4 111	4 223	4 463	4 584
1120 On capital gains	..	..	..	..	..	..	..	..	..	..
1200 Corporate	1 280	7 627	13 134	33 091	31 858	32 706	34 539	31 991	40 198	47 530
1210 On profits	1 280	7 627	13 134	33 091	31 858	32 706	34 539	31 991	40 198	47 530
Bauxite/alumina	134	430	446	866	0	1	0	0	0	0
Other companies	1 146	7 197	12 688	32 224	31 857	32 705	34 539	31 991	39 668	46 823
Minimum business tax	0	0	0	0	0	0	0	0	529	707
1220 On capital gains	..	..	..	..	..	..	..	..	..	..
1300 Unallocable between 1100 and 1200	977	14 209	20 718	30 820	28 103	29 419	29 130	31 224	35 254	38 704
Tax on dividends	68	854	248	1 059	1 028	1 080	1 175	1 904	980	1 408
Tax on interests	605	9 535	13 277	16 970	12 376	13 437	10 706	10 103	13 518	14 451
Education tax	305	3 821	7 193	12 792	14 699	14 903	17 249	19 217	20 756	22 845
2000 Social security contributions	**0**	**0**	**4 924**	**8 199**	**11 562**	**11 418**	**13 875**	**15 865**	**16 449**	**17 978**
2100 Employees	..	..	..	..	..	..	..	..	..	..
2110 On a payroll basis	..	..	..	..	..	..	..	..	..	..
2120 On an income tax basis	..	..	..	..	..	..	..	..	..	..
2200 Employers	..	..	..	..	..	..	..	..	..	..
2210 On a payroll basis	..	..	..	..	..	..	..	..	..	..
2220 On an income tax basis	..	..	..	..	..	..	..	..	..	..
2300 Self-employed or non-employed	..	..	..	..	..	..	..	..	..	..
2310 On a payroll basis	..	..	..	..	..	..	..	..	..	..
2320 On an income tax basis	..	..	..	..	..	..	..	..	..	..
2400 Unallocable between 2100, 2200 and 2300	..	..	4 924	8 199	11 562	11 418	13 875	15 865	16 449	17 978
National Insurance Scheme (NIS) contributions	..	..	4 924	8 199	11 562	11 418	13 875	15 865	16 449	17 978
2410 On a payroll basis	..	..	..	..	..	..	..	..	..	..
2420 On an income tax basis	..	..	..	..	..	..	..	..	..	..
3000 Taxes on payroll and workforce	**0**	**0**	**0**	**0**	**0**	**0**	**0**	**0**	**0**	**0**
4000 Taxes on property	**67**	**639**	**1 592**	**2 600**	**2 633**	**2 427**	**5 595**	**6 138**	**7 271**	**7 101**
4100 Recurrent taxes on immovable property	67	639	1 592	2 600	2 633	2 427	5 595	6 138	7 271	7 101
4110 Households	67	639	1 592	2 600	2 633	2 427	5 595	6 138	7 271	7 101
Property tax	67	0	0	0	0	0	0	0	0	0
Property tax (municipal)	0	639	1 592	2 600	2 633	2 427	5 595	6 138	7 271	7 101
4120 Others	0	0	0	0	0	0	0	0	0	0
4200 Recurrent taxes on net wealth	0	0	0	0	0	0	0	0	0	0
4210 Individual	..	..	..	..	..	..	..	..	..	..
4220 Corporate	..	..	..	..	..	..	..	..	..	..
4300 Estate, inheritance and gift taxes	0	0	0	0	0	0	0	0	0	0
4310 Estate and inheritance taxes	..	..	..	..	..	..	..	..	..	..
4320 Gift taxes	..	..	..	..	..	..	..	..	..	..
4400 Taxes on financial and capital transactions	0	0	0	0	0	0	0	0	0	0
4500 Non-recurrent taxes	0	0	0	0	0	0	0	0	0	0
4510 On net wealth	..	..	..	..	..	..	..	..	..	..
4520 Other non-recurrent taxes	..	..	..	..	..	..	..	..	..	..
4600 Other recurrent taxes on property	0	0	0	0	0	0	0	0	0	0
5000 Taxes on goods and services	**2 824**	**43 907**	**77 065**	**149 544**	**157 082**	**171 801**	**195 143**	**212 228**	**241 055**	**268 569**
5100 Taxes on production, sale, transfer, etc	2 760	43 107	75 954	147 500	154 981	169 408	192 380	209 293	237 849	265 064
5110 General taxes	297	22 356	45 602	84 409	90 937	97 135	109 819	121 073	138 222	149 111
5111 Value added taxes	293	22 356	45 602	82 407	88 720	95 032	107 660	118 755	135 857	146 030
5112 Sales tax	4	0	0	0	0	0	0	0	0	0
Sales tax on used cars	4	0	0	0	0	0	0	0	0	0
5113 Other	0	0	0	2 002	2 217	2 103	2 159	2 318	2 365	3 081
Environmental levy	0	0	0	2 002	2 217	2 103	2 159	2 318	2 365	3 081
5120 Taxes on specific goods and services	2 463	20 752	30 352	63 091	64 044	72 273	82 561	88 220	99 627	115 953
5121 Excises	1 158	9 751	12 387	38 112	36 569	40 105	37 827	41 347	49 283	59 327
Excise duty	44	0	0	0	0	0	0	0	0	0
Special consumption tax	1 115	9 751	12 387	38 112	36 569	40 105	37 827	41 347	49 283	59 327
5122 Profits of fiscal monopolies	0	0	0	0	0	0	0	0	0	0
5123 Customs and import duties	782	8 498	14 999	19 959	20 638	22 905	25 938	26 281	28 960	34 033
Custom duty	782	8 498	14 999	19 959	20 638	22 905	25 938	26 281	28 960	34 033
5124 Taxes on exports	0	0	0	0	0	0	0	0	0	0
5125 Taxes on investment goods	0	0	0	0	0	0	0	0	0	0

Table 5.17. Jamaica *(cont.)*
Details of tax revenue / Ingresos tributarios detallados

Million JAM

	1990	2000	2005	2010	2011	2012	2013	2014	2015	2016
5126 Taxes on specific services	523	2 503	2 966	5 020	6 837	9 264	18 796	20 592	21 384	22 593
Bank and trust	204	0	0	0	0	0	0	0	0	0
Entertainment tax	11	0	0	0	0	0	0	0	0	0
Betting, gaming and lottery	50	504	1 052	1 508	1 586	1 893	2 225	2 661	2 797	2 802
Accommodation tax	87	0	0	0	0	265	1 636	1 900	2 050	2 254
Telephone call tax	86	0	0	0	0	2 342	6 405	6 687	6 559	4 810
Travel tax	86	1 999	1 914	3 512	5 251	4 763	8 531	9 344	9 979	12 726
5127 Other taxes on internat. trade and transactions	0	0	0	0	0	0	0	0	0	0
5128 Other taxes	0	0	0	0	0	0	0	0	0	0
5130 Unallocable between 5110 and 5120	0	0	0	0	0	0	0	0	0	0
5200 Taxes on use of goods and perform activities	64	800	1 111	2 045	2 100	2 393	2 763	2 934	3 206	3 505
5210 Recurrent taxes	64	800	1 111	2 045	2 100	2 393	2 763	2 934	3 206	3 505
5211 Paid by households: motor vehicles	47	751	935	1 775	1 748	2 043	2 493	2 666	2 901	3 032
5212 Paid by others: motor vehicles	0	0	0	0	0	0	0	0	0	0
5213 Paid in respect of other goods	17	49	176	270	352	350	270	268	305	473
5220 Non-recurrent taxes	0	0	0	0	0	0	0	0	0	0
5300 Unallocable between 5100 and 5200	0	0	0	0	0	0	0	0	0	0
6000 Other taxes	**914**	**3 890**	**9 816**	**8 088**	**9 955**	**10 212**	**12 392**	**12 747**	**13 167**	**15 293**
6100 Paid solely by business	0	0	0	0	0	0	0	0	0	0
6200 Other	914	3 890	9 816	8 088	9 955	10 212	12 392	12 747	13 167	15 293
Contractors levy	16	266	475	748	1 139	1 198	1 091	909	994	1 245
Stamp duty (domestic)	898	3 623	9 341	7 339	8 815	9 014	11 301	11 838	12 174	14 048

Note: Data collected by fiscal year (1st April - 31st March) for 1990-2003, then by calendar year (year ending 31st December).
The data are on a cash basis.
Heading 1210: For this edition, a specific line for the minimum business tax has been added.
Heading 1300: For this edition, a specific line for the education tax has been added. General consumption taxes, special consumption taxes and stamp duties levied on imports have been reclassified based on their tax base rather than on the point of collection. This affects headings 5111, 5121 and 6200.

Source: Ministry of Finance and Planning.

StatLink http://dx.doi.org/10.1787/888933687012

Table 5.18. Mexico / México
Details of tax revenue / Ingresos tributarios detallados

Million MXN

	1990	2000	2005	2010	2011	2012	2013	2014	2015	2016
Total tax revenue	**102 005**	**804 206**	**1 136 968**	**1 771 992**	**1 929 636**	**2 046 939**	**2 211 513**	**2 453 028**	**2 953 156**	**3 159 084**
1000 Taxes on income, profits and capital gains	**34 673**	**276 548**	**402 036**	**683 604**	**772 704**	**803 071**	**957 213**	**979 251**	**1 230 555**	**1 427 114**
1100 Of individuals	..	..	195 869	313 473	352 386	397 701	425 621	514 208	609 384	681 784
Tax on income of individuals	..	..	195 869	313 473	352 386	397 701	425 621	514 208	609 384	681 784
1110 On income and profits	..	..	..	..	..	..	..	..	..	..
1120 On capital gains	..	..	..	..	..	..	..	..	..	..
1200 Corporate	..	..	135 840	246 745	303 176	288 360	392 199	441 317	592 443	700 925
Tax on income of corporations	..	..	135 840	246 745	303 176	288 360	392 199	441 317	592 443	700 925
1210 On profits	..	..	..	..	..	..	..	..	..	..
1220 On capital gains	..	..	..	..	..	..	..	..	..	..
1300 Unallocable between 1100 and 1200	34 673	276 548	70 327	123 386	117 143	117 010	139 393	23 726	28 728	44 405
Tax on income of other individuals and corporations	..	244 841	40 780	66 937	66 004	74 042	89 028	31 076	36 268	44 225
Tax on asset	..	13 913	12 033	-624	-1 120	-1 192	-1 325	-735	-502	-918
Credit on salary	..	17 794	17 514	9 708	2 076	1 387	1 274	2 423	993	1 144
Oil yields tax	..	0	0	2 296	3 019	573	3 210	4 669	0	0
IETU	..	0	0	45 069	47 165	42 199	47 205	-13 707	-11 777	-4 039
Imposed by Activity Exploration and extraction of hydrocarbon	..	0	0	0	0	0	0	0	3 746	3 994
2000 Social security contributions	**17 165**	**138 223**	**206 551**	**277 459**	**302 463**	**330 327**	**351 993**	**378 373**	**409 249**	**434 998**
2100 Employees	..	..	..	..	..	..	..	..	..	..
2110 On a payroll basis	..	..	..	..	..	..	..	..	..	..
2120 On an income tax basis	..	..	..	..	..	..	..	..	..	..
2200 Employers	..	..	..	..	..	..	..	..	..	..
2210 On a payroll basis	..	..	..	..	..	..	..	..	..	..
2220 On an income tax basis	..	..	..	..	..	..	..	..	..	..
2300 Self-employed or non-employed	..	..	..	..	..	..	..	..	..	..
2310 On a payroll basis	..	..	..	..	..	..	..	..	..	..
2320 On an income tax basis	..	..	..	..	..	..	..	..	..	..
2400 Unallocable between 2100, 2200 and 2300	17 165	138 223	206 551	277 459	302 463	330 327	351 993	378 373	409 249	434 998
2410 On a payroll basis	..	138 223	206 551	277 459	302 463	330 327	351 993	378 373	409 249	434 998
2420 On an income tax basis	..	0	0	0	0	0	0	0	0	0
3000 Taxes on payroll and workforce	**1 797**	**11 217**	**20 461**	**36 911**	**41 980**	**48 033**	**53 042**	**64 713**	**70 221**	**0**
Substitute tax on salary	..	0	0	0	0	0	0	0	0	..
Payroll tax	..	11 101	15 746	27 813	31 817	35 480	41 184	64 581	69 866	..
Tax on remuneration to the personal work	..	65	4 562	8 841	9 990	12 333	11 645	0	152	..
Tax on professions and fees	..	36	53	71	58	48	50	51	106	..
Tax on operations by contract	..	15	100	186	116	173	163	81	96	..
4000 Taxes on property	**1 914**	**13 964**	**26 796**	**38 955**	**41 186**	**45 186**	**46 238**	**54 978**	**57 673**	**0**
4100 Recurrent taxes on immovable property	1 036	9 948	16 641	25 724	28 728	31 544	31 338	37 751	37 961	..
4110 Households	0	0	0	0	0	0	0	0	0	..
4120 Others	1 036	9 948	16 641	25 724	28 728	31 544	31 338	37 751	37 961	..
Property tax	..	9 948	16 641	25 724	28 728	31 544	31 338	37 751	37 961	..
4200 Recurrent taxes on net wealth	0	0	0	0	0	0	0	0	0	..
4210 Individual	..	..	..	..	..	..	..	..	..	..
4220 Corporate	..	..	..	..	..	..	..	..	..	..
4300 Estate, inheritance and gift taxes	8	0	0	0	0	0	0	0	0	..
4310 Estate and inheritance taxes	8	..	..	..	..	..	..	..	..	..
4320 Gift taxes	0	..	..	..	..	..	..	..	..	..
4400 Taxes on financial and capital transactions	870	4 017	10 155	13 231	12 458	13 642	14 900	17 227	19 712	..
Alienation of immovable property	..	1 763	984	1 122	1 379	1 341	1 271	1 308	1 595	..
Transfer of ownership of real estate	..	2 236	5 528	5 027	3 923	4 575	4 518	5 008	6 671	..
Purchasing property	..	18	3 643	7 082	7 157	7 725	9 110	10 911	11 447	..
4500 Non-recurrent taxes	0	0	0	0	0	0	0	0	0	..
4510 On net wealth	..	..	..	..	..	..	..	..	..	..
4520 Other non-recurrent taxes	..	..	..	..	..	..	..	..	..	..
4600 Other recurrent taxes on property	0	0	0	0	0	0	0	0	0	..
5000 Taxes on goods and services	**44 837**	**356 603**	**469 430**	**707 664**	**738 891**	**783 241**	**761 823**	**938 945**	**1 140 849**	**1 268 163**
5100 Taxes on production, sale, transfer, etc	44 171	310 325	403 158	630 123	658 962	720 052	696 150	859 302	1 120 605	1 267 960
5110 General taxes	26 635	189 606	318 432	504 509	537 143	579 988	556 794	667 085	707 213	791 700
5111 Value added taxes	26 635	189 606	318 432	504 509	537 143	579 988	556 794	667 085	707 213	791 700
5112 Sales tax	0	0	0	0	0	0	0	0	0	0
5113 Other	0	0	0	0	0	0	0	0	0	0
5120 Taxes on specific goods and services	17 519	120 720	84 726	125 614	121 819	140 064	139 356	192 217	413 392	476 260
5121 Excises	10 072	86 163	55 286	86 098	94 623	98 490	104 111	160 754	361 538	420 448
Special tax on production and services	..	81 544	49 627	81 427	89 544	92 620	97 860	154 327	354 294	411 390
Tax on new automobiles	..	4 619	5 659	4 671	5 079	5 870	6 252	6 427	7 244	9 058
Tax on luxury goods and services	..	0	0	0	0	0	0	0	0	0
5122 Profits of fiscal monopolies	0	0	0	0	0	0	0	0	0	0

Table 5.18. Mexico / México (*cont.*)
Details of tax revenue / Ingresos tributarios detallados

Million MXN

	1990	2000	2005	2010	2011	2012	2013	2014	2015	2016
5123 Customs and import duties	6 998	33 285	27 512	26 602	29 946	31 161	32 324	36 841	45 361	51 915
Step customs officer	..	423	692	2 071	3 065	3 255	3 065	2 913	1 265	1 361
Import taxes	..	32 861	26 820	24 531	26 881	27 906	29 260	33 928	44 096	50 553
5124 Taxes on exports	75	4	0	0	2	1	1	1	1	0
Tax on exports	..	4	0	0	2	1	1	1	1	0
5125 Taxes on investment goods	0	0	0	0	0	0	0	0	0	0
5126 Taxes on specific services	132	1 042	1 578	10 958	-5 610	7 169	-967	-7 417	1 763	-1 262
IDE	..	0	0	8 022	-8 442	2 786	-5 988	-12 322	-3 323	-1 262
Tax on lodging	..	504	798	1 384	1 375	1 702	1 890	2 067	2 561	0
Public entertainment tax	..	240	349	462	360	625	566	543	689	0
Tax on lotteries, raffles and gambling	..	267	417	923	952	1 329	1 213	1 218	1 416	0
Tax on commercials	..	4	15	166	145	16	203	216	210	0
Various indirect taxes	..	28	0	1	0	711	1 149	861	209	0
5127 Other taxes on internat. trade and transactions	0	0	0	0	0	0	0	0	0	0
5128 Other taxes	242	226	350	1 956	2 858	3 243	3 886	2 040	4 730	5 159
Mining fees	..	226	350	1 956	2 858	3 243	3 886	2 040	4 730	5 159
5130 Unallocable between 5110 and 5120	17	0	0	0	0	0	0	0	0	0
5200 Taxes on use of goods and perform activities	666	46 278	66 272	77 541	79 930	63 189	65 674	79 643	20 245	203
5210 Recurrent taxes	666	46 278	66 272	77 541	79 930	63 189	65 674	79 643	20 245	203
5211 Paid by households: motor vehicles	567	8 878	15 237	21 319	22 186	16 464	19 174	20 370	19 880	0
Tax on motor vehicules	..	8 878	15 237	21 319	22 186	16 464	19 174	20 370	19 880	..
5212 Paid by others: motor vehicles	0	301	357	281	296	370	357	367	124	135
Tax on federal auto transport	..	301	357	281	296	370	357	367	124	135
5213 Paid in respect of other goods	99	37 099	50 678	55 942	57 447	46 355	46 143	58 906	240	68
Sport fishing	..	40	80	59	50	55	50	65	62	68
Sport hunting	..	3	0	0	0	0	0	0	0	0
Tax on commercial activities	..	63	113	50	66	42	26	33	64	0
Trade in books and magazines	..	0	0	0	0	0	3	1	1	0
Tax on industrial activities	..	2	0	82	38	145	49	13	93	0
Mining	..	0	0	1	0	0	1	2	21	0
Fee on use of public assets	..	36 991	50 485	55 749	57 292	46 113	46 013	58 792	0	0
5220 Non-recurrent taxes	0	0	0	0	0	0	0	0	0	0
5300 Unallocable between 5100 and 5200	0	0	0	0	0	0	0	0	0	0
6000 Other taxes	**1 619**	**7 651**	**11 693**	**27 398**	**32 412**	**37 080**	**41 204**	**36 767**	**44 608**	**28 809**
6100 Paid solely by business	0	0	0	0	0	0	0	0	0	0
6200 Other	1 619	7 651	11 693	27 398	32 412	37 080	41 204	36 767	44 608	28 809
Accessories	..	5 504	9 543	22 206	24 059	24 077	25 301	23 717	23 211	28 480
Unallocable between 1000 and 5000 caused in exercices fiscal previous liquidation slopes or of payment	..	374	-927	30	-118	2 260	1 618	504	4 168	329
Additional state and local taxes	..	1 773	3 077	5 162	8 471	10 743	14 285	12 546	17 228	0

Note: Year ending 31st December.

The data are on a cash basis.

The 2016 data for tax revenues of the state and local levels of government are not available. They comprise revenues in categories 3000, 4000, 5000 and 6000.

Heading 1000: In ECLAC data, income taxes are presented net of credit on salary figures.

Heading 2000: In ECLAC data, social security contributions are presented net of transfers from the Federal government for the payment of IMSS (Mexican Social Security Institute) pensions. Some amounts of social security contributions are now treated as non-tax revenue to align with the reporting to other international organisations.

Source: Ministry of Finance, Economic Department.

StatLink http://dx.doi.org/10.1787/888933687031

Table 5.19. Nicaragua

Details of tax revenue / Ingresos tributarios detallados

Million NIO

	1990	2000	2005	2010	2011	2012	2013	2014	2015	2016
Total tax revenue	..	**8 407**	**17 009**	**36 293**	**44 450**	**51 866**	**57 653**	**67 124**	**77 564**	**85 442**
1000 Taxes on income, profits and capital gains	..	**1 144**	**3 902**	**8 351**	**11 144**	**13 107**	**14 521**	**17 658**	**20 800**	**24 307**
1100 Of individuals	..	..	..	..	..	..	..	..	..	..
1110 On income and profits	..	..	..	..	..	..	..	..	..	..
1120 On capital gains	..	..	..	..	..	..	..	..	..	..
1200 Corporate	..	..	..	..	..	..	..	..	..	..
1210 On profits	..	..	..	..	..	..	..	..	..	..
1220 On capital gains	..	..	..	..	..	..	..	..	..	..
1300 Unallocable between 1100 and 1200	..	1 144	3 902	8 351	11 144	13 107	14 521	17 658	20 800	24 307
Income tax	..	1 144	3 902	8 351	11 144	13 107	14 521	17 658	20 800	24 307
2000 Social security contributions	..	**1 678**	**3 363**	**8 090**	**9 433**	**11 007**	**12 805**	**15 161**	**18 194**	**21 296**
2100 Employees	..	..	..	..	..	..	..	..	..	..
2110 On a payroll basis	..	..	..	..	..	..	..	..	..	..
2120 On an income tax basis	..	..	..	..	..	..	..	..	..	..
2200 Employers	..	..	..	..	..	..	..	..	..	..
2210 On a payroll basis	..	..	..	..	..	..	..	..	..	..
2220 On an income tax basis	..	..	..	..	..	..	..	..	..	..
2300 Self-employed or non-employed	..	..	..	..	..	..	..	..	..	..
2310 On a payroll basis	..	..	..	..	..	..	..	..	..	..
2320 On an income tax basis	..	..	..	..	..	..	..	..	..	..
2400 Unallocable between 2100, 2200 and 2300	..	1 678	3 363	8 090	9 433	11 007	12 805	15 161	18 194	21 296
2410 On a payroll basis	..	1 678	3 363	8 090	9 433	11 007	12 805	15 161	18 194	21 296
2420 On an income tax basis	..	0	0	0	0	0	0	0	0	0
3000 Taxes on payroll and workforce	..	**0**	**0**	**0**	**0**	**0**	**0**	**0**	**0**	**0**
4000 Taxes on property	..	**-11**	**2**	**130**	**191**	**239**	**311**	**374**	**513**	**604**
4100 Recurrent taxes on immovable property	..	0	0	0	0	0	0	0	0	0
4110 Households	..	..	..	..	..	..	..	..	..	..
4120 Others	..	..	..	..	..	..	..	..	..	..
4200 Recurrent taxes on net wealth	..	-11	2	130	191	239	311	0	0	0
4210 Individual	..	..	..	..	..	..	..	..	..	..
4220 Corporate	..	..	..	..	..	..	..	..	..	..
4300 Estate, inheritance and gift taxes	..	0	0	0	0	0	0	0	0	0
4310 Estate and inheritance taxes	..	..	..	..	..	..	..	..	..	..
4320 Gift taxes	..	..	..	..	..	..	..	..	..	..
4400 Taxes on financial and capital transactions	..	0	0	0	0	0	0	374	513	604
4500 Non-recurrent taxes	..	0	0	0	0	0	0	0	0	0
4510 On net wealth	..	..	..	..	..	..	..	..	..	..
4520 Other non-recurrent taxes	..	..	..	..	..	..	..	..	..	..
4600 Other recurrent taxes on property	..	0	0	0	0	0	0	0	0	0
5000 Taxes on goods and services	..	**5 584**	**9 725**	**19 032**	**22 885**	**26 611**	**28 975**	**32 597**	**36 537**	**38 339**
5100 Taxes on production, sale, transfer, etc	..	5 584	9 725	18 608	22 401	26 093	28 367	31 927	35 798	37 691
5110 General taxes	..	2 931	5 599	11 932	14 882	17 490	19 332	22 267	23 787	24 110
5111 Value added taxes	..	2 931	5 599	10 353	12 876	15 151	16 736	19 385	20 714	22 822
5112 Sales tax	..	0	0	0	0	0	0	0	0	0
5113 Other	..	0	0	1 579	2 006	2 339	2 596	2 883	3 073	1 289
5120 Taxes on specific goods and services	..	2 653	4 126	6 676	7 519	8 603	9 035	9 659	12 011	13 581
5121 Excises	..	2 034	3 227	5 541	6 070	6 884	7 254	7 755	9 773	10 950
Liquor	..	84	102	198	240	214	253	230	264	305
Beer	..	203	340	645	781	915	1 047	1 184	1 370	1 476
Cigarettes	..	70	143	45	0	0	174	1	0	0
Soft drinks	..	123	128	248	292	351	389	423	501	525
Petroleum products	..	1 359	1 756	2 699	2 700	3 045	3 418	3 938	4 396	5 021
Excise taxes on imports	..	196	734	1 559	1 901	2 233	1 924	1 902	3 105	3 505
Other specific excises on consumption	..	-1	25	148	156	126	49	78	136	117
5122 Profits of fiscal monopolies	..	0	0	0	0	0	0	0	0	0
5123 Customs and import duties	..	619	856	1 135	1 449	1 719	1 782	1 904	2 238	2 631
Custom duties	..	452	837	1 094	1 400	1 661	1 717	1 828	2 155	2 509
Temporary protection duty	..	96	0	0	0	0	0	0	0	0
On products originating in Colombia or Honduras	..	72	18	41	49	58	64	76	83	123
5124 Taxes on exports	..	0	0	0	0	0	0	0	0	0
5125 Taxes on investment goods	..	0	0	0	0	0	0	0	0	0
5126 Taxes on specific services	..	0	0	0	0	0	0	0	0	0
5127 Other taxes on internat. trade and transactions	..	0	43	0	0	0	0	0	0	0
5128 Other taxes	..	0	0	0	0	0	0	0	0	0
5130 Unallocable between 5110 and 5120	..	0	0	0	0	0	0	0	0	0
5200 Taxes on use of goods and perform activities	..	0	0	424	484	519	607	670	739	648
5210 Recurrent taxes	..	..	..	424	484	519	607	670	739	648

Table 5.19. Nicaragua *(cont.)*
Details of tax revenue / Ingresos tributarios detallados

Million NIO

	1990	2000	2005	2010	2011	2012	2013	2014	2015	2016
5211 Paid by households: motor vehicles	..	..	..	20	21	21	31	41	60	34
5212 Paid by others: motor vehicles	..	..	..	0	0	0	0	0	0	0
5213 Paid in respect of other goods	..	..	..	403	463	497	577	629	679	614
5220 Non-recurrent taxes	..	..	..	0	0	0	0	0	0	0
5300 Unallocable between 5100 and 5200	..	0	0	0	0	0	0	0	0	0
6000 Other taxes	**..**	**11**	**17**	**690**	**798**	**901**	**1 041**	**1 334**	**1 519**	**896**
6100 Paid solely by business	..	0	0	0	0	0	0	0	0	0
6200 Other	..	11	17	690	798	901	1 041	1 334	1 519	896
Stamp tax	..	11	17	20	22	24	77	87	90	90
Municipal tax	..	11	17	20	22	24	77	87	90	90

Note: Year ending 31st December.
The data are on a cash basis.
Comparable statistics for 1990 cannot be shown due to the devaluation of the Nicaraguan cordoba. For the first time, this edition includes tax revenues by local governments from 2010-16. This affects headings 5113, 5211, 5213 and 6200.

Source: Banco Central de Nicaragua y Ministerio de Hacienda y Crédito Público (Central Bank of Nicaragua and Ministry of Finance and Public Credit).

StatLink http://dx.doi.org/10.1787/888933687050

Table 5.20. Panama / Panamá
Details of tax revenue / Ingresos tributarios detallados

Million PAB

	1990	2000	2005	2010	2011	2012	2013	2014	2015	2016
Total tax revenue	**893**	**1 953**	**2 257**	**4 815**	**5 666**	**6 721**	**7 650**	**7 740**	**8 268**	**9 146**
1000 Taxes on income, profits and capital gains	**217**	**485**	**563**	**1 317**	**1 350**	**1 985**	**2 200**	**1 998**	**2 154**	**2 512**
1100 Of individuals	140	295	303	440	514	554	679	722	799	877
1110 On income and profits	140	295	303	440	514	554	679	722	799	877
Payroll	115	222	227	353	420	456	568	602	689	739
Personal income tax	14	20	24	35	28	38	52	58	45	54
Panama Canal Authority withholding	10	53	52	52	65	60	59	62	65	83
1120 On capital gains	..	..	..	..	..	..	..	..	..	..
1200 Corporate	66	159	213	603	539	1 068	970	896	938	1 137
1210 On profits	66	159	213	603	539	1 068	970	896	938	1 137
Colón Free Zone	5	3	4	20	24	51	39	43	36	36
Corporate income tax	61	155	208	584	515	1 017	931	853	902	1 101
1220 On capital gains	..	..	..	..	..	..	..	..	..	..
1300 Unallocable between 1100 and 1200	11	31	47	273	297	364	550	380	417	498
Dividends and complimentary tax	11	31	47	166	187	240	251	243	266	286
Capital gains	0	0	0	107	110	124	299	137	151	212
2000 Social security contributions	**271**	**742**	**827**	**1 637**	**2 042**	**2 186**	**2 677**	**2 794**	**3 049**	**3 380**
2100 Employees	..	..	..	..	..	..	..	..	..	..
2110 On a payroll basis	..	..	..	..	..	..	..	..	..	..
2120 On an income tax basis	..	..	..	..	..	..	..	..	..	..
2200 Employers	..	..	..	..	..	..	..	..	..	..
2210 On a payroll basis	..	..	..	..	..	..	..	..	..	..
2220 On an income tax basis	..	..	..	..	..	..	..	..	..	..
2300 Self-employed or non-employed	..	..	..	..	..	..	..	..	..	..
2310 On a payroll basis	..	..	..	..	..	..	..	..	..	..
2320 On an income tax basis	..	..	..	..	..	..	..	..	..	..
2400 Unallocable between 2100, 2200 and 2300	271	742	827	1 637	2 042	2 186	2 677	2 794	3 049	3 380
2410 On a payroll basis	..	..	..	..	..	..	..	..	..	..
2420 On an income tax basis	..	..	..	..	..	..	..	..	..	..
3000 Taxes on payroll and workforce	**0**	**36**	**36**	**59**	**65**	**70**	**82**	**134**	**111**	**111**
Education insurance	0	36	36	59	65	70	82	134	111	111
4000 Taxes on property	**43**	**62**	**109**	**212**	**229**	**261**	**338**	**337**	**319**	**333**
4100 Recurrent taxes on immovable property	28	34	57	108	110	120	181	176	151	168
4110 Households	28	34	56	108	110	120	181	176	151	168
4120 Others	0	0	0	0	0	0	0	0	0	0
4200 Recurrent taxes on net wealth	0	0	0	0	0	0	0	0	0	0
4210 Individual	..	..	..	..	..	..	..	..	..	..
4220 Corporate	..	..	..	..	..	..	..	..	..	..
4300 Estate, inheritance and gift taxes	0	0	0	0	0	0	0	0	0	0
4310 Estate and inheritance taxes	..	..	..	..	..	..	..	..	..	..
4320 Gift taxes	..	..	..	..	..	..	..	..	..	..
4400 Taxes on financial and capital transactions	3	9	21	30	36	41	49	45	48	41
4500 Non-recurrent taxes	0	0	0	0	0	0	0	0	0	0
4510 On net wealth	..	..	..	..	..	..	..	..	..	..
4520 Other non-recurrent taxes	..	..	..	..	..	..	..	..	..	..
4600 Other recurrent taxes on property	12	19	32	75	83	100	108	116	120	124
Commercial licences	12	19	32	75	83	100	108	116	120	124
5000 Taxes on goods and services	**335**	**573**	**692**	**1 513**	**1 894**	**2 124**	**2 253**	**2 384**	**2 539**	**2 712**
5100 Taxes on production, sale, transfer, etc	332	530	642	1 473	1 845	2 067	2 193	2 319	2 467	2 631
5110 General taxes	80	69	138	766	1 042	1 184	1 269	1 351	1 359	1 516
5111 Value added taxes	80	69	138	766	1 042	1 184	1 269	1 351	1 359	1 516
5112 Sales tax	0	0	0	0	0	0	0	0	0	0
5113 Other	0	0	0	0	0	0	0	0	0	0
5120 Taxes on specific goods and services	139	461	504	706	803	883	924	967	1 107	1 115
5121 Excises	0	141	106	239	310	356	397	452	581	586
Gasoline products	..	109	69	97	90	101	117	133	242	280
Beer	..	18	22	31	33	35	36	42	48	49
Wine and liquor	..	12	11	11	11	10	16	23	15	10
Soft drinks	..	2	3	6	6	7	7	7	7	6
Various products	..	0	1	95	171	45	53	48	53	36
Automobiles	..	0	0	0	0	133	141	176	182	183
Other	..	0	0	0	0	25	27	24	32	22
5122 Profits of fiscal monopolies	0	0	0	0	0	0	0	0	0	0
5123 Customs and import duties	125	298	364	390	394	420	409	381	391	355
5124 Taxes on exports	13	0	0	0	0	0	0	0	0	0
5125 Taxes on investment goods	0	0	0	0	0	0	0	0	0	0

Table 5.20. Panama / Panamá (*cont.*)
Details of tax revenue / Ingresos tributarios detallados

Million PAB

	1990	2000	2005	2010	2011	2012	2013	2014	2015	2016
5126 Taxes on specific services	0	17	27	65	80	86	96	109	111	149
Insurance premiums	..	17	19	47	52	54	60	63	48	54
Cable and telecommunications	..	0	6	17	28	31	34	45	39	41
Gambling	..	0	1	1	1	1	2	2	23	53
5127 Other taxes on internat. trade and transactions	1	5	7	12	18	21	22	25	25	26
Banks, financial institutions, and currency exchange	0	2	7	12	18	21	22	25	25	26
Other	1	3	0	0	0	0	0	0	0	0
5128 Other taxes	0	0	0	0	0	0	0	0	0	0
5130 Unallocable between 5110 and 5120	113	0	0	0	0	0	0	0	0	0
5200 Taxes on use of goods and perform activities	4	43	51	41	48	57	60	66	72	81
5210 Recurrent taxes	0	39	43	41	48	57	60	66	72	81
5211 Paid by households: motor vehicles	..	7	8	0	0	0	0	0	0	0
5212 Paid by others: motor vehicles	..	5	4	0	0	0	0	0	0	0
5213 Paid in respect of other goods	..	27	30	41	48	57	60	66	72	81
On commercial activities	..	25	29	38	46	54	57	62	69	77
On industrial activities	..	2	2	2	3	3	3	3	3	4
5220 Non-recurrent taxes	4	4	7	0	0	0	0	0	0	0
Building and construction	0	4	7	..	..	..	..	..	..	..
Ship registration	4	0	0	..	..	..	..	..	..	..
5300 Unallocable between 5100 and 5200	0	0	0	0	0	0	0	0	0	0
6000 Other taxes	**26**	**54**	**29**	**77**	**86**	**94**	**101**	**93**	**96**	**100**
6100 Paid solely by business	0	11	0	0	0	0	0	0	0	0
6200 Other	26	43	29	77	86	94	101	93	96	100
Legal services	17	42	28	41	47	45	46	41	37	35
Fiscal documents	9	1	1	36	39	49	55	52	59	65
Others	9	1	1	36	39	49	55	52	59	65

Note: Year ending 31st December.

The data are on a cash basis.

Heading 1110: Specific lines for personal income tax and Panama Canal Authority Withholding have been added .

Heading 3000: In ECLAC data, education insurance is classified as "Other taxes" (6000).

Heading 5127: In CIAT and ECLAC data, the tax on banks, financial institutions and currency exchange is classified as a property tax (4000).

Source: Contraloría General de la República y Ministerio de Economía y Finanzas (General Comptroller of the Republic of Panama and Ministry of Economics and Finance).

StatLink http://dx.doi.org/10.1787/888933687069

Table 5.21. Paraguay
Details of tax revenue / Ingresos tributarios detallados

Million PYG

	1990	2000	2005	2010	2011	2012	2013	2014	2015	2016
Total tax revenue	**348 889**	**3 587 451**	**7 434 024**	**15 637 675**	**17 727 016**	**19 261 951**	**20 540 296**	**24 472 900**	**25 833 690**	**27 272 588**
1000 Taxes on income, profits and capital gains	**73 726**	**470 388**	**938 886**	**2 096 498**	**2 607 282**	**2 902 725**	**3 100 223**	**3 678 392**	**3 922 384**	**4 429 169**
1100 Of individuals	..	41 021	82 086	184 361	228 802	254 965	283 915	398 570	457 693	396 573
1110 On income and profits	..	41 021	82 086	184 361	228 802	254 965	283 915	398 570	457 693	396 573
IRACIS - IRAGRO	..	41 021	82 086	183 211	228 648	254 458	270 540	314 649	331 856	256 019
Personal income tax	..	0	0	1 150	154	507	13 375	83 921	125 837	140 554
1120 On capital gains	..	..	..	..	..	..	..	..	..	..
1200 Corporate	..	429 367	856 800	1 912 137	2 378 480	2 647 760	2 816 308	3 279 822	3 464 691	4 032 596
1210 On profits	..	429 367	856 800	1 912 137	2 378 480	2 647 760	2 816 308	3 279 822	3 464 691	4 032 596
Income tax on small businesses	..	0	0	9 380	5 129	5 764	7 831	9 063	14 563	18 567
Single tax	..	4 238	5 802	715	544	317	32	72	5	3
Single tax on maquiladoras	..	0	289	3 310	3 182	4 570	4 669	9 783	10 892	12 087
IRACIS - IRAGRO	..	425 129	850 709	1 898 732	2 369 625	2 637 109	2 803 776	3 260 905	3 439 232	4 001 939
1220 On capital gains	..	..	..	..	..	..	..	..	..	..
1300 Unallocable between 1100 and 1200	73 726	0	0	0	0	0	0	0	0	0
Others	73 726	0	0	0	0	0	0	0	0	0
2000 Social security contributions	**28 882**	**919 533**	**1 591 980**	**3 552 640**	**3 979 252**	**4 844 110**	**5 158 072**	**6 336 260**	**7 044 316**	**7 048 846**
2100 Employees	..	..	..	..	..	..	..	..	..	..
2110 On a payroll basis	..	..	..	..	..	..	..	..	..	..
2120 On an income tax basis	..	..	..	..	..	..	..	..	..	..
2200 Employers	..	..	..	..	..	..	..	..	..	..
2210 On a payroll basis	..	..	..	..	..	..	..	..	..	..
2220 On an income tax basis	..	..	..	..	..	..	..	..	..	..
2300 Self-employed or non-employed	..	..	..	..	..	..	..	..	..	..
2310 On a payroll basis	..	..	..	..	..	..	..	..	..	..
2320 On an income tax basis	..	..	..	..	..	..	..	..	..	..
2400 Unallocable between 2100, 2200 and 2300	28 882	919 533	1 591 980	3 552 640	3 979 252	4 844 110	5 158 072	6 336 260	7 044 316	7 048 846
2410 On a payroll basis	28 882	919 533	1 591 980	3 552 640	3 979 252	4 844 110	5 158 072	6 336 260	7 044 316	7 048 846
2420 On an income tax basis	0	0	0	0	0	0	0	0	0	0
3000 Taxes on payroll and workforce	**0**	**0**	**0**	**0**	**0**	**0**	**0**	**0**	**0**	**0**
4000 Taxes on property	**17 162**	**0**	**0**	**272 385**	**289 456**	**310 237**	**350 169**	**390 102**	**430 034**	**566 117**
4100 Recurrent taxes on immovable property	17 162	..	..	254 306	266 371	289 493	..	..	398 251	529 479
4110 Households	17 162	..	..	254 306	266 371	289 493	..	..	398 251	529 479
Real estate tax	0	..	..	249 697	261 051	285 034	..	..	390 772	514 404
Tax on vacant lots	0	..	..	2 925	3 212	3 472	..	..	4 818	10 284
Other	17 162	..	..	1 684	2 109	987	..	..	2 661	4 792
4120 Others	0	..	..	0	0	0	..	..	0	0
4200 Recurrent taxes on net wealth	0	..	..	0	0	0	..	..	0	0
4210 Individual	..	..	..	..	..	..	..	..	..	..
4220 Corporate	..	..	..	..	..	..	..	..	..	..
4300 Estate, inheritance and gift taxes	0	..	..	0	0	0	..	..	0	0
4310 Estate and inheritance taxes	..	..	..	..	..	..	..	..	..	..
4320 Gift taxes	..	..	..	..	..	..	..	..	..	..
4400 Taxes on financial and capital transactions	0	..	..	16 316	22 406	20 061	..	..	30 987	35 259
Real estate transfer tax	..	..	..	11 766	16 362	14 704	..	..	22 406	22 978
Other	..	..	..	4 551	6 044	5 357	..	..	8 581	12 281
4500 Non-recurrent taxes	0	..	..	0	0	0	..	..	0	0
4510 On net wealth	..	..	..	..	..	..	..	..	..	..
4520 Other non-recurrent taxes	..	..	..	..	..	..	..	..	..	..
4600 Other recurrent taxes on property	0	..	..	1 762	679	682	..	..	796	1 378
5000 Taxes on goods and services	**179 312**	**2 080 878**	**4 309 832**	**9 460 962**	**10 749 735**	**11 081 105**	**11 808 277**	**13 919 885**	**14 416 197**	**15 207 133**
5100 Taxes on production, sale, transfer, etc	179 312	2 080 878	4 309 832	9 249 698	10 501 464	10 849 519	11 524 523	13 583 267	13 982 529	14 734 772
5110 General taxes	0	1 150 496	2 478 998	5 991 694	6 887 685	7 126 623	7 843 002	9 363 648	9 768 800	10 482 238
5111 Value added taxes	..	1 150 496	2 478 998	5 991 694	6 887 685	7 126 623	7 843 002	9 363 648	9 768 800	10 482 238
5112 Sales tax	..	0	0	0	0	0	0	0	0	0
5113 Other	..	0	0	0	0	0	0	0	0	0
5120 Taxes on specific goods and services	179 312	930 382	1 830 834	3 258 004	3 613 779	3 722 896	3 681 521	4 219 619	4 213 729	4 252 534
5121 Excises	41 087	456 561	949 962	1 710 531	1 892 587	2 063 020	2 048 143	2 442 895	2 391 628	2 575 775
Fuels	41 087	316 694	688 773	1 126 143	1 328 213	1 455 820	1 427 769	1 787 112	1 775 286	1 830 586
Other excises	0	136 194	249 239	537 887	564 374	607 200	620 374	655 783	616 342	745 189
Animal health and quality service	0	3 673	11 950	46 501	0	0	0	0	0	0
Livestock trade	0	0	0	0	0	0	0	0	0	0
5122 Profits of fiscal monopolies	0	0	0	0	0	0	0	0	0	0
5123 Customs and import duties	138 225	473 821	880 872	1 524 252	1 696 945	1 637 588	1 633 378	1 776 724	1 659 535	1 642 818
5124 Taxes on exports	0	0	0	0	0	0	0	0	0	0
5125 Taxes on investment goods	0	0	0	0	0	0	0	0	0	0

Table 5.21. Paraguay *(cont.)*
Details of tax revenue / Ingresos tributarios detallados

Million PYG

	1990	2000	2005	2010	2011	2012	2013	2014	2015	2016
5126 Taxes on specific services	0	0	0	23 221	24 247	22 288	0	0	162 566	33 942
Advertising	..	..	..	5 249	6 047	6 560	..	..	7 428	8 424
Public transport	..	..	..	4 363	4 649	4 121	..	..	4 297	4 316
Gambling	..	..	..	0	0	0	..	..	804	846
Other	..	..	..	13 609	13 551	11 607	..	..	150 037	20 356
5127 Other taxes on internat. trade and transactions	0	0	0	0	0	0	0	0	0	0
5128 Other taxes	0	0	0	0	0	0	0	0	0	0
5130 Unallocable between 5110 and 5120	0	0	0	0	0	0	0	0	0	0
5200 Taxes on use of goods and perform activities	0	0	0	211 027	208 542	230 890	283 754	336 618	389 482	444 952
5210 Recurrent taxes	..	..	..	211 027	208 542	230 890	283 754	336 618	389 482	444 952
5211 Paid by households: motor vehicles	..	..	..	0	0	0	..	..	0	0
5212 Paid by others: motor vehicles	..	..	..	52 365	64 667	67 399	..	..	94 393	106 200
Motor vehicle licences	..	..	..	52 365	64 667	67 399	..	..	94 393	106 200
5213 Paid in respect of other goods	..	..	..	158 662	143 875	163 491	..	..	295 090	338 752
Tax on construction	..	..	..	31 696	38 891	50 337	..	..	65 403	64 284
Licencing fees	..	..	..	126 965	104 983	113 153	..	..	229 686	274 468
5220 Non-recurrent taxes	..	..	..	0	0	0	0	0	0	0
5300 Unallocable between 5100 and 5200	0	0	0	237	39 730	696	0	0	44 186	27 409
6000 Other taxes	**49 807**	**116 652**	**593 326**	**255 190**	**101 291**	**123 774**	**123 554**	**148 260**	**20 758**	**21 323**
6100 Paid solely by business	0	0	0	0	0	0	0	0	0	0
6200 Other	49 807	116 652	593 326	255 190	101 291	123 774	123 554	148 260	20 758	21 323
Registration and stamp duties	0	71 777	192 393	332	159	168	179	106	91	82
Luxury automobile tax	0	0	3 897	91	129	153	218	57	54	152
Other	49 807	44 875	397 036	254 767	101 003	123 453	123 157	148 098	20 613	21 088

Note: Year ending 31st December.

The data are on a cash basis.

The figures for years up to and including 2004, as well as for 2013 and 2014, exclude local government tax revenues as the data are not available. This affects data in categories 4000, 5000 and 6000.

Heading 2000: Data on social security contributions collected by decentralised institutions are not available for 2011 to 2014, with the exception of the contributions made to the Instituto de Previsión Social (Social Security Institute).

Heading 1110: The proportion of data included in this category has been estimated from 1999 to 2014 based on the disaggregation provided in 2015.

Heading 1210: The proportion of data included in this category has been estimated from 1999 to 2014 based on the disaggregation provided in 2015.

Heading 5121: Data for animal health and quality service are not available from 2011.

Source: Subsecretaría de Estado de Tributación, Ministerio de Hacienda del Paraguay (Tax Undersecretary, Ministry of Finance of Paraguay).

StatLink http://dx.doi.org/10.1787/888933687088

Table 5.22. Peru / Perú
Details of tax revenue / Ingresos tributarios detallados

Million PEN

	1990	2000	2005	2010	2011	2012	2013	2014	2015	2016
Total tax revenue	**645**	**25 984**	**40 576**	**74 424**	**86 688**	**96 383**	**102 747**	**109 547**	**105 619**	**105 726**
1000 Taxes on income, profits and capital gains	**37**	**5 078**	**11 950**	**27 317**	**35 341**	**39 720**	**39 357**	**43 577**	**37 772**	**40 360**
1100 Of individuals	3	2 117	3 327	6 518	8 208	9 462	10 570	11 423	11 137	11 760
First category	..	167	181	160	196	253	310	374	443	504
Second category	..	7	250	869	1 291	1 136	1 275	1 214	1 287	1 536
Fourth category	..	234	395	521	567	637	744	834	783	871
Fifth category	..	1 641	2 369	4 735	5 877	7 054	7 820	8 473	8 044	8 248
Tax debt payments	..	68	130	233	277	382	421	529	581	601
1110 On income and profits	..	..	..	..	..	..	..	..	..	..
1120 On capital gains	..	..	..	..	..	..	..	..	..	..
1200 Corporate	32	2 526	8 391	19 561	26 036	28 453	26 207	26 593	24 266	24 786
1210 On profits	32	2 526	8 391	19 561	26 036	28 453	26 207	26 593	24 266	24 786
Third category	..	2 023	5 316	14 652	19 321	20 744	19 633	18 536	16 817	16 496
Income tax on mining	..	0	0	0	59	442	337	372	208	236
Income tax special regime	..	47	55	118	153	202	246	275	310	335
Other incomes corporate	..	18	41	148	224	229	187	193	167	215
Tax debt payments	..	438	1 908	2 856	3 987	4 397	3 029	3 703	3 066	3 204
Temporary tax on net assets	..	0	1 073	1 788	2 293	2 439	2 776	3 513	3 697	4 300
1220 On capital gains	..	..	..	..	..	..	..	..	..	..
1300 Unallocable between 1100 and 1200	1	436	232	1 239	1 097	1 804	2 579	5 561	2 369	3 814
Income tax on non-residents	1	487	542	1 511	1 735	2 244	2 848	6 027	3 248	5 205
Income tax refunds	0	-51	-310	-272	-638	-439	-269	-466	-879	-1 391
2000 Social security contributions	**50**	**3 175**	**4 012**	**7 930**	**8 947**	**10 142**	**11 260**	**11 847**	**12 681**	**13 186**
2100 Employees	..	566	692	2 434	2 672	2 897	3 160	3 158	3 451	3 585
2110 On a payroll basis	..	566	670	1 666	2 012	2 406	2 803	3 046	3 314	3 488
2120 On an income tax basis	..	0	23	768	661	491	357	112	137	97
Solidarity contribution for pension plan	..	..	23	768	661	491	357	112	137	97
2200 Employers	..	2 515	3 285	5 454	6 229	7 194	8 044	8 631	9 170	9 536
2210 On a payroll basis	..	2 432	3 140	5 216	6 015	6 979	7 827	8 413	8 926	9 282
2220 On an income tax basis	..	83	144	238	214	214	217	218	244	255
2300 Self-employed or non-employed	..	95	36	42	46	51	55	58	60	64
2310 On a payroll basis	..	..	..	..	..	..	..	..	..	..
2320 On an income tax basis	..	..	..	..	..	..	..	..	..	..
2400 Unallocable between 2100, 2200 and 2300	50	0	0	0	0	0	0	0	0	0
2410 On a payroll basis	50	..	..	..	..	..	..	..	..	..
2420 On an income tax basis	0	..	..	..	..	..	..	..	..	..
3000 Taxes on payroll and workforce	**0**	**1 149**	**7**	**1**	**0**	**2**	**0**	**-82**	**4**	**1**
4000 Taxes on property	**99**	**0**	**1 340**	**2 237**	**1 876**	**1 897**	**2 130**	**2 159**	**2 399**	**2 645**
4100 Recurrent taxes on immovable property	0	0	460	731	856	958	1 126	1 234	1 444	1 635
4110 Households	..	..	..	..	..	..	..	..	..	..
4120 Others	..	..	..	..	..	..	..	..	..	..
4200 Recurrent taxes on net wealth	61	0	0	0	0	0	0	0	0	0
4210 Individual	60	0	0	..	..	..	..	..	..	..
4220 Corporate	1	0	0	..	..	..	..	..	..	..
Revaluation of fixed assets	1	..	..	..	..	..	..	..	..	..
4300 Estate, inheritance and gift taxes	0	0	0	0	0	0	0	0	0	0
4310 Estate and inheritance taxes	..	..	..	..	..	..	..	..	..	..
4320 Gift taxes	..	..	..	..	..	..	..	..	..	..
4400 Taxes on financial and capital transactions	38	0	803	1 506	1 021	939	1 004	925	955	1 010
Financial transactions tax	0	..	706	944	395	126	134	153	161	168
Real estate transfer tax	0	..	97	561	625	813	870	772	795	842
Tax Law Decree 519	38	..	0	0	0	0	0	0	0	0
4500 Non-recurrent taxes	0	0	0	0	0	0	0	0	0	0
4510 On net wealth	..	..	..	..	..	..	..	..	..	..
4520 Other non-recurrent taxes	..	..	..	..	..	..	..	..	..	..
4600 Other recurrent taxes on property	0	0	76	0	0	0	0	0	0	0
5000 Taxes on goods and services	**423**	**15 952**	**22 721**	**36 354**	**39 438**	**42 511**	**46 264**	**49 934**	**51 099**	**48 247**
5100 Taxes on production, sale, transfer, etc	423	15 952	22 666	36 199	39 260	42 315	46 030	49 670	50 817	47 943
5110 General taxes	78	9 694	15 109	29 094	32 455	35 078	37 953	41 779	42 612	39 462
5111 Value added taxes	78	9 646	15 109	29 094	32 455	35 078	37 953	41 779	42 612	39 462
5112 Sales tax	0	0	0	0	0	0	0	0	0	0
5113 Other	0	47	0	0	0	0	0	0	0	0
5120 Taxes on specific goods and services	345	6 259	7 557	7 105	6 805	7 237	8 077	7 891	8 204	8 482
5121 Excises	232	3 518	4 193	4 875	4 965	5 212	5 787	5 488	5 796	6 175
Fuels	151	2 145	2 607	2 410	2 231	2 149	2 502	2 041	2 211	2 423
Gasoline sales tax	3	97	140	210	282	325	335	380	332	312
Other	78	1 304	1 459	2 258	2 487	2 769	2 978	3 094	3 284	3 479
Refunds on excise taxes	0	-28	-12	-4	-36	-31	-28	-27	-31	-39

Table 5.22. Peru / Perú (*cont.*)
Details of tax revenue / Ingresos tributarios detallados

Million PEN

	1990	2000	2005	2010	2011	2012	2013	2014	2015	2016
5122 Profits of fiscal monopolies	0	0	0	0	0	0	0	0	0	0
5123 Customs and import duties	64	2 741	3 143	1 803	1 380	1 529	1 706	1 790	1 775	1 606
5124 Taxes on exports	2	0	0	0	0	0	0	0	0	0
5125 Taxes on investment goods	0	0	0	0	0	0	0	0	0	0
5126 Taxes on specific services	0	0	220	428	460	496	585	613	634	701
Casinos and slot machines	..	..	49	187	195	219	269	279	279	298
Tourism tax	..	..	121	105	116	115	118	127	144	173
Municipal taxes on services	..	..	50	136	149	163	198	208	211	230
5127 Other taxes on internat. trade and transactions	48	0	0	0	0	0	0	0	0	0
5128 Other taxes	0	0	0	0	0	0	0	0	0	0
5130 Unallocable between 5110 and 5120	0	0	0	0	0	0	0	0	0	0
5200 Taxes on use of goods and perform activities	0	0	55	154	178	196	233	264	282	303
5210 Recurrent taxes	..	..	55	154	178	196	233	264	282	303
5211 Paid by households: motor vehicles	..	..	..	..	..	..	..	..	..	..
5212 Paid by others: motor vehicles	..	..	..	..	..	..	..	..	..	..
5213 Paid in respect of other goods	..	..	..	..	..	..	..	..	..	..
5220 Non-recurrent taxes	..	..	0	0	0	0	0	0	0	0
5300 Unallocable between 5100 and 5200	0	0	0	0	0	0	0	0	0	0
6000 Other taxes	**36**	**628**	**546**	**585**	**1 087**	**2 113**	**3 736**	**2 112**	**1 665**	**1 288**
6100 Paid solely by business	0	84	73	108	118	133	147	158	179	185
Single simplified regime	..	84	73	108	118	133	147	158	179	185
University Development Fund	..	0	0	0	0	0	0	0	0	0
6200 Other	36	544	473	477	969	1 980	3 590	1 954	1 486	1 102
Tax debt payments	9	543	397	714	709	857	893	814	922	1 068
Municipal fees	0	0	450	672	704	798	568	527	461	509
Other national level	28	20	178	254	528	1 372	3 133	2 034	1 771	1 091
Other local level	0	0	34	49	69	73	81	69	19	99
Other tax refund	0	-20	-587	-1 212	-1 041	-1 120	-1 085	-1 490	-1 686	-1 665

Note: Year ending 31st December.

The data are on a cash basis.

The figures for the years 2001-15 have been revised and updated. They exclude tax penalties considered as non-tax revenues by the OECD classification as set out in the OECD Interpretative Guide.

The figures for years up to and including 2001 exclude local government tax revenues as the data are not available.

The figures for tax refunds are based on tables by date of issuance.

Heading 2000: Social security contributions were reclassified compared to the previous edition. All contributions pertaining to pensions are only made by employees and contributions to healthcare are made by employers. The exceptions are special regimes which apply to self-employed and are levied on an income basis.

Heading 5123: These are gross of tax refunds on imports. These could not be distinguished from other tax refunds classified under 6200.

Source: Superintendencia Nacional de Aduanas y de Administración Tributaria y Banco Central de Reserva del Perú (National Superintendency for Customs and Tax Administrations and Central Reserve Bank of Peru).

StatLink http://dx.doi.org/10.1787/888933687107

Table 5.23. Trinidad and Tobago / Trinidad y Tobago
Details of tax revenue / Ingresos tributarios detallados

Million TTD

	1990	2000	2005	2010	2011	2012	2013	2014	2015	2016
Total tax revenue	**5 031**	**11 009**	**26 900**	**38 817**	**43 594**	**45 516**	**47 254**	**50 541**	**45 913**	**33 363**
1000 Taxes on income, profits and capital gains	**2 595**	**6 067**	**19 105**	**26 224**	**31 660**	**31 499**	**31 976**	**35 131**	**29 028**	**16 391**
1100 Of individuals	669	2 325	4 452	4 674	5 198	5 649	6 458	6 859	7 752	7 596
1110 On income and profits	669	2 325	4 452	4 674	5 198	5 649	6 458	6 859	7 752	7 596
Health surcharge	92	149	187	185	216	187	218	210	264	211
Insurance surrender tax	6	7	15	22	21	27	33	29	42	47
Individuals (Ch. 75:01)	571	2 169	4 250	4 467	4 961	5 435	6 207	6 620	7 445	7 337
1120 On capital gains	..	..	..	..	..	..	..	..	..	..
1200 Corporate	1 856	3 547	14 118	20 670	25 265	24 767	24 633	27 330	20 209	7 809
1210 On profits	1 856	3 547	14 118	20 670	25 265	24 767	24 633	27 330	20 209	7 809
Oil companies	1 439	2 441	10 806	13 834	16 023	15 827	14 772	16 970	10 513	1 017
Other companies	383	1 041	3 166	6 630	9 034	8 647	9 675	10 151	9 481	6 360
Business levy	0	65	146	206	209	294	187	210	215	433
National recovery impost	34	0	0	0	0	0	0	0	0	0
1220 On capital gains	..	..	..	..	..	..	..	..	..	..
1300 Unallocable between 1100 and 1200	70	195	536	881	1 197	1 084	885	942	1 067	986
2000 Social security contributions	**183**	**702**	**1 173**	**2 645**	**2 723**	**3 086**	**3 514**	**4 137**	**4 261**	**4 252**
2100 Employees	..	..	..	..	..	..	..	..	..	..
2110 On a payroll basis	..	..	..	..	..	..	..	..	..	..
2120 On an income tax basis	..	..	..	..	..	..	..	..	..	..
2200 Employers	..	..	..	..	..	..	..	..	..	..
2210 On a payroll basis	..	..	..	..	..	..	..	..	..	..
2220 On an income tax basis	..	..	..	..	..	..	..	..	..	..
2300 Self-employed or non-employed	..	..	..	..	..	..	..	..	..	..
2310 On a payroll basis	..	..	..	..	..	..	..	..	..	..
2320 On an income tax basis	..	..	..	..	..	..	..	..	..	..
2400 Unallocable between 2100, 2200 and 2300	183	702	1 173	2 645	2 723	3 086	3 514	4 137	4 261	4 252
2410 On a payroll basis	..	..	..	..	..	..	..	..	..	..
2420 On an income tax basis	..	..	..	..	..	..	..	..	..	..
3000 Taxes on payroll and workforce	**0**	**0**	**0**	**0**	**0**	**0**	**0**	**0**	**0**	**0**
4000 Taxes on property	**148**	**277**	**389**	**433**	**470**	**472**	**635**	**742**	**303**	**541**
4100 Recurrent taxes on immovable property	147	277	389	433	470	472	635	742	303	541
Lands and building taxes	39	64	63	22	11	5	4	3	3	3
House rate tax	108	213	326	411	459	468	631	738	300	538
4110 Households	..	..	..	..	..	..	..	..	..	..
4120 Others	..	..	..	..	..	..	..	..	..	..
4200 Recurrent taxes on net wealth	0	0	0	0	0	0	0	0	0	0
4210 Individual	..	..	..	..	..	..	..	..	..	..
4220 Corporate	..	..	..	..	..	..	..	..	..	..
4300 Estate, inheritance and gift taxes	1	0	0	0	0	0	0	0	0	0
4310 Estate and inheritance taxes	1	..	..	..	..	..	..	..	..	..
4320 Gift taxes	0	..	..	..	..	..	..	..	..	..
4400 Taxes on financial and capital transactions	0	0	0	0	0	0	0	0	0	0
4500 Non-recurrent taxes	0	0	0	0	0	0	0	0	0	0
4510 On net wealth	..	..	..	..	..	..	..	..	..	..
4520 Other non-recurrent taxes	..	..	..	..	..	..	..	..	..	..
4600 Other recurrent taxes on property	0	0	0	0	0	0	0	0	0	0
5000 Taxes on goods and services	**2 055**	**3 852**	**5 988**	**9 342**	**8 556**	**10 245**	**10 883**	**10 246**	**11 918**	**11 843**
5100 Taxes on production, sale, transfer, etc	1 928	3 559	5 690	8 924	8 077	9 663	10 273	9 614	11 271	11 163
5110 General taxes	980	1 890	2 963	6 032	4 917	6 337	6 658	5 745	7 223	7 016
5111 Value added taxes	927	1 890	2 963	6 032	4 917	6 337	6 657	5 745	7 223	7 016
5112 Sales tax	54	0	0	0	0	0	0	0	0	0
5113 Other	0	0	0	0	0	0	0	0	0	0
5120 Taxes on specific goods and services	948	1 669	2 727	2 891	3 160	3 326	3 616	3 869	4 048	4 147
5121 Excises	481	801	1 072	708	708	729	707	680	703	755
Rum and spirits	0	0	0	156	167	173	153	157	154	159
Alcohol and tobacco taxes	9	0	1	2	3	3	3	4	8	20
Beer duty	0	0	0	202	195	209	196	172	189	182
Oil (Petrol)	0	0	0	105	101	99	103	94	88	144
Cigarettes	0	0	0	241	240	241	236	231	235	219
Malt beverages	0	0	0	2	2	3	17	23	29	30
5122 Profits of fiscal monopolies	0	0	0	0	0	0	0	0	0	0
5123 Customs and import duties	260	748	1 473	1 905	2 168	2 319	2 588	2 861	3 014	3 003
5124 Taxes on exports	0	0	0	0	0	0	0	0	0	0
5125 Taxes on investment goods	0	0	0	0	0	0	0	0	0	0

Table 5.23. Trinidad and Tobago / Trinidad y Tobago *(cont.)*
Details of tax revenue / Ingresos tributarios detallados

Million TTD

	1990	2000	2005	2010	2011	2012	2013	2014	2015	2016
5126 Taxes on specific services	4	120	182	278	284	278	322	328	330	388
Insurance premium tax	0	56	98	167	172	174	194	197	191	182
Transaction tax on financial services	0	23	33	53	55	57	64	75	75	85
Hotel room tax	0	23	42	46	43	46	50	56	64	54
Betting and entertainment taxes	4	17	9	12	14	0	13	0	0	67
5127 Other taxes on internat. trade and transactions	202	0	0	1	0	0	0	0	0	0
5128 Other taxes	0	0	0	0	0	0	0	0	0	0
5130 Unallocable between 5110 and 5120	0	0	0	0	0	0	0	0	0	0
5200 Taxes on use of goods and perform activities	127	293	299	418	479	582	610	632	647	681
5210 Recurrent taxes	127	293	299	418	479	582	610	632	647	681
Motor vehicle taxes and duties	76	239	217	375	429	524	552	569	575	599
5211 Paid by households: motor vehicles	0	0	0	0	0	0	0	0	0	0
5212 Paid by others: motor vehicles	0	0	0	0	0	0	0	0	0	0
5213 Paid in respect of other goods	51	53	82	43	50	57	58	63	71	82
Liquor and miscellaneous business licence fees	5	10	10	10	11	10	11	11	11	10
Other taxes on the use of goods	45	44	72	33	39	47	47	52	61	72
5220 Non-recurrent taxes	0	0	0	0	0	0	0	0	0	0
5300 Unallocable between 5100 and 5200	0	0	0	0	0	0	0	0	0	0
6000 Other taxes	**49**	**111**	**245**	**172**	**185**	**214**	**246**	**285**	**403**	**336**
6100 Paid solely by business	0	0	0	0	0	0	0	0	0	0
6200 Other	49	111	245	172	185	214	246	285	403	336
Stamp duties	49	111	245	172	185	214	246	285	403	336

Note: Fiscal year ending on 30th September.
The data are on a cash basis.
Data for 2016 are revised revenue estimates for the fiscal year 2016/17 published by the House of Representatives.
Source: Ministry of Finance and IDB-CIAT (2015), *Equivalent Fiscal Pressure for Latin America and the Caribbean*, and House of Representatives.

StatLink http://dx.doi.org/10.1787/888933687126

Table 5.24. Uruguay
Details of tax revenue / Ingresos tributarios detallados

Million UYU

	1990	2000	2005	2010	2011	2012	2013	2014	2015	2016
Total tax revenue	**2 351**	**59 703**	**101 442**	**211 934**	**246 191**	**280 078**	**323 793**	**363 562**	**393 705**	**440 505**
1000 Taxes on income, profits and capital gains	**114**	**5 620**	**11 969**	**44 069**	**50 323**	**57 339**	**70 133**	**75 269**	**86 404**	**103 937**
1100 Of individuals	0	0	44	19 150	23 795	29 116	33 378	40 334	45 451	51 679
1110 On income and profits	..	..	44	16 792	20 849	25 353	29 100	35 367	39 613	44 817
Second category	..	..	..	14 644	18 422	22 534	26 048	31 365	34 881	39 883
Social security assistance	..	..	..	2 651	3 061	3 773	4 285	5 518	6 576	7 480
Tax refund	..	..	..	-504	-634	-955	-1 233	-1 517	-1 844	-2 545
1120 On capital gains	..	..	..	2 358	2 946	3 764	4 278	4 967	5 838	6 862
First category	..	..	..	2 358	2 946	3 764	4 278	4 967	5 838	6 862
1200 Corporate	114	5 620	11 925	23 257	23 940	26 169	34 076	31 698	37 078	47 734
1210 On profits	114	5 620	11 925	23 257	23 940	26 169	34 076	31 698	37 078	47 734
Corporate income tax (IRAE)	0	0	0	21 281	21 720	23 940	31 813	29 153	34 375	45 309
Corporate income tax (IRIC)	97	5 096	10 516	491	469	414	387	396	439	72
Small firms (minimum VAT)	0	296	457	586	600	631	686	741	796	850
Other	17	228	952	900	1 151	1 185	1 190	1 408	1 467	1 502
1220 On capital gains	..	..	..	..	..	..	..	..	..	..
1300 Unallocable between 1100 and 1200	0	0	0	1 662	2 588	2 053	2 679	3 237	3 875	4 523
Non resident taxpayers	0	0	0	1 662	2 588	2 053	2 679	3 237	3 875	4 523
2000 Social security contributions	**717**	**17 679**	**21 425**	**49 742**	**59 930**	**72 601**	**86 012**	**100 993**	**108 742**	**140 979**
2100 Employees	..	..	..	..	..	..	..	..	..	..
2110 On a payroll basis	..	..	..	..	..	..	..	..	..	..
2120 On an income tax basis	..	..	..	..	..	..	..	..	..	..
2200 Employers	..	..	..	..	..	..	..	..	..	..
2210 On a payroll basis	..	..	..	..	..	..	..	..	..	..
2220 On an income tax basis	..	..	..	..	..	..	..	..	..	..
2300 Self-employed or non-employed	..	..	..	..	..	..	..	..	..	..
2310 On a payroll basis	..	..	..	..	..	..	..	..	..	..
2320 On an income tax basis	..	..	..	..	..	..	..	..	..	..
2400 Unallocable between 2100, 2200 and 2300	717	17 679	21 425	49 742	59 930	72 601	86 012	100 993	108 742	140 979
2410 On a payroll basis	717	17 679	21 425	49 742	59 930	72 601	86 012	100 993	108 742	140 979
2420 On an income tax basis	0	0	0	0	0	0	0	0	0	0
3000 Taxes on payroll and workforce	**0**	**0**	**0**	**0**	**0**	**0**	**0**	**0**	**0**	**0**
4000 Taxes on property	**196**	**6 123**	**12 176**	**19 181**	**21 352**	**23 295**	**25 640**	**28 968**	**30 369**	**30 965**
4100 Recurrent taxes on immovable property	71	2 567	4 776	8 555	9 333	10 348	11 752	13 309	13 471	12 050
4110 Households	0	0	..	..	..	..	..	..	..	..
4120 Others	0	0	..	..	..	..	..	..	..	..
4200 Recurrent taxes on net wealth	94	2 076	4 943	8 948	10 030	11 067	11 892	13 714	14 776	16 652
4210 Individual	64	108	336	382	422	445	491	629	606	684
4220 Corporate	30	1 968	4 607	8 567	9 607	10 622	11 401	13 085	14 170	15 968
Corporate wealth	28	1 661	4 383	8 354	9 413	10 609	11 390	13 079	14 167	15 967
Other	1	307	224	213	194	13	11	6	3	1
4300 Estate, inheritance and gift taxes	0	0	0	0	0	0	0	0	0	0
4310 Estate and inheritance taxes	..	..	..	..	..	..	..	..	..	..
4320 Gift taxes	..	..	..	..	..	..	..	..	..	..
4400 Taxes on financial and capital transactions	0	372	886	1 350	1 545	1 414	1 516	1 442	1 601	1 724
Capital transfers	..	372	886	1 347	1 545	1 413	1 516	1 442	1 601	1 724
Capital transfers (additional)	..	0	0	3	0	0	0	0	0	0
4500 Non-recurrent taxes	0	0	0	0	0	0	0	0	0	0
4510 On net wealth	..	..	..	..	..	..	..	..	..	..
4520 Other non-recurrent taxes	..	..	..	..	..	..	..	..	..	..
4600 Other recurrent taxes on property	31	1 107	1 571	328	445	466	480	503	522	538
5000 Taxes on goods and services	**1 334**	**30 877**	**55 798**	**98 942**	**114 586**	**126 844**	**141 795**	**157 790**	**167 686**	**164 114**
5100 Taxes on production, sale, transfer, etc	1 270	28 301	52 727	94 990	110 473	122 310	136 035	151 001	160 146	155 836
5110 General taxes	660	18 009	34 641	69 365	79 672	88 338	98 758	108 260	113 651	123 262
5111 Value added taxes	660	17 995	34 601	69 365	79 672	88 338	98 758	108 260	113 651	123 262
5112 Sales tax	1	14	40	0	0	0	0	0	0	0
5113 Other	0	0	0	0	0	0	0	0	0	0
5120 Taxes on specific goods and services	610	10 291	18 086	25 625	30 801	33 972	37 278	42 741	46 495	32 574
5121 Excises	393	7 673	10 524	16 401	19 401	21 417	23 365	26 362	29 710	31 026
Fuels	203	4 067	4 900	6 551	8 447	9 147	10 269	11 816	14 096	15 222
Tobacco products	80	1 741	2 705	4 236	4 925	4 768	4 755	4 913	5 778	6 144
Alcoholic beverages	24	229	375	602	622	800	840	918	811	774
Beer	8	205	308	602	895	895	1 024	1 035	1 102	1 109
Non-alcoholic beverages	19	464	532	1 172	1 451	1 518	1 718	1 926	2 131	2 330
Motor vehicles	20	656	977	2 289	2 710	3 025	3 388	3 924	4 017	3 960
Sales of agricultural goods (MEVIR and INIA)	4	76	260	451	538	648	681	736	736	724
Other	35	235	468	497	-188	616	689	1 094	1 039	761
5122 Profits of fiscal monopolies	0	0	0	0	0	0	0	0	0	0

Table 5.24. Uruguay (cont.)
Details of tax revenue / Ingresos tributarios detallados

Million UYU

	1990	2000	2005	2010	2011	2012	2013	2014	2015	2016
5123 Customs and import duties	214	1 967	5 195	8 478	10 543	11 670	13 020	15 167	15 440	45
5124 Taxes on exports	1	92	287	371	446	432	422	520	582	658
5125 Taxes on investment goods	0	0	0	0	0	0	0	0	0	0
5126 Taxes on specific services	3	293	1 590	376	411	454	470	691	764	845
5127 Other taxes on internat. trade and transactions	0	265	489	0	0	0	0	0	0	0
5128 Other taxes	0	0	0	0	0	0	0	0	0	0
5130 Unallocable between 5110 and 5120	0	0	0	0	0	0	0	0	0	0
5200 Taxes on use of goods and perform activities	64	2 576	3 071	3 952	4 113	4 534	5 759	6 789	7 540	8 279
5210 Recurrent taxes	64	2 576	3 071	3 952	4 113	4 534	5 759	6 789	7 540	8 279
5211 Paid by households: motor vehicles	0	0	0	0	0	0	0	0	0	0
5212 Paid by others: motor vehicles	64	2 576	3 071	3 952	4 113	4 534	5 759	6 789	7 540	8 279
5213 Paid in respect of other goods	0	0	0	0	0	0	0	0	0	0
5220 Non-recurrent taxes	0	0	0	0	0	0	0	0	0	0
5300 Unallocable between 5100 and 5200	0	0	0	0	0	0	0	0	0	0
6000 Other taxes	**-10**	**-596**	**76**	**0**	**0**	**0**	**214**	**541**	**503**	**511**
6100 Paid solely by business	-10	-596	76	0	0	0	214	541	503	511
6200 Other	0	0	0	0	0	0	0	0	0	0

Note: Year ending 31st December.

The data are on a cash basis.

The figures for local government tax revenues have been estimated for 2016. This affects headings 4100 and 5212.

Headings 1110 and 1120: The data have been revised. The first category previously classified under heading 1110 is levied on capital gains and is therefore now classified under heading 1120. The second category previously classified under heading 1120 is levied on labour income and is now classified under heading 1110.

Heading 2000: Figures for 1990-98 are estimated by the Direction General of Taxes as the methodology they use to calculate social security contributions was not employed until 1999.

Headings 4000 and 5000: In ECLAC data, the tax on sales in public auctions is classified in category 4000.

Heading 5112: In ECLAC data, the tax on the sale of goods by public auctions is classified in category 4000.

Source: Dirección General Impositiva, Banco de Previsión Social e Instituto Nacional de Estadísticas (General Tax Directorate, Social Security Bank and National Statistics Institute).

StatLink http://dx.doi.org/10.1787/888933687145

Table 5.25. Venezuela
Details of tax revenue / Ingresos tributarios detallados

Million VEF

	1990	2000	2005	2010	2011	2012	2013	2014	2015	2016
Total tax revenue	**412**	**10 849**	**48 285**	**120 084**	**182 539**	**230 803**	**323 943**	**571 826**	**1 254 586**	**3 418 579**
1000 Taxes on income, profits and capital gains	**344**	**4 686**	**18 529**	**36 836**	**53 280**	**70 739**	**93 694**	**187 884**	**284 786**	**780 170**
1100 Of individuals	..	..	..	..	..	..	..	..	..	..
1110 On income and profits	..	..	..	..	..	..	..	..	..	..
1120 On capital gains	..	..	..	..	..	..	..	..	..	..
1200 Corporate	315	3 368	11 184	8 700	16 510	22 879	25 270	67 601	47 388	47 000
1210 On profits	315	3 368	11 184	8 700	16 510	22 879	25 270	67 601	47 388	47 000
Oil	315	3 368	11 184	8 700	16 510	22 879	25 270	67 601	47 388	47 000
1220 On capital gains	..	..	..	..	..	..	..	..	..	..
1300 Unallocable between 1100 and 1200	30	1 317	7 345	28 137	36 770	47 859	68 424	120 283	237 399	733 170
2000 Social security contributions	**20**	**591**	**1 890**	**9 690**	**12 936**	**15 585**	**21 422**	**28 600**	**38 200**	**45 000**
2100 Employees	..	..	..	..	..	..	..	..	..	..
2110 On a payroll basis	..	..	..	..	..	..	..	..	..	..
2120 On an income tax basis	..	..	..	..	..	..	..	..	..	..
2200 Employers	..	..	..	..	..	..	..	..	..	..
2210 On a payroll basis	..	..	..	..	..	..	..	..	..	..
2220 On an income tax basis	..	..	..	..	..	..	..	..	..	..
2300 Self-employed or non-employed	..	..	..	..	..	..	..	..	..	..
2310 On a payroll basis	..	..	..	..	..	..	..	..	..	..
2320 On an income tax basis	..	..	..	..	..	..	..	..	..	..
2400 Unallocable between 2100, 2200 and 2300	20	591	1 890	9 690	12 936	15 585	21 422	28 600	38 200	45 000
2410 On a payroll basis	..	..	..	..	..	..	..	..	..	..
2420 On an income tax basis	..	..	..	..	..	..	..	..	..	..
3000 Taxes on payroll and workforce	**0**	**0**	**0**	**0**	**0**	**0**	**0**	**0**	**0**	**0**
4000 Taxes on property	**1**	**400**	**2 834**	**222**	**273**	**346**	**530**	**1 046**	**2 946**	**9 088**
4100 Recurrent taxes on immovable property	0	0	0	0	0	0	0	0	0	0
4110 Households	..	..	..	..	..	..	..	..	..	..
4120 Others	..	..	..	..	..	..	..	..	..	..
4200 Recurrent taxes on net wealth	0	0	0	0	0	0	0	0	0	0
4210 Individual	..	..	..	..	..	..	..	..	..	..
4220 Corporate	..	..	..	..	..	..	..	..	..	..
4300 Estate, inheritance and gift taxes	1	19	55	222	273	346	530	1 046	2 946	9 088
4310 Estate and inheritance taxes	..	..	..	..	..	..	..	..	..	..
4320 Gift taxes	..	..	..	..	..	..	..	..	..	..
4400 Taxes on financial and capital transactions	0	381	2 779	0	0	0	0	0	0	0
Bank debits	..	292	2 743	..	..	..	..	..	..	..
Registration of immovable property rights	..	89	36	..	..	..	..	..	..	..
4500 Non-recurrent taxes	0	0	0	0	0	0	0	0	0	0
4510 On net wealth	..	..	..	..	..	..	..	..	..	..
4520 Other non-recurrent taxes	..	..	..	..	..	..	..	..	..	..
4600 Other recurrent taxes on property	0	0	0	0	0	0	0	0	0	0
5000 Taxes on goods and services	**46**	**5 173**	**25 032**	**73 336**	**107 059**	**140 203**	**203 894**	**346 272**	**912 820**	**2 558 015**
5100 Taxes on production, sale, transfer, etc	46	5 173	25 032	73 336	107 059	140 203	203 894	346 272	912 820	2 558 015
5110 General taxes	0	3 272	19 513	56 101	84 348	111 102	164 737	272 187	702 743	1 907 078
5111 Value added taxes	..	3 272	19 513	56 101	84 348	111 102	164 737	272 187	702 743	1 907 078
5112 Sales tax	..	0	0	0	0	0	0	0	0	0
5113 Other	..	0	0	0	0	0	0	0	0	0
5120 Taxes on specific goods and services	46	1 901	5 519	17 236	22 711	29 101	39 157	74 085	210 077	650 937
5121 Excises	16	774	1 604	8 872	8 774	11 247	16 371	30 525	116 575	439 925
Oil	6	468	472	1 280	0	0	0	0	0	0
Alcoholic beverages	6	85	427	2 192	2 762	3 542	5 975	10 888	44 498	156 878
Tobacco	4	220	704	5 401	6 011	7 706	10 397	19 636	72 077	283 047
Matches	0	1	1	0	0	0	0	0	0	0
5122 Profits of fiscal monopolies	0	0	0	0	0	0	0	0	0	0
5123 Customs and import duties	30	972	3 652	8 133	13 808	17 750	22 656	43 398	93 260	210 352
5124 Taxes on exports	0	0	0	0	0	0	0	0	0	0
5125 Taxes on investment goods	0	0	0	0	0	0	0	0	0	0
5126 Taxes on specific services	0	155	263	230	129	104	130	162	242	660
Telecommunications	0	151	237	0	0	0	0	0	0	0
Casinos, bingo and slot machines	0	5	26	230	129	104	130	162	242	660
5127 Other taxes on internat. trade and transactions	0	0	0	0	0	0	0	0	0	0
5128 Other taxes	0	0	0	0	0	0	0	0	0	0
5130 Unallocable between 5110 and 5120	0	0	0	0	0	0	0	0	0	0
5200 Taxes on use of goods and perform activities	0	0	0	0	0	0	0	0	0	0
5210 Recurrent taxes	..	..	..	..	..	..	..	..	..	..
5211 Paid by households: motor vehicles	..	..	..	..	..	..	..	..	..	..
5212 Paid by others: motor vehicles	..	..	..	..	..	..	..	..	..	..
5213 Paid in respect of other goods	..	..	..	..	..	..	..	..	..	..

Table 5.25. Venezuela *(cont.)*
Details of tax revenue / Ingresos tributarios detallados

Million VEF

	1990	2000	2005	2010	2011	2012	2013	2014	2015	2016
5220 Non-recurrent taxes	..	..	..	..	..	..	..	..	..	..
5300 Unallocable between 5100 and 5200	0	0	0	0	0	0	0	0	0	0
6000 Other taxes	**0**	**0**	**0**	**0**	**8 991**	**3 931**	**4 403**	**8 024**	**15 833**	**26 306**
6100 Paid solely by business	..	..	..	..	0	0	0	0	0	0
6200 Other	..	..	..	..	8 991	3 931	4 403	8 024	15 833	26 306

Note: The figures for 2015-16 should be interpreted with caution as they have been affected by the high rate of inflation over this period.
Year ending 31st December.
The data are on a cash basis.
The figures exclude state and local government tax revenues as the data are not available.
Heading 1210: The data on oil profits for 2015 and 2016 are estimated.
Heading 2000: The data on social security contributions are estimated from 2011.
Heading 5121: Data on oil excises are not available from 2011.

Source: Servicio Nacional Integrado de Administración Aduanera y Tributaria, Ministerio de Finanzas (National Integrated Service of Customs and Tax Administration, Ministry of Finance).

StatLink http://dx.doi.org/10.1787/888933687164

Chapter 6

Tax revenues by sub-sectors of general government

Capítulo 6

Ingresos tributarios por sub-sectores de gobierno general

Chapter 6 / Capítulo 6

Tax revenues by sub-sectors of general government

Revenues of both the Latin American and the OECD countries have been attributed to the different levels of government according to the revised guidelines set out in to the final version of the 2008 System of National Accounts (SNA). Under this, revenues are generally attributed to the level of government that exercises the authority to impose the tax or has the final discretion to set and vary the tax rate.

Ingresos tributarios por sub-sectores de gobierno general

Los ingresos de los países latinoamericanos y de los países de la OCDE se han atribuido a los diferentes niveles de gobierno de acuerdo con lo recogido en la versión final 2008 del Sistema de Cuentas Nacionales (SCN), según el cual, los ingresos se atribuyen por lo general al nivel de gobierno que ejerce la facultad de aplicar el impuesto o que puede a su discreción establecer y modificar la tasa del impuesto.

Table 6.1. Argentina, tax revenues by sub-sectors of government

Million ARS

	Federal government					State/Regional				
	1990	2000	2005	2010	2016	1990	2000	2005	2010	2016
1000 Taxes on income, profits and capital gains	**542**	**11 303**	**29 203**	**78 427**	**436 927**	**0**	**0**	**0**	**0**	**0**
1100 Of individuals	141	3 937	8 192	23 980	174 248	..	..	..	..	..
1200 Corporate	357	6 575	19 602	50 664	235 866	..	..	..	..	..
1300 Unallocable between 1100 and 1200	43	792	1 409	3 783	26 814	..	..	..	..	..
2000 Social security contributions	**0**	**0**	**0**	**0**	**0**	**0**	**0**	**0**	**0**	**0**
2100 Employees	..	..	..	..	..	..	..	..	..	..
2200 Employers	..	..	..	..	..	..	..	..	..	..
2300 Self-employed or non-employed	..	..	..	..	..	..	..	..	..	..
2400 Unallocable between 2100, 2200 and 2300	..	..	..	..	..	..	..	..	..	..
3000 Taxes on payroll and workforce	**0**	**0**	**0**	**0**	**0**	**0**	**0**	**0**	**0**	**0**
4000 Taxes on property	**616**	**1 254**	**11 439**	**32 674**	**153 697**	**549**	**2 614**	**4 558**	**10 864**	**66 317**
4100 Recurrent taxes on immovable property	0	0	0	0	0	419	1 809	2 837	5 035	29 066
4200 Recurrent taxes on net wealth	246	1 084	1 867	5 248	19 976	0	0	0	0	0
4300 Estate, inheritance and gift taxes	0	0	0	0	0	0	0	0	0	0
4400 Taxes on financial and capital transactions	330	100	9 550	27 423	133 721	130	804	1 722	5 829	37 251
4500 Non-recurrent taxes	40	70	21	3	0	0	0	0	0	0
4600 Other recurrent taxes on property	0	0	0	0	..	0	0	0	0	..
5000 Taxes on goods and services	**4 669**	**27 592**	**62 056**	**198 346**	**834 029**	**967**	**6 947**	**15 903**	**54 746**	**341 623**
5100 Taxes on production, sale, transfer, etc	4 671	28 174	63 941	201 402	849 012	791	6 114	14 613	51 148	318 582
5110 General taxes	1 594	19 009	36 853	116 386	583 217	791	6 114	14 613	51 148	318 582
5120 Taxes on specific goods and services	3 077	9 166	27 088	85 016	265 795	0	0	0	0	0
5130 Unallocable between 5110 and 5120	0	0	0	0	0	0	0	0	0	0
5200 Taxes on use of goods and perform activities[1]	0	0	0	0	0	177	833	1 289	3 598	23 042
5300 Unallocable between 5100 and 5200	-3	-583	-1 885	-3 056	-14 983	0	0	0	0	0
6000 Other taxes	**214**	**395**	**877**	**2 386**	**117 594**	**78**	**1 309**	**1 469**	**3 110**	**13 112**
6100 Paid solely by business	0	354	757	2 093	6 873	0	0	0	0	0
6200 Other[2]	214	41	120	294	110 721	78	1 309	1 469	3 110	13 112
Total tax revenue	**6 040**	**40 544**	**103 575**	**311 834**	**1 542 248**	**1 594**	**10 870**	**21 931**	**68 720**	**421 052**

Million ARS

	Local government[3]					Social Security Funds				
	1990	2000	2005	2010	2016	1990	2000	2005	2010	2016
1000 Taxes on income, profits and capital gains	..	..	..	..	..	**0**	**0**	**0**	**0**	**0**
1100 Of individuals	..	..	..	..	..	..	..	..	..	..
1200 Corporate	..	..	..	..	..	..	..	..	..	..
1300 Unallocable between 1100 and 1200	..	..	..	..	..	..	..	..	..	..
2000 Social security contributions	..	..	..	..	..	**2 583**	**9 670**	**17 400**	**102 460**	**556 067**
2100 Employees	..	..	..	..	..	..	2 486	3 690	37 990	219 274
2200 Employers	..	..	..	..	..	..	6 069	12 557	54 713	314 617
2300 Self-employed or non-employed	..	..	..	..	..	98	1 115	1 153	9 757	22 176
2400 Unallocable between 2100, 2200 and 2300	..	..	..	..	..	2 485	0	0	0	0
3000 Taxes on payroll and workforce	..	..	..	..	..	**0**	**0**	**0**	**0**	**0**
4000 Taxes on property	..	..	..	..	..	**0**	**0**	**0**	**0**	**0**
4100 Recurrent taxes on immovable property	..	..	..	..	..	..	..	..	..	..
4200 Recurrent taxes on net wealth	..	..	..	..	..	..	..	..	..	..
4300 Estate, inheritance and gift taxes	..	..	..	..	..	..	..	..	..	..
4400 Taxes on financial and capital transactions	..	..	..	..	..	..	..	..	..	..
4500 Non-recurrent taxes	..	..	..	..	..	..	..	..	..	..
4600 Other recurrent taxes on property	..	..	..	..	..	..	..	..	..	..
5000 Taxes on goods and services	..	..	..	..	..	**0**	**0**	**0**	**0**	**0**
5100 Taxes on production, sale, transfer, etc	..	..	..	..	..	..	..	..	..	..
5110 General taxes	..	..	..	..	..	..	..	..	..	..
5120 Taxes on specific goods and services	..	..	..	..	..	..	..	..	..	..
5130 Unallocable between 5110 and 5120	..	..	..	..	..	..	..	..	..	..
5200 Taxes on use of goods and perform activities[1]	..	..	..	..	..	..	..	..	..	..
5300 Unallocable between 5100 and 5200	..	..	..	..	..	..	..	..	..	..
6000 Other taxes	..	..	..	..	..	**0**	**0**	**0**	**0**	**0**
6100 Paid solely by business	..	..	..	..	..	..	..	..	..	..
6200 Other	..	..	..	..	..	..	..	..	..	..
Total tax revenue	..	..	..	..	..	**2 583**	**9 670**	**17 400**	**102 460**	**556 067**

1. In ECLAC data, tax on ownership of motor vehicles is classified in category 4000.
2. The tax debt payments in 2016 include revenue following the implementation of a new voluntary disclosure regime in July 2016 (Law 27260).
3. The figures exclude local government tax revenues as the data are not available.

StatLink http://dx.doi.org/10.1787/888933687183

Table 6.2. Bahamas, tax revenues by sub-sectors of government

Million BSD

	Federal government[1]					State/Regional				
	1990	2000	2005	2010	2016	1990	2000	2005	2010	2016
1000 Taxes on income, profits and capital gains	**0**	**0**	**0**	**0**	**0**	..	..	..	..	..
1100 Of individuals	0	0	0	0	0	..	..	..	..	..
1200 Corporate	0	0	0	0	0	..	..	..	..	..
1300 Unallocable between 1100 and 1200	0	0	0	0	0	..	..	..	..	..
2000 Social security contributions	**0**	**0**	**0**	**0**	**0**	..	..	..	..	..
2100 Employees	..	..	..	..	..	..	..	..	..	..
2200 Employers	..	..	..	..	..	..	..	..	..	..
2300 Self-employed or non-employed	..	..	..	..	..	..	..	..	..	..
2400 Unallocable between 2100, 2200 and 2300	..	..	..	..	..	..	..	..	..	..
3000 Taxes on payroll and workforce	**0**	**0**	**0**	**0**	**0**	..	..	..	..	..
4000 Taxes on property	**19**	**32**	**54**	**92**	**104**	..	..	..	..	..
4100 Recurrent taxes on immovable property	19	32	54	92	104	..	..	..	..	..
4200 Recurrent taxes on net wealth	0	0	0	0	0	..	..	..	..	..
4300 Estate, inheritance and gift taxes	0	0	0	0	0	..	..	..	..	..
4400 Taxes on financial and capital transactions	0	0	0	0	0	..	..	..	..	..
4500 Non-recurrent taxes	0	0	0	0	0	..	..	..	..	..
4600 Other recurrent taxes on property	0	0	0	0	0	..	..	..	..	..
5000 Taxes on goods and services	**386**	**723**	**736**	**795**	**1 472**	..	..	..	..	..
5100 Taxes on production, sale, transfer, etc	354	654	657	672	1 296	..	..	..	..	..
5110 General taxes	0	0	0	0	628	..	..	..	..	..
5120 Taxes on specific goods and services	354	654	657	672	668	..	..	..	..	..
5130 Unallocable between 5110 and 5120	0	0	0	0	0	..	..	..	..	..
5200 Taxes on use of goods and perform activities	32	69	78	123	177	..	..	..	..	..
5300 Unallocable between 5100 and 5200	0	0	0	0	0	..	..	..	..	..
6000 Other taxes	**33**	**95**	**135**	**223**	**100**	..	..	..	..	..
6100 Paid solely by business	0	0	0	0	0	..	..	..	..	..
6200 Other	33	95	135	223	100	..	..	..	..	..
Total tax revenue	**438**	**849**	**924**	**1 109**	**1 676**	..	..	..	..	..

Million BSD

	Local government[3]					Social Security Funds[1]				
	1990	2000	2005	2010	2016	1990	2000	2005	2010	2016
1000 Taxes on income, profits and capital gains	..	..	..	..	..	**0**	**0**	**0**	**0**	**0**
1100 Of individuals	..	..	..	..	..	..	..	..	..	..
1200 Corporate	..	..	..	..	..	..	..	..	..	..
1300 Unallocable between 1100 and 1200	..	..	..	..	..	..	..	..	..	..
2000 Social security contributions[2]	..	..	..	..	..	**66**	**115**	**136**	**167**	**280**
2100 Employees	..	..	..	..	..	..	..	..	60	105
2200 Employers	..	..	..	..	..	..	..	..	104	169
2300 Self-employed or non-employed	..	..	..	..	..	..	..	..	3	6
2400 Unallocable between 2100, 2200 and 2300	..	..	..	..	..	66	115	136	0	-1
3000 Taxes on payroll and workforce	..	..	..	..	..	**0**	**0**	**0**	**0**	**0**
4000 Taxes on property	..	..	..	..	..	**0**	**0**	**0**	**0**	**0**
4100 Recurrent taxes on immovable property	..	..	..	..	..	..	..	..	..	..
4200 Recurrent taxes on net wealth	..	..	..	..	..	..	..	..	..	..
4300 Estate, inheritance and gift taxes	..	..	..	..	..	..	..	..	..	..
4400 Taxes on financial and capital transactions	..	..	..	..	..	..	..	..	..	..
4500 Non-recurrent taxes	..	..	..	..	..	..	..	..	..	..
4600 Other recurrent taxes on property	..	..	..	..	..	..	..	..	..	..
5000 Taxes on goods and services	..	..	..	..	..	**0**	**0**	**0**	**0**	**0**
5100 Taxes on production, sale, transfer, etc	..	..	..	..	..	..	..	..	..	..
5110 General taxes	..	..	..	..	..	..	..	..	..	..
5120 Taxes on specific goods and services	..	..	..	..	..	..	..	..	..	..
5130 Unallocable between 5110 and 5120	..	..	..	..	..	..	..	..	..	..
5200 Taxes on use of goods and perform activities	..	..	..	..	..	..	..	..	..	..
5300 Unallocable between 5100 and 5200	..	..	..	..	..	..	..	..	..	..
6000 Other taxes	..	..	..	..	..	**0**	**0**	**0**	**0**	**0**
6100 Paid solely by business	..	..	..	..	..	..	..	..	..	..
6200 Other	..	..	..	..	..	..	..	..	..	..
Total tax revenue	..	..	..	..	..	**66**	**115**	**136**	**167**	**280**

1. The data for 2016 are preliminary as published by the Central Bank of Bahamas.
2. The data for social security contributions are estimated for 2016.
3. The figures exclude local government tax revenues as the data are not available.

StatLink http://dx.doi.org/10.1787/888933687202

Table 6.3. Barbados, tax revenues by sub-sectors of government

Million BAR

	Federal government[1]					State/Regional				
	1990	2000	2005	2010	2016	1990	2000	2005	2010	2016
1000 Taxes on income, profits and capital gains	**254**	**574**	**639**	**762**	**823**	..	..	..	..	..
1100 Of individuals	129	289	296	388	493	..	..	..	..	..
1200 Corporate	111	252	294	327	241	..	..	..	..	..
1300 Unallocable between 1100 and 1200	14	33	49	47	89	..	..	..	..	..
2000 Social security contributions	**0**	**0**	**0**	**0**	**0**	..	..	..	..	..
2100 Employees	..	..	..	..	..	..	..	..	..	..
2200 Employers	..	..	..	..	..	..	..	..	..	..
2300 Self-employed or non-employed	..	..	..	..	..	..	..	..	..	..
2400 Unallocable between 2100, 2200 and 2300	..	..	..	..	..	..	..	..	..	..
3000 Taxes on payroll and workforce	**0**	**0**	**0**	**0**	**0**	..	..	..	..	..
4000 Taxes on property	**39**	**92**	**127**	**114**	**191**	..	..	..	..	..
4100 Recurrent taxes on immovable property	26	60	76	98	175	..	..	..	..	..
4200 Recurrent taxes on net wealth	0	0	0	0	0	..	..	..	..	..
4300 Estate, inheritance and gift taxes	0	0	0	0	0	..	..	..	..	..
4400 Taxes on financial and capital transactions	0	0	0	0	0	..	..	..	..	..
4500 Non-recurrent taxes	13	32	51	16	16	..	..	..	..	..
4600 Other recurrent taxes on property	0	0	0	0	0	..	..	..	..	..
5000 Taxes on goods and services	**332**	**897**	**1 101**	**1 242**	**1 575**	..	..	..	..	..
5100 Taxes on production, sale, transfer, etc	332	793	974	1 092	1 425	..	..	..	..	..
5110 General taxes	197	501	610	753	948	..	..	..	..	..
5120 Taxes on specific goods and services	135	292	364	339	477	..	..	..	..	..
5130 Unallocable between 5110 and 5120	0	0	0	0	0	..	..	..	..	..
5200 Taxes on use of goods and perform activities	0	104	127	150	151	..	..	..	..	..
5300 Unallocable between 5100 and 5200	0	0	0	0	0	..	..	..	..	..
6000 Other taxes	**183**	**26**	**21**	**76**	**58**	..	..	..	..	..
6100 Paid solely by business	0	0	0	0	0	..	..	..	..	..
6200 Other	183	26	21	76	58	..	..	..	..	..
Total tax revenue	**808**	**1 589**	**1 889**	**2 194**	**2 647**	..	..	..	..	..

Million BAR

	Local government[2]					Social Security Funds[1]				
	1990	2000	2005	2010	2016	1990	2000	2005	2010	2016
1000 Taxes on income, profits and capital gains	..	..	..	..	..	**0**	**0**	**0**	**0**	**0**
1100 Of individuals	..	..	..	..	..	..	..	..	..	..
1200 Corporate	..	..	..	..	..	..	..	..	..	..
1300 Unallocable between 1100 and 1200	..	..	..	..	..	..	..	..	..	..
2000 Social security contributions	..	..	..	..	..	**134**	**295**	**408**	**525**	**288**
2100 Employees	..	..	..	..	..	..	..	..	..	..
2200 Employers	..	..	..	..	..	..	..	..	..	..
2300 Self-employed or non-employed	..	..	..	..	..	..	..	..	..	..
2400 Unallocable between 2100, 2200 and 2300	..	..	..	..	..	134	295	408	525	288
3000 Taxes on payroll and workforce	..	..	..	..	..	**0**	**0**	**0**	**0**	**0**
4000 Taxes on property	..	..	..	..	..	**0**	**0**	**0**	**0**	**0**
4100 Recurrent taxes on immovable property	..	..	..	..	..	..	..	..	..	..
4200 Recurrent taxes on net wealth	..	..	..	..	..	..	..	..	..	..
4300 Estate, inheritance and gift taxes	..	..	..	..	..	..	..	..	..	..
4400 Taxes on financial and capital transactions	..	..	..	..	..	..	..	..	..	..
4500 Non-recurrent taxes	..	..	..	..	..	..	..	..	..	..
4600 Other recurrent taxes on property	..	..	..	..	..	..	..	..	..	..
5000 Taxes on goods and services	..	..	..	..	..	**0**	**0**	**0**	**0**	**0**
5100 Taxes on production, sale, transfer, etc	..	..	..	..	..	..	..	..	..	..
5110 General taxes	..	..	..	..	..	..	..	..	..	..
5120 Taxes on specific goods and services	..	..	..	..	..	..	..	..	..	..
5130 Unallocable between 5110 and 5120	..	..	..	..	..	..	..	..	..	..
5200 Taxes on use of goods and perform activities	..	..	..	..	..	..	..	..	..	..
5300 Unallocable between 5100 and 5200	..	..	..	..	..	..	..	..	..	..
6000 Other taxes	..	..	..	..	..	**0**	**0**	**0**	**0**	**0**
6100 Paid solely by business	..	..	..	..	..	..	..	..	..	..
6200 Other	..	..	..	..	..	..	..	..	..	..
Total tax revenue	..	..	..	..	..	**134**	**295**	**408**	**525**	**288**

1. The data for 2016 are from the "Revised Estimates 2016-2017" published by parliament.
2. The figures exclude local government tax revenues as the data are not available.

StatLink http://dx.doi.org/10.1787/888933687221

Table 6.4. Belize, tax revenues by sub-sectors of government

Million BZD

	Federal government[1]					State/Regional				
	1990	2000	2005	2010	2016	1990	2000	2005	2010	2016
1000 Taxes on income, profits and capital gains	**37**	**76**	**129**	**248**	**265**	..	..	..	..	..
1100 Of individuals	21	19	35	52	84	..	..	..	..	..
1200 Corporate	12	51	90	189	170	..	..	..	..	..
1300 Unallocable between 1100 and 1200	4	6	4	7	10	..	..	..	..	..
2000 Social security contributions	**0**	**0**	**0**	**0**	**0**	..	..	..	..	..
2100 Employees	..	..	..	..	..	..	..	..	..	..
2200 Employers	..	..	..	..	..	..	..	..	..	..
2300 Self-employed or non-employed	..	..	..	..	..	..	..	..	..	..
2400 Unallocable between 2100, 2200 and 2300	..	..	..	..	..	..	..	..	..	..
3000 Taxes on payroll and workforce	**0**	**0**	**0**	**0**	**0**	..	..	..	..	..
4000 Taxes on property	**5**	**11**	**22**	**16**	**23**	..	..	..	..	..
4100 Recurrent taxes on immovable property	0	0	0	0	0	..	..	..	..	..
4200 Recurrent taxes on net wealth	0	0	0	0	0	..	..	..	..	..
4300 Estate, inheritance and gift taxes	0	0	0	0	0	..	..	..	..	..
4400 Taxes on financial and capital transactions	5	11	22	16	23	..	..	..	..	..
4500 Non-recurrent taxes	0	0	0	0	0	..	..	..	..	..
4600 Other recurrent taxes on property	0	0	0	0	0	..	..	..	..	..
5000 Taxes on goods and services	**126**	**211**	**289**	**412**	**656**	..	..	..	..	..
5100 Taxes on production, sale, transfer, etc	122	207	282	400	648	..	..	..	..	..
5110 General taxes	0	82	131	199	296	..	..	..	..	..
5120 Taxes on specific goods and services	122	125	151	200	352	..	..	..	..	..
5130 Unallocable between 5110 and 5120	0	0	0	0	0	..	..	..	..	..
5200 Taxes on use of goods and perform activities	4	4	7	13	7	..	..	..	..	..
5300 Unallocable between 5100 and 5200	0	0	0	0	0	..	..	..	..	..
6000 Other taxes	**0**	**0**	**0**	**0**	**0**	..	..	..	..	..
6100 Paid solely by business	..	..	..	..	..	..	..	..	..	..
6200 Other	..	..	..	..	..	..	..	..	..	..
Total tax revenue	**168**	**298**	**441**	**677**	**944**	..	..	..	..	..

Million BZD

	Local government[1]					Social Security Funds[1]				
	1990	2000	2005	2010	2016	1990	2000	2005	2010	2016
1000 Taxes on income, profits and capital gains	**0**	**0**	**0**	**0**	**0**	**0**	**0**	**0**	**0**	**0**
1100 Of individuals	..	..	..	..	..	..	..	..	..	..
1200 Corporate	..	..	..	..	..	..	..	..	..	..
1300 Unallocable between 1100 and 1200	..	..	..	..	..	..	..	..	..	..
2000 Social security contributions[2]	**0**	**0**	**0**	**0**	**0**	**10**	**18**	**50**	**60**	**82**
2100 Employees	..	..	..	..	..	..	..	..	..	..
2200 Employers	..	..	..	..	..	..	..	..	..	..
2300 Self-employed or non-employed	..	..	..	..	..	..	..	..	..	..
2400 Unallocable between 2100, 2200 and 2300	..	..	..	..	..	10	18	50	60	82
3000 Taxes on payroll and workforce	**0**	**0**	**0**	**0**	**0**	**0**	**0**	**0**	**0**	**0**
4000 Taxes on property	**1**	**2**	**6**	**7**	**6**	**0**	**0**	**0**	**0**	**0**
4100 Recurrent taxes on immovable property	1	2	6	7	6	..	..	..	..	..
4200 Recurrent taxes on net wealth	0	0	0	0	0	..	..	..	..	..
4300 Estate, inheritance and gift taxes	0	0	0	0	0	..	..	..	..	..
4400 Taxes on financial and capital transactions	0	0	0	0	0	..	..	..	..	..
4500 Non-recurrent taxes	0	0	0	0	0	..	..	..	..	..
4600 Other recurrent taxes on property	0	0	0	0	0	..	..	..	..	..
5000 Taxes on goods and services	**0**	**0**	**0**	**0**	**0**	**0**	**0**	**0**	**0**	**0**
5100 Taxes on production, sale, transfer, etc	..	..	..	..	..	..	..	..	..	..
5110 General taxes	..	..	..	..	..	..	..	..	..	..
5120 Taxes on specific goods and services	..	..	..	..	..	..	..	..	..	..
5130 Unallocable between 5110 and 5120	..	..	..	..	..	..	..	..	..	..
5200 Taxes on use of goods and perform activities	..	..	..	..	..	..	..	..	..	..
5300 Unallocable between 5100 and 5200	..	..	..	..	..	..	..	..	..	..
6000 Other taxes	**0**	**0**	**0**	**0**	**0**	**0**	**0**	**0**	**0**	**0**
6100 Paid solely by business	..	..	..	..	..	..	..	..	..	..
6200 Other	..	..	..	..	..	..	..	..	..	..
Total tax revenue	**1**	**2**	**6**	**7**	**6**	**10**	**18**	**50**	**60**	**82**

1. The data for 2016 are the expected outturn as presented by the Belize draft estimates of revenue and expenditures.
2. The data for social security contributions are estimated for 2016.

StatLink http://dx.doi.org/10.1787/888933687240

Table 6.5. Bolivia, tax revenues by sub-sectors of government

Million BOB

	Federal government					State/Regional				
	1990	2000	2005	2010	2016	1990	2000	2005	2010	2016
1000 Taxes on income, profits and capital gains	**68**	**1 209**	**2 383**	**6 294**	**10 876**	**..**	**..**	**..**	**..**	**..**
1100 Of individuals	68	214	214	263	497	..	..	..	..	..
1200 Corporate	0	995	2 169	6 031	10 379	..	..	..	..	..
1300 Unallocable between 1100 and 1200	0	0	0	0	0	..	..	..	..	..
2000 Social security contributions[1]	**0**	**0**	**0**	**0**	**0**	**..**	**..**	**..**	**..**	**..**
2100 Employees	..	..	..	..	..	..	..	..	..	..
2200 Employers	..	..	..	..	..	..	..	..	..	..
2300 Self-employed or non-employed	..	..	..	..	..	..	..	..	..	..
2400 Unallocable between 2100, 2200 and 2300	..	..	..	..	..	..	..	..	..	..
3000 Taxes on payroll and workforce	**0**	**0**	**0**	**0**	**0**	**..**	**..**	**..**	**..**	**..**
4000 Taxes on property	**1**	**3**	**640**	**367**	**455**	**..**	**..**	**..**	**..**	**..**
4100 Recurrent taxes on immovable property	0	0	0	0	0	..	..	..	..	..
4200 Recurrent taxes on net wealth	0	0	0	0	0	..	..	..	..	..
4300 Estate, inheritance and gift taxes	1	3	7	20	15	..	..	..	..	..
4400 Taxes on financial and capital transactions	0	0	633	347	440	..	..	..	..	..
4500 Non-recurrent taxes	0	0	0	0	0	..	..	..	..	..
4600 Other recurrent taxes on property	0	0	0	0	0	..	..	..	..	..
5000 Taxes on goods and services	**1 032**	**6 594**	**10 207**	**17 684**	**33 402**	**..**	**..**	**..**	**..**	**..**
5100 Taxes on production, sale, transfer, etc	1 032	6 594	10 207	17 684	33 402	..	..	..	..	..
5110 General taxes	708	3 892	6 768	12 434	24 288	..	..	..	..	..
5120 Taxes on specific goods and services	324	2 702	3 439	5 250	9 114	..	..	..	..	..
5130 Unallocable between 5110 and 5120	0	0	0	0	0	..	..	..	..	..
5200 Taxes on use of goods and perform activities	0	0	0	0	0	..	..	..	..	..
5300 Unallocable between 5100 and 5200	0	0	0	0	0	..	..	..	..	..
6000 Other taxes	**177**	**107**	**442**	**558**	**2 859**	**..**	**..**	**..**	**..**	**..**
6100 Paid solely by business	4	6	5	12	35	..	..	..	..	..
6200 Other	172	101	437	546	2 824	..	..	..	..	..
Total tax revenue	**1 277**	**7 913**	**13 671**	**24 903**	**47 592**	**..**	**..**	**..**	**..**	**..**

Million BOB

	Local government[2]					Social Security Funds				
	1990	2000	2005	2010	2016	1990	2000	2005	2010	2016
1000 Taxes on income, profits and capital gains	**..**	**0**	**0**	**0**	**0**	**..**	**0**	**0**	**0**	**0**
1100 Of individuals	..	..	..	..	..	..	..	..	..	..
1200 Corporate	..	..	..	..	..	..	..	..	..	..
1300 Unallocable between 1100 and 1200	..	..	..	..	..	..	..	..	..	..
2000 Social security contributions[1]	**..**	**0**	**0**	**0**	**0**	**..**	**666**	**936**	**1 645**	**10 251**
2100 Employees	..	..	..	..	..	..	..	..	..	..
2200 Employers	..	..	..	..	..	..	..	..	..	..
2300 Self-employed or non-employed	..	..	..	..	..	..	..	..	..	..
2400 Unallocable between 2100, 2200 and 2300	..	..	..	..	..	..	666	936	1 645	10 251
3000 Taxes on payroll and workforce	**..**	**0**	**0**	**0**	**0**	**..**	**0**	**0**	**0**	**0**
4000 Taxes on property	**..**	**0**	**0**	**0**	**0**	**..**	**0**	**0**	**0**	**0**
4100 Recurrent taxes on immovable property	..	..	..	..	..	..	..	..	..	..
4200 Recurrent taxes on net wealth	..	..	..	..	..	..	..	..	..	..
4300 Estate, inheritance and gift taxes	..	..	..	..	..	..	..	..	..	..
4400 Taxes on financial and capital transactions	..	..	..	..	..	..	..	..	..	..
4500 Non-recurrent taxes	..	..	..	..	..	..	..	..	..	..
4600 Other recurrent taxes on property	..	..	..	..	..	..	..	..	..	..
5000 Taxes on goods and services	**..**	**0**	**0**	**0**	**0**	**..**	**0**	**0**	**0**	**0**
5100 Taxes on production, sale, transfer, etc	..	..	..	..	..	..	..	..	..	..
5110 General taxes	..	..	..	..	..	..	..	..	..	..
5120 Taxes on specific goods and services	..	..	..	..	..	..	..	..	..	..
5130 Unallocable between 5110 and 5120	..	..	..	..	..	..	..	..	..	..
5200 Taxes on use of goods and perform activities	..	..	..	..	..	..	..	..	..	..
5300 Unallocable between 5100 and 5200	..	..	..	..	..	..	..	..	..	..
6000 Other taxes	**..**	**575**	**762**	**1 381**	**2 879**	**..**	**0**	**0**	**0**	**0**
6100 Paid solely by business	..	0	0	0	0	..	..	..	..	..
6200 Other	..	575	762	1 381	2 879	..	..	..	..	..
Total tax revenue	**..**	**575**	**762**	**1 381**	**2 879**	**..**	**666**	**936**	**1 645**	**10 251**

1. The figures for the heading 2000 have been revised from 2012 to account for the enforcement of renationalisation of the pension system.
2. The figures exclude local government tax revenues for the period 1990–1993 as the data are not available.

StatLink http://dx.doi.org/10.1787/888933687259

Table 6.6. Brazil, tax revenues by sub-sectors of government

Million BRL

	Federal government					State/Regional				
	1990	2000	2005	2010	2016	1990	2000	2005	2010	2016
1000 Taxes on income, profits and capital gains	**1**	**68 667**	**149 309**	**258 738**	**453 549**	**0**	**0**	**0**	**0**	**0**
1100 Of individuals[1]	0	3 406	6 981	87 828	162 255	..	..	..	..	..
1200 Corporate	0	25 430	73 071	128 255	197 941	..	..	..	..	..
1300 Unallocable between 1100 and 1200	0	39 831	69 257	42 656	93 353	..	..	..	..	..
2000 Social security contributions	**0**	**0**	**0**	**0**	**0**	**0**	**0**	**0**	**0**	**0**
2100 Employees	..	..	..	..	..	..	..	..	..	..
2200 Employers	..	..	..	..	..	..	..	..	..	..
2300 Self-employed or non-employed	..	..	..	..	..	..	..	..	..	..
2400 Unallocable between 2100, 2200 and 2300	..	..	..	..	..	..	..	..	..	..
3000 Taxes on payroll and workforce[2]	**0**	**6 749**	**14 468**	**33 090**	**53 537**	**0**	**0**	**0**	**0**	**0**
4000 Taxes on property	**0**	**17 726**	**35 282**	**27 038**	**34 771**	**0**	**5 623**	**11 282**	**23 885**	**46 275**
4100 Recurrent taxes on immovable property	0	234	288	485	1 126	0	0	0	0	0
4200 Recurrent taxes on net wealth	0	0	0	0	0	0	0	0	0	..
4300 Estate, inheritance and gift taxes	0	0	0	0	0	0	329	821	2 518	7 262
4400 Taxes on financial and capital transactions	0	17 492	34 994	26 553	33 645	0	0	0	0	0
4500 Non-recurrent taxes	0	0	0	0	0	0	0	0	0	0
4600 Other recurrent taxes on property	0	0	0	0	0	0	5 294	10 460	21 367	39 013
5000 Taxes on goods and services	**1**	**74 190**	**147 819**	**241 385**	**327 320**	**1**	**83 848**	**158 809**	**268 117**	**412 857**
5100 Taxes on production, sale, transfer, etc	1	74 190	147 819	241 385	327 320	1	82 279	153 437	268 117	412 857
5110 General taxes[2]	1	65 745	129 567	197 025	272 515	1	82 279	153 437	268 117	412 857
5120 Taxes on specific goods and services	0	8 445	18 252	44 360	54 805	0	0	0	0	0
5130 Unallocable between 5110 and 5120	0	0	0	0	0	0	0	0	0	0
5200 Taxes on use of goods and perform activities	0	0	0	0	0	0	1 569	5 372	0	0
5300 Unallocable between 5100 and 5200	0	0	0	0	0	0	0	0	0	0
6000 Other taxes[3]	**0**	**2 214**	**2 039**	**9 610**	**12 648**	**0**	**322**	**1 551**	**17 135**	**32 461**
6100 Paid solely by business	0	0	277	0	0	0	0	0	0	0
6200 Other[2]	0	2 214	1 761	9 610	12 648	0	322	1 551	17 135	32 461
Total tax revenue	**1**	**169 546**	**348 917**	**569 860**	**881 825**	**1**	**89 793**	**171 641**	**309 137**	**491 593**

Million BRL

	Local government					Social Security Funds				
	1990	2000	2005	2010	2016	1990	2000	2005	2010	2016
1000 Taxes on income, profits and capital gains	**0**	**0**	**0**	**0**	**0**	**0**	**0**	**0**	**0**	**0**
1100 Of individuals	..	..	..	..	..	..	..	..	..	..
1200 Corporate	..	..	..	..	..	..	..	..	..	..
1300 Unallocable between 1100 and 1200	..	..	..	..	..	..	..	..	..	..
2000 Social security contributions	**0**	**0**	**0**	**0**	**0**	**1**	**83 469**	**168 226**	**313 949**	**523 803**
2100 Employees	..	..	..	..	..	..	..	..	..	..
2200 Employers	..	..	..	..	..	0	18 709	32 248	64 271	124 713
2300 Self-employed or non-employed	..	..	..	..	..	..	..	..	..	..
2400 Unallocable between 2100, 2200 and 2300	..	..	..	..	..	1	64 760	135 978	249 679	399 090
3000 Taxes on payroll and workforce[2]	**0**	**0**	**0**	**0**	**0**	**0**	**0**	**0**	**0**	**0**
4000 Taxes on property	**0**	**5 469**	**9 710**	**23 454**	**47 201**	**0**	**0**	**0**	**0**	**0**
4100 Recurrent taxes on immovable property	0	4 519	8 117	17 448	37 562	..	..	..	..	..
4200 Recurrent taxes on net wealth	0	0	0	0	..	..	..	..	..	..
4300 Estate, inheritance and gift taxes	0	0	0	0	0	..	..	..	..	..
4400 Taxes on financial and capital transactions	0	950	1 593	6 005	9 639	..	..	..	..	..
4500 Non-recurrent taxes	0	0	0	0	0	..	..	..	..	..
4600 Other recurrent taxes on property	0	0	0	0	0	..	..	..	..	..
5000 Taxes on goods and services	**0**	**6 106**	**11 247**	**32 757**	**54 622**	**0**	**0**	**0**	**0**	**0**
5100 Taxes on production, sale, transfer, etc	0	6 106	11 247	32 757	54 622	..	..	..	..	..
5110 General taxes[2]	0	6 106	11 247	32 757	54 622	..	..	..	..	..
5120 Taxes on specific goods and services	0	0	0	0	0	..	..	..	..	..
5130 Unallocable between 5110 and 5120	0	0	0	0	0	..	..	..	..	..
5200 Taxes on use of goods and perform activities	0	0	0	0	0	..	..	..	..	..
5300 Unallocable between 5100 and 5200	0	0	0	0	0	..	..	..	..	..
6000 Other taxes[3]	**0**	**377**	**1 404**	**8 406**	**16 473**	**0**	**0**	**0**	**0**	**0**
6100 Paid solely by business	0	0	0	0	0	..	..	..	..	..
6200 Other[2]	0	377	1 404	8 406	16 473	..	..	..	..	..
Total tax revenue	**0**	**11 952**	**22 360**	**64 617**	**118 296**	**1**	**83 469**	**168 226**	**313 949**	**523 803**

1. In this edition, taxes on income and profits collected by state and local governments have been attributed to the central government. In previous editions these were attributed to state and local governments when they in fact pertained to the central government.
2. The PASEP (Program of Formation of the Patrimony of the Public Servants) contributions are added to the PIS (Social Integration Program) contributions in heading 5110 for the years prior to 2000.
3. The FUNDAF (Special Fund for Development and Improvement of Auditing Activities) contributions are included in heading 6200 from 2008.

StatLink http://dx.doi.org/10.1787/888933687278

Table 6.7. Chile, tax revenues by sub-sectors of government

Million CLP

	Federal government					State/Regional				
	1990	2000	2005	2010	2016	1990	2000	2005	2010	2016
1000 Taxes on income, profits and capital gains	**412 974**	**1 841 630**	**5 171 293**	**8 329 060**	**11 444 570**	**..**	**..**	**..**	**..**	**..**
1100 Of individuals[1]	99 154	604 100	738 620	1 492 837	2 990 653	..	..	..	..	..
1200 Corporate[1]	219 586	882 896	3 155 480	4 448 745	7 146 657	..	..	..	..	..
1300 Unallocable between 1100 and 1200	94 233	354 634	1 277 193	2 387 478	1 307 260	..	..	..	..	..
2000 Social security contributions	**66 738**	**232 728**	**287 422**	**371 386**	**483 065**	**..**	**..**	**..**	**..**	**..**
2100 Employees	61 200	209 907	249 526	310 558	415 423	..	..	..	..	..
2200 Employers	5 538	22 821	37 896	60 828	67 642	..	..	..	..	..
2300 Self-employed or non-employed	0	0	0	0	0	..	..	..	..	..
2400 Unallocable between 2100, 2200 and 2300	0	0	0	0	0	..	..	..	..	..
3000 Taxes on payroll and workforce	**0**	**0**	**0**	**0**	**0**	**..**	**..**	**..**	**..**	**..**
4000 Taxes on property	**59 682**	**255 371**	**490 120**	**245 044**	**576 802**	**..**	**..**	**..**	**..**	**..**
4100 Recurrent taxes on immovable property	10 331	3 578	4 909	8 805	16 478	..	..	..	..	..
4200 Recurrent taxes on net wealth	0	0	0	0	0	..	..	..	..	..
4300 Estate, inheritance and gift taxes	3 444	10 906	23 184	39 338	100 490	..	..	..	..	..
4400 Taxes on financial and capital transactions	45 907	240 886	462 027	196 901	459 834	..	..	..	..	..
4500 Non-recurrent taxes	0	0	0	0	0	..	..	..	..	..
4600 Other recurrent taxes on property	0	0	0	0	0	..	..	..	..	..
5000 Taxes on goods and services	**1 063 677**	**4 719 255**	**6 831 482**	**10 330 378**	**17 107 138**	**..**	**..**	**..**	**..**	**..**
5100 Taxes on production, sale, transfer, etc	1 060 304	4 684 525	6 811 389	10 294 165	17 055 497	..	..	..	..	..
5110 General taxes	664 421	3 306 350	5 391 285	8 399 926	14 073 050	..	..	..	..	..
5120 Taxes on specific goods and services[2]	395 883	1 378 175	1 420 104	1 894 239	2 982 447	..	..	..	..	..
5130 Unallocable between 5110 and 5120	0	0	0	0	0	..	..	..	..	..
5200 Taxes on use of goods and perform activities	3 374	34 730	20 094	36 213	51 641	..	..	..	..	..
5300 Unallocable between 5100 and 5200	0	0	0	0	0	..	..	..	..	..
6000 Other taxes	**-23 356**	**-112 195**	**-85 954**	**-61 117**	**-118 061**	**..**	**..**	**..**	**..**	**..**
6100 Paid solely by business	0	0	0	0	0	..	..	..	..	..
6200 Other	-23 356	-112 195	-85 954	-61 117	-118 061	..	..	..	..	..
Total tax revenue	**1 579 715**	**6 936 788**	**12 694 362**	**19 214 751**	**29 493 515**	**..**	**..**	**..**	**..**	**..**

Million CLP

	Local government					Social Security Funds				
	1990	2000	2005	2010	2016	1990	2000	2005	2010	2016
1000 Taxes on income, profits and capital gains	**0**	**0**	**0**	**0**	**0**	**0**	**0**	**0**	**0**	**0**
1100 Of individuals	0	0	0	0	0	0	0	0	0	0
1200 Corporate	0	0	0	0	0	0	0	0	0	0
1300 Unallocable between 1100 and 1200	0	0	0	0	0	0	0	0	0	0
2000 Social security contributions	**0**	**0**	**0**	**0**	**0**	**92 821**	**344 030**	**644 295**	**1 122 601**	**1 958 354**
2100 Employees	..	..	..	..	..	92 821	344 030	644 295	1 122 601	1 958 354
2200 Employers	..	..	..	..	..	0	0	0	0	0
2300 Self-employed or non-employed	..	..	..	..	..	0	0	0	0	0
2400 Unallocable between 2100, 2200 and 2300	..	..	..	..	..	0	0	0	0	0
3000 Taxes on payroll and workforce	**0**	**0**	**0**	**0**	**0**	**0**	**0**	**0**	**0**	**0**
4000 Taxes on property	**49 637**	**298 666**	**411 656**	**653 563**	**1 134 988**	**0**	**0**	**0**	**0**	**0**
4100 Recurrent taxes on immovable property	49 637	298 666	411 656	653 563	1 134 988	..	..	..	..	..
4200 Recurrent taxes on net wealth	0	0	0	0	0	..	..	..	..	..
4300 Estate, inheritance and gift taxes	0	0	0	0	0	..	..	..	..	..
4400 Taxes on financial and capital transactions	0	0	0	0	0	..	..	..	..	..
4500 Non-recurrent taxes	0	0	0	0	0	..	..	..	..	..
4600 Other recurrent taxes on property	0	0	0	0	0	..	..	..	..	..
5000 Taxes on goods and services	**55 045**	**322 514**	**514 952**	**854 778**	**1 512 659**	**0**	**0**	**0**	**0**	**0**
5100 Taxes on production, sale, transfer, etc	13 705	105 302	140 703	238 739	388 889	..	..	..	..	..
5110 General taxes	0	0	0	0	0	..	..	..	..	..
5120 Taxes on specific goods and services[2]	13 705	105 302	140 703	238 739	388 889	..	..	..	..	..
5130 Unallocable between 5110 and 5120	0	0	0	0	0	..	..	..	..	..
5200 Taxes on use of goods and perform activities	41 340	217 212	374 249	616 039	1 123 770	..	..	..	..	..
5300 Unallocable between 5100 and 5200	0	0	0	0	0	..	..	..	..	..
6000 Other taxes	**0**	**0**	**0**	**0**	**0**	**0**	**0**	**0**	**0**	**0**
6100 Paid solely by business	..	..	..	..	..	..	..	..	..	..
6200 Other	..	..	..	..	..	..	..	..	..	..
Total tax revenue	**104 682**	**621 180**	**926 608**	**1 508 341**	**2 647 647**	**92 821**	**344 030**	**644 295**	**1 122 601**	**1 958 354**

1. In this edition, further discrimination between taxes on dividends paid by individuals and corporations is provided, following the tax reform implemented in 2015.
2. ECLAC classifies Oil Prices Stabilisation Fund (FEPP) revenues as non-tax revenues.

StatLink http://dx.doi.org/10.1787/888933687297

Table 6.8. Colombia, tax revenues by sub-sectors of government

Million COP

	Federal government					State/Regional[1]				
	1990	2000	2005	2010	2016	1990	2000	2005	2010	2016
1000 Taxes on income, profits and capital gains	**771 694**	**7 103 525**	**17 348 618**	**26 218 852**	**54 326 726**	**0**	**0**	**0**	**0**	**0**
1100 Of individuals	47 210	1 499 345	3 594 441	5 192 384	10 378 965	..	..	..	..	..
1200 Corporate	359 758	5 119 828	13 044 361	20 405 209	41 966 610	..	..	..	..	..
1300 Unallocable between 1100 and 1200	364 726	484 352	709 816	621 258	1 981 152	..	..	..	..	..
2000 Social security contributions	**0**	**0**	**0**	**0**	**0**	**0**	**0**	**0**	**0**	**0**
2100 Employees	..	..	..	..	..	..	..	..	..	..
2200 Employers	..	..	..	..	..	..	..	..	..	..
2300 Self-employed or non-employed	..	..	..	..	..	..	..	..	..	..
2400 Unallocable between 2100, 2200 and 2300	..	..	..	..	..	..	..	..	..	..
3000 Taxes on payroll and workforce	**0**	**1 286 803**	**2 179 842**	**4 022 503**	**2 998 237**	**0**	**0**	**0**	**0**	**0**
4000 Taxes on property	**0**	**1 036 584**	**2 863 946**	**5 196 303**	**11 519 197**	**0**	**0**	**0**	**0**	**0**
4100 Recurrent taxes on immovable property	..	0	0	0	0	..	..	..	..	..
4200 Recurrent taxes on net wealth	..	0	462 720	1 970 530	4 440 142	..	..	..	..	..
4300 Estate, inheritance and gift taxes	..	0	0	0	0	..	..	..	..	..
4400 Taxes on financial and capital transactions	..	1 036 584	2 401 226	3 225 773	7 079 055	..	..	..	..	..
4500 Non-recurrent taxes	..	0	0	0	0	..	..	..	..	..
4600 Other recurrent taxes on property	..	0	0	0	0	..	..	..	..	..
5000 Taxes on goods and services	**1 035 934**	**11 022 878**	**21 393 776**	**34 882 447**	**51 027 299**	**263 429**	**1 204 940**	**1 966 325**	**2 752 254**	**4 720 288**
5100 Taxes on production, sale, transfer, etc	1 035 934	11 022 878	21 393 776	34 882 447	51 027 299	263 429	1 204 940	1 966 325	2 752 254	4 720 288
5110 General taxes	583 078	8 445 776	17 427 948	28 811 682	41 878 886	0	0	0	0	0
5120 Taxes on specific goods and services	452 856	2 577 102	3 965 828	6 070 765	9 148 413	263 429	1 204 940	1 966 325	2 752 254	4 720 288
5130 Unallocable between 5110 and 5120	0	0	0	0	0	0	0	0	0	0
5200 Taxes on use of goods and perform activities	0	0	0	0	0	0	0	0	0	0
5300 Unallocable between 5100 and 5200	0	0	0	0	0	0	0	0	0	0
6000 Other taxes	**78 306**	**480 784**	**682 084**	**483 762**	**455 355**	**0**	**518 253**	**1 117 016**	**2 029 017**	**3 634 853**
6100 Paid solely by business	0	0	0	0	0	..	0	0	0	0
6200 Other	78 306	480 784	682 084	483 762	455 355	..	518 253	1 117 016	2 029 017	3 634 853
Total tax revenue	**1 885 934**	**20 930 574**	**44 468 266**	**70 803 867**	**120 326 814**	**263 429**	**1 723 193**	**3 083 341**	**4 781 271**	**8 355 141**

Million COP

	Local government[1]					Social Security Funds[2]				
	1990	2000	2005	2010	2016	1990	2000	2005	2010	2016
1000 Taxes on income, profits and capital gains	**0**	**0**	**0**	**0**	**0**	**0**	**0**	**0**	**0**	**0**
1100 Of individuals	..	..	..	..	..	..	..	..	..	..
1200 Corporate	..	..	..	..	..	..	..	..	..	..
1300 Unallocable between 1100 and 1200	..	..	..	..	..	..	..	..	..	..
2000 Social security contributions	**0**	**0**	**0**	**0**	**0**	**203 596**	**4 989 000**	**7 845 000**	**11 478 085**	**21 694 000**
2100 Employees	..	..	..	..	..	..	..	..	..	..
2200 Employers	..	..	..	..	..	..	..	..	..	..
2300 Self-employed or non-employed	..	..	..	..	..	..	..	..	..	..
2400 Unallocable between 2100, 2200 and 2300	..	..	..	..	..	203 596	4 989 000	7 845 000	11 478 085	21 694 000
3000 Taxes on payroll and workforce	**0**	**0**	**0**	**0**	**0**	**0**	**0**	**0**	**0**	**0**
4000 Taxes on property	**56 160**	**991 070**	**1 974 213**	**3 338 935**	**6 747 288**	**0**	**0**	**0**	**0**	**0**
4100 Recurrent taxes on immovable property	56 160	991 070	1 974 213	3 338 935	6 747 288	..	..	..	..	..
4200 Recurrent taxes on net wealth	0	0	0	0	0	..	..	..	..	..
4300 Estate, inheritance and gift taxes	0	0	0	0	0	..	..	..	..	..
4400 Taxes on financial and capital transactions	0	0	0	0	0	..	..	..	..	..
4500 Non-recurrent taxes	0	0	0	0	0	..	..	..	..	..
4600 Other recurrent taxes on property	0	0	0	0	0	..	..	..	..	..
5000 Taxes on goods and services	**89 290**	**1 140 090**	**2 506 452**	**4 522 121**	**7 627 926**	**0**	**0**	**0**	**0**	**0**
5100 Taxes on production, sale, transfer, etc	89 290	1 140 090	2 506 452	4 522 121	7 627 926	..	..	..	..	..
5110 General taxes	89 290	1 140 090	2 506 452	4 522 121	7 627 926	..	..	..	..	..
5120 Taxes on specific goods and services	0	0	0	0	0	..	..	..	..	..
5130 Unallocable between 5110 and 5120	0	0	0	0	0	..	..	..	..	..
5200 Taxes on use of goods and perform activities	0	0	0	0	0	..	..	..	..	..
5300 Unallocable between 5100 and 5200	0	0	0	0	0	..	..	..	..	..
6000 Other taxes	**81 017**	**738 983**	**1 578 573**	**3 030 650**	**5 685 727**	**0**	**0**	**0**	**0**	**0**
6100 Paid solely by business	0	0	0	0	0	..	..	..	..	..
6200 Other	81 017	738 983	1 578 573	3 030 650	5 685 727	..	..	..	..	..
Total tax revenue	**226 467**	**2 870 144**	**6 059 238**	**10 891 707**	**20 060 941**	**203 596**	**4 989 000**	**7 845 000**	**11 478 085**	**21 694 000**

1. The data corresponds to the reported consolidated revenues of the territorial entities (departments and municipalities).
2. All of the health contributions pertaining to FOSYGA (Solidarity and Guarantee Fund) are classified as social security contributions from 2013. Prior to 2013, only the portion of the contributions used to finance the subsidised regime was included and the part to finance the contributory regime was classified in the social security sector as "other incomes".

StatLink http://dx.doi.org/10.1787/888933687316

Table 6.9. Costa Rica, tax revenues by sub-sectors of government

Million CRC

	Federal government					State/Regional				
	1990	2000	2005	2010	2016	1990	2000	2005	2010	2016
1000 Taxes on income, profits and capital gains	**11 820**	**128 805**	**324 224**	**748 093**	**1 416 218**	**..**	**..**	**..**	**..**	**..**
1100 Of individuals	..	..	16 438	202 849	414 247	..	..	..	..	..
1200 Corporate	..	..	288 355	450 312	742 011	..	..	..	..	..
1300 Unallocable between 1100 and 1200	11 820	128 805	19 430	94 932	259 961	..	..	..	..	..
2000 Social security contributions[1]	**1 345**	**18 677**	**30 854**	**61 193**	**145 909**	**..**	**..**	**..**	**..**	**..**
2100 Employees	..	..	..	..	..	..	..	..	..	..
2200 Employers	..	..	..	..	..	..	..	..	..	..
2300 Self-employed or non-employed	..	..	..	..	..	..	..	..	..	..
2400 Unallocable between 2100, 2200 and 2300	1 345	18 677	30 854	61 193	145 909	..	..	..	..	..
3000 Taxes on payroll and workforce	**0**	**0**	**0**	**0**	**0**	**..**	**..**	**..**	**..**	**..**
4000 Taxes on property	**366**	**3 007**	**10 846**	**18 270**	**40 561**	**..**	**..**	**..**	**..**	**..**
4100 Recurrent taxes on immovable property	0	0	0	3 527	4 098	..	..	..	..	..
4200 Recurrent taxes on net wealth	0	0	0	0	0	..	..	..	..	..
4300 Estate, inheritance and gift taxes	0	0	0	0	0	..	..	..	..	..
4400 Taxes on financial and capital transactions	366	3 007	10 846	14 743	36 462	..	..	..	..	..
4500 Non-recurrent taxes	0	0	0	0	0	..	..	..	..	..
4600 Other recurrent taxes on property	0	0	0	0	0	..	..	..	..	..
5000 Taxes on goods and services	**52 248**	**444 870**	**917 118**	**1 696 593**	**2 665 855**	**..**	**..**	**..**	**..**	**..**
5100 Taxes on production, sale, transfer, etc	49 867	425 630	884 359	1 598 789	2 504 674	..	..	..	..	..
5110 General taxes	21 326	222 775	485 168	920 298	1 420 938	..	..	..	..	..
5120 Taxes on specific goods and services[2]	28 541	202 856	399 192	678 491	1 083 735	..	..	..	..	..
5130 Unallocable between 5110 and 5120	0	0	0	0	0	..	..	..	..	..
5200 Taxes on use of goods and perform activities	2 380	19 240	32 758	97 804	161 181	..	..	..	..	..
5300 Unallocable between 5100 and 5200	0	0	0	0	0	..	..	..	..	..
6000 Other taxes[3]	**9 251**	**23 956**	**54 338**	**92 452**	**190 473**	**..**	**..**	**..**	**..**	**..**
6100 Paid solely by business	0	0	0	0	0	..	..	..	..	..
6200 Other	9 251	23 956	54 338	92 452	190 473	..	..	..	..	..
Total tax revenue	**75 030**	**619 314**	**1 337 380**	**2 616 600**	**4 459 015**	**..**	**..**	**..**	**..**	**..**

Million CRC

	Local government[4]					Social Security Funds				
	1990	2000	2005	2010	2016	1990	2000	2005	2010	2016
1000 Taxes on income, profits and capital gains	**0**	**0**	**0**	**0**	**0**	**0**	**0**	**0**	**0**	**0**
1100 Of individuals	..	..	..	..	..	..	..	..	..	..
1200 Corporate	..	..	..	..	..	..	..	..	..	..
1300 Unallocable between 1100 and 1200	..	..	..	..	..	..	..	..	..	..
2000 Social security contributions[1]	**0**	**0**	**0**	**0**	**0**	**29 198**	**230 505**	**466 487**	**1 078 072**	**1 839 242**
2100 Employees	..	..	..	..	..	..	..	..	..	..
2200 Employers	..	..	..	..	..	..	..	..	..	..
2300 Self-employed or non-employed	..	..	..	..	..	..	..	..	..	..
2400 Unallocable between 2100, 2200 and 2300	..	..	..	..	..	29 198	230 505	466 487	1 078 072	1 839 242
3000 Taxes on payroll and workforce	**0**	**0**	**0**	**0**	**0**	**7 484**	**59 129**	**112 082**	**248 259**	**435 328**
4000 Taxes on property	**1 200**	**5 390**	**14 264**	**45 436**	**93 771**	**0**	**0**	**0**	**0**	**0**
4100 Recurrent taxes on immovable property	1 200	5 390	14 264	45 436	93 771	..	..	..	..	..
4200 Recurrent taxes on net wealth	0	0	0	0	0	..	..	..	..	..
4300 Estate, inheritance and gift taxes	0	0	0	0	0	..	..	..	..	..
4400 Taxes on financial and capital transactions	0	0	0	0	0	..	..	..	..	..
4500 Non-recurrent taxes	0	0	0	0	0	..	..	..	..	..
4600 Other recurrent taxes on property	0	0	0	0	0	..	..	..	..	..
5000 Taxes on goods and services	**1 262**	**11 981**	**27 506**	**70 321**	**128 374**	**0**	**0**	**0**	**0**	**0**
5100 Taxes on production, sale, transfer, etc	0	83	94	1 513	3 512	..	..	..	..	..
5110 General taxes	..	0	0	0	0	..	..	..	..	..
5120 Taxes on specific goods and services[2]	..	83	94	1 513	3 512	..	..	..	..	..
5130 Unallocable between 5110 and 5120	..	0	0	0	0	..	..	..	..	..
5200 Taxes on use of goods and perform activities	1 262	11 898	27 411	68 808	124 862	..	..	..	..	..
5300 Unallocable between 5100 and 5200	0	0	0	0	0	..	..	..	..	..
6000 Other taxes[3]	**0**	**1 242**	**3 207**	**8**	**377**	**0**	**0**	**0**	**0**	**0**
6100 Paid solely by business	..	0	0	0	0	..	..	..	..	..
6200 Other	..	1 242	3 207	8	377	..	..	..	..	..
Total tax revenue	**2 461**	**18 613**	**44 976**	**115 765**	**222 522**	**36 682**	**289 634**	**578 568**	**1 326 332**	**2 274 570**

1. Social security contributions data presented by ECLAC include INA (National Institute of Apprenticeship), IMAS (Joint Social Aid Institute), and FODESAF (Social Development and Family Allowances Fund).
2. In ECLAC data, the tax on ownership of vehicles, aircraft and boats is classified in category 4000.
3. The figures have been improved and include the tax revenue of decentralised bodies (other than social security contributions) that was not accounted for in previous editions. The tax revenue of decentralised bodies is classified under the central government for this publication. In Costa Rica this revenue is classified under a separate unit (decentralised) considered to be different to the central government.
4. Local government tax revenue data have been expanded and start in 1990.

StatLink http://dx.doi.org/10.1787/888933687335

Table 6.10. Cuba, tax revenues by sub-sectors of government

Million CUP

	Federal government					State/Regional				
	1990	2000	2005	2010	2016	1990	2000	2005	2010	2016
1000 Taxes on income, profits and capital gains	**14**	**1 826**	**2 451**	**3 603**	**7 937**	..	..	..	..	..
1100 Of individuals	14	291	326	554	2 300	..	..	..	..	..
1200 Corporate	0	1 535	2 126	3 049	5 637	..	..	..	..	..
1300 Unallocable between 1100 and 1200	0	0	0	0	0	..	..	..	..	..
2000 Social security contributions	**0**	**0**	**0**	**0**	**0**	..	..	..	..	..
2100 Employees	..	..	..	..	..	..	..	..	..	..
2200 Employers	..	..	..	..	..	..	..	..	..	..
2300 Self-employed or non-employed	..	..	..	..	..	..	..	..	..	..
2400 Unallocable between 2100, 2200 and 2300	..	..	..	..	..	..	..	..	..	..
3000 Taxes on payroll and workforce	**0**	**970**	**2 962**	**4 414**	**2 420**	..	..	..	..	..
4000 Taxes on property	**0**	**0**	**0**	**0**	**0**	..	..	..	..	..
4100 Recurrent taxes on immovable property	..	..	..	..	..	..	..	..	..	..
4200 Recurrent taxes on net wealth	..	..	..	..	..	..	..	..	..	..
4300 Estate, inheritance and gift taxes	..	..	..	..	..	..	..	..	..	..
4400 Taxes on financial and capital transactions	..	..	..	..	..	..	..	..	..	..
4500 Non-recurrent taxes	..	..	..	..	..	..	..	..	..	..
4600 Other recurrent taxes on property	..	..	..	..	..	..	..	..	..	..
5000 Taxes on goods and services	**5 443**	**6 732**	**9 844**	**12 283**	**20 135**	..	..	..	..	..
5100 Taxes on production, sale, transfer, etc	5 443	6 732	9 844	12 283	20 135	..	..	..	..	..
5110 General taxes	5 017	6 131	9 036	10 525	17 550	..	..	..	..	..
5120 Taxes on specific goods and services	426	602	808	1 758	2 585	..	..	..	..	..
5130 Unallocable between 5110 and 5120	0	0	0	0	0	..	..	..	..	..
5200 Taxes on use of goods and perform activities	0	0	0	0	0	..	..	..	..	..
5300 Unallocable between 5100 and 5200	0	0	0	0	0	..	..	..	..	..
6000 Other taxes	**117**	**657**	**493**	**927**	**2 185**	..	..	..	..	..
6100 Paid solely by business	..	..	..	..	..	..	..	..	..	..
6200 Other	..	..	..	..	..	..	..	..	..	..
Total tax revenue	**5 574**	**10 185**	**15 750**	**21 227**	**32 677**	..	..	..	..	..

Million CUP

	Local government[1]					Social Security Funds				
	1990	2000	2005	2010	2016	1990	2000	2005	2010	2016
1000 Taxes on income, profits and capital gains	..	..	..	..	..	**0**	**0**	**0**	**0**	**0**
1100 Of individuals	..	..	..	..	..	..	..	..	..	..
1200 Corporate	..	..	..	..	..	..	..	..	..	..
1300 Unallocable between 1100 and 1200	..	..	..	..	..	..	..	..	..	..
2000 Social security contributions	..	..	..	..	..	**691**	**1 181**	**1 778**	**2 974**	**4 700**
2100 Employees	..	..	..	..	..	..	..	..	..	..
2200 Employers	..	..	..	..	..	..	..	..	..	..
2300 Self-employed or non-employed	..	..	..	..	..	..	..	..	..	..
2400 Unallocable between 2100, 2200 and 2300	..	..	..	..	..	691	1 181	1 778	2 974	4 700
3000 Taxes on payroll and workforce	..	..	..	..	..	**0**	**0**	**0**	**0**	**0**
4000 Taxes on property	..	..	..	..	..	**0**	**0**	**0**	**0**	**0**
4100 Recurrent taxes on immovable property	..	..	..	..	..	..	..	..	..	..
4200 Recurrent taxes on net wealth	..	..	..	..	..	..	..	..	..	..
4300 Estate, inheritance and gift taxes	..	..	..	..	..	..	..	..	..	..
4400 Taxes on financial and capital transactions	..	..	..	..	..	..	..	..	..	..
4500 Non-recurrent taxes	..	..	..	..	..	..	..	..	..	..
4600 Other recurrent taxes on property	..	..	..	..	..	..	..	..	..	..
5000 Taxes on goods and services	..	..	..	..	..	**0**	**0**	**0**	**0**	**0**
5100 Taxes on production, sale, transfer, etc	..	..	..	..	..	..	..	..	..	..
5110 General taxes	..	..	..	..	..	..	..	..	..	..
5120 Taxes on specific goods and services	..	..	..	..	..	..	..	..	..	..
5130 Unallocable between 5110 and 5120	..	..	..	..	..	..	..	..	..	..
5200 Taxes on use of goods and perform activities	..	..	..	..	..	..	..	..	..	..
5300 Unallocable between 5100 and 5200	..	..	..	..	..	..	..	..	..	..
6000 Other taxes	..	..	..	..	..	**0**	**0**	**0**	**0**	**0**
6100 Paid solely by business	..	..	..	..	..	..	..	..	..	..
6200 Other	..	..	..	..	..	..	..	..	..	..
Total tax revenue	..	..	..	..	..	**691**	**1 181**	**1 778**	**2 974**	**4 700**

1. The figures exclude local government tax revenues as the data are not available.

StatLink http://dx.doi.org/10.1787/888933687354

Table 6.11. Dominican Republic, tax revenues by sub-sectors of government

Million DOP

	Federal government					State/Regional				
	1990	2000	2005	2010	2016	1990	2000	2005	2010	2016
1000 Taxes on income, profits and capital gains	**1 670**	**10 782**	**30 042**	**53 643**	**134 804**	**..**	**..**	**..**	**..**	**..**
1100 Of individuals	..	4 088	7 588	17 088	40 193	..	..	..	..	..
1200 Corporate	..	4 679	16 222	21 475	69 362	..	..	..	..	..
1300 Unallocable between 1100 and 1200	1 670	2 015	6 232	15 080	25 249	..	..	..	..	..
2000 Social security contributions	**0**	**0**	**0**	**0**	**0**	**..**	**..**	**..**	**..**	**..**
2100 Employees	..	..	..	..	..	..	..	..	..	..
2200 Employers	..	..	..	..	..	..	..	..	..	..
2300 Self-employed or non-employed	..	..	..	..	..	..	..	..	..	..
2400 Unallocable between 2100, 2200 and 2300	..	..	..	..	..	..	..	..	..	..
3000 Taxes on payroll and workforce	**0**	**0**	**0**	**0**	**0**	**..**	**..**	**..**	**..**	**..**
4000 Taxes on property	**74**	**689**	**6 749**	**13 315**	**19 809**	**..**	**..**	**..**	**..**	**..**
4100 Recurrent taxes on immovable property	9	115	1 710	555	1 871	..	..	..	..	..
4200 Recurrent taxes on net wealth	0	0	0	2 449	3 544	..	..	..	..	..
4300 Estate, inheritance and gift taxes	11	96	84	231	388	..	..	..	..	..
4400 Taxes on financial and capital transactions	40	377	4 716	8 658	13 265	..	..	..	..	..
4500 Non-recurrent taxes	3	32	89	488	681	..	..	..	..	..
4600 Other recurrent taxes on property	11	70	151	934	61	..	..	..	..	..
5000 Taxes on goods and services	**4 483**	**32 442**	**91 152**	**175 069**	**294 161**	**..**	**..**	**..**	**..**	**..**
5100 Taxes on production, sale, transfer, etc	4 413	31 724	89 434	168 570	281 259	..	..	..	..	..
5110 General taxes	970	9 912	40 983	81 226	159 212	..	..	..	..	..
5120 Taxes on specific goods and services[1]	3 444	21 812	48 451	87 345	122 047	..	..	..	..	..
5130 Unallocable between 5110 and 5120	0	0	0	0	0	..	..	..	..	..
5200 Taxes on use of goods and perform activities	69	718	1 718	6 498	12 902	..	..	..	..	..
5300 Unallocable between 5100 and 5200	0	0	0	0	0	..	..	..	..	..
6000 Other taxes[2]	**159**	**495**	**1 661**	**0**	**1**	**..**	**..**	**..**	**..**	**..**
6100 Paid solely by business	0	0	0	..	0	..	..	..	..	..
6200 Other	159	495	1 661	..	1	..	..	..	..	..
Total tax revenue	**6 386**	**44 408**	**129 604**	**242 027**	**448 776**	**..**	**..**	**..**	**..**	**..**

Million DOP

	Local government[3]					Social Security Funds[4]				
	1990	2000	2005	2010	2016	1990	2000	2005	2010	2016
1000 Taxes on income, profits and capital gains	**..**	**..**	**..**	**..**	**..**	**0**	**0**	**0**	**0**	**0**
1100 Of individuals	..	..	..	..	..	..	..	..	..	..
1200 Corporate	..	..	..	..	..	..	..	..	..	..
1300 Unallocable between 1100 and 1200	..	..	..	..	..	..	..	..	..	..
2000 Social security contributions	**..**	**..**	**..**	**..**	**..**	**53**	**490**	**35**	**1 845**	**1 550**
2100 Employees	..	..	..	..	..	..	..	..	..	1 392
2200 Employers	..	..	..	..	..	..	..	..	..	158
2300 Self-employed or non-employed	..	..	..	..	..	..	..	..	..	0
2400 Unallocable between 2100, 2200 and 2300	..	..	..	..	..	53	490	35	1 845	0
3000 Taxes on payroll and workforce	**..**	**..**	**..**	**..**	**..**	**0**	**0**	**0**	**0**	**0**
4000 Taxes on property	**..**	**..**	**..**	**..**	**..**	**0**	**0**	**0**	**0**	**0**
4100 Recurrent taxes on immovable property	..	..	..	..	..	..	..	..	..	..
4200 Recurrent taxes on net wealth	..	..	..	..	..	..	..	..	..	..
4300 Estate, inheritance and gift taxes	..	..	..	..	..	..	..	..	..	..
4400 Taxes on financial and capital transactions	..	..	..	..	..	..	..	..	..	..
4500 Non-recurrent taxes	..	..	..	..	..	..	..	..	..	..
4600 Other recurrent taxes on property	..	..	..	..	..	..	..	..	..	..
5000 Taxes on goods and services	**..**	**..**	**..**	**..**	**..**	**0**	**0**	**0**	**0**	**0**
5100 Taxes on production, sale, transfer, etc	..	..	..	..	..	..	..	..	..	..
5110 General taxes	..	..	..	..	..	..	..	..	..	..
5120 Taxes on specific goods and services[1]	..	..	..	..	..	..	..	..	..	..
5130 Unallocable between 5110 and 5120	..	..	..	..	..	..	..	..	..	..
5200 Taxes on use of goods and perform activities	..	..	..	..	..	..	..	..	..	..
5300 Unallocable between 5100 and 5200	..	..	..	..	..	..	..	..	..	..
6000 Other taxes[2]	**..**	**..**	**..**	**..**	**..**	**0**	**0**	**0**	**0**	**0**
6100 Paid solely by business	..	..	..	..	..	..	..	..	..	..
6200 Other	..	..	..	..	..	..	..	..	..	..
Total tax revenue	**..**	**..**	**..**	**..**	**..**	**53**	**490**	**35**	**1 845**	**1 550**

1. In ECLAC data, the tax on transfer of movable goods is classified as a property tax (4000).
2. In ECLAC data, the vehicle transfer tax is classified as a property tax (4000).
3. The figures exclude local government tax revenues as the data are not available.
4. The figures exclude social security contributions to general government managed by the private sector.

StatLink http://dx.doi.org/10.1787/888933687373

Table 6.12. Ecuador, tax revenues by sub-sectors of government

Million USD

	Federal government[1]					State/Regional				
	1990	2000	2005	2010	2016	1990	2000	2005	2010	2016
1000 Taxes on income, profits and capital gains	**138**	**293**	**936**	**2 348**	**4 315**	..	..	..	..	..
1100 Of individuals	..	10	27	80	224	..	..	..	..	..
1200 Corporate	..	53	342	485	1 377	..	..	..	..	..
1300 Unallocable between 1100 and 1200	138	231	567	1 783	2 714	..	..	..	..	..
2000 Social security contributions	**0**	**0**	**0**	**0**	**0**	..	..	..	..	..
2100 Employees	..	..	..	..	..	..	..	..	..	..
2200 Employers	..	..	..	..	..	..	..	..	..	..
2300 Self-employed or non-employed	..	..	..	..	..	..	..	..	..	..
2400 Unallocable between 2100, 2200 and 2300	..	..	..	..	..	..	..	..	..	..
3000 Taxes on payroll and workforce	**0**	**0**	**0**	**0**	**0**	..	..	..	..	..
4000 Taxes on property	**0**	**0**	**1**	**5**	**365**	..	..	..	..	..
4100 Recurrent taxes on immovable property	..	..	0	0	8	..	..	..	..	..
4200 Recurrent taxes on net wealth	..	..	0	0	202	..	..	..	..	..
4300 Estate, inheritance and gift taxes	..	..	1	5	15	..	..	..	..	..
4400 Taxes on financial and capital transactions	..	..	0	0	0	..	..	..	..	..
4500 Non-recurrent taxes	..	..	0	0	141	..	..	..	..	..
4600 Other recurrent taxes on property	..	..	0	0	0	..	..	..	..	..
5000 Taxes on goods and services	**668**	**1 330**	**2 802**	**6 152**	**9 910**	..	..	..	..	..
5100 Taxes on production, sale, transfer, etc	665	1 319	2 742	5 997	9 603	..	..	..	..	..
5110 General taxes	302	836	1 975	3 886	6 042	..	..	..	..	..
5120 Taxes on specific goods and services	363	483	767	2 110	3 561	..	..	..	..	..
5130 Unallocable between 5110 and 5120	0	0	0	0	0	..	..	..	..	..
5200 Taxes on use of goods and perform activities	3	11	60	156	307	..	..	..	..	..
5300 Unallocable between 5100 and 5200	0	0	0	0	0	..	..	..	..	..
6000 Other taxes	**27**	**0**	**2**	**289**	**97**	..	..	..	..	..
6100 Paid solely by business	0	..	0	0	0	..	..	..	..	..
6200 Other	27	..	2	286	97	..	..	..	..	..
Total tax revenue	**833**	**1 623**	**3 741**	**8 794**	**14 686**	..	..	..	..	..

Million USD

	Local government[1,2]					Social Security Funds[1]				
	1990	2000	2005	2010	2016	1990	2000	2005	2010	2016
1000 Taxes on income, profits and capital gains	**0**	**0**	**0**	**0**	**0**	**0**	**0**	**0**	**0**	**0**
1100 Of individuals	..	..	..	..	..	..	..	..	..	..
1200 Corporate	..	..	..	..	..	..	..	..	..	..
1300 Unallocable between 1100 and 1200	..	..	..	..	..	..	..	..	..	..
2000 Social security contributions	**0**	**0**	**0**	**0**	**0**	**243**	**228**	**1 109**	**2 549**	**4 741**
2100 Employees	..	..	..	..	..	..	..	..	..	..
2200 Employers	..	..	..	..	..	..	..	..	..	..
2300 Self-employed or non-employed	..	..	..	..	..	..	..	..	..	..
2400 Unallocable between 2100, 2200 and 2300	..	..	..	..	..	243	228	1 109	2 549	4 741
3000 Taxes on payroll and workforce	**0**	**0**	**0**	**0**	**0**	**0**	**0**	**0**	**0**	**0**
4000 Taxes on property	**14**	**11**	**44**	**82**	**225**	**0**	**0**	**0**	**0**	**0**
4100 Recurrent taxes on immovable property	13	10	38	66	141	..	..	..	..	..
4200 Recurrent taxes on net wealth	0	0	0	0	0	..	..	..	..	..
4300 Estate, inheritance and gift taxes	0	0	0	0	0	..	..	..	..	..
4400 Taxes on financial and capital transactions	1	2	6	15	84	..	..	..	..	..
4500 Non-recurrent taxes	0	0	0	0	0	..	..	..	..	..
4600 Other recurrent taxes on property	0	0	0	0	0	..	..	..	..	..
5000 Taxes on goods and services	**14**	**20**	**85**	**143**	**368**	**0**	**0**	**0**	**0**	**0**
5100 Taxes on production, sale, transfer, etc	6	11	43	81	220	..	..	..	..	..
5110 General taxes	4	4	15	39	82	..	..	..	..	..
5120 Taxes on specific goods and services	1	6	29	42	138	..	..	..	..	..
5130 Unallocable between 5110 and 5120	0	0	0	0	0	..	..	..	..	..
5200 Taxes on use of goods and perform activities	5	2	9	12	47	..	..	..	..	..
5300 Unallocable between 5100 and 5200	3	8	33	49	101	..	..	..	..	..
6000 Other taxes	**2**	**2**	**50**	**1**	**0**	**0**	**0**	**0**	**0**	**0**
6100 Paid solely by business	0	0	0	0	0	..	..	..	..	..
6200 Other	2	2	50	1	0	..	..	..	..	..
Total tax revenue	**29**	**33**	**179**	**225**	**593**	**243**	**228**	**1 109**	**2 549**	**4 741**

1. The 2016 figures include solidarity contributions enforced in this year to finance the reconstruction efforts in the aftermath of the 2015 earthquake. These affect headings 1100, 1200, 4200, 4500, 4600 and 5111.
2. The figures for local government tax revenues have been estimated for 2016.

StatLink http://dx.doi.org/10.1787/888933687392

Table 6.13. El Salvador, tax revenues by sub-sectors of government

Million USD

	Federal government					State/Regional				
	1990	2000	2005	2010	2016	1990	2000	2005	2010	2016
1000 Taxes on income, profits and capital gains	**95**	**407**	**637**	**995**	**1 659**	..	..	..	..	..
1100 Of individuals	..	..	312	571	695	..	..	..	..	..
1200 Corporate	..	..	356	423	763	..	..	..	..	..
1300 Unallocable between 1100 and 1200	95	407	-31	0	202	..	..	..	..	..
2000 Social security contributions	**0**	**0**	**0**	**0**	**0**	..	..	..	..	..
2100 Employees	..	..	..	..	..	..	..	..	..	..
2200 Employers	..	..	..	..	..	..	..	..	..	..
2300 Self-employed or non-employed	..	..	..	..	..	..	..	..	..	..
2400 Unallocable between 2100, 2200 and 2300	..	..	..	..	..	..	..	..	..	..
3000 Taxes on payroll and workforce	**0**	**0**	**0**	**0**	**0**	..	..	..	..	..
4000 Taxes on property	**26**	**12**	**16**	**16**	**107**	..	..	..	..	..
4100 Recurrent taxes on immovable property	0	0	0	0	0	..	..	..	..	..
4200 Recurrent taxes on net wealth	16	0	0	0	0	..	..	..	..	..
4300 Estate, inheritance and gift taxes	0	0	0	0	0	..	..	..	..	..
4400 Taxes on financial and capital transactions	10	12	16	16	107	..	..	..	..	..
4500 Non-recurrent taxes	0	0	0	0	0	..	..	..	..	..
4600 Other recurrent taxes on property	0	0	0	0	0	..	..	..	..	..
5000 Taxes on goods and services	**259**	**903**	**1 447**	**1 855**	**2 400**	..	..	..	..	..
5100 Taxes on production, sale, transfer, etc	259	903	1 447	1 847	2 387	..	..	..	..	..
5110 General taxes	133	714	1 104	1 433	1 813	..	..	..	..	..
5120 Taxes on specific goods and services	127	189	344	415	574	..	..	..	..	..
5130 Unallocable between 5110 and 5120	0	0	0	0	0	..	..	..	..	..
5200 Taxes on use of goods and perform activities	0	0	0	0	14	..	..	..	..	..
5300 Unallocable between 5100 and 5200	0	0	0	0	0	..	..	..	..	..
6000 Other taxes	**58**	**0**	**0**	**0**	**0**	..	..	..	..	..
6100 Paid solely by business	0	0	..	..	..	..	..	..	..	..
6200 Other	58	0	..	..	..	..	..	..	..	..
Total tax revenue	**438**	**1 322**	**2 100**	**2 865**	**4 166**	..	..	..	..	..

Million USD

	Local government[1]					Social Security Funds[2]				
	1990	2000	2005	2010	2016	1990	2000	2005	2010	2016
1000 Taxes on income, profits and capital gains	..	..	**0**	**0**	**0**	**0**	**0**	**0**	**0**	**0**
1100 Of individuals	..	..	..	..	..	..	..	..	..	..
1200 Corporate	..	..	..	..	..	..	..	..	..	..
1300 Unallocable between 1100 and 1200	..	..	..	..	..	..	..	..	..	..
2000 Social security contributions	..	..	**0**	**0**	**0**	**67**	**263**	**282**	**369**	**539**
2100 Employees	..	..	..	..	..	..	75	76	99	143
2200 Employers	..	..	..	..	..	..	176	181	238	347
2300 Self-employed or non-employed	..	..	..	..	..	..	13	25	33	48
2400 Unallocable between 2100, 2200 and 2300	..	..	..	..	..	67	0	0	0	0
3000 Taxes on payroll and workforce	..	..	**0**	**0**	**0**	**0**	**0**	**0**	**0**	**0**
4000 Taxes on property	..	..	**0**	**0**	**0**	**0**	**0**	**0**	**0**	**0**
4100 Recurrent taxes on immovable property	..	..	..	..	..	..	..	..	..	..
4200 Recurrent taxes on net wealth	..	..	..	..	..	..	..	..	..	..
4300 Estate, inheritance and gift taxes	..	..	..	..	..	..	..	..	..	..
4400 Taxes on financial and capital transactions	..	..	..	..	..	..	..	..	..	..
4500 Non-recurrent taxes	..	..	..	..	..	..	..	..	..	..
4600 Other recurrent taxes on property	..	..	..	..	..	..	..	..	..	..
5000 Taxes on goods and services	..	..	**0**	**0**	**0**	**0**	**0**	**0**	**0**	**0**
5100 Taxes on production, sale, transfer, etc	..	..	..	..	..	..	..	..	..	..
5110 General taxes	..	..	..	..	..	..	..	..	..	..
5120 Taxes on specific goods and services	..	..	..	..	..	..	..	..	..	..
5130 Unallocable between 5110 and 5120	..	..	..	..	..	..	..	..	..	..
5200 Taxes on use of goods and perform activities	..	..	..	..	..	..	..	..	..	..
5300 Unallocable between 5100 and 5200	..	..	..	..	..	..	..	..	..	..
6000 Other taxes	..	..	**37**	**63**	**89**	**0**	**0**	**0**	**0**	**0**
6100 Paid solely by business	..	..	0	0	0	..	..	..	..	..
6200 Other	..	..	37	63	89	..	..	..	..	..
Total tax revenue	..	..	**37**	**63**	**89**	**67**	**263**	**282**	**369**	**539**

1. Local government tax revenues have been expanded and start in 2003.
2. Social security contributions are those paid to the Salvadoran Institute of Social Security (ISSS) and exclude contributions to the privately managed regime.

StatLink http://dx.doi.org/10.1787/888933687411

Table 6.14. Guatemala, tax revenues by sub-sectors of government

Million GTQ

	Federal government					State/Regional				
	1990	2000	2005	2010	2016	1990	2000	2005	2010	2016
1000 Taxes on income, profits and capital gains	**507**	**3 295**	**6 049**	**10 319**	**20 572**	**..**	**..**	**..**	**..**	**..**
1100 Of individuals	25	143	645	1 225	2 082	..	..	..	..	..
1200 Corporate	482	3 149	3 756	6 520	14 418	..	..	..	..	..
1300 Unallocable between 1100 and 1200	0	2	1 647	2 574	4 072	..	..	..	..	..
2000 Social security contributions	**0**	**0**	**0**	**0**	**0**	**..**	**..**	**..**	**..**	**..**
2100 Employees	..	..	..	..	..	..	..	..	..	..
2200 Employers	..	..	..	..	..	..	..	..	..	..
2300 Self-employed or non-employed	..	..	..	..	..	..	..	..	..	..
2400 Unallocable between 2100, 2200 and 2300	..	..	..	..	..	..	..	..	..	..
3000 Taxes on payroll and workforce	**0**	**0**	**0**	**0**	**0**	**..**	**..**	**..**	**..**	**..**
4000 Taxes on property	**0**	**17**	**9**	**11**	**24**	**..**	**..**	**..**	**..**	**..**
4100 Recurrent taxes on immovable property	..	6	1	1	1	..	..	..	..	..
4200 Recurrent taxes on net wealth	..	0	0	0	0	..	..	..	..	..
4300 Estate, inheritance and gift taxes	..	0	0	0	0	..	..	..	..	..
4400 Taxes on financial and capital transactions	..	12	8	10	23	..	..	..	..	..
4500 Non-recurrent taxes	..	0	0	0	0	..	..	..	..	..
4600 Other recurrent taxes on property	..	0	0	0	0	..	..	..	..	..
5000 Taxes on goods and services	**1 709**	**10 317**	**16 402**	**23 259**	**33 105**	**..**	**..**	**..**	**..**	**..**
5100 Taxes on production, sale, transfer, etc	1 681	10 131	16 083	22 754	31 355	..	..	..	..	..
5110 General taxes	762	6 259	10 753	16 980	24 215	..	..	..	..	..
5120 Taxes on specific goods and services	919	3 872	5 330	5 773	7 140	..	..	..	..	..
5130 Unallocable between 5110 and 5120	0	0	0	0	0	..	..	..	..	..
5200 Taxes on use of goods and perform activities	28	186	319	505	1 750	..	..	..	..	..
5300 Unallocable between 5100 and 5200	0	0	0	0	0	..	..	..	..	..
6000 Other taxes	**104**	**186**	**315**	**572**	**370**	**..**	**..**	**..**	**..**	**..**
6100 Paid solely by business	0	0	0	0	..	..	..	..	..	..
6200 Other	104	186	315	572	370	..	..	..	..	..
Total tax revenue	**2 320**	**13 816**	**22 775**	**34 161**	**54 071**	**..**	**..**	**..**	**..**	**..**

Million GTQ

	Local government[1]					Social Security Funds[2]				
	1990	2000	2005	2010	2016	1990	2000	2005	2010	2016
1000 Taxes on income, profits and capital gains	**..**	**0**	**0**	**0**	**0**	**0**	**0**	**0**	**0**	**0**
1100 Of individuals	..	..	..	..	..	..	..	..	..	..
1200 Corporate	..	..	..	..	..	..	..	..	..	..
1300 Unallocable between 1100 and 1200	..	..	..	..	..	..	..	..	..	..
2000 Social security contributions	**..**	**0**	**0**	**0**	**0**	**436**	**2 569**	**4 072**	**6 408**	**10 974**
2100 Employees	..	..	..	..	..	..	..	..	..	..
2200 Employers	..	..	..	..	..	..	..	..	..	..
2300 Self-employed or non-employed	..	..	..	..	..	..	..	..	..	..
2400 Unallocable between 2100, 2200 and 2300	..	..	..	..	..	436	2 569	4 072	6 408	10 974
3000 Taxes on payroll and workforce	**..**	**0**	**0**	**0**	**0**	**0**	**0**	**0**	**0**	**0**
4000 Taxes on property	**..**	**147**	**341**	**620**	**564**	**0**	**0**	**0**	**0**	**0**
4100 Recurrent taxes on immovable property	..	147	341	620	564	..	..	..	..	..
4200 Recurrent taxes on net wealth	..	0	0	0	0	..	..	..	..	..
4300 Estate, inheritance and gift taxes	..	0	0	0	0	..	..	..	..	..
4400 Taxes on financial and capital transactions	..	0	0	0	0	..	..	..	..	..
4500 Non-recurrent taxes	..	0	0	0	0	..	..	..	..	..
4600 Other recurrent taxes on property	..	0	0	0	0	..	..	..	..	..
5000 Taxes on goods and services	**..**	**0**	**0**	**0**	**0**	**0**	**0**	**0**	**0**	**0**
5100 Taxes on production, sale, transfer, etc	..	..	..	..	..	..	..	..	..	..
5110 General taxes	..	..	..	..	..	..	..	..	..	..
5120 Taxes on specific goods and services	..	..	..	..	..	..	..	..	..	..
5130 Unallocable between 5110 and 5120	..	..	..	..	..	..	..	..	..	..
5200 Taxes on use of goods and perform activities	..	..	..	..	..	..	..	..	..	..
5300 Unallocable between 5100 and 5200	..	..	..	..	..	..	..	..	..	..
6000 Other taxes	**..**	**0**	**0**	**0**	**0**	**0**	**0**	**0**	**0**	**0**
6100 Paid solely by business	..	..	..	..	..	..	..	..	..	..
6200 Other	..	..	..	..	..	..	..	..	..	..
Total tax revenue	**..**	**147**	**341**	**620**	**564**	**436**	**2 569**	**4 072**	**6 408**	**10 974**

1. Revenues from the municipal property tax (IUSI) are recorded at the local government level.
2. Corresponds to social security contributions to the Guatemalan Social Security Institute (IGSS) and payments by public employees to the government's pension fund.

StatLink http://dx.doi.org/10.1787/888933687430

Table 6.15. Guyana, tax revenues by sub-sectors of government

Million GYD

	Federal government[1]					State/Regional				
	1990	2000	2005	2010	2016	1990	2000	2005	2010	2016
1000 Taxes on income, profits and capital gains	**1 752**	**16 179**	**23 843**	**39 561**	**60 914**	**..**	**..**	**..**	**..**	**..**
1100 Of individuals	333	7 734	11 139	17 816	26 439	..	..	..	..	..
1200 Corporate	1 375	8 266	12 555	21 427	33 965	..	..	..	..	..
1300 Unallocable between 1100 and 1200	43	179	149	317	510	..	..	..	..	..
2000 Social security contributions	**0**	**0**	**0**	**0**	**0**	**..**	**..**	**..**	**..**	**..**
2100 Employees	..	..	..	..	..	..	..	..	..	..
2200 Employers	..	..	..	..	..	..	..	..	..	..
2300 Self-employed or non-employed	..	..	..	..	..	..	..	..	..	..
2400 Unallocable between 2100, 2200 and 2300	..	..	..	..	..	..	..	..	..	..
3000 Taxes on payroll and workforce	**0**	**0**	**0**	**0**	**0**	**..**	**..**	**..**	**..**	**..**
4000 Taxes on property	**53**	**701**	**828**	**1 593**	**3 297**	**..**	**..**	**..**	**..**	**..**
4100 Recurrent taxes on immovable property	40	681	807	1 562	3 258	..	..	..	..	..
4200 Recurrent taxes on net wealth	0	0	0	0	0	..	..	..	..	..
4300 Estate, inheritance and gift taxes	13	20	21	31	39	..	..	..	..	..
4400 Taxes on financial and capital transactions	0	0	0	0	0	..	..	..	..	..
4500 Non-recurrent taxes	0	0	0	0	0	..	..	..	..	..
4600 Other recurrent taxes on property	0	0	0	0	0	..	..	..	..	..
5000 Taxes on goods and services	**2 200**	**20 798**	**27 940**	**59 360**	**84 156**	**..**	**..**	**..**	**..**	**..**
5100 Taxes on production, sale, transfer, etc	2 162	20 530	27 414	58 846	83 147	..	..	..	..	..
5110 General taxes	1 399	14 861	21 396	27 044	36 968	..	..	..	..	..
5120 Taxes on specific goods and services	763	5 669	6 019	31 802	46 179	..	..	..	..	..
5130 Unallocable between 5110 and 5120	0	0	0	0	0	..	..	..	..	..
5200 Taxes on use of goods and perform activities	38	268	525	514	1 009	..	..	..	..	..
5300 Unallocable between 5100 and 5200	0	0	0	0	0	..	..	..	..	..
6000 Other taxes	**1 037**	**204**	**370**	**1 233**	**1 150**	**..**	**..**	**..**	**..**	**..**
6100 Paid solely by business	0	0	0	0	0	..	..	..	..	..
6200 Other	1 037	204	370	1 233	1 150	..	..	..	..	..
Total tax revenue	**5 041**	**37 882**	**52 981**	**101 746**	**149 517**	**..**	**..**	**..**	**..**	**..**

Million GYD

	Local government[1]					Social Security Funds[1]				
	1990	2000	2005	2010	2016	1990	2000	2005	2010	2016
1000 Taxes on income, profits and capital gains	**..**	**..**	**0**	**0**	**0**	**0**	**0**	**0**	**0**	**0**
1100 Of individuals	..	..	..	..	..	..	..	..	..	..
1200 Corporate	..	..	..	..	..	..	..	..	..	..
1300 Unallocable between 1100 and 1200	..	..	..	..	..	..	..	..	..	..
2000 Social security contributions[2]	**..**	**..**	**0**	**0**	**0**	**191**	**4 868**	**6 670**	**10 047**	**18 468**
2100 Employees	..	..	..	..	..	..	..	..	..	..
2200 Employers	..	..	..	..	..	..	..	..	..	..
2300 Self-employed or non-employed	..	..	..	..	..	..	..	..	..	..
2400 Unallocable between 2100, 2200 and 2300	..	..	..	..	..	191	4 868	6 670	10 047	18 468
3000 Taxes on payroll and workforce	**..**	**..**	**0**	**0**	**0**	**0**	**0**	**0**	**0**	**0**
4000 Taxes on property	**..**	**..**	**0**	**0**	**0**	**0**	**0**	**0**	**0**	**0**
4100 Recurrent taxes on immovable property	..	..	..	..	..	..	..	..	..	..
4200 Recurrent taxes on net wealth	..	..	..	..	..	..	..	..	..	..
4300 Estate, inheritance and gift taxes	..	..	..	..	..	..	..	..	..	..
4400 Taxes on financial and capital transactions	..	..	..	..	..	..	..	..	..	..
4500 Non-recurrent taxes	..	..	..	..	..	..	..	..	..	..
4600 Other recurrent taxes on property	..	..	..	..	..	..	..	..	..	..
5000 Taxes on goods and services	**..**	**..**	**0**	**0**	**0**	**0**	**0**	**0**	**0**	**0**
5100 Taxes on production, sale, transfer, etc	..	..	..	..	..	..	..	..	..	..
5110 General taxes	..	..	..	..	..	..	..	..	..	..
5120 Taxes on specific goods and services	..	..	..	..	..	..	..	..	..	..
5130 Unallocable between 5110 and 5120	..	..	..	..	..	..	..	..	..	..
5200 Taxes on use of goods and perform activities	..	..	..	..	..	..	..	..	..	..
5300 Unallocable between 5100 and 5200	..	..	..	..	..	..	..	..	..	..
6000 Other taxes	**..**	**..**	**668**	**113**	**164**	**0**	**0**	**0**	**0**	**0**
6100 Paid solely by business	..	..	0	0	0	..	..	..	..	..
6200 Other	..	..	668	113	164	..	..	..	..	..
Total tax revenue	**..**	**..**	**668**	**113**	**164**	**191**	**4 868**	**6 670**	**10 047**	**18 468**

1. The data for 2016 are revised budget estimates published by the Ministry of Finance.
2. Social security figures for 2015 and 2016 are estimated.

StatLink http://dx.doi.org/10.1787/888933687449

Table 6.16. Honduras, tax revenues by sub-sectors of government

Million HNL

	Federal government					State/Regional				
	1990	2000	2005	2010	2016	1990	2000	2005	2010	2016
1000 Taxes on income, profits and capital gains	**431**	**2 907**	**7 037**	**13 232**	**29 584**	**..**	**..**	**..**	**..**	**..**
1100 Of individuals	157	991	2 312	4 528	10 173	..	..	..	..	..
1200 Corporate	274	1 916	4 725	8 705	19 411	..	..	..	..	..
1300 Unallocable between 1100 and 1200	0	0	0	0	0	..	..	..	..	..
2000 Social security contributions	**0**	**0**	**0**	**0**	**0**	**..**	**..**	**..**	**..**	**..**
2100 Employees	..	..	..	..	..	..	..	..	..	..
2200 Employers	..	..	..	..	..	..	..	..	..	..
2300 Self-employed or non-employed	..	..	..	..	..	..	..	..	..	..
2400 Unallocable between 2100, 2200 and 2300	..	..	..	..	..	..	..	..	..	..
3000 Taxes on payroll and workforce	**0**	**0**	**0**	**0**	**0**	**..**	**..**	**..**	**..**	**..**
4000 Taxes on property	**16**	**266**	**631**	**994**	**2 362**	**..**	**..**	**..**	**..**	**..**
4100 Recurrent taxes on immovable property	0	0	0	0	0	..	..	..	..	..
4200 Recurrent taxes on net wealth	0	0	0	0	0	..	..	..	..	..
4300 Estate, inheritance and gift taxes	0	0	0	0	0	..	..	..	..	..
4400 Taxes on financial and capital transactions	0	0	0	0	1 738	..	..	..	..	..
4500 Non-recurrent taxes	0	0	316	381	0	..	..	..	..	..
4600 Other recurrent taxes on property	16	266	315	613	624	..	..	..	..	..
5000 Taxes on goods and services	**1 405**	**11 445**	**19 032**	**28 937**	**58 611**	**..**	**..**	**..**	**..**	**..**
5100 Taxes on production, sale, transfer, etc	1 405	11 445	19 032	28 937	58 611	..	..	..	..	..
5110 General taxes	344	5 146	9 565	16 050	36 521	..	..	..	..	..
5120 Taxes on specific goods and services	1 061	6 299	9 468	12 887	22 090	..	..	..	..	..
5130 Unallocable between 5110 and 5120	0	0	0	0	0	..	..	..	..	..
5200 Taxes on use of goods and perform activities	0	0	0	0	0	..	..	..	..	..
5300 Unallocable between 5100 and 5200	0	0	0	0	0	..	..	..	..	..
6000 Other taxes	**1**	**2**	**7**	**9**	**18**	**..**	**..**	**..**	**..**	**..**
6100 Paid solely by business	0	0	0	0	0	..	..	..	..	..
6200 Other	1	2	7	9	18	..	..	..	..	..
Total tax revenue	**1 853**	**14 620**	**26 708**	**43 173**	**90 574**	**..**	**..**	**..**	**..**	**..**

Million HNL

	Local government[1]					Social Security Funds				
	1990	2000	2005	2010	2016	1990	2000	2005	2010	2016
1000 Taxes on income, profits and capital gains	**..**	**..**	**..**	**..**	**..**	**0**	**0**	**0**	**0**	**0**
1100 Of individuals	..	..	..	..	..	..	..	..	..	..
1200 Corporate	..	..	..	..	..	..	..	..	..	..
1300 Unallocable between 1100 and 1200	..	..	..	..	..	..	..	..	..	..
2000 Social security contributions	**..**	**..**	**..**	**..**	**..**	**179**	**1 727**	**4 416**	**8 671**	**14 402**
2100 Employees	..	..	..	..	..	..	..	..	..	..
2200 Employers	..	..	..	..	..	..	..	..	..	..
2300 Self-employed or non-employed	..	..	..	..	..	..	..	..	..	..
2400 Unallocable between 2100, 2200 and 2300	..	..	..	..	..	179	1 727	4 416	8 671	14 402
3000 Taxes on payroll and workforce	**..**	**..**	**..**	**..**	**..**	**0**	**0**	**0**	**0**	**0**
4000 Taxes on property	**..**	**..**	**..**	**..**	**..**	**0**	**0**	**0**	**0**	**0**
4100 Recurrent taxes on immovable property	..	..	..	..	..	..	..	..	..	..
4200 Recurrent taxes on net wealth	..	..	..	..	..	..	..	..	..	..
4300 Estate, inheritance and gift taxes	..	..	..	..	..	..	..	..	..	..
4400 Taxes on financial and capital transactions	..	..	..	..	..	..	..	..	..	..
4500 Non-recurrent taxes	..	..	..	..	..	..	..	..	..	..
4600 Other recurrent taxes on property	..	..	..	..	..	..	..	..	..	..
5000 Taxes on goods and services	**..**	**..**	**..**	**..**	**..**	**0**	**0**	**0**	**0**	**0**
5100 Taxes on production, sale, transfer, etc	..	..	..	..	..	..	..	..	..	..
5110 General taxes	..	..	..	..	..	..	..	..	..	..
5120 Taxes on specific goods and services	..	..	..	..	..	..	..	..	..	..
5130 Unallocable between 5110 and 5120	..	..	..	..	..	..	..	..	..	..
5200 Taxes on use of goods and perform activities	..	..	..	..	..	..	..	..	..	..
5300 Unallocable between 5100 and 5200	..	..	..	..	..	..	..	..	..	..
6000 Other taxes	**..**	**..**	**..**	**..**	**..**	**0**	**0**	**0**	**0**	**0**
6100 Paid solely by business	..	..	..	..	..	..	..	..	..	..
6200 Other	..	..	..	..	..	..	..	..	..	..
Total tax revenue	**..**	**..**	**..**	**..**	**..**	**179**	**1 727**	**4 416**	**8 671**	**14 402**

1. The figures exclude local government tax revenues since they included non-tax revenues and central government transfers for the period 1990-2015. Local government tax revenue is only available for the year 2016 and is not included in this edition to allow comparability over time.

StatLink http://dx.doi.org/10.1787/888933687468

Table 6.17. Jamaica, tax revenues by sub-sectors of government

Million JAM

	Federal government					State/Regional				
	1990	2000	2005	2010	2016	1990	2000	2005	2010	2016
1000 Taxes on income, profits and capital gains	**3 944**	**39 277**	**69 894**	**118 708**	**158 409**	..	..	..	..	..
1100 Of individuals	1 687	17 441	36 043	54 798	72 175	..	..	..	..	..
1200 Corporate	1 280	7 627	13 134	33 091	47 530	..	..	..	..	..
1300 Unallocable between 1100 and 1200	977	14 209	20 718	30 820	38 704	..	..	..	..	..
2000 Social security contributions	**0**	**0**	**0**	**0**	**0**	..	..	..	..	..
2100 Employees	..	..	..	..	..	..	..	..	..	..
2200 Employers	..	..	..	..	..	..	..	..	..	..
2300 Self-employed or non-employed	..	..	..	..	..	..	..	..	..	..
2400 Unallocable between 2100, 2200 and 2300	..	..	..	..	..	..	..	..	..	..
3000 Taxes on payroll and workforce	**0**	**0**	**0**	**0**	**0**	..	..	..	..	..
4000 Taxes on property	**67**	**0**	**0**	**0**	**0**	..	..	..	..	..
4100 Recurrent taxes on immovable property	67	..	..	..	..	..	..	..	..	..
4200 Recurrent taxes on net wealth	0	..	..	..	..	..	..	..	..	..
4300 Estate, inheritance and gift taxes	0	..	..	..	..	..	..	..	..	..
4400 Taxes on financial and capital transactions	0	..	..	..	..	..	..	..	..	..
4500 Non-recurrent taxes	0	..	..	..	..	..	..	..	..	..
4600 Other recurrent taxes on property	0	..	..	..	..	..	..	..	..	..
5000 Taxes on goods and services	**2 824**	**43 907**	**77 065**	**149 544**	**268 569**	..	..	..	..	..
5100 Taxes on production, sale, transfer, etc	2 760	43 107	75 954	147 500	265 064	..	..	..	..	..
5110 General taxes	297	22 356	45 602	84 409	149 111	..	..	..	..	..
5120 Taxes on specific goods and services	2 463	20 752	30 352	63 091	115 953	..	..	..	..	..
5130 Unallocable between 5110 and 5120	0	0	0	0	0	..	..	..	..	..
5200 Taxes on use of goods and perform activities	64	800	1 111	2 045	3 505	..	..	..	..	..
5300 Unallocable between 5100 and 5200	0	0	0	0	0	..	..	..	..	..
6000 Other taxes	**914**	**3 890**	**9 816**	**8 088**	**15 293**	..	..	..	..	..
6100 Paid solely by business	0	0	0	0	..	..	..	..	..	..
6200 Other	914	3 890	9 816	8 088	15 293	..	..	..	..	..
Total tax revenue	**7 748**	**87 074**	**156 775**	**276 340**	**442 271**	..	..	..	..	..

Million JAM

	Local government[1]					Social Security Funds				
	1990	2000	2005	2010	2016	1990	2000	2005	2010	2016
1000 Taxes on income, profits and capital gains	..	**0**	**0**	**0**	**0**	..	..	**0**	**0**	**0**
1100 Of individuals	..	..	..	..	..	..	..	..	..	..
1200 Corporate	..	..	..	..	..	..	..	..	..	..
1300 Unallocable between 1100 and 1200	..	..	..	..	..	..	..	..	..	..
2000 Social security contributions	..	**0**	**0**	**0**	**0**	..	..	**4 924**	**8 199**	**17 978**
2100 Employees	..	..	..	..	..	..	..	..	..	..
2200 Employers	..	..	..	..	..	..	..	..	..	..
2300 Self-employed or non-employed	..	..	..	..	..	..	..	..	..	..
2400 Unallocable between 2100, 2200 and 2300	..	..	..	..	..	..	..	4 924	8 199	17 978
3000 Taxes on payroll and workforce	..	**0**	**0**	**0**	**0**	..	..	**0**	**0**	**0**
4000 Taxes on property	..	**639**	**1 592**	**2 600**	**7 101**	..	..	**0**	**0**	**0**
4100 Recurrent taxes on immovable property	..	639	1 592	2 600	7 101	..	..	..	..	..
4200 Recurrent taxes on net wealth	..	0	0	0	0	..	..	..	..	..
4300 Estate, inheritance and gift taxes	..	0	0	0	0	..	..	..	..	..
4400 Taxes on financial and capital transactions	..	0	0	0	0	..	..	..	..	..
4500 Non-recurrent taxes	..	0	0	0	0	..	..	..	..	..
4600 Other recurrent taxes on property	..	0	0	0	0	..	..	..	..	..
5000 Taxes on goods and services	..	**0**	**0**	**0**	**0**	..	..	**0**	**0**	**0**
5100 Taxes on production, sale, transfer, etc	..	..	..	..	..	..	..	..	..	..
5110 General taxes	..	..	..	..	..	..	..	..	..	..
5120 Taxes on specific goods and services	..	..	..	..	..	..	..	..	..	..
5130 Unallocable between 5110 and 5120	..	..	..	..	..	..	..	..	..	..
5200 Taxes on use of goods and perform activities	..	..	..	..	..	..	..	..	..	..
5300 Unallocable between 5100 and 5200	..	..	..	..	..	..	..	..	..	..
6000 Other taxes	..	**0**	**0**	**0**	**0**	..	..	**0**	**0**	**0**
6100 Paid solely by business	..	..	..	..	..	..	..	..	..	..
6200 Other	..	..	..	..	..	..	..	..	..	..
Total tax revenue	..	**639**	**1 592**	**2 600**	**7 101**	..	..	**4 924**	**8 199**	**17 978**

1. The figures exclude local and state/regional government tax revenues as they are not available.

StatLink http://dx.doi.org/10.1787/888933687487

Table 6.18. Mexico, tax revenues by sub-sectors of government

Million MXN

	Federal government					State/Regional				
	1990	2000	2005	2010	2016	1990	2000	2005	2010	2016
1000 Taxes on income, profits and capital gains[1]	**34 668**	**276 548**	**402 036**	**683 604**	**1 427 114**	**3**	**0**	**0**	**0**	..
1100 Of individuals	..	..	195 869	313 473	681 784	..	..	..	..	..
1200 Corporate	..	..	135 840	246 745	700 925	..	..	..	..	..
1300 Unallocable between 1100 and 1200	34 668	276 548	70 327	123 386	44 405	3	..	..	..	..
2000 Social security contributions[2]	**0**	**0**	**0**	**0**	**0**	**0**	**0**	**0**	**0**	..
2100 Employees	..	..	..	..	..	..	..	..	..	..
2200 Employers	..	..	..	..	..	..	..	..	..	..
2300 Self-employed or non-employed	..	..	..	..	..	..	..	..	..	..
2400 Unallocable between 2100, 2200 and 2300	..	..	..	..	..	..	..	..	..	..
3000 Taxes on payroll and workforce	**818**	**0**	**0**	**0**	**0**	**972**	**11 215**	**20 429**	**36 818**	..
4000 Taxes on property	**3**	**0**	**0**	**0**	**0**	**894**	**7 018**	**10 905**	**13 137**	..
4100 Recurrent taxes on immovable property	0	..	..	..	..	482	5 238	6 544	8 522	..
4200 Recurrent taxes on net wealth	0	..	..	..	..	0	0	0	0	..
4300 Estate, inheritance and gift taxes	0	..	..	..	..	7	0	0	0	..
4400 Taxes on financial and capital transactions	3	..	..	..	..	405	1 781	4 361	4 615	..
4500 Non-recurrent taxes	0	..	..	..	..	0	0	0	0	..
4600 Other recurrent taxes on property	0	..	..	..	..	0	0	0	0	..
5000 Taxes on goods and services	**44 605**	**355 056**	**467 019**	**701 372**	**1 268 163**	**118**	**1 346**	**2 124**	**5 805**	..
5100 Taxes on production, sale, transfer, etc	44 029	309 283	401 580	627 187	1 267 960	45	910	1 364	2 470	..
5110 General taxes	26 635	189 606	318 432	504 509	791 700	0	0	0	0	..
5120 Taxes on specific goods and services	17 394	119 677	83 148	122 678	476 260	30	910	1 364	2 470	..
5130 Unallocable between 5110 and 5120	0	0	0	0	0	15	0	0	0	..
5200 Taxes on use of goods and perform activities	576	45 773	65 439	74 185	203	73	436	760	3 335	..
5300 Unallocable between 5100 and 5200	0	0	0	0	0	0	0	0	0	..
6000 Other taxes	**1 340**	**5 878**	**8 616**	**22 236**	**28 809**	**165**	**907**	**1 537**	**2 546**	..
6100 Paid solely by business	0	0	0	0	0	0	0	0	0	..
6200 Other	1 340	5 878	8 616	22 236	28 809	165	907	1 537	2 546	..
Total tax revenue	**81 434**	**637 482**	**877 671**	**1 407 212**	**2 724 086**	**2 152**	**20 485**	**34 995**	**58 307**	..

Million MXN

	Local government					Social Security Funds				
	1990	2000	2005	2010	2016	1990	2000	2005	2010	2016
1000 Taxes on income, profits and capital gains[1]	**2**	**0**	**0**	**0**	..	**0**	**0**	**0**	**0**	**0**
1100 Of individuals	..	..	..	..	..	..	..	..	..	..
1200 Corporate	..	..	..	..	..	..	..	..	..	..
1300 Unallocable between 1100 and 1200	2	..	..	..	..	..	..	..	..	..
2000 Social security contributions[2]	**0**	**0**	**0**	**0**	..	**17 165**	**138 223**	**206 551**	**277 459**	**434 998**
2100 Employees	..	..	..	..	..	..	..	..	..	..
2200 Employers	..	..	..	..	..	..	..	..	..	..
2300 Self-employed or non-employed	..	..	..	..	..	..	..	..	..	..
2400 Unallocable between 2100, 2200 and 2300	..	..	..	..	..	17 165	138 223	206 551	277 459	434 998
3000 Taxes on payroll and workforce	**7**	**2**	**32**	**93**	..	**0**	**0**	**0**	**0**	**0**
4000 Taxes on property	**1 017**	**6 946**	**15 891**	**25 818**	..	**0**	**0**	**0**	**0**	**0**
4100 Recurrent taxes on immovable property	554	4 710	10 098	17 202	..	..	..	..	..	..
4200 Recurrent taxes on net wealth	0	0	0	0	..	..	..	..	..	..
4300 Estate, inheritance and gift taxes	1	0	0	0	..	..	..	..	..	..
4400 Taxes on financial and capital transactions	462	2 236	5 793	8 616	..	..	..	..	..	..
4500 Non-recurrent taxes	0	0	0	0	..	..	..	..	..	..
4600 Other recurrent taxes on property	0	0	0	0	..	..	..	..	..	..
5000 Taxes on goods and services	**114**	**202**	**288**	**487**	..	**0**	**0**	**0**	**0**	**0**
5100 Taxes on production, sale, transfer, etc	97	133	214	466	..	..	..	..	..	..
5110 General taxes	0	0	0	0	..	..	..	..	..	..
5120 Taxes on specific goods and services	95	133	214	466	..	..	..	..	..	..
5130 Unallocable between 5110 and 5120	2	0	0	0	..	..	..	..	..	..
5200 Taxes on use of goods and perform activities	17	69	74	21	..	..	..	..	..	..
5300 Unallocable between 5100 and 5200	0	0	0	0	..	..	..	..	..	..
6000 Other taxes	**114**	**866**	**1 539**	**2 616**	..	**0**	**0**	**0**	**0**	**0**
6100 Paid solely by business	0	0	0	0	..	..	..	..	..	..
6200 Other	114	866	1 539	2 616	..	..	..	..	..	..
Total tax revenue	**1 254**	**8 016**	**17 750**	**29 014**	..	**17 165**	**138 223**	**206 551**	**277 459**	**434 998**

Note: The 2016 data for tax revenues of the state and local levels of government are not available. They comprise revenues in categories 3000, 4000, 5000 and 6000.

1. In ECLAC data, income taxes are presented net of credit on salary figures.
2. Some amounts of social security contributions are now treated as non-tax revenue to align with reporting to other international organisations. In ECLAC data, social security contributions are presented net of transfers from the Federal government for the payment of IMSS (Mexican Social Security Institute) pensions.

StatLink http://dx.doi.org/10.1787/888933687506

Table 6.19. Nicaragua, tax revenues by sub-sectors of government

Million NIO

	Federal government					State/Regional				
	1990	2000	2005	2010	2016	1990	2000	2005	2010	2016
1000 Taxes on income, profits and capital gains	..	**1 144**	**3 902**	**8 351**	**24 307**	..	..	..	..	..
1100 Of individuals	..	..	..	..	..	..	..	..	..	..
1200 Corporate	..	..	..	..	..	..	..	..	..	..
1300 Unallocable between 1100 and 1200	..	1 144	3 902	8 351	24 307	..	..	..	..	..
2000 Social security contributions	..	**0**	**0**	**0**	**0**	..	..	..	..	..
2100 Employees	..	..	..	..	..	..	..	..	..	..
2200 Employers	..	..	..	..	..	..	..	..	..	..
2300 Self-employed or non-employed	..	..	..	..	..	..	..	..	..	..
2400 Unallocable between 2100, 2200 and 2300	..	..	..	..	..	..	..	..	..	..
3000 Taxes on payroll and workforce	..	**0**	**0**	**0**	**0**	..	..	..	..	..
4000 Taxes on property	..	**-11**	**2**	**130**	**604**	..	..	..	..	..
4100 Recurrent taxes on immovable property	..	0	0	0	0	..	..	..	..	..
4200 Recurrent taxes on net wealth	..	-11	2	130	0	..	..	..	..	..
4300 Estate, inheritance and gift taxes	..	0	0	0	0	..	..	..	..	..
4400 Taxes on financial and capital transactions	..	0	0	0	604	..	..	..	..	..
4500 Non-recurrent taxes	..	0	0	0	0	..	..	..	..	..
4600 Other recurrent taxes on property	..	0	0	0	0	..	..	..	..	..
5000 Taxes on goods and services	..	**5 584**	**9 725**	**17 029**	**36 403**	..	..	..	..	..
5100 Taxes on production, sale, transfer, etc	..	5 584	9 725	17 029	36 403	..	..	..	..	..
5110 General taxes	..	2 931	5 599	10 353	22 822	..	..	..	..	..
5120 Taxes on specific goods and services	..	2 653	4 126	6 676	13 581	..	..	..	..	..
5130 Unallocable between 5110 and 5120	..	0	0	0	0	..	..	..	..	..
5200 Taxes on use of goods and perform activities	..	0	0	0	0	..	..	..	..	..
5300 Unallocable between 5100 and 5200	..	0	0	0	0	..	..	..	..	..
6000 Other taxes	..	**11**	**17**	**20**	**90**	..	..	..	..	..
6100 Paid solely by business	..	0	0	0	0	..	..	..	..	..
6200 Other	..	11	17	20	90	..	..	..	..	..
Total tax revenue	..	**6 729**	**13 646**	**25 530**	**61 403**	..	..	..	..	..

Million NIO

	Local government[1]					Social Security Funds				
	1990	2000	2005	2010	2016	1990	2000	2005	2010	2016
1000 Taxes on income, profits and capital gains	..	..	..	**0**	**0**	..	**0**	**0**	**0**	**0**
1100 Of individuals	..	..	..	..	..	..	..	..	..	..
1200 Corporate	..	..	..	..	..	..	..	..	..	..
1300 Unallocable between 1100 and 1200	..	..	..	..	..	..	..	..	..	..
2000 Social security contributions	..	..	..	**0**	**0**	..	**1 678**	**3 363**	**8 090**	**21 296**
2100 Employees	..	..	..	..	..	..	..	..	..	..
2200 Employers	..	..	..	..	..	..	..	..	..	..
2300 Self-employed or non-employed	..	..	..	..	..	..	..	..	..	..
2400 Unallocable between 2100, 2200 and 2300	..	..	..	..	..	..	1 678	3 363	8 090	21 296
3000 Taxes on payroll and workforce	..	..	..	**0**	**0**	..	**0**	**0**	**0**	**0**
4000 Taxes on property	..	..	..	**0**	**0**	..	**0**	**0**	**0**	**0**
4100 Recurrent taxes on immovable property	..	..	..	..	..	..	..	..	..	..
4200 Recurrent taxes on net wealth	..	..	..	..	..	..	..	..	..	..
4300 Estate, inheritance and gift taxes	..	..	..	..	..	..	..	..	..	..
4400 Taxes on financial and capital transactions	..	..	..	..	..	..	..	..	..	..
4500 Non-recurrent taxes	..	..	..	..	..	..	..	..	..	..
4600 Other recurrent taxes on property	..	..	..	..	..	..	..	..	..	..
5000 Taxes on goods and services	..	..	..	**2 003**	**1 936**	..	**0**	**0**	**0**	**0**
5100 Taxes on production, sale, transfer, etc	..	..	..	1 579	1 289	..	..	..	..	..
5110 General taxes	..	..	..	1 579	1 289	..	..	..	..	..
5120 Taxes on specific goods and services	..	..	..	0	0	..	..	..	..	..
5130 Unallocable between 5110 and 5120	..	..	..	0	0	..	..	..	..	..
5200 Taxes on use of goods and perform activities	..	..	..	424	648	..	..	..	..	..
5300 Unallocable between 5100 and 5200	..	..	..	0	0	..	..	..	..	..
6000 Other taxes	..	..	..	**670**	**806**	..	**0**	**0**	**0**	**0**
6100 Paid solely by business	..	..	..	0	0	..	..	..	..	..
6200 Other	..	..	..	670	806	..	..	..	..	..
Total tax revenue	..	..	..	**2 673**	**2 742**	..	**1 678**	**3 363**	**8 090**	**21 296**

Note: Comparable statistics for 1990 cannot be shown due to the devaluation of the Nicaraguan cordoba.

1. The figures exclude local government tax revenues for the period 1990-2010 as the data are not available. For the first time, this edition includes tax revenues by local governments from 2010-16. This affects headings 5113, 5211, 5213 and 6200.

StatLink http://dx.doi.org/10.1787/888933687525

Table 6.20. Panama, tax revenues by sub-sectors of government

Million PAB

	Federal government					State/Regional				
	1990	2000	2005	2010	2016	1990	2000	2005	2010	2016
1000 Taxes on income, profits and capital gains	**217**	**485**	**563**	**1 317**	**2 512**	..	..	..	..	..
1100 Of individuals	140	295	303	440	877	..	..	..	..	..
1200 Corporate	66	159	213	603	1 137	..	..	..	..	..
1300 Unallocable between 1100 and 1200	11	31	47	273	498	..	..	..	..	..
2000 Social security contributions	**0**	**0**	**0**	**0**	**0**	..	..	..	..	..
2100 Employees	..	..	..	..	..	..	..	..	..	..
2200 Employers	..	..	..	..	..	..	..	..	..	..
2300 Self-employed or non-employed	..	..	..	..	..	..	..	..	..	..
2400 Unallocable between 2100, 2200 and 2300	..	..	..	..	..	..	..	..	..	..
3000 Taxes on payroll and workforce[1]	**0**	**36**	**36**	**59**	**111**	..	..	..	..	..
4000 Taxes on property	**43**	**62**	**109**	**212**	**333**	..	..	..	..	..
4100 Recurrent taxes on immovable property	28	34	56	108	168	..	..	..	..	..
4200 Recurrent taxes on net wealth	0	0	0	0	0	..	..	..	..	..
4300 Estate, inheritance and gift taxes	0	0	0	0	0	..	..	..	..	..
4400 Taxes on financial and capital transactions	3	9	21	30	41	..	..	..	..	..
4500 Non-recurrent taxes	0	0	0	0	0	..	..	..	..	..
4600 Other recurrent taxes on property	12	19	32	75	124	..	..	..	..	..
5000 Taxes on goods and services	**335**	**530**	**642**	**1 473**	**2 631**	..	..	..	..	..
5100 Taxes on production, sale, transfer, etc	332	530	642	1 473	2 631	..	..	..	..	..
5110 General taxes	80	69	138	766	1 516	..	..	..	..	..
5120 Taxes on specific goods and services[2]	139	461	504	706	1 115	..	..	..	..	..
5130 Unallocable between 5110 and 5120	113	0	0	0	0	..	..	..	..	..
5200 Taxes on use of goods and perform activities	4	0	0	0	0	..	..	..	..	..
5300 Unallocable between 5100 and 5200	0	0	0	0	0	..	..	..	..	..
6000 Other taxes	**26**	**54**	**29**	**41**	**35**	..	..	..	..	..
6100 Paid solely by business	0	11	0	0	0	..	..	..	..	..
6200 Other	26	43	29	41	35	..	..	..	..	..
Total tax revenue	**622**	**1 167**	**1 379**	**3 102**	**5 621**	..	..	..	..	..

Million PAB

	Local government					Social Security Funds				
	1990	2000	2005	2010	2016	1990	2000	2005	2010	2016
1000 Taxes on income, profits and capital gains	..	**0**	**0**	**0**	**0**	**0**	**0**	**0**	**0**	**0**
1100 Of individuals	..	..	..	..	..	..	..	..	..	..
1200 Corporate	..	..	..	..	..	..	..	..	..	..
1300 Unallocable between 1100 and 1200	..	..	..	..	..	..	..	..	..	..
2000 Social security contributions	..	**0**	**0**	**0**	**0**	**271**	**742**	**827**	**1 637**	**3 380**
2100 Employees	..	..	..	..	..	..	..	..	..	..
2200 Employers	..	..	..	..	..	..	..	..	..	..
2300 Self-employed or non-employed	..	..	..	..	..	..	..	..	..	..
2400 Unallocable between 2100, 2200 and 2300	..	..	..	..	..	271	742	827	1 637	3 380
3000 Taxes on payroll and workforce[1]	..	**0**	**0**	**0**	**0**	**0**	**0**	**0**	**0**	**0**
4000 Taxes on property	..	**0**	**0**	**0**	**0**	**0**	**0**	**0**	**0**	**0**
4100 Recurrent taxes on immovable property	..	0	0	..	..	..	..	..	..	..
4200 Recurrent taxes on net wealth	..	0	0	..	..	..	..	..	..	..
4300 Estate, inheritance and gift taxes	..	0	0	..	..	..	..	..	..	..
4400 Taxes on financial and capital transactions	..	0	0	..	..	..	..	..	..	..
4500 Non-recurrent taxes	..	0	0	..	..	..	..	..	..	..
4600 Other recurrent taxes on property	..	0	0	..	..	..	..	..	..	..
5000 Taxes on goods and services	..	**43**	**51**	**41**	**81**	**0**	**0**	**0**	**0**	**0**
5100 Taxes on production, sale, transfer, etc	..	0	0	0	0	..	..	..	..	..
5110 General taxes	..	0	0	..	..	..	..	..	..	..
5120 Taxes on specific goods and services[2]	..	0	0	..	..	..	..	..	..	..
5130 Unallocable between 5110 and 5120	..	0	0	..	..	..	..	..	..	..
5200 Taxes on use of goods and perform activities	..	43	51	41	81	..	..	..	..	..
5300 Unallocable between 5100 and 5200	..	0	0	0	0	..	..	..	..	..
6000 Other taxes	..	**0**	**0**	**36**	**65**	**0**	**0**	**0**	**0**	**0**
6100 Paid solely by business	..	0	0	0	..	..	..	..	..	..
6200 Other	..	0	0	36	65	..	..	..	..	..
Total tax revenue	..	**43**	**51**	**76**	**146**	**271**	**742**	**827**	**1 637**	**3 380**

1. In ECLAC data, education insurance is classified as "Other taxes" (6000).
2. In CIAT and ECLAC data, the tax on banks, financial institutions and currency exchange is classified as a property tax (4000).

StatLink http://dx.doi.org/10.1787/888933687544

Table 6.21. Paraguay, tax revenues by sub-sectors of government

Million PYG

	Federal government					State/Regional				
	1990	2000	2005	2010	2016	1990	2000	2005	2010	2016
1000 Taxes on income, profits and capital gains	**73 726**	**470 388**	**938 886**	**2 096 498**	**4 429 169**	**..**	**..**	**..**	**..**	**..**
1100 Of individuals	..	41 021	82 086	184 361	396 573	..	..	..	..	..
1200 Corporate	..	429 367	856 800	1 912 137	4 032 596	..	..	..	..	..
1300 Unallocable between 1100 and 1200	73 726	0	0	0	0	..	..	..	..	..
2000 Social security contributions[1]	**28 882**	**300 451**	**541 310**	**1 140 654**	**1 915 971**	**..**	**..**	**..**	**..**	**..**
2100 Employees	..	..	..	..	..	..	..	..	..	..
2200 Employers	..	..	..	..	..	..	..	..	..	..
2300 Self-employed or non-employed	..	..	..	..	..	..	..	..	..	..
2400 Unallocable between 2100, 2200 and 2300	28 882	300 451	541 310	1 140 654	1 915 971	..	..	..	..	..
3000 Taxes on payroll and workforce	**0**	**0**	**0**	**0**	**0**	**..**	**..**	**..**	**..**	**..**
4000 Taxes on property	**17 162**	**0**	**0**	**0**	**0**	**..**	**..**	**..**	**..**	**..**
4100 Recurrent taxes on immovable property	17 162	..	..	..	..	..	..	..	..	..
4200 Recurrent taxes on net wealth	0	..	..	..	..	..	..	..	..	..
4300 Estate, inheritance and gift taxes	0	..	..	..	..	..	..	..	..	..
4400 Taxes on financial and capital transactions	0	..	..	..	..	..	..	..	..	..
4500 Non-recurrent taxes	0	..	..	..	..	..	..	..	..	..
4600 Other recurrent taxes on property	0	..	..	..	..	..	..	..	..	..
5000 Taxes on goods and services	**179 312**	**2 080 878**	**4 309 832**	**9 226 477**	**14 701 676**	**..**	**..**	**..**	**..**	**..**
5100 Taxes on production, sale, transfer, etc	179 312	2 080 878	4 309 832	9 226 477	14 701 676	..	..	..	..	..
5110 General taxes	0	1 150 496	2 478 998	5 991 694	10 482 238	..	..	..	..	..
5120 Taxes on specific goods and services	179 312	930 382	1 830 834	3 234 783	4 219 438	..	..	..	..	..
5130 Unallocable between 5110 and 5120	0	0	0	0	0	..	..	..	..	..
5200 Taxes on use of goods and perform activities	0	0	0	0	0	..	..	..	..	..
5300 Unallocable between 5100 and 5200	0	0	0	0	0	..	..	..	..	..
6000 Other taxes	**49 807**	**116 652**	**238 134**	**109 424**	**13 371**	**..**	**..**	**..**	**..**	**..**
6100 Paid solely by business	0	0	0	0	0	..	..	..	..	..
6200 Other	49 807	116 652	238 134	109 424	13 371	..	..	..	..	..
Total tax revenue	**348 889**	**2 968 370**	**6 028 162**	**12 573 052**	**21 060 187**	**..**	**..**	**..**	**..**	**..**

Million PYG

	Local government[2]					Social Security Funds[3]				
	1990	2000	2005	2010	2016	1990	2000	2005	2010	2016
1000 Taxes on income, profits and capital gains	**..**	**..**	**0**	**0**	**0**	**..**	**0**	**0**	**0**	**0**
1100 Of individuals	..	..	..	..	..	..	..	..	..	..
1200 Corporate	..	..	..	..	..	..	..	..	..	..
1300 Unallocable between 1100 and 1200	..	..	..	..	..	..	..	..	..	..
2000 Social security contributions[1]	**..**	**..**	**0**	**0**	**0**	**..**	**619 082**	**1 050 670**	**2 411 987**	**5 132 875**
2100 Employees	..	..	..	..	..	..	..	..	..	..
2200 Employers	..	..	..	..	..	..	..	..	..	..
2300 Self-employed or non-employed	..	..	..	..	..	..	..	..	..	..
2400 Unallocable between 2100, 2200 and 2300	..	..	..	..	..	..	619 082	1 050 670	2 411 987	5 132 875
3000 Taxes on payroll and workforce	**..**	**..**	**0**	**0**	**0**	**..**	**0**	**0**	**0**	**0**
4000 Taxes on property	**..**	**..**	**0**	**272 385**	**566 117**	**..**	**0**	**0**	**0**	**0**
4100 Recurrent taxes on immovable property	..	..	..	254 306	529 479	..	..	..	..	..
4200 Recurrent taxes on net wealth	..	..	..	0	0	..	..	..	..	..
4300 Estate, inheritance and gift taxes	..	..	..	0	0	..	..	..	..	..
4400 Taxes on financial and capital transactions	..	..	..	16 316	35 259	..	..	..	..	..
4500 Non-recurrent taxes	..	..	..	0	0	..	..	..	..	..
4600 Other recurrent taxes on property	..	..	..	1 762	1 378	..	..	..	..	..
5000 Taxes on goods and services	**..**	**..**	**0**	**234 485**	**505 457**	**..**	**0**	**0**	**0**	**0**
5100 Taxes on production, sale, transfer, etc	..	..	..	23 221	33 096	..	..	..	..	..
5110 General taxes	..	..	..	0	0	..	..	..	..	..
5120 Taxes on specific goods and services	..	..	..	23 221	33 096	..	..	..	..	..
5130 Unallocable between 5110 and 5120	..	..	..	0	0	..	..	..	..	..
5200 Taxes on use of goods and perform activities	..	..	..	211 027	444 952	..	..	..	..	..
5300 Unallocable between 5100 and 5200	..	..	..	237	27 409	..	..	..	..	..
6000 Other taxes	**..**	**..**	**355 192**	**145 766**	**7 952**	**..**	**0**	**0**	**0**	**0**
6100 Paid solely by business	..	..	0	0	0	..	..	..	..	..
6200 Other	..	..	355 192	145 766	7 952	..	..	..	..	..
Total tax revenue	**..**	**..**	**355 192**	**652 636**	**1 079 526**	**..**	**619 082**	**1 050 670**	**2 411 987**	**5 132 875**

1. Data on social security contributions collected by decentralised institutions are not available from 2011, with the exception of the contributions made to the Instituto de Previsión Social (Social Security Institute).
2. The figures for years up to and including 2004, as well as for 2013 and 2014, exclude local government tax revenues as the data are not available.
3. The figures for years up to and including 1998 exclude decentralised institutions as the data are not available.

StatLink http://dx.doi.org/10.1787/888933687563

Table 6.22. Peru, tax revenues by sub-sectors of government

Million PEN

	Federal government					State/Regional				
	1990	2000	2005	2010	2016	1990	2000	2005	2010	2016
1000 Taxes on income, profits and capital gains	**37**	**5 078**	**11 950**	**27 317**	**40 360**	**..**	**..**	**..**	**..**	**..**
1100 Of individuals	3	2 117	3 327	6 518	11 760	..	..	..	..	..
1200 Corporate	32	2 526	8 391	19 561	24 786	..	..	..	..	..
1300 Unallocable between 1100 and 1200	1	436	232	1 239	3 814	..	..	..	..	..
2000 Social security contributions	**0**	**0**	**0**	**0**	**0**	**..**	**..**	**..**	**..**	**..**
2100 Employees	..	..	..	..	..	..	..	..	..	..
2200 Employers	..	..	..	..	..	..	..	..	..	..
2300 Self-employed or non-employed	..	..	..	..	..	..	..	..	..	..
2400 Unallocable between 2100, 2200 and 2300	..	..	..	..	..	..	..	..	..	..
3000 Taxes on payroll and workforce	**0**	**1 149**	**7**	**1**	**1**	**..**	**..**	**..**	**..**	**..**
4000 Taxes on property	**99**	**0**	**783**	**944**	**168**	**..**	**..**	**..**	**..**	**..**
4100 Recurrent taxes on immovable property	0	0	0	0	0	..	..	..	..	..
4200 Recurrent taxes on net wealth	61	0	0	0	0	..	..	..	..	..
4300 Estate, inheritance and gift taxes	0	0	0	0	0	..	..	..	..	..
4400 Taxes on financial and capital transactions	38	0	706	944	168	..	..	..	..	..
4500 Non-recurrent taxes	0	0	0	0	0	..	..	..	..	..
4600 Other recurrent taxes on property	0	0	76	0	0	..	..	..	..	..
5000 Taxes on goods and services	**423**	**15 952**	**22 615**	**36 064**	**47 713**	**..**	**..**	**..**	**..**	**..**
5100 Taxes on production, sale, transfer, etc	423	15 952	22 615	36 064	47 713	..	..	..	..	..
5110 General taxes	78	9 694	15 109	29 094	39 462	..	..	..	..	..
5120 Taxes on specific goods and services	345	6 259	7 506	6 970	8 251	..	..	..	..	..
5130 Unallocable between 5110 and 5120	0	0	0	0	0	..	..	..	..	..
5200 Taxes on use of goods and perform activities	0	0	0	0	0	..	..	..	..	..
5300 Unallocable between 5100 and 5200	0	0	0	0	0	..	..	..	..	..
6000 Other taxes	**36**	**628**	**62**	**-136**	**679**	**..**	**..**	**..**	**..**	**..**
6100 Paid solely by business	0	84	73	108	185	..	..	..	..	..
6200 Other	36	544	-11	-244	494	..	..	..	..	..
Total tax revenue	**595**	**22 808**	**35 416**	**64 191**	**88 921**	**..**	**..**	**..**	**..**	**..**

Million PEN

	Local government[1]					Social Security Funds				
	1990	2000	2005	2010	2016	1990	2000	2005	2010	2016
1000 Taxes on income, profits and capital gains	**..**	**..**	**0**	**0**	**0**	**0**	**0**	**0**	**0**	**0**
1100 Of individuals	..	..	..	..	..	..	..	..	..	..
1200 Corporate	..	..	..	..	..	..	..	..	..	..
1300 Unallocable between 1100 and 1200	..	..	..	..	..	..	..	..	..	..
2000 Social security contributions	**..**	**..**	**0**	**0**	**0**	**50**	**3 175**	**4 012**	**7 930**	**13 186**
2100 Employees	..	..	..	..	..	..	566	692	2 434	3 585
2200 Employers	..	..	..	..	..	..	2 515	3 285	5 454	9 536
2300 Self-employed or non-employed	..	..	..	..	..	..	95	36	42	64
2400 Unallocable between 2100, 2200 and 2300	..	..	..	..	..	50	0	0	0	0
3000 Taxes on payroll and workforce	**..**	**..**	**0**	**0**	**0**	**0**	**0**	**0**	**0**	**0**
4000 Taxes on property	**..**	**..**	**557**	**1 293**	**2 477**	**0**	**0**	**0**	**0**	**0**
4100 Recurrent taxes on immovable property	..	..	460	731	1 635	..	..	..	..	..
4200 Recurrent taxes on net wealth	..	..	0	0	0	..	..	..	..	..
4300 Estate, inheritance and gift taxes	..	..	0	0	0	..	..	..	..	..
4400 Taxes on financial and capital transactions	..	..	97	561	842	..	..	..	..	..
4500 Non-recurrent taxes	..	..	0	0	0	..	..	..	..	..
4600 Other recurrent taxes on property	..	..	0	0	0	..	..	..	..	..
5000 Taxes on goods and services	**..**	**..**	**106**	**290**	**533**	**0**	**0**	**0**	**0**	**0**
5100 Taxes on production, sale, transfer, etc	..	..	50	136	230	..	..	..	..	..
5110 General taxes	..	..	0	0	0	..	..	..	..	..
5120 Taxes on specific goods and services	..	..	50	136	230	..	..	..	..	..
5130 Unallocable between 5110 and 5120	..	..	0	0	0	..	..	..	..	..
5200 Taxes on use of goods and perform activities	..	..	55	154	303	..	..	..	..	..
5300 Unallocable between 5100 and 5200	..	..	0	0	0	..	..	..	..	..
6000 Other taxes	**..**	**..**	**484**	**721**	**609**	**0**	**0**	**0**	**0**	**0**
6100 Paid solely by business	..	..	0	0	0	..	..	..	..	..
6200 Other	..	..	484	721	609	..	..	..	..	..
Total tax revenue	**..**	**..**	**1 147**	**2 303**	**3 619**	**50**	**3 175**	**4 012**	**7 930**	**13 186**

Note: The figures for the years 2001-15 have been revised and updated. These exclude tax penalties considered as non-tax revenues by the OECD classification as set out in the OECD Interpretative Guide.

1. The figures for years up to and including 2001 exclude local government tax revenues as the data are not available.

StatLink http://dx.doi.org/10.1787/888933687582

Table 6.23. Trinidad and Tobago, tax revenues by sub-sectors of government

Million TTD

	Federal government[1]					State/Regional				
	1990	2000	2005	2010	2016	1990	2000	2005	2010	2016
1000 Taxes on income, profits and capital gains	**2 595**	**6 067**	**19 105**	**26 224**	**16 391**	..	..	..	..	..
1100 Of individuals	669	2 325	4 452	4 674	7 596	..	..	..	..	..
1200 Corporate	1 856	3 547	14 118	20 670	7 809	..	..	..	..	..
1300 Unallocable between 1100 and 1200	70	195	536	881	986	..	..	..	..	..
2000 Social security contributions	**0**	**0**	**0**	**0**	**0**	..	..	..	..	..
2100 Employees	..	..	..	..	..	..	..	..	..	..
2200 Employers	..	..	..	..	..	..	..	..	..	..
2300 Self-employed or non-employed	..	..	..	..	..	..	..	..	..	..
2400 Unallocable between 2100, 2200 and 2300	..	..	..	..	..	..	..	..	..	..
3000 Taxes on payroll and workforce	**0**	**0**	**0**	**0**	**0**	..	..	..	..	..
4000 Taxes on property	**41**	**64**	**63**	**22**	**3**	..	..	..	..	..
4100 Recurrent taxes on immovable property	39	64	63	22	3	..	..	..	..	..
4200 Recurrent taxes on net wealth	0	0	0	0	0	..	..	..	..	..
4300 Estate, inheritance and gift taxes	1	0	0	0	0	..	..	..	..	..
4400 Taxes on financial and capital transactions	0	0	0	0	0	..	..	..	..	..
4500 Non-recurrent taxes	0	0	0	0	0	..	..	..	..	..
4600 Other recurrent taxes on property	0	0	0	0	0	..	..	..	..	..
5000 Taxes on goods and services	**2 055**	**3 852**	**5 988**	**9 342**	**11 843**	..	..	..	..	..
5100 Taxes on production, sale, transfer, etc	1 928	3 559	5 690	8 924	11 163	..	..	..	..	..
5110 General taxes	980	1 890	2 963	6 032	7 016	..	..	..	..	..
5120 Taxes on specific goods and services	948	1 669	2 727	2 891	4 147	..	..	..	..	..
5130 Unallocable between 5110 and 5120	0	0	0	0	0	..	..	..	..	..
5200 Taxes on use of goods and perform activities	127	293	299	418	681	..	..	..	..	..
5300 Unallocable between 5100 and 5200	0	0	0	0	0	..	..	..	..	..
6000 Other taxes	**49**	**111**	**245**	**172**	**336**	..	..	..	..	..
6100 Paid solely by business	0	0	0	0	0	..	..	..	..	..
6200 Other	49	111	245	172	336	..	..	..	..	..
Total tax revenue	**4 740**	**10 094**	**25 401**	**35 760**	**28 574**	..	..	..	..	..

Million TTD

	Local government[1]					Social Security Funds[1]				
	1990	2000	2005	2010	2016	1990	2000	2005	2010	2016
1000 Taxes on income, profits and capital gains	**0**	**0**	**0**	**0**	**0**	**0**	**0**	**0**	**0**	**0**
1100 Of individuals	..	..	..	..	..	..	..	..	..	..
1200 Corporate	..	..	..	..	..	..	..	..	..	..
1300 Unallocable between 1100 and 1200	..	..	..	..	..	..	..	..	..	..
2000 Social security contributions	**0**	**0**	**0**	**0**	**0**	**183**	**702**	**1 173**	**2 645**	**4 252**
2100 Employees	..	..	..	..	..	..	..	..	..	..
2200 Employers	..	..	..	..	..	..	..	..	..	..
2300 Self-employed or non-employed	..	..	..	..	..	..	..	..	..	..
2400 Unallocable between 2100, 2200 and 2300	..	..	..	..	..	183	702	1 173	2 645	4 252
3000 Taxes on payroll and workforce	**0**	**0**	**0**	**0**	**0**	**0**	**0**	**0**	**0**	**0**
4000 Taxes on property	**108**	**213**	**326**	**411**	**538**	**0**	**0**	**0**	**0**	**0**
4100 Recurrent taxes on immovable property	108	213	326	411	538	..	..	..	..	..
4200 Recurrent taxes on net wealth	0	0	0	0	0	..	..	..	..	..
4300 Estate, inheritance and gift taxes	0	0	0	0	0	..	..	..	..	..
4400 Taxes on financial and capital transactions	0	0	0	0	0	..	..	..	..	..
4500 Non-recurrent taxes	0	0	0	0	0	..	..	..	..	..
4600 Other recurrent taxes on property	0	0	0	0	0	..	..	..	..	..
5000 Taxes on goods and services	**0**	**0**	**0**	**0**	**0**	**0**	**0**	**0**	**0**	**0**
5100 Taxes on production, sale, transfer, etc	..	..	..	..	..	..	..	..	..	..
5110 General taxes	..	..	..	..	..	..	..	..	..	..
5120 Taxes on specific goods and services	..	..	..	..	..	..	..	..	..	..
5130 Unallocable between 5110 and 5120	..	..	..	..	..	..	..	..	..	..
5200 Taxes on use of goods and perform activities	..	..	..	..	..	..	..	..	..	..
5300 Unallocable between 5100 and 5200	..	..	..	..	..	..	..	..	..	..
6000 Other taxes	**0**	**0**	**0**	**0**	**0**	**0**	**0**	**0**	**0**	**0**
6100 Paid solely by business	..	..	..	..	..	..	..	..	..	..
6200 Other	..	..	..	..	..	..	..	..	..	..
Total tax revenue	**108**	**213**	**326**	**411**	**538**	**183**	**702**	**1 173**	**2 645**	**4 252**

1. Data for 2016 are revised revenue estimates for the fiscal year 2016/17 published by the House of Representatives.

StatLink http://dx.doi.org/10.1787/888933687601

Table 6.24. Uruguay, tax revenues by sub-sectors of government

Million UYU

	Federal government					State/Regional				
	1990	2000	2005	2010	2016	1990	2000	2005	2010	2016
1000 Taxes on income, profits and capital gains	**114**	**5 620**	**11 969**	**44 069**	**103 937**	**..**	**..**	**..**	**..**	**..**
1100 Of individuals	0	0	44	19 150	51 679	..	..	..	..	..
1200 Corporate	114	5 620	11 925	23 257	47 734	..	..	..	..	..
1300 Unallocable between 1100 and 1200	0	0	0	1 662	4 523	..	..	..	..	..
2000 Social security contributions[1]	**0**	**0**	**0**	**0**	**0**	**..**	**..**	**..**	**..**	**..**
2100 Employees	..	..	..	..	..	..	..	..	..	..
2200 Employers	..	..	..	..	..	..	..	..	..	..
2300 Self-employed or non-employed	..	..	..	..	..	..	..	..	..	..
2400 Unallocable between 2100, 2200 and 2300	..	..	..	..	..	..	..	..	..	..
3000 Taxes on payroll and workforce	**0**	**0**	**0**	**0**	**0**	**..**	**..**	**..**	**..**	**..**
4000 Taxes on property	**125**	**3 709**	**7 400**	**11 690**	**19 767**	**..**	**..**	**..**	**..**	**..**
4100 Recurrent taxes on immovable property	0	153	0	1 064	852	..	..	..	..	..
4200 Recurrent taxes on net wealth	94	2 076	4 943	8 948	16 652	..	..	..	..	..
4300 Estate, inheritance and gift taxes	0	0	0	0	0	..	..	..	..	..
4400 Taxes on financial and capital transactions	0	372	886	1 350	1 724	..	..	..	..	..
4500 Non-recurrent taxes	0	0	0	0	0	..	..	..	..	..
4600 Other recurrent taxes on property	31	1 107	1 571	328	538	..	..	..	..	..
5000 Taxes on goods and services	**1 270**	**28 301**	**52 727**	**94 990**	**155 836**	**..**	**..**	**..**	**..**	**..**
5100 Taxes on production, sale, transfer, etc	1 270	28 301	52 727	94 990	155 836	..	..	..	..	..
5110 General taxes	660	18 009	34 641	69 365	123 262	..	..	..	..	..
5120 Taxes on specific goods and services	610	10 291	18 086	25 625	32 574	..	..	..	..	..
5130 Unallocable between 5110 and 5120	0	0	0	0	0	..	..	..	..	..
5200 Taxes on use of goods and perform activities	0	0	0	0	0	..	..	..	..	..
5300 Unallocable between 5100 and 5200	0	0	0	0	0	..	..	..	..	..
6000 Other taxes	**-10**	**-596**	**76**	**0**	**511**	**..**	**..**	**..**	**..**	**..**
6100 Paid solely by business	-10	-596	76	0	511	..	..	..	..	..
6200 Other	0	0	0	0	0	..	..	..	..	..
Total tax revenue	**1 500**	**37 034**	**72 171**	**150 750**	**280 050**	**..**	**..**	**..**	**..**	**..**

Million UYU

	Local government[2]					Social Security Funds				
	1990	2000	2005	2010	2016	1990	2000	2005	2010	2016
1000 Taxes on income, profits and capital gains	**0**	**0**	**0**	**0**	**0**	**0**	**0**	**0**	**0**	**0**
1100 Of individuals	..	..	..	..	..	..	..	..	..	..
1200 Corporate	..	..	..	..	..	..	..	..	..	..
1300 Unallocable between 1100 and 1200	..	..	..	..	..	..	..	..	..	..
2000 Social security contributions[1]	**0**	**0**	**0**	**0**	**0**	**717**	**17 679**	**21 425**	**49 742**	**140 979**
2100 Employees	..	..	..	..	..	..	..	..	..	..
2200 Employers	..	..	..	..	..	..	..	..	..	..
2300 Self-employed or non-employed	..	..	..	..	..	..	..	..	..	..
2400 Unallocable between 2100, 2200 and 2300	..	..	..	..	..	717	17 679	21 425	49 742	140 979
3000 Taxes on payroll and workforce	**0**	**0**	**0**	**0**	**0**	**0**	**0**	**0**	**0**	**0**
4000 Taxes on property	**71**	**2 414**	**4 776**	**7 491**	**11 198**	**0**	**0**	**0**	**0**	**0**
4100 Recurrent taxes on immovable property	71	2 414	4 776	7 491	11 198	..	..	..	..	..
4200 Recurrent taxes on net wealth	0	0	0	0	0	..	..	..	..	..
4300 Estate, inheritance and gift taxes	0	0	0	0	0	..	..	..	..	..
4400 Taxes on financial and capital transactions	0	0	0	0	0	..	..	..	..	..
4500 Non-recurrent taxes	0	0	0	0	0	..	..	..	..	..
4600 Other recurrent taxes on property	0	0	0	0	..	..	..	..	..	..
5000 Taxes on goods and services	**64**	**2 576**	**3 071**	**3 952**	**8 279**	**0**	**0**	**0**	**0**	**0**
5100 Taxes on production, sale, transfer, etc	0	0	0	0	0	..	..	..	..	..
5110 General taxes	..	..	..	..	..	..	..	..	..	..
5120 Taxes on specific goods and services	..	..	..	..	..	..	..	..	..	..
5130 Unallocable between 5110 and 5120	..	..	..	..	..	..	..	..	..	..
5200 Taxes on use of goods and perform activities	64	2 576	3 071	3 952	8 279	..	..	..	..	..
5300 Unallocable between 5100 and 5200	0	0	0	0	0	..	..	..	..	..
6000 Other taxes	**0**	**0**	**0**	**0**	**0**	**0**	**0**	**0**	**0**	**0**
6100 Paid solely by business	..	..	..	..	..	..	..	..	..	..
6200 Other	..	..	..	..	..	..	..	..	..	..
Total tax revenue	**135**	**4 990**	**7 846**	**11 443**	**19 476**	**717**	**17 679**	**21 425**	**49 742**	**140 979**

1. The figures for 1990-98 are estimated by the Direction General of Taxes as the methodology they use to calculate social security contributions was not employed until 1999.
2. The figures for local government tax revenues have been estimated for 2016.

StatLink http://dx.doi.org/10.1787/888933687620

Table 6.25. Venezuela, tax revenues by sub-sectors of government

Million VEF

	Federal government[3]					State/Regional[4]				
	1990	2000	2005	2010	2016	1990	2000	2005	2010	2016
1000 Taxes on income, profits and capital gains[1]	**344**	**4 686**	**18 529**	**36 836**	**780 170**	..	..	..	..	..
1100 Of individuals	..	..	..	..	..	..	..	..	..	..
1200 Corporate	315	3 368	11 184	8 700	47 000	..	..	..	..	..
1300 Unallocable between 1100 and 1200	30	1 317	7 345	28 137	733 170	..	..	..	..	..
2000 Social security contributions[2]	**0**	**0**	**0**	**0**	**0**	..	..	..	..	..
2100 Employees	..	..	..	..	..	..	..	..	..	..
2200 Employers	..	..	..	..	..	..	..	..	..	..
2300 Self-employed or non-employed	..	..	..	..	..	..	..	..	..	..
2400 Unallocable between 2100, 2200 and 2300	..	..	..	..	..	..	..	..	..	..
3000 Taxes on payroll and workforce	**0**	**0**	**0**	**0**	**0**	..	..	..	..	..
4000 Taxes on property	**1**	**400**	**2 834**	**222**	**9 088**	..	..	..	..	..
4100 Recurrent taxes on immovable property	0	0	0	0	0	..	..	..	..	..
4200 Recurrent taxes on net wealth	0	0	0	0	0	..	..	..	..	..
4300 Estate, inheritance and gift taxes	1	19	55	222	9 088	..	..	..	..	..
4400 Taxes on financial and capital transactions	0	381	2 779	0	0	..	..	..	..	..
4500 Non-recurrent taxes	0	0	0	0	0	..	..	..	..	..
4600 Other recurrent taxes on property	0	0	0	0	0	..	..	..	..	..
5000 Taxes on goods and services	**46**	**5 173**	**25 032**	**73 336**	**2 558 015**	..	..	..	..	..
5100 Taxes on production, sale, transfer, etc	46	5 173	25 032	73 336	2 558 015	..	..	..	..	..
5110 General taxes	0	3 272	19 513	56 101	1 907 078	..	..	..	..	..
5120 Taxes on specific goods and services	46	1 901	5 519	17 236	650 937	..	..	..	..	..
5130 Unallocable between 5110 and 5120	0	0	0	0	0	..	..	..	..	..
5200 Taxes on use of goods and perform activities	0	0	0	0	0	..	..	..	..	..
5300 Unallocable between 5100 and 5200	0	0	0	0	0	..	..	..	..	..
6000 Other taxes	**0**	**0**	**0**	**0**	**26 306**	..	..	..	..	..
6100 Paid solely by business	..	..	..	..	0	..	..	..	..	..
6200 Other	..	..	..	..	26 306	..	..	..	..	..
Total tax revenue	**391**	**10 258**	**46 395**	**110 394**	**3 373 579**	..	..	..	..	..

Million VEF

	Local government[4]					Social Security Funds[3]				
	1990	2000	2005	2010	2016	1990	2000	2005	2010	2016
1000 Taxes on income, profits and capital gains	..	..	..	..	..	**0**	**0**	**0**	**0**	**0**
1100 Of individuals	..	..	..	..	..	..	..	..	..	..
1200 Corporate	..	..	..	..	..	..	..	..	..	..
1300 Unallocable between 1100 and 1200	..	..	..	..	..	..	..	..	..	..
2000 Social security contributions[2]	..	..	..	..	..	**20**	**591**	**1 890**	**9 690**	**45 000**
2100 Employees	..	..	..	..	..	..	..	..	..	..
2200 Employers	..	..	..	..	..	..	..	..	..	..
2300 Self-employed or non-employed	..	..	..	..	..	..	..	..	..	..
2400 Unallocable between 2100, 2200 and 2300	..	..	..	..	..	20	591	1 890	9 690	45 000
3000 Taxes on payroll and workforce	..	..	..	..	..	**0**	**0**	**0**	**0**	**0**
4000 Taxes on property	..	..	..	..	..	**0**	**0**	**0**	**0**	**0**
4100 Recurrent taxes on immovable property	..	..	..	..	..	..	..	..	..	..
4200 Recurrent taxes on net wealth	..	..	..	..	..	..	..	..	..	..
4300 Estate, inheritance and gift taxes	..	..	..	..	..	..	..	..	..	..
4400 Taxes on financial and capital transactions	..	..	..	..	..	..	..	..	..	..
4500 Non-recurrent taxes	..	..	..	..	..	..	..	..	..	..
4600 Other recurrent taxes on property	..	..	..	..	..	..	..	..	..	..
5000 Taxes on goods and services	..	..	..	..	..	**0**	**0**	**0**	**0**	**0**
5100 Taxes on production, sale, transfer, etc	..	..	..	..	..	..	..	..	..	..
5110 General taxes	..	..	..	..	..	..	..	..	..	..
5120 Taxes on specific goods and services	..	..	..	..	..	..	..	..	..	..
5130 Unallocable between 5110 and 5120	..	..	..	..	..	..	..	..	..	..
5200 Taxes on use of goods and perform activities	..	..	..	..	..	..	..	..	..	..
5300 Unallocable between 5100 and 5200	..	..	..	..	..	..	..	..	..	..
6000 Other taxes	..	..	..	..	..	**0**	**0**	**0**	**0**	**0**
6100 Paid solely by business	..	..	..	..	..	..	..	..	..	..
6200 Other	..	..	..	..	..	..	..	..	..	..
Total tax revenue	..	..	..	..	..	**20**	**591**	**1 890**	**9 690**	**45 000**

1. Tax revenues on taxes on income, profits and capital gains, particularly those arising from oil profits have been estimated for 2015 and 2016.
2. Data on social security contributions are estimated from 2011 to 2016.
3. The figures for 2015-16 should be interpreted with caution as they have been affected by the high rate of inflation over this period.
4. The figures exclude state and local government tax revenues as the data are not available.

StatLink http://dx.doi.org/10.1787/888933687639

Annex A

The OECD Classification of Taxes and Interpretative Guide[1]

Table of contents

A.1. The OECD Classification of Taxes

1000 *Taxes on income, profits and capital gains*

- 1100 Taxes on income, profits and capital gains of individuals
  - 1110 On income and profits
  - 1120 On capital gains
- 1200 Corporate taxes on income, profits and capital gains
  - 1210 On income and profits
  - 1220 On capital gains
- 1300 Unallocable as between 1100 and 1200

2000 *Social security contributions*

- 2100 Employees
  - 2110 On a payroll basis
  - 2120 On an income tax basis
- 2200 Employers
  - 2210 On a payroll basis
  - 2220 On an income tax basis
- 2300 Self-employed or non-employed
  - 2310 On a payroll basis
  - 2320 On an income tax basis
- 2400 Unallocable as between 2100, 2200 and 2300
  - 2410 On a payroll basis
  - 2420 On an income tax basis

3000 *Taxes on payroll and workforce*

4000 *Taxes on property*

- 4100 Recurrent taxes on immovable property
  - 4110 Households
  - 4120 Other
- 4200 Recurrent taxes on net wealth
  - 4210 Individual
  - 4220 Corporate
- 4300 Estate, inheritance and gift taxes
  - 4310 Estate and inheritance taxes
  - 4320 Gift taxes
- 4400 Taxes on financial and capital transactions
- 4500 Other non-recurrent taxes on property
  - 4510 On net wealth
  - 4520 Other non-recurrent taxes
- 4600 Other recurrent taxes on property

5000 *Taxes on goods and services*

5100 Taxes on production, sale, transfer, leasing and delivery of goods and rendering of services

5110 General taxes

5111 Value added taxes

5112 Sales taxes

5113 Turnover and Other general taxes on goods and services

5120 Taxes on specific goods and services

5121 Excises

5122 Profits of fiscal monopolies

5123 Customs and import duties

5124 Taxes on exports

5125 Taxes on investment goods

5126 Taxes on specific services

5127 Other taxes on international trade and transactions

5128 Other taxes on specific goods and services

5130 Unallocable as between 5110 and 5120

5200 Taxes on use of goods, or on permission to use goods or perform activities

5210 Recurrent taxes

5211 Paid by households in respect of motor vehicles

5212 Paid by others in respect of motor vehicles

5213 Other recurrent taxes

5220 Non-recurrent taxes

5300 Unallocable as between 5100 and 5200

6000 *Other taxes*

6100 Paid solely by business

6200 Paid by other than business or unidentifiable

The OECD Interpretative Guide[1]

A.2. Coverage

General criteria

1. In the OECD classification the term "taxes" is confined to compulsory unrequited payments to general government. Taxes are unrequited in the sense that benefits provided by government to taxpayers are not normally in proportion to their payments.

2. The term 'tax' does not include fines, penalties and compulsory loans paid to government. Borderline cases between tax and non-tax revenues in relation to certain fees and charges are discussed in §11–14.

3. General government consists of the central administration, agencies whose operations are under its effective control, state and local governments and their administrations, certain social security schemes and autonomous governmental entities, excluding public enterprises. This definition of government follows that of the 2008 *System of National Accounts* (SNA).[2] In that publication, the general government sector and its sub-sectors are defined in Chapter 4, paragraphs 4.117 to 4.165.

4. Extra-budgetary units are part of the general government system. These are general government entities with individual budgets that are not fully covered by the main or general budget. These entities operate under the authority or control of a central, state, or local government. Extra-budgetary entities may have their own revenue sources, which may be supplemented by grants (transfers) from the general budget or from other sources. Even though their budgets may be subject to approval by the legislature, similar to that of budgetary accounts, they have discretion over the volume and composition of their spending. Such entities may be established to carry out specific government functions, such as road construction, or the nonmarket production of health or education services. Budgetary arrangements vary widely across countries, and various terms are used to describe these entities, but they are often referred to as "extra-budgetary funds" or "decentralised agencies."

5. Compulsory payments to supra-national bodies and their agencies are no longer included as taxes as from 1998, with some exceptions. However, custom duties collected by EU member states on behalf of the European Union are still identified as memorandum items and included in overall tax revenue amounts in the country tables (Chapter 4) of the country in which they are collected. (See §99). In countries where the church forms part of general government church taxes are included, provided they meet the criteria set out in §1 above. As the data refer to receipts of general government, levies paid to non-government bodies, welfare agencies or social insurance schemes outside general government, trade unions or trade associations, even where such levies are compulsory, are excluded. Compulsory payments to general government earmarked for such bodies are, however, included, provided that the government is not simply acting in an agency capacity.[3] Profits from fiscal monopolies are distinguished from those of other public enterprises and are treated as taxes because they reflect the exercise of the taxing power of the state by the use of monopoly powers (see §65–67), as are profits received by the government from the purchase and sale of foreign exchange at different rates (see §74).

6. Taxes paid by governments (e.g. social security contributions and payroll taxes paid by governments in their capacity as an employer, consumption taxes on their purchases or taxes on their property) are not excluded from the data provided. However, where it is

possible to identify the amounts of revenue involved,[4] they are shown in Chapter 4.2 of this Report.

7. The relationship between this classification and that of the System of National Accounts (SNA) is set out in Sections A.9 and A.11 below. Because of the differences between the two classifications, the data shown in national accounts are sometimes calculated or classified differently from the practice set out in this guide. These and other differences are mentioned where appropriate (e.g. in §30 below) but it is not possible to refer to all of them. There may also be some differences between this classification and that employed domestically by certain national administrations (e.g. see §12 below), so that OECD and national statistics data may not always be consistent: any such differences, however, are likely to be very slight in terms of amounts of revenues involved.

Social security contributions

8. Compulsory social security contributions, as defined in §39, and paid to general government, are treated here as tax revenues. Being compulsory payments to general government they clearly resemble taxes. They may, however, differ from other taxes in that the receipt of social security benefits depends, in most countries, upon appropriate contributions having been made, although the size of the benefits is not necessarily related to the amount of the contributions. Better comparability between countries is obtained by treating social security contributions as taxes, but they are listed under a separate heading so that they can be distinguished in any analysis.

9. The strict dividing line between tax revenues (compulsory unrequited payments to general government) and non-tax compulsory payments (NTCPs) (payments that are either requited or made to other institutions) is clearly defined. However, within the range of different compulsory payments to governments existing across countries, it is not always straightforward in practice to decide whether specific payments are either taxes or NTCPs. For example, compulsory pension savings that are controlled by general government and that accumulate on an individual account earning a market return or a rate that compensates for inflation would at first sight be categorised as NTCPs as opposed to taxes. However, even these payments might still be 'unrequited' and therefore classify as taxes instead of NTCPs (for example if these pension savings are not paid out when the taxpayer dies before reaching the pension age and the funds are then used to provide a minimum pension to all taxpayers that are insured). These issues result in the social security revenue figures reported for most countries being based on the premise that all types of compulsory payments to general government are judged to some extent to have a re-distributional element. It should be noted that this conclusion is based on a typically broad interpretation of the term 'unrequited' in the tax definition.

10. Social security contributions which are either voluntary or not payable to general government (see §1) are not treated as taxes, though in some countries, as indicated in the country footnotes, there are difficulties in completely eliminating voluntary contributions and certain compulsory payments to the private sector from the revenue figures. Imputed social security contributions are also not treated as taxes.

Fees, user charges and licence fees

Apart from vehicle licence fees, which are universally regarded as taxes, it is not easy to distinguish between those fees and user charges which are to be treated as taxes and those which are not, since, whilst a fee or charge is levied in connection with a specific service or activity, the strength of the link between the fee and the service provided may vary considerably, as may the relation between the amount of the fee and the cost of providing the service. Where the recipient of a service pays a fee clearly related to the cost of providing the service, the levy may be regarded as requited and under the definition of §1 would not be considered as a tax. In the following cases, however, a levy could be considered as 'unrequited':

a. where the charge greatly exceeds the cost of providing the service;
b. where the payer of the levy is not the receiver of the benefit (e.g. a fee collected from slaughterhouses to finance a service which is provided to farmers);
c. where government is not providing a specific service in return for the levy which it receives even though a licence may be issued to the payer (e.g. where the government grants a hunting, fishing or shooting licence which is not accompanied by the right to use a specific area of government land);
d. where benefits are received only by those paying the levy but the benefits received by each individual are not necessarily in proportion to his payments (e.g. a milk marketing levy paid by dairy farmers and used to promote the consumption of milk).

12. In marginal cases, however, the application of the criteria set out in §1 can be particularly difficult. The solution adopted – given the desirability of international uniformity and the relatively small amounts of revenue usually involved – is to follow the predominant practice among tax administrations rather than to allow each country to adopt its own view as to whether such levies are regarded as taxes or as non-tax revenue.[5]

13. A list of the main fees and charges in question and their normal[6] treatment in this publication is as follows:

Non-tax revenues:	court fees; driving licence fees; harbour fees; passport fees; radio and television licence fees where public authorities provide the service.
Taxes within heading 5200:	permission to perform such activities as distributing films; hunting, fishing and shooting; providing entertainment or gambling facilities; selling alcohol or tobacco; permission to own dogs or to use or own motor vehicles or guns; severance taxes.

14. In practice it may not always be possible to isolate tax receipts from non-tax revenue receipts when they are recorded together. If it is estimated that the bulk of the receipts derive from non-tax revenues, the whole amount involved is treated as a non-tax revenue; otherwise, such government receipts are included and classified according to the rules provided in §32 below.

Royalties

15. The ownership of subsoil assets in the form of deposits of minerals or fossil fuels (coal, oil, or natural gas) depends upon the way in which property rights are defined by law and also on international agreements in the case of deposits below international waters. In some cases, either the ground below which the mineral deposits are located, the deposits themselves or both may belong to a local or central government unit.

16. In such cases, these general government units may grant leases to other institutional units that permit them to extract these deposits over a specified period of time in return for a payment or series of payments. These payments are often described as 'royalties' but they are essentially rent that accrues to owners of natural resources in return for putting these assets at the disposal of other units for specified periods of time. The rent may take the form of periodic payments of fixed amounts, irrespective of the rate of extraction, or, more commonly, they may be a function of the quantity, volume, or value of the asset extracted. Enterprises engaged in exploration on government land may make payments to general government units in exchange for the right to undertake test drilling or otherwise investigate the existence and location of subsoil assets. Such payments are also recorded as rents even though no extraction may take place. These payments are therefore classified as non-tax revenues.

17. The same principles apply when other institutional units are granted leases that permit them to fell timber in natural forests on land owned by general government units. These payments are also classified as non-tax revenues.

18. These rents or royalties paid to general government should not be confused with taxes on income and profits, severance taxes, business licenses, or other taxes. If the payments are levied on the profits from the extraction activity, then they should be classified as taxes on incomes, profits and gains (1000). In addition, any severance payments that are imposed on the extraction of minerals and fossil fuels from reserves owned privately or by another government should be classified as taxes. Payments related to the gross value of production should be classified as other taxes on goods and services (5128). Payments for a license or permit to conduct extraction operations should be classified as taxes on use of goods and on permission to use goods or perform activities (5213).

Fines and penalties

19. In principle, fines and penalties charged on overdue taxes or penalties imposed for the attempted evasion of taxes should not be recorded as tax revenues. However it may not be possible to separate payments of fines or other penalties from the revenues from the taxes to which they relate. In this case the fines and penalties relating to a particular tax are recorded together with the revenues from that tax and fines and penalties paid with revenue from unidentifiable taxes are classified as other taxes in Category 6000. Fines not relating to tax offences (e.g. for parking offences), or not identifiable as relating to tax offences, are also not treated as tax revenues.

A.3. Basis of reporting

Accrual reporting

20. The data reported in this publication for recent years are predominantly recorded on an accrual basis, i.e. recorded at the time that the tax liability was created. Further information is provided in the footnotes to the country table in Chapter 4 of the Report.

21. However, data for earlier years are still predominantly recorded on a cash basis, i.e. at the time at which the payment was received by government. Thus, for example, taxes withheld by employers in one year but paid to the government in the following year and taxes due in one year but actually paid in the following year are both included in the receipts of the second year. Corrective transactions, such as refunds, repayments and drawbacks, are deducted from gross revenues of the period in which they are made.

22. Data on tax revenues are recorded without offsets for the administrative expenses connected with tax collection. Similarly, where the proceeds of tax are used to subsidise particular members of the community, the subsidy is not deducted from the yield of the tax, though the tax may be shown net of subsidies in the national records of some countries.

23. As regards fiscal monopolies (heading 5122), only the amount actually transferred to the government is included in government revenues. However, if any expenditures of fiscal monopolies are considered to be government expenditures (e.g. social expenditures undertaken by fiscal monopolies at the direction of the government) they are added back for the purpose of arriving at tax revenue figures (see §65 below).

The distinction between tax and expenditure provisions[7]

24. Because this publication is concerned only with the revenue side of government operations, no account being taken of the expenditure side, a distinction has to be made between tax and expenditure provisions. Normally there is no difficulty in making this distinction as expenditures are made outside the tax system and the tax accounts and under legislation separate from the tax legislation. In borderline cases, cash flow is used to distinguish between tax provisions and expenditure provisions. Insofar as a provision affects the flow of tax payments from the taxpayer to the government, it is regarded as a tax provision and is taken into account in the data shown in this publication. A provision which does not affect this flow is seen as an expenditure provision and is disregarded in the data recorded in this publication.

25. Tax allowances, exemptions and deductions against the tax base clearly affect the amount of tax paid to the government and are therefore considered as tax provisions. At the other extreme, those subsidies which cannot be offset against tax liability and which are clearly not connected with the assessment process, do not reduce tax revenues as recorded in this publication. Tax credits are amounts deductible from tax payable (as distinct from deductions from the tax base). Two types of tax credits are distinguished, those (referred to here as wastable tax credits) which are limited to the amount of the tax liability and therefore cannot give rise to a payment by the authorities to the taxpayer, and those (referred to as non-wastable tax credits) which are not so limited, so that the excess of the credit over the tax liability can be paid to the taxpayer.[8] A wastable tax credit, like a tax allowance, clearly affects the amount of tax paid to the government, and is therefore considered as a tax provision. The practice followed for non-wastable tax credits[9] is to distinguish between the 'tax expenditure component',[10] which is that portion of the credit that is used to reduce or eliminate a taxpayer's liability, and the 'transfer component', which is the portion that exceeds the taxpayer's liability and is paid to that taxpayer. Reported tax revenues should be reduced by the amount of the tax expenditure component but not by the amount of the transfer component. In addition, the amounts of the tax expenditure and transfer components should be reported as memorandum items in the country tables. Countries that are unable to distinguish between the tax expenditure and transfer components should indicate whether or not the tax revenues have been reduced by the total of these components, and provide any available estimates of the amounts of the two components. Further information is given in Chapter 1 of the Report, which illustrates the effect of alternative treatments of non-wastable tax credits on tax to GDP.

Calendar and fiscal years

26. National authorities whose fiscal years do not correspond to the calendar year show data, where possible, on a calendar year basis to permit maximum comparability with the data of other countries. There remain a few countries where data refer to fiscal years. For these the GDP data used in the comparative tables also correspond to the fiscal years.

A.4. General classification criteria

The main classification criteria

27. The classification of receipts among the main headings (1000, 2000, 3000, 4000, 5000 and 6000) is generally governed by the base on which the tax is levied: 1000 income, profits and capital gains; 2000 and 3000 earnings, payroll or number of employees; 4000 property; 5000 goods and services; 6000 multiple bases, other bases or unidentifiable bases. Where a tax is calculated on more than one base, the receipts are, where possible, split among the various headings (see §32 and §81). The headings 4000 and 5000 cover not only taxes where the tax base is the property, goods or services themselves but also certain related taxes. Thus, taxes on the transfer of property are included in 4400[11] and taxes on the use of goods or on permission to perform activities in 5200. In headings 4000 and 5000 a distinction is made in certain sub-headings between recurrent and non-recurrent taxes: recurrent taxes are defined as those levied at regular intervals (usually annually) and non-recurrent taxes are levied once and for all (see also §47 to §50, §53, §54 and §79 for particular applications of this distinction).

28. Earmarking of a tax for specific purposes does not affect the classification of tax receipts. However, as explained in §39 on the classification of social security contributions, the conferment of an entitlement to social benefits is crucial to the definition of the 2000 main heading.

29. The way that a tax is levied or collected (e.g. by use of stamps) does not affect classification.

Classification of taxpayers

30. In certain sub-headings distinctions are made between different categories of taxpayers. These distinctions vary from tax to tax:

a. *Between individuals and corporations in relation to income and net wealth taxes*

The basic distinction is that corporation income taxes, as distinct from individual income taxes, are levied on the corporation as an entity, not on the individuals who own it, and without regard to the personal circumstances of these individuals. The same distinction applies to net wealth taxes on corporations and those on individuals. Taxes paid on the profits of partnerships and the income of institutions, such as life insurance or pension funds, are classified according to the same rule. They are classified as corporate taxes (1200) if they are charged on the partnership or institution as an entity without regard to the personal circumstances of the owners. Otherwise, they are treated as individual taxes (1100). Usually, there is different legislation for the corporation taxes and for the individual taxes.[12] The distinction made here between individuals and corporations does not follow the sector classification between households, enterprises, and so on of the System of National Accounts for income and outlay accounts. The SNA classification requires certain unincorporated businesses[13] to be excluded from the household sector and included with non-financial enterprises and financial institutions. The tax on the profits of these businesses, however, cannot always be separated from the tax on the other income of their owners, or can be separated only on an arbitrary basis. No attempt at this separation is made here and the whole of the individual income tax is shown together without regard to the nature of the income chargeable.

b. *Between households and others in relation to taxes on immovable property*

Here the distinction is that adopted by the SNA for the production and consumption expenditure accounts. The distinction is between households as consumers (i.e. excluding non-incorporated business) on the one hand and producers on the other hand. However, taxes on dwellings occupied by households, whether paid by owner-occupiers, tenants or landlords, are classified under households. This follows the common distinction made between taxes on domestic property versus taxes on business property. Some countries are not, however, in a position to make this distinction.

c. *Between households and others in relation to motor vehicle licences*

Here the distinction is between households as consumers on the one hand and producers on the other, as in the production and consumption expenditure accounts of the SNA.

d. *Between business and others in relation to the residual taxes (6000)*

The distinction is the same as in c) above between producers on the one hand and households as consumers on the other hand. Taxes which are included under the heading 6000 because they involve more than one tax base or because the tax base does not fall within any of the previous categories but which are identifiable as levyable only on producers and not on households are included under 'business'. The rest of the taxes which are included under the heading 6000 are shown as 'other' or non-identified.

Surcharges

31. Receipts from surcharges in respect of particular taxes are usually classified with the receipts from the relevant tax whether or not the surcharge is temporary. If, however, the surcharge has a characteristic which would render it classifiable in a different heading of the OECD list, receipts from the surcharge are classified under that heading separately from the relevant tax.

Unidentifiable tax receipts and residual sub-headings

32. A number of cases arise where taxes cannot be identified as belonging entirely to a heading or sub-heading of the OECD classification and the following practices are applied in such cases:

a. The heading is known, but it is not known how receipts should be allocated between sub-headings: receipts are classified in the appropriate residual sub-heading (1300, 2400, 4520, 4600, 5130, 5300 or 6200).
b. It is known that the bulk of receipts from a group of taxes (usually local taxes) is derived from taxes within a particular heading or sub-heading, but some of the taxes in the group whose amount cannot be precisely ascertained may be classifiable in other headings or sub-headings: receipts are shown in the heading or sub-heading under which most of the receipts fall.
c. Neither the heading nor sub-heading of a tax (usually local) can be identified: the tax is classified in 6200 unless it is known that it is a tax on business in which case it is classified in 6100.

A.5. Commentaries on items of the list

1000 — *Taxes on income, profits and capital gains*

33. This heading covers taxes levied on the net income or profits (i.e. gross income minus allowable tax reliefs) of individuals and enterprises. Also covered are taxes levied on the capital gains of individuals and enterprises, and gains from gambling.

34. Included in the heading are:

a. taxes levied predominantly on income or profits, though partially on other bases. Taxes on various bases which are not predominantly income or profits are classified according to the principles laid down in §32 and §81;

b. taxes on property, which are levied on a presumed or estimated income as part of an income tax (see also §47(a), (c) and (d));

c. compulsory payments to social security fund contributions that are levied on income but do not confer an entitlement to social benefits. When such contributions do confer an entitlement to social benefits, they are included in heading 2000 (see §39);

d. receipts from integrated scheduler income tax systems are classified as a whole in this heading, even though certain of the scheduler taxes may be based upon gross income and may not take into account the personal circumstances of the taxpayer.

35. The main subdivision of this heading is between levies on individuals (1100) and those on corporate enterprises (1200). Under each subdivision a distinction is made between taxes on income and profits (1110 and 1210), and taxes on capital gains (1120 and 1220). If certain receipts cannot be identified as appropriate to either 1100 or 1200, or if in practice this distinction cannot be made (e.g. because there are no reliable data on the recipients of payments from which withholding taxes are deducted) they are classified in 1300 as not-allocable.

Treatment of credits under imputation systems

36. Under imputation systems of corporate income tax, a company's shareholders are wholly or partly relieved of their liability to income tax on dividends paid by the company out of income or profits liable to corporate income tax. In countries with such systems,[14] part of the tax on the company's profits is available to provide relief against the shareholders' own tax liability. The relief to the shareholder takes the form of a tax credit, the amount of which may be less than, equal to, or more than the shareholder's overall tax liability. If the tax credit exceeds this tax liability the excess may be payable to the shareholder. As this type of tax credit is an integral part of the imputation system of corporate income tax, any payment to the shareholders is treated as a repayment of tax and not as expenditure (compare the treatment of other tax credits described in §25).

37. As the tax credit under imputation systems (even when exceeding tax liability) is to be regarded as a tax provision, the question arises whether it should be deducted from individual income tax receipts (1110) or corporate income tax receipts (1210). In this Report, the full amount of corporate income tax paid is shown under 1210 and no imputed tax is included under 1110. Thus, the full amount of the credit reduces the amount of 1110 whether the credit results in a reduction of personal income tax liability or whether an actual refund is made because the credit exceeds the income tax liability. (Where, however, such tax credits are deducted from corporation tax in respect of dividends paid to corporations the amounts are deducted from the receipts of 1210).

1120 and 1220 — *Taxes on capital gains*

38. These sub-headings comprise taxes imposed on capital gains, 1120 covering those levied on the gains of individuals and 1220 those levied on the gains of corporate enterprises, where receipts from such taxes can be separately identified. In many countries this is not the case and the receipts from such taxes are then classified with those from the income tax. Heading 1120 also includes taxes on gains from gambling.

2000 — *Social security contributions*

39. Classified here are all compulsory payments that confer an entitlement to receive a (contingent) future social benefit. Such payments are usually earmarked to finance social benefits and are often paid to institutions of general government that provide such benefits. However, such earmarking is not part of the definition of social security contributions and is not required for a tax to be classified here. However, conferment of an entitlement is required for a tax to be classified under this heading. So, levies on income or payroll that are earmarked for social security funds but do not confer an entitlement to benefit are excluded from this heading and shown under personal income taxes (1100) or taxes on payroll and workforce (3000). Taxes on other bases, such as goods and services, which are earmarked for social security benefits are not shown here but are classified according to their respective bases because they generally confer no entitlement to social security benefits.

40. Contributions for the following types of social security benefits would, *inter alia*, be included: unemployment insurance benefits and supplements, accident, injury and sickness benefits, old-age, disability and survivors' pensions, family allowances, reimbursements for medical and hospital expenses or provision of hospital or medical services. Contributions may be levied on both employees and employers.

41. Contributions may be based on earnings or payroll ('on a payroll basis') or on net income after deductions and exemptions for personal circumstances ('on an income tax basis'), and the revenues from the two bases should be separately identified if possible. However, where contributions to a general social security scheme are on a payroll basis, but the contributions of particular groups (such as the self-employed) cannot be assessed on this basis and net income is used as a proxy for gross earnings, the receipts may still be classified as being on a payroll basis. In principle, this heading excludes voluntary contributions paid to social security schemes. When separately identifiable these are shown in the memorandum item on the financing of social security benefits. In practice, however, they cannot always be separately identified from compulsory contributions, in which case they are included in this heading.

42. Contributions to social insurance schemes which are not institutions of general government and to other types of insurance schemes, provident funds, pension funds, friendly societies or other saving schemes are not considered as social security contributions. Provident funds are arrangements under which the contributions of each employee and of the corresponding employer on his/her behalf are kept in a separate account earning interest and withdrawable under specific circumstances. Pension funds are separately organised schemes negotiated between employees and employers and carry provisions for different contributions and benefits, sometimes more directly tied to salary levels and length of service than under social security schemes. When contributions to these schemes are compulsory or quasi-compulsory (e.g. by virtue of agreement with professional and union organisations) they are shown in the memorandum item (refer to Chapter 4.2 of the Report).

43. Contributions by government employees and by governments in respect of their employees, to social security schemes classified within general government are included in this heading. Contributions to separate schemes for government employees, which can be regarded as replacing general social security schemes, are also regarded as taxes.[15] Where, however, a separate scheme is not seen as replacing a general scheme and has been negotiated between the government, in its role as an employer, and its employees, it is not regarded as social security and contributions to it are not regarded as taxes, even though the scheme may have been established by legislation.

44. This heading excludes 'imputed' contributions, which correspond to social benefits paid directly by employers to their employees or former employees or to their representatives (e.g. when employers are legally obliged to pay sickness benefits for a certain period).

45. Contributions are divided into those of employees (2100), employers (2200), and self-employed or non-employed (2300), and then further sub-divided according to the basis on which they are levied. Employees are defined for this purpose as all persons engaged in activities of business units, government bodies, private non-profit institutions, or other paid employment, except the proprietors and their unpaid family members in the case of unincorporated businesses. Members of the armed forces are included, irrespective of the duration and type of their service, if they contribute to social security schemes. The contributions of employers are defined as their payments on account of their employees to social security schemes. Where employees or employers are required to continue the payment of social security contributions when the employee becomes unemployed these contributions, data permitting, are shown in 2100 and 2200 respectively. Accordingly, the sub-heading 2300 is confined to contributions paid by the self-employed and by those outside of the labour force (e.g. disabled or retired individuals).

3000 — *Taxes on payroll and workforce*

46. These consist of taxes payable by enterprises assessed either as a proportion of the wages or salaries paid or as a fixed amount per person employed. They do not include compulsory social security contributions paid by employers or any taxes paid by employees themselves out of their wages or salaries

4000 — *Taxes on property*

47. This heading covers recurrent and non-recurrent taxes on the use, ownership or transfer of property. These include taxes on immovable property or net wealth, taxes on the change of ownership of property through inheritance or gift and taxes on financial and capital transactions. The following kinds of tax are excluded from this heading:

a. taxes on capital gains resulting from the sale of a property (1120 or 1220);

b. taxes on the use of goods or on permission to use goods or perform activities (5200); see §76;

c. taxes on immovable property levied on the basis of a presumed net income which take into account the personal circumstances of the taxpayer. They are classified as income taxes along with taxes on income and capital gains derived from property (1100);

d. taxes on the use of property for residence, where the tax is payable by either proprietor or tenant and the amount payable is a function of the user's personal circumstances (pay, dependants, and so on). They are classified as taxes on income (1100);

e. taxes on building in excess of permitted maximum density, taxes on the enlargement, construction or alteration of certain buildings beyond a permitted value and taxes on building construction. They are classified as taxes on permission to perform activities (5200);

f. taxes on the use of one's own property for special trading purposes like selling alcohol, tobacco, meat or for exploitation of land resources (e.g. United States severance taxes). They are classified as taxes on permission to perform activities (5200).

4100 — *Recurrent taxes on immovable property*

48. This sub-heading covers taxes levied regularly in respect of the use or ownership of immovable property.

- these taxes are levied on land and buildings;
- they can be in the form of a percentage of an assessed property value based on a national rental income, sales price, or capitalised yield; or in terms of other characteristics of real property, (for example size or location) from which a presumed rent or capital value can be derived.
- such taxes can be levied on proprietors, tenants, or both. They can also be paid by one level of government to another level of government in respect of property under the jurisdiction of the latter.
- debts are not taken into account in the assessment of these taxes, and they differ from taxes on net wealth in this respect.

49. Taxes on immovable property are further sub-divided into those paid by households (4110) and those paid by other entities (4120), according to the criteria set out in §30(*b*) above.

4200 — *Recurrent taxes on net wealth*

50. This sub-heading covers taxes levied regularly (in most cases annually) on net wealth, i.e. taxes on a wide range of movable and immovable property, net of debt. It is sub-divided into taxes paid by individuals (4210) and taxes paid by corporate enterprises (4220) according to the criteria set out in §30(*a*) above. If separate figures exist for receipts paid by institutions, the tax payments involved are added to those paid by corporations.

4300 — *Estate, inheritance and gift taxes*

51. This sub-heading is divided into taxes on estates and inheritances (4310) and taxes on gifts (4320).[16] Estate taxes are charged on the amount of the total estate whereas inheritance taxes are charged on the shares of the individual recipients; in addition the latter may take into account the relationship of the individual recipients to the deceased.

4400 — *Taxes on financial and capital transactions*

52. This sub-heading comprises, *inter alia*, taxes on the issue, transfer, purchase and sale of securities, taxes on cheques, and taxes levied on specific legal transactions such as validation of contracts and the sale of immovable property. The heading does not include:

a. taxes on the use of goods or property or permission to perform certain activities (5200);

b. fees paid to cover court charges, charges for birth, marriage or death certificates, which are normally regarded as non-tax revenues (see §11);

c. taxes on capital gains (1000);

d. recurrent taxes on immovable property (4100);

e. recurrent taxes on net wealth (4200);

f. once-and-for-all levies on property or wealth (4500).

4500 — *Other non-recurrent taxes on property*[16]

53. This sub-heading covers once-and-for-all, as distinct from recurrent, levies on property. It is divided into taxes on net wealth (4510) and other non-recurrent taxes on property (4520). Heading 4510 would include taxes levied to meet emergency expenditures, or for redistribution purposes. Heading 4520 would cover taxes levied to take account of increases in land value due to permission given to develop or provision of additional local facilities by general government, any taxes on the revaluation of capital and once-and-for-all taxes on particular items of property.

4600 — *Other recurrent taxes on property*

54. These rarely exist in OECD member countries, but the heading would include taxes on goods such as cattle, jewellery, windows, and other external signs of wealth.

5000 — *Taxes on goods and services*

55. All taxes and duties levied on the production, extraction, sale, transfer, leasing or delivery of goods, and the rendering of services (5100), or in respect of the use of goods or permission to use goods or to perform activities (5200) are included here. The heading thus covers:

a. multi-stage cumulative taxes;

b. general sales taxes — whether levied at manufacture/production, wholesale or retail level;

c. value-added taxes;

d. excises;

e. taxes levied on the import and export of goods;

f. taxes levied in respect of the use of goods and taxes on permission to use goods, or perform certain activities;

g. taxes on the extraction, processing or production of minerals and other products.

56. Borderline cases between this heading and heading 4000 (taxes on property) and 6100 (other taxes on business) are referred to in §47, §52 and §78. Residual sub-headings (5300) and (5130) cover tax receipts which cannot be allocated between 5100 and 5200 and between 5110 and 5120, respectively; see §32.

5100 — *Taxes on the production, sale, transfer, leasing and delivery of goods and rendering of services*

57. This sub-heading consists of all taxes, levied on transactions in goods and services on the basis of their intrinsic characteristics (e.g. value, weight of tobacco, strength of alcohol, and so on) as distinct from taxes imposed on the use of goods, or permission to use goods or perform activities, which fall under 5200.

5110 — *General taxes on goods and services*

58. This sub-heading includes all taxes, other than import and export duties (5123 and 5124), levied on the production, leasing, transfer, delivery or sales of a wide range of goods and/ or the rendering of a wide range of services, irrespective of whether they are domestically produced or imported and irrespective of the stage of production or distribution at which they are levied. It thus covers value-added taxes, sales taxes and multi-stage cumulative

taxes. Receipts from border adjustments in respect of such taxes when goods are imported are added to gross receipts for this category, and repayments of such taxes when goods are exported are deducted. These taxes are subdivided into 5111 value-added taxes, 5112 sales taxes, 5113 turnover and other general taxes on goods and services.

59. Borderline cases arise between this heading and taxes on specific goods (5120) when taxes are levied on a large number of goods, for example, the United Kingdom purchase tax (repealed in 1973) and the Japanese commodity tax (repealed in 1988). In conformity with national views, the former United Kingdom purchase tax is classified as a general tax (5112) and the former Japanese commodity tax as excises (5121).

5111 — *Value-added taxes*

60. All general consumption taxes charged on value-added are classified in this sub-heading, irrespective of the method of deduction and the stages at which the taxes are levied. In practice, all OECD countries with value-added taxes normally allow immediate deduction of taxes on purchases by all but the final consumer and impose tax at all stages. In some countries the heading may include certain taxes, such as those on financial and insurance activities, either because receipts from them cannot be identified separately from those from the value-added tax, or because they are regarded as an integral part of the value-added tax, even though similar taxes in other countries might be classified elsewhere (e.g. 5126 as taxes on services or 4400 as taxes on financial and capital transactions).

5112 — *Sales taxes*

61. All general taxes levied at one stage only, whether at manufacturing or production, wholesale or retail stage are classified here.

5113 — *Turnover and other general taxes on goods and services*

62. These are multi-stage cumulative taxes and taxes where elements of consumption taxes are combined with multistage taxes. These taxes are levied each time a transaction takes place without deduction for taxes paid on inputs. Multi-stage taxes can be combined with elements of value-added or sales taxes.

5120 — *Taxes on specific goods and services*

63. Excises, profits generated and transferred from fiscal monopolies, and customs and imports duties as well as taxes on exports, foreign exchange transactions, investment goods and betting stakes and special taxes on services, which do not form part of a general tax of 5110, are included in this category.

5121 — Excises

64. Excises are taxes levied as a product specific unit tax on a predefined limited range of goods. Excises are usually levied at differentiated rates on nonessential or luxury goods, alcoholic beverages, tobacco, and energy. Excises may be imposed at any stage of production or distribution and are usually assessed as a specific charge per unit based on characteristics by reference to the value, weight, strength, or quantity of the product. Included are special taxes on individual products such as sugar, sugar beets, matches, and chocolates; taxes levied at varying rates on a certain range of goods; and taxes levied on tobacco goods, alcoholic drinks, motor fuels, and hydrocarbon oils. If a tax collected principally on imported goods also applies, or would apply, under the same law to comparable domestically produced goods, then the revenue from this tax is classified as arising from excises rather than from import duties. This principle applies even if there is no comparable domestic production

or no possibility of such production. Taxes on the use of utilities such as water, electricity, gas, and energy are regarded as excises rather than taxes on specific services (5126). Excises exclude those taxes that are levied as general taxes on goods and services (5110); profits of fiscal monopolies (5122); customs and other import duties (5123); or taxes on exports (5124).

5122 — *Profits of fiscal monopolies*

65. This sub-heading covers that part of the profits of fiscal monopolies which is transferred to general government or which is used to finance any expenditures considered to be government expenditures (see §23). Amounts are shown when they are transferred to general government or used to make expenditures considered to be government expenditures.

66. Fiscal monopolies reflect the exercise of the taxing power of government by the use of monopoly powers. Fiscal monopolies are non-financial public enterprises exercising a monopoly in most cases over the production or distribution of tobacco, alcoholic beverages, salt, matches, playing cards and petroleum or agricultural products (i.e. on the kind of products which are likely to be, alternatively or additionally, subject to the excises of 5121), to raise the government revenues which in other countries are gathered through taxes on dealings in such commodities by private business units. The government monopoly may be at the production stage or, as in the case of government-owned and controlled liquor stores, at the distribution stage.

67. Fiscal monopolies are distinguished from public utilities such as rail transport, electricity, post offices, and other communications, which may enjoy a monopoly or quasi-monopoly position but where the primary purpose is normally to provide basic services rather than to raise revenue for government. Transfers from such other public enterprises to the government are considered as non-tax revenues. The traditional concept of fiscal monopoly is not generally extended to include state lotteries, the profits of which are usually accordingly regarded as non-tax revenues. However, they can be included as tax revenues if the prime reason for their operation is to raise revenues to finance government expenditure. Fiscal monopoly profits are distinguished from export and import monopoly profits (5127) transferred from marketing boards or other enterprises dealing with international trade.

5123 — *Customs and other import duties*

68. Taxes, stamp duties and surcharges restricted by law to imported products are included here. Also included are levies on imported agricultural products which are imposed in member countries of the European Union and amounts paid by certain of these countries under the Monetary Compensation Accounts (MCA) system.[17] Starting from 1998, customs duties collected by European Union member states on behalf of the European Union are no longer reported under this heading in the country tables (in Chapter 4 of the Report). Excluded here are taxes collected on imports as part of a general tax on goods and services, or an excise applicable to both imported and domestically produced goods.

5124 — *Taxes on exports*

69. In the 1970s, export duties were levied in Australia, Canada and Portugal as a regular measure and they have been used in Finland for counter-cyclical purposes. Some member countries of the European Union pay, as part of the MCA system, a levy on exports (see note 16 to §68). Where these amounts are identifiable, they are shown in this heading. This heading does not include repayments of general consumption taxes or excises or customs duties on exported goods, which should be deducted from the gross receipts under 5110, 5121 or 5123, as appropriate.

5125 — *Taxes on investment goods*

70. This sub-heading covers taxes on investment goods, such as machinery. These taxes may be imposed for a number of years or temporarily for counter-cyclical purposes. Taxes on industrial inputs which are also levied on consumers [e.g. the Swedish energy tax which is classified under (5121)] are not included here.

5126 — *Taxes on specific services*

71. All taxes assessed on the payment for specific services, such as taxes on insurance premiums, banking services, gambling and betting stakes (e.g. from horse races, football pools, lottery tickets), transport, entertainment, restaurant and advertising charges, fall into this category. Taxes levied on the gross income of companies providing the service (e.g. gross insurance premiums or gambling stakes received by the company) are also classified under this heading. Tax revenues from bank levies and payments to deposit insurance and financial stability schemes are provisionally included here for the 2012 edition. The detailed classification is set out in §108.

72. Excluded from this sub-heading are:

a. taxes on services forming part of a general tax on goods and services (5110);

b. taxes on electricity, gas and energy (5121 as excises);

c. taxes on individual gains from gambling (1120 as taxes on capital gains of individuals and non-corporate enterprises) and lump-sum taxes on the transfer of private lotteries or on the permission to set up lotteries (5200);[18]

d. taxes on cheques and on the issue, transfer or redemption of securities (4400 as taxes on financial and capital transactions).

5127 — *Other taxes on international trade and transactions*

73. This sub-heading covers revenue received by the government from the purchase and sale of foreign exchange at different rates. When the government exercises monopoly powers to extract a margin between the purchase and sales price of foreign exchange, other than to cover administrative costs, the revenue derived constitutes a compulsory levy exacted in indeterminate proportions from both purchaser and seller of foreign exchange. It is the common equivalent of an import duty and export duty levied in a single exchange rate system or of a tax on the sale or purchase of foreign exchange. Like the profits of fiscal monopolies and import or export monopolies transferred to government, it represents the exercise of monopoly powers for tax purposes and is included in tax revenues.

74. The sub-heading covers also the profits of export or import monopolies, which do not however exist in OECD countries, taxes on purchase or sale of foreign exchange, and any other taxes levied specifically on international trade or transactions.

5128 — *Other taxes on specific goods and services*

75. This item includes taxes on the extraction of minerals, fossil fuels and other exhaustible resources from deposits owned privately or by another government together with any other unidentifiable receipts from taxes on specific goods and services. Taxes on the extraction of exhaustible resources are usually a fixed amount per unit of quality or weight, but can be a percentage of value. The taxes are recorded when the resources are extracted. Payments from the extraction of exhaustible resources from deposits owned by the government unit receiving the payment are classified as rent.

5200 — *Taxes on use of goods or on permission to use goods or perform activities*

76. This sub-heading covers taxes which are levied in respect of the use of goods as distinct from taxes on the goods themselves. Unlike the latter taxes – reported under 5100 –, they are not assessed on the value of the goods but usually as fixed amounts. Taxes on permission to use goods or to perform activities are also included here, as are pollution taxes not based upon the value of particular goods. It is sometimes difficult to distinguish between compulsory user charges and licence fees which are regarded as taxes and those which are excluded as non-tax revenues. The criteria which are employed are noted in §11–12.

77. Although the sub-heading refers to the 'use' of goods, registration of ownership rather than use may be what generates liability to tax, so that the taxes of this heading may apply to the ownership of animals or goods rather than their use (e.g. race horses, dogs and motor vehicles) and may apply even to unusable goods (e.g. unusable motor vehicles or guns).

78. Borderline cases arise with:

a. taxes on the permission to perform business activities which are levied on a combined income, payroll or turnover base and, accordingly, are classified following the rules in §81;

b. taxes on the ownership or use of property of headings 4100, 4200 and 4600. The heading 4100 is confined to taxes on the ownership or tenancy of immovable property and – unlike the taxes of 5200 – they are related to the value of the property. The net wealth taxes and taxes on chattels of 4200 and 4600 respectively are confined to the ownership rather than the use of assets, apply to groups of assets rather than particular goods and again are related to the value of the assets,

5210 — *Recurrent taxes on use of goods and on permission to use goods or perform activities*

79. The principal characteristic of taxes classified here is that they are levied at regular intervals and that they are usually fixed amounts. The most important item in terms of revenue receipts is vehicle licence taxes. This sub-heading also covers taxes on permission to hunt, shoot, fish or to sell certain products and taxes on the ownership of dogs and on the performance of certain services, provided that they meet the criteria set out in §11–12. The sub-divisions of 5210 are user taxes on motor vehicles paid by households (5211) and those paid by others (5212).[19] Sub-heading 5213 covers dog licences and user charges for permission to perform activities such as selling meat or liquor when the levies are on a recurring basis. It also covers recurrent general licences for hunting, shooting and fishing where the right to carry out these activities is not granted as part of a normal commercial transaction (e.g. the granting of the licence is not accompanied by the right to use a specific area which is owned by government).

5220 — *Non-recurrent taxes on use of goods and on permission to use goods or perform activities*

80. This section covers non-recurrent taxes levied on the use of goods or on permission to use goods or perform activities and taxes levied each time goods are used. It includes taxes levied on the emission or discharge into the environment of noxious gases, liquids or other harmful substances.

- Payments for tradable emission permits issued by governments under cap and trade schemes should be recorded here at the time the emissions occur. No revenue should be recorded for permits that governments issue free of charge. The accrual basis of recording means that there can be a timing difference between the cash being received by government for the permits and the time the emission occurs. In the national accounts, this timing gives rise to a financial liability for government during the period.

- Payments made for the collection and disposal of waste or noxious substances by public authorities should be excluded as they constitute a sale of services to enterprises.

81. Other taxes falling under heading 5200 that are not levied recurrently are also included here. Thus, once-and-for-all payments for permission to sell liquor or tobacco or to set up betting shops are included provided they meet the criteria set out in §11–12.

6000 — *Other taxes*

82. Taxes levied on a base, or bases, other than those described under headings 1000, 3000, 4000 and 5000, or on bases of which cannot be considered to be related to any one of these headings, are included here. Where taxes are levied on a multiple base and it is possible to estimate the receipts related to each base the separate amounts are included under the appropriate headings. If separate amounts cannot be estimated and it is known that most of the receipts are derived from one base, the whole of the receipts are classified according to that base. Otherwise, they are classified here. Other revenues included here are presumptive taxes not included elsewhere in the classification system, taxes on individuals in the form of a poll tax or capitation tax, stamp taxes not related to financial and capital transactions nor falling exclusively on a single category of transaction, expenditure taxes where personal deductions or exemptions are applied and unidentifiable tax receipts. A subdivision is made between taxes levied wholly or predominantly on business (6100) and those levied on others (6200).

A.6. Conciliation with national accounts

83. This section of the tables provides a re-conciliation between the OECD calculation of total tax revenues and the total of all taxes and social contributions paid to general government as recorded in the country's National Accounts. Where the country is a member of the European Union (EU), the comparison is between the OECD calculation of total tax revenues and the sum of tax revenues and social contributions recorded in the combination of the general government and the institutions of the EU sectors of the National Accounts.

A.7. Memorandum item on the financing of social security benefits

84. In view of the varying relationship between taxation and social security contributions and the cases referred to in §39 to §45, a memorandum item collects together all payments earmarked for social security-type benefits, other than voluntary payments to the private sector. Data are presented as follows (refer Chapter 4.2 of the Report):

a. Taxes of 2000 series.

b. Taxes earmarked for social security benefits.

c. Voluntary contributions to the government.

d. Compulsory contributions to the private sector.

Guidance on the breakdown of (a) to (d) above is provided in §39 to §45.

A.8. Memorandum item on identifiable taxes paid by government

85. Identifiable taxes actually paid by government are presented in a memorandum item classified by the main headings of the OECD classification of taxes. In the vast majority of countries, only social security contributions and payroll taxes paid by government can be identified. These are, however, usually the most important taxes paid by governments (refer to Chapter 4.2 of the Report).

A.9. Relation of OECD classification of taxes to national accounting systems

86. A system of national accounts (SNA) seeks to provide a coherent framework for recording and presenting the main flows relating respectively to production, consumption, accumulation and external transactions of a given economic area, usually a country or a major region within a country. Government revenues are an important part of the transactions recorded in SNA. The final version of the 2008 SNA was jointly published by five international organisations: the United Nations, the International Monetary Fund, the European Union, the Organisation for Economic Co-operation and Development, and the World Bank in August 2009. The *System* is a comprehensive, consistent and flexible set of macroeconomic accounts. It is designed for use in countries with market economies, whatever their stage of economic development, and also in countries in transition to market economies. The important parts of the SNA's conceptual framework and its definitions of the various sectors of the economy have been reflected in the OECD's classification of taxes.

87. There are, however, some differences between the OECD classification of taxes and SNA concepts that are listed below. They arise because the aim of the former is to provide the maximum disaggregation of statistical data on what are generally regarded as taxes by tax administrations.

a. OECD includes compulsory social security contributions paid to general government in total tax revenues. Imputed and voluntary contributions plus those paid to private funds are not treated as taxes (§8 and §10 above);
b. there are different points of view on whether or not some levies and fees are classified as taxes (§11 and §12 above);
c. OECD excludes imputed taxes or subsidies resulting from the operation of official multiple exchange rates or from the central bank paying a rate of interest on required reserves that is different from other market rates;
d. there are differences in the treatment of non-wastable tax credits

88. As noted in §1 and §2, headings 1000 to 6000 of the OECD list of taxes cover all unrequited payments to general government, other than compulsory loans and fines. Such unrequited payments including fines, but excluding compulsory loans can be obtained from adding together the following figures in the 2008 SNA

- value-added type taxes (D.211);
- taxes and duties on imports, excluding VAT (D.212);
- export taxes (D.213);
- taxes on products, excluding VAT, import and export taxes (D.214);
- other taxes on production (D.29);
- taxes on income (D.51);
- other current taxes (D.59);

- social contributions (D.61), excluding voluntary contributions;
- capital taxes (D.91).

A.10. The OECD classification of taxes and the International Monetary Fund (GFS) system

89. The coverage and valuation of tax revenues in the GFS system and the 2008 SNA are very similar. Therefore, the differences between the OECD classification and that of the 2008 SNA (see §87 above) also apply to the GFS. In addition the International Monetary Fund subdivides the OECD 5000 heading into section IV (Domestic Taxes on Goods and Services) and section V (Taxes on International Trade and Transactions). This reflects the fact that while the latter usually yield insignificant amounts of revenue in OECD countries, this is not the case in many non-OECD countries.

A.11. Comparison of the OECD classification of taxes with other international classifications

90. The table below describes an item by item comparison of the OECD classification of taxes and the classifications used in the following:

i) System of National Accounts (2008 SNA);

ii) European System of Accounts (2010 ESA);

iii) IMF *Government Finance Statistics Manual* (GFSM2014).

91. These comparisons represent those that would be expected to apply in the majority of cases. However in practice some flexibility should be used in their application. This is because in particular cases, countries can adopt varying approaches to the classification of revenues in National Accounts.

	OECD Classification	2008 SNA	2010 ESA	GFSM2014
1000	Taxes on income, profits and capital gains			
	1100 Individuals			
	1110 Income and profits	D51-8.61a	D51A	1111
	1120 Capital gains	D51-8.61c, d	D51C, D	1111
	1200 Corporations			
	1210 Income and profits	D51-8.61b	D51B	1112
	1220 Capital gains	D51-8.61c	D51C	1112
	1300 Unallocable as between 1100 and 1200			1113
2000	Social security contributions			
	2100 Employees	D613-8.85	D613	1211
	2200 Employers	D611-8.83	D611	1212
	2300 Self-employed, non-employed	D613-8.85	D613	1213
	2400 Unallocable as between 2100, 2200 and 2300			1214
3000	Taxes on payroll and workforce	D29-7.97a	D29C	112
4000	Taxes on property			
	4100 Recurrent taxes on immovable property			
	4110 Households	D59-8.63a	D59A	1131
	4120 Other	D29-7.97b	D29A	1131
	4200 Recurrent net wealth taxes			
	4210 Individual	D59-8.63b	D59A	1132
	4220 Corporations	D59-8.63b	D59A	1132
	4300 Estate, inheritance and gift taxes			
	4310 Estate and inheritance taxes	D91-10.207b	D91A	1133
	4320 Gift taxes	D91-10.207b	D91A	1133
	4400 Taxes on financial and capital transactions	D59-7.96d; D29-7.97e	D214B, C	114114; 1161
	4500 Other non-recurrent taxes on property	D91-10.207a	D91B	1135
	4600 Other recurrent taxes on property	D59-8.63c	D59A	1136
5000	Taxes on goods and services			
	5100 Taxes on production, sale and transfer of goods and services			
	5110 General taxes on goods and services			
	5111 Value-added taxes	D211-7.89	D211; D29G	11411
	5112 Sales taxes	D2122-7.94a; D214-7.96a	D21224; D214I	11412
	5113 Other general taxes on goods and services	D214-7.96a	D214I	11413
	5120 Taxes on specific goods and services			
	5121 Excises	D2122-7.94b; D214-7.96b	D21223; D214A, B, D	1142
	5122 Profits of fiscal monopolies	D214-7.96e	D214J	1143
	5123 Customs and other import duties	D2121-7.93	D2121; D21221, 2	1151
	5124 On exports	D213-7.95a	D214K	1152-4
	5125 On investment goods			
	5126 On specific services	D2122-7.94c; D214-7.96c	D21225; D214E, F, G, H; D29F	1144; 1156
	5127 Other taxes on international trade and transactions	D2122-7.94d D29-7.95b D29-7.97g D59-8.64d	D21226; D29D; D59E	1153; 1155-6
	5128 Other taxes on specific goods and services			1146
	5130 Unallocable between 5110 and 5120			
	5200 Taxes on use of goods and on permission to use goods or perform activities			
	5210 Recurrent taxes on use of goods and on permission to use goods or perform activities			
	5211 Motor vehicle taxes households	D59-8.64c	D59D	11451
	5212 Motor vehicles taxes others	D29-7.97d	D214D; D29B	11451
	5213 Other recurrent taxes on use of goods and on permission to use goods or perform activities	D29-7.97c, d, f D59-8.64c	D29B, E, F; D59D	11452
	5220 Non-recurrent taxes on permission to use goods or perform activities			11452
	5300 Unallocable as between 5100 and 5200			
6000	Other taxes			
	6100 Payable solely by business			1161
	6200 Payable by other than business, or unidentifiable	D59-8.64a, b	D59B, C	1162

A.12. Attribution of tax revenues by sub-sectors of general government

92. The OECD classification requires a breakdown of tax revenues by sub-sectors of government. The definition of each sub-sector and the criteria to be used to attribute tax revenues between these sub-sectors are set out below. They follow the guidance of the 2008 SNA and GFSM 2014.

Sub-sectors of general government to be identified

a) Central government

93. The central government sub-sector includes all governmental departments, offices, establishments and other bodies which are agencies or instruments of the central authority whose competence extends over the whole territory, with the exception of the administration of social security funds. Central government therefore has the authority to impose taxes on all resident and non-resident units engaged in economic activities within the country.

b) State, provincial or regional government

94. This sub-sector consists of intermediate units of government exercising a competence at a level below that of central government. It includes all such units operating independently of central government in a part of a country's territory encompassing a number of smaller localities, with the exception of the administration of social security funds. In unitary countries, regional governments may be considered to have a separate existence where they have substantial autonomy to raise a significant proportion of their revenues from sources within their control and their officers are independent of external administrative control in the actual operation of the unit's activities.

95. At present, federal countries comprise the majority of cases where revenues attributed to intermediate units of government are identified separately. Spain is the only unitary country in this position. In the remaining unitary countries, regional revenues are included with those of local governments.

c) Local government

96. This sub-sector includes all other units of government exercising an independent competence in part of the territory of a country, with the exception of the administration of social security funds. It encompasses various urban and/or rural jurisdictions (e.g. local authorities, municipalities, cities, boroughs, districts).

d) Social security funds

97. Social security funds form a separate sub-sector of general government. The social security sub-sector is defined in the 2008 SNA by the following extracts from paragraphs 4.124 to 4.126 and 4.147:

"Social security schemes are social insurance schemes covering the community as a whole or large section of the community that are imposed and controlled by government units. The schemes cover a wide variety of programmes, providing benefits in cash or in kind for old age, invalidity or death, survivors, sickness and maternity, work injury, unemployment, family allowance, health care, etc. There is not necessarily a direct link between the amount of the contribution paid by an individual and the benefits he or she may receive." (Paragraph 4.124).

"When social security schemes are separately organised from the other activities of government units and hold their assets and liabilities separately from the latter and engage in financial transactions on their own account they qualify as institutional units that are described as social security funds." (Paragraph 4.125).

"The amounts raised, and paid out, in social security contributions and benefits may be deliberately varied in order to achieve objectives of government policy that have no direct connection with the concept of social security as a scheme to provide social benefits to members of the community. They may be raised or lowered in order to influence the level of aggregate demand in the economy, for example. Nevertheless, so long as they remain separately constituted funds, they must be treated as separate institutional units in the SNA. (Paragraph 4.126).

"The social security funds sub-sector (of general government) consists of the social security funds operating at all levels of government. Such funds are social insurance schemes covering the community as a whole or large section of the community that are imposed by government units." (Paragraph 4.147).

98. This definition of social security funds is followed in the OECD classification with the two following exceptions which are excluded

- Schemes imposed by government and operated by bodies outside the general government sector, as defined in §3 of this manual; and
- Schemes to which all contributions are voluntary.

Supra-national authorities

99. This sub-sector covers the revenue-raising operations of supra-national authorities within a country. In practice, the only relevant supra-national authority in the OECD area is that of the institutions of the European Union (EU). As from 1998, supra-national authorities are no longer included in the *Revenue Statistics*, to achieve consistency with the SNA definition of general government which excludes them. For example, income taxes and social security contributions collected by European Institutions and paid by European civil servants who are resident of EU member countries should not be included. However the specific levies paid by the member states of the EU continue to be included in total tax revenues and they are shown under this heading.

Criteria to be used for the attribution of tax revenues

100. When a government collects taxes and pays them over in whole or in part to other governments, it is necessary to determine whether the revenues should be considered to be those of the collecting government which it distributes to others as grants, or those of the beneficiary governments which the collecting government receives and passes on only as their agent. The criteria to be used in the attribution of revenues are set out in §101 to §104 which replicate paragraphs 3.70 to 3.73 from the 2008 SNA.

101. In general, a tax is attributed to the government unit that

a. exercises the authority to impose the tax (either as a principal or through the delegated authority of the principal),

b. has final discretion to set and vary the rate of the tax

102. Where an amount is collected by one government for and on behalf of another government, and the latter government has the authority to impose the tax, and set and vary its rate, then the former is acting as an agent for the latter and the tax is reassigned. Any amount retained by the collecting government as a collection charge should be treated as a payment for a service. Any other amount retained by the collecting government, such as under a tax-sharing arrangement, should be treated as a current grant. If the collecting government was delegated the authority to set and vary the rate, then the amount collected should be treated as tax revenue of this government.

103. Where different governments jointly and equally set the rate of a tax and jointly and equally decide on the distribution of the proceeds, with no individual government having ultimate overriding authority, then the tax revenues are attributed to each government according to its respective share of the proceeds. If an arrangement allows one government unit to exercise ultimate overriding authority, then all of the tax revenue is attributed to that unit.

104. There may also be the circumstance where a tax is imposed under the constitutional or other authority of one government, but other governments individually set the tax rate in their jurisdictions. The proceeds of the tax generated in each respective government's jurisdiction are attributed as tax revenues of that government.

Levies paid by member states of the European Union

105. The levies paid by the member states of the EU take the form specific levies which include

a. custom duties and levies on agricultural goods (5123),

b. gross monetary compensation accounts (5123 if relating to imports and 5124 if relating to exports); and

c. Steel, coal, sugar and milk levies (5128).

106. The custom duties collected by member states on behalf of the EU are recorded

- on a gross of collection fee basis;
- using figures adjusted so that duties are shown on a 'final destination' as opposed to a 'country of first entry' basis where such adjustments can be made. These adjustments concern in particular duties collected at important (sea) ports. Although the EU duties are collected by the authorities of the country of first entry, when possible these duties should be excluded from the revenue of the collecting country and be included in the revenue of the country of final destination.

107. This is the specific EU levy that most clearly conforms to the attribution criterion described in §99 above. Consequently as from 1998, these amounts are footnoted as a memorandum item to the EU member state country tables (in Chapter 4) and no longer shown under heading 5123. However the figures are included in the total tax revenue figures on the top line for all the relevant years shown in the tables.

A.13. Provisional classification of revenues from bank levies and payments to deposit insurance and financial stability schemes

108. The OECD have adopted the following interim approach to reporting revenue from bank levies plus deposit insurance and stability fees for the 2012 and subsequent editions of *OECD Revenue Statistics*. It is recommended that the amounts should be recorded under category 5126.

- Compulsory payments of stability fees, bank levies and deposit insurance should generally be treated as tax revenues where the payments are made to General Government and allocated to the governments' consolidated or general funds so that the Government is free to make immediate use of the money for the purposes that it chooses. This principle would apply regardless of whether the Government is promising to make payments to guarantee the banks' customer deposits in some future contingency.
- If the compulsory payments are made to general government and placed in funds that are earmarked to be entirely channelled back to the sector of the economy that comprises the companies that are subject to the payment, they would still generally be treated as tax revenues on the grounds that the funds would be available for the government and would reduce its budget deficit, the fee is unrequited for an individual entity and the amounts raised could be unrelated to any eventual pay out to depositors or expenditure on wider support for the financial sector.
- Payments to made to the smaller long-standing schemes for insuring 'retail' deposits, where the payment levels are consistent with the costs of insurance should be classified as fee for service.
- Any payments which involve governments realising the assets of a failed institution or receiving a priority claim on its assets in liquidation in order to fund payments of compensation to customers for their lost deposits would be treated as a fee for a service as opposed to tax revenues.
- Compulsory payments that are made to funds operated outside the government sector and non-state institutions backed by the deposit takers and all payments to voluntary schemes should not be treated as tax revenues.

Notes

1. References in this OECD Interpretative Guide to Sections or Parts of "this Report" refer to OECD (2017), *Revenue Statistics 2017*, OECD Publishing, Paris.
2. All references to SNA are to the 2008 edition.
3. See section A.12 of this guide for a discussion of the concept of agency capacity.
4. It is usually possible to identify amounts of social security contributions and payroll taxes, but not other taxes paid by government.
5. If, however, a levy which is considered as non-tax revenue by most countries is regarded as a tax — or raises substantial revenue — in one or more countries, the amounts collected are footnoted at the end of the relevant country tables, even though the amounts are not included in total tax revenues.
6. Names, however, can frequently be misleading. For example, though a passport fee would normally be considered a non-tax revenue, if a supplementary levy on passports (as is the case in Portugal) were imposed in order to raise substantial amounts of revenue relative to the cost of providing the passport, the levy would be regarded as a tax under 5200.

7. A more detailed explanation of this distinction can be found in the special feature, 'Current issues in reporting tax revenues', in the 2001 edition of the *Revenue Statistics*.
8. Sometimes the terms 'non-refundable' and 'refundable' are used, but it may be considered illogical to talk of 'refundable' when nothing has been paid.
9. A different treatment, however, is accorded to non-wastable tax credits under imputation systems of corporate income tax (§36–38).
10. This is not strictly a true tax expenditure in the formal sense. Such tax expenditures require identification of a benchmark tax system for each country or, preferably, a common international benchmark. In practice it has not been possible to reach agreement on a common international benchmark.
11. Unless based on the profit made on a sale, in which case they would be classified as capital gains taxes under 1120 or 1220.
12. In some countries the same legislation applies to both individual and corporate enterprises for particular taxes on income. However, the receipts from such taxes are usually allocable between individuals and enterprises and can therefore be shown in the appropriate sub-heading.
13. For example, "...sufficiently self-contained and independent that they behave in the same way as corporations....... (including) keeping a complete set of accounts" (2008 SNA, section 4.44).
14. In Canada — a country also referred to as having an imputation system — the (wastable) tax credit for the shareholder is in respect of domestic corporation tax deemed to have been paid whether or not a corporation tax liability has arisen. As there is no integral connection between the corporation tax liability and the credit given against income tax under such systems, these credits for dividends are treated, along with other tax credits, on the lines described in §25.
15. This may also apply where a scheme for government employees existed prior to the introduction of a general social security scheme.
16. In the 2008 SNA these are regarded as capital transfers and not as taxes (see section A.8).
17. This is the system by which the European Union adjusts for differences between the exchange rates used to determine prices under the Common Market Agricultural Policy and actual exchange rates. Payments under the system may relate to imports or exports and where these amounts are separately identifiable they are shown under the appropriate heading (5123 or 5124). In this Report, these amounts are shown gross (i.e. without deducting any subsidies paid out under the MCA system).
18. Transfers of profits of State lotteries are regarded as non-tax revenues (see also §67).
19. See §30(c) as regards this distinction.

Anexo A

Guía de interpretación de la OCDE[1]

Índice

A.1. Clasificación de impuestos de la OCDE

1000 *Impuestos sobre la renta, las utilidades y las ganancias de capital*

1100 Impuestos sobre la renta, utilidades y ganancias de capital de personas físicas

1110 Renta y utilidades

1120 Ganancias de capital

1200 Impuesto sobre la renta, utilidades y ganancias de capital de sociedades.

1210 Renta y utilidades

1220 Ganancias de capital

1300 No clasificables entre 1100 y 1200

2000 *Contribuciones a la seguridad social*

2100 Empleados

2110 Sobre la base de la nómina

2120 Sobre la base del impuesto sobre la renta

2200 Empleadores

2300 Trabajadores por cuenta propia o no empleados

2400 No clasificables entre 2100, 2200 y 2300

3000 *Impuestos sobre la nómina y la fuerza de trabajo*

4000 *Impuestos sobre la propiedad*

4100 Impuestos recurrentes sobre la propiedad inmueble

4110 Hogares

4120 Otros

4200 Impuestos recurrentes sobre la riqueza neta

4210 Personas físicas

4220 Sociedades

4300 Impuestos sobre sucesiones, herencias y donaciones

4310 Impuestos sobre sucesiones y herencias

4320 Impuestos sobre donaciones

4400 Impuestos sobre transacciones financieras y de capital

4500 Otros impuestos no recurrentes sobre la propiedad

4600 Otros impuestos recurrentes sobre la propiedad

5000 *Impuestos sobre los bienes y servicios*

5100 Impuestos sobre la producción, venta, transferencia, arrendamiento y entrega de bienes y prestación de servicios

5110 Impuestos generales

5111 Impuestos sobre el valor agregado

5112 Impuestos sobre las ventas

5113 Otros impuestos generales sobre ingresos brutos y sobre bienes y servicios

5120 Impuestos sobre bienes y servicios específicos

5121 Impuestos selectivos

5122 Utilidades de los monopolios fiscales

5123 Derechos de aduanas y otros derechos de importación

5124 Impuestos sobre las exportaciones

5125 Impuestos sobre los bienes de inversión

5126 Impuestos sobre servicios específicos

5127 Otros impuestos sobre el comercio y las transacciones internacionales

5128 Otros impuestos sobre bienes y servicios específicos

5130 No clasificables entre 5110 y 5120

5200 Impuestos sobre el uso de bienes y sobre el permiso para usar bienes y realizar actividades

5210 Impuestos recurrentes

5211 Pagados por los hogares sobre vehículos automotores.

5212 Pagados por otros sobre vehículos automotores

5213 Otros impuestos recurrentes

5220 Impuestos no recurrentes

5300 No clasificables entre 5100 y 5200

6000 *Otros impuestos*

6100 Pagados únicamente por empresas

6200 Pagados por otros distintos de las empresas o no identificables

Guía de Interpretación de la OCDE

A.2. Cobertura

Criterios generales

1. En la clasificación de la OCDE, el término "impuestos" se circunscribe exclusivamente a los pagos sin contraprestación efectuados al gobierno general. Los impuestos carecen de contraprestación en el sentido en que, normalmente, las prestaciones proporcionadas por el gobierno a los contribuyentes no guardan relación directa con los pagos realizados por estos.

2. El término "impuestos" no incluye las multas, sanciones pecuniarias, ni préstamos obligatorios pagados al gobierno. La delimitación entre ingresos tributarios y no tributarios en relación con ciertas tasas y cargos se abordan en los § 11–14.

3. El gobierno general comprende la Administración central y los organismos que se hallan bajo su control efectivo, los gobiernos estatales y locales y sus respectivas administraciones, y ciertos regímenes de seguridad social y entidades gubernamentales autónomas, excluidas las empresas públicas. Esta definición del gobierno proviene del *Sistema de Cuentas Nacionales* (SCN) 2008;[2] en esa publicación, el sector del gobierno general y sus subsectores se hallan definidos en el capítulo 4, párrafos 4.117 a 4.165 de la versión en inglés.

4. Las unidades extrapresupuestarias son parte del sistema de gobierno general. Estas son entidades del gobierno general con presupuestos individuales que no están completamente cubiertos por el presupuesto principal o general. Estas entidades operan bajo la autoridad o el control de un gobierno central, estatal o local. Las entidades extrapresupuestarias pueden tener sus propias fuentes de ingresos, que pueden complementarse con subvenciones (transferencias) del presupuesto general o de otras fuentes. A pesar de que sus presupuestos pueden estar sujetos a la aprobación de la legislatura, similar a la de las cuentas presupuestarias, tienen discreción sobre el volumen y la composición de sus gastos. Dichas entidades pueden establecerse para llevar a cabo funciones gubernamentales específicas, como la construcción de carreteras o la producción de servicios de salud o educación pública. Los arreglos presupuestarios varían ampliamente entre países, y se utilizan diversos términos para describir estas entidades, pero a menudo se los denomina "fondos extrapresupuestarios" o "agencias descentralizadas".

5. Los pagos obligatorios a autoridades supranacionales y a los organismos vinculados a ellas no se incluyen como impuestos desde 1998, con contadas excepciones; sin embargo, los derechos de aduana recaudados por los estados miembros de la Unión Europea en nombre de esta siguen registrándose como partidas informativas y se incluyen en los cuadros de países (Capítulo 4 de la publicación *Revenue Statistics* de la OCDE), concretamente en la recaudación tributaria total del país en el que se cobran (véase el § 99). Por otra parte, en los países en los que la Iglesia forma parte del gobierno general, se computan los impuestos eclesiásticos, siempre que reúnan los criterios establecidos en el § 1. Además, habida cuenta de que los datos hacen referencia a las entradas que recibe el gobierno general, quedan excluidos los gravámenes abonados a órganos no gubernamentales, organismos de bienestar o regímenes de seguro social externos al gobierno general, y sindicatos u organizaciones profesionales, aun cuando dichos gravámenes sean obligatorios; sin embargo, los pagos obligatorios al gobierno general asignados a esos entes sí están incluidos aquí siempre que el gobierno no actúe como mero agente de estos.[3] Las utilidades de los monopolios fiscales se diferencian de las de otras empresas

públicas, y se tratan como impuestos porque reflejan el ejercicio del poder tributario del Estado mediante el uso de prerrogativas monopolísticas (véanse los §§ 65–67), al igual que las utilidades percibidas por el gobierno por la compra y la venta de divisas a diferentes tipos de cambio (véase el § 74).

6. Los impuestos pagados por el gobierno (p. ej., contribuciones a la seguridad social e impuestos sobre la nómina pagados por el gobierno en su calidad de empleador, impuestos sobre el consumo en sus compras o impuestos sobre sus propiedades) no se han excluido de los datos presentados. Sin embargo, cuando ha sido posible identificar las cantidades de ingreso implicadas,[4] se han mostrado en el Capítulo 4.2 de la publicación Estadísticas Tributarias en países de la OCDE.

7. La relación entre esta clasificación y la del Sistema de Cuentas Nacionales (SCN) se aclara en los apartados A.9 y A.11 *infra.*; dado que estas dos clasificaciones no coinciden en todos sus aspectos, en ocasiones, los datos presentados en las cuentas nacionales se calculan o clasifican de forma diferente a lo establecido en la presente guía y, aunque esas y otras diferencias se han mencionado en determinados casos (p. ej., en el § 30 *infra.*), no ha sido posible hacer referencia a todas ellas. Por otra parte, pueden darse asimismo ciertas disparidades entre la presente clasificación y la empleada internamente por algunas administraciones nacionales (véase el § 12), por lo que quizá las estadísticas de la OCDE y las nacionales no siempre concuerden; sin embargo, es más que probable que esas diferencias sean mínimas en lo que a la cuantía de ingresos se refiere.

Contribuciones a la seguridad social

8. Las contribuciones obligatorias a la seguridad social, tal y como se definen en el § 39, abonadas al gobierno general, se tratan aquí como ingresos tributarios, ya que, al tratarse de pagos preceptivos al gobierno general, se asemejan claramente a los impuestos. No obstante, pueden diferir de otros impuestos por el hecho de que la recepción de prestaciones de la seguridad social depende, en numerosos países, de que se hayan aportado las debidas contribuciones, aunque la magnitud de dichas prestaciones no tiene por qué estar supeditada obligatoriamente al importe de las contribuciones. Al tratar las contribuciones sociales como impuestos, se obtiene un mayor grado de comparabilidad entre países, aunque se han consignado en una categoría separada para poder distinguirlas en cualquier análisis.

9. La estricta distinción entre los ingresos tributarios (pagos obligatorios sin contraprestaciones directas a los gobiernos generales) y los pagos obligatorios no tributarios (NTCPs por sus siglas en inglés) (pagos que con derechos a contraprestaciones o que se realizan a otras instituciones) está claramente definida. Sin embargo, dentro del rango de diferentes pagos obligatorios realizados a los gobiernos en todos los países, no siempre es sencillo en la práctica decidir si los pagos específicos son impuestos o NTCPs. Por ejemplo, los ahorros de pensión obligatorios que son controlados por el gobierno general y que se acumulan en una cuenta individual obteniendo una rentabilidad del mercado o una tasa que compensa la inflación se clasificarían a primera vista como NTCPs en lugar de impuestos. Sin embargo, incluso estos pagos podrían no dar origen a "reembolsos" y clasificarse como impuestos en lugar de NTCPs (por ejemplo, si estos ahorros no se pagan cuando el contribuyente muere antes de alcanzar la edad de jubilación y los fondos se utilizan para proporcionar una pensión mínima a todos los contribuyentes que están asegurados). Estos problemas hacen que las cifras de ingresos de la seguridad social reportadas para la mayoría de los países se basen en la premisa de que todos los tipos de pagos obligatorios a las administraciones públicas se consideran en cierta medida como elementos de redistribución. Cabe señalar

que esta conclusión se basa en una interpretación generalmente amplia del término "no correspondido" en la definición del impuesto.

10. Por el contrario, las contribuciones a la seguridad social voluntarias o no pagaderas al gobierno general (véase el § 1) no se tratan como impuestos, aunque en ciertos países, tal y como se indica debidamente en cada caso en las notas que figuran al pie de los cuadros, plantea dificultades el eliminar tanto las contribuciones voluntarias como algunos pagos obligatorios al sector privado de las cifras de recaudo tributario. Las contribuciones a la seguridad social imputadas tampoco son considerados impuestos.

Tasas, cargos a usuarios y licencias

11. Aparte de las tasas por licencia de vehículos, universalmente consideradas como impuestos, no resulta fácil distinguir entre las tasas y cargos a usuarios que deben tratarse como impuestos y las que no, ya que, aunque toda tasa o cargo se impone en conexión con un servicio o una actividad específicos, la intensidad del vínculo entre el derecho cobrado y el servicio prestado puede variar considerablemente, al igual que puede hacerlo la relación entre la cuantía de la tasa y el costo que supone proporcionar el servicio en cuestión. En todo caso, cuando el beneficiario del servicio pague una tasa claramente relacionada con el costo que supone prestar un servicio, puede inferirse que el gravamen tiene contraprestación y, de acuerdo con la definición reseñada en el § 1, no se considerará como impuesto. En sentido contrario, puede estimarse que el gravamen "carece de contraprestación" cuando:

a. el cargo exceda con creces el costo que supone prestar el servicio;

b. el pagador o sujeto pasivo del gravamen no sea el beneficiario del servicio (p. ej., tasas recaudadas de los mataderos para financiar un servicio proporcionado a los titulares de explotaciones agropecuarias);

c. el gobierno no proporcione un servicio específico a cambio del pago del gravamen, aun y cuando se emita un permiso en beneficio del sujeto pasivo (p. ej., cuando el gobierno concede licencias de caza, pesca o tiro que no otorgan el derecho a usar una zona específica propiedad del gobierno);

d. los servicios beneficien únicamente a los pagadores del gravamen, pero las utilidades recibidas por cada persona no guarden necesariamente proporción con sus pagos (p. ej., el gravamen sobre la comercialización de la leche que recae en los criadores de ganado lechero y que se utiliza para fomentar el consumo de la leche).

12. Pese a las anteriores consideraciones, en ciertos casos excepcionales la aplicación de los criterios plasmados en el § 1 puede resultar particularmente compleja. La solución adoptada –dada la conveniencia de uniformidad internacional y las cantidades de ingreso relativamente bajas implicadas por lo general– ha consistido en seguir la práctica dominante en la mayoría de las administraciones, en lugar de permitir que cada país aplique su propia visión sobre si estos gravámenes deben considerarse como ingresos tributarios o no tributarios.[5]

13. Seguidamente, se ofrece una lista de las principales tasas y cargos en cuestión, y su tratamiento normal[6] en esta publicación:

Ingresos no tributarios:	tasas procesales, permisos de conducir, tasas portuarias, tasas por expedición de pasaportes, licencias de radio y televisión cuando las autoridades públicas proporcionan el servicio de difusión.

Impuestos de la partida 5200: permiso para realizar actividades tales como distribución cinematográfica; caza, pesca o tiro; suministro de instalaciones para actividades recreativas o de ocio o juegos de azar; venta de bebidas alcohólicas o tabaco; posesión de animales domésticos o uso de vehículos automotores; derechos sobre la extracción.

14. En la práctica, puede que no siempre resulte posible aislar las entradas tributarias de las no tributarias cuando estas se registran conjuntamente. En ese caso, si se considera que la mayoría de las entradas proviene de ingresos no tributarios, se tratará el importe total como tal; de lo contrario, esas entradas del gobierno se incluirán y clasificarán según las normas recogidas en el § 27.

Regalías

15. La propiedad de los activos del subsuelo en forma de depósitos de minerales o combustibles fósiles (carbón, petróleo o gas natural) depende de la forma en que los derechos de propiedad están definidos por la ley y también de los acuerdos internacionales en el caso de depósitos bajo aguas internacionales. En algunos casos, ya sea en el terreno por debajo del cual se encuentran los depósitos minerales, los depósitos en sí o ambos pueden pertenecer a una unidad del gobierno local o central.

16. En tales casos, estas unidades del gobierno general pueden otorgar arrendamientos a otras unidades institucionales que les permitan extraer estos depósitos durante un período de tiempo específico a cambio de un pago o una serie de pagos. Estos pagos a menudo se describen como "regalías", pero son esencialmente rentas que se acumulan a los propietarios de los recursos naturales a cambio de poner estos activos a disposición de otros agentes durante períodos de tiempo específicos. El alquiler puede tomar la forma de pagos periódicos de cantidades fijas, independientemente de la tasa de extracción, o, más comúnmente, pueden ser una función de la cantidad, el volumen o el valor del activo extraído. Las empresas dedicadas a la exploración en tierras del gobierno pueden hacer pagos a las unidades del gobierno general a cambio del derecho a realizar perforaciones de prueba o investigar de otro modo la existencia y ubicación de los activos del subsuelo. Dichos pagos también se registran como rentas aunque no se realice ninguna extracción. Por lo tanto, estos pagos se clasifican como ingresos no tributarios.

17. Los mismos principios se aplican cuando a otras unidades institucionales se les conceden arrendamientos que les permiten talar madera en bosques naturales en tierras que son propiedad de unidades del gobierno general. Estos pagos también se clasifican como ingresos no tributarios.

18. Estas rentas o regalías pagadas al gobierno general no deben confundirse con los impuestos sobre los ingresos y las ganancias, los impuestos sobre la extracción de recursos naturales, las licencias comerciales u otros impuestos. Si los pagos se aplican a las ganancias de la actividad de extracción, entonces deben clasificarse como impuestos sobre ingresos, utilidades y ganancias (1000). Además, cualquier pago que se imponga a la extracción de minerales y combustibles fósiles de las reservas de propiedad privada o de otro gobierno se debe clasificar como impuestos. Los pagos relacionados con el valor bruto de la producción deben clasificarse como otros impuestos sobre bienes y servicios (5128). Los pagos de una licencia o permiso para realizar operaciones de extracción se deben clasificar como impuestos sobre el uso de bienes y sobre el permiso para usar bienes o realizar actividades (5213).

Multas y sanciones pecuniarias

19. En principio, las multas y sanciones pecuniarias impuestas por el pago tardío de los impuestos o por el intento de evasión de los impuestos no deben registrarse como ingresos tributarios. Sin embargo, en ocasiones no es posible distinguir y separar los pagos por multas y penalidades del recaudo del impuesto a los que estos están relacionados. En este caso, las multas y sanciones pecuniarias vinculadas a un determinado impuesto se registran con los ingresos de ese impuesto. Las multas y penalidades pagadas sobre el recaudo de impuestos no identificados se clasifican como otros impuestos en la partida 6000. Las multas que no están relacionadas con delitos tributarios (por ejemplo, las infracciones por estacionamiento indebido), o que no puedan ser identificadas como ofensas tributarias, no serán tratadas como ingresos tributarios.

A.3. Principios de registro

Criterio de devengo

20. Los datos recogidos en esta publicación relativos a los últimos años se han registrado predominantemente según el criterio de devengo, esto es, se han computado en el momento en que nace la obligación. Se ofrece más información al respecto en las notas que figuran al pie de los cuadros de países en el Capítulo 4 del informe.

21. Sin embargo, los datos relativos a años anteriores han seguido registrándose principalmente según el criterio de caja, es decir, en el momento en que el gobierno recibió el pago. Por lo tanto, por ejemplo, los impuestos descontados por los empleadores en un año pero pagados al gobierno al año siguiente y los impuestos debidos un año pero liquidados el año después constan ambos en las entradas del segundo año. Las transacciones correctoras, tales como devoluciones, reembolsos y reintegros, se deducen de los ingresos brutos del periodo en que se realizan.

22. Los datos sobre ingresos tributarios se registran sin deducción de los gastos administrativos propios de la recaudación impositiva. De igual modo, cuando los recursos generados por un impuesto se emplean para subvencionar a miembros particulares de la comunidad, el subsidio no se descuenta del producto impositivo, aunque puede que el impuesto aparezca sin los subsidios en los registros nacionales de algunos países.

23. En lo que a los monopolios fiscales se refiere (5122), únicamente se incluye en los ingresos del gobierno el importe realmente transferido a este. Sin embargo, si cualquier gasto de los monopolios fiscales se considera gasto del gobierno (p. ej., gastos sociales emprendidos por los monopolios fiscales en beneficio del gobierno), se añadirán posteriormente con el fin de llegar a cifras de ingreso tributario (véase el § 65 *infra.*).

Distinción entre disposiciones tributarias y disposiciones relativas al gasto[7]

24. Dado que la presente publicación aborda únicamente la actividad del gobierno desde el punto de vista del ingreso, sin tener en cuenta los aspectos relacionados con el gasto, resulta preciso realizar una distinción entre las disposiciones que rigen estos dos elementos. Por lo general, no existe dificultad alguna en diferenciar ambos aspectos, ya que los gastos operan en un ámbito externo al sistema tributario y sus cuentas, y se rigen por una legislación separada de la impositiva. En los casos de difícil delimitación, se emplea el flujo de caja para distinguir entre disposiciones tributarias y disposiciones relativas al gasto. En la medida en que una disposición incida en el flujo de pagos tributarios del contribuyente al gobierno, se entenderá que reviste un carácter tributario y se tendrá en cuenta en los datos recogidos en

esta publicación. Cualquier disposición que no afecte a ese flujo se reputará como relativa al gasto y no se tendrá en consideración en la información plasmada en la publicación.

25. Las desgravaciones, exenciones y deducciones tributarias sobre la base imponible afectan claramente a la cantidad transferida al gobierno y, por ende, se consideran disposiciones de naturaleza tributaria. En el extremo opuesto, los subsidios o exoneraciones que no compensen la obligación tributaria y que estén claramente desvinculados del proceso de evaluación, no reducen los ingresos tributarios consignados en esta publicación. De particular interés en este ámbito resultan los créditos fiscales, que son cantidades deducibles del impuesto liquidable (lo que los diferencia de las deducciones sobre la base imponible). Cabe distinguir dos tipos de créditos fiscales: los créditos fiscales no exigibles (a veces denominados desaprovechables), limitados al importe de la obligación tributaria y que, por ende, no pueden generar un pago de las autoridades al contribuyente; y los créditos fiscales exigibles (o no desaprovechables), que no están sometidos a dicho límite, de forma que toda cantidad que exceda la obligación tributaria puede abonarse al contribuyente.[8] Al igual que las desgravaciones, un crédito fiscal no exigible afecta claramente a la cantidad transferida al gobierno y, por ende, se considerará como tributario. La práctica seguida para los créditos fiscales exigibles[9] consiste en distinguir entre "el componente de gasto tributario"[10] que es la porción del crédito empleada en reducir o eliminar la obligación del contribuyente" y el "componente de transferencia", constituido por la parte que excede la obligación del contribuyente y que se paga a este. Al registrar los ingresos tributarios deberá restarse la parte equivalente al componente de gasto tributario, pero no la correspondiente al componente de transferencia. Además, las cantidades de ambos componentes deberán figurar como partidas informativas en los cuadros de países. Los países que no puedan diferenciar entre estos dos componentes deberán indicar si se ha restado de los ingresos tributarios el total de ellos y presentar las evaluaciones disponibles del valor que ambos representan. Para mayor información, consúltese el Capítulo 1 de la publicación *Revenue Statistics* de la OCDE, que examina el efecto de los diversos tratamientos de los créditos fiscales exigibles en la relación impuestos sobre PIB.

Calendario y ejercicio fiscal

26. Las autoridades nacionales cuyos ejercicios fiscales no coinciden con el año calendario deben presentar los datos, siempre que sea posible, sobre la base del año calendario, a fin de permitir el mayor grado posible de comparación con la información de otros países. Subsisten algunos países en los que los datos hacen referencia a los ejercicios fiscales; para ellos, los datos relativos al PIB utilizados en los cuadros comparativos corresponden igualmente a los ejercicios fiscales.

A.4. Criterios generales de clasificación

Principales criterios de clasificación

27. El desglose de las entradas fiscales en las diversas categorías (1000, 2000, 3000, 4000, 5000 y 6000) se rige en general por la base sobre la cual recae el impuesto: 1000, renta, utilidades y ganancias de capital; 2000 y 3000, remuneraciones, nómina o número de empleados (fuerza de trabajo); 4000, propiedad; 5000, bienes y servicios; 6000, bases múltiples, otras bases o bases no identificables. Cuando un impuesto se calcula sobre más de una base, las entradas que genera se distribuyen, en la medida de lo posible, entre las diversas categorías (véanse los §§ 32 y 81). Las categorías 4000 y 5000 no sólo cubren aquellos impuestos en los que la base tributaria está constituida por la propiedad, los bienes o los servicios en sí mismos,

sino también ciertos impuestos afines; y así, por ejemplo, los impuestos sobre transmisiones patrimoniales se incluyen en la partida 4400,[11] y los impuestos sobre el uso de bienes y sobre el permiso para realizar actividades, en la 5200. En las categorías 4000 y 5000, se distingue en ocasiones entre impuestos recurrentes y no recurrentes: son impuestos recurrentes los que se recaudan a intervalos regulares (por lo general, anualmente), y no recurrentes, los que se imponen una sola vez (véanse los § 47-§50, §53–§54 y §79 para profundizar en las aplicaciones particulares de esta distinción).

28. La asignación de un impuesto a fines específicos no afecta a la clasificación de las entradas fiscales que genera. Sin embargo, tal y como se explica en el § 39 en relación con la clasificación de las contribuciones a la seguridad social, el hecho de que estas confieran un derecho a recibir prestaciones sociales es decisivo para la definición de la categoría 2000.

29. La forma en que se establece o recauda un impuesto (p.ej., mediante el uso de timbres) no afecta a su clasificación.

Clasificación de los contribuyentes

30. En ocasiones, se distingue entre diversas clases de contribuyentes. Esas distinciones dependen de cada impuesto.

a. *Entre personas físicas y sociedades en relación con los impuestos sobre la renta y sobre la riqueza neta*

La distinción básica aquí es que los impuestos sobre la renta de las sociedades (impuesto de sociedades), a diferencia de los impuestos sobre la renta de las personas físicas, gravan a la sociedad como entidad y no a sus propietarios, independientemente de las circunstancias personales de estos; la misma distinción se aplica a los impuestos sobre la riqueza neta de las sociedades y de las personas físicas. Los impuestos liquidados sobre las utilidades de las asociaciones y sobre la renta de las instituciones, tales como seguros de vida o fondos de pensiones, se clasifican siguiendo la misma regla, y así, se considerarán impuestos sobre las sociedades (1200) si se cargan a la asociación o institución como persona jurídica sin tener en cuenta las circunstancias personales de sus propietarios, o impuestos sobre las personas físicas en el caso contrario (1100). Por lo general, los impuestos aplicados a las sociedades y a las personas físicas se rigen por legislaciones diferentes.[12] La distinción realizada aquí entre personas físicas y sociedades no sigue la categorización por sectores entre hogares, empresas, etcétera, del Sistema de Cuentas Nacionales para las cuentas de ingresos y desembolsos. La clasificación del SCN requiere que ciertas empresas no constituidas en sociedad[13] se excluyan del sector de los hogares y vengan a sumarse a las empresas no financieras y las instituciones financieras. Sin embargo, el impuesto sobre las utilidades de esos negocios no siempre puede separarse del impuesto sobre la renta de sus propietarios o, como mucho, puede deslindarse sólo arbitrariamente. Por ello, no se ha intentado reproducir aquí esa separación, y la totalidad del impuesto sobre la renta de las personas físicas se ha recogido en un solo bloque, independientemente de la naturaleza del ingreso imponible.

b. *Entre hogares y otros en relación con los impuestos sobre la propiedad inmueble*

Esta distinción es la misma que la adoptada por el SCN para las cuentas de gasto del consumo final de los hogares y de producción. Se trata pues de diferenciar a los hogares como consumidores (esto es, excluidas las empresas no constituidas en sociedad), por una parte, y a los productores, por otra. Los impuestos sobre las viviendas ocupadas por los hogares, tanto a cargo de los propietarios-ocupantes como de los arrendatarios o de los arrendadores, se incluyen en los hogares, lo que coincide con la diferenciación que suele hacerse comúnmente entre los impuestos sobre la propiedad doméstica y los impuestos sobre la propiedad empresarial. No obstante, algunos países no se hallan en situación de operar esta distinción.

c. *Entre hogares y otros en relación con las licencias de vehículos automotores*

Se distingue aquí entre los hogares como consumidores, por una parte, y los productores, por otra, al igual que en las cuentas de gasto del consumo final de los hogares y de producción del SCN.

d. *Entre empresas y otros en relación con los impuestos residuales (6000)*

La distinción es la misma que en c), esta vez, entre los productores, por una parte, y los hogares como consumidores, por otra. Los impuestos recogidos en la categoría 6000 bien porque gravan más de una base tributaria, o bien porque su base no entra dentro del ámbito de ninguna de las categorías anteriores pero es identificable como imponible sobre los productores, y no sobre los hogares, se incluyen en 'empresas'. El resto de los impuestos de la categoría 6000 se imputan a 'otros' o no identificables.

Recargos

31. Las entradas procedentes de recargos relacionados con impuestos particulares se clasifican por lo general en base al impuesto correspondiente, ya sea el recargo temporal o no. Pero si el recargo posee una característica que lo califica para ser clasificada en una categoría diferente de la lista de la OCDE, las entradas generadas por el recargo se recogen en dicha categoría, separadas de las del correspondiente impuesto.

Entradas tributarias no identificables y partidas residuales

32. En un cierto número de casos, no logra determinarse que los impuestos pertenezcan enteramente a una categoría o partida de la clasificación de la OCDE y, en esos casos, se aplican las siguientes pautas:

a. Se conoce la categoría, pero no la forma de distribuir las entradas entre las diversas subdivisiones: las entradas se clasifican en la correspondiente partida o subpartida residual (1300, 2400, 4520, 4600, 5130, 5300 o 6200).

b. Se sabe que la mayor parte de las entradas procedentes de un grupo de impuestos (normalmente, impuestos locales) proviene de impuestos de una categoría o una partida particulares, pero algunos de los impuestos del grupo cuya cuantía no puede determinarse con exactitud pueden clasificarse en otras categorías o partidas: las entradas se consignan en la categoría o partida a la que pertenezca la mayoría de ellas.

c. No puede identificarse ni la categoría ni la partida correspondiente al impuesto (normalmente, local): el impuesto se incorpora a la partida 6200, a menos que se conozca que se trata de un impuesto sobre las empresas, en cuyo caso se incluye en la partida 6100.

A.5. Comentarios sobre ítems de la lista

1000 – *Impuestos sobre la renta, las utilidades y las ganancias de capital*

33. Esta categoría cubre los impuestos aplicados a la renta o a las utilidades netas (esto es, la renta bruta menos las deducciones permitidas) de las personas físicas y las sociedades, así como los impuestos a los que se someten las ganancias de capital de esos mismos sujetos pasivos, y las ganancias obtenidas en juegos de azar.

34. Se incluyen en esta categoría:

a. los impuestos que gravan predominantemente la renta o las utilidades, aunque recaigan parcialmente sobre otras bases; los impuestos aplicados a varias bases que no sean mayoritariamente la renta o las utilidades se clasifican de acuerdo con los principios establecidos en los §§ 32 y 81;

b. los impuestos sobre la propiedad aplicados a un ingreso presunto o estimado como parte de un impuesto sobre la renta (véase el § 47(*a*), (*c*) y (*d*));

c. los pagos obligatorios al fondo de contribuciones de la seguridad social impuestos sobre la renta que no confieran un derecho a prestaciones sociales; si esas contribuciones otorgan derecho a prestaciones sociales, se incluyen en la categoría 2000 (véase el § 39);

d. el producto de los sistemas integrados de impuestos sobre la renta de régimen cedular se clasifican como un todo en esta categoría, aunque algunos de los impuestos cedulares puedan basarse en la renta bruta y no tener en cuenta las circunstancias personales del contribuyente.

35. La principal división de esta categoría se efectúa entre los gravámenes a personas físicas (1100) y aquellos a sociedades (1200). A su vez, en cada partida, se separa entre impuestos sobre la renta y las utilidades (1110 y 1210) e impuestos sobre las ganancias de capital (1120 y 1220). Si algunas entradas no pueden atribuirse pertinentemente a la partida 1100 o a la 1200, o si no puede realizarse esta distinción en la práctica (p. ej., por falta de datos fiables sobre los receptores de los pagos de los que se deducen los impuestos con retención en la fuente), las entradas se incorporan a la partida 1300 como "no clasificables".

Tratamiento de los créditos fiscales en los sistemas de imputación

36. En los sistemas de imputación del impuesto de sociedades, los accionistas están exentos, total o parcialmente, de responder en concepto del impuesto sobre la renta por los dividendos abonados por la compañía a partir de la renta o de las utilidades sometidas al impuesto de sociedades. En los países con este sistema,[14] una parte del impuesto sobre las utilidades de la sociedad está disponible para exonerar a los accionistas de su propia obligación tributaria. La exoneración del accionista reviste la forma de un crédito fiscal, cuyo importe puede ser inferior, igual o superior al pasivo tributario total del accionista. Si el crédito fiscal excede al pasivo tributario, puede que ese exceso sea pagadero al accionista. Dado que este tipo de crédito fiscal es parte integrante del sistema de imputación del impuesto sobre la renta de las sociedades, cualquier pago a los accionistas se trata como devolución tributaria, y no como gasto (compárese con el tratamiento de otros créditos fiscales descrito en el § 25).

37. Puesto que en los sistemas de imputación el crédito fiscal (incluso cuando excede la obligación tributaria) debe considerarse como disposición tributaria, se plantea la cuestión de determinar si deberá deducirse de las entradas en concepto de impuesto sobre la renta de las personas físicas (1110) o de las entradas atribuibles al impuesto sobre la renta de las sociedades (1210). En este informe, la cantidad total pagada a título del impuesto sobre la renta de las sociedades se recoge en la subpartida 1210, y el impuesto no imputado en la subpartida 1110. Por lo tanto, la cuantía total del crédito se resta de esta última subpartida, tanto si el crédito da lugar a una reducción de la obligación tributaria por renta personal, como si se realiza un reembolso porque el crédito fiscal excede el pasivo tributario por este concepto. (No obstante, si los créditos fiscales se deducen del impuesto de sociedades por dividendos repartidos a otras sociedades, las correspondientes cantidades se descuentan de las entradas registradas en la subpartida 1210.)

1120 y 1220 – *Impuestos sobre las ganancias de capital*

38. Como su nombre indica, estas subpartidas engloban los impuestos sobre las ganancias de capital, ya de las personas físicas (1120), ya de las sociedades (1220), siempre que las entradas procedentes de estos impuestos puedan identificarse por separado. Ese no es el caso en numerosos países, y las entradas de estos impuestos se clasifican junto con las del impuesto sobre la renta. La subpartida 1120 contiene asimismo los impuestos sobre las ganancias obtenidas en juegos de azar.

2000 – *Contribuciones a la seguridad social*

39. Entran en esta categoría todos los pagos obligatorios que confieran un derecho a recibir una prestación social futura (contingente). Esos pagos suelen estar asignados al financiamiento de prestaciones sociales y, a menudo, se pagan a las instituciones del gobierno general que proporcionan dichas prestaciones. Sin embargo, esa asignación no forma parte de la definición de las contribuciones a la seguridad social y no es necesaria para que un impuesto sea clasificado en esta categoría, pero, para que un impuesto se incluya aquí, sí será preciso que confiera un derecho. Y así, los gravámenes sobre la renta o la nómina asignados a los fondos de seguridad social pero que no confieran el derecho a recibir prestaciones sociales quedan excluidos de la presente categoría y se registran bien entre los impuestos sobre la renta de las personas físicas (1100), bien junto con los impuestos sobre la nómina y la fuerza de trabajo (3000). Los impuestos aplicados sobre otras bases, como los bienes y servicios, no se consignarán aquí aunque estén asignados a prestaciones de la seguridad social, sino que se catalogarán según sus respectivas bases, ya que por lo general no otorgarán derecho alguno a prestaciones sociales.

40. Entre otras, se incluirán aquí las contribuciones a los siguientes tipos de prestaciones de la seguridad social: prestaciones y suplementos por seguro de desempleo; prestaciones por accidente, lesión o enfermedad; pensiones por jubilación, invalidez y supervivencia; ayudas familiares; reembolsos de gastos médicos u hospitalarios o prestación de servicios médicos u hospitalarios. Las contribuciones pueden recaudarse tanto de los empleados como de los empleadores.

41. Las contribuciones pueden tener como base bien las remuneraciones o la nómina ('sobre la base de la nómina'), bien la renta neta tras deducciones y exenciones por circunstancias personales ('sobre la base del impuesto sobre la renta'), y el producto de ambas bases deberá identificarse separadamente en la medida de lo posible. Cuando las contribuciones al régimen general de la seguridad social se basen en la nómina, pero las de grupos particulares (tales como los trabajadores por cuenta propia) no puedan evaluarse en función de esta base y se emplee en ese caso la renta neta como una aproximación de las remuneraciones brutas, las entradas seguirán clasificándose sobre la base de la nómina. En principio, esta categoría excluye las contribuciones voluntarias aportadas a los regímenes de seguridad social, que, cuando sea posible identificarlas de forma separada, se recogerán en la partida informativa sobre el financiamiento de las prestaciones sociales; sin embargo, en la práctica, estas aportaciones no siempre pueden desvincularse de las contribuciones obligatorias, en cuyo caso se incluirán igualmente en esta categoría.

42. Las contribuciones a los regímenes de seguro social no vinculados a instituciones del gobierno general, así como las aportaciones a otros tipos de sistemas de seguro, tales como planes de previsión o planes de pensiones, mutualidades u otros planes de ahorro, no se consideran contribuciones a la seguridad social. Los planes de previsión son acuerdos por los que las contribuciones de cada empleado y la parte correspondiente del empleador en

nombre de aquél se conservan en una cuenta separada que genera interés, de la que pueden retirarse en circunstancias específicas. Por su parte, los planes de pensiones son regímenes organizados separadamente, negociados entres empleados y empleadores, que conllevan disposiciones sobre diversas contribuciones y prestaciones, a veces más directamente vinculadas a los niveles salariales y a la duración del servicio que en otros esquemas sociales. Cuando las contribuciones a esos regímenes son obligatorias o cuasiobligatorias (p. ej., en virtud de un acuerdo con sindicatos u organizaciones profesionales), se hacen constar en la partida informativa (véase el Capítulo 4.2 de este Reporte).

43 Las contribuciones de los empleados del gobierno y de este con respecto a sus empleados a los regímenes de seguridad social incluidos en el gobierno general se clasifican en esta categoría. También se consideran impuestos las contribuciones de los empleados del gobierno a regímenes diferentes que puedan reputarse sustitutivos de los regímenes generales de seguridad social.[15] Por el contrario, cuando un régimen diferente no pueda considerarse sustitutivo de uno general y haya sido negociado entre el gobierno, en su papel de empleador, y sus empleados, no se estimará como régimen de seguridad social y, por lo tanto, las contribuciones a él no se tendrán como impuestos, aunque el régimen haya sido instaurado por la legislación.

44. Esta categoría excluye las contribuciones 'imputadas', que corresponden a las prestaciones sociales pagadas directamente por los empleadores a sus empleados, antiguos empleados o personas a cargo de estos (p. ej., cuando los empleadores están legalmente obligados a correr con las prestaciones por enfermedad durante cierto tiempo).

45. Las contribuciones se dividen en tres partidas principales – empleados (2100), empleadores (2200) y trabajadores por cuenta propia o no empleados (2300) – y se subdividen posteriormente en función de la base que gravan. A efectos de la presente publicación, se entiende por empleados todas las personas contratadas en actividades de unidades empresariales, órganos gubernamentales, instituciones privadas sin ánimo de lucro u otro tipo de empleo remunerado, con excepción de los dueños de empresas no constituidas en sociedad y de los miembros no remunerados de sus familias. También se consideran empleados los miembros de las Fuerzas Armadas, independientemente de la duración y del tipo de su servicio, siempre que coticen a regímenes de la seguridad social. Por su parte, las contribuciones de los empleadores se definen como las aportaciones que estos realizan por cuenta de sus empleados a los sistemas de seguridad social. Si los empleados o los empleadores tienen la obligación de continuar cotizando a la seguridad social en el caso de desempleo de un empleado, esas contribuciones se muestran en las partidas 2100 y 2200, respectivamente, siempre que los datos lo permitan. En consecuencia, la partida 2300 queda reservada a las contribuciones abonadas por los trabajadores por cuenta propia y por quienes no se hallan incluidos en la población activa (p. ej., incapacitados o jubilados).

3000 – *Impuestos sobre la nómina y la fuerza de trabajo*

46. Consiste en los impuestos pagados por las firmas o empresas, ya sea como una proporción de los salarios o la nómina, ya como una cantidad fija por persona empleada. No incluyen pagos a la seguridad social obligatorios pagados por empleadores u otros impuestos pagados por los empleados mismos de sus salarios o remuneraciones.

4000 – *Impuestos sobre la propiedad*

47. Esta categoría engloba los impuestos, recurrentes y no recurrentes, sobre el uso, la titularidad o la transmisión de la propiedad, lo que incluye impuestos sobre la propiedad inmueble y la riqueza neta, sobre el cambio de titularidad en la propiedad por herencia o

donación, y sobre transacciones financieras y de capital. Quedan excluidas de esta categoría los siguientes tipos de impuestos:

a. los impuestos sobre las ganancias de capital procedentes de la venta de propiedad (1120 o 1220);
b. los impuestos sobre el uso de bienes y sobre el permiso para usar bienes o realizar actividades (5200): véase el § 76;
c. los impuestos sobre los bienes inmuebles gravados sobre la base de un ingreso neto presunto que tiene en cuenta las circunstancias personales del contribuyente: se clasifican como impuestos sobre la renta junto con los impuestos sobre la renta y sobre las ganancias de capital derivadas de la propiedad (1100);
d. los impuestos sobre el uso de la propiedad con fines residenciales, tanto si debe responder del impuesto el propietario como el arrendatario, siempre que la cantidad debida tenga en cuenta las circunstancias personales del usuario (ingresos, personas a cargo, etcétera): se integran en los impuestos sobre la renta (1100);
e. los impuestos sobre los edificios con una densidad máxima superior a la permitida; sobre la ampliación, construcción o modificación de ciertos edificios más allá de un valor umbral; y sobre la construcción de edificios: todos ellos se integran en los impuestos sobre el permiso para realizar actividades (5200);
f. los impuestos sobre el uso de la propiedad propia para fines comerciales especiales, tales como la venta de bebidas alcohólicas, tabaco o carne, o para la explotación de tierras (p. ej., impuestos sobre la extracción en Estados Unidos): se integran en los impuestos sobre el permiso para realizar actividades (5200).

4100 – *Impuestos recurrentes sobre la propiedad inmueble*

48. Esta partida comprende los impuestos con que se grava de forma regular el uso o la titularidad de bienes inmuebles.

- Estos impuestos gravan las tierras y los edificios.
- Pueden consistir en un porcentaje del valor tasado de una propiedad, basado a su vez en un ingreso por alquiler hipotético, en el precio de venta, en un rendimiento capitalizado o en otras características de la propiedad inmueble (por ejemplo, el tamaño o la ubicación) de las que quepa inferir un alquiler o un valor de capital hipotéticos.
- Estos impuestos pueden aplicarse a los propietarios, a los arrendatarios o a ambos. También pueden pagarse de un nivel de gobierno a otro en relación con los bienes bajo jurisdicción de este último.
- Para la evaluación de estos impuestos, no se tienen en cuenta las deudas y, en ese sentido, difieren de los impuestos sobre la riqueza neta.

49. Los impuestos recurrentes sobre la propiedad inmueble se subdividen a su vez en los pagados por los hogares (4110) y los abonados por otros sujetos pasivos (4120), de acuerdo con los criterios establecidos en el § 30(*b*) *supra*.

4200 – *Impuestos recurrentes sobre la riqueza neta*

50. Esta partida abarca los impuestos con que se grava periódicamente (por lo general, anualmente) la riqueza neta, esto es, los impuestos sobre un amplio abanico de bienes muebles e inmuebles, descontadas sus deudas. Esta partida se subdivide a su vez en los impuestos pagados por las personas físicas (4210) y los abonados por las sociedades (4220),

de acuerdo con los criterios establecidos en el § 30(*a*) *supra*. Si existen cifras separadas para las entradas correspondientes a pagos realizados por instituciones, se añaden a la subpartida de las sociedades.

4300 – *Impuestos sobre sucesiones, herencias y donaciones*

51. Esta partida se divide entre impuestos sobre sucesiones o herencias (4310) e impuestos sobre donaciones (4320).[16] Los impuestos sobre sucesiones gravan el valor total de la sucesión o del caudal hereditario, mientras los impuestos sobre herencias se aplican a las cuotas recibidas por los causahabientes individualmente considerados o en función de la relación de estos con el difunto.

4400 – *Impuestos sobre transacciones financieras y de capital*

52. Esta partida incluye, entre otros, los impuestos sobre la emisión, transmisión, compra y venta de valores, sobre los cheques, y sobre transacciones legales específicas, tales como la validación de contratos o la venta de bienes inmuebles. La partida no incluye:

a. los impuestos sobre el uso de bienes y sobre el permiso para realizar ciertas actividades (5200);
b. las tasas abonadas en concepto de costos procesales o expedición de actas de nacimiento, matrimonio o defunción, que suelen considerarse como ingresos no tributarios (véase el § 11);
c. los impuestos sobre ganancias de capital (1000);
d. los impuestos recurrentes sobre la propiedad inmueble (4100);
e. los impuestos recurrentes sobre la riqueza neta (4200);
f. otros impuestos no recurrentes sobre la propiedad o la riqueza (4500).

4500 – *Otros impuestos no recurrentes sobre la propiedad*[16]

53. Esta partida cubre los gravámenes sobre la propiedad que, a diferencia de los impuestos recurrentes, se recaudan una sola vez. Se divide en impuestos no recurrentes sobre la riqueza neta (4510) y otros impuestos no recurrentes sobre la propiedad (4520). La subpartida 4510 contiene los impuestos que se recaudan a fin de hacer frente a gastos excepcionales o de redistribuir la riqueza. Por su parte, la subpartida 4520 comprende los impuestos que gravan los incrementos de valor de la tierra, debido, por ejemplo, a permisos para su desarrollo concedidos por el gobierno general o a la provisión por parte de este de instalaciones locales adicionales; cualesquiera impuestos sobre la reevaluación del capital; y aquellos impuestos gravados una sola vez sobre determinados tipos de propiedad.

4600 – *Otros impuestos recurrentes sobre la propiedad*

54. Aunque este tipo de impuestos rara vez se dan en los países miembros de la OCDE, esta partida incluye los impuestos sobre bienes tales como ganado bovino, joyas, ventanas y otros signos externos de riqueza.

5000 – *Impuestos sobre los bienes y servicios*

55. Se incluyen en esta categoría todos los impuestos y derechos sobre la producción, extracción, venta, transmisión, arrendamiento y entrega de bienes, así como sobre la prestación de servicios (5100), y también los impuestos aplicados al uso de bienes y al permiso para usar bienes o realizar actividades (5200). Por lo tanto, esta categoría comprende:

a. los impuestos acumulativos de etapas múltiples;
b. los impuestos generales sobre las ventas aplicados, ya sea en la fabricación/producción, ya sea en la venta al por mayor o al por menor;

c. los impuestos sobre el valor agregado;
d. los impuestos selectivos;
e. los impuestos sobre las importaciones y exportaciones de bienes;
f. los impuestos sobre el uso de bienes y sobre el permiso para usar bienes o realizar ciertas actividades;
g. los impuestos sobre la extracción, el procesamiento o la producción de minerales y otros productos.

56. Los casos de difícil delimitación entre esta categoría y la categoría 4000 (impuestos sobre la propiedad) o la partida 6100 (otros impuestos pagados únicamente por empresas) se tratan en los § 47, §52 y §78. La partida 5300 y la subpartida 5130, ambas residuales, incluyen, respectivamente, las entradas tributarias que no hayan podido clasificarse entre las partidas 5100 y 5200 o entre las subpartidas 5110 y 5120, respectivamente, veáse §32.

5100 – *Impuestos sobre la producción, venta, transmisión, arrendamiento y entrega de bienes, y la prestación de servicios*

57. Esta partida comprende todos los impuestos aplicados a transacciones de bienes y servicios por las características intrínsecas de estos (p. ej., valor, peso del tabaco, graduación de las bebidas alcohólicas, etcétera) a diferencia de los impuestos determinados por el uso de bienes o por el permiso para usar bienes o realizar actividades, que entran dentro del ámbito de la partida 5200.

5110 – *Impuestos generales*

58. En esta subpartida, se incluyen todos los impuestos, aparte de los derechos de importación y exportación (5123 y 5124, respectivamente), que gravan la producción, el arrendamiento, la transmisión, la entrega o la venta de un amplio abanico de bienes o la prestación de una gran variedad de servicios, independientemente de que sean de producción nacional o importados, o de la etapa de producción o de distribución en la que recaigan. Por ende, comprende los impuestos sobre el valor agregado, los impuestos sobre las ventas y los impuestos acumulativos de etapas múltiples. A las entradas brutas generadas, se añaden las entradas por ajustes fronterizos en concepto de esos impuestos cuando se importan bienes, y se restan las devoluciones de dichos impuestos cuando se exportan bienes. Esta subpartida se divide a su vez en los epígrafes 5111, impuestos sobre el valor agregado; 5112, impuestos sobre las ventas; y 5113, otros impuestos generales sobre los ingresos brutos y sobre bienes y servicios.

59. Suelen plantearse dificultades de delimitación entre esta subpartida y la dedicada a los impuestos sobre bienes y servicios específicos (5120) cuando los impuestos se aplican a un gran número de bienes, como, por ejemplo, en el caso del impuesto sobre las compras del Reino Unido (abolido en 1973) o el impuesto sobre mercancías de Japón (abolido en 1988). De acuerdo con las respectivas perspectivas nacionales, el antiguo impuesto sobre las compras británico se ha clasificado como impuesto general (5112), mientras el desaparecido impuesto sobre mercancías japonés se ha incluido entre los impuestos selectivos (5121).

5111 – *Impuestos sobre el valor agregado*

60. Todos los impuestos generales al consumo cargados sobre el valor agregado entran dentro de este epígrafe, independientemente del método de deducción y de las etapas en las que recaiga el impuesto. En la práctica, todos los países de la OCDE con este tipo de impuestos permiten que todos los intermediarios, excepto el consumidor final, se deduzcan inmediatamente los impuestos sobre las compras e imponen tributación en todas las etapas.

Para algunos países, puede que se incluyan en este epígrafe otros impuestos, tales como los aplicados sobre actividades financieras y de seguros, o bien porque las entradas que generan no pueden identificarse separadamente de las procedentes del impuesto sobre el valor agregado, o bien porque se considera que forman parte de este último, aunque esos mismos impuestos puedan clasificarse diferentemente en terceros países (p. ej., como impuestos sobre servicios específicos (5126) o impuestos sobre transacciones financieras y de capital (4400).

5112 – *Impuestos sobre las ventas*

61. Se clasifican aquí todos los impuestos generales aplicados a una sola etapa, ya sea en la fabricación/producción, o en la venta al por mayor o al por menor.

5113 – *Otros impuestos generales sobre los ingresos brutos y sobre bienes y servicios*

62. Estos son impuestos acumulativos de etapas múltiplese impuestos en los que el impuesto al consumo se combina con otros impuestos multifásicos. Estos impuestos se aplican cada vez que se realiza una transacción sin deducción del valor de los impuestos pagados sobre los insumos. Los impuestos multifásicos pueden combinarse con elementos de los impuestos sobre el valor agregado o sobre las ventas.

5120 – *Impuestos sobre bienes y servicios específicos*

63. Se incluyen en esta subpartida los impuestos selectivos, las utilidades generadas y transferidas por los monopolios fiscales, y los derechos de aduana y otros derechos de importación, así como los impuestos sobre las exportaciones, las transacciones de divisas, los bienes de inversión y las apuestas, y los impuestos especiales sobre los servicios que no formen parte de uno de los impuestos generales de la subpartida 5110.

5121 – *Impuestos selectivos*

64. Los impuestos selectivos gravan la unidad de un producto específico de una gama predefinida y limitada de bienes. Los impuestos generalmente se aplican a tasas diferenciadas sobre bienes no esenciales o de lujo, bebidas alcohólicas, tabaco y la energía. Los selectivos pueden imponerse en cualquier etapa de la producción o distribución y generalmente se aplican como un cargo específico por unidad en función de las características del bien con referencia al valor, peso, intensidad o cantidad del producto. Se incluyen impuestos especiales sobre productos como el azúcar, la remolacha azucarera, fósforos y chocolates; e impuestos que gravan a tasas variables una cierta gama de bienes; e impuestos aplicados a los productos de tabaco, bebidas alcohólicas, combustibles para motores e hidrocarburos. Si un impuesto recaudado principalmente sobre bienes importados también se aplica, o se aplicaría, bajo la misma ley a bienes comparables de producción nacional, entonces los ingresos de este impuesto se clasifican como impuestos selectivos más que de derechos de importación. Este principio se aplica incluso si no hay producción nacional comparable o no hay posibilidad de tal producción. Los impuestos sobre el uso de servicios como agua, electricidad, gas y energía se consideran como impuestos selectivos más que impuestos sobre servicios específicos (5126). Los selectivos no incluyen los gravámenes que se aplican como impuestos generales sobre bienes y servicios (5110); beneficios de los monopolios fiscales (5122); derechos de aduana y otros derechos de importación (5123); o impuestos a las exportaciones (5124).

5122 – *Utilidades de los monopolios fiscales*

65. Este epígrafe comprende la parte de las utilidades de los monopolios fiscales transferida al gobierno general o usada para financiar gastos considerados como gastos del gobierno (véase el § 23). Las cantidades implicadas se registran cuando se transfieren al gobierno general o cuando se usan para gastos considerados como gastos del gobierno.

66. Los monopolios fiscales reflejan el ejercicio del poder tributario del gobierno mediante el uso de prerrogativas monopolísticas. Se trata de empresas públicas no financieras que ejercen un monopolio, en la mayoría de los casos sobre la producción o la distribución de tabaco, bebidas alcohólicas, sal, fósforos, cartas de juego, productos derivados del petróleo y productos agrícolas (es decir, sobre el tipo de productos susceptibles de estar sometidos, alternativa o adicionalmente, a los impuestos selectivos del epígrafe 5121), con el fin de recaudar ingresos para el gobierno que en otros países se obtienen gravando las operaciones que sobre dichos bienes efectúan las unidades empresariales privadas. El monopolio del gobierno puede intervenir en la etapa de producción o, en el caso de los establecimientos de licores propiedad del gobierno o bajo control de éste, en la etapa de distribución.

67. Cabe distinguir los monopolios fiscales de los servicios públicos, tales como el transporte ferroviario, la electricidad, los servicios de correos y otras comunicaciones, que pueden gozar también de una posición monopolística o cuasi-monopolística, pero cuyo fin primero suele ser la prestación de servicios básicos y no la obtención de ingresos para el gobierno; las transferencias de esas otras empresas públicas al gobierno se consideran ingresos no tributarios. Generalmente, el concepto tradicional de monopolio fiscal no abarca a las loterías estatales, cuyas utilidades usualmente se consideran, en consecuencia, ingresos no tributarios. No obstante, se pueden considerar como ingresos tributarios si su función principal es la de recaudar para financiar gasto gubernamental. Las utilidades de los monopolios fiscales se han separado de las de los monopolios de importación y exportación (5127) transferidas de juntas de comercialización u otras empresas dedicadas al comercio internacional.

5123 – *Derechos de aduana y otros derechos de importación*

68. Se incluyen aquí los impuestos, derechos de timbre y sobrecargas limitados por ley a los productos importados, así como los gravámenes sobre los productos agrícolas importados impuestos en los países miembros de la Unión Europea y las cantidades satisfechas por algunos de esos países a tenor del sistema de montantes compensatorios monetarios (MCM).[17] Desde 1998, los derechos de aduana recaudados por los Estados miembros de la Unión Europea en nombre de ésta ya no se registran en este epígrafe en los cuadros de países (Capítulo 4 de la publicación *Revenue Statistics* de la OCDE). Quedan excluidos aquí los impuestos recaudados de las importaciones como parte de un impuesto general sobre los bienes y servicios, así como los impuestos selectivos aplicables tanto a bienes importados como a bienes de producción nacional.

5124 – *Impuestos sobre las exportaciones*

69. En los años 1970, los derechos de exportación se aplicaban en Australia, Canadá y Portugal como una medida de carácter regular, y en Finlandia se han utilizado con fines contracíclicos. Algunos países miembros de la Unión Europea pagan un gravamen sobre las exportaciones, en el marco del sistema MCM (véase la nota a pie de página §16 en el § 68). Cuando las cantidades recaudadas son identificables, se integran en este epígrafe, que no incluye, sin embargo, las devoluciones de impuestos generales al consumo, de impuestos selectivos o de derechos de aduana sobre los bienes exportados, que se deducirán de las entradas brutas de 5110, 5121 o 5123, según corresponda.

5125 – *Impuestos sobre los bienes de inversión*

70. Este epígrafe cubre los impuestos sobre los bienes de inversión, tales como la maquinaria. Estos impuestos pueden cargarse por un cierto número de años o temporalmente con fines contracíclicos. No se incluyen aquí aquellos impuestos sobre los insumos industriales que

recaen también en los consumidores (p. ej., el impuesto sobre la energía en Suecia, que se clasifica en 5121).

5126 – *Impuestos sobre servicios específicos*

71. Todos los impuestos sobre el pago por servicios específicos, tales como los impuestos sobre las primas de seguro, los servicios bancarios, los juegos de azar y las apuestas (p. ej., carreras de caballos, quinielas de fútbol, lotería), el transporte, las actividades recreativas o de ocio, los restaurantes y la publicidad, entran dentro de este epígrafe. También se clasifican aquí los impuestos sobre el ingreso bruto de las empresas que prestan el servicio (p. ej., primas de seguro o apuestas brutas recibidas por una empresa). Los ingresos tributarios procedentes de gravámenes bancarios y pagos a sistemas de seguro de depósitos y de estabilidad financiera se han incluido provisionalmente en este epígrafe para la edición de 2012. La clasificación detallada figura en § 108.

72. Se excluyen de este epígrafe:

a. los impuestos sobre servicios que formen parte de un impuesto general sobre los bienes y servicios (5110);

b. los impuestos sobre la electricidad, el gas y la energía (5121, impuestos selectivos);

c. los impuestos sobre las ganancias de las personas físicas en los juegos de azar (1120, impuestos sobre las ganancias de capital de las personas físicas o de las empresas no constituidas en sociedad) y los impuestos fijos sobre la transferencia de loterías privadas o sobre el permiso para crear loterías (5200);[18]

d. los impuestos sobre los cheques y sobre la emisión, transmisión o compra y venta de valores (4400, impuestos sobre transacciones financieras y de capital).

5127 – *Otros impuestos sobre el comercio y las transacciones internacionales*

73. Este epígrafe abarca los ingresos percibidos por el gobierno por la compra y la venta de divisas a diferentes tipos de cambio. Cuando el gobierno ejerce poderes monopolísticos para obtener un margen entre los precios de compra y de venta de divisas superior al que sería necesario para cubrir los costos administrativos, el ingreso generado constituye un gravamen obligatorio impuesto en proporciones indeterminadas tanto sobre el comprador como sobre el vendedor de divisas. Es un equivalente común de los derechos de importación y exportación cargados en un sistema con tipo de cambio único o de un impuesto sobre la compraventa de divisas. Al igual que las utilidades de los monopolios fiscales o de los monopolios de importación y exportación transferidas al gobierno, representa el ejercicio de las prerrogativas monopolísticas con fines fiscales y, por lo tanto, se incluye en los ingresos tributarios.

74. El epígrafe engloba asimismo las utilidades de los monopolios de importación y exportación, que, sin embargo, son inexistentes en los países de la OCDE; los impuestos sobre la compraventa de divisas; y cualesquiera otros impuestos que recaigan sobre el comercio o las transacciones internacionales.

5128 – *Otros impuestos sobre bienes y servicios específicos*

75. Este epígrafe incluye los impuestos sobre la extracción de minerales, combustibles fósiles y otros recursos agotables de yacimientos de propieddad privada o de otro nivel de gobierno, así como cualesquiera otras entradas no identificables procedentes de impuestos sobre bienes y servicios específicos. Los impuestos sobre la extracción de recursos agotables suelen traducirse en un importe fijo por cantidad o peso, pero también pueden adoptar un valor porcentual. Los impuestos se registran en el momento de extracción de los recursos.

Los pagos por extracción de recursos agotables de yacimientos propiedad de la unidad de gobierno que recibe el pago se clasifican como alquiler.

5200 – *Impuestos sobre el uso de bienes y sobre el permiso para usar bienes o realizar actividades*

76. Esta partida incluye los impuestos aplicados al uso de bienes a diferencia de los impuestos sobre los propios bienes. Al contrario que los impuestos de este último tipo (registrados en la partida 5100), los impuestos considerados aquí no se basan en el valor de los bienes, sino que suelen revestir la forma de importes fijos. Los impuestos sobre el permiso para usar bienes o realizar actividades entran asimismo en esta partida, como, por ejemplo, los impuestos sobre la contaminación que no se basan en el valor de bienes particulares. En ocasiones, resulta complejo distinguir entre cargos obligatorios a los usuarios y tasas de licencia que se consideran como impuestos y aquellos que quedan excluidos por reputarse como ingresos no tributarios; los criterios de deslinde empleados se explican en los § 11 y §12.

77. Aunque el título de esta partida menciona el "uso" de bienes, es posible que sea el registro de la propiedad, y no el uso, lo que dé lugar a la obligación tributaria, y que los impuestos contenidos aquí se apliquen más al hecho de ser titular de ciertos animales o bienes (p. ej., caballos de carreras, perros y vehículos automotores) que al uso que se hace de ellos, o que recaigan incluso en bienes inutilizables (p. ej., vehículos automotores o armas inservibles).

78. Se plantean casos de difícil delimitación con respecto a:

a. los impuestos sobre el permiso para realizar actividades empresariales que parten de una base combinada de renta, nómina o volumen de ventas, que se clasifican de acuerdo con las normas del § 81;

b. los impuestos sobre la propiedad o el uso de la propiedad de las partidas 4100, 4200 y 4600; la partida 4100 se dedica exclusivamente a los impuestos sobre la titularidad o la posesión de bienes inmuebles y, a diferencia de los impuestos de la partida 5200, recaen siempre sobre el valor de la propiedad; los impuestos sobre la riqueza neta (4200) y otros impuestos recurrentes sobre la propiedad (4600) se circunscriben al hecho de ser titular de propiedades, y no al uso de activos; se aplican a grupos de activos, y no a bienes particulares; y están en todo caso relacionados con el valor de los activos en cuestión.

5210 – *Impuestos recurrentes*

79. La principal característica de los impuestos consignados aquí es que se recaudan a intervalos regulares y se cobran por lo general según una cantidad fija. En términos de ingresos, el elemento más importante está constituido por los impuestos por licencia de vehículos, aunque también integran esta subpartida los impuestos sobre los permisos de caza, pesca o tiro o sobre la venta de ciertos productos, así como los impuestos sobre la propiedad de animales domésticos y sobre la prestación de ciertos servicios siempre que estos reúnan los criterios establecidos en los § 11 y §12. Los epígrafes en que se divide la partida 5210 son: los impuestos sobre vehículos automotores pagados por los hogares (5211) y los satisfechos por otros sujetos pasivos (5212);[19] por su parte, el epígrafe 5213 abarca las licencias a propietarios de animales domésticos y los cargos a usuarios por el permiso de realizar actividades, tales como la venta de carne o de bebidas alcohólica cuando los gravámenes se imponen de forma recurrente, así como las licencias generales periódicas de caza, pesca y tiro cuando el derecho a emprender esas actividades no se otorga como parte de una transacción comercial normal (p. ej., la concesión de la licencia no implica el derecho a usar una zona específica propiedad del gobierno).

5220 – *Impuestos no recurrentes*

80. Se incluyen aquí los impuestos no recurrentes aplicados sobre el uso de bienes y sobre el permiso para utilizar bienes o realizar actividades, así como los impuestos aplicados cada vez que se utilizan los bienes.

- Entran en esta subpartida los impuestos sobre la emisión o liberación en el medio ambiente de gases y líquidos nocivos y otras sustancias peligrosas. Los pagos por permisos negociables de emisión expedidos por los gobiernos en el marco de programas de límites máximos y comercio de emisiones deberán registrarse aquí en la fecha en que se produzcan las emisiones. No se computarán ingresos por los permisos que los gobiernos expidan a título gratuito. El registro según el criterio de devengo implica que habrá una diferencia temporal entre el momento en que el gobierno reciba el pago por los permisos y el momento en que se produzca la emisión. En las cuentas nacionales, esta diferencia genera un pasivo para el gobierno durante ese periodo.
- Se excluirán los pagos efectuados por la recogida y eliminación de desechos o sustancias nocivas por parte de los poderes públicos, ya que constituyen una venta de servicios a las empresas.

81. También se incluyen aquí otros impuestos que entren dentro del ámbito de aplicación de la partida 5200 y que no se recauden recurrentemente. Por lo tanto, quedarán comprendidos los pagos únicos por permisos para la venta de alcohol o tabaco o para la creación de centros de apuestas, siempre que cumplan los criterios de los § 11–12.

6000 – *Otros impuestos*

82. Esta categoría recoge los impuestos que reposan en una o varias bases diferentes de las descritas en las categorías 1000, 3000, 4000 y 5000, o en bases que no puedan considerarse relacionadas a ninguna de estas categorías, se incluyen aquí. Los impuestos de base múltiple, y si es posible estimar las entradas relacionadas con cada base las cantidades desglosadas se repartirán en las correspondientes categorías de acuerdo a su base. Si no pueden calcularse los valores por separado y se sabe que la mayoría de las entradas proceden de una base determinada, el total de estas se atribuirán de acuerdo con dicha base. En caso contrario, las entradas se clasificarán aquí. Otros ingresos incluidos aquí son los impuestos presuntos no incluidos en el sistema de clasificación, los impuestos a las personas en forma de impuesto de capitación, impuestos de sellos no relacionados con las transacciones financieras y de capital que no pertenecen exclusivamente a una sola categoría de transacción, impuestos a los gastos donde se aplican deducciones o exenciones personales y recibos de impuestos no identificables. Esta categoría se subdivide entre los impuestos pagados completa o principalmente por las empresas (6100) y los abonados por otros sujetos pasivos (6200).

A.6. Conciliación con las cuentas nacionales

83. Esta sección de los cuadros reconcilia el cálculo de la recaudación tributaria total realizado por la OCDE y el total de todos los impuestos y contribuciones sociales pagados al gobierno general tal y como figuran en el registro de las cuentas nacionales de cada país. Cuando el país es miembro de la Unión Europea (UE), la comparación se establece entre el cálculo de la recaudación tributaria total realizado por la OCDE y la suma de los ingresos tributarios y contribuciones sociales registrado en la combinación del gobierno general y de las instituciones de los sectores de la UE de las cuentas nacionales.

A.7. Partida informativa sobre el financiamiento de las prestaciones sociales

84. A la vista de la variedad de relaciones entre la tributación y las contribuciones a la seguridad social y de los casos mencionados en los § 39 al §45, se ha previsto una partida informativa que recopile todos los pagos asignados a las prestaciones tipo de la seguridad social, aparte de los pagos voluntarios al sector privado. Los datos se presentan de la forma siguiente (véase el Capítulo 4.2 de este Reporte):

a. Impuestos de la categoría 2000.

b. Impuestos asignados a las prestaciones de la seguridad social.

c. Contribuciones voluntarias al gobierno.

d. Contribuciones obligatorias al sector privado.

Los § 39al §45 ofrecen las debidas orientaciones para efectuar el desglose entre las rúbricas (*a*) a (*d*).

A.8. Partida informativa sobre impuestos identificables pagados por el gobierno

85. Los impuestos identificables realmente pagados por el gobierno se presentan en una partida informativa, desglosados según las principales categorías de la clasificación de impuestos de la OCDE. En la vasta mayoría de los países, sólo pueden identificarse las contribuciones a la seguridad social y los impuestos sobre la nómina satisfechos por el gobierno, que, sin embargo, suelen ser los gravámenes más importantes liquidados por los gobiernos (véase el Capítulo 4.2 de este Reporte).

A.9. Relación de la clasificación de impuestos de la OCDE con el Sistema de Cuentas Nacionales

86. El Sistema de Cuentas Nacionales (SCN) pretende proporcionar un marco coherente para registrar y presentar los principales flujos relacionados con la producción, el consumo, la acumulación y las transacciones con el exterior de una determinada zona económica, por lo general, un país o una región destacada de un país, y, en este sentido, los ingresos del gobierno constituyen una importante parte de las transacciones registradas en todo sistema de cuentas nacionales. En agosto de 2009, la versión final del SCN 2008 se publicó conjuntamente por cinco organizaciones internacionales: la Organización de las Naciones Unidas, el Fondo Monetario Internacional, la Unión Europea, la Organización para la Cooperación y el Desarrollo Económicos, y el Banco Mundial. La publicación está diseñada para ser empleada en países con economías de mercado, sea cual sea su estadio de desarrollo económico, así como en países en transición hacia economías de mercado. Las principales partes del marco conceptual y las definiciones de los diversos sectores económicos del SCN se han plasmado en la clasificación de impuestos de la OCDE.

87. Sin embargo, existen ciertas diferencias, reseñadas seguidamente, entre la clasificación de impuestos de la OCDE y los conceptos del SCN, debidas a que la finalidad de la clasificación de la OCDE consiste en lograr la máxima desagregación posible de los datos estadísticos en relación con lo que, por lo general, las Administraciones tributarias consideran como impuestos. Y así:

a. la OCDE incluye las contribuciones a la seguridad social obligatorias, pagadas al gobierno general en la recaudación tributaria total. No se consideran como impuestos las contribuciones imputadas y voluntarias, además de aquellas pagadas a fondos privados (véanse los § 8 y §10 *supra*.);

b. los puntos de vista sobre la calificación de algunos gravámenes y tasas como impuestos son diferentes (§ 11y §12 *supra.*);

c. la OCDE excluye los impuestos imputados o los subsidios procedentes de la aplicación de múltiples tipos de cambio oficiales, o del pago de una tasa diferente a otras del mercado sobre reservas requeridas que pueda hacer el banco central;

d. los créditos fiscales exigibles se tratan de forma diferente.

88. Tal y como se ha apuntado en los § 1 y §2, las categorías 1000 a 6000 de la lista de impuestos de la OCDE cubren todos los pagos sin contraprestación al gobierno general, aparte de las multas y los préstamos obligatorios. Esos pagos sin contraprestación, incluidas las multas pero excluidos los préstamos obligatorios, pueden obtenerse añadiendo los siguientes valores del SCN 2008:

- impuestos sobre el valor agregado (D211);
- impuestos y derechos sobre las importaciones, IVA no incluido (D212);
- impuestos sobre las exportaciones (D213);
- impuestos sobre los productos, IVA e impuestos sobre las importaciones y exportaciones no incluidos (D214);
- otros impuestos sobre la producción (D29);
- impuestos sobre la renta (D51);
- otros impuestos corrientes (D59);
- contribuciones sociales (D61), excluidas las contribuciones voluntarias;
- impuestos sobre el capital (D91).

A.10. Relación de la clasificación de impuestos de la OCDE con el sistema de estadísticas de finanzas públicas del Fondo Monetario Internacional

89. La cobertura y la valoración de los ingresos tributarios en el sistema de estadísticas de finanzas públicas (EFP) y en el SCN 2008 son muy similares. Por lo tanto, a excepción del tratamiento dado a los créditos fiscales exigibles, las diferencias entre la clasificación de la OCDE y la del SCN 2008 (véase el § 87 *supra.*) son de aplicación igualmente al sistema de EFP. Además, el Fondo Monetario Internacional (FMI) escinde la categoría única 5000 de la OCDE en dos categorías distintas dedicadas a los impuestos nacionales sobre bienes y servicios (114) y a los impuestos sobre el comercio y las transacciones internacionales (115). Esto refleja el hecho de que, mientras estos últimos impuestos suelen generar insignificantes cantidades de ingresos en la zona de la OCDE, ese no es el caso en la mayoría de los países no pertenecientes a la Organización.

A.11. Comparación de la clasificación de impuestos de la OCDE con otras clasificaciones internacionales

90. El cuadro siguiente recoge una comparación ítem por ítem entre la clasificación de impuestos de la OCDE y las clasificaciones empleadas en:

i. el Sistema de Cuentas Nacionales (SCN 2008);

ii. el Sistema Europeo de Cuentas (SEC 1995);

iii. el *Manual de estadísticas de finanzas públicas* del FMI (MEFP 2001).

91. Estas comparaciones representan equivalencias que podrán aplicarse en la mayoría de los casos. Con todo, deberán emplearse con cierta flexibilidad, ya que, en casos particulares, los países pueden adoptar enfoques diferentes para la clasificación de los ingresos en las cuentas nacionales.

	Clasificación de la OCDE	SNA 2008	ESA 2010	GFSM2014
1000	Impuestos sobre los ingresos, utilidades y ganancias de capital			
	1100 Personas			
	1110 Ingresos y utilidades	D51-8.61a	D51A	1111
	1120 Ganancias de capital	D51-8.61c, d	D51C, D	1111
	1200 Corporaciones			
	1210 Ingresos y ganancias	D51-8.61b	D51B	1112
	1220 Ganancias de capital	D51-8.61c	D51C	1112
	1300 No clasificables entre 1100 y 1200			1113
2000	Contribuciones a la seguridad social			
	2100 Empleados	D613-8.85	D613	1211
	2200 Empleadores	D611-8.83	D611	1212
	2300 Auto-empleados y no empleados	D613-8.85	D613	1213
	2400 No asignables entre 2100, 2200 y 2300			1214
3000	Impuestos sobre la nómina y fuerza de trabajo	D29-7.97a	D29C	112
4000	Impuesos sobre la propiedad			
	4100 Impuestos recurrentes sobre la propiedad inmueble			
	4110 Hogares	D59-8.63a	D59A	1131
	4120 Other	D29-7.97b	D29A	1131
	4200 Impuestos recurrentes sobre la riqueza neta			
	4210 Hogares	D59-8.63b	D59A	1132
	4220 Corporaciones	D59-8.63b	D59A	1132
	4300 Impuestos sobre sucesiones, herencias y donaciones			
	4310 Impuestos sobre sucesiones y herencias	D91-10.207b	D91A	1133
	4320 Impuestos sobre donaciones	D91-10.207b	D91A	1133
	4400 Impuestos sobre transacciones financieras y de capital	D59-7.96d; D29-7.97e	D214B, C	114114; 1161
	4500 Otros impuestos no recurrentes sobre la propiedad	D91-10.207a	D91B	1135
	4600 Otros impuestos recurrentes sobre la propiedad	D59-8.63c	D59A	1136
5000	Impuestos sobre los bienes y servicios			
	5100 Impuestos sobre la producción, venta y transmisión de bienes y prestación de servicios			
	5110 Impuestos generales sobre bienes y servicios			
	5111 Impuestos sobre el valor agregado	D211-7.89	D211; D29G	11411
	5112 Impuestos sobre las ventas	D2122-7.94a; D214-7.96a	D21224; D214I	11412
	5113 Otros impuestos generales sobre los ingresos brutos y sobre bienes y servicios	D214-7.96a	D214I	11413
	5120 Impuestos sobre bienes y servicios específicos			
	5121 Impuestos selectivos	D2122-7.94b; D214-7.96b	D21223; D214A, B, D	1142
	5122 Utilidades de los monopolios fiscales	D214-7.96e	D214J	1143
	5123 Derechos de aduanas y otros derechos de importación	D2121-7.93	D2121; D21221, 2	1151
	5124 Sobre las exportaciones	D213-7.95a	D214K	1152-4
	5125 Sobre los bienes de inversión			
	5126 Sobre servicios específicos	D2122-7.94c; D214-7.96c	D21225; D214E, F, G, H; D29F	1144; 1156
	5127 Otros impuestos sobre el comercio y las transacciones internacionales	D2122-7.94d D29-7.95b D29-7.97g D59-8.64d	D21226; D29D; D59E	1153; 1155-6
	5128 Otros impuestos sobre bienes y servicios específicos			1146
	5130 No clasificables entre 5110 y 5120			
	5200 Impuestos sobre el uso de bienes y sobre el permiso para usar bienes y realizar actividades			
	5210 Impuestos recurrentes			
	5211 Sobre vehículos automotores: hogares	D59-8.64c	D59D	11451
	5212 Sobre vehículos automotores: otros	D29-7.97d	D214D; D29B	11451
	5213 Otros impuestos recurrentes en el uso de bienes y en el permiso para el uso de bienes y la realización de actividades	D29-7.97c, d, f D59-8.64c	D29B, E, F; D59D	11452
	5220 Impuestos no recurrentes sobre el permiso para el uso de bienes o la realización de actividades			11452
	5300 No clasificables entre 5100 y 5200			
6000	Otros impuestos			
	6100 Pagados únicamente por empresas			1161
	6200 Pagados por otros distintos de las empresas o no identificables	D59-8.64a, b	D59B, C	1162

A.12. Atribución de ingresos tributarios por subsectores del gobierno general

92. La clasificación de la OCDE requiere un desglose de los ingresos tributarios por subsectores del gobierno general. Seguidamente, se establecen la definición de cada subsector y los criterios que deben emplearse para atribuir los ingresos tributarios entre ellos, que siguen las orientaciones del SCN 2008 y del MEFP 2014.

Identificación de los subsectores del gobierno general

a) Gobierno central

93. El subsector del gobierno central incluye todos los departamentos, oficinas y establecimientos del gobierno, así como otros órganos que constituyen organismos o instrumentos de la autoridad central, cuya competencia se extiende a todo el territorio, con excepción de la administración de los fondos de seguridad social. En consecuencia, el gobierno central tiene la facultad de someter a tributación a todas las unidades residentes y no residentes que emprendan actividades económicas en el país.

b) Gobierno estatal, provincial o regional

94. Este subsector está compuesto por unidades intermedias del gobierno que ejercen su competencia a un nivel inferior al del gobierno central. Incluye a todas las unidades que operan independientemente del gobierno central en una parte del territorio de un país que engloba numerosas pequeñas localidades, con la excepción de la administración de los fondos de seguridad social. En los países unitarios, puede considerarse que los gobiernos regionales tienen una existencia separada, en la que cuentan con la suficiente autonomía como para recaudar sus ingresos de fuentes bajo su control, y sus funcionarios son independientes del control administrativo externo en el ejercicio de las actividades de la unidad.

95. En la actualidad, los países federales representan la mayoría de los casos en los que los ingresos atribuidos a unidades intermedias del gobierno se identifican de forma separada. España es el único país unitario en ese caso; en el resto de los países unitarios, los ingresos regionales se computan junto con los de los gobiernos locales.

c) Gobierno local

96. Este subsector incluye todas las demás unidades del gobierno que ejercen una competencia independiente en parte del territorio de un país, con excepción de la administración de los fondos de seguridad social. Engloba varios entes urbanos o rurales (p. ej., autoridades locales, municipios, ciudades, delegaciones, distritos).

d) Fondos de seguridad social

97. Los fondos de seguridad social forman un subsector separado del gobierno general. El SCN 2008 define el subsector de la seguridad social según lo expuesto en sus párrafos 4.124 a 4.126 y 4.147, citados seguidamente:

> "Los regímenes de seguridad social son sistemas de seguros sociales que cubren a la comunidad en su conjunto o a amplios sectores de la misma, y que son impuestos y controlados por unidades del gobierno. Los sistemas abarcan una gran variedad de programas, y ofrecen prestaciones en dinero o en especie por vejez, invalidez o muerte, supervivencia, enfermedad y maternidad, accidentes de trabajo, desempleo, ayudas familiares, asistencia sanitaria, etc. No existe necesariamente una relación directa entre la cuantía de la contribución pagada por un individuo y las prestaciones que este pueda recibir." (Párrafo 4.124)

"Cuando los sistemas de seguridad social se organizan por separado de las demás actividades de las unidades del gobierno, mantienen sus activos y pasivos separados de estas últimas, y realizan operaciones financieras por cuenta propia, se califican de unidades institucionales, que reciben el nombre de fondos de seguridad social." (Párrafo 4.125)

"Las cantidades recaudadas y pagadas por contribuciones y prestaciones de la seguridad social pueden modificarse deliberadamente con el fin de alcanzar determinados objetivos de la política del gobierno que no tengan relación directa con el concepto de la seguridad social como sistema destinado a ofrecer prestaciones sociales a los miembros de la comunidad. Pueden aumentarse o disminuirse, por ejemplo, con el fin de influir en el nivel de la demanda agregada de la economía. No obstante, mientras se mantengan como fondos constituidos por separado, han de ser tratados, en el SCN, como unidades institucionales diferentes." (Párrafo 4.126)

"El subsector de los fondos de seguridad social [del gobierno general] está conformado por los fondos de seguridad social que operan en todos los niveles del gobierno. Dichos fondos son sistemas de seguros sociales que cubren a la comunidad en su conjunto o a amplios sectores de la misma, y que son impuestos por unidades del gobierno." (Párrafo 4.147)

98. La clasificación de la OCDE sigue esta definición de los fondos de seguridad social con las dos siguientes excepciones, por las se excluyen:

- los sistemas impuestos por el gobierno pero administrados por órganos externos al sector del gobierno general, tal y como se ha definido en el § 3 de este manual, y
- los sistemas en los que todas las contribuciones son voluntarias.

Autoridades supranacionales

99. Este subsector engloba las operaciones de recaudación fiscal de autoridades supranacionales dentro de un país. En la práctica, la única autoridad supranacional que cabe tener en cuenta en la zona de la OCDE es la que conforman las instituciones de la Unión Europea (UE). Desde 1998, las autoridades supranacionales no se incluyen en *Revenue Statistics*, a fin de ser coherentes con la definición que el SCN da del gobierno general, que las excluye. Por ejemplo, los impuestos sobre la renta y las contribuciones a la seguridad social recaudados por instituciones europeas y pagados a empleados públicos europeos que residen en países miembros de la OCDE no deberían incluirse. Pese a todo, ciertos gravámenes específicos pagados por los Estados miembros de la UE siguen incorporándose a la recaudación tributaria total y, en ese caso, se muestran bajo esta denominación.

Criterios de atribución de los ingresos tributarios

100. Cuando un gobierno recauda impuestos y los transfiere, en todo o en parte, a otros gobiernos, es necesario determinar si esos ingresos se imputarán al gobierno recaudador que los distribuye a otros en forma de donaciones, o si se atribuirán a los gobiernos beneficiarios para los que el gobierno recaudador actúa como mero agente, recibiendo el producto de los impuestos y transfiriéndolos posteriormente. Los criterios de atribución de los ingresos se establecen en los § 101–§104 siguientes, y siguen lo dispuesto en los puntos 3.70 a 3.73 del SCN 2008.

101. Por regla general, un impuesto se atribuye a la unidad de gobierno que:

a. ejerce la facultad de aplicar el impuesto (como entidad principal o a través de la autoridad delegada por la entidad principal), y

b. puede a su discreción establecer y modificar la tasa del impuesto.

102. Cuando un gobierno recauda impuestos para y en nombre de otro, y este último tiene la facultad de aplicar el impuesto y establecer y modificar su tasa impositiva, entonces el gobierno recaudador actúa como agente de este, y el impuesto se reasigna. Cualquier cantidad retenida por el gobierno recaudador como cargo por la recaudación deberá tratarse como pago por un servicio. Cualquier otra cantidad retenida por el gobierno recaudador, por ejemplo, en el marco de un arreglo de coparticipación de impuestos, deberá tratarse como una donación corriente. Si se delegó al gobierno recaudador la autoridad para establecer y modificar la tasa impositiva entonces las cantidades recaudadas deberán tratarse como ingresos tributarios de este gobierno.

103. Cuando diferentes gobiernos establecen conjuntamente y por igual la tasa de un impuesto y el uso de los recursos, sin que ninguno de ellos tengan la autoridad final y exclusiva, entonces los ingresos tributarios se atribuyen a cada gobierno según la proporción de recursos que le corresponda; si el acuerdo permite a una unidad del gobierno ejercer el control final y exclusivo, entonces todos los ingresos tributarios se atribuirán a dicha unidad.

104. También puede ocurrir que un gobierno tenga la autoridad constitucional o de otra índole de aplicar un impuesto, pero que otros gobiernos establezcan individualmente la tasa de ese impuesto en sus jurisdicciones; los recursos generados por el impuesto en cuestión en la jurisdicción de cada gobierno se atribuirán como ingresos tributarios a los respectivos gobiernos.

Gravámenes satisfechos por los Estados miembros de la Unión Europea

105. Los gravámenes satisfechos por los Estados miembros de la Unión Europea (UE) revisten la forma de:

a. derechos de aduana y gravámenes sobre los bienes agrícolas (5123),
b. cuentas de compensación monetaria brutas (5123 en relación con las importaciones y 5124 en relación con las exportaciones), y
c. gravámenes sobre el acero, el carbón, el azúcar y la leche (5128).

106. Los derechos de aduana recaudados por los Estados miembros de la UE en nombre de esta se registran de la siguiente forma:

- sobre la base de un coeficiente de recaudación bruta;
- ajustando los resultados, siempre que sea posible, de forma que esos derechos se muestren en relación con una base de "destino final", por oposición a la base de "país de primera entrada"; estos ajustes atañen particularmente a los derechos colectados en importantes puertos (marítimos); aunque los derechos de la UE se perciben por las autoridades del país de primera entrada, siempre que sea posible cabrá excluir esos derechos del ingreso del país recaudador e incluirlos en el ingreso del país de destino final.

107. Este es el gravamen específico de la UE que más claramente se ciñe al criterio de atribución consignado en el § 99. En consecuencia, desde 1998, las cantidades en relación con este gravamen se registran como partida informativa en los cuadros de países de los Estados miembros de la UE (en el Capítulo 4 de la publicación *Revenue Statistics* de la OCDE) y no se integran ya en la partida 5123. Sin embargo, se incluyen en las cifras de recaudación tributaria total de la línea superior para los años correspondientes mostrados en los cuadros.

A.13. Clasificación provisional de los ingresos tributarios procedentes de gravámenes bancarios y pagos a sistemas de seguro de depósitos y de estabilidad financiera

108. La OCDE ha adoptado el siguiente enfoque provisional para el registro de los ingresos procedentes de gravámenes bancarios, así como de seguro de depósitos y tasas de estabilidad para la edición 2012 y las posteriores publicaciones de *Revenue Statistics* de la OCDE. Se recomienda que los importes sean registrados bajo la subpartida5126.

- Los pagos obligatorios de tasas de estabilidad, gravámenes bancarios y primas de seguro de depósitos se tratarán por lo general como ingresos tributarios cuando se abonen al gobierno general y se asignen a los fondos consolidados o generales de este, de forma que el gobierno pueda utilizar libre e inmediatamente el dinero para los fines que elija. Este principio se aplicará independientemente de que el gobierno prometa revertir esos pagos para garantizar los depósitos de los clientes de los bancos en caso de necesidad futura.
- Si los pagos obligatorios se abonan al gobierno general y se destinan a fondos afectados exclusivamente a volver al sector de la economía que engloba a las sociedades sujetas a dichos pagos, éstos seguirán considerándose ingresos tributarios dado que los fondos estarán disponibles para el gobierno y podrán reducir su déficit presupuestario, que la tasa no conlleva contraprestación para una entidad individual y que las cantidades recaudadas no tienen relación con cualquier pago posterior a los depositantes o cualquier gasto realizado como medio de respaldo más amplio al sector financiero.
- Se clasificarán como tasa por servicio los pagos que deban aportarse a sistemas permanentes más reducidos para garantizar los depósitos de "particulares" cuando los niveles de pago concuerden con el coste del seguro.
- También se clasificarán como tasa por servicio, y no como ingreso tributario, los pagos que impliquen que el gobierno ejecute los activos de una institución en quiebra o tenga un derecho prioritario sobre la liquidación de activos de esta con objeto de financiar los pagos de compensación a los clientes por la pérdida de sus depósitos.

No se tratarán como ingresos tributarios los pagos obligatorios destinados a fondos externos al sector de gobierno y a instituciones no estatales respaldadas por los tomadores de depósitos, ni los pagos hechos a sistemas voluntarios.

Notas

1. Las referencias a la publicación *Revenue Statistics* de la OCDE en esta Guía Interpretativa, aluden a OECD (2017), *Revenue Statistics 2017*, OECD Publishing, Paris.
2. Todas las referencias al SCN deberán entenderse hechas a la edición de 2008.
3. Véase el apartado K de la presente guía para el análisis del concepto de agente.
4. Por lo general, es posible identificar la cuantía de las contribuciones a la seguridad social y de los impuestos sobre la nómina, pero no otros impuestos asumidos por el gobierno.
5. Sin embargo, si un gravamen considerado como ingreso no tributario en la mayoría de los países se califica de tributario –o permite recaudar sustanciales ingresos– en uno o más países, las entradas en concepto de dicho gravamen se indican en las notas que figuran al pie de los cuadros de países, pero no se incluyen en la recaudación tributaria total.
6. Obsérvese, no obstante, que los nombres pueden dar lugar a confusión. Por ejemplo, aunque una tasa sobre los pasaportes se trataría normalmente como ingreso no tributario, si se impone un gravamen suplementario sobre los pasaportes (como en el caso de Portugal) con el fin de conseguir un ingreso

sustancialmente mayor que el costo que supone proporcionar el pasaporte, dicho gravamen deberá considerarse como un impuesto sobre el uso de bienes (5200).

7. Para una explicación más detallada de esta distinción, consúltese el estudio especial sobre cuestiones de actualidad en relación con el registro de los ingresos tributarios *Current issues in reporting tax revenues*, en la edición 2001 de *Revenue Statistics*.

8. En ocasiones, se emplean asimismo los términos "no reembolsable" y "reembolsable", pero puede parecer ilógico hablar de "reembolsable" cuando no se ha pagado nada.

9. Con la excepción del diferente tratamiento dado a los créditos fiscales exigibles en los sistemas de imputación del impuesto sobre sociedades (§§ 36–38).

10. No se trata aquí de verdaderos gastos tributarios en sentido formal, ya que tales gastos requieren que se identifique un sistema tributario de referencia para cada país o, mejor si cabe, una referencia internacional común y, en la práctica, no se ha logrado acuerdo sobre esta última.

11. A menos que se basen en la plusvalía obtenida con la venta, en cuyo caso se clasificarían como impuestos sobre las ganancias de capital, en las subpartidas 1120 o 1220.

12. Con todo, algunos países aplican la misma legislación a ambos en impuestos particulares sobre la renta, aunque las entradas procedentes de dichos impuestos suelen ser fácilmente atribuibles a uno u otro caso y pueden, por lo tanto, consignarse en la debida partida.

13. Por ejemplo, "[...] que son suficientemente autónomas e independientes y se comportan como si fueran sociedades [...] (incluido en el hecho de llevar) conjuntos completos de cuentas" (SCN 2008, 4.44).

14. En Canadá, país en el que se considera que rige un sistema de imputación, el crédito fiscal (no exigible) para el accionista nace en relación con el impuesto nacional sobre sociedades que se reputa haber pagado, tanto si ha surgido una obligación tributaria para la sociedad como si no. Habida cuenta de que no existe una conexión íntegra entre la obligación tributaria de la sociedad y el crédito concedido en relación con el impuesto sobre la renta en esos sistemas, los créditos por dividendos se tratan, junto con otros créditos fiscales, según lo descrito en el § 25.

15. Esto puede darse, por ejemplo, cuando ya existía un régimen para los empleados del gobierno previo a la introducción de un régimen general de seguridad social.

16. En el SCN 2008, se consideran transferencias de capital y no impuestos (véase la sección A.8.).

17. Mediante este sistema, la Unión Europea ajusta las diferencias entre los tipos de cambio empleados para determinar los precios de la política agrícola común (PAC) y los tipos de cambio reales. Los pagos realizados en este sistema pueden estar relacionados con importaciones o exportaciones y, cuando ha sido posible identificar por separado las respectivas cantidades, se han mostrado en el correspondiente epígrafe (5123 o 5124). En el presente informe, esas cantidades se han consignado en valores brutos (esto es, sin deducir ningún subsidio otorgado en el marco del sistema MCM).

18. Las transferencias de las utilidades de las loterías del Estado se consideran ingresos no tributarios (véase el § 67).

19. Véase el § 30(c) en relación con esta distinción.

OECD PUBLISHING, 2, rue André-Pascal, 75775 PARIS CEDEX 16
(23 2018 15 3 P) ISBN 978-92-64-29222-2 – 2018

www.ingramcontent.com/pod-product-compliance
Ingram Content Group UK Ltd.
Pitfield, Milton Keynes, MK11 3LW, UK
UKHW051458290926
15471UKWH00008B/1269

9 789264 292222